D1602426

ADVANCE PRAISE FOR

Russia in War and Revolution: The Memoirs of Fyodor Sergeyevich Olferieff

"Fedor Sergeevich Olfer'ev, a former Imperial Page and officer of the Russian General Staff, has gifted to us a remarkably forthright and captivating account of the first thirty years of his life (which also happened to be imperial Russia's last). Yet, as Professor Gary M. Hamburg reminds the readers in his insightful and lucid prolegomenon, Olfer'ev did not write his memoirs to settle old scores or 'to be understood by his contemporaries.' His goal was loftier—'to understand himself and to record his broken life for posterity.' Masterfully translated by his American-born granddaughter and splendidly contextualized in Hamburg's extraordinary learned historical essays, Olfer'ev's reflections on the challenges and choices of his generation, which was groomed to serve the monarch but ended up abandoning His Majesty to save the country, offer an indispensable guide to life and polity of old Russia during its last and most consequential years of wars and revolutions."

—**Semion Lyandres**, professor of modern European/Russian history, University of Notre Dame

"Accurate, clear-eyed, and unsentimental, Fyodor Olferieff's memoirs provide valuable insights into the last years of imperial Russia, World War I, the Revolution, and the civil strife that followed. Gracefully translated and augmented by Gary Hamburg's insightful companion essay, these recollections can be read with pleasure and profit by specialists and the general public."

—**Richard Robbins**, professor emeritus, University of New Mexico

"Fyodor Olferieff's memoir is a fascinating account of a tsarist officer's life and journey through Russia's revolutionary era. Olferieff was a perceptive observer who witnessed a host of important events and figures, and Gary Hamburg's detailed introduction enhances his memoir's value as historical source."

—**Sam Ramer**, associate professor of history,
Tulane University

"This memoir of a Russian nobleman and officer, not titled but of high rank, who lived through the entire drama of the decline of the monarchy, war, revolution, and civil war, to a classic escape through Odessa in 1919 and eventual American exile and citizenship, fluently translated into English by his granddaughter, tells a story that is familiar—the landed gentry childhood, the Corps of Pages, the Horse Grenadiers, the Imperial Military Academy, active duty in the imperial army, and then survival in the incredible confusion of Kiev in 1918—yet one that is extraordinarily textured, detailed, and thoughtful. The background is expertly set in Gary Hamburg's historiographically up-to-date introductory review of the decline of the old regime, the war, revolution, and civil war, followed at the end of the memoir by his meticulously well-informed running commentary on the contents of the memoir (best consulted, I should think, in a back-and-forth with the reading of the memoir itself). Altogether, a remarkable contribution to historical knowledge."

—**Terence Emmons**, professor of history emeritus,
Stanford University

RUSSIA IN WAR AND REVOLUTION

Portrait of Fyodor Sergeyevich Olferieff, 1905.

RUSSIA IN WAR AND REVOLUTION

The Memoirs of Fyodor Sergeyevich Olferieff

BY

FYODOR SERGEYEVICH OLFERIEFF

EDITED BY

GARY M. HAMBURG

TRANSLATED BY

TANYA ALEXANDRA CAMERON

HOOVER INSTITUTION PRESS

Stanford University • Stanford, California

With its eminent scholars and world-renowned library and archives, the Hoover Institution seeks to improve the human condition by advancing ideas that promote economic opportunity and prosperity, while securing and safeguarding peace for America and all mankind. The views expressed in its publications are entirely those of the authors and do not necessarily reflect the views of the staff, officers, or Board of Overseers of the Hoover Institution.

hoover.org

Hoover Institution Press Publication No. 710
Hoover Institution at Leland Stanford Junior University,
Stanford, California 94305-6003

All photographs and illustrations are from the Olferieff Collection, Hoover Institution Library & Archives, Stanford University. Maps were hand drawn by Fyodor Olferieff.

First printing 2020
27 26 25 24 23 22 21 20 9 8 7 6 5 4 3 2 1

Manufactured in the United States of America
Printed on acid-free, archival-quality paper.

Library of Congress Control Number: 2020944426

ISBN: 978-0-8179-2364-8 (cloth)
ISBN: 978-0-8179-2366-2 (epub)
ISBN: 978-0-8179-2367-9 (mobi)
ISBN: 978-0-8179-2368-6 (PDF)

Contents

Foreword

It is always a pleasure to bring the treasures of the Hoover Institution Library & Archives to a broad audience in the form of documentary publications. The memoirs of Fyodor Olferieff are a particularly enticing example. Like all memoirs, they give a subjective view of events, in this case from the point of view of an Imperial Russian Army officer, a member of Russia's enlightened aristocracy, a careful observer of the final decades of imperial rule. These memoirs offer an unusual glimpse into the author's world, unusual in its breadth and depth, where the expected "Let them eat cake" attitude is replaced by a more subtle, complex, and sympathetic view of prerevolutionary Russia, along with adequate attention to the failings of both government and society.

The memoirs describe Olferieff's childhood and upbringing, his family and education, and then his military experiences, with particular attention paid to his service during the First World War. A graduate of the Russian Imperial Corps of Pages, Olferieff first served in the Life Guard Horse Grenadier Regiment. During World War I, Olferieff was highly decorated and advanced to the rank of lieutenant colonel of the General Staff. The collapse of discipline following the February 1917 revolution in Russia and the disintegration of the army vividly convey the sense of coming doom felt by the author. After the storm broke, Olferieff served in the anti-Bolshevik (White) army of South Russia, eventually emigrating with his family to California.

For many decades, the Theo Olferieff papers at the Hoover Institution consisted of one brief typescript entitled "Soviet Russia in the Orient" (1932). In 2016, Olferieff's granddaughter Tanya Alexandra Cameron contacted us with information about her grandfather's remaining papers and artifacts, including these memoirs. The publication of the memoirs in connection with the acquisition of the entire collection seemed an ideal fit. His collection includes biographical materials, his writings, photographs depicting members of the Olferieff family in Russia and California (1884–1967), and memorabilia (1866–1916), such as an icon presented to Olferieff on the fiftieth anniversary of his service in the Horse Grenadier Regiment. The entire Olferieff collection is now in the Hoover Library & Archives, and the memoirs are now in your hands, for which we thank Tanya Cameron and her family.

Anatol Shmelev
Robert Conquest Curator for Russia and Eurasia
Hoover Institution Library & Archives
Stanford University

Translator's Foreword

TANYA ALEXANDRA CAMERON

The translation of my grandfather's memoirs has been a labor of love ever since he pulled the manuscript out of a closet in his home in San Francisco and showed it to me. He asked that I do something with it because he was too old and worn out. That was in 1969. I promised I would, but I had to learn Russian first. I also had two young toddlers who needed my attention.

It wasn't till 1986, while living in Bozeman, Montana, where my husband taught biology at Montana State University, that I finally had the opportunity to begin my studies. The class was only offered for one year because only two of the initial nine students wanted to continue. That next year we studied at my kitchen table with our teacher, Laulette Malchik. Then the following year, 1988, I traveled to the Soviet Union for almost three months to visit all the places my grandfather wrote about, including the area of the original family estate near Rzhev. Laulette accompanied me, because she was married to a Russian whom she had met while on a Fulbright scholarship. Her in-laws lived in St. Petersburg, and other relatives of her husband's lived in Moscow.

Traveling alone without Intourist guides made us an oddity. Our travels were extensive, from Petrozavodsk in the north, south to St. Petersburg, Tver, Moscow, Kiev, Odessa, and Yalta, and east on the Trans-Siberian Railroad as far as Lake Baikal, Irkutsk, and Listvyanka. When I returned, I enjoyed giving a couple of lectures accompanied by slides in the Russian history class of Dr. David Large. Before I left he allowed me to audit his popular class, which was almost standing room only because of his excellent command of the subject and outstanding teaching skills.

Finally, in 1989, I began the task that has led to this book. Over the many years since then, I have been encouraged by my husband, David, children Julie and Seth, and many friends to continue. I especially thank Seth for his help with computer and program problems. My aunt Alexandra Olferieff Grieco Hodapp also encouraged me, and was able to share the history of the family's time in this country and her early recollections of their escape from Russia, as she was eight years old when they arrived in the United States.

My mother passed away in 1970, before my grandfather, and as she was only five when they arrived here, her memories were not as clear. When I was growing up, the Second World War was foremost, as my father was a naval officer in the Pacific and the tragic loss of my uncle as a Japanese prisoner of war in the Philippines cast a pall on my youth. I was really too young to appreciate as I was growing up the historical significance of my dear grandfather's life.

This book is dedicated to my grandfather.

Introduction: The End of Imperial Russia

GARY M. HAMBURG

This book presents for the first time the memoirs of Fedor Sergeevich Olfer'ev (1885–1971). They are lucidly translated from an unpublished Russian manuscript and annotated by his granddaughter Tanya A. Cameron, who has added a moving postscript on the lives of Fedor Sergeevich and his wife, Marusia, after their emigration to the United States. I have contributed an essay on the historical context of Olfer'ev's Russian life.

Born into a noble family in Tver' province, Olfer'ev grew up in the last decades of Russia's old regime. In childhood he became familiar with rural life by befriending peasant boys and listening to his peasant nanny, by attending services at country churches, by watching neighboring gentry socialize with each other, and by observing his father's behavior in local society. In young adulthood, Olfer'ev attended two of Russia's most elite educational institutions: the Petersburg School of Pages and the General Staff Academy. Matriculation in the School of Pages gave him many opportunities to meet members of Russia's royal family. At court and at public celebrations involving the pages, he watched and interacted with Emperor Nicholas II and Empress Aleksandra. At court, in military service, and in other venues, he also encountered other members of the Romanov family. He therefore formed impressions of the Romanovs at a critical juncture in Russia's political history and began to develop his own critical analysis of the country's political prospects. At the General Staff Academy, where he studied from 1911 to 1914, he saw the Empire's best military minds in action and did his best to understand elements of military strategy that would later be employed in the Great War.

Between 1905 and 1907, Olfer'ev undertook his first military assignments. He helped guard the magnificent palace at Peterhof against revolutionaries in 1905. His unit of Grenadiers controlled crowds on Petersburg streets in that same revolutionary year, and in 1906 it suppressed a rebellion by sailors at the Kronstadt Naval Base. In 1907, his squadron arrested members of the Latvian Forest Brothers, and he served on a tribunal that sentenced one of those arrestees to death. His activity in the military from 1905 to 1907 raised moral and political questions that would come to obsess him in the writing of his memoirs. He wondered whether his own advantages in status and education could be justified, given the peasants' poverty and their resentment of the nobility. He asked whether future Russian common soldiers were likely to maintain military discipline when ordered to confront protestors from their own class. In meditating on the accident of his birth, he asked whether he, if born a peasant, might have thrown himself into the revolutionary movement.

These questions became more urgent for Olfer'ev after he enrolled in the General Staff Academy. He quickly realized that if Russia found itself embroiled in a European war, the psychology of Russia's oppressed classes might affect the military outcome of that conflict. He wondered whether peasant soldiers would stay loyal to their units under the duress of total war. In the tense atmosphere of the prewar years, Olfer'ev also speculated on the viability of the Russian monarchy, an institution inextricably linked to the maintenance of social arrangements that were then under challenge in the Empire. Olfer'ev began to suspect that the royal house would not long survive, that Russia's body politic was a "living corpse."

Olfer'ev devotes the heart of his book to his own experiences in the Great War. He painstakingly recounts the rout of General Aleksandr Vasil'evich Samsonov's II Army in August 1914. He describes a series of battles on the Polish front and also several incidents of troop demoralization attending the army's great retreat in 1915. He records political discussions among officers in 1915 and 1916: he overheard some of these conversations and participated in others. From his perspective at Army Headquarters (Stavka), he traces and tries to explain the army's rapid politicization in 1917. During the war, Olfer'ev seemingly managed to be everywhere, especially during the climactic days of the February/March revolution of 1917, when he served at Stavka and intermittently visited the front.

By virtue of his many military assignments and his role on the army General Staff, Olfer'ev had the opportunity to gauge the effectiveness of Russia's military leaders. He closely scrutinized the orders of Grand Duke Nikolai Nikolaevich and his chief of staff General Nikolai Nikolaevich Ianushkevich. At Stavka in 1916 and early 1917, he served Nicholas II and his chief of staff General Mikhail Vasil'evich Alekseev. He tracked the activity, military and political, of General Nikolai Vladimirovich Ruzskii, particularly during Nicholas II's abdication. In summer 1917, Olfer'ev served for a short time under General Lavr Georgievich Kornilov, whose desire to reimpose military discipline in the army and the capital led to confrontation with the Provisional Government in late August/early September 1917. Later in the year, he was an aide to General Nikolai Nikolaevich Dukhonin, the acting Supreme Commander of the Russian army, and was on duty the day that Bolshevik sailors murdered Dukhonin in December 1917.

The memoirs offer various assessments of these leaders' military prowess: for example, Olfer'ev is critical of Ianushkevich and of Emperor Nicholas, but is more tempered in his views of Grand Duke Nikolai Nikolaevich. The memoirs show how deeply political were the tactics of each of these leaders, even when they purported to stand "above politics." To Russian historians, Olfer'ev's memoirs raise the structural problems of the army as ultimate guarantor of the imperial political order, and of the General Staff as competitor with the civil government for sovereign control during wartime. By late 1917, it seemed to Olfer'ev that army and state were one, so that for him the end of Stavka in December 1917 was also the end of Russian statehood.

Olfer'ev's war memories are vivid, intelligently told, and almost always accurate. In a few instances, they provide concrete details that cannot be found in other accounts. A handful of passages in Olfer'ev's memoirs run events together, lack discrete temporal references, or reveal confusion over the revolutionary process. These moments are, paradoxically, among its most valuable, because they reflect the chaos of the Great War and the Russian revolution. Such passages illustrate how memory works, or doesn't work, in turbulent historical situations. In general, Olfer'ev's treatment of the war years provides profound insight into the gradual disintegration of the imperial army, the virtual collapse of the imperial economy, the social psychology of catastrophic military defeat, and Russia's consequent revolution.

The concluding chapters of Olfer'ev's memoirs discuss the early phases of the civil war (or wars) that followed the Russian revolution. Olfer'ev worked with many of the generals who helped organize the Volunteer Army in late 1917/early 1918. He was a subordinate of General Alekseev at Mogilev, and after the revolution, met with Alekseev at Novocherkassk. He had admired General Kornilov's devotion to Russia, but he criticized Kornilov's conduct in the showdown with Aleksandr Fedorovich Kerenskii's government in late August/early September 1917. Olfer'ev regarded General Anton Ivanovich Denikin as a man of great talent and as one of the finest memoirists of the civil war, but did not praise Denikin's political acumen. Nor did he think highly of General Petr Nikolaevich Vrangel, a man of keen intelligence and good military sense who was, in Olfer'ev's opinion, also a supreme egoist and fantasist. Olfer'ev's frank portraits of these and other White leaders are set forth in carefully crafted paragraphs devoted to the persons in question. However, aspects of his impressions of them also emerge gradually, as Olfer'ev's narrative touches on key episodes in the civil war.

Among the best pages in the memoirs are those that analyze the politics and fighting in Kiev in 1918, and in Odessa in 1919. Olfer'ev was part of the exodus from the military and from the displaced propertied classes that moved into Kiev in 1918. His cohort of army veterans and privileged Russian landowners lived as exiles in this great metropolis, once regarded by Great Russians as a "purely Russian city" despite its location in Ukraine. Natives of Kiev either barely tolerated their presence or actively sought to drive them out of the city, so that Olfer'ev and his wife sheltered in Kiev as semi-fugitives, as "persecuted" people [*gonimye*]. Olfer'ev records difficult episodes in his underground life in Kiev, and also comments on the city's politics under German occupation. After the fall of the Ukrainian government, the hetmanate, he and his family left for Odessa, where they encountered renewed political instability and dealt with the French occupation. By the time the Olfer'evs evacuated Odessa in April 1919, Fedor Sergeevich had reached the conclusion that future foreign intervention in the Russian civil war was unlikely, and if it did occur, it would be futile.

In this section of the memoirs, Olfer'ev sketches the desultory fighting outside Kiev between supporters and opponents of hetman Pavlo Petrovych

Skoropads'kyi. He then alludes to the brutal killings of officers inside the city by forces directed by Symon Vasylyovich Petliura. In the chapter on Odessa, Olfer'ev describes the murder of thirteen White generals in Piatigorsk, an atrocity recounted to him by the wife of one of the victims. Olfer'ev does not hide his indignation over these developments, but he stipulates that all parties in the civil war had *les mains sales.* He explains the sordidness of such incidents as the result of class hatred, of the manifest failure of Russia's government and educated classes to properly educate the country's peasants and workers.

Internal evidence in the narrative suggests that Olfer'ev composed his reminiscences between 1946 and 1962 and that he relied largely but not exclusively on memory to do so. Tanya A. Cameron translated the memoirs at the request of Fedor Sergeevich himself. She provides biographical annotations on most of the individuals mentioned in the memoirs. My companion essay incorporates additional information about some of these historical actors. The essay frames the historical context of various occurrences, especially when the events in question are important to Russian history and to Olfer'ev. It identifies points in the narrative where Olfer'ev was unclear about exact dates of events or about the relationships among them. The essay is a self-standing meditation on a fascinating historical source, but also (and mainly) it is a supplement to that source. A reader should therefore attend first to Olfer'ev's memoirs, and should consult the companion essay if needed.

In her translation, Cameron transliterates Russian names phonetically, often giving common English variants; she suppresses the soft sign that some translators render as an apostrophe. Cameron refers to her grandfather by his American name, Fyodor Sergeyevich Olferieff, and in the postscript refers to her grandmother as Mary Olferieff. In the preface and companion essay, I adhere to the standard scholarly convention for transliteration of Russian names and terms. I sometimes note variant spellings in Russian, Ukrainian, or other languages. When the context demands, I give Ukrainian rather than Russian spellings of names. Inevitably, there are inconsistencies: for example, I transliterate the name of the Ukrainian capital city as "Kiev" instead of "Kyiv," principally because that was Olfer'ev's preference.

Unless otherwise noted, I use dates in the Russian Old Style—twelve days behind the Western European calendar in the nineteenth century, and thirteen days behind in the twentieth. For references to European statecraft and to dates during the Great War, I have provided double entries: the first to the Russian Old Style calendar, the second to the European calendar (example: October 25/November 7, 1917).

Russia and the Revolution of 1905

The last half-century of Russia's old regime offers us a stunning contrast between an agrarian polity, largely traditional in social structure and economy, and an urbanizing society in the process of rapid economic growth. In spite of the legal abolition of serfdom in 1861, most early twentieth-century Russians still lived on the land in small villages and farmed their communal plots with horse-drawn ploughs, just as their ancestors had done. Not till the late 1880s did a steady stream of young people begin to leave their villages to work in big-city factories, and even then most of these workers identified with the countryside as closely as with their urban environments. Initially after serfdom ended the landed nobility continued to dominate rural life in terms of wealth and social prestige. But as peasant standards of living slowly improved in parts of Russia, and as young peasants moved to the cities, the nobility's social control weakened and the nobility's relative status declined, gradually but seemingly ineluctably, especially in the eyes of the younger generation of villagers.[1] As of 1914, the portion of land owned by nobles had fallen significantly compared to a half-century earlier.

The contradiction between Russia's swiftly changing economy and what remained of its traditional social makeup accounted in large measure for the polarization of its politics. As the historian Abraham Ascher rightly notes, "the country seemed to be divided into two camps, one defending the old order and the other pressing for fundamental change." And yet these two camps were themselves fragmented, such that the forces of order "failed to speak with one voice," while up to 1917 the forces of change "failed to mount a unified onslaught on the old regime."[2]

The tsars Aleksandr III (ruled 1881–94) and Nicholas II (ruled 1894–1917) embodied traditional authority during the twilight of the regime. They possessed sovereignty, or, as the 1832 Fundamental Laws put it, "autocratic and unlimited powers . . . ordained by God Himself."[3] Yet the writ of majesty was constrained by many factors: the notorious inefficiency and corruption of the Russian bureaucracy, the sheer vastness of the Empire, the complexities of local customs, and the differences among the Empire's constituent nationalities. Beginning in the early 1860s, the central government helped create a series of semi-autonomous institutions of elective local self-government—the zemstvos (land councils) in the central provinces, and municipal councils in larger cities. The idea behind these councils was to enlist representatives from Russian society—from the nobility, from the merchantry, from the peasantry, and from urban guilds—to resolve pressing problems. Yet the newly reformed local governments proved difficult for the central government to manage, partly because delegates often thought differently about local problems than Petersburg officials did, and partly because the most liberal among them favored the adoption of a European-style constitution, or at least a national-level council to advise the tsar on important policy matters. By roughly 1900, therefore, the central government faced a dilemma: whether to rein in—or even suppress—the activities of the local self-governing entities it had established in the 1860s, or to collaborate with these new institutions in the making of a broader representative system. The former would guarantee the survival of the autocratic system, at least in the short term; the latter would undercut autocracy but perhaps preserve the monarchy in the long term.

After the turn of the twentieth century, conservatives sought to prop up the failing monarchy by various means. For example, policeman Sergei Vasil'evich Zubatov organized a government-sponsored union in Moscow, the Society for Mutual Aid of Workers in the Mechanical Trades, to mitigate protests by that city's workers. He wanted to persuade workers that the government was "on their side." In 1902, Zubatov added another union in Petersburg.[4] Meanwhile, Minister of Internal Affairs Viacheslav Konstantinovich Plehve advocated minor reforms in rural administration but also sought to control liberal activism by blocking members of the zemstvo from attending national meetings and by arresting its dissident leaders.[5] Minister of Finance Sergei Iul'evich Vitte introduced elements of a transformative economic system mixing major investments in industry, tariff protectionism, and artificially balanced trade, while supporting the autocracy against its critics from the zemstvos.[6] In a notorious memorandum in 1903, Vitte argued that the zemstvos, which he regarded as "the first step toward constitutional government," had proven incompatible with the autocracy.[7]

Starting in 1900, conservatives inside and outside the government established new political groups, such as the Russian Assembly (*Russkoe sobranie*) and the Union of Russian People (*Soiuz russkogo naroda*), to defend the monarchy through the writing of petitions and, after 1905, through formation of electoral political parties. These groups were bitterly critical of Russian constitutionalists. They upheld the interests of Great Russians against other nationalities in the Empire; members of the Union of Russian People blamed the Empire's Jews for much of the country's upheaval.[8] For their part, from the late 1890s, liberals and socialists established organizations aimed at Russia's political and social transformation. Terence Emmons has shown how liberals moved from small informal groups, like the Colloquy (*Beseda*) circle, to the building of political parties in 1905, such as left-liberal Constitutional Democrats (the so-called "Kadets") and centrist Union of October 17 (the "Octobrists").[9] The liberal parties supported the introduction of civil rights for all Russian citizens without distinction, the promulgation of a constitutional charter, and introduction of the rule of law in the Empire. The Kadets favored social reforms to ameliorate dire social inequalities, including the granting to peasants of additional lands and the protection of urban laborers against dangerous working conditions. To achieve these ends, the Kadets were willing to seek allies on the extreme left and to overlook, or tacitly to approve, leftist political terrorism if doing so would make the central government more likely to reform itself. The Kadets tended to distrust the central government as a partner in building a Russian *Rechtsstaat*, whereas the Octobrists initially believed a constitutional monarchy might be quickly created.

Parties of the left, such as the Socialist-Revolutionaries (the "SRs") and Social Democrats, adopted a more militant posture toward the regime and toward the underlying Russian social order. The SRs and their parliamentary faction, the Trudoviks, wanted to construct a socialist society based on the peasant land communes. They disagreed with one another over how to move toward this agenda and over how fast it could be reached.[10] The SR "Battle Group" adopted terrorism to intimidate the people's purported "enemies" on the right. The group was responsible for killing hundreds of officials before, during, and after 1905.[11] Relying on the Battle Group, the Left SRs sought a swift transition to public ownership of land and redistribution of goods according to need—they called this program the "nationalization and socialization of production." The Right SRs and Trudovik group tended not to support violence against government officials, although they did not rule out its use against landowners in a revolutionary situation. They took seriously the "democratic" nature of revolution, and so wanted to foster a revolutionary program with as broad as possible popular support. Although the SRs were agrarian socialists, they thought of their party as representing all Russia's toilers, including urban workers.[12]

When the Social Democrats started to organize themselves before the turn of the century, they considered themselves an anti-capitalist, pro-working-class group, the true Russian heirs to Marx's and Engels's German socialism. By 1903, they had split into three groups. The first group was the Bund, Jewish workers mostly living in the Pale of Settlement on the Empire's western periphery. The second was the Mensheviks, who brandished the banner of "classical Marxism"—that is, they aligned themselves temporarily with Russian liberals until the "bourgeois revolution" had occurred, then they planned to build a democratic workers movement over the decades until capitalism had prepared the conditions for a proletarian revolution. The third group, and ultimately most important of them, was the Bolsheviks, a faction that advocated a more immediate proletarian revolution under the party's guidance. The Bolsheviks' theoretical leader, Vladimir Il'ich Ulianov (Lenin), believed that, left to their own devices, Russian workers could never make a revolution because they could not rise above "trade union consciousness." He laid so much emphasis on the inculcation in workers of revolutionary consciousness through the "vanguard of the proletariat" that he seemed at times to break from Marx's belief that consciousness arises from the human relationship to productive forces, not from political convictions as such. The historian Andrzej Walicki has argued that Lenin did not deliberately abandon classical Marxist theory so much as fear that, without the Bolsheviks' decisive intervention, the opportunity for a proletarian revolution in Russia might be missed.[13]

Compared to politics in Western Europe, politics in early twentieth-century Russia was more polarized and more fragmented. The dividing line between left and right in Russia was more to the left of the political spectrum, because the existing order had historically been less accommodating to reform-minded groups and more resistant to civil rights, and so the wide expectation in Russia was the entire system would have to change. The threat of revolution therefore was in the air almost constantly in the two decades before 1917. Meanwhile, divisions between political factions of the left and right made the political situation more treacherous for the central government and less predictable for everyone; in such an unstable environment, nobody could accurately gauge the country's immediate political future.

Between late 1904 and spring 1907, the Empire experienced the dramatic series of events known as the Revolution of 1905. Historians have focused on different moments as the symbolic beginning of this revolution: the assassination of Minister of Internal Affairs Plehve on July 15, 1904; the national meeting of zemstvo activists in Petersburg from November 6 to 9, 1904; the meeting of the regime's critics in a series of public banquets in the last two months of the year; and the violent suppression of Petersburg workers on January 9, 1905—so-called "Bloody Sunday." From the perspective of the liberal opposition, what tied these moments together was educated society's desire to supplant autocracy by the rule of law, and indeed many succeeding events in 1905 derived their significance from that objective. For example, liberals stood behind the resolution on June 16 by the Congress of City Council Representatives calling for national elections to a bicameral legislature, and most liberals also supported the draft Fundamental Laws circulated by the July Congress of Zemstvo and City Council Representatives demanding civil liberties and an elective legislature.[14] Liberals criticized the government's tame concession on August 6, 1905—the "Bulygin constitution"—for promising national elections while leaving the monarch in office, with his autocratic functions essentially intact.[15]

The most important development of 1905, again from the liberals' perspective, was the tsar's Manifesto of October 17, which granted civil liberties, ordered elections to a State Duma on the basis of universal male suffrage, and mandated that no law could become effective without the Duma's approval. This document did not explicitly mention a constitution, but it did seem to acknowledge that autocracy had come to an end in Russia. In the wake of the manifesto, the liberals formally split into the two parties mentioned above: the Kadets and Octobrists—the former awaiting details about its implementation and hoping for promulgation of a constitution, the latter trusting that the tsar would now act prudently in fleshing out the new system.

From the viewpoint of Russian factory workers, events in 1905 looked different. In Petersburg, the radical Orthodox priest Father Georgii Apollonovich Gapon founded the Assembly of Russian Factory and Mill Workers, and on January 9, 1905, led them in procession to the Winter Palace to present a petition to the tsar. This petition combined requests for political change (national elections to a constituent assembly based on universal suffrage; the establishment of civil rights and equality before the law) and social change (the promulgation of an eight-hour day, the legalization of unions, state insurance for workers).[16] The government's decision to meet the petitioners with force had the effect of increasing workers' determination to change labor laws; indeed, according to Ascher, "the memory of Bloody Sunday kept workers in a state of agitation for some time." Late in the spring, the sheer force of labor militancy drew Social Democrats into the workers movement, and by summer even liberals were trying to attract workers' support for their program.[17] By September and October of 1905, there were widespread strikes in Moscow, Petersburg, and other cities. In the second week of October, there was a general strike that may have involved as many as two million workers. Ascher has argued that Russian workers had undergone "a notable process of politicization [since January]."[18] The politicized labor movement alarmed the central government, and thus contributed to its decision to publish the Manifesto of October 17.

From 1905 to 1907, peasants from various parts of the Empire also expressed their unhappiness with the existing order. The Soviet historian Sergei Mitrofanovich Dubrovskii has calculated over seven thousand instances of peasant protest in those years; about three-quarters involved actions against landowners (the burning of estate buildings, illegal cutting of woods, seizure of arable land, etc.), and another 15 percent involved conflicts with state officials, the police, or soldiers.[19] The protests were strongest in central Russia, in the fertile Central Black Earth provinces, but also in Ukraine, Belorussia, and the Southwest.[20] Ascher has noted that, in 1905 alone, there were more than three thousand incidents of peasant protest, with the peak months being May, June, and July, then November and December.[21] The big driver in most of these incidents was peasant economic distress, but the hostility to local nobles and officials was palpable. By late spring, some peasants made unmistakably political demands: in Kherson province, for example, villagers from Tashino called on the government to grant civil liberties and to convene a constituent assembly. In August 1905, this demand was repeated by the "Constitutional Assembly of the All-Russian Peasants Union," whose delegates met secretly near Moscow.[22] Most peasants probably acted without coordinating their protests with the Socialist-Revolutionary Party, but in certain cases the SRs may have shaped their tactics.

In a study of rural unrest in Kursk province, the historian Burton Richard Miller counted nearly two hundred incidents in calendar year 1905, most of them in February or in November and December.[23] Many of these involved armed clashes with local authorities, including the police and even armed forces. Others involved destruction of landed estates that reminded observers of the eighteenth-century Pugachev rebellion.[24] In Kursk, there were relatively few incidents that Miller can classify as having a "political character," but here and there peasants circulated inflammatory proclamations. Attacks on police stations and unlawful replacements of local officials also occurred, and these attacks might be called "political."[25] Miller found little evidence that outside agitators provoked peasant protests, but abundant evidence that peasants knew (through newspapers, soldiers' letters, workers returning home from other parts of Russia, and zemstvo liberals) what was happening elsewhere in the Empire.[26] He also discovered ties between peasants and the local intelligentsia, including teachers, who may have been inspired by the Socialist-Revolutionaries.[27]

Complicating this picture of 1905 were popular sentiments in Poland and the Baltic provinces. Following the Polish insurrection of 1863–64, the Russian government had adopted repressive policies in Poland; indeed, it administered Russian Poland under emergency rules. As the historian Robert Blobaum has noted, Aleksandr II effectively incorporated Polish provinces into the Russian Empire, and later, Aleksandr III attempted to Russify the population of Poland. Both tsars mandated Russian as the official language of instruction in Poland's schools.[28] The government made rules restricting Roman Catholic instruction in state schools and forbidding proselytizing in border regions. Those rules, widely resented in Poland, contributed to the anti-Russian sentiment of Józef Pilsudski and his Polish Socialist Party, which sought to reestablish Polish independence. In late 1904/early 1905, the PSP sponsored protests against the Russian Empire's war against Japan, and the antiwar campaign helped "prepare the ground" for revolution in 1905.[29]

Most Polish worker demonstrations in early 1905 were responses to local economic conditions, but the Warsaw general strike in January, in which the government killed sixty-four civilians, fueled outrage against the Russian authorities.[30] The April and May strike in Lodz pitted workers against Russian troops; in May, twenty thousand Russian troops imposed martial law in the Lodz region, and over one hundred fifty people were killed in skirmishes with the army.[31] According to Blobaum, the October–November Warsaw general strike was both a protest against factory conditions and a vehicle for socialist political demands.[32]

In the Baltic provinces, Latvian and Estonian peasants resented Russian officials for enforcing the use of Russian language in local schools and for limiting the free exercise of religion in the region through anti-proselytization laws. The peasants also chafed against German landlords' economic privilege and their virtual monopoly over land ownership. As Ascher has noted, one thousand five hundred landlords in Latvia owned more land than did 1.3 million Latvian peasants. The collapse of the social order that occurred in the Baltic area in early 1905 resulted in a de facto civil war between landlords and peasants, a war that prompted the Russian central government to send troops to suppress the rebellious peasantry.[33] This rural strife took the character of partisan warfare, in which Latvian peasants organized in bands called the Forest Brothers.

National Elections, the Duma System, and Petr Stolypin

If the strongest urban, rural, and national protests against Russia's central government had all occurred simultaneously, the regime might have completely collapsed. The army, already taxed by its commitment of troops in the Russo-Japanese War, would have been too thinly stretched to help the police suppress universal disorder. Even absent an Empire-wide crisis, the scale of popular protests in 1905 was sufficient to force the government to offer political concessions. Nicholas II signed the Manifesto of October 17 to extricate the government from danger, but he did so only because he had no other choice. One of his closest advisors, his uncle Grand Duke Nikolai Nikolaevich, told him that anything short of granting political liberties would not resolve the crisis. The grand duke rejected categorically the only other option on the table—the imposition of dictatorship.[34] In his diary entry for October 17, the tsar wrote: "I signed the manifesto at 5 p.m. After such a day, my head was spinning and my thoughts became confused. Lord, help us, make Russia tranquil again."[35]

The Manifesto of October 17 was a first step toward restoring the government's badly shaken authority, but it did not succeed at once. As Ascher has noted, "from October 18 until early December, Russian society enjoyed so much freedom that some observers actually considered the new conditions dangerous because extremists would now be able to increase their support among the masses."[36] The government finally drove the revolution into retreat by March 1906, mostly by using force.[37] A pivotal element of the government's political strategy was to sponsor national elections, the first in the Empire's long history.

The government mandated that the elections occur in four *curiae* (nobility, merchantry, peasantry, and workers), and that delegates to the legislature or Duma be selected indirectly. In most places, voters cast their ballots between late February and mid-April 1906. Because the government had arranged the franchise to avoid direct balloting, and because it trusted that peasant electors would support the monarchy and take conservative positions, it anticipated that the elections would contribute to restoration of political order.[38] Richard Pipes has asserted that Nicholas II expected national elections to produce a cooperative Duma: "It was the same mistake the French monarchy had committed in 1789 when it doubled the representation of the Third Estate in the Estates General."[39]

The government also took the precaution of rewriting Russia's Fundamental Laws. The new document affirmed the emperor's "supreme autocratic power," power purportedly derived from God. It dropped the notion that this autocratic power was "unlimited"—a crucial part of earlier conceptions of the monarchy. Unspoken but implicit in the insistence on the emperor's "autocratic power" was the claim that, since he was the source of the new Fundamental Laws, he had the right to abrogate them, if necessary.

The document created a two-chambered legislature, rather than the unicameral system promised in the Manifesto of October 17. The upper house, the State Council [*Gosudarstvennyi sovet*], consisted of appointed officials and of representatives of public bodies (notably the Church and noble assemblies). The idea was an upper house that would block any radical initiatives from the popularly elected Duma. The Fundamental Laws preserved most of emperor's key prerogatives (appointing ministers, declaring war and peace), and also granted the government the right to issue emergency decrees when the Duma was not in session. Incidentally, the government did not publicize the Fundamental Laws until *after* the Duma elections had occurred—a tactic that indicated its bad faith, but that also prevented the shape of the new political system from surfacing as the main issue in the Duma elections. On the other side of the ledger, the Fundamental Laws gave Duma members the prerogatives to vote for legislation, including the budget, to speak on political matters with immunity from prosecution, and to ask questions of ministers. These prerogatives constituted significant advances in political rights, even though they did not subordinate ministers to the Duma's authority.

But the First Duma was more radical than expected. The Kadets were the largest political group in it, with one hundred eighty-five out of four hundred seventy-eight delegates, but there were also ninety-four Trudoviks and seventeen declared socialists. According to Ascher, "the government and its supporters were stunned by the victory of the opposition."[40] The Duma had scarcely begun to meet when Prime Minister Ivan Logginovich Goremykin directed his assistant minister of internal affairs, Sergei Efimovich Kryzhanovskii, to start preparing new legislation that would change the electoral law to produce a more conservative outcome. Goremykin privately decided the Duma would have to be dismissed, and in the meantime he neither attended its sessions nor cooperated with its requests for information from ministers.[41]

Duma delegates confronted rather than collaborated with the government. In early May, they sent Nicholas II a list of demands, including items they knew to be unacceptable: abolition of the State Council; making ministers responsible to the Duma rather than to the executive; and agrarian reforms that would entail confiscating certain privately owned lands for redistribution to the peasantry. Thus, the possibility of a working relationship between Duma and government soured from both ends. In June and July 1906, a Duma commission issued an "Appeal to the People" calling for some land from private owners to be expropriated for redistribution to the peasants. The determination of many Duma members to resolve the agrarian problem in this manner alarmed the government and finally provoked it to dissolve the legislature on July 8. In response to the dissolution, the Kadets wrote a resolution—nicknamed the "Vyborg Manifesto"—asking the people not to pay taxes and not to fulfill their military obligations. The authors of the resolution misjudged the popular mood: whatever support existed for the Duma did not translate into resistance of this sort.[42] Yet the Vyborg Manifesto illustrated the gap between the government and the people's elected representatives.

After the dissolution of the First Duma, which had met for just seventy-three days of its maximum five-year term, there was no hope for a quick resolution to Russia's political crisis and no obvious way to restore even a semblance of tranquility in the shaken Empire. The Emperor pledged elections to a Second Duma, but some of his advisors suggested dictatorship as an alternative. In this fraught situation, Nicholas II asked the minister of internal affairs, Petr Arkad'evich Stolypin, a relatively obscure outsider, to act as prime minister. Stolypin remained in office from July 8, 1906 to his death on September 5, 1911, and during those five years, he dominated Russian politics. He used military courts to try revolutionaries and violent protestors. Meanwhile, he sought, albeit on his own terms, to cooperate with the Duma, and he put forward a series of reforms aimed at transforming the peasantry into a class of conservative property owners. The Socialist-Revolutionaries and Social Democrats despised him, mainly on ideological grounds but also because they feared his effectiveness. Octobrists such as Aleksandr Ivanovich Guchkov praised his intelligence and courage, and initially supported much of his program. In his vast novel on the Russian revolution, *Red Wheel* [*Krasnoe koleso*], Aleksandr Isaevich Solzhenitsyn devotes an entire chapter to Stolypin, in which he portrays the prime minister as a man of extraordinary character whose death constituted the real end of the Romanov dynasty.[43]

The most controversial measure of Stolypin's first months in office was the establishment of military field courts [*zakon o voenno-polevykh sudakh*], instituted by emergency decree on August 19, 1906. A ruthless response to the country's lawlessness, the law gave guilty parties no right to appeal their sentences. It mandated that in cases where guilt of serious criminal activity was "obvious," the case must be submitted to a field court within twenty-four hours, the military tribunal must render its verdict within forty-eight hours of the deed, and in the event of a guilty verdict, execution of the sentence must occur in twenty-four hours. The government justified this legislation by asserting that it had no choice but to respond to the country's lawlessness. Indeed, there was a wave of assassinations in late summer 1906, and robberies swept the country in fall 1906. As Ascher has noted, between spring and fall of 1906, assassinations, attacks on government buildings and sabotage destabilized Latvia; meanwhile, in Warsaw citizens lived under assault by radicals and the government was under a state of siege.[44] The decree remained in force for eight months, until April 19, 1907, and during that time field courts ordered the execution of over a thousand men. Over seven hundred more were sentenced to hard labor or prison.[45] The main effects of the field courts were to end the worst of the lawlessness in the Empire and to force the revolutionary parties to be more selective in resorting to terrorism. In the long run, as Ascher has observed, "pacification achieved by such means was bound to widen the chasm between state and society."[46]

In November 1906, acting by emergency decree, Stolypin instituted agrarian reforms designed to make Russian agriculture more efficient by encouraging intensive cultivation of consolidated plots, on the French and American models of farming. He expected that, over time, the most industrious and skillful peasant farmers would purchase lands from less committed and skillful ones, which might further raise agricultural yields. And, finally, he desired to transform peasants from dissatisfied potential insurgents into stout defenders of private property and of the government. He expected that this transformation would entail a change in peasants' *mentalité*—from seeking security within the commune through shared risk to small-scale entrepreneurship. The prime minister's "wager on the strong" thus bolstered rural capitalism and undercut agrarian socialism, striking directly at the SR's program for land socialization and nationalization based on the commune.

Stolypin knew that his agrarian program could only be implemented gradually, and that it would therefore require decades to have the desired impact. Most historians have pointed to the modest changes in land ownership and land consolidation over the reform's decade of operation. For example, according to Ascher, by 1914 roughly 20 percent of peasants had obtained ownership of their land.[47] The Soviet historian of agriculture Dubrovskii has estimated that by 1917, about 10 percent of Russian farmers tilled consolidated plots.[48] However, David Macey has argued that by 1916, over half of peasant households and two-thirds of communal households had requested the government's assistance in reordering their holdings. Macey therefore maintains that the reform was much more successful than previously thought. Many more peasants proved willing to trust the government than has been supposed, and peasant responsiveness to market conditions was more positive than many scholars have posited.[49]

The third major initiative of Stolypin entailed the dismissal of the Second Duma and the proclamation of new electoral rules on June 3, 1907. The Second Duma convened on February 20, 1907, and was dismissed on June 3 of that year—that is, just over a hundred days from its inaugural session. Its delegates included two hundred twenty-two socialists (counting over a hundred Trudoviks and sixty-five Social Democrats), but only ninety-eight Kadets (their representation decreased by more than 50 percent) and fifty-four Octobrists and Rightists. Because the Kadets lacked the political clout that they had obtained in the First Duma, and because they were chastened by the failure of the Vyborg Manifesto to mobilize popular support behind them, they adopted a less confrontational line in the Second Duma. The government for its part wanted to work with the new Duma insofar as that was consistent with the Fundamental Laws. Ascher makes the case that "both the Court and the opposition resolved to avoid the dissension that had characterized the First Duma." He adds: "Stolypin's interest in cooperating with the Duma was not based simply on his desire to institutionalize the structure of government established by the Fundamental Laws. The prime minister was convinced that his own political fate was closely linked to the fate of the Duma."[50]

Unfortunately, the Duma did not survive a series of political missteps, some by the government and others by the Duma. Stolypin waited too long to abolish the field tribunals, and he was firm in his commitment to the agrarian law of November 9, 1906. He did not communicate clearly enough the limits of his support for the Duma. At the same time, the Duma seemed hostile, rather than receptive, to Stolypin's legislative agenda, even though some of his proposals (for example, laws supporting civil liberties and religious toleration) ought to have elicited wide support. The Duma refused to renounce terror as a political weapon, for fear that doing so would open its members to criticism for not immediately ridding the country of military field tribunals. On April 16, the Armenian Social Democrat Arshak Gerasimovich Zurabov criticized the Russian army as "unfit" for the Empire's defense—a criticism that the right wing and the tsar interpreted as an insult to the army.[51] In April and May, the Duma debated whether private land should be confiscated for distribution to the peasants. This debate led Stolypin to defend his decree of November 9, 1906 and to warn the Duma that nationalization of land would provoke "social revolution."[52] The pretext for the Duma's dissolution was a meeting on May 5 of Duma Social Democrats with soldiers. The government interpreted the meeting as evidence of the SD deputies' willingness to facilitate armed insurrection. Many Duma members, while not in sympathy with the Social Democrats, objected to police raids prompted by the government's suspicion of the SDs: in their view, these raids violated the immunity of Duma members from arrest.[53]

The government announced the Duma's dissolution and the new electoral rules simultaneously. The new electoral law, issued not as an emergency decree but as an imperial manifesto, reduced the number of future Duma delegates by cutting representatives from border regions—particularly those from Central Asia, Russian Poland, and Armenia. It decreased the number of urban workers and peasants, and increased the number of property owners, particularly landed nobles. The goal was to ensure that the Third Duma would be a more conservative body and therefore more loyal to the monarchy.

Historians have offered various characterizations of Stolypin's law of June 3, 1907. Stolypin's critics have described it as a coup d'état, because it violated the Fundamental Laws and established a less democratic electoral regime than the one obtaining in 1906. Even his sympathizers admit that the law represented a change of the constitutional order, although they emphasize that the tsar, in promulgating the Fundamental Laws, had reserved the right to change them. To Stolypin, these legal questions probably mattered little. From his perspective, the First and Second Dumas had failed abysmally, so the electoral law that had created them had to be altered.

From 1907 onward, Russian national elections followed Stolypin's new rules—that is, they adhered to the "June 3 system." His gamble that the new rules would produce more conservative Dumas paid off. In the Third Duma (which remained in session, with interruptions, from November 1, 1907 to June 9, 1912), his main allies were ninety-six moderate rightists and one hundred fifty-four Octobrists; in all, according to Ascher, the "government could reasonably count on the support of about three hundred deputies out of a total of four hundred forty-one."[54] Many delegates to the Third Duma owned substantial property, either landed estates or factories. Other delegates were former military men or retired civil servants. There were fifty members of the clergy, most (but not all) of them monarchists advocating a strong central government.[55] In the Fourth Duma (which met in five sessions, with long interruptions, from November 15, 1912 to February 25, 1917), the government's support initially came from two hundred eighteen Nationalists, moderate rightists, and Octobrists—that is, its natural supporters constituted about half of the Duma's deputies. However, during the Great War, many Octobrists expressed dissatisfaction with the government's handling of the Duma. After 1915, a number of them joined the Progressive Bloc—a group critical of the executive branch—thus diminishing the pro-government forces.[56]

In both the Third and Fourth Dumas, there was a substantial group of "hard" rightists—fifty of them in the Third Duma, and as many as sixty-five in the Fourth Duma. As a general rule, the hard rightists followed Nicholas II's political program when he explicitly signaled his desires, but during the Third Duma, they sometimes sharply criticized Stolypin and elements of his program. In the Third and Fourth Dumas, the hard rightists often collaborated with conservatives in the upper house of the legislature, the State Council, which gave them a political weight greater than their numbers in the Duma itself.[57] In certain cases, therefore, the hard rightists had enough clout to block the government's programs. In debates, they often clashed with the left, polarizing Duma discourse in the process. Thus, the moderately conservative Duma chambers did not necessarily make life easier for Stolypin and his successors.

Stolypin positioned himself as a reformer and simultaneously as defender of the Russian monarchy, of a strong central government, and of a "great Russia." Although he made dozens of policy speeches to the Duma, he was likely most candid about his plans for reforming Russia in 1911, when he disclosed his program to Aleksandr Vladimirovich Zenkovskii.[58] His ideas included improving conditions of the working class, especially through social insurance; expanding zemstvo activities and making the zemstvos more inclusive; working to create universal education and universal medical care; improving relations among the nationalities in Russia, and simultaneously improving relations among different religious groups, including the Jews. He wanted to increase the prime minister's authority over ministers by building a "unified government." He cautioned Russian diplomats against military interventions in Europe and Asia, and called for an international organization to adjudicate disputes among nations.[59] It is easy to see why this program alarmed certain conservatives and the hard rightists: in their view, it was dangerous to make concessions to workers, the zemstvos, the non-Orthodox. Many of them, however, tended to agree with Stolypin's pacific foreign policy: after the debacle of the Russo-Japanese War, they were not eager to embark on another foreign adventure.

The biggest test of Stolypin's political program occurred in 1910–11, when he introduced a bill extending zemstvo self-government to the western provinces that lacked it. The prime minister wanted greater uniformity of administration across the Empire, and he rightly viewed the situation on the western periphery as anomalous. To accomplish his goal, he was willing to change the zemstvo electoral formula in the western provinces to produce zemstvos with more noble landowners than peasant delegates, and more Great Russians than delegates from other nationalities. He worried that, without certain stipulations, the western zemstvos might include too many peasants, and might be dominated by Polish landowners instead of Russian ones. However, in the view of many Russian conservatives, Stolypin's concessions did not go far enough to protect noble landowners and Great Russian interests. Although the Duma voted to adopt Stolypin's bill, the State Council, mobilized by conservatives and the ultra-right, defeated it in March 1911. Stolypin responded to this defeat by tendering his resignation to the tsar. When Nicholas refused to accept it, the prime minister demanded that the tsar allow him to prorogue the Duma and to issue the government's plan for western zemstvos as an emergency decree. He also asked Nicholas to authorize the temporary exile from Petersburg of the bill's two most vocal conservative critics. This ultimatum may have been a political blunder, but Stolypin thought it necessary to bolster his position.

In the backroom showdown over Stolypin's resignation, the dowager empress Maria Fedorovna supported him against the tsar, while Nicholas's wife Aleksandra Fedorovna took the tsar's part against the prime minister.[60] In the end, Nicholas bowed to Stolypin's ultimatum, but perhaps never forgave the prime minister for it, even though in April 1911 he bestowed on Stolypin the Aleksandr Nevskii medal for service to the Empire.[61] By late summer the prime minister was suffering from bad health and anxiety over his political enemies. He told the Octobrist Aleksandr Ivanovich Guchkov and State Secretary Vladimir Nikolaevich Kokovtsov that he expected to be assassinated.

On September 1, 1911, Stolypin was shot at the Kiev Municipal Theater. The police immediately apprehended the assassin, Dmitrii Grigor'evich Bogrov. Bogrov was an anarchist with ties to Socialist-Revolutionaries, but also had been on the payroll of the political police, the *Okhrana*. To many contemporaries, it seemed suspicious that Bogrov had received a ticket admitting him to the theater from a minder in the *Okhrana*.[62] We do not know whether the assassin acted on his own initiative or in collaboration with authorities. The Soviet historian Aron Iakovlevich Avrekh has asserted that the assassination was the work of the police.[63] Taking the contrary view, Ascher has argued that Bogrov perhaps "decided once and for all to throw in his lot with the radical left." Ascher ascribes the police role in providing Bogrov with a ticket solely to the "gullibility" of Bogrov's minder.[64] In 1911–12, a government commission under the chairmanship of Maksimilian Ivanovich Trusevich investigated security arrangements in Kiev surrounding Stolypin's assassination and accused four officials of criminal negligence in the affair.[65] In 1912, the tsar blocked the trial of these officials. From available evidence, Nicholas II was "indifferent to Stolypin's fate" and Empress Aleksandra was "relieved" over his disappearance from the country's leadership.[66]

Stolypin's assassination demonstrated that the Third of June System had only incompletely masked the Empire's profound polarization under a veneer of normality. Historians of the Old Regime have long debated whether or not prewar Russia was headed for revolution. Leopold Haimson maintains that workers were alienated from the government and society, that workers mobilized themselves to confront the regime beginning in 1905, and again in 1914 in a general strike, and that their political protests were intensified by the revival of the opposition to the regime "among the higher strata of urban society."[67] Haimson also notes that in June 1914, in the wake of the general strike, the government was preparing to dissolve the Duma and to transform it into a consultative body.[68] In reaction to the government's threatened "coup," opinion in the Kadet party split between left Kadets, who recommended confronting the government by revolutionary means, and right Kadets, who sought to avoid militancy on the grounds that it would precipitate the Duma's dissolution.[69] Meanwhile, Wayne Dowler has argued that Russian society on the eve of the war was in fact pluralistic and not starkly divided between state and society in the ways that Haimson had supposed.[70] Dowler was therefore an "optimist" regarding the possibility of Russia's peaceful evolution. More recently, Irina Glebova has asserted: "The entire period from 1907 to 1913 can be treated as a reaction to the revolution [of 1905–07]. The country's peaceful renewal advanced under the banner of reformism. . . . The scope of liberty expanded, encompassing various spheres and social strata. Liberty in Russia was starting to assume a critical mass, to affect our stubbornly unfree society. At the same time, a tendency toward prohibition, toward limitation of liberty made itself evident (the government regarded the reestablishment of order as tantamount to return to the prerevolutionary situation of 'all-powerful autocracy'). In general, these [two] tendencies balanced each other."[71] In spite of this "balance" between freedom and unfreedom, Glebova considered the Empire's direction on the whole positive, with 1905 "pointing the way forward to the future"—that is, toward liberty and progress.[72]

War and Revolutions

By 1914, Russia had been a Great Power for two centuries. Over that stretch of time, imperial statesmen had concluded that the requirements of waging war on a large scale included heavy taxation of the populace; brutal, if not efficient, conscription of troops and military materiel; extensive military planning and organization; and the ability to sustain popular morale. The sheer growth of government had led to effective taxation, conscription, and strategic planning mechanisms; but however much energy the government devoted to propagandizing its military objectives, it possessed no magic elixir to guarantee popular support in wartime. During the Russo-Japanese war of 1904–05, military reversals quickly diminished the government's prestige—a process that accelerated the 1905 revolution.[73] We know from many sources, including Olfer'ev, that the loss of the Russian fleet at Tsushima produced deep mourning, even in the Winter Palace. The ongoing military disaster reminded acute observers of a deep pattern in Russian history—namely, that wars had often led to domestic reforms. Examples abounded from the time of Peter I and Catherine II, which generated wide-ranging administrative reforms; from the early days of Aleksandr I, who instituted the ministerial system of administration and who contemplated abolishing serfdom; the post-Crimean trauma that led to the abolition of serfdom; and the turbulence following the Russo-Turkish war of 1877–78 that contributed to the reformer Loris-Melikov's "dictatorship of the heart." There had also been moments, such as the early days of the Napoleonic invasion in 1812, when the government had feared military defeat would trigger social revolution. Therefore, the rapid succession of events after 1904—unsuccessful war against Japan, revolution against autocratic rule, the Stolypin reforms—constituted a confirmation of an old pattern, but also a warning of what might await Russia in the event of a European war in 1914.

In spite of the domestic dangers, on March 19, 1909, following Austria's high-handed 1908 decision to annex Bosnia and Herzegovina, the Russian Council of Ministers debated the advisability of going to war against Austria and Germany. As the historian Dominic Lieven notes, "all of those present were aware of the domestic political dangers of war, but in the absence of the minister responsible—in other words, Stolypin, the minister of the interior—this issue was not raised." Instead, the Russian ministers decided against confronting Austria. The decision rested on financial grounds (the war would be expensive), on military grounds (the Russian army was in no condition to fight the Germans), and diplomatic ones (Russian intervention would not be supported by the British or French governments).[74]

The Bosnian annexation crisis left the Russians chastened, but also determined to ready their army for a future confrontation with Austria and Germany. Lieven has concluded that the results of the annexation crisis were "catastrophic, wrecking Russo-Austrian relations to a degree that cast a shadow right down to July 1914."[75] Indeed, during the Balkan crises of 1912–13, senior Austrian and German diplomats understood that the Russian leadership would probably have accepted war if it were necessary to avoid a repetition of the earlier humiliation.[76]

The Russian decision to fight Austria and Germany in 1914 has been exhaustively analyzed by historians of the Empire. In the Soviet era, scholars tended to see the 1914 Russian leadership as participants in the imperialist competition to master Europe and to identify the Russians' protection of Serbia as a flashpoint in relations with Austria and Germany, but also to stress Germany's special responsibility for initiating the conflict in July 1914 through its "blank check" supporting Austrian intervention against Serbia.[77] As Joshua Sanborn notes, the Soviet approach to the war's origins is broadly consistent with that of the important German scholar Fritz Fischer, who lays a heavy onus on German imperialism in triggering the war.[78] Among historians of Russia in the West, at least until recently, the dominant interpretation has been the one championed by Dominic Lieven, who stresses the Russian leadership's acute anxiety over being forced by Germany and Austria to fight. In Sanborn's summary, Lieven contends: "They [the Russians] went to war reluctantly, because they felt that any further failures [after 1908 and 1912] to protect client states or [Russia's] own prestige would unacceptably and permanently damage Russia's imperial prestige and place at the table of the Great Powers.[79]

In 2011, Lieven's view fell under challenge by Sean McMeekin, who contends that Russian leaders were aggressors, that they manipulated events in 1914 in order to achieve the long-term objective of seizing control of the Turkish Straits and establishing Russia as the preeminent power in southern Europe and the Middle East.[80] McMeekin's interpretation harmonizes, though not perfectly, with that of Christopher M. Clark, who contends that responsibility for the Great War was widely shared, especially by Serbia, Austria, and Germany, but also by Russia and its Western allies.[81] The notion that responsibility for the war was dispersed has seemingly become established among scholars, but not everyone has accepted the proposition that Russian policy makers triggered the war by their decision on July 24 and 26 to begin partial mobilization of the armed forces.[82]

In 2015, Lieven published another book, this one based on new archival research in post-Soviet Russia. As in his earlier volume, he stresses Russian anxiety generated by the Empire's humiliation during the Bosnian annexation crisis and the Balkan wars. Lieven also underlines Russian nervousness over the future of Ukraine, where a secessionist movement rooted in Austrian Galicia threatened to spread to Russian-held territory. Furthermore, he acknowledges that in early 1914—that is, before the July crisis—the tsar gave "priority to Ottoman affairs and in particular to the Straits." In this respect, according to Lieven, Nicholas II "was typical of the Russian policy makers, to all of whom the Turkish situation seemed unstable and unpredictable."[83] However, Lieven still places the major responsibility for the July events on Austria, whose ultimatum to Serbia made confrontation with Russia likely, and on Germany, which supported the Austrian ultimatum.[84]

For our purposes, the crucial consideration is the interconnections between Russian domestic circumstances and its 1914 decision to fight. In February 1914, the rightist Petr Nikolaevich Durnovo wrote a memorandum warning that one cost of European war might be revolution at home. In Durnovo's opinion, a long European war would undermine the morale of the Russian army and thereby make it ineffective in resisting revolution at home. Thus, he put other policy makers in Petersburg on notice that a conflict with Germany and Austria might be fatal to the Empire.[85] In July 1914, Durnovo's warning was not so much forgotten as ignored. The Russian ambassador to Sweden, Anatolii Vasil'evich Nekliudov, suspected that war with Germany would lead to defeat and revolution; nevertheless, he concluded that Russia could not bow to the Austrian-German ultimatum.[86] Minister of Internal Affairs Nikolai Alekseevich Maklakov was convinced that war against Germany would bolster the socialist cause in Russia, because "revolutionary ideas are dearer to the masses than a victory over Germany." However, Maklakov resigned himself to the prospect of war, because "one cannot escape one's fate."[87] These contemporary assessments suggest that in July 1914, Russian policy makers knew that European war was an enormous risk to a fragile domestic order—a risk they accepted because they could not contemplate the alternative of repeated international humiliation.

How to explain this behavior? Minister of Agriculture Aleksandr Vasil'evich Krivoshein, at the pivotal June 24 meeting of the conference of ministers, argued that Russia's earlier policy of accommodation with the

Germans and Austria had not succeeded, and therefore the only way to deter war was to risk it by standing up to the Central Powers. It would be worse for Russia domestically and internationally to pursue accommodation, only to be dragged into war later.[88] Another explanation may be that Russian leaders attached more importance to foreign policy considerations than to domestic ones. A final explanation may be Nicholas II's tendency toward a kind of mysticism: he believed God would show Russia how to escape disaster. Perhaps the presence of Grigorii Efimovich Rasputin in the empress's entourage and the Empress Aleksandra's own religious disposition bolstered the tsar's mysticism.

In the event, the war's sheer destructiveness strained Russia's fragile social order to its limit. According to the French historian Alexandre Sumpf, between 1914 and 1918 Russian authorities conscripted fifteen and a half million men between eighteen and forty-three years old to fight, out of twenty-six million men of service age—that is, nearly 60 percent of the eligible citizens. Over five million men were mobilized in 1914, with five million more in 1915. Because the authorities worried about the loyalty of the troops, they avoided conscription of people from the Caucasus, the Far North, and Central Asia; and they limited the number of Tatars, Bashkirs, and troops drawn from the Baltic provinces.[89] Thus, the conscription burden fell disproportionately on inhabitants of central Russia, Ukraine, and Belorussia. By 1918, Russians had sustained over nine hundred thousand military deaths, and over five million casualties (2.8 million wounded and 2.3 million felled by disease). Of the casualties, probably over a million were completely disabled.[90] Among the disabled, many suffered from mental illnesses, and virtually all of these went untreated.[91]

To the devastation mentioned above, we must add the economic and social losses incurred from the imprisonment in various countries of between two and a half million and three million Russian soldiers. Some were held for short periods, but many remained in detention from September 1914 through 1917. In many cases, Russian authorities and Russian civilian organizations such as the Red Cross had no access to the names of Russian prisoners, and communication with these POWs was virtually impossible. Sumpf has suggested that Russian POWs became "uprooted" or "forcibly excised" [*déracinés*] from their homeland.[92] Given the horrific losses of human resources due to death, injury, disability, and imprisonment, it was unlikely that Russia could have endured the war without significant social change. Even if we make the counterfactual assumption that the imperial army should have won the war, the fruits of this victory would have been but ashes in the mouths of the populace.

In the western periphery, the occupying Russian army created a stream of refugees consisting partly of groups assumed to be hostile to Russia, primarily ethnic Germans and Jews, and partly of peasants, who were regarded as inconvenient to the war effort. These refugees abandoned their homes and loaded their belongings into carts, clogging the roads in a vain attempt to escape persecution and deprivation. Sumpf has estimated that peasants across the Empire lost as much as 5 percent of their mobile wealth in the process of flight.[93] Soldiers in the army not infrequently treated ethnic Germans as enemies of Russia, and regarded Jews as enemies, parasites, or spies.[94] The military authorities removed Germans from certain areas in the Baltic provinces; the Petrograd military district was the site of ethnic cleansing on supposed security grounds.[95]

Needless to say, the army's treatment of minority nationalities and, for that matter, of adherents of non-Orthodox religious confessions, did nothing to endear these groups to the Empire. Ukraine had long had its share of nationalists agitating for either autonomy within or independence from Russia. During the war, the German government did everything it could, short of stirring up a revolution, to bolster Ukrainian separatist consciousness. By early 1917, pro-independence nationalism had taken strong root, so that by mid-summer 1917 Ukrainian leaders were in a position to resist Petrograd's control. Similarly in Poland, pressure for independence increased sharply after the great retreat of the Russian army in 1915. Under Józef Pilsudski, as many as twenty-five thousand Poles gathered to take arms against Russia. In July 1916, Pilsudski's legions confronted Russian troops at Kostiuchnówka, after which he asked the Central Powers to support Polish independence from Russia. The Baltic provinces and Finland also witnessed burgeoning nationalist movements. In the Baltics, until mid-1917 the emphasis was on political autonomy from Russia, but later a strong pro-independence campaign developed. In Finland, a powerful independence movement had surfaced even before 1914, although the tsarist government had suppressed it with difficulty. The nationalist faction reasserted itself in 1917 as the authority of the Russian central government diminished.[96] The appearance during the war of nationalist movements on the western periphery of the Russian Empire was both an accelerant of the revolutionary activity in Russia (because it facilitated the collapse of the central governmental authority) and a pre-condition of the Russian civil war, or civil wars, after 1917. Joshua Sanborn provocatively but probably rightly describes the Russian revolution as a process of "decolonization," in which, particularly after mid-1917, nationalities across Russia sought some form of local sovereignty.[97] Nationalist independence movements helped shape the civil war in many places in the Empire, but especially in Poland, Ukraine, and the Caucasus; regional autonomy movements also impacted Siberia and other areas where the central government's control had historically been weak.

According to Lieven, even as these fissiparous tendencies developed, the Russian army showed itself to be "in general superior to the Austrian," but also "inferior to the German [army]." Although the Russian army suffered a number of defeats (the Tannenberg debacle in 1914, the Gorlice-Tarnów rout of 1915), and although it endured dark days during the "great retreat" of 1915, the army did not lose the war in battle. Instead, support for the military gradually collapsed behind the lines. Economic factors, such as inflation in the cities, the inadequacy of railroad stock, and the food shortages of late 1916/early 1917 hastened this collapse. After a respite in labor unrest at the beginning of the war, the labor movement revived in the first half of 1915, with a wave of economic strikes.[98] Labor unrest was driven by many developments, but the fall of real wages during the war was an important factor.[99] Over time, political causes joined economic ones: in the cities, anger developed over the continuing war, especially from mid-1915 on.

Bad political decisions by the government further poisoned the atmosphere. By mid-1915, the military situation had deteriorated, as Russian troops retreated under fire. Duma delegates argued that, under the circumstances, the executive should treat the Duma as a full partner in the war effort—a position bolstered by the fact that since 1914, public organizations like the Union of Zemstvos and Union of Towns had been supplying medical care and auxiliary war service.[100] Liberals in the Duma argued that educated society had come of age, that it had fully supported the war effort and therefore deserved the government's trust. Kadets, Octobrists, and some moderate conservatives joined the Progressive Bloc, whose main demand was for a government acceptable to the Duma and to the broader public. The tsar's failure in August and September 1915 to install such a government, his dismissal of three ministers who sought to collaborate with the Progressive Bloc, and his simultaneous decision to assume command of the armed forces destroyed the hope of a wartime partnership between the Duma and the government. By preventing an alliance between the government and the Duma in August 1915, Nicholas "made a revolution virtually unavoidable."[101] According to Sumpf, the government "appeared more and more isolated and defenseless against the powerful currents that assailed it from every side."[102]

From 1915 onward, certain Duma members no longer sought compromise with the government. Even before the August showdown, Aleksandr Ivanovich Guchkov had campaigned to discredit war minister Sukhomlinov as a traitor. In September 1915, the conservative Kadet Vasilii Alekseevich Maklakov published an allegorical article accusing Russia's "mad chauffeur" (the tsar) of incompetence in maneuvering his "automobile" (Russia) down a dangerous mountain road.[103] The tale implied both the peril of revolution and the helplessness of responsible people in the Duma to head it off. In November 1916, Pavel Nikolaevich Miliukov denounced Russian war decisions as "stupidity or treason." Meanwhile, the 1916 appointment by Nicholas of Aleksandr Dmitrievich Protopopov as minister of internal affairs was strongly criticized by Duma's liberals, who considered Protopopov "insane."[104] As Mel'gunov has noted, in 1916 opposition to the government sometimes took the shape of conspiracy against Nicholas and Aleksandra.[105] Thus in the period from late summer 1915 to winter 1916, the political climate went from bad to worse.

The February/March 1917 revolution issued from the economic and political causes enumerated above but also from related sources: mutinies against the established order on the part of reserve soldiers in the capital, the incompetence of Petrograd security units, and finally, the decision by senior army generals to support the idea of the tsar's abdication or forcible removal from office.[106] In a general way, as Lieven observes, "Russia's World War I went roughly as Petr Durnovo, Russia's most intelligent 'reactionary' leader, had predicted in his February 1914 memorandum"—that is, the war weakened political authority and thereby opened the door to revolution. "A dynasty that had ruled for three hundred years departed almost overnight and with a whimper rather than a bang, because very few Russians were willing to defend it."[107]

Like every major political event with a wide spectrum of participants, the February/March revolution had different meanings, depending upon the angle of judgment. As the historian S. A. Smith observes, "for the lower classes, liberty and democracy signaled nothing short of a social revolution that would entail the comprehensive destruction of the old order and the construction of a new way of life in accordance with justice and freedom." For them, the first order of business was resolving social and economic problems, such as the bread shortages in Petrograd and the rampant inflation affecting the cities; or in the case of soldiers and sailors, ending "degrading treatment" by officers. As Smith has noted, the revolution was for the masses "only secondarily about questions of law and political representation."[108] The lower classes pursued their aims through national councils or "soviets" [*sovety*], like the Petrograd Soviet of Workers, Peasants and Soldiers Deputies, and through hundreds of local and regional councils. They also availed themselves of public agencies like the zemstvos, which they sought to "democratize," as well as of sympathetic ministers in the Provisional Government.

For Duma delegates, the achievement of justice and political agency were central objectives. Duma leaders engineered the emperor's abdication because they sought to take control of a war effort that, in their opinion, had been badly misdirected. They also saw Nicholas II as a symbol of the autocracy that many of them had sought to abolish in 1905–07. Although the Duma leadership undoubtedly viewed itself as a truly patriotic elite legitimated by elections and therefore sanctioned by the voice of the people, its attitudes had also been shaped by years of frustrated powerlessness, inept conspiracy, and hatred of the government. People like the Duma chairman Mikhail Vladimirovich Rodzianko now hoped to exercise power at long last, in the name of democracy and the rule of law. Among the eleven ministers in the first cabinet of the Provisional Government, the chairman was Georgii Evgen'evich L'vov, the leader of the All-Russia Zemstvo Union. The strongest of the others were probably the foreign minister Pavel Nikolaevich Miliukov, the long-time leader of the Kadets, and the war minister Aleksandr Ivanovich Guchkov, the Octobrist. Although

L'vov had a reputation as a "democrat," he, like Miliukov and Guchkov, was strong-willed and no stranger to political conspiracy. As the historian Vitalii Ivanovich Startsev demonstrates, members of the first cabinet of the Provisional Government did not take power "with shaking hands," but did so eagerly. In Startsev's view, the Provisional Government was nothing less than a "bourgeois dictatorship."[109]

In Petrograd early in 1917, there was an informal power-sharing arrangement—"dual power" [*dvoevlastie*]—in which the Petrograd Soviet and Provisional Government vied for dominance. This contentious power constellation rather took the edge off the "bourgeois dictatorship," if there actually was such a thing. Outside the capital, Smith notes, "dual power was less in evidence." In the provinces and towns of Russia, the Provisional Government had more parties with which to negotiate and therefore had a more complex task in implementing its decisions. By late 1917 in the countryside, "the revolution substantially reduced the degree of interference in village life by external authority."[110] Put another way, the February/March revolution was but an earlier stage in the disintegration of the old order, a step toward what some Russians considered "anarchy."

From a legal perspective, the key documents in the history of the February/March revolution were Nicholas II's abdication on March 2/15 and the "Provisional Government's Declaration of Its Composition and Tasks" on March 3/16, 1917.

In the abdication decree, Nicholas, "in agreement with the State Duma, recognized it as proper to abdicate the throne of the Russian state and to lay down sovereign authority." Nicholas abdicated in favor of his brother, Grand Duke Mikhail Aleksandrovich, who, Nicholas declared, should "guide affairs of the state in complete and inviolable unity with representatives of the people in legislative institutions, on principles that will be established by them [these institutions] in the form of an inviolable oath."[111] This decree, if it had been respected by the grand duke, would have created a constitutional monarchy; however, Mikhail Aleksandrovich refused to take the throne, thereby making possible a different arrangement of power.

The Declaration of March 3 was issued by the Provisional Committee of Members of the State Duma [*Vremennyi komitet chlenov Gosudarstvennoi Dumy*], "with the assistance and sympathy of the capital's soldiers and populace in this moment of victory over the dark forces of the old regime." The declaration promised "a more stable arrangement of executive authority." It named the ministers who would serve in the new cabinet. It also pledged the cabinet would "be guided by the following principles:

1. Full and immediate amnesty for everyone accused of political or religious offenses, including terrorist attacks, military mutinies, rural crimes and so on;
2. Freedom of speech, of the press, of association, of meetings, and of strikes, and freedom to disseminate political liberties to soldiers within limits permitted by military operations;
3. Abolition of all forms of discrimination based on Estate, confessional, and national identity;
4. Immediate preparations to summon a Constituent Assembly on the basis of universal, equal, secret, and direct voting, which will determine the future form of government and of the country's constitution;
5. Replacement of the police by a popular militia with an elective element, subordinated to organs of local self-government;
6. Elections to bodies of local self-government on the basis of universal, direct, equal, and secret voting;
7. Non-disarmament and non-expulsion from Petrograd of military units that had participated in the revolutionary movement;
8. Under conditions of strict observance of military discipline in authorized units and during the discharge of military service, the lifting of all restrictions for soldiers in the exercise of civil rights afforded other citizens. The Provisional Government considers its duty to take into account, but not to delay because of military circumstances, the implementation of the above reforms and measures."[112]

According to Startsev, the eight points of the Declaration of March 3 "were not the result of unilateral action by ministers," but were rather the product of negotiations between the Petrograd Soviet and the Temporary Duma Committee. However, the introduction to the declaration was "in all probability" the consequence of the Duma Committee's desire to establish a cabinet independent of the Petrograd Soviet.[113] In other words, the declaration was both one of the earliest fruits of dual power and an illustration of its danger. According to historian Andrei Borisovich Nikolaev, the Declaration of March 3 was also a constitutional document in that it established the lineaments of what he has termed the "Third of March" system. In Nikolaev's opinion, that system consisted of five characteristics:

1. Preservation of the principle of governmental continuity, insofar as Prime Minister L'vov had been appointed prime minister by Nicholas II, and also insofar as the new government pledged to maintain the Fundamental Laws;
2. Recognition of the legitimacy of the Provisional Government by the Temporary Duma Committee and also by the Executive Committee of the Petrograd Soviet;
3. The existence of the Provisional Government without legal responsibility to any other entity;
4. Acceptance in principle of a constitutional monarchy and parliamentary system;
5. Resolution of the future form of Russian government by the Constituent Assembly.

In April, the system was altered by attribution of sovereign authority to the Temporary Committee of the State Duma, subject to the action of the State Duma and the State Council and under the operation of a cabinet responsible to the Temporary Committee, until the convocation of the Constituent Assembly.[114]

The Third of March system began to fall apart virtually from the moment of its genesis. In April, it lost the support of Rodzianko and of the Temporary Committee of the State Duma. When L'vov was forced to resign as prime minister in mid-summer, the system lost whatever continuity with the tsar it had preserved. On September 1, the new prime minister Aleksandr Kerenskii departed sharply from the system's original assertion of political legitimacy by proclaiming Russia a republic. This proclamation violated the continuity of the state by severing any ties with the monarchy and with the elected Duma. The final blow to the March 3 system was the October/November revolution.[115]

Nikolaev's model of the Third of March system alerts us to the kind of political compromise that might have been possible a decade earlier, in the revolutionary years of 1905–07. If Nicholas II had renounced his autocratic prerogatives fully and completely in 1905, a constitutional monarchy might have taken shape around a bicameral system, with political leadership in the legislature coming from the Kadets and Octobrists. Installation of this system might have required establishment of a cabinet responsible to the Duma, and it might also have entailed conceding sovereignty to the lower house of the legislature, which represented *vox populi*. Probably the convocation of a constitutional convention, of the Constituent Assembly, would have been an impossible concession in 1905–07; however, stipulating circumstances for the assembly's convocation might have been in the realm of possibility. (Think here of American rules for amendment of the constitution, which include procedures for calling a constitutional convention.) By highlighting this missed opportunity, Nikolaev has underlined the tsar's earlier stubbornness and even political blindness.

At the same time, Nikolaev's model illustrates how evanescent was support for the arrangement of March 3. That the Third of March system came undone within a few months makes sense, because the forces of change in Russia had never been united. The transformation of sovereignty in February/March 1917 licensed nearly unlimited political expression and assembly, and therefore enabled Russians to speak in their own names authoritatively as they could not have done earlier. Because the "center" of the political spectrum in Russia was revolutionary, pressure from below pushed the Provisional Government, the Petrograd Soviet, and popular sentiment to the left in the months following the February/March events. The October/November 1917 revolution that put the Bolsheviks in power was a manifestation of that natural shifting of sentiment. It is therefore a serious mistake to suppose, as certain historians have done, that the October revolution can best be interpreted as a "coup d'état."

Smith argues that, "for the privileged classes, the overthrow of autocracy had been an act of self-preservation necessitated by the need to bring victory in war and engender a renaissance of the Russian people."[116] On the basis of the Third of March model, the thinness of this claim is obvious: the Temporary Committee of the State Duma tried to find a parliamentary path forward consistent with public aspirations since 1905, and it took immense risks in doing so (negotiating with the Executive Committee of the Petrograd Soviet, pledging to convoke a constitutional convention). One can call the Third of March system "an act of self-preservation" in the tautological sense that every political plan is self-regarding, but the description is false if it is meant to imply the Third of March system was "conservative."

Nikolaev's model of the first revolutionary "constitution" of 1917 is not so much mistaken, as it is incomplete. The Petrograd politicians who fashioned the Third of March system incorrectly assumed that, because they constituted the Duma leadership and parleyed with the Petrograd Soviet, they could claim legitimacy across the Empire. As we have shown above, however, the military presence in the western periphery had alienated much of the populace in Ukraine, the Baltic provinces, and Poland. The degree of this alienation was a new development that undercut the manufactured consensus of the prewar Duma election.

Nikolaev's model also fails to reckon with the army. The tsar's abdication decree had mentioned the revolutionary transformation of common soldiers: points 1, 2, 7, and 8 had all demanded recognition, in various ways, of soldiers' rights, including the propriety of mutinies before February/March 1917. The decree had therefore broadened the body politic in a fashion unprecedented in wartime. Nicholas's abdication, perhaps his final "legacy" to Russian military men, had belatedly extended to them a share in the country's sovereignty. At the same time, the abdication decree implicitly recognized that the country's generals in Stavka had acted as protectors of the nation in compelling him to abdicate. The decree linked "the fate of Russia, the honor of our heroic army, the people's welfare, and the entire future of our Fatherland" as justifications for his action.[117] Therefore, Nikolaev's model of the early revolutionary "constitutional" arrangement should have specified that the army high command acted as "co-sovereigns" with the Temporary Committee of the Duma and that common soldiers stood in it as both symbols of national greatness and repositories of political rights.

Between late summer and early fall 1917, the Provisional Government's authority collapsed in Latvia and at the Kronstadt Naval Base, and then in Petrograd. This set of developments cannot be attributed to Bolshevik initiatives alone, or, for that matter, to the efforts of any single political faction or social group. Everywhere popular sentiment had shifted against the war, and common people had become exasperated with Aleksandr Fedorovich Kerenskii's leadership. This disaffection, intensely felt in urban areas, also strongly affected the army and naval forces, which increasingly lost their cohesion and no longer served as reliable partners with the Provisional Government. The historian Martin Malia has described the situation in late 1917 as a "descent into political anarchy."[118] The collapse of the Third of March system and the splintering of authority in Petrograd and elsewhere, which was its symptom, were preconditions of October/November revolution but also of the civil wars that followed it.

Civil Wars

The civil wars waged in the former Russian Empire from the October/November revolution to 1921 had their origins in the process of decolonization begun earlier, the struggle over sovereignty between civil society and the army high command that commenced in February/March 1917, and political disagreements among the forces of change that had been unresolved since the revolutions of 1905–07. All these causes were manifest in the struggle for mastery in Ukraine and Crimea from late 1917 onward, with the added complication that the struggle occurred in appalling conditions: a failed economy, military defeat, disintegration of the army, German occupation of Ukraine from March to November 1918, and French occupation of Crimea from December 1918 to April 1919. By every account, the civil wars entailed catastrophic demographic losses. The historian Boris Vadimovich Sokolov has calculated the number of excess deaths in the civil war at over five million; meanwhile, the demographer Boris Tsesarevich Urlanis has estimated that there were eight hundred thousand military deaths, and roughly eight million civilian deaths.[119]

From our point of view, the civil conflicts can be seen as mechanisms for settling early twentieth-century social and ideological disputes. It is a mistake to define the wars exclusively as Red–White struggles (there were many other forces at arms), and erroneous to think of the White Army as resisting revolution in the name of the "old order." Only extreme rightist elements in the White Army would have defended prerevolutionary political institutions or antebellum social arrangements. Many prominent White leaders had taken part in forcing Nicholas II to abdicate the throne, and supported something like a return to the March 3 declaration as a basis for political life. It is of course reductive to regard the overall outcome of the civil wars as a "Red" victory, even if by 1922 the Bolshevik government had managed to consolidate authority in their wake. Even in 1922, many questions underlying the civil wars remained unanswered; indeed, that was why Bolshevik leaders thought Soviet power was still insecure after the civil wars had come to an end.

Olfer'ev observed firsthand the violence of the 1905–07 revolution, the fashioning of the Stolypin system, the coming of the Great War, the collapse of the imperial state in early 1917, and the first episodes of civil wars in Ukraine and Crimea. He watched as these events unfolded and tried to understand their historical logic. His memoirs are precious because of his personal perspective on events, and because of his reflections concerning his own motivations. Like Lev Tolstoy's fictional character Pierre Bezukhov, Olfer'ev was a privileged observer of a bloody, historically pivotal era, one that has forever altered Russia and has also left its indelible mark on us.

Notes

1. For an overview of the nuances in rural relations, see David Moon, "Peasants and Agriculture," in *The Cambridge History of Russia*, vol. 2, ed. Dominic Lieven, *Imperial Russia, 1689–1917* (Cambridge, New York: The Cambridge University Press, 2006), 369–93.
2. Abraham Ascher, *The Revolution of 1905: Russia in Disarray* (Stanford, CA: Stanford University Press, 1988), 11–12.
3. Quoted in Ascher, *Russia in Disarray,* 12.
4. On the so-called "Zubatovshchina," see Jeremiah Schneiderman, *Sergei Zubatov and Revolutionary Marxism: The Struggle for the Working Class in Tsarist Russia* (Ithaca, NY: Cornell University Press, 1976); and Sergei Vladimirovich Medvedev, *Eksperiment Zubatova: legalizatsiia rabochego dvizheniia v pervye gody XX v.* (Moscow: Universitet Dmitriia Pozharskogo, 2018).
5. See Edward H. Judge, *Plehve: Repression and Reform in Imperial Russia, 1902–1904* (Syracuse: NY: Syracuse University Press, 1983).
6. For the "Vitte system," see Theodore H. Von Laue, *Sergei Witte and the Industrialization of Russia* (New York: Columbia University Press, 1963); for Vitte as a statesman, see Boris Vasil'evich Anan'ich and Rafael Sholomovich Ganelin, *Sergei Iul'evich Vitte i ego vremia* (Sankt-Peterburg: Dmitrii Bulanin, 1999). A very interesting biography of

Vitte is Francis W. Wcislo, *Tales of Imperial Russia: The Life and Times of Sergei Witte, 1849–1915* (Oxford: Oxford University Press, 2011).

7. Sergei Iul'evich Vitte, *Samoderzhanie i zemstvo: Konfidentsial'naia zapiska Ministra finansov Stats-Sekretaria S. Iu. Vitte (1899)*, 2nd ed. (Stuttgart: Verlag und Druck von J.H.W. Dietz, 1903), 1–224, here 198.
8. See Iurii Il'ich Kir'ianov, *Russkoe sobranie. 1900–1917* (Moscow: ROSSPEN, 2003); idem., *Pravye partii v Rossii. 1911–1917* (Moscow: ROSSPEN, 2001); and idem., editor, *Pravye partii. Dokumenty i materialy. 1905–1917 gg., v dvukh tomakh* (Moscow: ROSSPEN, 1998).
9. Terence Emmons, "The Beseda Circle, 1899–1905," *Slavic Review* 32:3 (1973), 461–90; Emmons, *The Formation of Political Parties and the First National Elections in Russia* (Cambridge, MA: Harvard University Press, 1983). See also Valentin Valentinovich Shelokhaev, *Partiia oktiabristov v period pervoi russkoi revoliutsii* (Moscow: Nauka, 1987).
10. On the history of the SRs, see Manfred Hildermeier, *The Russian Socialist Revolutionary Party before the First World War* (New York: St. Martin's Press, 2000); Maureen Perrie, *The Agrarian Policy of the Russian Socialist-Revolutionary Party: From its Origins through the Revolution of 1905–1907* (Cambridge: Cambridge University Press, 2009); Oliver H. Radkey, *The Agrarian Foes of Bolshevism: Promise and Default of the Russian Socialist Revolutionaries, February to October 1917* (New York: Columbia University Press, 1958).
11. On the wave of terrorism in Russia during Nicholas II's reign, see Anna Geifman, *Thou Shalt Kill: Revolutionary Terrorism in Russia: 1894–1917* (Princeton, NJ: Princeton University Press, 1993).
12. Michael S. Melancon, *Stormy Petrels: The Socialist Revolutionaries in Russia's Labor Organizations, 1905–1914* (Pittsburgh, PA: University of Pittsburgh Center for Russian and East European Studies, 1988).
13. See Andrzej Walicki, *Marxism and the Leap to the Kingdom of Freedom: The Rise and Fall of the Communist Utopia* (Stanford, CA: Stanford University Press, 1995), 269–397, especially 274–75.
14. Ascher, *Russia in Disarray*, 176–77.
15. Ascher, *Russia in Disarray*, 179–81.
16. See the text in Walter Sablinsky, *The Road to Bloody Sunday: Father Gapon and the St. Petersburg Massacre of 1905* (Princeton, NJ: Princeton University Press, 1976), 344–49. On the labor movement in 1905, see Gerald D. Suhr, *1905 in St. Petersburg: Labor, Society and Revolution* (Stanford, CA: Stanford University Press, 1989).
17. Ascher, *Russia in Disarray*, 140, 150–51.
18. Ascher, *Russia in Disarray*, 219.
19. See Sergei Mitrofanovich Dubrovskii, *Krest'ianskoe dvizhenie v revoliutsii 1905–1907 gg.* (Moscow: Izdatel'stvo Akademii nauk SSSR, 1956), 65–76; Maureen Perrie, *The Agrarian Policy of the Russian Socialist-Revolutionary Party from Its Origins through the Revolution of 1905* (Cambridge: Cambridge University Press, 1977), 119.
20. Perrie, *The Agrarian Policy of the Russian Socialist-Revolutionary Party*, 119–20.

21. Ascher, *Russia in Disarray*, 162.
22. Ascher, *Russia in Disarray*, 165, 167.
23. Burton Richard Miller, *Rural Unrest during the First Russian Revolution: Kursk Province, 1905–1906* (Budapest: Central European University Press, 2013), 138, 141–47, 160–75.
24. Miller, *Rural Unrest*, 228–31.
25. Miller, *Rural Unrest*, 233–34.
26. Miller, *Rural Unrest*, 239.
27. Miller, *Rural Unrest*, 241.
28. Robert E. Blobaum, *Rewolucja: Russian Poland, 1904–1907* (Ithaca, NY and London: Cornell University Press, 1995), 4–8.
29. Blobaum, *Rewolucja,* 51.
30. Ascher, *Russia in Disarray*, 157.
31. Blobaum, *Rewolucja,* 97–98.
32. Blobaum, *Rewolucja,* 103–4.
33. Ascher, *Russia in Disarray*, 159–60.
34. Ascher, *Russia in Disarray*, 227–28; Sergei Iul'evich Vitte, *Vospominaniia v trekh tomakh. Tom 2* (Berlin: Slovo, 1922–1924), 13.
35. *Dnevnik Imperatora Nikolaia II* (Berlin: Slovo, 1923), 222.
36. Ascher, *Russia in Disarray*, 275.
37. Ascher, *Russia in Disarray*, 335.
38. Abraham Ascher, *The Revolution of 1905. Authority Restored* (Stanford, CA: Stanford University Press, 1992), 50.
39. Richard Pipes, *The Russian Revolution* (New York: Vintage Books, 1990), Kindle version, location 4318.
40. Ascher, *Authority Restored,* 53.
41. Ascher, *Authority Restored,* 101–2.
42. Ascher, *Authority Restored,* 209–10.
43. Aleksandr Isaevich Solzhenitsyn, *Krasnoe koleso. Uzel pervyi. Avgust Chetyrnadtsogo,* in *Sobranie sochinenii v tridtsati tomakh, Tom vos'moi* (Moscow: Vremia, 2006), *glava 65,* 225.
44. Ascher, *Authority Restored,* 242–43.
45. Ascher, *Authority Restored,* 247–48.
46. Ascher, *Authority Restored,* 249.
47. Ascher, *Authority Restored,* 273–74.
48. Dubrovskii, *Stolypinskaia zemel'naia reforma: iz istorii sel'skogo khoziaistva i krest'ianstvo Rossii v nachale XX veka* (Moscow: Izdatel'stvo Akademii nauk SSSR, 1963), 305.
49. David Macey, "Reflections on Peasant Adaptation in Rural Russia at the Beginning of the Twentieth Century: The Stolypin Agrarian Reforms," *Journal of Peasant Studies* 31: 3–4 (2004), 400–26, here 407, 416.
50. Ascher, *Authority Restored,* 297–98.
51. Ascher, *Authority Restored,* 314–17.
52. Ascher, *Authority Restored,* 319–21.
53. Ascher, *Authority Restored,* 340–47.

54. Ascher, *P. A. Stolypin. The Search for Stability in Late Imperial Russia* (Stanford, CA: Stanford University Press, 2001), 210. On Stolypin's management of the Third Duma, see Geoffrey A. Hosking, *The Russian Constitutional Experiment: Government and Duma, 1907–1914* (Cambridge, England: University Press, 1973).
55. Ascher, *P. A. Stolypin*, 215.
56. The classic Soviet book on the Fourth Duma and war is Valentin Semenovich Diakin, *Russkaia burzhuaziia i tsarizm v gody pervoi mirovoi voiny (1914–1917)* (Leningrad: Nauka, Leningradskoe otdelenie, 1967). For a more recent treatment, see Fedor Aleksandrovich Gaida, *Liberal'naia oppozitsiia na putiiakh k vlasti: 1914–1917 g.* (Moscow: ROSSPEN, 2003).
57. See Andrei Aleksandrovich Ivanov, "Pravyi spektr Gosudarstvennoi dumy i Gosudarstvennogo soveta Rossii v gody Pervoi mirovoi voiny: 1914–fevral' 1917 gg.," Dissertatsiia na soiskanie uchenoi stepeni doktora istoricheskikh nauk, Rossiiskii gosudarstvennyi pedagogicheskii universitet im. A. I. Gertsena, 2011.
58. See Aleksandr Vladimirovich Zenkovskii, "Proekt P. A. Stolypina o nekotoroi reorganizatsii sushchestvovavshikh togda Ministerstv," *Pravda o Stolypine*, 87–114; and Zenkovskii, "Proekty P. A. Stolypina v oblasti vneshnei politiki," in *Pravda o Stolypine*, ed. Zenkovskii, 115–30.
59. For a convenient summary of Stolypin's program, see Ascher, *P. A. Stolypin*, 365–68.
60. Ascher, *P. A. Stolypin*, 331–48.
61. Ascher, *P. A. Stolypin*, 355.
62. For Bogrov's final testimony to the police after the assassination, see "Protokol doprosa D. G. Bogrova ot 10 sentiabria 1911 goda," in Russkii Gosudarstvennyi Voennyi Istoricheskii Arkhiv [RGVIA], fond 1769 [Voenno-okruzhnoi sud Kievskoi voennoi oblasti], opis' 13, delo 11, ll. 133–35 verso; published by *Arkhivi Ukraini*, 1990, no. 4, 11–14.
63. Aron Iakovlevich Avrekh, "Stolypin, liberaly, revoliutsiia," in *Gosudarstvennaia deiatel'nost" P. A. Stolypina*, ed. Nadezhda Konstantinovna Figurovskaia i Aleksandr Davidovich Stepanskii (Moscow: Izdatel'stvo MGOU: A/O "Rosvuznauka," 1994), 34–66.
64. Ascher, *P. A. Stolypin*, 379, 381–82.
65. For documents on Stolypin's death, including documents relating to the official investigation by Trusevich, see Sergei Aleksandrovich Stepanov, *Zagadki ubiistva Stolypina* (Moscow: Progress-Akademiia, 1995).
66. These are the conclusions in Ascher, *P. A. Stolypin*, 374.
67. Leopold Haimson, "The Problem of Social Stability in Urban Russia, 1905–1917," *Slavic Review* (Part 1) 23:4 (December 1964), 619–42; (Part 2) 24:1 (March 1965), 1–22); and Haimson, "The Problem of Political and Social Stability in Urban Russia on the Eve of the Revolution, Revisited," *Slavic Review* 59:4 (Winter 2000), 848–75, here 854.
68. Haimson, "Urban Russia on the Eve of the Revolution, Revisited," 858–59.
69. Haimson, "Urban Russia on the Eve of the Revolution, Revisited," 862–63.
70. Wayne Dowler, *Russia in 1913* (DeKalb: Northern Illinois University Press, 2010).
71. Irina Igor'evna Glebova, "Pervaia revoliutsiia kak lokomotiv russkoi istorii. (Tezisy),"

Trudy po rossievedeniiu. Sbornik nauchnykh trudov, vypusk 6 (Moscow: RAN. INION, 2016) 262–76, especially 272–76, here 272.

72. Glebova, "Pervaia revoliutsiia kak lokomotiv russkoi istorii," 274.
73. See the terse remarks by David Van der Oye, "Russian Foreign Policy, 1815–1917," in *Cambridge History of Russia,* vol. 2, *Imperial Russia*, ed. Dominic Lieven (Cambridge: Cambridge University Press), 554–74, here 569.
74. Dominic Lieven, *The End of Tsarist Russia: The March to World War I and Revolution* (New York: Penguin Books, 2016), 222.
75. Lieven, *The End of Tsarist Russia*, 210.
76. Lieven, *The End of Tsarist Russia*, 225.
77. See Joshua Sanborn, "Russian Historiography on the Origins of the First World War since the Fischer Controversy," *Journal of Contemporary History* 48:2 (2013), 350–62.
78. See Fritz Fischer, *Griff nach der Weltmacht: die Kriegszielpolitik des kaiserlichen Deutschland 1914–18* (Düsseldorf: Droste, 1961); and Sanborn, "Russian Historiography," 353–55.
79. Joshua A. Sanborn, "Russian Imperialism, 1914–2014: Annexationist, Adventurist, or Anxious?" *Revolutionary Russia* 27:2 (2014), 92–108, here 94.
80. Sean McMeekin, *The Russian Origins of the First World War* (Cambridge, MA: Harvard University Press, 2011).
81. Christopher M. Clark, *The Sleepwalkers: How Europe Went to War in 1914* (London: Allen Lane, 2012).
82. See the excellent review article by Annika Mombauer, "Guilt or Responsibility? The Hundred-Year Debate on the Origins of World War I," *Central European History* 48 (2015), 541–64, here 558–59.
83. Lieven, *The End of Tsarist Russia*, 307.
84. Lieven, *The End of Tsarist Russia,* 316.
85. Lieven, *The End of Tsarist Russia,* 302–7.
86. Lieven, *The End of Tsarist Russia,* 320; Nekliudoff, *Diplomatic Reminiscences before and during the World War, 1911–1917* (New York: E. P. Dutton, 1920), 297–99.
87. Quoted in Lieven, *The End of Tsarist Russia,* 323.
88. K. A. Krivoshein, *A. V. Krivoshein (1857–1921 g.). Ego znachenie v istorii Rossii nachala XX veka* (Paris: 1973), 199–200. See also finance minister Petr L'vovich Bark's account of the July 24 meeting in "Iiul'skie dni 1914 g.," *Vozrozhdenie* 91 (iiul' 1959), 19–23.
89. Alexandre Sumpf, *La grande guerre oubliée: Russie, 1914–1918* (Paris: Perrin, 2014), 32.
90. Alexandre Sumpf, "War Losses (Russian Empire)," *1914–1918 online. International Encyclopedia of the First World War,* 1–10, here 2–3.
91. Sumpf, "War Losses (Russian Empire)," 3.
92. Sumpf, *La grande guerre oubliée*, 212–13.
93. Sumpf, *La grande guerre oubliée*, 218–19.
94. Sumpf, *La grande guerre oubliée*, 222–23.
95. Sumpf, *La grande guerre oubliée*, 224–25. For a monograph on this important subject, see Eric Lohr, *Nationalizing the Russian Empire: The Campaign against Enemy Aliens during World War I* (Cambridge, MA: Harvard University Press, 2003).

96. There is a huge literature on nationalism in each of these venues. For a convenient summary of developments during the war, see Sumpf, *La grande guerre oubliée*, 333–56.
97. See Sanborn, *Imperial Apocalypse: The Great War and the Destruction of the Russian Empire* (Oxford: Oxford University Press, 2014), 205–38.
98. Haimson, "Urban Russia on the Eve of the Revolution, Revisited," 864. For a monographic treatment of labor disputes during the war, see Leopold H. Haimson and Eric Brian, "Labor Unrest in Imperial Russia during the First World War: A Quantitative Analysis and Interpretation," in *Strikes, Social Conflict and the First World War: An International Perspective*, ed. Leopold Haimson and Giulio Sapelli (Milan: Feltrinelli, 1992), 389–452.
99. Sumpf, *La grande guerre oubliée*, 152.
100. For the history of the Union of Zemstvos and the organization "Zemgor," see Thomas Earl Porter, Lawrence W. Langer, *Prince George E. Lvov: The Zemstvo, Civil Society, and Liberalism in Late Imperial Russia* (Lanham, MD: Lexington Books, 2017).
101. Pipes, *The Russian Revolution,* online version, location 5917.
102. Sumpf, *La grande guerre oubliée*, 315.
103. See *Russkii vestnik,* No. 221 (27 sentiabria 1915), 2; quoted in and discussed by Pipes, *The Russian Revolution,* online version, location 5889.
104. Lieven, *The End of Tsarist Russia,* 343–50.
105. Mel'gunov, *Na put'iakh k dvortsovomu perevorotu: (Zagovory pered revoliutsiei 1917 goda)* (Paris: Knizhnoe delo "Rodnik", 1931).
106. For the best of recent scholarship on the February revolution, see Semion Lyandres, *The Fall of Tsarism: Untold Stories of the February 1917 Revolution* (Oxford: Oxford University Press, 2014); Tsuyoshi Hasegawa, *The February Revolution in Petrograd 1917: The End of the Tsarist Regime and the Birth of Dual Power* (Leiden, Boston: Brill, 2017); Andrei Borisovich Nikolaev, *Dumskaia revoliutsiia: 27 fevralia–3 marta 1917, v dvukh tomakh* (St. Petersburg: Rossiiskii gosudarstvennyi pedagogicheskii universitet im. A. I. Gertsena, 2017). The best of the earlier scholarship dealing with politics can be found in Sergei Petrovich Mel'gunov, *Martovskie dni* (Paris: 1961) George Katkov, *Russia, 1917: The February Revolution* (New York: Harper & Row, 1967); and Vitalii Ivanovich Startsev, *Rossiiskoe samoderzhavie v 1905–1917 gg.: Bor'ba vokrug "Otvetstvennogo ministerstva" i "Pravitel'stva doveriia"* (Leningrad: Nauka, Leningradskoe otdelenie, 1977).
107. Lieven, *The End of Tsarist Russia,* 343, 350.
108. S. A. Smith, "The Revolutions of 1917–1918," *The Cambridge History of Russia. Volume 3: The Twentieth Century*, ed. Ronald Grigor Suny (Cambridge: Cambridge University Press, 2006), 114–39, here 119–20.
109. See Startsev, *Russkaia burzhuaziia i samoderzhavie*; idem., *Revoliutsiia i vlast': Petrogradskii Sovet i Vremennoe pravitel'stvo v marte-aprele 1917 g.* (Moscow: Mysl', 1978); and Startsev, *Vnutrenniaia politika Vremennogo pravitel'stva pervogo sostava* (Leningrad: Leningradskoe otdelenie izdatel'stva "Nauka", 1980).
110. Smith, "The Revolutions of 1917–1918," 117.
111. A photograph of the abdication decree can be found in "Akt otrecheniia ot prestola imperatora Nikolaia II," *100 glavnykh dokumentov rossiiskoi istorii*, at doc.histrf.ru.

The signed decree was the second variant of the abdication: Nicholas had originally abdicated in favor of his son Aleksei.

112. See "Deklaratsiia Vremennogo pravitel'stva o ego sostave i zadachakh, 3 marta 1917 goda," in *Dokumenty XX veka* at doc20vek.ru.
113. Startsev, "Deklaratsiia Vremennogo pravitel'stva ot 3 marta 1917 goda," *Tainy istorii*, at secrethistory.su; original in *Nestor*, no. 3, 2000.
114. See Andrei Borisovich Nikolaev, "Politicheskaia sistema Rossii v marte–oktiabre 1917 g.: osnovnye cherty i etapy istorii," *Journal of Modern Russian History and Historiography*, no. 12 (2019), 1–36, here 35.
115. Nikolaev, "Politicheskaia sistema Rossii v marte–oktiabre 1917 g.," 35–36.
116. Smith, "The Revolutions of 1917–1918," 119.
117. "Akt otrecheniia ot prestola imperatora Nikolaia II," cited above.
118. Martin Malia, *Comprendre la Révolution russe* (Paris: Éditions du Seuil, 1980), 112–14.
119. See the graphs in Boris Vadimovich Sokolov, "Liudskie poteri Rossii I SSSR v voinakh, vooruzhennykh konfliktakh i inykh demograficheskikh katastrofakh XX v.," *Pravda o Velikoi Otechestvennoi voine (Sbornik statei)* (St. Petersburg: Aleteiia, 1989); and in Boris Tsesarevich Urlanis, "Grazhdanskaia voina," *Istoriia voennykh poter'. Voiny i narodonaselenie Evropy. Liudskie poteri voruzhennykh sil evropeiskikh stran v voinakh XVII–XX vv. (Istoriko-statistichekoe issledovanie* (St. Petersburg: Poligon, 1994).

THE MEMOIRS OF

Fyodor Sergeyevich Olferieff

Translated by Tanya Alexandra Cameron

Childhood

Early Remembrances

It is night. Mother and I are seated on the sofa by the lamp. I have a sore throat. Apparently to stop my crying and keep me occupied, Mother leafs through a magazine and shows me the pictures. In one of the pictures, a man is carrying a woman in his arms as he wades to the shore. In the background is an abandoned boat. Mother reads the sentence beneath the picture: "He pulled her out of the boat."

I remember that picture to this day. Much later I wondered why the picture made such an impression on me, and I found it in an old issue of *Niva* for the year 1888. Thus, my first recollection goes back to when I was three years old.

I am lying on some rocks over which water is rippling, and the cold current is soaking my clothing. There is a sort of roof over my head. I begin to shiver . . .

What happened just before or after this, I do not recall. Later, my mother told us that once the carriage in which we were fording a river hit a rock and overturned. I landed right under the carriage.

I am being carried in someone's arms as we push through a crowd of people to the altar in the church. The priest and the deacon, clad in shining robes, hold a golden chalice. I cry with all my might and struggle to escape from the arms, not wanting to approach these figures. Yet, I am brought to them.

I make a last effort to escape, but the deacon already is gripping my head firmly, and the priest pours into my mouth a sweet liquid with a bit of bread. After that I am immediately removed from the church. My nurse says, "For somebody else's sin, the child is suffering."

My surroundings are gradually coming into focus. I have a sister, Lilia. She is a little older than I am and is always teasing me. If I become angry and hit her, she complains to the nurse . . .

There is also another little girl, Vera. She is not my sister, but lives with us because she is an orphan. I play more with Vera than with Lilia . . .

Mama is always concerned that we be well fed and warmly dressed so as not to catch cold. Each evening we go with her to the cattle yard where she makes us drink fresh, warm milk. For me this is great torture because I don't like milk. But I mustn't disobey: I must suffer and drink . . .

My father has black hair, a black beard, and large, melancholy brown eyes. When he enters, everyone treats him with special respect. Even though he rarely pays attention to us, I am afraid of him. Yet, I am very happy when he talks or jokes with me. But sadly, this seldom happens . . .

Our house is built on a high bank of the Volga, where a small rivulet called Shutinka joins the big river. The junction can be seen from our window. The peasant children often play and swim there. We are not allowed to go there alone, but sometimes Vera and I manage to run off and swim, too. When they catch us, we are punished.

One time, when we were banished to the nurse's room for punishment, we committed yet another crime: we got the *prosfora*[1] out from behind the icon and ate it up. When the nurse found out, she made us kneel before the image of the saint; she herself kneeled beside us, and we all prayed that God would forgive our sin. When she saw that we were fully aware of our guilt, we were forgiven.

Once, trying to hide a sunflower seed from Vera, I stuck it into my nose. She could not find it, but when I tried to get it out to show how cleverly I had hidden it, the seed wouldn't come out. Vera tried to help, but she just pushed it in further. We ran to the servant girl's room. There, Akulina, the

1. Orthodox Christian holy bread.

dishwasher, sat me on her knee, took my nose in her mouth and tried to suck the seed out. But it was no use. I had to admit everything to the nurse and Mother. They sent for the doctor, who could come only after several days. By that time, my nose was already badly swollen. He pulled the seed out with forceps.

Once we stuffed ourselves with cherries overhanging the roof of the clay barn by reaching out through a broken window. Afterwards, we were very sick.

However, the greatest event was our disappearance from home one day, when we were lost in the forest till late at night and everyone living on the estate was out looking for us. We were picking wild strawberries and didn't notice when it was getting dark. We suddenly got scared, and in our fright, ran in the opposite direction from home. Soon we stopped, clung to each other, and began to shout. There was no answer except the echo. We walked slowly, crying. Every rustle, the crunch of branches beneath our feet, even the bird we spooked frightened us more. Finally, we came to the bank of the river, ran along it, and found our way back home. Everybody was so happy about our return that we were not even punished. Sonia, the maid, said that probably Leshy, the woods goblin, had led us astray. But Mother said that there is no woods goblin; that's just a fairytale, but there really are wolves, and they could easily have eaten us.

This event was the last drop that caused the cup of Mama's and my nurse's patience to run over. Before I even had a chance to say good-bye to her, Vera was sent to a Moscow orphanage school. I never saw her again. Aunt Volkonskaya wrote from Moscow that Vera was a good student. Later on, Mother said that she saw Vera in Moscow, and that she had already become a dressmaker. Later, news arrived that she had married.

After Father took Vera to school, he brought back with him from Moscow a young French governess, Mademoiselle Blanche, who had recently arrived from Paris. She was a very cheerful and talkative young woman and was surprised by everything: the quantity of snow, the sledges, the peasants in their bast shoes. Often, however, she would become sad, and I would see tears in her eyes. I quickly learned to chatter in French, and we became fast friends. She would tell me fairy tales, tell me about France, about her mother and brother, and then she would begin to cry again. Her main responsibility was to look after me. She called me "Mon joujou" or "Mon poulet en sucre," kissed me, and taught me to read French. I learned how to read French before I learned to read Russian.

I also remember how one night my sister and I stood at the window of the house belonging to our village elder, Sergei Yakovlevich, and watched as our big house was enveloped in flame. The courtyard, which was lit up by the fire, was full of people. On the roof of the kitchen next to the house, people were pouring water out of buckets which were being passed to them from below. My teeth were chattering from excitement.

As they told us later, the fire was discovered late, and those of us who were sleeping on the second floor were carried out with great difficulty down an already-burning staircase. The house and all that was in it burned to the ground. Our favorite dog, Narcissus, perished in the fire.

Rzhev: 1891–93

I.

We are living in a big stone house, which stands between other identical houses built in a row. In the back of the house there is a small garden, and in front, is the street, paved with cobblestones. Along this street, with a big clatter, go carriages and coachmen. On the opposite side of the street is a large parade ground with soldiers' quarters in the back. On the parade ground, the soldiers have their drills; they ride horses, first singly, then three in a row. Their horses jump the obstacles; then the soldiers assemble in a line. All of this they do on the commands of an officer.

On holidays, all the soldiers dress up in splendid uniforms and gather by the small church, which stands right in the corner of the parade ground. There they stand in a square formation and respond loudly and precisely to the greetings of their commanders. After that, they march to music past the most important commander, keeping their neat line formations.

Father says that these soldiers have recently come from fighting the Turks. And that, in general, soldiers exist to protect us from enemies who might otherwise attack us. All this sounds so exciting that I firmly resolve to become a soldier, ride on horseback, jump over obstacles, and go to war against the Turks. Deep in my soul, I have a dream that someday I may even become an officer and command other people. Thus, my career is decided although I am only six years old.

The officers frequently visit our home, and their presence brings animation, noise, and cheer. After dinner they play the piano and sing; sometimes, if there are other guests, there is dancing. I love one of the officers because he always plays with me. He sings beautifully and accompanies himself on a zither. His name is Aleksandr Aleksandrovich Selivanov. Could I have imagined then that this cheerful, big, wonderful man had a niece who was destined to become my wife?

II.

In addition to my sister Lilia, I also have a little sister Vava and a brother Sasha. Sasha is only two years old. Once Sasha was very ill, and after his fever came down and he wanted to get up on his feet, he couldn't stand. He had completely lost the use of one of his legs. The doctor called it infantile paralysis and advised that he be taken at once to Moscow. Father and Mother left with Sasha, and they lived in Moscow for some time.

After they left, the house fell silent. We children lived with our nurse, Tatiana Ivanovna, Mademoiselle Blanche, and Yulia Pavlovna Koltypina, who taught us Russian. We went for walks, studied, and on holidays, the nurse took us to the regimental church for vigil and divine liturgy.

In the church the soldiers stood in orderly lines on one side, and the officers and the public stood on the other. The singing was done very well by young soldiers who were called cantonists. I loved the evening service. Seeing how earnestly my nurse was praying, I also prayed: I prayed that God would send health to Sasha, prayed for Father and Mother, my nurse, my sisters, and all people, especially for those who did not believe in God and did not go to church. I never prayed for myself; my nurse taught me that God would not forget me if I would think of others. I knew that you cannot see God, that He is everywhere, but that in church it is easier to communicate with Him, and when I felt His presence, I was so happy and at peace. Only those who have at some time experienced this feeling can understand how fortunate are those who keep their faith to the end of their days. For these happy moments of my life, I am indebted to my nurse, Tatiana Ivanovna.

She was born in the province of Perm and spoke with a typical Ural accent, stressing the letter *o*. She came to St. Petersburg when she was very young with the family of a rich gold dealer. After his children had been placed in various schools, Tatiana Ivanovna came to our family and remained with us.

Tatiana Ivanovna not only became part of the family, but in questions concerning us children, her voice carried almost the same weight as our mother's. Not infrequently she disagreed and even quarreled with Mother, and Mother, who never gave in to anyone, would agree and make peace with the nurse.

She trusted in God like a child, and she transmitted this faith to me. She believed in universal forgiveness, saying that God taught us to pardon the sins of men. She renounced possessions and money, giving everything she had to others, not asking or questioning their need. She never married, and told us frequently, "Were it not for you, children, I would long ago have entered a monastery. My place is there." But she did not believe that she had the right to carry out this desire, as she knew that we needed her.

Finally, they brought Sasha home. He could walk and even run, but for the rest of his life, one of his legs was shorter than the other, and he walked with a slight limp.

The New Location: 1893

I was eight years old when it was announced to us children that we were moving back to the country where a new house had been built. But this time it was not at Stolypino, but at another estate which was located close to my father's place of service. He had been appointed *zemsky nachal'nik*, provincial head, of the Rzhev District.

I was sorry to leave the soldiers, whom I knew well by now and visited often in the barracks. They took me to the stables, sat me on the horses, taught me proper form in the saddle, and, occasionally even allowed me to ride behind the stables. It's well known that no one is more friendly with children than soldiers, and I had made many friends among them.

Seeing how sad I was, Father promised to give me a horse and a saddle as soon as we got to Kurchino, as our new estate was called. He also said that the soldiers would be bringing their horses for grazing one month each year, and that I would be able to see them again there.

Our move to Kurchino is imprinted clearly on my mind. On the previous day, our cook Nikanor Nikitich, a former serf of my mother's family, and his helper Mishka, who had worked in the celebrated restaurant Cubat, in St. Petersburg, and because of that, knew a few French words, were sent ahead. One was to prepare dinner at Kurchino, the other breakfast for us at a rest stop halfway there.

We proceeded in two carriages. At the head of the train, in a carriage drawn by three horses, a troika, were Father, Mother, and the two younger children. Following on the *dolgusha*, a vehicle with eight seats, four on each side, rode the nurse with Lilia, Mademoiselle Blanche, Yulia Pavlovna, the maid Sonia, and myself. I was sitting on the box seat next to the coachman, Ferapont. We were also drawn by a troika of horses.

Our way lay along the right shore of the Volga, upstream, following the so-called Toropets Road. The road was wide and very dusty. The traffic was brisk, and our carriage did not attract any particular attention. After riding about twenty versts,[2] we stopped at the entrance to one of the villages where we were met by some fifteen peasants. At their head was the *volostnoi starshina*, the district chief, dressed in a handsome, blue *poddevka*[3] and shiny boots. Around his neck, he wore a chain with a large badge. He was a completely round, pleasant man of about thirty-five, with a little black beard and sleek, smoothly combed hair. Next to him, dressed in a city jacket, stood the district clerk. Other peasants were either wearing bast shoes or were barefoot, and all wore homespun checkered shirts and pants. Most of them were wearing warm winter caps, which they respectfully removed. They all had very long hair which they shook back from their faces as they talked. This was a delegation which had come out to meet their new provincial head.

I learned later that the position of provincial head, zemsky nachal'nik, had just been reinstated, and Father was the first to take the job in this district. This position replaced the institution of the *mirovye posredniki*, village

2. A verst, an obsolete Russian unit of length, is equal to 0.6629 miles (1.0668 kilometers; 3,500 feet).

3. A variant of a coat or overdress with long sleeves.

legal consultants. This change was considered one of the so-called reactionary reforms associated with the reign of Alexander III, which were severely criticized by the liberal elements of our intelligentsia. The very vehemence with which this measure was condemned indicated that it was an obstacle to the realization of their liberal goals, if the intelligentsia even considered these goals as such at the time. However, as the cause of the storm which was inevitably moving toward Russia lay not in the country's administrative nor even political structure, but completely within its economic order, this reform was just one more blow from the existing powers that fell "upon the shaft and not the horse."[4] Of course, it could have no effect upon the events that followed. Judging from the enormous and difficult task which my father carried out and the respect which he commanded among the peasants, I believed that even in the position of zemsky nachal'nik a man could make a difference.

Upon our arrival, Father went with the peasants to the district seat, and we proceeded to the bank of the river, where Mishka, surrounded by a crowd of inquisitive children, awaited us with a samovar and zakuska.[5]

After that, we turned and left the Toropets Road and followed a cart track. The countryside was becoming more and more rugged. The small groves gave way to larger and larger sections of forest, and the road became noticeably worse. As we were passing through the villages, in accordance with our tradition, the coachman would speed up, which always produced great confusion in the village. The children raced to open the gates, dogs came running from all sides to bark at the horses, chickens flew squawking out of the way, and even the pigs lost their customary placidity, lifting their noses from the mud to stare at us. At the gates, we tossed specially prepared baranki and prianiki[6] to the children.

About five versts before reaching Kurchino, we entered into a tall timber forest where the sun's rays never penetrated. There it smelled of damp humus and fresh pitch, and puddles on the road did not dry up by winter. This was our own Kurchino forest, and as we emerged from it, we could see on the hill our newly built estate with its large, one-story house. To the

4. Russian proverb: *Koli ne po koniu, tak po ogloble.*

5. Tea and a snack.

6. Little bagels and spice cookies.

right, about half a verst away, a small village surrounded by tilled fields came into view. Beyond it and a little to the left was another. Behind the estate and to the left stretched another forest as far as the eye could see.

In front of the estate, we were met by a crowd of peasants, who had gathered to greet their new masters. In those times, even though serfdom had long ceased to exist, it is doubtful that the peasantry could imagine life without masters. On the steps of our new house, we were met by an old friend of our family, Andrei Andreevich Shteinman, a Russian Swiss agricultural specialist, who presented us with the traditional bread and salt. Following the suggestion of Andrei Andreevich and with his help, my father decided to cultivate a tract of virgin land, which was called in the deed of purchase Kurchino or Govorukhino. This tract consisted of 885 desiatins (2.7 acres), which were almost completely covered by forest.

Next to Andrei Andreevich stood the priest, his wife and daughter, and the psalm reader. A lectern had been set up, and after our parents made the rounds, the short service began, and the house was sprinkled with holy water both inside and out. After the rites, our father chatted again with the peasants. In the meanwhile, two small barrels of vodka and zakuska were brought out for the peasants, and we went into the house and began our dinner. We children did not get to stay to the end of dinner. Instead, we were sent to our new bedrooms, where we fell asleep to the songs of the peasants as they continued to sing beneath our windows.

My Friends: 1893–98

Our life at Kurchino flowed on, I suppose, very much as it did for most landowners of moderate means. We soon established neighborly relations with the peasantry. Both men and women were constantly coming to the estate for medical help, or with requests to settle family quarrels, or invitations to be their babies' godparents, or to bless a bride. Both Father and Mother were very hospitable. It made no difference whether it was a peasant, the priest's wife, the wife of the chief police officer, or a neighboring landowner—everybody was invited to sit down, and offered refreshment; everyone was listened to, and every effort was made to be of assistance.

I was allowed to go to the village and get to know and play with the peasant children, and I took full advantage of this. I became friends with many boys: Os'ka Matveev, Van'ka Enamushka, Van'ka Sinev, Pet'ka Kokorev, Iuda Pavlov, Van'ka Baranenok . . .[7] They all were somewhat older than I and came from two neighboring villages, Poltino and Lodygino.

At first, they were a little afraid to come to the estate house, but they soon got used to being there with me. We swung on the swings, ran playing at the Pas de Géant,[8] went to the forest to gather mushrooms, caught pike in deep pools using a looped rope, built a raft on our pond, and went swimming. Our leader was Pet'ka Kokorev because he was older and stronger than the rest of us and was both the bravest and most brash. None of us would ever have dared to steal an egg from the neighbor's chicken's nest, but Kokorev did. No one could swim or dive as well as he could; no one could run as fast or climb a tree as quickly. He was cruel: nothing gave him more pleasure than to twist the head of a chicken and leave it half dead to perish. Nobody knew so many "dirty stories" as he did. All these inevitably included the priest and his spouse; and the priest always turned out to be a fool. When at first I did not quite get the hang of these stories, there was a great deal of laughter and jeering over my naiveté. Pet'ka Kokorev did not quite like me because I was dressed better than he was and was the master's son, but he tolerated me, hoping at some time to use me for his own ends. He was an orphan and lived in the home of his uncle. He himself owned nothing, and perhaps because of this, believed that everything in the world was his. When he turned fifteen, he went to Moscow to work in a factory. I saw him again only when he came back to the village to report for military service. When he saw me he smiled, but never came up to the house. I heard that he became destructive when he drank. After he left for the service, I lost track of him.

Os'ka Matveev was a modest, tow-headed boy with gray eyes. He was the son of the village elder. His mother, who had become close friends with my mother, brought him one day to our house and told him in no uncertain terms to behave himself in the home of his masters. He did just that.

7. Os'ka=Iosif, Van'ka=Ivan, Pet'ka=Petr.

8. "Pas de Géant" or "Giant Steps"—a suspension device used to perform a gymnastic game.

As the oldest son in the family, he was exempt from military service. His parents saw to it that he married at an early age, and he became a good and honest peasant.

Van'ka Enamushka was a smart and inquisitive sort of boy. He was the son of the poorest family in the village, and when he came to the house, he was always hungry. I would run to the kitchen to get a piece of bread and butter for him. He had a difficult family life. His father, who was always drunk, beat his wife and children. For this reason, Van'ka became fearful and very sensitive to blows. My mother was very concerned with this unfortunate family. Not infrequently both Van'ka and his sister would spend the night at our house, and he would greedily study my books and the magazine *Niva*, and as soon as he saw a picture of a car, a locomotive, or a bicycle, he would try to figure out what makes a steam engine move, and why a bicycle doesn't fall. His entire mind was directed towards mechanics, and my mother was very glad that she was later able to help him enter a trade school in Moscow. What became of him, I do not know.

Van'ka Sinev used to come to visit our house to see his sister, Aniuta, who spent several months there almost completely immobilized by dropsy. He, too, appeared sick; he was a little blind and was deaf in one ear, which he kept stopped with a rag as it was running. His entire body was covered with sores. It was said that his father had brought a "bad illness" with him from Moscow and infected the whole family. The boy seldom played with us as he was becoming more ill and did not survive his sister by long. He died before he was fourteen.

Iuda Pavlov and Van'ka Baranenok belonged to what might be called the village aristocracy. They wore cotton print shirts, and for church on Sundays, they would don boots and broadcloth pants over the boot tops. Iuda was the son of a doorman at the Moscow Philharmonic by the name of Pavel Filimonych,[9] who lived in Moscow. It was said that he had another family there; however, he continued to maintain his village family in high style.

Baranenok, the son of a mill-owner, was a handsome boy. He could play the harmonica, and before he was sixteen years old, was the idol of the local

9. Colloquial, reduced form of the patronymic Filimonovich.

girls. Both Iuda and Van'ka, when they grew up, were considered very good catches. Baranenok even inspired couplets which were sung by the girls of the neighborhood, such as:

On the pathways of our fields
Ivan Egorovich runs by,
Shirt with stitching on the collar,
Silken kerchief on his neck . . .

Both Iuda and Van'ka were always very polite to me, and even though they were more independent than most, they always called me either "master," or Fyodor Sergeyevich.

However, a great obstacle to my playing with the village boys was the fact that all boys in rural areas, after reaching their tenth birthday, were considered part of the work force. They already had definite responsibilities, and especially in summer these responsibilities were so numerous that there was no time for games. To begin with, they had to look after the horses. They would unharness them and take them to the field at night, hobble them, bring them back in the morning and harness them. In addition, they drove the horse carts, hauling manure out to the fields in summer, and filling the carts with hay, rye, or oats. In winter, they hauled lumber, firewood, and grain. Thus, in order to be with my friends, I had to learn to do all these things, and do them as well as they did. It was especially difficult to learn to mow. You not only had to make a precise swath, but also had to maintain a certain speed so as not to hold up the person mowing behind you.

Besides all this, I already had some responsibilities of my own, of which I was very proud. Twice a week I had to ride ten versts to the post office on my horse, Zadornyi,[10] who had been given to me by my father as promised. I also was charged with the task of dividing the stacks of hay with the peasants when they were sharecropping on our land.

However, the sailor blouse and short pants in which I was dressed were not appropriate for these activities. It took great persistence to get my parents to make me some long pants and give me a pair of high boots. I still remember my first pants: they were made out of some striped pants of my

10. "Perky."

father's that went with his old morning coat. Those first boots with the high tops cost ten rubles.

But even such clothing did not always solve the problem. Once we were swimming in the river where the shore was covered with gravel. The other boys ran barefoot across it as if it were soft grass, but when I took off my boots, I had to crawl on all fours until I reached the sandy bottom. Pet'ka Kokorev didn't miss this chance to tease me. "You should have asked your papa to buy you another pair of boots—one for water and one for land." I put up with his teasing, but decided then and there to toughen my soles until they were as hard as the others'. To the horror of both my nurse and Mademoiselle Blanche, I would constantly take off my boots and run barefoot, often to return home with bleeding feet. This was reported to my father who simply commented, "Let him run barefoot if he wants to. Just see to it that he washes his feet more often." As a result, the soles of my feet had become like leather by the end of summer.

Some years later, when I was already a cadet in military school, the doctor noticed my soles while giving me a medical exam and asked, "Are you allowed to go barefoot in the country?" "Yes, Sir," I answered. "Up to a certain point that is even good for your health," said the physician. "But we forbid it in the Corps for fear of infection, and for this same reason, we don't recommend it during vacation."

My comrades, who had overheard this conversation, gathered around me, stared at my feet, and started teasing me. "What are you, a fool or a peasant boy?" At first, I tried to laugh it off, but when this didn't help, I gave one particularly irritating effeminate mama's boy such a good country punch in the nose that it started bleeding. After that, my feet were left in peace. And when vacation time came, I made no effort to grow back that delicate pink skin on my heels.

Sashutka: 1894–1902[11]

All in tears, Avdotia Enamushka was sitting in Mama's bedroom. Mama was trying to give her some medication. Just then, her husband appeared in the

11. Sashutka is one of the diminutive forms for Aleksandr.

yard of our estate. He was yelling and brandishing a scythe. Mama went out to talk to him. I was behind her, holding her skirt, fearing that something frightening might happen.

"Barynia,"[12] shouted the man, "give me back my Dunia or there will be trouble."

"I'm not holding your Dunia, Ivan," answered my mother in a quiet voice, "but I shall talk to you only if you put down that scythe and take off your cap."

Ivan became somewhat embarrassed. Apparently, the tone of Mother's voice had an effect. He took off his cap and laid down the scythe.

"Aren't you ashamed, Ivan, to beat your wife and children? And such a good wife as Avdotia and such fine children. Don't you know, you drunken fool, that you could kill them?"

"What kind of wife is she?" Ivan became furious again. "She brings me home somebody else's children, and I'm supposed to feed them! You know Sashutka isn't mine. And I've got my doubts about the rest of them, too." His voice trembled, and he was on the verge of tears. His shirt was in shreds, and his hair hung in long, black curls across his forehead. In his rage he was pitiful.

"That is not true," said my mother confidently and severely, "and if you wouldn't drink so much, you wouldn't dream up all kinds of rubbish."

"Rubbish?" he asked, fixing on Mama with his penetrating, black, crazy eyes. Then suddenly he switched his aggressive tone to a whining one. "I won't do it anymore, Barynia. As God's my witness, I won't. I'll repent at the confession. I'll quit drinking for good . . . Only, give me back my Dunia."

"Maman, comment ce fait-il que Sashutka ne lui appartient pas?"[13] I asked, surprised.

"Tais-toi, ce n'est pas ton affaire!"[14] Mother cut off my words. "You go now, Ivan. Avdotia and I will go to the village together."

These were the busiest days of summer field work—haying time. So even though the family drama was at its height, Ivan went off to the fields. Mother and Avdotia went to the village, and I ran behind them, trying not to draw attention to myself, so that I wouldn't be sent home.

12. "Madam."
13. "Mom, how is it that Sashutka isn't his?"
14. "Shut up, it's not your business."

The Enamushkas lived at the farthest edge of the village, and although I was used to the poverty of peasant homes, Ivan's house amazed even me with its squalor. The straw roof, which Ivan probably never changed, only adding straw where it leaked, was weighing down one of the walls of the shed, and hung almost to the ground, threatening to bring the whole thing down. Because of the crooked wall, the shed door would not close.

Inside the shed, between the gate and the porch, there weren't even planks to cover the manure, so you had to jump carefully so as not to step in the wet dung. Inside, the house smelled; an unchanged baby, who was lying in his cradle which hung from a pole fastened to the ceiling, was crying loudly. His oldest sister, Dunia, was trying in vain to rock him to sleep. Dunia looked very much like her father; she had the same black curls, and round, black eyes. Another baby came crawling across the floor, his mouth smeared with dirt, and strings of mucous dripping from his nose.

Sashutka, a little girl of ten, threw herself on her mother as soon as she saw us, trying to hide in her skirt. My friend, Van'ka, was not at home. Part of the curtain around the bed was torn, and the blanket was trailing on the floor. Obviously, nobody was even thinking about cleaning up the house. A hunk of bread was lying on the table. A hopelessly large number of flies swarmed over it, while others buzzed loudly, beating against the remaining glass in the windows, which in places had been pasted over with paper. In the garden, a cow, which probably hadn't been milked in a long time, was mooing impatiently.

Mother asked whether or not the children had eaten, and learned that there was no food in the house save for the hunk of bread and a small barrel of kvas.[15] She sent Dunia up to the estate house for food, and sat down next to Avdotia, putting her arm around her.

"Let me take Sashutka, Avdotia," Mother said, "and have her live at the big house until everything settles down here. Do you want to, Sashutka?" Sashutka only looked down and clung more closely to her mother.

It was decided that if Sashutka wanted to, she would come live with us. We didn't have to wait long. The next day she was already playing with us in the garden. Sashutka was put to bed in the maids' room, and some of Lilia's dresses were altered to fit her.

---

15. A lightly fermented drink made from barley, malt, and rye.

During this period, I was very taken by military games. I would outfit my brother and both sisters in caps, which Mademoiselle Blanche had made out of paper, dress them in military capes, crisscrossed in front like the ones I had seen the soldiers wearing, arm them with sticks, and march with them along the corridor which ran through our house, singing military songs at the top of our lungs: "Hurrah, hurrah, hurrah! Brothers, hurrah! We are ready to die for our Father, the Tsar," sang my soldiers, making my grandfather, Nikolai Ivanovich, who was living with us, very annoyed: he needed the long corridor for his morning constitutional.

Sashutka was my best soldier, the most obedient and most disciplined. Other soldiers usually began deserting me as soon as they got bored with the game, but Sashutka would stay, leaving only after I had dismissed her. In general, this little girl was the complete opposite of Vera. Vera had been small, dark, and full of initiative. In all our undertakings and pranks, she had been the leader, while I had followed submissively. Sashutka, on the contrary, liked to be led, and was happy only when someone was commanding her. She was a pink-cheeked, blond little girl with gray-green eyes and hair that was soft like flax.

The military exercises in the house were only the warm-up for serious battle maneuvers in the vegetable garden and around the outbuildings of the estate. The yard here was overgrown with burdock, which I mowed down with concentrated fury, slashing off burrs to the right and left with my stick. My faithful soldier, Sashutka, always fought directly behind me, and I knew that she was always ready to come to the rescue of her commander.

Autumn came. It grew colder. We spent more time sitting indoors, and my lessons grew longer and longer. Mademoiselle Blanche gladly taught Sashutka, whom she called Cendrillon,[16] too, and she proved to have a great ability to learn.

When playing outdoors, we would run to the threshing barn, where they were threshing flax, and listen to the songs which the working girls sang as they toiled. Sashutka had a good ear, and she taught me many songs. We would also run to visit her mother, Avdotia, bringing her all the things my mother sent her. We played with Van'ka and Dun'ka, sometimes bringing them up to the estate.

---

16. "Cinderella."

When it grew cold, after the snow fell, the grown-ups built us an ice slide, which ended in a long coast down from the top of the hill on which our house stood. We would all go sledding on it, usually getting buried in a snowdrift, and run home happy and freezing.

After a while, I stopped playing with my friends completely and played only with Sashutka. Everyone grew used to seeing us together, and Zina, the priest's daughter, who wanted to play with us herself, sneered enviously at us, calling us "bride and groom."

But everything comes to an end. It was decided that it was time for Sashutka to go away to school, and I was to start my studies in earnest. Sashutka was taken to the same school in Moscow which Vera was attending. Our parting was very sad; and many tears were shed on both sides.

At first, after she left, I waited impatiently for letters from our Aunt Volkonskaya with news about Sashutka, and even wrote a few letters to her myself, with Mama telling me what to write. But time, especially in childhood, heals all sorrows. As Mademoiselle Blanche used to say of these matters, "Loin des yeux, loin du coeur."[17] Other games and other friends led me to forget even Sashutka.

Then once in St. Petersburg, when I was some seventeen years old, a carriage drove up to our house, and a lady, dressed in an expensive fur cloak, got out and came up to the door. I opened the door, and at first I didn't recognize her. Only when she smiled, and the familiar dimple appeared on her cheek, I cried out, "Sashutka?"

"Yes, it is I, Fyodor Sergeyevich."

We stood looking at each other, not knowing what to say. Except for the joy of seeing each other, we no longer had anything in common, even aside from the fact that she was now a grown young woman, while I was still a boy. We went into the dining room, where my nurse, Tatiana Ivanovna, was sitting.

"It is nice to see you, Sashutka. How well dressed you are! Are you married now?"

"Not yet," answered Sashutka, looking down.

"Ah, how heavy are our sins," sighed my nurse, Nyanya.

There was a long pause.

---

17. "Out of sight, out of mind."

"And where do you . . . where are you living now?" I asked, not knowing whether to address her in the familiar "*ty*"[18] or not.

"I live in Moscow. I just came here for a short time."

Another long pause.

"And here Tatiana Fedorovna just recently went to Kurchino." Nyanya wouldn't be stopped. "And she said that Avdotia is ailing and complains that you don't write her."

Sashutka said nothing, dropping her head still lower.

"Well, I'm going now, Tatiana Ivanovna," she murmured, after a new pause. "I just came by to look at Fyodor Sergeyevich." She would not lift her eyes to look at my nurse.

"But why don't you wait for Mother?" I said. "She'll be back any minute, and she'll be sorry that she missed you."

"No, I have to leave now. What a beautiful uniform you have, Fyodor Sergeyevich." She lifted her eyes, which were full of tears, to look at me, and ran out down the staircase.

After she left, Nyanya never said a word about her. I didn't bring up the subject. From that time on, I heard nothing about Sashutka.

Mens Sano in Corpore Sano[19]

An izba,[20] in which the peasants in our parts lived, was a one-room log structure about twenty by thirty feet, and some seven or eight feet high, as I recall it now. The roof was either straw or covered with boards. Light came in through two or three tiny square windows, which were tightly covered by a pane of glass. Fresh air came in only through the door. Occupying approximately one-quarter of the room, in one of the back corners, was a large Russian stove. In the other rear corner there was usually a two-person plank bed concealed by a curtain. Between the stove and the bed was the entrance door. In the front of the house, in the commonly called

18. Russian has two personal pronouns that can be used when addressing one person: *ty* (familiar, informal; singular) or *vy* (polite, respectful, formal; plural).

19. "A healthy mind in a healthy body."

20. Hut.

red corner,[21] under the icon, stood the dining table with benches around it. The rest of the space was occupied by a rack for a splinter,[22] a weaving loom, and a spinning wheel.

As I remember when I was a child in the village of Poltino, which had some fifty households, only the two most prosperous families could afford kerosene lamps. I believe kerosene cost about ten kopecks a pound, and of course only a rich peasant could permit himself such luxury.

The entrance door was preceded by a large anteroom, usually full of household goods. Beyond was the so-called "cold izba," approximating in size the front part of the house, but without a stove, so that you could sleep here only in summer.

Flush to one side of the izba there was a shed for livestock, which usually held a cow, a horse, a pig, two or three sheep, and about ten chickens. This part of the property, together with the room for human habitation, was called the *dvor*.[23] The walls of both parts were covered over with dung approximately one foot thick for winter, in order to keep in the heat, with openings left for the doors and windows. Usually by February so much snow would blow in that the whole building looked like a snowdrift. It was impossible to distinguish the roof from the walls, and the path along the street was at the level of the windowsills. It was a daily job to clear the snow from the gate and windows.

Beyond the house was the vegetable garden, the barn with a dibble,[24] and in the well-to-do houses, a bathhouse. The entire piece of property belonged to one family, and was about one-quarter of a desiatina in size.

One such peasant household usually consisted of a family of five or six. Sometimes older members of the family who were no longer able to work lived here, too, or a married son who had not yet left for military service. In this case, when he was called for duty, his young wife would remain with his family. Frequently a boy was married off just before leaving for service in order to provide the family with an extra pair of working hands.

---

21. Beautiful corner or icon corner.

22. Peasant huts were often illuminated by flame contained within narrow splinters of wood fixed at an angle in an iron holder.

23. A homestead.

24. A small, curved, hand-held implement for making holes in the ground for planting seeds and bulbs.

The large bed in an izba was occupied by the married son or, if there was none, by the head of the family. The rest of the family, old and young, had to sleep either on the stove or in front of it. The Russian peasant slept without undressing, often in his sheepskin coat.

A peasant washed in the bathhouse, or if there was no such place, then in the Russian stove. First he would remove all the coal and ashes, and then crawl into the stove. After he had worked up a good sweat, he would emerge, lash himself with a birch switch, and run into the open to roll in the snow, then again return to the stove. The congested living quarters, plus the fact that people slept in the same clothes they wore during the day, was conducive to the existence of bed bugs, fleas, and lice. Preparation of food in the living quarters led to cockroaches; while the presence of cattle brought flies.

In such izbas people lived, ate, drank, sickened, and, in front of the entire family, multiplied and died. The lack of fresh air in an izba made it almost impossible for a person not used to it to remain there any length of time.

The staple item of the peasant's diet was black rye bread. Without bread, he could not work. After bread came potatoes, peas, cabbage, cucumbers, turnips, radishes, carrots, onions, milk, and eggs. Meat was a rare luxury on the peasant's table. A cow was kept as long as it gave milk, after which the peasant would sell it and buy a younger one. When a cow was slaughtered at the estate, there was usually a line of women from the village eager to get the head, hoofs, heart, and intestines—all the parts which we didn't eat. Water and kvas were almost the only drinks the peasants had. Tea, so beloved by the Russians, was a luxury, and the famous samovar could be found in only one out of ten izbas.

But it was not so much the kind of food, as the scarcity of any food that was the real problem of the peasants. In the course of the long winter, a peasant family usually consumed all its store of vegetables and most of the bread; while during summer, working from sunup to sundown, a peasant lived exclusively on bread and kvas. The few eggs which his chickens laid served in lieu of money, and therefore, eggs were used for food only with great prudence.

Because of the scarcity of food, the quality of food suffered too. In the village, they ate the very same kind of rye bread which we did, but it was baked from contaminated flour; it was damp, heavy, and didn't taste good.

A cheap type of potatoes, called plodovka, was used. These potatoes were harvested late and were smaller, less tasty, and less nutritious than the ones we planted.

The fact that the workers did not get an adequate diet resulted in lower productivity, which in turn meant that the fields were not worked as well as they might have been. This was one reason the land became exhausted.

At the same time, the rate of increase in population in Russia, according to the 1897 census, was equal to almost 2 percent, exceeding the rate of increase in both Europe and America. Evidently, the natural law to which every living thing on earth is subject—in its conception, growth, bloom, and decay—is so much stronger than mankind's genius with its civilization, that, even in the absence of civilization, the development of a nation proceeds at its own pace. In this degree of natural growth our faith in the Russian people resided, and continues to reside.

When I was eleven years old, I happened to witness the way in which this increase takes place. One day the peasants from the village Lodygino were helping clear out the manure from the cattle yard. Children were standing on the carts, which entered the yard one after another by one gate; the loaded carts went out by the opposite gate. The children's parents were using pitchforks to heap manure onto the carts. After loading one of the carts, Grishka's[25] pregnant young wife, Aniuta, bent over and grabbed her stomach with both hands, moaned, and went into the shed. At first, no one paid any attention, but soon her groans brought the other women. In the meanwhile, the procession of carts in the yard continued, and the work went right along.

In the shed, Aniuta was on her back by the wall and groaned continuously. The women made a tight circle around her, and one of them sent me to get Mama. It took some time for me to find her, and when we finally arrived, Aniuta was already sitting on the manure leaning against the wall. In her skirts a newborn baby was making little cries.

"Now, thank God, everything's all right; I've bitten off the cord for her," said Natalia.

"Is it a boy?" asked Mama.

25. Grishka is one of the diminutive forms for Grigory.

"Yes, Mistress," said the young mother, looking tenderly at the tiny, red bundle in her skirt.

Mama helped her get on one of the carts and took her to the village.

I already had an idea of how babies are born, so I was surprised not so much by the birth itself, as by the casual way in which the peasants reacted to this event. It was as if the appearance of a new human life in a cowshed was the most natural thing in the world. I couldn't help but compare this with how it had been only a few months ago when my new sister, Tanya, had come into the world. Long before the birth, a midwife, Praskovia Fedorovna, came to stay with us. Our family doctor, Petr Spiridonovich Brio, was present during the delivery, and after giving birth, Mother remained in bed for nine days.

The peasantry regarded death as simply as they did birth. The big Russian stove in the izba where people prepared their food, bathed, slept, and on which they lay when they were sick, also served as their deathbed. I remember the old man Arkhip, who lay for months on the stove and moaned. Everyone around him had grown so used to his moans that they paid attention to Arkhip only when the noise ceased. When they went to look, he was dead.

I remember how Aniuta Sineva died of dropsy while staying in a wing of our house. When she became very sick, her mother brought her a clean linen gown in which Aniuta was to appear before Our Lord after her death. The gown was put on before the arrival of the priest. Before beginning the prayers, the priest placed a lighted wax candle in her hands. Aniuta started to make the sign of the cross, but her hand never reached her forehead; her arm fell, and she expired.

Soon after that, her brother, my friend Van'ka, died. It was summertime; his bed was in the cold izba, where I brought him medicines and bouillon from our kitchen. He was always glad to see me. He knew that he was dying and didn't regret the end of his suffering, but kept repeating that in the next world he would pray to God to send good health to Mama and myself.

One morning when I came, I saw Van'ka's father fitting together a coffin out of boards. Inside, Van'ka lay on the table, covered with a linen cloth. On his eyes lay two copper five-kopeck pieces, to help keep the lids closed. His mother stood nearby, fanning the flies away from the scabs which covered his face. She was praying and wept aloud from time to time.

The peasants mourned aloud not so much because they could not bear the loss of their loved one, but because tradition required them to do so. The absence of wailing women at a funeral, or when sending a young soldier off to military service, was considered a breach of etiquette. In the cities, at the funerals of merchants, lamenters or "weepers," as they were called, were usually hired to do the job. This is where the term "weepers" comes from, referring to people who serve on the staff of funeral bureaus.

It would seem that the congested living in the village, with all of life's natural functions carried on in front of everybody, would have had a negative influence on the younger generation. But evidently nature itself arose in their defense. Also, heavy labor from their early years, and the fact that they had barely enough to eat, did not dispose the young people to idle indulgences.

True, there were crimes and murders. I remember Makhalova, a worker from the sawmill, who together with his son knifed an entire family to death to take seven rubles which were tied up in a corner of a kerchief. I remember Akim Svistunov, who ripped open his neighbor Ilia's stomach out of jealousy. I remember drunken brawls and knife fights. Prostitution was also present in the persons of Agrafena Shinkarka[26] and Palashka[27] Soldatka,[28] who charged ten kopecks a night. There was adultery and perversion when a woman of around forty, Maria Skotnichikha, gave birth to a baby by a fourteen-year-old boy.

Still, all of these were the exceptions. For the vast majority of the peasantry there were solid constraints which, unfortunately, have been lost in our civilized world. There was religion, the teachings of which were accepted unquestioningly, and social opinion, ready to cruelly punish anyone who overstepped the bounds. Then there was the esprit de corps of each village, which ensured that the village lads would defend the honor of their girls against the young men of another village. And a young woman had to guard her reputation carefully, so that her gate would not be smeared with tar, and she would not lose her chance to get married.

There was also syphilis, which was carried from Moscow. The nature of this infection, and the absence of timely medical care, aided its spread. But

26. Probably unofficial, a descriptive name that means hostess of the inn.
27. Palashka is one of the diminutive forms for Pelageia.
28. Unofficial, descriptive name that means wife or widow of a soldier.

indeed, even with all our cultural achievements, syphilis continues to flourish, and the specialists continue to get rich on it.

The most common epidemics were smallpox (even though vaccination was a legal requirement), spotted typhus, called "the fever," and among the children, scarlet fever, diphtheria, and in summer months, dysentery. Yet, to be fair, in the course of almost twenty years during which I lived in the country, I do not recall any serious epidemics in the Tver Province.

In the second sector of the Rzhev District, where my father served as chief administrator, there were thirty thousand inhabitants, and only two local doctors with one ten-bed hospital, which was located about ten versts from Kurchino. It stood to reason that one doctor could not possibly care for the medical needs of fifteen thousand people scattered over an area forty versts[29] in diameter. It is clear, too, that although vaccination for smallpox was required, it was far from reaching one hundred percent of the population. Quarantine of the sick was, of course, impossible in practice. Our doctor, Ivan Vladimirovich Lavrov, was trained in the St. Petersburg Military Medical Academy, which was considered the best medical school in Russia. He was young and energetic, but, having access to only the simplest medical supplies and only ten beds for the severely ill, he could rely only upon fresh air and the muzhik's strong constitution in healing the peasants.

"*Mens sano in corpore sano*"—how often that expression could be read and heard in Russia! At the same time, nowhere but in Russia was so little done to create and maintain healthful conditions for the overworked, half-starved bodies of our peasants. But from where, then, came the high morale of the victorious Imperial Orthodox Russian Army which, as we all knew, had caused neighboring lands to tremble since the Battle of Kulikovo?[30]

We will return to the question of the spirit of the Russian Army. Here, I would say only that the hungry, cold, and poverty-stricken life of the muzhik, without any hope for the future, made the Russian peasant the most undemanding soldier in the world, able to adapt and endure under the most unbelievable conditions. This endurance was generally confused with the soldiers' lofty spiritual qualities.

29. Forty versts is approximately twenty-seven miles.
30. In 1380.

Not Enough Land

One day we were visited by the land surveyor Aleksei Dmitrievich Yakimansky. He was a big, red-headed man, with a tic in one cheek, who spoke in a stentorian voice, stuttering slightly and blinking his bloodshot eyes. He was a virtuoso swearer, choosing terms of abuse like a poet choosing rhymes; he never repeated himself. Meeting him for the first time while he was working in the field, you could believe that he was a terribly violent man. In reality, none of his subordinates were afraid of him because they knew that he was a kind man who, because of his coarse nature, was unable to behave differently.

Seeing my mother in the yard, he got himself and his considerable body out of the carriage with youthful dexterity, doffed his cap, and kissed her hand with a provincial flourish. Then, taking one or two steps backward, he bawled out:

"Tatiana Fedorovna, where on earth are your peasants? Didn't I write and tell you that they should be here?" He stuck his finger out towards the ground near his feet, indicating precisely where the peasants were supposed to be.

"Yes, according to your letter, you should have been here yourself yesterday, and not today. Knowing you, Aleksei Dmitrievich, I didn't have the peasants gather," said Mama, laughing. "Now let's go into the house and have carp; then you and Sergei Nikolaevich can decide when to call the peasants."

"Humph, humph," snorted the surveyor, blinking his eyes. "Maybe that's right . . . Well, carp with a glass of vodka wouldn't go badly."

Next morning the peasants gathered by the fence, which was supposed to represent the boundary between the peasants' lands and ours. Yakimansky arrived with his chain and telescopic sighting compass, which he called an astrolabe; my father was there, and I came with him. The problem was to establish precisely the boundary between our holdings, as Father had just sold the timber rights to the forest bordering on the peasants' land.

"So you consider that to be the boundary line?" asked the surveyor, addressing the peasants and pointing to the fence.

"It must be. This fence has been here since olden times, and nobody ever objected to it."

Yakimansky got out his map and some other papers, unwound his chain, and set out at a rapid pace for the nearest crossroads. Then, garnishing his words with some three-story curses, he ordered them to bring the instrument and drag over the chain. Inasmuch as he had neither the patience nor the vocabulary to explain what he wanted, it took a long time for the peasants to do what was needed with the stakes and the chain. He shouted, swore, took off his cap and threw it on the ground, and spit in every direction. Finally, after measuring with the chain in the direction of the fence, bypassing it a little ways, he pointed to the spot where the peasants should start digging in order to find the iron boundary marker. To his great satisfaction, the mark was found, located several paces from the fence towards the peasants' land. Fixing his instrument at this point, he used his compass to direct it along the boundary line. Finally, indicating a tall tree in the distance, he declared the line between the marker and the tree to be the actual boundary line, at the end of which a second marker would be found. Thus, the peasants had been using a strip of land some three or four paces wide and extending for about a verst which actually belonged to us.

The peasants became agitated. Old Kornei declared that from the oldest times remembered they had had an agreement with the previous landowner, Petr Aleksandrovich Potemkin, the former master of Kurchino, that the boundary line was supposed to fall on the fence line.

"I don't give a hang where you agreed to put the fence," yelled Yakimansky. "I am showing you SOBs where the line goes that marks the official boundary."

The location of the boundary line was important to us not only in order to meet the terms set for the sale of the forest section, but also because of the principle: If the line were not decisively established now, the peasants might, at some future time, move the fence even further onto our holdings.

For the peasants, the establishment of the boundary would call for a complete reapportioning of all their fields, since the area was divided into strips of land parallel to the boundary line, and the man whose strip was closest to us would lose more than half of his land.

The surveyor measured the boundary, found the second marker at the far end, and took his leave. We left, too, but the peasants gathered into a circle, sat down on the grass, and began to discuss what had occurred.

The question of land was the question most crucial to the life of the Russian peasant. There was not sufficient land for the peasants to grow enough to live on until the following harvest. If I remember correctly, each male individual was allotted about two and a half desiatins of land, according to the last census. Inasmuch as the number of women was roughly equal to that of the men, this made a little over one desiatin for each mouth. Taking into account the fact that each year for every hundred individuals, two new mouths were added, the future appeared increasingly dim.

The peasants' land belonged to the community, but each peasant worked individually that strip of land which had been assigned to him for the given year at the village meeting. From this strip, he harvested his crop, but he was obliged to turn a certain portion of this into the common reserve to insure seed for next year's crops. The peasant never knew ahead of time which strip would be assigned to him in the following year, nor who would get the strip he was working this year. This was not conducive to improving the land's productivity; as the current worker was not concerned about the land's future, he did not plow deeply enough or fertilize the soil sufficiently.

The land shortage meant that the better part of the land had to be used for cereal grains,[31] which, in turn, precluded the sowing of other grains used in the so-called multiple-field system of crop rotation. All of the peasants' land was divided into three types of fields, with one part remaining fallow while it was fertilized and allowed to rest; the second part being seeded to rye, and the third to spring oats and flax. On one hand, this system left one-third of the total area idle; on the other, seeding rye on the same soil every third year was exhausting the land.

When we came to Kurchino in 1893, there were no plows in the villages. Instead, everything was plowed using the ancient *sokha*, a light wooden plow which required great physical effort from both man and horse. It was also time consuming and did not break up the soil adequately. As time went on, with the help of the county government, the peasants bought plows on credit, which added an extra financial burden, leaving them further in arrears.

31. Wheat and rye.

The crop was divided in the following manner: the part due to the community for seed grain was taken out first; the remainder was then hauled to the miller who took out his payment in grain and returned the balance in the form of flour to the peasant for food. The mill was a very profitable enterprise; water and wind energy were freely available, and the miller became richer and richer, holding power over the local peasants. The flour the peasants obtained had to last for twelve months. Naturally, the supply often was not large enough, and the peasants had to buy more flour from the same miller at his price, paying for it either out of wages for winter work, or by selling their cow.

Judging only from the fact that the peasants were continually in arrears with their taxes, with the debt increasing from year to year, public opinion could not ignore the need for increasing the peasants' holdings. Conversations about increasing their land were heard constantly. The census of 1897 indicated that there were 3.3 desiatins for each inhabitant of the Tver Province (I quote these figures from memory). Inasmuch as there were no government lands in Tver Province, it follows that about two-thirds of the entire area belonged to the landed gentry.

I am not familiar with the proposal for land reapportionment since this belonged to that category of "meaningless daydreams," advocated only by the most advanced men of the period; there was little hope for their actual realization. Another solution to the problem of land scarcity, used in many provinces where there was insufficient land, was to relocate the excess population to Siberia. Since this was not done in our province, I know very little about it.

Finally, the third method of relieving congestion in the countryside was the flood of peasants to the factories in Moscow. This movement, which arose spontaneously from the peasants' need for income, laid the foundation for the class that was to become the working proletariat.

There was also an attempt to increase the productivity of the peasants' lands, and thus avert the rapidly approaching storm. This was the time after the Russo-Japanese War,[32] during the so-called Stolypin period.[33] The peasant holdings were divided into pieces and assigned to individual

32. 1904–05.

33. Petr Arkadevich Stolypin was Premier and Minister of the Interior from 1906 to 1911.

households. Where it was feasible, such holdings were consolidated into farms. This measure, like most of the measures introduced by Stolypin, had a number of positive aspects, but like everything which was undertaken from above, it was belated. Furthermore, it failed to resolve the basic problem of the lack of land. This measure was aimed at eliminating the somewhat socialistic principle of rural *obschina*,[34] and creating in its stead a class of landed farmers. However, it completely ignored the fact that at this time in the world market, Russia was up against the massive, mechanized output of American agriculture. It was only possible to compete with it by introducing the same production methods. The peasant who had been moved to an individual farm became a private entrepreneur, but, as we shall see, like the owner of an estate, he was faced with insurmountable obstacles.

As Father and I were returning home from the surveying, I started to ask him to let the peasants have the strip of land which was, after all, of no use to us. Father replied that if he let the Poltino peasants have this piece of land, he would have to give a similar strip to the Lodygino, Kashino, and Zadnevo peasants, and all others who lived on the surrounding lands. Besides, he explained, we had to pay taxes on the land, and still owed money on it to the bank—which would hardly agree to such a handout.

On the following day, it was decided at the village meeting that the boundary established by the surveyor where the markers had been found should be considered valid. All the forest on the Kurchino side of this line was to be given to the purchaser who bought the land for timber, while the narrow strip of land which had been cultivated by the peasants was to be left in their hands until the next annual redistribution.

However, this redistribution never took place. The year 1905 was approaching, after which it would be unwise to speak of redistribution.

The Landed Gentry

In describing our remote corner of Tver Province, I do not mean to imply that all of Russia was exactly like our area. On the other hand, I am equally

34. Rural community ownership.

sure that we were far from being an exception, and that in central Russia there were many other sections similar to ours.

In all of the works written after the revolution, the landowner is described as a parasite who, having sucked all the life-force from the peasants, and enriched himself at their expense, proceeded to throw his money away, either in the dens of the capital, or at foreign resorts. There were no such landowners in our parts, not if they lived on their income from the land. True, the landowners' homes were cleaner than those of the peasants; they dressed better, and were generally able to provide more education for their children. Still, in order to live on the income from their estates, they had to work just as hard as peasants. That rich Russian aristocracy, which was famed throughout Europe, either belonged to the great landed families of the South; owned lands and natural resources in Siberia, the Far East, or the Caucasus; or, finally, had sources of income which had nothing to do with their estates.

Immediately adjoining the land of the village Lodygino was the estate of Riazantsevo. It belonged to a landlady Kossopolianskaia. Tall, slender, and probably once very beautiful, she was now silent and gloomy, but polite. She lived in an old house with geraniums in the windows; a lamp always burned in the corner before the icons; there was a canary in a cage, and small scatter rugs were spread on the immaculate, white floors. She would never leave her estate to go anywhere except for church services, visiting us rarely, and then only if she had some important business to discuss.

She had a husband, a quick, dark-haired, little Pole, with a short beard and gold-framed glasses. I am inclined to believe that he probably married not so much the lady as her five hundred desiatins, which he diligently farmed by himself with the aid of his son. The son looked like his mother, and knew how to read and write, but did not receive any further education. He was married to a peasant girl, who was the third working person in the household.

Thus, there were three persons working in the family, and together with two hired hands, they were able to plow and harvest a sufficient number of acres to feed themselves. This was a family which lived exclusively on the income from their land, and which—thanks, evidently, to the appearance of the Pole, Kossopoliansky—didn't lose their heads over the loss of free labor after the liberation of the serfs, but cut their needs to the minimum, and, rolling up their sleeves, set to work themselves. Kossopoliansky soon died, but his family continued to work. They didn't become rich, but they were not in need either. The education of the son's children no longer differed in any way from that of the peasants', since sending them to school in Moscow was considered an inadmissible luxury. Their farming, too, showed no further progress, since the greatest part of the land remained uncultivated.

Next to the Riazantsevo estate was the small estate of Dame Aleksandra Nikolaevna Zagarina. She was an old maid, the daughter of a general, who had been educated at the Smolny Institute, and, according to her, had danced there with the Emperor himself. Aleksandra Nikolaevna, who was not yet an old woman, lived alone in a small but neat little house, wore a bustle, and a little hat that sat on the top of her head, with ribbons that tied under her chin. In church, her place was on the left kliros, at the head of the congregation; and woe to him who dared to come up to kiss the cross before her at the close of the service.

The estate of Miss Zagarina was relatively small, and in charge of everything on it, including the mistress herself, was an old coachman, a former serf of her father's, by the name of Pavel Matveevich. It was rumored that when the old man was angry, he would not hesitate to hit even his mistress. In the presence of others, he treated her with deference; she in turn was haughty. The land of Dame Zagarina's estate was worked by her neighbors, the Ermolinskys, who paid a nominal lease fee. What she herself lived on, only she knew.

Beyond the lands of Zagarina was the farmstead of a noble family, the Ermolinskys. Several families, all belonging to the same old, aristocratic clan lived on this estate. By the time we knew them, they had come to resemble the peasants completely: they were illiterate, worked in the fields, and some went to Moscow to work in the factories. Their households differed in no way from those of the peasants, except that they owned a little more land, and had no village organization. In all, this group consisted of four or five families.

Further along the perimeter was the estate of a true gentleman-landowner, Sergei Leonidovich Ivin. Later, when I read Turgenev's description of Russian landowners such as Chertopkhanov or Nedopiuskin, in my imagination Chertopkhanov always bore the face of our Ivin. He was just such a petty tyrant, just as impatient, and just as cruel as Turgenev's hero, and like Chertopkhanov, liked to ride a horse with a Cossack saddle, and use his whip on everyone he could reach with it. He was still a young man, and his most prominent feature was his eyes, which seemed to protrude in anger. It was said that he had been expelled from his regiment for cruel treatment of his soldiers. He tried the same cruelty with his peasants, but it was rumored that in turn the muzhiks had beaten him up more than once. I myself once noticed a blue bruise under one of his crazy eyes. He was single, and often hung around the village girls, for which he was severely beaten. From us, he stole Mademoiselle Blanche.

How it happened, I don't know. I remember only that while I was confined to my room sick with measles, Mademoiselle Blanche came to my window with tears in her eyes and cried through the glass, "Adieu mon cheri, adieu mon enfant. Je ne sais pas si jamais je te reverrai." Just then the nurse entered the room, and Mademoiselle Blanche retreated from the window. I fell into tears and begged the nurse to tell me what had happened. The nurse only shook her fist after Mademoiselle Blanche, and said that she had gone to work for Ivin. My grief knew no bounds.

I do not know how Ivin managed his estate, since after the episode with Mademoiselle Blanche, our family discontinued its acquaintance with him. I know, however, that he was constantly involved in lawsuits with everyone, especially with the peasants. I do not know what became of Mademoiselle Blanche, but she soon left Ivin.

Adjoining Ivin's estate were the Chertolino lands, belonging to Count Aleksei Pavlovich Ignatev, at that time Governor General of Kiev Province. Later on, he became a member of the Imperial Council; he was killed by a terrorist in Tver in 1906.

This relatively small estate of Ignatev's was of course not really a source of income for him; it was rather a summer residence for his family, who came there for two or three months each year. The peasants respected the Count as one of the Tsar's high officials and always rejoiced at his coming: he was famous for his generous gifts and help to those in need. My parents exchanged visits with the Ignatevs, but it always seemed to me that my father didn't particularly like the Count, due to the difference in their political views. It was well known that Count Ignatev belonged to the far-right wing of the most reactionary group of nobility in the reign of Tsar Alexander III.

Not so long ago I came into possession of the memoirs, translated into English, of the oldest son of Count Ignatev, Aleksei, who became a general in the Red Army. He is about ten years older than I am. Like me, he was educated in the Page Corps and like me, became a Kamer-Page of the Empress; like me, too, he first served in the cavalry of the Guards, and subsequently became an officer of the General Staff. But at this point, the parallel ends: he remained behind to serve under Soviet power; I left the country. I presume he wrote his memoirs chiefly to explain why the son of one of the Tsar's courtiers who was killed by the revolution remained behind to serve this revolution. I am writing my memoirs chiefly to explain why I left my native land.

Anyone at some future time comparing these two documents should first of all keep in mind the following factor: Count Ignatev was writing within the territory of Soviet Russia, and had to weigh every phrase in order not to be brought to account by the censors, while I, in my exile, have for a censor only my own conscience. If in order to be printed my writing must be subjected to change, I shall leave it in manuscript form until happier days, when we can speak the truth.

Next to the Ignatevs, and completing the perimeter of the boundaries of our estate, was the estate of Petr Aleksandrovich Potemkin, the same man from whom my father had purchased Kurchino. Petr Aleksandrovich was an older man, with a long graying beard and very kindly eyes. My father spoke of him as a highly educated and humane individual. He was a bachelor, and his sister lived with him. He did not farm his estate, but leased the land to the peasants, and lived on the income he received from selling timber or selling off sections of land. In other words, again, he was living on his capital.

The picture would not be complete if I failed to mention two other neighboring families. They could not actually be considered landowners, because they did not have enough land to be counted in the census. What they had were summer homes, or dachas, where these families came for the summer. These people took nothing from the land, but on the contrary, brought money with them to spend locally, which made them popular with the peasants.

One of these families, that of the retired Colonel Mitrofan Vasilevich Ivanitsky-Vasilenko, lived very close to us, and we were good friends with them. They had two sons, Kolia[35] and Pasha,[36] who were young cadets; we spent the entire summer together, and my memory of them remains one of the brightest of my childhood.

The other family, by the name of Zhdanov, was very large. The father was an inspector in some school. The children were of various ages, and it is possible that one of the younger boys was the recently deceased Soviet bigwig Andrei Zhdanov.[37] In Zhdanov's biography, it mentions that he originated from Tver Province.

Our Establishment

My father was born in St. Petersburg into the family of a Penza landowner. The latter never lived in the countryside himself, but served in the army, and held a very high post in the Synod. My father was the younger of two sons, and when his brother died at an early age, all the attention of both parents, and the tenderness of his mother, was concentrated on him. He was raised wanting for nothing, educated in the Corps of Pages, and served in the Preobrazhensky Regiment. He advanced quickly in the service; was sociable, witty, and well-liked, both in his regiment and in society. It seemed that his career in the Guards was guaranteed. His health, however, was never particularly strong.

He married the daughter of a landowner with estates in Tver and Saratov, Tatiana Fedorovna Salova. Unlike my father, she had never lived in the capital, and disliked it. I remember how Mama would say that she was counting the days until she could go home to the country, and how my father said that she felt suffocated in Petersburg. Nonetheless, he remained in the service, and my older sister was born in Petersburg.

It happened, however, that my grandfather, who was straightforward, very outspoken, and sharp-tongued, unexpectedly lost his position, which

35. Nickname for Nikolai.

36. Nickname for Pavel.

37. A. A. Zhdanov was a member of the Politburo, Secretary of the Central Committee of the Communist Party, and the Party boss of Leningrad. He served Stalin faithfully and was a leader in the restoration of Communist orthodoxy from 1946 until his death, in August 1948.

was the main source of income for the family. He was retired with great honor and a good pension; none the less, his resignation was forced. Mama seized this opportunity, and insisted that my father also go into the reserves, and move to the estate at Stolypino, which she had received as a dowry. There, my father was soon elected Justice of the Peace, and took to farming with the same conscientiousness he brought to everything he did. He was fortunate: a series of harvests brought in a good profit, and when my grandfather Salov died, and Mama received her inheritance, they decided to invest it in land. Not just any land—my parents were looking for unbroken, virgin land, because it was their idea to set up a new estate themselves, one which would have all new, modern equipment. My father was looking, in his own words, for a place where he could "beat a return out of their investment."

Kurchino was just such a piece of land. My parents were considered to have bought it very cheaply—they paid something like 35,000 rubles for 885 desiatins of land, three-quarters of which was covered by a good fir forest. There was no farmhouse on the estate, but there was a livestock yard, with a hundred head of cattle in it. They began to see a return on their investment and planted flax. My parents visited Kurchino frequently, and when they returned, they called it "a gold mine." That is why, when the Stolypino estate burned down, the new house was built at Kurchino.

The house and all the other structures around it were built out of timber from our own forest and bricks made in our own, newly renovated brick yard and kilns. A fruit orchard was planted, earth-sheltered sheds were constructed, the encroaching forest was transformed into a park, while behind it the brook was dammed for a pond. On this dam they planned to put a mill. All this took two years and a considerable sum of money. In addition to this, they purchased ordinary (single-shared) plows, three-shared plows, harrows, a thresher, mowers, etc. My father was the first in the region to plant clover and to introduce the regular, seven-field system of crop rotation. The results were soon evident: his yield was more than twice that of the peasants. I remember the figures for the yield from spring wheat: while the peasants' yield rarely exceeded five or six to one we came out with thirteen or fifteen to one.

But all these harvests still fell far short of giving the return on these expenditures of money and labor that could have been obtained by investing them in any other enterprise rather than agriculture. There were three reasons for this: a steady decline in the grain market, the absence of an economical way to transport the grain to market, and, most important, a shortage of working hands when they were needed. This was the middle of the eighteen-nineties when American grain first appeared on the European market in such quantities that the cost per pood[38] fell from one ruble to fifty kopecks. The price of other grains fell proportionately.

Kurchino was forty versts from the nearest railroad station, and there were no navigable waterways to move its produce. The grain had to be transported by cart. This cartage was expensive, and was made more so because we had to compete with the Morozov factory of Moscow which at this time was hauling lumber from our region, and even from our own forest. The entire community felt the urgent need for a railroad. Finally, in 1900, the rail tracks were laid about ten versts from us. This, the so-called Moscow-Windau line,[39] was built expressly for the direct exchange of goods between the Moscow industrial region and Europe by way of Riga and Windau. This railway proved a great help to us, but soon a new problem appeared: Germany, in return for her neutrality in the Russo-Japanese War, demanded a preferential trade treaty from Russia. As a result of this treaty, the price of flax, our chief cash crop, fell drastically.

But the greatest problem of all was obtaining labor. I remember the time when a worker, who was hired in April and discharged on October first, was given full maintenance, thirty rubles in cash, and a pair of boots. In other terms, it was forty rubles in cash or forty poods of bread. In time, however, even before the Russo-Japanese War, when the doors to foreign capital were thrown open wide, secondary industries began developing at full steam; factories, plants, power stations, and railroads were being constructed. The cost of labor more than doubled; one pair of working hands would cost not forty but one hundred and forty poods of bread, calculated by its declining market value. As the area of agricultural development was increasing, it called for a proportionately larger number of workers which meant additional expense. Moreover, not every working hand knew how to

38. Forty Russian or 36 English pounds.
39. Today Windau is called Ventspils.

handle machinery, let alone how to repair it. For that purpose, one had to employ Latvians and Estonians whose wages exceeded one hundred rubles.

The shortness of the growing season and the time consuming, primitive work methods employed by the peasants in their own small fields made it hard to count on their help when the big-scale operations called for about two days' work from a large number of hands such as at the time of haying or clearing dung. Ordinarily, it was necessary to go to the village personally and persuade the peasants to come give a hand.

Leasing the land to the peasants resulted in poor handling of soil and its eventual depletion. Usually it was done only by those landowners who had lost hope of ever solving these problems themselves. The more common practice was working for half the crop. We, too, used this method in our holdings. We usually discovered that after deducting the expenses, such as sowing, purchasing, maintaining and repairing machines, and paying taxes, one-half the crop would dwindle down to approximately one-quarter. It occurs to me that the American farmer would readily understand the Russian landowner if he were to lose his Negro and Mexican help. This state of affairs forced the landowner to sell his timber or sections of his land in order to manage, as our friend Potemkin did. Or, as a last resort, he would begin to do agricultural work himself, plowing as much of the land as he was able working with his own hands. This was the case of our other neighbor Kossopoliansky. In the first instance, the landowner was headed into ruin, in the second the establishment just slowly sickened.

My father did not lose faith; he deeply believed that hard work and an honest regard towards the business would sooner or later justify themselves. He took risks, invested all he had in the business, and vainly expected that in the course of time all these expenditures would be returned to him a hundred-fold. He worked day and night, and while he was still living, our establishment managed to make ends meet. But as already mentioned, he did not possess good health. Work and worry were gradually undermining his strength. After one of his trips to the country in the spring, he returned quite ill to St. Petersburg, where we were then living. He went to bed, and after three days, died from pneumonia. He was merely forty-eight years old. This was March 1905. A few years later the agony of Kurchino began, and soon afterwards, the agony of the country's entire old order.

Faith, Tsar, and Fatherland

According to Russian Orthodox catechism, faith is a firm belief in the unseen as well as in the seen; belief in things that are desired and sought for as if they were actual. This was the faith in God which we professed. We believed in the Holy Virgin and the Saints. Our faith was a part of ourselves. There were no unbelievers in the countryside.

Our Lord was steadfast and most generous. He was omnipotent. The trouble was that He dwelled too high up, and sometimes our prayers did not reach Him. We firmly believed in life everlasting, in the last judgment, in heaven and in hell. All this was visually represented in a country-style picture (publishing house of I. D. Sytin of Moscow), and we believed that representation—the ascending and descending stairways, tortures in hell for various trespasses, etc. We also believed that all our pains and sorrows are due to the great distance from earth to heaven. We believed that if suffering ends in death, the death is in accord with God's will, and that we shall be rewarded in heaven for our pains on earth. The soul appears before God Almighty. We knew only about our Orthodox religion. Belonging to another faith or other denomination was considered a criminal heresy. However, people of other faiths were not persecuted; instead, they were pitied. You did not marry them, but they could enter your house, and it was permissible to share your meals with them.

Just as faith was part of ourselves, so religion was an integral part of our everyday life. A newborn infant could not be named without participation of the church. A christening certificate was just as indispensable as a vaccination certificate for smallpox when you got married, entered service, or applied for a passport. Only a church marriage was considered a lawful marriage; and in order to have one, a certificate of penitence and communion was required. The priest blessed the dying, and the body was attended and prayed for in church. The church was responsible for issuing the death certificate.

We did not blame God for the fact that the clergy, His representatives on earth, were not always equal to the task. The devil was mighty and vigilant, and we all were sinners subject to his temptation. If the priest, in his humanity, would sin with us, his failing would not be worse than ours. The priest of our *pogost*,[40] called Zaiach'i Gory,[41] was especially subject to the devil's temptation. This was a man about thirty-five years of age, of small stature and stocky build, with a short, light-colored braid of thinning hair gathered from all sides of his head, and a narrow band of beard framing his round face and passing under his chin. He constantly blinked his squinty, inflamed eyes, and he talked so quickly and indistinctly that you were frequently obliged to ask him to repeat himself. He had a meager education, and my grandfather, who was well versed in church matters and knew the service by heart, often instructed him in how to pronounce the proclamations in Church Slavonic and how to preach. The priest's wife was a stern, silent woman, with a face pitted with smallpox scars, and his daughter, Zina, was a great gossip.

Father Mefody, which was his name, lived in poverty as our parish was poor. He was a kindly man, and did not show evidence of greed. Frequently he gave his services gratis, and the peasants even took advantage of this. To his misfortune, he was a compulsive drinker. As his drinking sprees sometimes lasted more than a week, he was not always in a condition to perform the services.

On our estate, we followed the tradition from year to year of allowing our peasants to fish for carp in our ponds before All Saints' Day. Once Father Mefody joined the group. He took off his robes, tucked up his braid, and entered the water. He was very excited, shouted, and ordered those around him where to throw the net. The catch, as usual, was good. The peasants divided the fish, leaving some for our kitchen, and happy with their take, departed; but Father Mefody stayed for dinner, and in the course of it became so besotted with vodka that in the end he had to be loaded into a carriage and delivered home.

The following day members of the congregation, who were all dressed up for the holiday, gathered for the liturgy. However, Father Mefody wasn't there to begin the service. Finally, very late and with great difficulty, his psalm reader brought him to the church, where he donned his robes and began the divine service. As attested by Dame Zagarina, who, as always, stood in front on the left in the choir, Father Mefody vomited on the

40. *Pogost* is a parish center (church and cemetery).

41. "Hares' Hills."

altar, and she observed with her own eyes how the psalm reader, Andrei Andreevich, wiped up after him with a rag. The service ended without a sermon, and due to the indisposition of the priest, without coming to the cross.

From church, Dame Zagarina came directly to our house, and in spite of every effort on the part of my grandfather to rescue Father Mefody, declared that she was going to report it all to the bishop. After a while my grandfather, who was acquainted with the bishop, received a request from him to give his opinion about the priest. Grandfather did so, making every effort to temper the poor fellow's shortcomings, and for the time being the bishop confined himself to issuing a reprimand.

However, the enmity between the lady and the priest was just beginning. On another occasion, she reported him again, saying that Father Mefody, being drunk while she was kissing the cross at the close of the service, hit her teeth so hard with it that he almost knocked them out. This time she was able to produce witnesses and for the second time filed a complaint. As a result, Father Mefody was exiled to a monastery for penitence, and another priest, who was more humble, was assigned to our church.

Just as we could not conceive of the universe without God, we could not imagine our country without our Tsar. Not knowing how to think in abstract terms, we pictured God Almighty as a bearded person, with a kindly and wise face, sitting on a cloud. For the same reason, the expression of the national genius was imagined to be embodied in God's chosen Tsar, who was assigned by God to rule over us. In the person of the Tsar was concentrated all the wisdom of this earth. Thus, there was a saying when speaking about an intelligent individual: "He has a Tsar in his head."

This tendency to personify abstract ideas apparently is continuing with the Russian populace today. Stalin is just such a figure representing the might of the working men.

Some time ago, during the Second World War, I met a Soviet merchant marine in San Francisco and invited him to my house for dinner. He was a young man who had a secondary education and was a member of the Communist Party. He could read English, and our American freedom of criticizing everything and everybody apparently was annoying to him.

"Tell me," he asked, "how is it allowed that such a genius as your President Roosevelt is subject to such abuse and criticism in the newspapers?"

"In America there is only one genius," I answered, "that of the American people. President Roosevelt is a servant of the people, and we all support him as long as he fulfills our will."

My guest was most surprised.

The Tsar, very much as our religion, was part and parcel of our existence. The laws by which we lived were given by His Majesty's Manifesto or by ukase to the Governing Senate, and every court decree was issued "By Order of His Imperial Majesty." In the corner of every cottage of the land where the peasants hung their icon and picture of the Last Judgment, there also hung portraits of the Tsar, in a red hussar's dolman, and the Tsarina, in a traditional Russian *sarafan*[42] and headdress.[43]

Thus, if God was too high to hear us though still able to see our sins from His heavenly heights, and the Tsar too far away to see us, as the folk wisdom had it, it stood to reason that he would not know much about us. If the representative of the Lord Almighty so frequently was not equal to it, likewise the agents of the Tsar, his governors, local judges, police force and officers were liable to commit sins against the laws of the land and misuse the power delegated to them by the Tsar. And very much like the image of God, the image of the Tsar remained immaculate and the wrath of the population did not affect it.

In early October of 1894, the last of our summer crop was being threshed on the barn floor. The days were getting shorter; it was half dark, and just a kerosene lamp weakly flickered in the corner. My father had just returned from the city and went directly to the barn.

"News has just arrived that our Tsar has died," he announced.

The peasants stopped working, laid aside their flails, took off their caps, and made the holy sign of the cross. At the time I was only nine years old, but I shall never forget this solemn and mournful moment. Their sorrow was simple and sincere. Tsar Alexander III never sought popularity, and in a personal sense, the peasants never knew him. They were grieved by the loss of the Tsar as a symbol, as the supreme head of the Russian family. Work was immediately stopped, and as the peasants were dispersing towards their homes in groups, they were discussing the untimely death of the Tsar in

42. A Russian national dress for women.

43. Both portraits were printed by the same publishing house of I. D. Sytin.

the bloom of his life and saying that even the Tsar could not be saved by doctors.

On the following day, the manifesto came to the church, and the community gathered for the memorial service and an oath of allegiance to the new Tsar, Nikolai Aleksandrovich. There was a service in the evening as well, and again the church was overflowing. Neither the poverty of our church, nor the old, worn robes of the priest, nor the meager chorus, in which the snuffling voice of the psalm reader resounded above the rest, could disturb the solemnity of that service. After the memorial service, a lectern was placed in the middle of the church with the Bible and the cross on it. Father Mefody emerged and read aloud the manifesto declaring the accession to the throne of the young Emperor. After that, all present raised their right hands with fingers forming the sign of the cross and intoned after the priest the words of the oath:

"I solemnly swear and affirm before God Almighty and the Holy Bible that I willingly must serve truly and sincerely, without sparing my own life, and to the last drop of my blood, His Imperial Majesty, my sole and all-powerful Tsar Emperor Nikolai Aleksandrovich." I do not recall the whole wording of the oath, but it concluded as follows: "May God Almighty help me fulfill this solemn oath; as a token of this, I kiss the cross, and the words of my Savior. Amen."

Upon leaving the church, the peasants surrounded my father and listened as he talked about the young monarch, with whom he had served in the same regiment. Father stated that the Tsar was a simple, humble man, who would not permit special treatment while on the march or in the officer's club. He spoke of the broad education Nikolai Aleksandrovich had received and of his many travels. He mentioned that the Tsar was of small stature and ended by saying, "Yes, in size he is not great, but we firmly believe that his deeds will be great." Father never thought when he made this statement that soon after this discussion, as one of Tver's nobility expressing to the new Tsar the hope of implementing urgent reforms, he would hear the historical phrase "meaningless dreams" applied by the Tsar to the most serious ideas of his loyal subjects.

Fatherland, national pride, devotion to one's country, civic duty, and the like—all these abstract concepts were inculcated principally by the firmly established state schools. But as there were no such facilities outside of large cities, these concepts were understood by the population in their own way. Our Fatherland was so big, its frontiers so far removed, that because of our then available means of communication, it was popularly believed that the people were beyond reach. For an individual who has never seen a geographical map, it was indeed difficult or impossible to conceive of the size and the position of our land among other countries. We knew in a very general way that somewhere over there, at the edge of the earth and beyond our fence, which separates us from the abyss, lived Germans, French, Turks, and Chinese. Way, way beyond the seas were the English, and that was about all there was to it. Russia is so vast, so we thought, that even if the Germans would want to fight a war with us, our soldiers would immediately stop them at the frontier. True enough, the old men were telling us that there was the time when the French came to Russia and went as far as Moscow. Well, that was the time when our peasants picked up their axes and pitchforks and chased them all out. The French had nowhere to take refuge, and many of them froze to death in our land. Moreover, our climate does not suit them, their clothing has no warmth in it, and our food is not agreeable to them. On the other hand, if a Frenchman or a German would come to us in a peaceful way, and would want to live with us, we would welcome him. We shall not share our bread with him, but if he has his own, he may live with us as long as he chooses.

Perhaps there was no other nation in the world which was less self-conscious nationally than Russia. Russians never snubbed either a Chinaman, a Turk, or a Negro. They did not care for the Jews, it is true, because they crucified Christ, and because they believed Jews were earning their money not by their work, but by speculation.

Love for one's Fatherland was expressed by attachment to one's own house, to the place where one was born. This focus was understandable due to the dimensions of Russia and the diversity of its integral parts. In Turkestan, for instance, a peasant would not feel more at home than he would in Romania or Poland. His civic duty was understood to be his taxes, outstanding debts, military service, water fees, etc. In that respect he did not differ from people in other lands in his inclination to lighten or even avoid such obligations. The only difference was that our peasant was able to exist without cash, and in order to pay his taxes, it was sometimes necessary to either sell his cow or some of the grain which was kept to feed the family.

The payment of taxes was insured by the community's mutual trust, and if in the long run a household was unable to pay what was owed, the village had to be responsible for such payment.

I remember how on one occasion in November my father and I were returning home from Rzhev. On the way, he decided to stop in at the district's community headquarters. The chief met us there with hot tea and some zakuska, after which my father asked him to open the "cold room." This was the name for the local jail, because as a rule, it was unheated. However, when the door was opened, steam poured out of it just as from a bathhouse. When the steam cleared, before my eyes appeared all of our Poltino peasants—there were twenty-five men in there. They either stood leaning against the wall or crouched on the floor in their short, winter fur coats and warm bast shoes. When my father entered, they all stood up and joyously greeted him. Amongst the peasants, I particularly remember one, Nikanor Pavlov, a man who was well regarded by his village, an honest worker, and a good family man. He liked me very much, always teaching me this and that, and giving me fatherly advice. He remained leaning against the wall, greeted me, and I got the impression that he was unhappy that I saw him incarcerated. I, too, was embarrassed that I found myself in this room.

The reason for this mass detention was the community's mutual responsibility for the outstanding taxes which were not paid by some of them. My father came to offer them a proposal that he would pay these debts on condition that they make it up by effecting delivery of our flax to Rzhev. It would have seemed that this offer would be highly acceptable to them. But no, the peasants began to argue about it. The discussion which followed was not completely clear to me, and my father, without reaching any agreement, left the jail, and we resumed our sledge voyage towards home. Then he explained to me that the peasants calculated that it was more profitable to search for a method themselves to pay the debts of those in arrears; but transport of our flax was work for which the whole village was paid, and they felt it unjust to yield that amount for those peasants who failed in their obligations. The thought of a needy public treasury and their civic responsibility never crossed their minds. As we were nearing our residence, we encountered a peasant's sledge which was followed by a cow being driven forward by a lamenting woman. The cow, apparently her only one, was destined to be sold to pay her taxes.

The Orthodox faith, the Tsar, and the Fatherland—these were the three bases of the foundation which upheld the old order in Russia. What has become of them now?

"They have been destroyed and are no more," an immigrant would say.

"They have never mattered much and were not understood by the general population," a Soviet historian would say.

In my own opinion, neither is correct. The underpinnings weren't destroyed but have only changed their aspect: the newly revived secular clergy has made its own modifications to the law, again maintaining the same dependence on the primary foundation of the land: absolute autocratic authority.

The new schooling in Russia over the past twenty-five years has given the younger generation a fanatical patriotism which the masses lacked in the past, and it has also inspired them with a spirit of leadership among the peoples of the world in the direction of rebuilding life in accord with the so-called new ideas. The three bases, which in the course of many centuries have helped Russia liberate herself from under the Asiatic yoke, unite, and grow into one of the greatest powers of the world, have again helped her protect herself for the foreseeable future from the intrusion of the Western World.

Instruction Is Light, and Ignorance Is Darkness

According to the census of 1897, three out of every four persons in Russia were illiterate. This ratio related to the generation which preceded my own. But in my experience, managing young soldiers in the regiment ten years later, I found just 10 percent were illiterate. True, my statistic covered only young males who were of draft age, while the census of the whole population also included women and the older and younger generations. But even allowing that all women in my age bracket were illiterate, which indeed they were not, the percentage of illiteracy in one generation was reduced more than twofold. I also cannot think of any children in our village who would not have gone for at least one winter to our country school. True enough, our village school was far from perfect and left much to be desired. All I want to underline is the peasants' eager interest and desire to get some education in the course of the first decade of this century.

We did not have a permanent school building in either Poltino or Lodygino. The nearest school was located ten versts away, and obviously nobody could go to study there. In Lodygino, Andrei Andreevich, the psalm reader of the church, taught, transferring his class in turns from one peasant's house to another. And in Poltino, his daughter, a local beauty, Olga Andreevna, who had received a fourth-grade education, gave the instruction. As a matter of fact, in Poltino the classes took place in an unfinished cottage, which the children themselves heated up before classes began. Father and daughter were paid for their work in kind, receiving eggs, flour, potatoes, linen, and the like. Children were taught the alphabet and how to read and write. The only equipment a school child had consisted of a small slate, a broken piece of chalk for writing, and a much-used alphabet book. Children were taught between the ages of eight and ten. By the age of ten, a boy was already considered a working member of the family, and continuing with his studies in school was thought to be a luxury.

Learning how to read and write was done entirely on the initiative of the peasants themselves. Everybody, including even the drunk Enamushka, believed firmly that children should be instructed in order not to suffer in life, as they themselves had suffered. The zemstvo[44] gave them every assistance, and the schools were constantly increasing in number and in size. As far as the Ministry of National Education was concerned, before you could begin to raise the educational level, it was necessary to train a contingent of politically dependable teachers. The preparation of such teachers, however, was practically impossible because all graduates of educational institutions, with the exception of the military schools and a minimal number of schools for the privileged in the capitals, on the one hand were already acquainted with the existing unrest in the land, and on the other were considered by those in power as potential revolutionaries.

In the meanwhile, the time had come when I began to prepare in earnest for examinations and entrance to the Page Corps. The age of entry was thirteen years, and the classes began at the third level. Right after my birth, my father, just as his father before him, entered me as a Candidate Page of the Court of His Imperial Majesty. The Page Corps was open to the sons and grandsons of generals and the corresponding ranks in civilian service.

44. County council.

Education was given at the expense of the crown, and each graduate was duty bound to serve in the officers' ranks of the military for three years. The subject matter of the third-class level of the Corps corresponded to the third form of the Real Schools[45] in the country, with the addition of the requirement to learn to speak, read, and write in French and German.

After Mademoiselle Blanche left us, I had a succession of governesses and governors—among them was the German master, Herr Martin Stein, who was popularly called by our servants, Martyn Martynych.[46] None of them, however, succeeded in teaching me to speak German, and as a result, the German language was my Achilles heel in the Corps and in the General Staff Academy which I attended later on.

Two years prior to my entrance examination, it was decided that I should have a teacher to instruct me in all other subjects, instead of my former teacher Yulia Pavlovna, who had returned to her home. This new teacher, Nikolai Nikolaevich Turchaninov, was a student from the University of St. Petersburg who was banished from the capital because of his politically suspect views. He was a young man of about twenty-five who never shaved or cut his hair. Before his arrival, Father told us that Turchaninov was a very educated, well-read man, and a harmless dreamer; and Father hoped that as he was conscientious in regard to his work, he would be very helpful in getting me ready for school.

As time went on, it proved that he did not provide me much help, either in my grasp of grammar, arithmetic, or the Holy Scriptures. He was indeed an interesting individual, but he remained quite indifferent to my progress and assimilation of knowledge: when I knew my lessons, he did not praise me; when I was negligent in preparing my lessons, he would forget to ask me for a report. He used to talk at length about his childhood, about how difficult it was for him, a child who grew up in poverty, to enter the university, and how unfair it was that he was expelled from it. He firmly believed that the time would come when truth would prevail, when neither God nor Tsar nor soldiers would be needed, when the poor would live as well as the rich, and when people would not be afraid to hear and speak the truth.

---

45. Schools at which science and modern languages were taught instead of classical languages.

46. Colloquial, reduced form of the patronymic Martynovich.

All this commanded my respect and affection for him, but it hurt when he ridiculed the things which I held sacred, which were inculcated in my soul so lovingly by my nurse, Tatiana Ivanovna, and which I then so jealously and carefully preserved. He laughed at my prayers, the church, our conception of the Trinity, and he was rather casual about my lessons relating to the Holy Scriptures. While studying the Old Testament, I occasionally had questions, and I would turn to him for an explanation. One such question was:

"Cain and Abel had children. But who were the mothers of these children, Nikolai Nikolaevich?"

"Don't ask me about that, my friend," he would answer. "You better ask the priest this question when he gets drunk—he will tell you."

I held the authority of my grandfather in very high esteem. I considered him the most intelligent and the most educated man in the world. True enough, the limits of Kurchino were the limits of my knowledge of the world. In all events, I considered everything my grandfather said to be the irrefutable truth. It so happened that at that time a Jew by the name of Veniamin Pukh lived on our estate. He was about to lose his right to reside outside the Pale of Settlement, and he was trying to get a deferment. My mother permitted him to stay temporarily in the house of the manager of our estate. Pukh was an elderly, whiny, shabby-looking, pitiful individual. In the mornings he would put a hood on his head, turn his face to the east and pray, murmuring something which he was reading out of a small book. We were very curious and watched him from afar. Grandfather did not care for him and would call him a rogue if not a crook. On one occasion when I was talking about him with Turchaninov, I too called him a crook. Turchaninov stopped me short:

"Listen, Fyodor, my dear fellow. You are a good boy, and I very much want you to remember what I shall say: Never repeat accusations made by others until you are personally sure that they are justified. According to what you know, what has he actually done?"

"He is a Jew; Jews betrayed Christ, and so he cannot be an honest man."

"That Veniamin Pukh is a Jew, this fact he cannot change. Indeed, as a person, he has never betrayed Christ. And, for that matter, Jesus Christ himself was a Jew. You just think about it all and remember my words."

It is said that the psyche of a child is like a sponge—it absorbs everything that goes on around it. The words of my teacher, Nikolai Nikolaevich, remained forever in my memory.

At mealtime, Nikolai Nikolaevich talked loudly, drank lots of vodka, and quarreled audaciously with my grandfather. Grandfather enjoyed arguing, and did it well. Usually he remained cool, made his comments with a smile and in a kindly spirit. I didn't understand the subjects of their controversies, but it seemed to me that Grandfather always had the last word. Once I heard Grandfather saying to Mother, "Turchaninov is a typical nihilist." This word was not in my vocabulary, but it has remained with me ever since, associated with the image of my teacher. Later on, when we were taught literature in the Corps and were discussing nihilism in connection with Turgenev's *Fathers and Sons*, I again recalled Nikolai Nikolaevich, and I even pictured Bazarov in his form.

Nikolai Nikolaevich had another foible—he courted all our maids one after another. My mother was always receiving complaints from the maids' room and even from the village. One evening Olga Andreevna, daughter of the church psalm reader, came to talk to Mother. When she left for home, Nikolai Nikolaevich also disappeared. After a while Olga Andreevna came running back all in tears. Mother ordered the carriage and sent her home under the supervision of the coachman. Early next morning, Turchaninov left for Rzhev never to return.

After his departure, my new teacher was the instructor from the nearby country school, Mikhail Vasilevich Sadikov, who was a married man with two children. He was the complete opposite of Turchaninov: good-looking, with short cut hair, neatly dressed, and polite. He would sit respectfully on the edge of his chair responding to my parents' questions, *Da-s* and *Net-s.*[47]

He applied himself conscientiously to the lessons, meticulously followed the program of classes, and with great patience explained all that it required. One day when I raised the same question about the wives of Cain and Abel, which Turchaninov didn't want to answer, he quickly said, "Why do you

47. *Da-s* means "yes, sir/madam." *Net-s* means "no, sir/madam." The Russian words *sudar'* (sir) and *sudarynia* (madam) routinely added after an utterance were reduced to a single fricative -s.

want to know? This is not a question which will be asked on your examination. Meanwhile, if we do not waste our time on irrelevant matters, you may pass it that much better."

And indeed I did pass my entrance examination successfully. I owed it to my teacher Mikhail Vasilevich who was the first to instill in me a sense of the need when approaching all matters, to first grasp the essentials, to as they say, "grab the bull by the horns." He gave me a solid base for my school program, and ever since, it has been easy for me to continue my education.

It is probable that in Russia during this period there were relatively few teachers such as Sadikov. And yet it seems to me that stopping the propagation of schools in the search for suitable teachers was like prohibiting breathing for fear of spreading an infection.

My departure to St. Petersburg marks the end of my childhood. In the capital I found myself in an environment which had nothing in common with the one in which I grew up during my first thirteen years of life. The first thing which amazed me was the complete ignorance about village life I encountered there. And yet from this class of society came the people who governed Russia. That is probably why the most noble and well-meaning among them frequently did not know what they were creating.

As the years went by, I was grateful to my parents for having given me the chance to grow up so intimately connected with the way life was actually lived in Russia. This gave me the background to adjust to the most unexpected situations which later came my way, and frequently helped me avoid making faulty judgments.

I did not leave Kurchino never to return. I spent all my leaves and vacations there. And my close bond with the inhabitants of the countryside continued when I later taught them as soldiers in the military service.

Youth

Page Corps: The First Steps

Behind a beautiful iron fence on Sadovaia Street across from the Gostinyi Dvor stood a large, dark-red building on which was written in big letters: Page Corps of His Imperial Majesty. The building was constructed during Elizabeth's time by the architect Rastrelli[1] for Count Vorontzov.[2] Subsequently, Emperor Paul I gave shelter here to the Maltese Knights who were fleeing from Napoleon from the island of Malta. For them, a Roman Catholic Church was built at the rear of the building, which was still there during our time and had the most fashionable Catholic congregation in Petersburg. The last grandmaster of the order of the Knights of Malta was buried in the church. Around the tomb and under the altar was a cave which, according to legend, served as an exit to the underground walk which led to the Engineering Castle where Paul I lived. For us, this cave served as a hiding place to get away from our studies.

The history of the Corps says that with the appearance of the Knights in Petersburg, the Russian aristocracy began to send their sons to be educated by them. The Knights lived idly; they were supported by the court, and nothing was refused them. The legend says nothing about the results of the education of our youth by the Knights. I also do not know what happened to them in the course of time. All that is known is that in 1802,

1. Francesco Bartolomeo Rastrelli.

2. The building was originally built for Count Mikhail Illarionovich Vorontzov as his residence.

Emperor Alexander I organized a military school in this building which became known as the Page Corps.

In this Corps I spent seven years of my youth. I remember my anxiety upon entering the gates one morning in May when my father was taking me to introduce me to his former tutor, who now was the inspector of classes, General Anatoly Alekseevich Danilovsky, whom the Pages called Totoshka.[3] After going through the gates, the cabbie turned right and drove up to the corner wing of the building, which was the apartment quarters of the inspector. At the time it seemed to me that Father was wrong in trying to obtain some sort of favoritism for me, and I sighed with great relief when Danilovsky, a small, good-looking General with graying sideburns and kind, laughing eyes, received Father with open arms, and as if to answer my apprehension, sat me down in the corner and did not even deign to honor me with a single question.

Subsequently, during my whole stay in the Corps, I tried to keep my head down so that Totoshka would not notice me, and only once did I happen to meet with him. This was when I recited my lessons in his presence. As usual, I knew my lesson, but this day I answered especially well, and after class Danilovsky approached me and said, "I am very pleased with your progress. Your father was also a good student, and the most outstanding pupil in my class. Try to follow his example."

After our meeting with the inspector, Father took me to the premises of the Corps. It was a holiday, and the Pages were on leave; so we walked freely through the classrooms, reception rooms, and bedrooms. Father showed me the desks where he had sat, the beds where he had slept; greeted the doormen, Kazakevich and Nazarov, who remembered him as a Page; and came across the gym instructor, Fedor Evdokimovich Bordakov, who embraced him. It was obvious that even though a quarter century had passed since my father's graduation from the Corps, very little had changed, and I did not feel like a stranger entering it.

I remember my entrance examinations: French, in which the Frenchman Milliarde dictated a story to me, "Les Dix Sous du Petit Pierre";

3. Nickname for a totalizator, a pari-mutuel betting machine that was first introduced at the hippodrome in Tsarskoe Selo in 1876.

Russian, in which I wrote a composition on the "Captain's Daughter"[4] for the old man Sheremetev; and Bible study, in which I gave an answer about Jonah's sojourn in the belly of a whale. I remember the old, thin, meticulous German man, Lang, who was always dressed in formal uniform of a full dress coat with gold buttons—to him I recited, "Eine Kleine Beenefloh." I remember my arithmetic teacher, Sobolev, commending me for my ability to quickly add and subtract in my head. I scored well in all the examinations, and I began to realize that my preparations at home were above average as compared to my comrades entering the school with me. Because of this, when I returned home, Mikhail Vasilevich received a silver cigarette case from my parents, and he joyfully lifted me with outstretched arms so that I was looking down on him and said, "When you grow up and become a general, do not forget the old man."

One condition almost interfered with such a successful beginning to my military career. After the entrance examinations, we had our physicals. I was diagnosed as having myopia, which was a surprise to me because it seemed that I always saw everything that was necessary. During the examination, however, I was unable to read through the designated line, and Dr. Danini told my father that I was unfit for military duty. He said that the question of eyesight had begun to have a bearing on entrance, and the requirements had become especially rigid with the appointment of War Minister Rediger,[5] who issued new instructions on the acceptance of children into military schools.

This was when the primary influence on battle preparations for the army was General Adjutant Mikhail Ivanovich Dragomirov.[6] The military regulations at that time were permeated with his theory, which advocated the revival of Suvorov's *The Science of Victory* in opposition to the new European method calling for improvements in firearms and in general techniques. No one will deny that the fundamental premise in *The Science of Victory* by the

4. Historical novel by A. S. Pushkin.

5. Aleksandr Fedorovich Rediger was Russian Minister of War in 1905–09.

6. Mikhail Ivanovich Dragomirov (1830–1905) was a Russian general and military writer. In 1859 he served as professor of tactics at the General Staff Academy. After distinguishing himself in the Russo-Turkish War of 1877–78, he returned to become chief of the General Staff Academy. During his eleven years in this position, he collated and introduced into the Russian Army all the best military literature of Europe. He was instrumental in improving the morale and technical efficiency of the Russian officer corps.

great military philosopher was and continues to be the foundation not only of strategy, but of all of life's battles. But his great sayings, such as "Judgment of eye, speed, and attack," or "The bullet is a fool, but the bayonet is a fine chap," could not be literally applied. Unfortunately, in those days we happily embraced these sayings, rejected the necessity of developing techniques, and only learned how to tightly close ranks with the yell, "Hurrah," impetuously throwing ourselves into bayonet charges. The war minister at that time, Rediger, purportedly said: We do not need learned officers in glasses. It is important first of all that they be physically fit.

You cannot deny the necessity of requiring physical fitness of the officers, but to compare health to learning was rather dubious. By the cruel irony of fate, we were soon defeated by the Japanese, among whom it is known are many myopics, and it is even difficult to visualize a Japanese officer not wearing glasses.

In any event, Father and I were preparing to return home when unexpectedly a note came from the Corps that I had been accepted and was to return to the school at the beginning of the term.

I never knew who interceded in my case. Even if he wanted to, Father did not have time to make any move in this direction. It could not have been anybody but Danilovsky, but he never admitted this.

My Page Comrades

One day while roaming through the world, I came upon a volume of a magnificent 1903 edition of the *History of the Page Corps* in Hollywood. It was written by a famous military historian and biographer of our time, Shilder, for the 100th anniversary of the Corps. In it was a photograph of the Pages of the Second Company, and with the permission of the owner, I made a copy of the picture which is now hanging in front of me. It allows me to incorporate some numbers to cast light on the personnel not only of the Page Corps but also of our governing classes and especially the representatives of the old army's high command whose sons and grandsons were my Page comrades. Of the seventy-seven people in the photograph, only forty-three had Russian surnames, eighteen German, four Swedish, seven Polish, and one of each of the following: English, Lithuanian, Latvian, Georgian, and Tartar.

Page Corps, Second Company (sixth and seventh year), 1902. Fyodor is sitting fourth from the left in the front row.

Out of the twenty-one Germans and Swedes, only six were Orthodox; the remaining fifteen were Lutheran. The latter indicated that the Germans serving in Russia continued primarily to marry German women. All seven Poles were Catholics and mainly belonged to the high Polish aristocracy. Among these were Prince Radziwill, Count Velepolsky, Count Grabovsky, etc. Out of the forty-three Russian names, eighteen belonged to the old princes' and boyars' families, fifteen to the families who had served in Peter's and Catherine's time, and the ten younger ones were hereditary noblemen. All the German and Swedish surnames belonged to the Baltic and Finnish aristocracy. More than a quarter of the men represented in the photograph had titles of Prince, Count, or Baron.

The closed society replenishing the ranks of the Pages sent sons to the Corps from generation to generation. For this reason, a number was added to the surname of each Page on admittance, which specified the number of kin educated in the military academy. Thus, in the Corps with me were: Leontev the 17th, Belokopytov the 3rd, Count Velepolsky the 2nd, Baron Fredericks the 12th and 13th, Prince Trubetskoi the 7th and 8th, Count Gendrikov the 2nd. I was Olferieff the 2nd.

The following table of figures, put together on the basis of the same photograph, gives a clear understanding of how greatly out of proportion the German element was in the commanding ranks of the old army and generally in the old government.

	In the Group of Pages	**In Russia (from the census of 1897)**
Russians	57%	65.5%
Germans	28%	1.7%
Poles	9%	6.5%
Others	6%	26.3%

It would be careless to continue to analyze these figures basing them on an incidental photograph of the Pages, but in a manner of speaking they only confirm a long-known fact. To this one can add that included in the 26.3 percent of "other" nationalities in Russia were 4 percent Jews and 15 percent Asiatics: Turko-Tartars, Mongolians, Finns, and others who were not represented at all in the Page Corps.

[Compared to my village friends, with whom my friendship had never ended, my new comrades were taller and generally larger than the half-hungry peasant children. But if a fight occurred in the village, they would stand up for themselves, because life taught them to be resourceful in purely physical combat in order to survive. By the age of ten, a peasant boy had already become a laborer and knew well that he had to work to obtain a slice of bread. At the same time, the Pages had no doubt that they were born to be waited upon.][7]

At home I was brought up to do everything for myself. I was helped with making my bed, changing linen, and cleaning my boots. The rest I did myself. I remember how in the military school I was presented with a servant, who in spite of my protests called me, "Your Grace," made my bed, cleaned my boots and clothing, and—what especially embarrassed me—gave me a bath, and dressed and undressed me, as my nurse used to do when I was four years old. However, I must confess that very soon I became used to this and accepted it all as my due.

[We also looked down on our educators, in the same way as families saw the governess as being hardly one step higher than the servants. In spite of this, it did not interfere with our respect and sincere love for some of them.]

It seemed to me that life in the exclusive environment of a military school had many psychological similarities to life in a correctional institution. In both, people were separated from the superiors, in whose hands lay all the power over the powerless subordinates; in both, the subordinates considered their superiors sworn enemies; in both, the subordinates cultivated the so-called convict conscience, which permitted them to lie to the superiors, and to deceive and not listen to them. Besides this, among themselves the subordinates demanded complete solidarity, mutual assistance, the concealment of their comrades' escapades, and even taking blame on themselves if a comrade was threatened with a severe punishment. In both, there was an organized internal life, limits to freedom of action, and in this internal life, a propagation of traditions which gave the right of "primogeniture" or seniority to the oldest residents in the institution. This was the right to use all the given freedom at the expense of the new students, who had to wait their turn in order to become full members of the community.

7. Bracketed text here and immediately following was crossed out by the author.

The Corps in its internal organization was divided into three companies. Company 1 consisted of two so-called special classes. The Pages in it were considered to be on active military duty, and took the oath of allegiance. The order of life within it strictly adhered to the statute of Internal Service Regulations and Army Regulation on Discipline. Company 2, the so-called front line, armed with guns of the old model, consisted of Pages from the sixth and seventh classes. Finally, Company 3, which included third, fourth, and fifth classes, was limited to military education and discipline. In each Company, according to tradition, the senior class was considered to have full rights, and the juniors were the "animals," who were required to pass through a stern probation period before they could progress to the senior class. In this way, everyone in his time passed the course in the Corps, three times as an animal and three times in the honorable state of cornet. In this situation it was more difficult for the animals in the Second Company than in the Third, and in the First, considerably more difficult than in the Second. The whole burden of animal life revolved around the requirement of a notorious order in the pace of the community's life. For example, in the morning everyone lined up to use the wash basins, called "tower." Naturally, the junior class had to use the facilities first, so the seniors could sleep a little longer. The continual demand on the juniors was that they had to jump out of bed immediately at the sound of the bell, dress quickly, and run to prayer service. And the seniors allowed themselves to be late for prayers. It was necessary to keep order in formation, and that is why the juniors kept in step.

On the premises were many corridors and passageways; in the garden and on the parade ground were many paths and sidewalks. Some of them were more convenient and shorter, but, of course, not everyone could simultaneously make use of them. For this reason they were closed to the animals. And so it went. Gradually, the aristocratic license of the senior class reached its limits, and the juniors were forced to hold themselves more and more in check, toe the line, not gather in groups of more than three, refrain from speaking loudly, and watch vigilantly in order not to miss saluting a Page somewhere in hiding. Sometimes, throughout the whole long day, the juniors were only able to breathe freely during lectures in their own classes. But here there appeared a new concern: the necessity to know the lesson; or should it be otherwise, to avoid being called upon by the teacher.

In maintaining all these drills, I do not remember one occurrence of

A few of Fyodor's classmates in the Page Corps class of 1905.

physical force by the seniors. True, the juniors carried out their orders with greater exactness than the orders of the officers. It was explained that every attempt at protest and disobedience by the recalcitrant animals would be nipped in the bud by their own comrades in the class. Life for those who tried stubbornly to resist became unbearable, and they finally were compelled to abandon the Corps. There were also many occasions when the boys who were spoiled by their families could not cope with the drills and left. All this hazing had long ago become customary in our boarding school and was so firmly established that the command did not attempt to eradicate it. Even the Chief of all military schools, Grand Duke Konstantin Konstantinovich, who was loved by all, was not able to fight against it.

Was there friendship between the Pages in the Corps both before and after graduation? There absolutely was a comradeship in the Corps. All for one and one for all was put in practice in full force. The classes were not large, and having lived together for seven years, we knew each other very well and lived like brothers. But our friendship ordinarily did not go beyond the Corps and could not, for instance, be compared with the relationships which were established in the Guards Regimental family. Before graduation from the Corps, following one of its oldest traditions, we were given stainless steel rings lined on the inside with gold. On the exterior was written, "One of the many"/the number of graduates in the class/, and on the inside, the name of the wearer and year of graduation. The motto on the ring was very beautiful: "Strong as steel and noble as gold." Among themselves, all the Pages from youngest to eldest, from third-class Page to commander of the forces used the familiar term of "thou." A former Page could always be recognized by his unaffected manner and by his ability to get along in all circles of life. Except in these purely external common traits, the resemblance of the Pages after leaving the Corps ends, for not one privileged educational institution produced in their alumni such a diversity of life attainments and political convictions as the Page Corps.

[Naturally, we were all educated to be devoted to the throne, but perhaps because of our closeness to the court, we didn't deify the Monarch and have a slavish attachment to him as did many monarchists who knew the Tsar only by his portraits or through newspaper articles. It is also possible that the families who had preserved remnants of the old gentry traditions inculcated a healthier respect towards the Monarch.]

The former Pages had divided political views: On one side were the extreme monarchists and members of the Russian People's Alliance such as Aleksei Ignatev (the father), Vladimir Bezobrazov, and Fedor Trepov; on the other side were the moderate Octobrist members of the Duma, Mikhail Rodzianko and Engelgardt, who stood on the side for the abdication of the Tsar at the very beginning of the revolution. On one side were the devoted servants of the Tsar, like Count Fredericks or Khan Nakhichevansky; on

Page Corps class of 1905 upon its first commission, April 22, 1905, at its building's main entrance. In the center is Grand Duke Konstantin, head of the military schools. Fyodor is in the front row, third from left.

the other side, the hero of the Galician victory, Aleksei Brusilov, who audaciously called for the Tsar's abdication and went to serve on the side of the revolutionaries. On one side were the sly slaves like Voeikov, and on the other side, those who did not desert their own sovereign until the very end—his faithful servants, Prince Dolgorukov and Tatischev.

In the civil war we see Mikhail Diterikhs, one of the distinguished generals of the White Movement; Pavel Skoropadsky on the side of the Ukrainians; Getman, the traitor to Great Russia; and finally, Aleksei Ignatev (the son), and Aleksandr Verkhovsky in the Red Army.

In the old days, the Page Corps contributed to the ranks of eminent Decembrists, and finally in the '60s of the last century appeared a world-renowned preacher of anarchism, the former Kamer-Page of the Emperor Alexander II, Prince Petr Kropotkin. "Les extrémités ce touchant," the French were saying. It is impossible not to be moved by Anarchist Kropotkin, who gave up his whole career for an ideal. On the other side, one cannot feel anything but reverence for the memory of Vasily Dolgorukov and Ilia Tatischev, surrendering their lives in the service of their monarch, who already had been arrested by the people. One may not be in agreement with Rodzianko or Bezobrazov and suchlike, but they cannot be condemned because their actions came out of a sincere feeling of duty towards their homeland. It is impossible however not to admit that Marshal of the Court Voeikov treated his own position at court and his friendship with the Emperor only in terms of what other advantages they would bring him in addition to his personal career and profits. The moment his benefactor was no longer useful to him, he did not hesitate to renounce him. One cannot tolerate the action of former Kamer-Page and member of His Majesty's retinue General Skoropadsky, who did not realize the harm he was doing to his homeland when, with the help of Germany, he proclaimed the separatist movement in the Ukraine. The Pages could not be proud of such men as Voeikov and Skoropadsky.

There was, however, another category of Pages who crossed over to the side of revolution and joined the ranks of the Red Army. These were Aleksei Brusilov (the father), Aleksei Ignatev (the son), and Aleksandr Verkhovsky. I knew all three of them well, and the situation which induced them to join the Reds is clear to me. Later I will give you the characteristics of Brusilov. Regarding Ignatev, he can be judged by his memoirs. Here I will speak of Verkhovsky.

Aleksandr Verkhovsky

In 1902, a new cadet by the name of Aleksandr Verkhovsky was transferred from the Aleksandrovsky Corps[8] to our sixth class. They assigned him a seat next to mine. He could be described as a small boy of rather insignificant appearance, skinny, nervous, with a kind of metallic glow in his colorless eyes and an unpleasant, dissonant voice. We did not like him from the beginning. But apparently he already was used to the feeling that his appearance was not in his favor, and he seemed not to mind it. He did not converse much with anyone, except on the occasions when he needed certain information, then he would question you politely, and always, just

8. Emperor Alexander II Cadet Corps.

as politely, insist on a direct answer to his question, and very politely thank you for it. In class he absorbed every word of the teacher like a sponge, carefully took orderly notes in legible handwriting, and stood out at once as a brilliant student. He quickly grasped the rules of our life and the demands imposed by the seniors, conducted himself discretely, walked the straight and narrow, and did his best to remain inconspicuous. If it happened that in spite of all this caution he was penalized by the seniors and had to stand at attention in the "tower," he would do it just as conscientiously as he prepared his lessons. [As I was of an exactly opposite temperament, I usually would take part in all the pranks and undertakings and, without thinking of the outcome, would freely and loudly express my views.][9] At times I was under the impression that Verkhovsky tried to imitate me, in order to be somewhat more popular. This was something he did not know how to do, and apparently it felt so unnatural to him that he would resume his usual ways. I was soon tired of sitting with him, and I moved to the back bench. Verkhovsky remained alone on his bench, and only when there was a lack of space in the class would someone sit next to him.

Two years passed, and Verkhovsky was so much ahead of his class in all subjects that he began to be a topic of conversation. He grew up, matured, was more sure of himself, and his comrades gave him credit for his superiority. But he was not able to gain love and prestige. By the end of the year we were all transferred to the senior Special Class and were promoted to status of Kamer-Pages, with appointments to be personal pages to members of the imperial family. Verkhovsky, as our best student, was made sergeant major, and was appointed to be the Page of the Tsar. From that point on, one could notice in the tone of his voice a note of self-confidence. He began to express his views freely, and at times was critical not only of our own environment, but also of the events outside our walls.

These were the years when our army suffered one defeat after another in Manchuria, and we all were reacting painfully, trying to guess the reasons for these failures. At the same time, the mob was looting the Gostinyi Dvor, situated outside our gates, and there was bloodshed in the streets of St. Petersburg on January 9. The mood was foreboding, and amongst

9. Bracketed text here was crossed out by the author.

ourselves we were definitely against revolution and anything which might foreshadow it. We believed what we read in the newspaper *Novoe Vremia*,[10] which attributed our lack of success at the front primarily to revolutionary propaganda. There were terrorist acts here and there; then there was the unfortunate shot fired at the Blessing of the Waters ceremony followed by a demonstration, and we were all under the impression that the life of the Tsar was threatened. It was natural, therefore, that every comment, even one that would otherwise seem to be an innocent remark, made casually in conversation, would appear to have a special significance. This is why any critical remarks made at that time by Verkhovsky, who continued to remain somewhat alien to us all, would evoke a sharp reaction on our part. Personally I was unable to find any subject of conversation in common with him. I remember only on one occasion when we were returning from Tsarskoe Selo, after Court service, Verkhovsky, who was in the same carriage with us, said, "I am glad that I am Kamer-Page of the Tsar, and I do not have to drag around women's skirts." What he meant was the trains on the gowns of the Empress and the Grand Duchesses, on ceremonial occasions. Rebinder, who was my partner in my duty to carry the train of the Empress, remarked, "Nobody invited you to do Court service, there are enough military academies besides the Page Corps." Verkhovsky said nothing. In the meantime, if this same remark about ladies' trains was made by Rebinder himself or by one of us other Pages, it would produce only laughter and jest. Somehow, though, it was not proper for Verkhovsky to make this statement.

Once during the period of unrest in St. Petersburg, a squadron of Mounted Grenadiers was stationed at our Corps manege. We all visited the manege frequently to look at the horses, to talk to the soldiers, and to discuss with them their service and country living. The servicemen in turn, inasmuch as they knew that we were getting ready to become officers, were interested in our work. On one occasion, Verkhovsky asked the soldiers, "Tell me, do officers hit you on occasion?" To which the head of the platoon who stood nearby answered, "Of course they do, if we deserve it." "Nobody has the right to hit a soldier," remarked Verkhovsky. The top sergeant who was present, an old veteran of the Turkish War, cleared his throat, threw

10. Russian newspaper published in St. Petersburg from 1868 to 1917.

back his shoulders and ordered the soldiers to disperse. This tactless remark of Verkhovsky aroused great indignation in our midst, and it was agreed then and there to make him change his way of doing things.

By a strange coincidence, when I was commissioned to officer's rank in the Mounted Grenadiers, I was appointed to this same Second Squadron. Once during night duty on field maneuvers, a time when the differences between the chief and the subordinate are at a minimum and human relationships prevail, I asked the leader of the platoon, whose name was Zavrazhnyi, and who as I recalled was the one who replied to Verkhovsky when they were stationed at the Page Corps, "Do you remember last year, when you were at the Page Corps manege, and we Pages came to get acquainted with the boys?"

"Yes, Your Honor, I do remember. And I remember you also. You were the chief of the squad."

"And do you recall how you replied to our sergeant when he asked whether the officers hit the soldiers? Why did you answer that way? Nobody hits you here."

"But why would the sergeant ask us? It was not proper for the sergeant to ask this question, Your Honor. I answered as I did on purpose."

"Well in all events, it was not a good thing to answer as you did. One would believe that we beat our men."

"Right you are, Sir, now I understand it. After that, the commander of the squadron made an investigation. I got plenty for it. And Mitrofan Antonych[11] scolded me also."

"Well, well," said I laughingly, "did anyone hit you?"

"Ney, Your Honor." He smiled back. "They were inquiring mostly about what else Kamer-Page Verkhovsky had said."

On the evening of the day when the conversation between Verkhovsky and the Mounted Grenadiers had taken place, we all gathered in the smoking room and discussed how we could restrain Verkhovsky before he got his officers' commission, which was due in approximately two months. It transpired that everyone present could cite an example of his objectionable way of saying things, but on the other hand, none of these actions could be

11. Colloquial, reduced form of the patronymic Antonovich.

considered a serious misdemeanor. They indeed could be considered tactless, or perhaps indicative of future unreliability, but no more than that. For all of us, who were getting ready for the most solemn moment of our life, that is, promotion to the rank of an officer (in our estimation an officer being a knight without fear and above reproach), his failings were such that we thought they completely justified our decisive action. Meanwhile, we fully realized that putting pressure on our sergeant major would be judged a breach of discipline. However, we did not plan to take it to our superiors before we had notified Verkhovsky himself.

The following morning the whole class gathered in the smoking room. There were several individuals particularly inimical to Verkhovsky, who proposed a motion to advise him to immediately leave the Corps. Those who agreed with this plan were to stand by the wall; those who opposed it were to remain by the window. Out of twenty-seven present, only one, Vasia[12] Buturlin, remained standing by the window. There was an exclamation from the opposite side, "Does this mean, Buturlin, that you want to leave us, too?" But this question hung in the air unanswered. We all loved Buturlin, and in every sense he was one of "us." He quietly announced that he was against such an approach to the question and protested it, and if the rest of his classmates did not agree, he was ready to leave the Corps. Vasia's bold approach produced a strong impression. As I remember, it was I who offered the following solution: To call Verkhovsky, to confront him with all the evidence against him, to suggest that he recognize his wrongdoing, and promise that in the future he would carry on in consonance with the high office of Kamer-Page of the Tsar. For our part, we would promise that all would remain unrevealed till our death. Should Verkhovsky insist that he was right, he should leave the Corps at once. This manner of posing the problem was accepted by all concerned, and one of the Pages, Kreits, was charged to call him in and relay this to him in our presence. Verkhovsky listened with his head bowed. After Kreits was through, he raised his head and with a metallic firmness said, "I do not consider myself guilty in any way. Neither now nor in the future shall I change or deny my convictions. I shall not take back my words." Having said this, he rapidly left the room.

12. Nickname for Vasily.

We returned to our classes for study. Verkhovsky was not in class. During the following recess, Karpinsky, the company's commander, came in, Verkhovsky accompanying him. Following his command, we formed lines. He commanded, "Attention." Karpinsky began talking sternly but with nervousness in his voice, saying that we had erred against discipline, and if we did not come to our senses, we all would be severely punished. He advised us to apologize. After that, Verkhovsky commanded, "Disperse." It was obvious from the expressions on our faces that we were ready to be punished in whatever manner, but there was no way of reconciling us with Verkhovsky. Verkhovsky left with Karpinsky, and we never saw him again within the walls of the Corps. He was given a leave of absence. The director of the Corps, General Epanchin, came to talk to us, and said not a few rather sour words regarding our basic lack of understanding of discipline. Subsequent to that, many Pages were called in for questioning. I was not among those called. The Grand Duke Konstantin Konstantinovich also came, and in contrast to his usual ways, was very cold with us; but he would not talk to us about the incident, either collectively or individually. After he left, it became known that he did not find anything unacceptable in the way Verkhovsky behaved, and that most likely the whole affair should be dropped, and we should be penalized.

In the meanwhile, the rumor of the scandal reached beyond the Corps' walls. People were talking in St. Petersburg about a plot in the Page Corps, in which the Kamer-Page of the Emperor played the cardinal role. Old alumni became involved, and the senior among them, General Rikhter, summoned representatives of our class for an investigation. At the same time, we received a letter from Verkhovsky's mother in which she appealed to us to forget personal grudges, and to let her son continue his career. The letter was very convincing, and it was obvious that we had caused her a great deal of pain. But we remained relentless.

On March 5, my father died, and thus I was not present at the final phase of the Verkhovsky affair. When I returned to the Corps, I read in the military publication *Russky Invalid* the Order of His Majesty the Tsar on the reassignment of Verkhovsky to the 35th Artillery Brigade as a fire-master at the theater of war. I learned also that, in spite of the report of the Grand Duke which had exonerated Verkhovsky, the Tsar, after consultation with Rikhter, had sided with the Pages.

During the war, in his first battle, Verkhovsky was awarded the soldier's Cross of St. George and very soon was promoted to the rank of officer in one of the artillery brigades quartered in Finland.

A few years later I met Verkhovsky again, in the General Staff Academy. We both avoided encounters and conversations up until we were close to the end of our studies. As in the Corps, Verkhovsky was leading the class. But apparently he was not sure that he would be accepted for service in the General Staff. On one occasion, when we were approaching the time when his class was to be presented to the Tsar, he came to me and asked, "Say, Olferieff, why did your class expel me? If I had known what the accusations actually were, I would have tried to explain, and if I had erred in my younger years, I regret it, and would have begged the class to forgive me. Could you take it upon yourself to convey these words to our class?" I told him that I personally remembered very well the accusations in question, but that he refused to humble himself and chose to ignore the milieu from which he had derived all his privileges. I also promised to relay our conversation to the comrades, which I did a few days later at our graduation dinner. The comrades approved my reply to Verkhovsky, and wanted me to tell him that they would in no way interfere with his future service.

In another few days, when Verkhovsky was presented to the Tsar with his graduating class, the Tsar said to him, "I am pleased, Verkhovsky, that you have thought it over and are on the right path now. I want to congratulate you with the completion of your work in the Academy, and I wish you success in your future career."

"I trust, Your Imperial Majesty, that I shall be able to demonstrate by deed my devotion to You, Your Imperial Majesty, and to the Fatherland," Verkhovsky answered.

And then came the war. Verkhovsky, from the beginning, was appointed the Senior Adjutant of the General Staff in one of the army divisions, and demonstrated his valor by one exploit after another. He was awarded the St. George's Arms, the Order of St. George, and after being badly wounded, was evacuated to the rear. After he recovered, he was appointed to the Aviation School on the Black Sea. The revolution found him acting in this capacity.

Following the example of the Baltic Fleet, the sailors in Sevastopol had surrounded the officers' mess, where most of the officers were present, at the time, and demanded that they come out to the plaza. Verkhovsky tried to make use of his past record to save himself and his comrades. He came out to talk to the sailors from the balcony and told them that all the officers were on the side of revolution, and that he, as an individual who had suffered under the Tsarist regime, was willing to answer for all who were now in the quarters. Thus the danger was averted, and no terrorist acts occurred. Verkhovsky was elected as a member of a delegation from the Black Sea Fleet to the Petrograd Soviet of Workers and Soldiers. On his way, he stopped at Mogilev, at the Staff of the Supreme Commander, where I met him again. He was burning with a desire to serve the revolution, and in response to our pessimistic outlook, he affirmed that now our army should without doubt conquer Germany.

Then followed the Kerensky period, and Verkhovsky was made a general and was appointed Military Commander of the Moscow Region. In the course of the Kornilov Rebellion, he was temporarily present at his staff, and had consultations with Kornilov. But it was in vain that Kornilov trusted him. When Verkhovsky returned to Moscow, he switched sides and backed Kerensky, and together with him betrayed Kornilov.

When the Bolsheviks took over, he was in Petrograd and was arrested. However, he soon was released and entered the ranks of the Red Army.

Later, when I was already in America, I read that Verkhovsky was going around Moscow on a bicycle and lecturing in all the military schools. Finally, and that was before the case of Tukhachevsky, I heard that he was the Aide to the Commander in Chief of the Caucasus Military Region.

His subsequent fate is unknown to me.[13]

More on the Page Corps

We acquired some knowledge in the many subjects we were taught, but it seemed that not one of them gave us the chance to apply that knowledge practically [or even enable us to enter a school of higher learning without obtaining additional education and taking preliminary tests. It sometimes

13. On August 19, 1938 he was shot at the firing ground Kommunarka, NKVD mass execution site near Moscow (now within Moscow).

appeared that our program was purposely put together to keep us from leaving the military service.][14] The mathematics course, for instance, was very comprehensive; it included a whole year of arithmetic theory, which required not only knowing that two and two equal four, but proving why precisely four, and not five. We were taught analytical geometry, but not descriptive geometry, which did not qualify us even to become draftsmen in the future. We were taught to understand mathematical functions, but not how to make use of them. We were taught the political history of all times and people, the history of literature (Russian, French, German), art history, church history, and finally military history. There was so little time spent on the latter that we knew nothing about the history of war. We were taught jurisprudence, mechanics, chemistry, cosmography, geography, topography, theory of shading and perspective, fencing, horseback riding, ballroom dancing, and finally, so-called manual labor, in which we had to learn elementary carpentry and steel trades. This began and ended by teaching us to whittle small sticks with a sharp knife to make them as round as possible.

In addition to the allocation of money from the Department of Military Schools, the Corps of Pages also received an allocation from the Palace, which together amounted to 500 rubles per person per year, or a total of 100,000–125,000 rubles for the whole Corps. During those times, such a considerable sum made it possible to spend more money on our teachers as compared to the Cadet Corps, and the Corps of Pages took advantage of this in full measure. Everyone who stood out in the educational community at that time was invited to teach us, and thanks to the enlightened assistance of the Grand Duke, even the political convictions of the instructors did not act as a hindrance to employment in the Corps. For example, the priest Grigory Petrov, who was known for his rhetoric and very liberal sermons, was allowed to serve. We loved to listen to him in class; his lectures rarely touched on the church history which he taught—for this there was a book—but he spoke on the theme of everyday life in the officers' circles, which we were preparing to join. His speech flowed like a mountain spring, a clear crystal stream of the magnificent Russian language. Neither before nor after him have I heard such a preacher.

14. Bracketed text here was crossed out by the author.

A professor from the Artillery Academy, Colonel Persky, taught us mechanics. He was an outstanding mathematician at that time. With his lively comparisons and cleverly chosen examples from life, he was able to turn such a dry subject as mechanics into an interesting study.

The professor of chemistry, Colonel Ipatev, already a well-known scholar, gave us lectures on organic and inorganic chemistry. Later, when living in America, he became world famous for his achievements in the field of gasoline production.

An astronomer, who came specially from the Pulkovo Observatory, lectured us in cosmography; a famous lawyer, Professor Prince Drutskoi-Sokolinsky, lectured on the foundations of military legislation; and finally, Professor Petrov, who as an outstanding teacher was invited to Tsarskoe Selo to teach the Tsar's daughters, taught us Russian.

There were also weak teachers who followed long-since obsolescent methods, such as Rudolf Ignatevich Menzhinsky, teacher of history, who had taught all the classes for more than twenty-five years. He taught my father and me using the same textbook, gave the same lectures—page by page, asked the same questions, and dispensed grades according to tradition: if the father was a poor student then the son could not possibly receive a good mark. He was kept in the school only because no one could imagine the Corps without him.

There were also some teachers who were not too bad, but they had no tact and fared poorly. We played tricks on them in class, and the Pages drove them out in a short time. Finally, there were some like the Frenchman Du Lou, who came to class in a naval officer's uniform that did not fit him and told us obscene anecdotes. However, he did not remain long—he was sentenced to hard labor for the corruption of a minor.

Striving to give us as broad an education as possible, they invited to the Corps great scholars who they discovered were visiting the capital. I remember one dark-haired Italian who was rushing from hall to hall with a small box in his hands demonstrating his invention of the wireless telegraph. It was none other than Marconi. I remember our excursions to the museum, to the underground mine shaft of the Institute of Mines under the Neva, to the factories, and to the military ships. I remember how we were taken to Kronstadt to view the launching of the handsome cruiser

Variag,[15] sparkling white as snow. It was leaving for the Far East and would soon be abandoned (in battle at Chempulo).

In addition, the Corps spent much money to develop our musical and artistic talents. Every day after supper, musicians from the orchestra of the Court Chapel arrived to teach us to play various instruments, beginning with piano and concluding with balalaika and drums. A choir and three orchestras were organized. In the evening there were also classes in painting and sculpture.

In general, our school days, beginning at six in the morning and finishing at ten in the evening, were crammed with all sorts of studies, and when I came home on Saturdays, I was sincerely happy to be able to get enough sleep and rest. I felt how quickly I was growing and becoming a man, how my strength was increasing, and how youth was blossoming; and in full measure I drank up that worry-free joy of life which by good fortune falls to youth.

Artists from the Imperial Theater were frequently invited to the Corps: Davydov, Varlamov, Savina, Michurina; and from the opera: Kuza, Figner, Yakovlev. They read, sang, recited, and performed plays for us. Before graduation, an historical play, *Izmail*, was presented in costume. Yurev, the artist, produced it, and the roles were played by the Pages.

It always makes me sad when I recollect how much was given to us and how little we grasped. Like swine trampling on pearls, we took everything for granted, and only accepted that which amused us. We studied poorly and lazily, and lacking natural artistic talent, never became artists. [The main cause probably was that we were accepted into the Corps not for our personal abilities, but on the merit of our ancestors, and very often these abilities were insufficient for receiving an education.][16]

There were godforsaken professions such as veterinary medicine, dentistry, and drafting, which for one reason or another were made up primarily of men unable to become medical doctors or engineers. (Of course there are exceptions to this observation.) One such profession was the teachers in military schools, most of whom were officers who had graduated from one

15. "Varangian."

16. Bracketed text here was crossed out by the author.

of the second-class military academies. These were good, deserving, and highly moral people who conscientiously dedicated themselves to difficult, responsible, and thankless work. But among them there were no brilliant people to be found.

Among my educators, I remember with great respect and gratitude three colonels. One was Vladimir Vladimirovich Kvadri, whose very kind heart was hidden under his austere exterior. Then there was Aleksei Alekseevich Orlov, large, clumsy, and baldheaded, who had difficulty keeping step in formation, but at the same time had a good ear for music and played the cello exceptionally well. Looking at him I always asked myself how did this man enter military service? In spite of this there was not one of us who did not remember him with a kind word. And there was Vladimir Filipovich Potekhin, Commander of the Second Company, nicknamed "Zhamais" from the word *jamais*, which he once read from the class blackboard pronouncing all the letters. He was an old bachelor and philosopher, who gave his whole life to the military training of his pupils, deeply believing that Russia would be happy only when our forces occupied "Berlin on the river Spree." When we complained of exhaustion after extremely long drills or military excursions through the city during severe frosts, we knew that the reminder about "Berlin" would follow without fail. In spite of his exceedingly plain appearance and visible austerity, everyone loved him.

My first director of the Corps was Count Fedor Eduardovich Keller, who was a former Page, Horse Guardsman, officer of the General Staff, Adjutant to Skobelev, Commander of the Imperial Family Rifle Guards Regiment, member of the English Club, and a friend of the Emperor. His nickname was "Pegashka"[17] because he had one patch of gray whiskers. How knowledgeable Keller was in military subjects I do not know. I only know that among us he was one of our own—we loved him and were proud of him. I remember how every Friday late in the evening returning from the club he would quickly walk through our bedroom to the infirmary, where a nurse served who was not in her prime of life, but still a beautiful woman. We gossiped about the Count's love which had begun long ago, going back to the war with Turkey, and for this love we gave him an even bigger halo.

17. "Piebald" (of two colors).

Whether it was merely a coincidence or the direct result of the appointment of Grand Duke Konstantin Konstantinovich as chief of all military schools, I do not know, but immediately after the Grand Duke assumed the office, Count Keller gave up his position with the Corps and was appointed Governor of Ekaterinoslav. It is hard to say what his former experience had in common with the administrative responsibilities of a governor. With the declaration of the Japanese War, Keller asked to be assigned to the fighting army. His request was granted, and he received command of the 10th Infantry Division. This appointment was not uncharacteristic of that time. Count Keller had not served in the ranks from the time he relinquished his command of the Rifle Battalion. In spite of all his brilliant, knightly conduct and personal bravery, which he had proven with Skobelev, it was completely predictable that he was not prepared to lead sixteen thousand men into battle in a country which was totally unfamiliar to him and under incomprehensible contemporary battle conditions.

Historians of this war say that the Russian generals, in searching for solutions to the problems of up-to-date battle management, either went to the deep rear, giving their orders by telephone and thus losing the necessary personal contact with their subordinates, or threw themselves into the front lines, thus losing touch with the remaining units. Count Keller belonged to the latter. He was killed while they were advancing in lines as he rode out ahead on his white horse.

My second director was General Nikolai Alekseevich Epanchin, an officer of the Preobrazhensky Regiment, participant in the Turkish war, officer of the General Staff, and war historian. The hostility and coldness we felt towards Epanchin was as great as our liking was for Keller. But since the director was not close to us and the vicissitudes in our lives at that time were not influenced by him, but rather by the much more colorful, high standing Grand Duke Konstantin Konstantinovich, we paid very little attention to Epanchin.

Again I remembered
the land of my dear country.
And the sorrow of the past
struck deeply in my heart.

—K. R. [KONSTANTIN ROMANOV]

How often in my exile I recalled this verse, when I experienced longing for my homeland to the point of physical pain. Suddenly I remembered the author of it, our beloved Grand Duke Konstantin Konstantinovich, and asked myself: How could a person who had so little Russian blood, and who by his position was obliged to remain at a distance from the mass of ordinary Russian people, appear inseparable from and so understanding of those people? And the recollection of him answered my question: in Konstantin Romanov beat the heart of a poet, which helped him divine the Russian soul, penetrate the Russian love for the homeland, and stand together with them as an indivisible part.

When I was in the fifth grade, we were having Bible study. The class had not prepared the lesson, and as the monitor of the class I asked the priest, by the name of B[elogostitsky], not to ask us questions. The lazy, cynical, and absolutely incompetent teacher had no objections to this. He sat down at the desk, opened up the catechism and began to read in a monotone. We all quickly sank into a state very close to sleep except those in the back benches who were playing an audacious game of tic-tac-toe, and from time to time, the disgruntled shriek of the loser could be heard.

At that moment, the Grand Duke entered the classroom. It was impossible not to recognize him because his portrait hung in our presence. Besides his height, his eyes, with their sorrowful expression, drew one's attention. I reported to him. He greeted the priest and us and went to an empty seat in the back of the room and asked us to continue the lesson.

The priest closed the book and announced to the Grand Duke that he would quiz the students. This was perhaps the best way possible to hide his lack of talent. He called on me to give an answer to the lesson, probably hoping that I was prepared. He asked the question. I repeated it in an affirmative tone, as it happens when a student doesn't know the answer. The priest reiterated the question again and included the answer. I paraphrased the answer. He asked another question with an imbedded answer. I repeated the answer. And thus we began, as they say, to "pull the wool over the eyes" of the Grand Duke.

But here, from the back of the room resounded the voice of the Grand Duke, "And from what Gospel is that answer which you just repeated after Father Belogostitsky?" I realized that my downfall had come. I could have taken a risk—there was a 25 percent chance of success. But I decided that it was necessary to accept my embarrassment with honor and answered, "I do not know, Your Imperial Highness."

"From all that you said, this was the only good and honest answer," stated the Grand Duke and left the classroom.

Afterwards Matveev, who was sitting next to him, told me that the Grand Duke asked him, "Who is this fellow?" Matveev gave him my name. "Is he the son of a Preobrazhenets?[18]" he asked. "Yes, he is."

When we were left alone in the classroom, there was a burst of indignation against the priest. In the back of the room they started pounding on the desks, and cries of "We cannot be let down" erupted. Belogostitsky had a difficult time trying to quiet everyone and said that the Grand Duke was still within our premises and was able hear us. Soon, however, everything returned to the previous rut of lethargy, but I could not overcome the mental distress I felt thinking my career had been destroyed so early in life.

Belogostitsky, the teacher of religion, did not remain for long. He was swept out in the house cleaning which came about with the appointment of the Grand Duke, who dismissed many teachers.

Besides changes in personnel, the physical punishment practiced in some of the Corps had been prohibited, and there were glaring changes in physical health education. For instance, before the Grand Duke's time, students younger than sixteen who contracted venereal disease were immediately expelled from school. Those who became ill between sixteen and eighteen were transferred to the third discipline category, and were sometimes subjected to shameful punishment by having their epaulets removed so that everyone saw the unfortunate sick students walking in the back of the line. At the same time, no measures were taken to prevent the possibility of contagion in the schools. Naturally, those who became ill concealed the infection until it was too late, and frequently their health was impaired for the rest of their lives. I remember that I did not know where such a disease came from, and I was furious when my friend was expelled because he became ill. On Saturday, I arrived home and while sitting at the table shared my indignation with my parents and our guests, naming the disease. My father changed the subject, and after supper, explained to me what the

18. An officer of the Preobrazhensky Regiment.

problem was and suggested that in the future I not repeat words picked up from the Corps unless I knew what they meant.

The Grand Duke made fundamental changes in the situation—he abolished all punishment of those who became ill, and demanded that the Corps not expel but treat them. A venereal disease division was organized in the infirmary. This was a very bold decision for these times, which only the Grand Duke could bring about.

With the same wisdom, a solution regarding smoking was established. The sixteen- to seventeen-year-olds in the Corps were permitted to smoke, and in the lower divisions, the punishment was reduced to a minimum.

Never before had there been such significant changes as there were under the Grand Duke as chief of military schools. He visited the Corps often, went into all the details of our life, and knew all of us. He did not boast knowledge of our last names as others did; but he knew more about each of us, and which ones had shortcomings and who needed help. It was astonishing that even people outside the Corps had the same impression of him.

He remembered me well from the time of my unsuccessful answers about the Bible. Once on a Saturday when I was a senior, and just before my departure for vacation, I was called to the duty room, where the Adjutant of the Grand Duke, Colonel Rittikh, informed me that Her Royal Highness the Greek Queen, Olga Konstantinovna, the sister of the Grand Duke, to whom I was attached during the christening of the heir, desired to see me on Sunday after the ten o'clock liturgy in the Marble Palace. Dress uniform was required. This call flattered me, but considering an event which I shall speak of later, I did not want her to recall the details of the christening ceremony and set out for the palace reluctantly.

In the church of the Marble Palace, as in all palace churches, the men stood on the left side and the women on the right. By the old Russian tradition, it was just the opposite: the men stood on the right and the women on the left. I came early and stood in a secluded corner on the left side of this very small church. Gradually about twenty-five people gathered, seemingly those serving in the palace. Just before the beginning of the service, the Grand Duke entered with the Queen and his daughter, Tatiana. After them came his long-necked brother, Dmitry Konstantinovich. The liturgy began. A small choir sang very harmoniously, exceptionally simple songs, and their simplicity produced the best melodies, which so rarely were heard in the big churches. The plain surroundings brought me back to the main town of our district, Rzhev, to the days of my childhood, and to my deep belief.

After the liturgy, the Grand Duke, who noticed me immediately on his entrance into the church, approached me and said, "It is good that I found you. The Queen wants to see you before you leave for home."

I kissed the Queen's hand, and she gave me a small case which contained a gold medal on a sky-blue ribbon. On the front side of the medal was an image, a profile of her husband, King George, and on the other side, Mercury, gracefully running naked with wings in the place of spurs. "Take this in memory of our meeting at the christening of the heir—this is the medal of the Greek Order of the Savior." I bowed deeply and again kissed her outstretched hand. "And now you will go to lunch with us," said the Grand Duke, who was standing next to us.

In the dining room, everyone except me was a member of the family: the Grand Duke with his wife Elisaveta Mavrikievna, who, being a Lutheran, had not been in church. The Grand Duke sat at the head of the table and on his right sat the Queen, and I was seated next to her. To the right of me sat Dmitry Konstantinovich. Across from me, to the left of the Grand Duke sat his daughter, Tatiana, further down next to the hostess sat her sister-in-law, Duchess Vera Konstantinovna of Württemberg. The hostess sat between her and Dmitry Konstantinovich. During lunch, as in all such family settings, there were free and easy discussions on family affairs. They were deliberating on the departure of the Queen; often everyone spoke at the same time, interrupting each other. Then, all at once, everyone became silent and ate quickly. Dmitry Konstantinovich asked me in what regiment I was planning to enlist. It was necessary to answer diplomatically, because Dmitry commanded the Horse Grenadiers, which I intended to join, but I had not yet been accepted by the officers of the regiment. "I hope, Your Imperial Highness, that the Horse Grenadiers will deem me worthy of acceptance." "Oh, what a coincidence," said the Grand Duke. "You like horses?" The subject of horses, as I learned later, was one of the two subjects on which Dmitry Konstantinovich could sustain a conversation. (The other was religion.) And for me it was more familiar than for many others. He talked about the Orlov-Rostopchin breed of horses, and the fact that unfortunately not all shared his good opinion of it. My responses were appropriate and the twenty minutes at the table passed very quickly. Before lunch ended, Konstantin Konstantinovich asked me to show him my medal, and upon examining it said as he pointed to Mercury, "Look, don't make a mistake. This is not the King—but maybe it is. However, maybe they look alike in this form. But to learn the truth you will have to ask the Queen." "You are always saying foolish things, Konstantin," Olga said, laughing and hitting him on the shoulder.

After lunch, the Grand Duke took me to his study—a large room densely furnished with many pieces of upholstered furniture. Its windows looked out on the Neva. There was a large table bearing visible signs that the owner behind it did a lot of work. All around on the shelves were many books and pictures. The Grand Duke sat me down in a deep chair and began to question me about where I had lived before entering the Corps. Learning that I had lived in obscurity in a village, he became very interested, and inquired about the peasants and their religion. He, of course, did not know of our village adversities, and he did not touch upon them. His questions concerned their spiritual life, and not once did I hear dissonance in them.

Before the end of my audience with Konstantin Konstantinovich, he drew back the heavy drapes in the corner, behind which appeared a small chapel with a great number of heavily ornamented icons. "Here," he said, "when you get married, I shall bless you."

Then he remembered my father, with whom at one time he had played in amateur theater, and asked me to give him his regards. As a result, my father came with me to the palace on New Year's Day and we signed the book of holiday greetings.

Upon dismissing me, Konstantin Konstantinovich said, "I hope that I did not take too much of your holiday time. Go and take your rest." "Your Imperial Highness, I will never forget this day," I answered.

My visit to the Marble Palace was not an exception but the rule in the routine of the Grand Duke. A Sunday seldom passed without a cadet having lunch with him. In the course of time, I exchanged impressions concerning these meetings with other former cadets, and found out that the Grand Duke never asked them where they received their education.

It is fair to rebuke the old regime, which placed irresponsible people in responsible positions. Konstantin Konstantinovich represented a fortunate exception, and if he took advantage of being unaccountable, he did it only for good deeds. In many instances no one else could surmount the traditions and stagnation of those times. The Grand Duke conducted reforms thanks only to his direct access to the Emperor.

As the war approached, all the sons of Konstantin Konstantinovich remained at their posts in the front lines. One of them, Oleg, was killed in one of the first battles. The war found the Grand Duke in Germany; and not wishing to avail himself of the privileges presented to him by Wilhelm II, with great difficulty he walked part of the way accompanied by other Russians, crossed the border, and returned home. He was married to a German woman, and probably the ethical shock of the war was especially painful for him. The death of his son [in battle] depressed him even more, damaged his health, and quickly sent him to his grave.

The Arrival of the Emperor

"What use are dances, when I am good at the 'front,'" the pupils in the military schools were saying. This expression was brought to us by the cadets who transferred to the Corps. Its meaning can be explained as follows: Dancing, drill, which was called the *front*, and gymnastics were compulsory components of our physical education. Grades received in them were combined, and an average grade was worked out. This average was taken into consideration together with the marks earned in academic subjects for evaluating our progress. Thus, if one's grade in the *front* was good, then it was not necessary to try too hard in dancing. And vice versa, if we were weak in the *front*, then we had to be successful in dancing in order to receive an average grade. There was little masculinity in dancing, and for boys our age, heroism and masculinity were everything we could wish for. Therefore, in dancing we were only fulfilling our duty; most of us did not like it; and as a rule, we did not shine at the grand balls.

This was the first year of my residence in the Corps. In the White Hall, the stage manager of the ballet troupe of the Imperial Theaters, Nikolai Sergeevich Aistov, taught us dancing. Tall, well-built, with long gray curls, he dressed in a formal frock coat and impeccably supple half boots, and was strict with us to the point of rudeness. But since we knew that in fulfilling his compulsory military service he rose to the rank of Feldwebel, we were inspired with respect for him, and considering him one of us, tolerated his rudeness.

He taught us ballet—first of all the positions, then classical dances: polonaise, minuet, lancers, and quadrille. After that came the mazurka and the waltz. On that day, as always, we began with the positions. He stood in front of us gracefully separating his long legs like a compass demonstrating the various positions, and we stood opposite trying hard to imitate him. At the same time, a pianist, a sullen man of about thirty-five, wearing an exceptionally long frock coat, was beating out the tempo with familiar motifs on a grand piano in the corner.

Suddenly, from the side of Georgievsky Hall towards the direction of the special classes, Kamer-Page Engelke ran through shouting, "The Emperor, the Emperor." Trembling seized me as I realized that now I would see the Emperor himself. A lump stuck in my throat. My legs, which were still in third position, felt as though weights hung from them. Not a minute had passed when the stentorian voice of Aistov resounded, "Ten-hut!" We drew our legs together and became silent. At the door of the hall appeared a group of five or six generals and officers resplendent in dress uniforms. All of them were tall. But observing attentively I saw the Emperor in the back of this group. He resembled his well-known portraits, but he was a head shorter than all those who entered with him; and this unexpected contrast had an unfavorable effect on me. Every man knows how a boy of twelve admires height and strength. Even all adults want to be tall or appear taller than they are. But this little disappointment was displaced by the exultant feeling of happiness to be in the same room with the Emperor, to see and hear him. When he drew nearer, I noticed that on his simple Preobrazhensky frock coat he had more pleats than I would have allowed my tailor to make for me. His wide trousers and boots resembled government issues. This impression came quickly, and again quickly disappeared. He neither shaved nor trimmed his beard, probably following the custom of the Russian common people, and a considerable part of his cheeks was covered with hair.

"Good day, Gentlemen," resounded the voice of the Tsar.

I nearly began to sob, and in a high soprano together with the others I yelled: "Good day, Your Imperial Majesty."

The Emperor, arranging his unmanageable mustache with his right hand and holding his head high in a somewhat peculiar manner, passed so closely in front of us that it was awe-inspiring, and looked directly into our eyes with an affectionate regard, as if he had long known each of us personally.

After passing in front of us, the Emperor moved to the side. At this point Count Keller entered the hall with rapid strides. The Emperor extended his hand to him and said, "Today I decided to make use of a few free hours which I was given unexpectedly, and stopped by to see you, Count." It seemed as if he was trying to make an excuse for not forewarning the director of his arrival.

The Count made a low bow and stood next to the Emperor but a quarter step back. Aistov ordered us to pair off for a polonaise. The pianist began to play the polonaise from *A Life for the Tsar*, and we proceeded to dance around the hall. It was very distasteful having to present ourselves to the Emperor for the first time by passing him with a dance instead of with a ceremonial march. After performing all the required steps of the dance, we again returned to our beginning positions. The Emperor shook hands with Aistov and proceeded to the special classes.

After his departure, our enthusiasm was so overwhelming that no one could think of continuing the lesson. We all gathered around Aistov and compared notes on what had just occurred. It seemed to us that the Tsar saw and perhaps would remember each one of us.

Soon an order came for all those who had seen the Emperor to assemble in front of the building across from the main entrance. Here awaiting the Emperor was one lone, sturdy, gray trotter harnessed to a small so-called German sled, which was covered with a warm bearskin rug. In the coach box sat the bearded driver, in a tightly fitting coachman's overcoat with medals on his chest. Behind the first sled stood a troika, a sled harnessed with three horses abreast, for the Tsar's retinue.

When the Emperor had made the rounds of all the classes, he exited by the main entrance, sat down in the sled, and putting on his gloves, gestured to his acquaintances and to everyone who could see him, and started towards the gates. With a deafening roar, "Hurrah!" rang out from the three hundred young Pages gathered at the entrance, and we all ran toward the gates after the Tsar. Those who were closer caught hold of the back of the sled, and jumped on the runners, on the coachman's box, and even in the area where the Emperor had his legs. Looking at us he smiled, clearly sharing our need to observe the old traditions established during the time of Alexander II.

We ran after the Emperor until we reached the public library, at which point the coachman turned left onto Nevsky Prospect. The Emperor waved at us; those who clung to the sled jumped off, and the horse, relieved of the load, dashed in the direction of the Winter Palace.

The Emperor's visit to the Corps was marked by a three-day holiday. I ran home and breathlessly told everyone of my great fortune to have seen the Tsar. When I came to my senses a little bit, my disappointment in the outward appearance of the Emperor resurfaced. And I asked my father, "Why does the Emperor have so many pleats on his frock coat? And why such baggy trousers, and strange, unattractive boots?" Father smiled and said, "Because the Emperor is wearing a uniform, not like all of you with your chests puffed out who wear French trousers. What other way can the Tsar dress, but in a uniform?"

The Emperor visited us every year. We saw him in parades, and when we were on guard duty, and in Court service. Meetings with him became routine, and they no longer threw me into such a state of wild enthusiasm. The joy of seeing him gradually faded to the background, and was replaced with the joy of getting a leave. I remember counting the days to the approaching vacations. As a rule, we counted thus: Christmas, two weeks; Maslenitsa,[19] three days; fasting, one week; Emperor, three days; Easter, ten days; etc. The meetings with him were so similar, one to the next, that a great many completely vanished from my memory. But the impression of the first meeting remained with me all my life.

The Heir Is Born

On August 4, 1904, the long-awaited heir was born. This event, so joyous for their Majesties, served, as one would expect, to lift the spirit of the entire country and especially of the Manchurian Army, which in those days

19. Also known as Butter Week, Crepe Week, and other names, celebrated before Great Lent.

suffered defeat after defeat; and low morale from those losses pervaded all spheres of society.

During this time, I was on summer vacation in Kurchino, and eagerly devoured all news of the war, trying to find in it at least a tiny ray of hope for a favorable turning point. But in vain. Even *Novoe Vremia* revealed nothing to advance this hope. The neighboring peasants, knowing that I read the papers, gathered on the country estate in order to find out what was happening and talk about the ills of the day.

"Have you heard anything good about the war Fyodor Sergeevich?" asked Osip Zadnevsky, who was a dedicated, honest village police captain with an inquisitive mind.

"No, things look bad. We must be patient," I answered.

"When will this damned war end? It has already destroyed many people. And they continue to take more and more into the service. Nikanor from Kashin, who lost his leg, arrived home a few days ago and was saying that it's impossible to defeat the Japanese. He said that just as we dragged the cannon into position on a hill, the cursed enemy immediately destroyed it before we could get off a shot. Their cannon, such an evil one, can fire from somewhere and not even be seen. So, Sir, is it possible that we do not have such guns?"

"Yes, we have." I lied involuntarily, not admitting that we did not know how to shoot from covered positions. "It is just necessary to wait. Maybe they did not have time to bring in the guns. You see Manchuria is so far from us."

"Since it's such a great way off, why fight for her?" Osip wasn't appeased. "Here messengers from Siberia are saying that immense quantities of land exist there, but there's no one to cultivate it. It would be better to plow it first and march on Manchuria from there."

Trying to defend our Far Eastern policy, I said, "But we need an outlet to the sea in order to carry on trade."

"How can we carry on trade, Sir? We ourselves have nothing to eat."

"You are so impatient, Osip. Look at our happiness. An heir has been born. Now we'll quickly defeat the Japanese."

"But, Master, you know he's a little tyke. We'll have to wait about twenty years for him to rescue us. No, Fyodor Sergeyevich, according to my simple reasoning, it's necessary to end the war quickly, or it will be bad for us all."

As Osip spoke, it was clear that all who had gathered around shared his view. With a heavy heart, I left to have my supper.

During that summer our home was filled with young people. Cousins, neighboring friends, and their guests spent days and nights with us. There was a great deal of noise in the dining room, and I was met by shouts coming from all directions. "Well how is everything, Fyodor?" yelled Grisha[20] Ivanov, a student at Petersburg University who was visiting with our neighbors. "You promised that we would not retreat further, but suddenly we seem to be losing ground again. Now we cannot believe you. It is clear that we have to go ourselves to save the cause."

I did not answer him. It seemed to me that Grisha was right, that every honest man should be there now. And I would have to accomplish this quickly before it was too late. After supper I went back to my suite. It was already dark, a myriad of August stars were twinkling in the sky. Here and there meteors were flying, and I reflected upon how many little stars were being destroyed, yet it did not seem that there were fewer of them. [From the maidservants' quarters drifted the sound of several voices in song. One of them stood out with its strength and freshness. A thought flew through my mind, "This dark-eyed Grusha[21] knows that I like her and will send news of herself." I did not go there.][22]

For a long time that evening I was unable to fall asleep, because I kept trying to figure out how I could go to war without waiting for promotion to an officer's rank, which would take another year. This is the condition I was in when I received a telegram in the morning from the Corps ordering my immediate return to carry out court duty.

When I arrived at the Corps, preparations for the christening of the heir were in progress. Court uniforms were hastily being fitted for us. And since the senior class had already been promoted to officers, we were quickly taught the Pages' duties to the Royal individuals, the most complicated of which was carrying the trains of the Tsarina and the Grand Duchesses. The Empress had a train that trailed nine feet along the ground, and the Grand Duchesses—six feet. The result of all the instruction was to teach us that

20. Nickname for Grigory.
21. Nickname for Agrafena and Agrippina.
22. Bracketed text here was crossed out by the author.

every place where there was room, the train had to be smoothed out on the floor; and at turns and stops, it had to be rearranged or draped around their legs. During all these operations, under no circumstance should one impede the free movement of its wearer.

The teaching itself was conducted in this manner: In turn each of us wore a blanket in the form of a skirt, and fastened to it with pins was another blanket, which dragged along the floor. We depicted an imaginary woman, who was making all sorts of grimaces and wiggling her behind as she walked from one end of the hall to the other, making unexpected turns, stopping, and reversing direction. At the same time the trainees were carrying, straightening, and turning the trailing appendage. Training was accompanied by all sorts of witty remarks and finally was concluded with the least successful student, by virtue of his inability to keep up with his lady, having to treat the rest to sweet tea pies. For this we sent a servant to a confectioner's shop called Ballet, on the corner of Ekaterininskaia Street and Nevsky Prospect, who brought us one hundred tea pies which we immediately devoured, stuffing our young stomachs.

During one of our exercises Vasia Gershel'man, who had just been promoted to the cornets in the Nezhinsky Dragoon Regiment, came to visit us on his way to the battlefront, where his regiment and his father were stationed. Appearing cheerful and happy and not for a minute doubting that we would have a quick victory, he aroused in us both envy and the desire to drop everything and run off to the front. I shared my plans with him to ask for an assignment from the Corps to the war, but he told me that an order had just been issued not to promote any more officers to units stationed in Manchuria, on account of the great scarcity of officers in European Russia. In spite of everything, I still maintained hope, and decided to submit my report to the supervisors.

In the meantime, we pages were being assigned to the imperial personages by their seniority and by our class standing. Thus, the first-place student was assigned to the Emperor, the second and third to the Empress, the fourth and fifth to the other Empress,[23] the sixth and others following to the Grand Duchesses. Those remaining without designation were regarded as reserves and were appointed to the visiting royalty.

23. Empress Maria Fedorovna, mother of Nicholas II.

I was assigned as a constant Page to Empress Aleksandra Fedorovna, but since she did not appear at the christening,[24] I was appointed to the Greek Queen Olga Konstantinovna, who at this time was visiting her brother in the Marble Palace.

On the day of the christening we were driven to the Baltic train station in court carriages. In New Peterhof we were again met by carriages and were conveyed to the large Peterhof Palace. This palace, built during the reign of Elizaveta Petrovna,[25] impressed me because it was the oldest building I had ever seen. It had low ceilings, narrow doors, and a row of small passage rooms, of no use to anyone, which were furnished with old, uncomfortable furniture. No one had lived in this palace for a long time, and it had been turned into a museum.

We were arrayed in one of these small rooms from which a door led to the so-called Internal Chambers, where only the Tsar's family and their intimate friends could gain access. The doors to these chambers were always closed, and stationed outside were the so-called *Araps*—Abyssinians or simply Negroes draped in embroidered red kaftans, baggy silk trousers, stockings, and soft slippers, which were turned up at the toes. These slippers allowed them to move around without making any noise. The first Negro was brought here by Peter the Great from the Turkish campaign. Since that time, they have always been a presence in the palace. One of the descendants of the Arap Gannibal[26] was, as is well-known, our poet Aleksandr Sergeevich Pushkin.

Sometime later the door opened, the Araps moved to each side and Empress Maria Fedorovna appeared on the arm of Grand Duke Aleksei Aleksandrovich—she was the godmother and he represented the entire Manchurian Army, its officers and soldiers, who were proclaimed their heir's godfathers. After the Empress came her Pages. Next in the procession was the Queen of Greece on the arm of Grand Duke Mikhail Aleksandrovich, who had just lost his title as heir to the throne. On her way past me, the Queen gave me her rather heavy ermine cape, which I placed on my left arm as we were taught, and followed her, totally concentrating on her royal,

24. A mother could not attend church for forty days after the birth of a child.

25. Empress Elizaveta Petrovna, daughter of Peter the Great.

26. Abram Petrovich Gannibal (1696–1781), General of Peter the Great and Pushkin's great-grandfather, of African descent.

nine-foot train. It was the same length as the Empress's, but according to protocol, she was entrusted with only one Page. I focused all my attention on seeing that her train did not get caught on something, or that the Grand Duke Vladimir Aleksandrovich, who was walking behind me, did not step on it. Suddenly the cape slipped from my arm and was caught on a doorknob which we were passing, and its lace trimming tore. I quickly dropped the train, disentangled the cape from the knob, and successfully proceeded ahead. But to my great shame, the cape again was caught on the next doorknob and made an even more violent ripping noise. The powerful voice of Vladimir Aleksandrovich rang out from behind. "Olga, what is all this ripping noise that your Page is making?" The Queen did not look around. I was saved probably because everyone was used to Vladimir Aleksandrovich's continual joking.

At this moment we were entering the church. Olga Konstantinovna stood in her place. I arranged her train around her legs and moved back. Before doing anything else, I examined the lace on her cape, and to my horror, saw that a six-inch piece of lace was hanging from it. I was so disturbed by what had happened that the ceremony passed without my noticing it. I only heard the baby as he cried out weakly when he was immersed in water, as all babies would do in his situation.

When the ceremony ended, the procession retraced its steps to the Internal Chambers, and I parted with the Queen and her train in the area where the Araps stood, but the cape remained on my arm. When we were drawn up again in two ranks, I tried to tear off the hanging piece of lace, but it was risky to do this because the tear could have gone further. The servant who came with us from the Corps and who was standing in the rear saw my difficulty, produced a pair of scissors from his pocket, and cut it off. This piece was in my possession for a long time as a remembrance of my clumsiness and all the worry which I had lived through on this ill-fated day of my first court duty. I comforted myself at the time by my firm decision to request a voluntary transfer to the active army immediately upon my return to the Corps. This would be duty that I knew and liked. Out there would be service befitting a soldier's rank.

Soon from the Interior Chambers came a footman wearing a hat with a plume, short breeches, stockings, and shoes, who loudly proclaimed: "Her Royal Majesty, the Queen of Greece wishes to see her Page."

"Page to the Queen of Greece," voices were transmitting from one to the other. I stepped out, feeling like someone who is about to be condemned to death, and followed the footman.

In the center of one of the rooms to which I was brought stood a child's crib. Around it were only ladies and probably the heir's nurse. Among them I saw Olga Konstantinovna, who took the cape from me, threw it on the nearest chair, thanked me, and then taking me by the hand, led me to the crib, saying, "I want you to see your heir." In the crib lay a small, nice, and red lump, who was trying with great effort to straighten out his arms and legs, continually throwing off his sheet, with which his nurse was repeatedly covering him. I looked intently at the baby, trying to remember his face and find in it something different from other babies which would remain in my memory; but it was futile—he looked just like any other infant. After letting me go, Olga Konstantinovna said, "I hope to see you again soon." I kissed her extended hand and joined my group.

On my way back to the Corps, I was dreaming only of how I could distinguish myself in the war, how everyone, including Olga Konstantinovna, would know of my heroic deeds, and how she would forgive me for the torn cape. I then remembered Osip Zadnevsky, and after the victory I would go to him and say, "You see Osip, I told you that it was just necessary to be patient." I was wishing for even much more, but to my great disappointment, upon my request, which I gave on my return to the Corps, General Epanchin imposed the decision: "Everyone has his turn. There is no basis for complying with this request." But coming to congratulate us on our promotion to Kamer-Pages, he told me that I had already spent a lot of time and effort on my preparation, that there were so few officers in European Russia now, that the unnecessary dispatch to the fighting army of an officer who had not as yet completed his training would serve no use, but rather would do harm. He approved of my aspiration and said that I would still have time to serve my country.

I did not want to go to Kurchino for the remaining two weeks of leave and with pleasure accepted my classmate's invitation to accompany him to Pskov Province.

A Shot Fired

In St. Petersburg, the last quarter of 1904 seemed to follow its normal course. Receptions and state dinners were taking place as usual in the Winter Palace. With the gathering of society from foreign hot springs and from their own country estates, the social season of informal parties, balls, operas, and concerts was under way. The Guards were celebrating their squadron and company holidays with overflowing rivers of champagne and drunken orgies. Only those who had kin at the front or a few others who understood that Russia was in the midst of a tragedy were thinking about the war. When war was mentioned, the majority railed against Kuropatkin,[27] the Commander in Chief, heaping all the blame on him and expressing their surprise that so much confidence was placed in this "parvenue" as to entrust him with the command of the army. One of the principal abettors of our troubles, military educator Mikhail Ivanovich Dragomirov, could think of nothing better than to make witty remarks and puns to the effect that "in Manchuria macaques fight with bunglers," and that he was able to eat most dishes except partridges in sugar, which he couldn't stomach, alluding to the names of the two chief officers of the war, General Kuropatkin[28] and War Minister Sakharov.[29]

Meanwhile, with each day, impatience and discontent were mounting in the common people throughout the land. Grisha Ivanov was saying that in open meetings at the university, they were invited to take up arms to put an end to the oppression under which the populace lived. For Christmas I went to Moscow. While there I visited a childhood friend of mine, Pasha Ivanitsky, who then served in one of the Grenadiers' Regiments of the Moscow garrison. We went together to the Moscow Art Theater to see Kachalov

27. Aleksei Nikolaevich Kuropatkin (1848–1925) was a Russian General and Minister of War. He was highly regarded in peace and war as being one of the foremost soldiers in Europe until his losses in the Russo-Japanese War. His lack of success in that war was largely attributable to his subjugation to the command of Admiral Alekseev, the Tsar's Viceroy in the Far East, and to internal dissension among the generals. In his later writings, he admitted his own mistakes and gave nothing but praise to the troops who had been committed to battle in conditions that could bring nothing but failure.

28. Russian surname originating from the first name or nickname Kuropatka, "partridge."

29. Russian surname derived from the word *sakhar*, "sugar."

in one of his crowning roles as Ibsen's hero Brand, the prototype of a future Bolshevik. In addition to the marvelous and thoroughly realistic performance of the actors, I was also struck by the genuine, everyday crowd filling the spectators' hall—there were no shiny military uniforms nor opulent ladies' costumes in the loges, such as lit up the theaters of St. Petersburg. In Moscow, it seemed, the bulk of the crowd consisted of students, both men and women, who wore their everyday clothes, and bought cheap seats. Doctors, lawyers, and Muscovite merchants of the new-style "high finance" occupied the parterre. I felt ill at ease in my gold-embroidered uniform, and tried to remain as inconspicuous as possible.

In the theater, Pasha introduced me to one of his regimental comrades and two women college students, who invited us to their place of residence for a cup of tea, apologizing endlessly to me for the simplicity of their surroundings and the meagerness of the things served. The girls lived in the same part of town where the Grenadiers were stationed, beyond the Moscow River, occupying a small, clean room with mats on the floor and geraniums at the windows. Both girls attended dental courses. It was obvious that Pasha was in love with one of them, a tall girl with brown hair and light-gray, melancholy eyes, whose name was Olga Alekseevna Obukhova. Later I learned that she was the illegitimate daughter of my own distant relative, Aleksei Obukhov, who served in the Horse Guards Regiment at one time. He used to visit us at our estate when I was a child. As I recall, he, too, was quite tall and had a somewhat cold facial expression. I remember that my grandfather did not particularly care for him.

The other girl, Anna Vasilevna, whose last name I don't remember now, was a little older than Olga. She was small, dark-haired, and gay, but visibly very nervous. At teatime we talked about the theater of Stanislavsky, about the actors Kachalov and Germanova, and about the authors Ibsen and Leonid Andreev. All that was unfamiliar matter to me, and I kept my peace. Then the conversation switched to the latest news of the war, and I got the impression that Lieutenant Mikhail Mikhailovich Novikov, Pasha's comrade, was openly rejoicing at our mishaps. I noted rather sharply, that now is not the time to be critical, that it is our misfortune that we don't all recognize the necessity to concentrate all our powers to achieve victory. And I thought to myself that the authorities were too lenient with expressions of revolution, which should be suppressed with a firm hand.

"Oh, that's where you stand," shouted Mikhail Mikhailovich. "So much red color in your uniform, but personally you are rather on the black side." I felt like I was beginning to choke. Blood was rushing to my head. At this point Pasha intervened, saying that of course no one wants our army to be defeated. "But," he said, "if it is unavoidable, that defeat should be utilized in a manner which shall make such dishonor impossible in the 'New Russia.' "

"And how shall it be possible to avoid defeat, Pavel Mitrofanovich?" Novikov asked. "Do you believe we can conquer the Japs by launching icons, which are being sent to the front instead of cannons? Or shall we use the gold which the aristocracy has plundered there? But even if this gold could ransom us out of this deal, would these brigands ever give it up?"

Thus in these trying days spoke a lieutenant of one of our oldest regiments, a regiment which from the time of Suvorov had been famed as an exemplar of steadfastness in defense of the native land. As I looked at him, my apprehensions mounted.

"I think, Lieutenant Sir," I said, wanting to sound official, "that in a time of battle no one, and especially not ourselves, the military, has the right to lose hope of achieving success."

"Ah so, I am hoping too," sighed Anna Vasilevna with sadness, looking into space. Then suddenly she burst out laughing nervously. Pasha told me later that two years previously her fiancé, who had a bad political record, was exiled to Siberia, and that after finishing her course, she was to join him there.

As we were returning home with Pasha late that night, I asked him, "How come you are friends with revolutionaries? Even last year you were thinking very much as I think now. What can an officer have in common with revolution?"

"Much has changed since," he answered. "I have learned many truths, discovered the other side of many medals. Novikov is not the only one in the regiment. Most people are thinking more or less along the same lines."

I remembered this conversation a year later when the government, in order to quash riots in Moscow, had to send the Guards there. The Moscow garrison was clearly unreliable.

On January 6, 1905, as usual, on the feast of Theophany, there was a parade in the Winter Palace and the Blessing of the Waters ceremony in the presence of the Tsar's family. As was the custom, right across from the Jordan entrance to the Palace, a so-called Jordan basin was cut in the Neva's ice.[30] The Tsar and the Grand Dukes, after viewing the military forces, joined the ecclesiastical procession[31] at the Jordan, but the Empresses and Grand Duchesses were watching the ceremony from the second-story windows of the Palace. On the opposite bank of the Neva by the Stock Exchange, an artillery battery was positioned to fire a salute whenever the cross was immersed into the water of the Jordan basin.

The Empress took her place right by the window and was attentively watching every motion of her husband, who stood ahead of the rest of the group, directly behind the clergy. Rebinder and I were standing right behind the Empress. We heard the salvo from the side of the Stock Exchange; apparently the cross had been lowered into the water, after which we heard another volley. At the moment of the second salute, the sound of splintering glass rang out right by us, and my first thought was that the violent vibration of the air shattered it. But just then, something fell to the floor and rolled. At that time, a third and last salvo was heard. The Master of Ceremonies, Count Apraksin, picked up the little ball rolling on the floor and was carefully examining it. I was closely watching Her Majesty, who turned pale and grasped the window frame, as if getting ready to tear away and run at any instant. At that time, I was not able to see what was happening on the river at the site of the Jordan. As I learned later, the divine service continued in an orderly fashion, and only after it was over did the Tsar proceed to the Palace. Seeing that he was approaching, Her Majesty turned around abruptly, seized her train herself, and rapidly ran down to meet her husband. We barely were able to follow her, and I remember that when she was descending the stairs, with her train lifted, I could see her legs. In those

30. "An open temple, painted and gilded, supported by pillars, surmounted by a golden cross and embellished with icons of John the Baptist was erected [on the Neva] . . . and in the middle of the sacred enclosure a hole was cut in the ice and called the Jordan . . . [The Blessing of the Waters] ceremony, a sanctification based on the immersion of Jesus in the Jordan, was a rite dating far back into antiquity." (Suzanne Massie, *Land of the Firebird: The Beauty of Old Russia* [New York: Simon and Schuster, 1980], 363.)

31. Typically with the cross, banners, and icons.

days, to see a woman's legs was a great rarity. And to observe the legs of the Tsarina was even more unusual.

At the entrance, she took the Tsar's arm with a brisk motion, and they both headed quickly for their private quarters. We remained at the door with the Araps, apparently being completely forgotten, and stood there for a very long time. My partner Rebinder told me that he saw shrapnel on the floor in the room, and there was no doubt that the shot was authentic.

Finally Captain Malashenko came to us. He apologized that he had forgotten to take us to lunch and ordered us to remain at our posts to await His Imperial Majesty's appearance, which would proceed as scheduled. And indeed, the ceremony took place soon afterwards. The Empress evidently, at least outwardly, succeeded in controlling her emotions, and only red splotches on her cheeks betrayed her inner feelings.

In the westernmost part of the Palace, in a large room, the name of which I now don't recall, with garden-facing windows through which the cold sun of the Theophany was brightly shining, the most handsome crowd I had ever seen was gathering: foreign embassy members in full state dress, courtiers in gilded uniforms, ladies-in-waiting and maids of honor in elegant Russian sarafans. The Emperor, wearing the uniform of his Hussars, with a red jacket and a white pelisse, and the Empress in a rich sarafan, placed themselves in one of the corners of the room, and the official representatives and dignitaries began approaching them in accord with their seniority, the ambassadors and their wives first—French, German, British, etc. Each exchanged a few courteous sentences with the Tsar and Tsarina, as only an accomplished diplomat could carry off, and the routine of the ceremony fully captured everyone's attention.

At this point, the Governor of the City, General Fullon,[32] entered the room at a rapid pace, approached the Tsar, and reported: "Your Imperial Majesty, the shooting was done by the First Battery of the Mounted Artillery of the Guards."

"Ah, so my own battery was shooting at me?" said the Tsar.

Fullon stood with his head down. Then he quickly departed, and the reception continued as if nothing had happened. It was inconceivable that the news brought by Fullon about his beloved Mounted Artillery did not

32. Ivan Aleksandrovich Fullon (1844–1920).

sadden the Tsar. However, neither his facial expression nor those words he was exchanging with the ambassadors betrayed his reaction.

That same day Fullon was pensioned off, and the officers of the battery in question were incarcerated in the Fortress of Peter and Paul. Among them was a modest young man, Kolia Rot,[33] with whom I had spent five years in the Corps.

Why the Governor of the City, who did not have any relation to the troops, was so severely dealt with, while the Commander in Chief, Grand Duke Vladimir Aleksandrovich, remained unpunished, was difficult to comprehend.[34]

The affair of this shot was quickly hushed up. The official version was that there was a training projectile stuck in one of the cannons; but another rumor was that this cannon was attended to by two non-commissioned volunteers, who bore all the responsibility for the event.

Some time passed. The commander of the battery, Colonel Davydov, was released from duty and pensioned off, and the officers were transferred to the field artillery. The events which followed three days later, with bloodshed in the streets of the capital, were considerably more serious and quickly obscured the incident of the shot.

In those painful days for the Tsar of crushing the first revolution, when the Guards who remained on the side of the old order saved his throne for him, four insignificant incidents occurred in the Guards' units, and all four in detachments which were closest to the monarch: the shot directed at him from a battery which he himself had commanded while he was heir to the throne; disturbances in the First Battalion of the Preobrazhensky Regiment, which he also had commanded. His personal Kamer-Page was accused of free thinking and expelled from the Corps. Finally, His Majesty's Hussars—the regiment which was closest to his heart, in which he had spent all his youth, and which he was in command of when he ascended the throne—declared a mass protest about something, which occurred during summer maneuvers.

Was all that just a coincidence, or was it the result of some special effort

---

33. Nikolai Rot was a distant relative of Fyodor S. Olferieff.

34. It was said that General Fullon was punished not so much for the shot but for his use of a system of double spying in covering the security of the imperial family.

on the part of the revolution directed towards people most faithful to the Tsar?

It is difficult to say.

Tsarskoe Selo

After the events of January 6 and 9, the Tsar left the Winter Palace and moved his permanent residence to the small Aleksandrovsky Palace located at Tsarskoe Selo. This was necessary for better surveillance and the greater security of that palace.

Formal receptions and the palace ball were canceled, reducing to a bare minimum the ceremonies which took place in the big palace of Tsarskoe Selo, or even at times in the house where the Tsar's family lived, called the Aleksandrovsky Palace. St. Petersburg outwardly grew calm, all gaiety being suspended. And the reason for this change was not the distressing news from the war front, but rather the unrest in the streets of the capital, making residence there not without danger. Many decided it was better to leave St. Petersburg and went abroad.

Only three Kamer-Pages assigned to Their Majesties, namely, Verkhovsky, Rebinder, and myself, had to report every week to Tsarskoe Selo; and sometimes the Kamer-Pages of the Empress Dowager were called to Gatchina. As a rule, we were brought to Tsarskoe Selo at ten o'clock in the morning for the reception of foreign envoys and ambassadors, persons coming to congratulate Their Majesties, and the reception of Court ladies and so-called City ladies. The latter was the appellation given the wives of the superior ranks of St. Petersburg's bureaucracy who did not possess a Court title. Also there were receptions of various delegations, such as noblemen, territorial organizations, the Eastern vassal princes and khans, members of legislative institutions, and so on.

Our duty was to stand behind Their Majesties during more solemn occasions, or by the door of the chamber in times of less formal receptions. At the conclusion of the ceremony, the Empress usually said a few gracious words to us, and we were taken upstairs, fed lunch, inevitably with the Russian champagne Abrau Durso, and then driven home.

Aleksandrovsky Palace was a two-storied, middle-sized residential home, standing in the middle of a park. It was furnished much more modestly than the opulent individual residences of St. Petersburg and especially those of Moscow. You were struck by an odd allocation of space and rooms. For instance, a door right from the vestibule led to a room with a play slide such as there are on children's playgrounds, and on the floor around it were scattered dolls and other toys. Clearly it was a nursery, and the children were ushered from it at the time of receptions because all who arrived had to pass through it to attend the reception. It was obvious, too, that in this house children were given first priority, in spite of the fact that sometimes visitors had to step over their toys. On the other side of the children's playroom was a fairly long, carpeted room filled with bookcases. The following room was covered with a Persian rug and completely empty. In it, as one of the servants explained to me, Their Majesties dined. A dining table was brought in during mealtimes and removed immediately after the meal was over. Still further was the corner drawing room, which was considerable in size, furnished with French furniture. Receptions were usually held in this drawing room. From this room, and also from the preceding dining room, there were doors to a room where I had never been; but judging by the fact that the Tsar would sometimes come out of it accompanied by ministers and high officials, I assumed that it was his study. I do not know of any other rooms on the first floor.

Upstairs, in the portion of the building with which I was familiar, there was a narrow corridor, with doors opening into a number of small rooms on both sides of it. One of these apparently served as a classroom, as I had once seen the Russian language teacher, Petrov, coming out of it with the Tsar's children. Another room, where we usually were given our lunch, was a work room of Princess Orbeliani, a personal lady-in-waiting of the Empress. The princess was a cripple, and could move from place to place only in a wheelchair. I did not know the location of the imperial bedrooms and the children's other rooms. However, I was under the impression that in this palace there was no separation of state rooms from private quarters because the structure was too small for this. I did not see any Araps there either. In order to avoid a surprise appearance of Their Majesties in a room where a visitor was waiting, a courier preceded them, announcing to the

The royal family and officers.

bystanders that Their Majesties followed after him. I felt that, inasmuch as we were in this house only at the time of receptions when the palace was prepared for that purpose, the everyday functioning and arrangement of it escaped us. At any rate, the house where the Tsar was living was not large; he lived very modestly, and seemed quite indifferent to the impression that his dwelling made on visitors.

In the course of my visits to the palace I had an opportunity—as much as my limited experience and youth allowed—to observe, to have trivial conversations with, and to study the mannerisms of the Empress Aleksandra Fedorovna, the woman who went down in history, whether deservedly or not, as the individual who, more than any other, brought about the fall of the old order in Russia. It is to be noted that in those days her reputation was above reproach. She was considered to be an outstanding mother and a devoted, loving wife. The Tsar, who, as it is known, married for love, was still in love with her. Nevertheless, the Russians were not fond of her, as she was, or at least appeared to be, haughty, and apparently sought to avoid any communication with St. Petersburg society. She was usually compared with the Dowager Empress, who was easy to approach and always friendly; and on that basis a breach arose between the two courts.

The comparison of the young Tsarina with her mother-in-law did not go in her favor. I remember that on one occasion I was sent to Gatchina to substitute for a Page who was ill, and after serving duty there, I was honored with a fairly lengthy conversation with Maria Fedorovna. In the first place, she conversed in our native tongue; in the second, she was more familiar with Russian people, and knew how to talk to them and say things both understandably and pleasantly. Moreover, she always smiled in a charming way, which right away made her very likable. The young Tsarina usually spoke French, a language which was clearly foreign to both her and the person to whom she was talking. Her native tongues were German and English, but very few Russians spoke these languages. The topic of her conversation was usually suggested to her, and therefore her questions were rather awkward. You got the feeling while talking to her that she was fulfilling a burdensome and uninteresting task. At the same time, I never saw a smile on her face. She would blush frequently and suddenly cease speaking. [People said that she was beautiful, but in my opinion she was too heavy for that. It was especially noticeable when she stood next to the Tsar. Her large,

The Tsar and Tsarina with officers.

red hands, her thin, never-smiling lips, and her cold-sounding voice were not in her favor.][35] Perhaps she was more sociable in the company of people whom she knew and understood. In any case, that is how I saw her and how she appeared to the overwhelming majority of her subjects.

I was presented to the Empress by her first Master of Ceremonies, a friend of my father who graduated with him from the Corps, Count Gendrikov. Introducing me, he said that he was very happy to welcome into the service of Her Majesty the son of his friend from the Corps. The Tsarina extended her large hand, to which I pressed my lips, and asked me the question which everyone usually asked all of us that year—what regiment did I intend to join?

"Au regiment des Grenadiers-à-Cheval, Madame," I answered.

"Ah, c'est a Peterhoff qu'ils sont logés. Connaissez-vous Peterhoff? Moi je l'aime beaucoup."[36]

We were taught to not answer questions in a monosyllable, yes or no, but to try to put in the answer a thought which would serve as the topic for a new question.

"Oui, Madame, surtout les jardins et les fontaines."

"Savez-vous que mes Lanciers sont aussi logés a Peterhoff?"[37]

This sentence, as all the others, certainly didn't have any objective in mind, but I thought that implied in it was the question of why then didn't I join her Lancers?

"Oui, Madame, les Grenadiers-à-Cheval et les Lanciers forment la première brigade de la deuxième division de la guarde montée,"[38] I reported to her.

The Empress made a demi-bow to me indicating the end of the conversation, and uttered: "J'espére de vous rencontrer a Peterhoff."[39] She then turned to Rebinder.

---

35. Bracketed text here was crossed out by the author.

36. "The Horse Grenadiers Regiment, Madam."

"Ah, they are billeted at Peterhof. Are you acquainted with Peterhof? I like it very much."

37. "Yes, Madam, mainly the gardens and fountains."

"Do you know my Ulans are also billeted at Peterhof?"

38. "Yes, Madam, the Horse Grenadiers and the Ulans make up the First Brigade of the Second Division of the mounted guard."

39. "I hope to meet you at Peterhof."

How often, as I stood behind her during receptions, did I hear how difficult it was for Russian people who were introduced to her to respond in French. How many were the embarrassments, incomplete sentences, and unwillingly hindered conversations. At that time, I was thinking how difficult it was to be the wife of the Tsar in a land whose language she did not know. In those days that I am recounting, she not only did not know the language, but completely failed to know or understand the Russian people. Only after having lived half my life outside my native land, did I appreciate what the German Princess Alix must have lived through as the foreign wife of the Russian Tsar.

On one occasion after lunch while waiting upstairs for our carriage, we noticed an opened notebook on Princess Orbeliani's desk. It clearly contained her daily journal. On the opened page we read the following phrase: "She was again out of sorts. She came back all red in the face, and did not utter a word to anyone to the end of the day." We really wanted to turn the page and read further. But we didn't dare.

During the Holy Week before Easter in all the regiments of the Guards the following order was customarily given: "Assigned to the palace on Holy Easter Sunday to bring good wishes to Their Majesties are: Colonel . . . Rotmistr . . . Vakhmistr . . . Appear at 11:00 a.m. in such and such hall to await further instructions from the Hofmarschal office. Uniform should be full dress. To perfume or dye one's mustache is not allowed."[40]

The holiday greetings were beginning in the front hall where the reception took place. There stood a long line of officers and soldiers, who each in turn approached the Tsar, exchanged kisses with him three times, and kissed the hand of the Tsarina. From her we each received a porcelain egg with a crown and her initials. The Tsar endured this ceremony stoically. We pages approached him last and he likewise conscientiously kissed each of us three times.

This was my last service duty at the palace before becoming an officer. The Tsarina was notified about this, but on that day she evidently wasn't in a frame of mind to converse with us. [On that occasion we had our new

---

40. Vakhmistr = cavalry sergeant major; rotmistr = cavalry and infantry colonel. These terms had their origins in German lands. *Wachtmeister* designated a cavalry or artillery junior officer. *Rittmeister* referred to a senior cavalry officer.

Fyodor on the parade grounds at the palace.

Sergeant Major Svetozarov. This represented his only active duty with the Tsar.][41] On April 22, the day of my promotion, I received an imperial order from the hand of the Empress, and she repeated her wish to see me again at Peterhof. When in the following year this was realized on the day of the regimental holiday, she recognized me, and being delighted at seeing a familiar face, spent more time in conversation with me than with the others.

[As far as we were concerned, the Tsarina was always cool but amiable to us. Yet, after our last round of duty when Gendrikov told her that my father had recently died, she was warmly sympathetic and wished me success. She closed her conversation again saying, "J'espére de vous revoir à Peterhof." ("I hope you return to Peterhof.") And from that time on whenever she saw me at Peterhof, she always exchanged a few words with me.]

In the course of my duty in the palace, I saw the following persons who were close to the Tsar's family: Count Frederiks, who was Minister of the Court, and to whom Tsar Alexander III entrusted his heir before he

41. Bracketed text here and immediately following was later added by the author.

died; Lord High Marshal Count Benkendorf; Lady Governess of the Court Her Royal Highness Princess Golitsyna; and Grand Master of Ceremonies Count Gendrikov. Besides these, on several occasions I saw in the palace the Commander of the Ulans, General Aleksandr Afinogenovich Orlov, a comrade of the Tsar by service in the Hussar Regiment; and his favorite aide-de-camp Drenteln,[42] an officer of the Preobrazhensky Regiment.

Whenever people find out that I served in the Palace, they ask me if I ever saw Rasputin. No, I never met Rasputin. In the first place, he was not in St. Petersburg at that time. He appeared five years later. In the second place, while I was there I did not know about the private life of the Tsar's family, and exactly all that was happening "on the other side of the Araps" was known to only a very limited circle of people. This is why it is my conviction that much of what was said about Rasputin was greatly distorted and exaggerated, and if that ill-fated adventurer was able to profit from all these rumors, the fault lay not at Tsarskoe Selo, but rather with that corrupt Petersburg society itself, which placed Rasputin on a pedestal, and together with him fell into the abyss.

42. Aleksandr Aleksandrovich Drenteln (1868–1925).

My Youth in the Horse Grenadier Regiment

To Drink to Russia Is a Joy

The most outstanding event of the first twenty years of my life was my promotion to the rank of an officer. My cherished wish from early childhood had been realized—I was a cavalry officer. Soldiers would be under my command, and I would teach them how to serve the Tsar and the Fatherland. And I felt that I knew how to teach them. On this day I was so full of my own personal experience and paid so little attention to what was happening around me that the procedure of promotion has nearly vanished from my memory. I remember that the pages and cadets were in formation on the square in front of the palace at Tsarskoe Selo, and remember that upon the greetings of the Emperor, we, for the last time as soldiers, replied in a soldierly fashion, "Good day, Your Imperial Highness!" But when he congratulated us as officers, we silently saluted. It seems that after that we yelled, "Hurrah!" Then Rebinder and I were called to the entrance steps, where the Empress stood. She, as usual without a smile, extended her hand for us to kiss and awarded us a copy of the Order of Promotion. I was greatly flattered that she remembered the regiment which I was joining and reiterated her desire to see me in Peterhof.

From Tsarskoe Selo, I went directly to the tailor, changed into my officer's uniform, and from there left for home. I shared my happiness with my mother, and our only sadness was that my father had not lived to see me become an officer. How pleased he would have been. In the evening our class graduation supper was held at Ernest.[1] We all had been preparing for this event for a long time; the details of who would sit with whom and who would say what had been decided. But the supper was colorless and even boring. We all became introspective and were preoccupied with our own thoughts.

"Your Excellency," I reported, "Cornet[2] Olferieff presents himself upon promotion for acceptance into Your Excellency's Life Guards Horse Grenadier Regiment."

This happened at noon in the lounge of the regimental officer assembly at Peterhof in the presence of nearly all the officers of the regiment, who had gathered for a farewell luncheon honoring Cornet Baron Engelgardt, who was leaving for the academy.

The Commander of the Regiment, Baron Nikolai Aleksandrovich Budberg, a slight, well-built general with a kind smile, wearing the St. Vladimir Order on his chest and the Page Corps' Maltese Cross on the side, shook my hand and the hand of my fellow graduating classmate, Karlusha[3] Gartman, wished us good luck, and then ordered us to the duty room to remove our dress uniforms. Much to our surprise, Zelik, the Jew, already awaited us there with our requisite shoulder straps in his hands. How Zelik knew where or when he was needed in the regiment was known only by him.

Meanwhile, in the dining room the officers crowded about the hors d'oeuvre table, behind which stood soldiers in immaculate white shirts serving as waiters and pouring vodka for the gentlemen. The officer in charge of the gathering, Lieutenant Baron Vrangel, led us to the table, and told us that from now on we were considered members of the mess and were to make ourselves feel at home. He offered us a shot of vodka. I had just reached the age of 20, disliked vodka, and had never been intoxicated in my life. We were served in silver drinking cups, extremely large and frightening, which, as I learned later, were a gift to the officer assembly from our neighbors, the Kaspiisky Regiment, who had left for war. To refuse a drink, however, was out of the question. This I knew long before joining the regiment. With great effort, suppressing a grimace, I drank my first cup. After

1. The restaurant Ernest was opened by entrepreneur Ernst G. Hiegel in 1909.
2. Equivalent to Second Lieutenant.
3. Nickname for Karl.

Vrangel, others approached me in turns and in groups. Everyone proposed the same: drink vodka. I drank one cup after another, and quickly lost count. I became giddy, then began to get dizzy, so I firmly resolved to control myself by eating as much as possible in order not to get drunk.

Trumpeters appeared in the billiard room, which was adjacent to the dining room. The Commander of the Regiment sat at a long table, where lunch was being served. We all followed suit and sat down. Triumphal sounds from *Tannhäuser*[4] wafted through the air, replaced by the march from *Les Huguenots*.[5] Then they played a sentimental waltz and ended with a lively tune from the operetta *The Merry Widow*.[6]

Champagne was being served. The Commander stood up, gave a short speech honoring Engelgardt, took out a gold cigarette case, and raised a glass of the sparkling wine in salute as he approached him. Engelgardt stood and everyone began to sing the jubilant tune "Charochka,"[7] to the well-known text of Aleksei Tolstoy. Engelgardt drank the proffered glass of champagne. The trumpeters played "The March of the Sixth Squadron," and a short "Hurrah" completed the ceremony. A lighted candle appeared in front of the Commander, and this was the signal to permit smoking.

During this time the balalaika players appeared in the dining room and filled the air with the supple sounds of the Third Waltz by Andreev, which in those days, along with the Andreev Chorus, toured around the world and met with enormous success.

The ritual of libation continued. The first glass was served to the Commander, then to each of the staff officers. After that, the drinking continued by squadrons, accompanied by squadron marches, and in the end by ranks. The final ceremony went like this: to the chanting of "No drinking without the generals," the Commander stood up and drank his goblet dry. Then, "No drinking without the colonels," who thereupon drank two goblets each. The rotmistrs drank three, one after the other. The staff rotmistrs, in like manner, four. The lieutenants drank five. Finally, the cornets, who were ten in number, formed a line, each holding a tray with six goblets, which equaled the contents of one bottle. Upon the command of the senior

4. Full title *Tannhäuser und der Sängerkrieg auf Wartburg*, an opera by Richard Wagner.
5. A French opera by Giacomo Meyerbeer.
6. An Austro-Hungarian operetta by Franz Lehár.
7. A drinking song.

cornet, "On your mark, get set, drink: One," we drank the first goblet. "Two," the second, and so on. When I downed the sixth glass, my head was spinning and gas was exploding from my nostrils. Making an incredible effort, I reached a chair. But after sitting down, I lost consciousness.

I woke up on a sofa in the room of the duty officer. It was dark. My legs, encased in high tight boots, were aching. My head was splitting at the seams, and it was very painful to move it. I tried to get up but fell back helplessly on the pillow. Nevertheless, after a few minutes, I forced myself to get up, buttoned my uniform, and walked into the anteroom.

It was well after midnight. At the entrance, a regimental cabman dozed. All trains to Petersburg had left, and there was nowhere to go. Voices were audible from the mess hall. The whole place reeked of champagne. Hoping to find Gartman, I walked into the mess. There at the cornets' end of the table under dim candlelight sat about five men drinking cognac. Tired soldiers with sphinx-like expressions on their faces were serving black coffee. Gartman was not there. Engelgardt, morosely leaning against the back of his forward-facing chair, was singing:

I shall don a black habit
In a nunnery I shall live

The rest joined in on the refrain, beating the table out of rhythm with their fists, probably to indicate their firm decision to become nuns.

I loved, I suffered
But the scoundrel forgot me.

It was obvious that no one present knew what had happened to me and where I had been. They counted me as one of the heroes who stood his ground on the battlefield, greeted me with joyous enthusiasm, and there and then poured into me several glasses of cognac. On account of this, my head felt better, but again I became intoxicated. Soon the carousing ended; and one of those present, Staff Rotmistr Shults, who had known me before my entrance into the regiment, took me to his place to spend the night.

Before going to bed, we were emphatically informed by the orderly that in accordance with the order of the regiment, all officers must report at 11 a.m. to the officers' assembly to meet the Commander of the Corps.

Shults, in a fatherly manner, patted the orderly on the shoulder saying, "Admit you are lying." But denying this, the orderly continued to repeat himself. Finally, when we reached our beds, he removed our boots and left.

I suffered all night as though I were on a tossing ship. In the morning, in spite of a headache and the pain racking my entire body, I jumped out of bed at the first call of the orderly, woke Shults, and we reached the officers' assembly in time.

Soon, escorted by the Commander of the Regiment, the Commander of the Corps, old Prince Vasilchikov, entered the mess in Hungarian Hussar of the Life Guards uniform. Making a tour around the group, he addressed us and explained the whole purpose of his visit. From his concise, simple speech, we understood that the high command doubted the political reliability of the soldiers in connection with the discovery of an attempt in some regiments to spread revolutionary propaganda among them. In view of this, orders were given to strictly watch where the lower ranks went, to forbid outsiders in the barracks, and to inspect the soldiers' mail. To facilitate surveillance, a command was given to immediately erect gates at all entrances to the barracks and place sentries at them. After this we jokingly named them accordingly—"The Gates Against Revolution."

During this speech I had a headache. My thoughts flowed slowly, and I couldn't concentrate. The recollection of my drunken behavior the night before in the presence of the Commander, the officers, and the soldiers preyed on my mind. It seemed to me that my service in the regiment was all over, and everything that was said about the gates seemed so far away and so insignificant. I was annoyed to see that no one except myself was suffering, physically or morally.

We went to lunch. It was a repetition of the day before, drinking vodka and eating zakuskas. The soldiers were just as impeccably dressed and serious as before; nothing but expressionless faces stretched before me. They were as respectful to me as to the others.

After lunch, when the Commander of the Corps and the Commander of the Regiment had left, champagne again appeared on the table, and Engelgardt called forth the singers. I made ready to leave, but Engelgardt, who had drunk Brüderschaft with me, persuaded me to stay and promised that both of us would go to the city that evening.

Soon we could hear a stamping at the doors, and marching soldiers entered the dining hall singing the traditional song.

I love, I love, and shall love
I shall never forget
My own first love.

The singing came to a halt. Darkly handsome young men formed a semicircle at the front and began singing. The one standing in the center put his hand to his cap and ordered, "Attention!" They all exuded an aura of youth, health, and strength. Joyous smiles beamed from their faces. It was obvious that they were happy to be asked to sing.

The senior officer of the Horse Grenadiers greeted them, and answering the welcome, they sang out with all their youthful might:

From the edge of midnight to the distant midday,
The mighty, majestic eagle flew in,
Cast an eagle-sharp eye
O'er the wide realm's distant frontier,
The expanse of the steppes and snowy peaks,
The vanquished borders of the mountainous battlements
And in the valley met Your Cossacks
All appeared with the welcoming cry.
Long life to the glory of Orthodox Russia,
To the joy, to the prosperity of Your falcons.
You, our Sovereign, we expected long ago
Wishing to see Your eagle eye,
Cleared the fields from rapacious vultures
In order to receive You fully.
Accept, Ataman, our Mighty Sovereign,
The joyous cries of Your Cossacks.
Hurrah! Hurrah! To the Great Tsar.
Hurrah! Hurrah! To You our hero.

Hurrah! To the hope of our days, and
Hurrah! To all Your family.

This song, as the legend goes, was composed by a prisoner in a Caucasian jail upon a visit of Alexander III to the Caucasus. It is said that on account of it, he was set free. It came to us, as many others, from the choral singing master, His Majesty's guard.

The singers themselves, with hats cocked dashingly to one side, in well-fitted uniforms, reminded one of young eagles. The leader of the choir cut short the song with a terse stroke of his hand, and then, after a brief pause, waved again, and a dancing tune began.

Beets are growing in the garden.
A scrivener fell in love with me,
Gave me high-heeled shoes.
But the heels aren't so good.
But the heels aren't so good.
Dear Sirs, they are broken down.
For it's me, the young one, the Grenadiers are wooing.

Leo Tolstoy thought that music could often push people into sin and crime. It is known that martial music promotes heroism in men. I can attest to the fact that there is no better stimulus than a soldier's song for the purpose of getting drunk.

Songs were exchanged for drinks; the soldiers lifted the officers to the ceiling. From that position, the officers were giving speeches, emptying their glasses, and shattering them on the floor. They paid the soldiers money and gave them beer and vodka, which from time to time the soldiers wandered off to drink.

The "fir tree," the name given in the regiment for this type of a drinking spree, dragged on till the wee hours. Finally, the singers left, and Engelgardt, again in a melancholy mood, sang his favorite song:

I shall kneel
And ask forgiveness.

"*Vin Triste*," as the French saying goes, fit Engelgardt. It was obvious that he regretted leaving the regiment.

That night I again was drunk and once more remained in Peterhof. This time I spent the night with my future roommates and best friends, Batezatul and Krichinsky.

But the next day, exhausted, with a swollen face and feeling terrible remorse, I returned home and, with tears in my eyes, told my mother what had happened to me. What impressed me the most was the quantity of liquor people were able to consume and at the same time find pleasure in it.

One more situation which I couldn't entirely explain then, but which I didn't allow to defeat me, was the relationship of the officers to the soldiers. It seemed that the abolition of serfdom had had no effect whatsoever. The lower ranks were called "people," as though making a distinction between them and horses. But the officers who got drunk in their presence cared just as little about the impressions their conduct made on the soldiers as men who do not worry about what animals think of them.

Those who read about my childhood would clearly understand the reaction our regimental circle provoked in me. My father was too proud and independent to stress his social class by looking down on those beneath him, and being obliged in turn to concede his inferiority to those who occupied a higher position.

In our village house one could see a peasant in a homespun coat drinking tea in the dining room with my mother, and in that same room on other occasions, a nobleman would be our guest. A priest used to visit us, as well as a Jewish man by the name of Veniamin Pukh, whom Mother protected from being exiled to a frontier settlement. My friends were peasant children among whom I grew up, and with whom I shared both joy and sorrow, and who, in the course of time, made up the ranks of those same soldiers who sang in the officers' mess and lifted my intoxicated body to the ceiling.

While I was in the army corps among my comrades and in uniform, I was compelled to behave as befit a person of my station. Here I realized that gentlemen and servants could not intermingle. Among those who did not belong in our circle were the petty bourgeois, the merchants, and the civil service officials. Among the latter were guardsmen and soldiers in the line. Finally, and the most important thing, was who belonged or did not belong to what was called "society." I accepted all of this as inevitable, but because of my early days, I could not suppress my feelings of protest. And now after all that had happened to me, I truly suffered in remembering that I was drunk and that probably the soldiers carried me to the sofa when I lost consciousness. I felt that my prestige was damaged in their eyes and that all my dreams of becoming a good commander had ended.

My mother and I had a long discussion on how to correct the mistakes I had made. At the time, Mother was mostly concerned about my becoming an alcoholic. Again, as always upon making a serious decision, we thought of my father, and as before, felt lost without his advice. To leave military service would be a step backward and would mean starting all over in preparation for a new career. This required a strong will, which I did not have. I decided to remain in the regiment.

Soon my first impressions began to fall into place. I started to understand that my fellow officers were people like everyone else and that their understanding of good and evil did not differ too much from my own. Among them I found good comrades and faithful friends. The very same Engelgardt, who was leaving the regiment, a man who had behaved like a beast for a whole week, proved to be not only a modest, good, compassionate person but also a capable military lawyer. Less than a year had passed before the Horse Grenadier Regiment became "Our Regiment," and the family of officers was as close to me as my own family. I learned to look only on the bright side of regimental life and closed my eyes to its ugly side. I learned to drink and quickly became an integral part of the regiment, and was just as responsible as all the others for those faults that, it seemed to me later, brought us to catastrophe. When this catastrophe shook our very foundation, I thought that our troubles had occurred because we felt obliged to preserve the so-called long-standing tradition necessary to uphold "the spirit of the regiment" and its "old fighting glory." From these traditions we maintained those external expressions of military valor and unity between officers and soldiers, which in time of war occur as a natural reaction to dangerous battle conditions. In the absence of this setting, all our drinking bouts, drunken speeches, flourishes of trumpets, and songs of "Hurrah" did not in themselves carry sincerity; and in our day, the officers and soldiers were distant from each other. Contributing to this alienation, it is said, was the fact that the officers substituted outward severity for sensible discipline, and held such an elevated opinion of themselves that it didn't permit them to condescend to the soldiers and speak with them in an ordinary, human way.

It seemed to me that this very same tradition of conducting ourselves just as our "glorious ancestors" had prevented us from going along with our progressive civic population. Instead of that we built "gates against revolution," endeavoring to hold back the old serf order behind them. At the same time we drafted soldiers from among the people who had already savored a knowledge of good and evil. In this contradiction, in spite of the outward appearance of stability, lay the germ of the approaching catastrophe.

This I believed, as did many others among us, when the chopping down of the "old forest" began in Russia, and we, like splinters, flew off all over the world.

It was necessary to reside on foreign soil for many years, to observe the people living in a so-called "democratic" country, to taste together with them happiness and grief, and at the same time to examine the evolution of the new regime in the Fatherland in order to arrive at the conviction that the division of people into classes of the weak and the strong is not the result of either a political or economic structure, but the consequence of human nature; and revolution against the exploitation of the weak by the strong appears as an indispensable element in the cyclic development of every living being on earth. Revolution occurs when the governing class begins to have doubts and to recognize its own bankruptcy. Russia needed a philosophy like Tolstoy's in order to overthrow our old regime and put it in the hands of new people, who, in their turn, would start the newest cycle.

In Defense of the Throne

At the entrances to the barracks of the squadrons, large wooden-plank gates were hastily constructed, which for some reason remained unpainted for a long time and gaped like white stains against the dark-red background of the brick buildings. At the gates were posted our own fully armed Kirilenkos and Shevchuks, who could not figure out why this had happened, since no one had guarded the barracks for many years, and not one thief had ever broken into them; and now, not only were the gates locked, but Guards were stationed there. However, our servants said that there were certain students who were internal enemies, and one had to fear them and defend the Tsar and the Fatherland from them. But in the first place, there were no students in Peterhof, and in the second, why should a student offend a soldier? The soldier is a person of low status.

But Kirilenko did not like to ponder too long. "That is the way it should be. The authorities know best." And he continued to stand, watching through the night the empty streets of old Peterhof, where from time to time a pack of dogs ran by in a fit of heat, a tardy coachman passed by, or a homeward-bound officer walked along, returning from a spree, trying to keep upright and follow a straight line.

We read the soldiers' letters from home, which only contained greetings. The senders, perhaps, would have written more, but they lacked the skill to formulate a thought, and had little knowledge of the fancy words of the village scribe. Frequently the letters contained a greasy three-ruble note. I knew well how difficult it was in the village household to save this money. But even if someone had told a mother that her son ate much better and worked much less in the regiment than at home, she would still not believe this, and it is doubtful whether the son would try to convince her.

At the same time, the Russian nation was experiencing a bitter insult delivered to it by a small Asiatic country which heretofore had been little known. The squadron of Admiral Rozhdestvensky[8] was annihilated; Port Arthur was falling, and our army, till that time having been well supplied and replenished, and physically prepared for combat, was now demoralized and forced to surrender as it stood on the Siping positions like a slaughtered animal decomposing under the scorching Manchurian sun.

Throughout the country, in factories and mills, strikes became more frequent among the workers, and their demands were not economic but political: the establishment of legislative chambers and the creation of an accountable government. Students in higher education institutions cast aside their books and took up politics. Their demands were more extreme: immediate abdication of the Tsar and the proclamation of a republic. At the same time, voices were raised for the creation of a labor government.

---

8. Admiral Zinovy Rozhdestvensky was commander of the fleet that was sent to the Far East all the way from the Baltic during the Russo-Japanese War. His fleet was destroyed during the Battle of Tsushima Strait, May 27–29, 1905.

Here and there on the landlords' country estates, the peasants flung a "red rooster."[9] And in the southwest beyond the frontier settlement, people, in their misguided pursuit of God, began to attack the Jews. There was a feeling of foreboding and approaching decisive events. Almost everywhere a state of emergency was declared, in which troops were called out to help the civil authorities restore law and order.

During these days it was the Guards' duty to protect the Tsar, his throne, his family, and the capital. Our regiment was frequently called to Petersburg in full military readiness with ammunition carts and was stationed there according to squadron in the Guards' barracks, the riding schools, and the palaces.

At that time, however, the revolutionaries seldom walked out onto the street with weapons in their hands, and usually our first appearance was enough to calm everyone. Our duty was to patrol the streets or simply to stand in battle preparedness in case of an emergency. Accordingly, we were never under the authority of the police, and when the police were unable to handle the situation, the area was turned over to the senior army chief, and he took control.

I remember my first guard duty. Once, an agitated police inspector arrived in the barracks of the Finland Guard Regiment, where our squadron was stationed, and asked for help in stopping the mob from walking to the Birzhevoi Bridge. I was sent with the platoon. The commander of the squadron, Pavel Vladimirovich Filosofov, a very humane and cultured man, and the son of the famous feminist Filosofova,[10] dispatched us with strict orders that we not draw our swords unless we saw that the mob was armed.

Approaching the university, I saw a crowd of roughly two hundred or more moving towards the Birzhevoi Bridge. It consisted of young people in students' caps, high school students, many civilians, laborers, and quite a few young women. Approximately ten police officers were trying to stop them. You could hear singing coming from the crowd.

"Cornet," the approaching officer said, "attack them, and we shall block their way to the bridge."

I drew up the platoon in formation and walked towards the crowd.

---

9. They set fire to the estates.

10. Anna Pavlovna Filosofova (1837–1912).

From the mob came the cries, "Oprichniki![11] We are not afraid of your whips." And from the direction of several young girls, who were walking quite close to me, I heard a squeaky voice yell, "So young, yet such a villain." It was clearly directed towards me. I looked their way. Their faces expressed malice. The back lines shoved forwards, and they drew close up against my stirrups. The soldiers, moving immediately behind me, guided their horses straight towards them, and they gave way. In such a manner we were able to push through the crowd, which already was beginning to disperse in front of us. When, however, I turned and looked back, I again saw the crowd closing in. I felt very foolish not knowing what to do next. As hard as I tried to remember what the regulations were, I could not come up with anything applicable to such a situation in my military training. I considered it beneath my dignity to enter into a conversation with the demonstrators. I went back through the crowd. They again separated and let me ride through. I turned around again. The crowd was now used to me. There was no more swearing. Here and there you could hear laughter. The only thing I achieved by my maneuvers was to prevent the organizers from moving toward the bridge. Thus, visibly embodying the law that "a charge does not withstand an interruption," the crowd began to disperse, and soon the task of preventing it from crossing the bridge was accomplished. The police informed me that my help was no longer needed. I returned to the barracks where Filosofov fully approved of my achievement.

As a rule, the behavior of the police towards us was very proper. However, there were occasions when the officers tried to reprimand us. This took place in summer, perhaps the day of dismissal of the Second Duma. I stood with the platoon in the courtyard of police headquarters, behind which was the Kazan Cathedral. It was one of the infrequent sultry July days in Petersburg when the air smelled of hot asphalt, and from time to time a drowsy *sbiten'*[12] vendor would pass by along the thinly populated streets with a wooden jug perched on his head containing the suspicious liquid,

11. The *oprichniki* were the hated Life-Guardsmen created by Ivan the Terrible in the late sixteenth century whose purpose was to destroy those whom the Tsar considered to be his enemies. In reality, they were a political or secret police who ushered in a reign of terror. They dressed in black and rode black horses. (See Nicholas Riasanovsky, *A History of Russia*, 8th ed. [New York: Oxford University Press, 2011], 150–51.)

12. *Sbiten'* is a popular Russian drink consisting of hot water, honey, capsicum, and spices.

and Tartars who dealt in old clothes would wander through the yards crying out in a monotone, "Khalat, khalat."[13] Many of Petersburg's residents were away for the summer at their dachas.

At the entrance gates of the police station, a yard keeper appeared with a harmonica in his hands, sat on a bench, and began to play. Several fellows from my platoon sat down beside him; two or three kitchen maids from the neighboring apartments assembled and began to flirt, accompanied by hysterical female giggles as they exerted themselves shelling sunflower seeds.

A police inspector approached me and asked in a commanding voice, "Cornet, don't you know that soldiers in uniform assisting civil authorities should not lower their dignity by associating with the local residents?"

Of course, I was wrong, but I did not like the police officer's tone and answered, "I did not know Mr. Colonel. If I am doing something unlawful, I ask you to inform my squadron commander in the Marble Palace."

The words *Marble Palace* made a big impression, and the inspector tried to convince me that he did not intend to reprimand me but just wanted to remind me of the instructions. He promptly left, I withdrew the soldiers, and the gaieties ended.

There were more difficult situations. Once I was ordered with half of the squadron to escort a large ammunition transport from the Vyborg side to Selo Ivanovskoe, which was located halfway between Shlisselburg and Petersburg. Here were the quarters of the 22nd Artillery. This event occurred during winter. There was such a snowstorm that on Nevsky the streetlamps were invisible. The transport was very long; when its head appeared on Nevsky, its tail was just moving down the Liteinyi Bridge. In the vanguard was a lone Horse Grenadier. The rest were divided by twos for every ten horse-drawn carts. The platoon trailed behind. I continually let the train of carts get ahead of me. We successfully passed the Aleksandr Nevsky Monastery, and the glass factory, which at this time was on strike, and the workers walked in groups through the streets. One such group flung invective as well as rocks and chunks of ice in my direction. My spirited stallion Svoiak[14] suddenly reared up. The platoon commander approached me and asked for the order

13. A *khalat* is an oriental-style dressing gown, and also the Tartar expression for buying and selling old clothes.

14. A nickname with two meanings: brother-in-law or a strike, in Russian billiards.

to surround the group who were throwing rocks. "Honorable Sir, I saw those who were hurling them. Please allow me to arrest them." I got off my horse, and several soldiers dismounted around me. I commanded the rest to keep moving, and to watch vigilantly in order to protect the transport from attack. I ordered them not to be distracted by the arrests, for my feeling was that the workers' objective was to attack the transport. After the soldiers surrounded me, rocks were no longer hurled, and finally we successfully escaped past the factory, and our lines stretched out beyond the city.

There, another difficulty awaited us: the snowstorm had covered the road, and the main detachment was continually getting lost in the snow-drifts. Sometimes the transport would spread out in the wrong direction, and it was necessary to wait for the rear line. At the same time, the carts were filling up with snow, and if we had to wait for half an hour, it would be impossible to move them. In one place a sled overturned, and it was necessary to transfer the ammunition. Darkness approached. We slowly continued to crawl along like a worm, drawing out our head and pulling up our tail. My hands and feet were numb. My moist breath froze the small opening in the *bashlyk*[15] that was wrapped around my head.

We arrived at the barracks park quite late in the evening. In spite of our forewarning, they didn't expect us there, and no preparations had been made for lodging either people or horses. The duty officer was not present. Finally we found him. He arrived from the country house where the officers' quarters were located, and apologized profusely to me, stating that they were having a small "flight"—in plain language, a drinking spree.

Having settled the people and horses with great difficulty, and having put the baggage train, to which the duty officer placed his own sentry, in the square, I traveled with him to the Pella Palace, which stood two versts from the barracks.

This country house had formerly been used as a hunting lodge of Empress Catherine II. By its appearance, one could believe that the house, where the officers lived, had never been maintained since that time. Inside it was so damp that water ran down the filthy walls. Clearly there was no heating. The wretchedness and misery of the officers' dwelling was manifest to everyone.

15. Caucasian hood.

In the dining room around a table sat officers who had consumed too many drinks; seated at the head was a large, long-bearded colonel—the commander of the park. Because of his great size and his beard, he stood out among them.

On the table were vodka, sardines, and pickles; the tablecloth was soiled. It was evident that much had been drunk, and the "flight" was coming to an end.

The colonel seated me next to him and offered me vodka, which I drank with pleasure for the first time. For a while, the drunken assembly became silent; then everyone came to life again. But soon after, a heavy woman with a shawl thrown over her shoulders walked in, and paying no attention to anyone yelled, "Again you are getting my husband drunk," approached the commander of the park, grabbed him by the shirt sleeve and ordered, "March home." The colonel looked pitiful and seemed to shrink in size. He stood up and obediently followed his commandress.

My presence at this incident embarrassed the officers. After the commander's departure, they outdid each other praising him and said his only weakness was his total submission to his wife.

Not taking off my coat, I slept in this same dining room on a dirty sofa, and because of the cold, I didn't even remove my cap. In the morning the snowstorm subsided, and after saying good-bye to my amiable hosts, I changed pace and went to the Marble Palace where our squadron was stationed, had dinner with Grand Duke Dmitry Konstantinovich, and entertained everyone with the tale of my adventures.

From this small incident, I was left with a deep impression of the contrast between the luxury of the capital and the poverty and misery of the provincial garrison, which was only twenty-five versts from Petersburg. Barracks Park was cold and grimy; its soldiers, with unkempt hair and obviously poorly nourished, wandered through the park like drowsy flies. The stables where the horses lived were mucky, and the horses themselves had manure plastered to their flanks. The duty officer, with pince-nez askew on a crooked nose and uncombed hair sticking out from under his rumpled cap—all this was such a sharp contrast to my bold, fine-looking Horse Grenadiers, who even after a difficult crossing in the hard frost maintained their brave appearance. On my way back, the platoon commander told me that the soldiers' food at the park was so poor that in the morning he had to send the caterer of the mess to the village to purchase bread.

Poverty ridden, cold . . . Great Russia, on the shoulders of which bloomed one of the magnificent capitals in the world! Not I, nor those to whom I related what I had seen while dining with the Grand Duke, could then comprehend this contradiction.

———

One autumn evening, after dining in the officers' club on stufat and macaroni, we arranged ourselves comfortably around a small green table in the library, established stakes, and began playing Preference, a card game. Outside it was pouring rain and beginning to get dark. On this particular evening, my partner and I were not having much luck. Batezatul, as always, was kidding Slovitsky; and Petrun, witty as ever, wanted to increase the stakes and rebuked me for not observing his demand bid. All of a sudden an orderly entered, walking quickly, and addressing Petrzhkevich said, "Honorable Sir, there is an alarm for the Second Squadron." We went to the front hall. Our horses stood at the entrance, and at the door was an orderly with field equipment. My orderly informed me that our new squadron commander, Rotmistr Navrotsky, had stopped at our quarters and ordered that I overtake the squadron on the road to Oranienbaum.

Having mounted our horses, we galloped in the direction of Oranienbaum and soon came upon the squadron. Navrotsky informed us in secret that he had received orders to load the squadron on a barge, and on arrival at Kronstadt, occupy the barracks of the 10th Naval Crew, and to act at our own discretion while awaiting the arrival of General Ivanov, at whose disposal the squadron had been designated.

Disembarking in Kronstadt, the squadron drew up on the wharf in complete darkness. The electric plant was not working. When we were all in place, Navrotsky addressed the squadron with the words, "Men, remember your oath and obey the officers. If anyone dares to deviate from the full performance of his duty, he will not go unpunished."

The patrol was sent ahead, and we moved in the direction of the naval depot in darkness along deserted streets. Deadly silence reigned throughout the city. Soon the sound of shattering glass attracted our attention, and we saw a mob of sailors looting a liquor store. Some of them were drunk and were lying on the sidewalk. The others, upon seeing us, took to their heels with their pockets stuffed with bottles and disappeared in darkness. Navrotsky ordered us to surround the remaining ones. From the crowd someone yelled, "Comrades, do not surrender." The sailors rushed to force their way through our encirclement. One shouted, "Oprichniki, blood suckers," while grabbing the stirrup of a Horse Grenadier. About ten others were trying to break through to him as he hollered, "The damned SOBs will kill us anyway." One of the soldiers hit him with a riding crop. After that blow, others followed, and the thrashing of the intoxicated sailors by the enraged soldiers began in earnest. The sailors surrendered, and with lowered heads stood gathered in a group in their unbuttoned greatcoats and caps minus their ribbons while surrounded by the Horse Grenadiers. We did not know what to do with them because the authorities could not be located at that moment. So we had to drive them along with us.

When we arrived at the naval depot, the bodies of seven slain officers were just being removed by relatives. Our soldiers who witnessed this shook with anger. During the first days of our stay at the stronghold, the misfortune turned on the sailors, who were caught in the streets and beaten unmercifully with riding crops—whether innocent or guilty—and after that brought to the depot.

In the course of the entire first night we did not remove our weapons and ammunition nor unsaddle our horses. Several horse patrols were dispatched to warn the peaceful citizens of possible violence. During this night, in the whole fortress with a garrison of several thousand, there was just one part, our squadron, on which the authorities could lean. But, where these authorities were, we did not know.

In the morning the infantry arrived in the city from Petersburg with the celebrated General Nikolai Iudovich Ivanov. Police appeared in the streets, and the lamps were lit. The city resumed its normal appearance. The squadron remained in Kronstadt for about a month.

By the way, recalling this incident brings to mind an encounter I had in San Francisco about fifteen years ago. At that time we were all unemployed, and everyone was short of money. Since the banks would not issue loans for homes, one friend directed me to an old timer, a Russian, who gave mortgage loans. In one of the working-class hotels of the city, I found a very decent, intelligent elderly gentleman who was employed as a janitor in the commercial district of the city. Living as an ascetic and denying himself everything from his life in America, he had accumulated a small sum of money and was giving loans with interest at the legal rate. He listened to me attentively and asked, "Are you an officer?" "Yes," I answered, "and who are you?" "I am a sailor. Do you remember when there was a mutiny in Kronstadt? During that time I was on the revolutionary committee. When the land forces arrived, and we saw that our battle was lost, we fled to Petersburg. There, another committee transferred us abroad." "Yes, I remember that very well," I said. "I myself was part of those land forces." He smiled and said, "Ah well, who is to know who was right at that time. And now we are here and must help each other." He gave me the loan. And we are still in touch.

Nicholas Our Tsar-Father

The dining room of the club is in semi-darkness. A gypsy chorus under the direction of Nikolai Ivanovich Shishkin has just entered through the side door. Behind them are gypsy women in bright gold-embroidered dresses followed by guitar players in equally bright costumes. In front of all of them with his guitar is Nikolai Ivanovich himself, baldheaded, well-fed, and appearing more like a merchant from Gostinyi Dvor.

The gypsies are not sitting down, they are waiting for some sort of signal.

We, the officers of the regiment, are sitting in front of them, and amongst us is the Tsar.

Shishkin, having lowered his head in readiness to strike up the performance and having become all ears, stands facing the Tsar. The Tsar, with a smile, nods, and in a blast of fortissimo the incomparable gypsy chord resounds:

Hey! Comrade lads
The Horse Grenadiers are our brothers
Together, strongly we shall sing
We are living in a glorious regiment
Forever dear and new to us
Hail to old Peterhof

Hail to Mother Russia
How is Aleksandra? [We all stand up.]
And Nicholas, our Tsar-Father
The end has come to all our enemies
And how could you wish for more
Having the Tsarina as our mother
Before the Heir, himself
How steadfast we are.

The Tsar, with an unsuppressed smile, twists his mustache. He is obviously pleased and relaxed. With us he is in his own circle and knows that even though we continue to watch his every step, movement, and opinion, we are doing this just to fully remember the happy moments we spend together with him.

After this song, everyone sits down except the gypsy guitar players, who stand behind their wives, sisters, and daughters the entire evening.

Some who hadn't heard the gypsies, either in the setting of a private room in the choral Gypsy settlement on the Black River or the Aquarium Restaurant in Petersburg, or at the Yar Restaurant in Moscow, or in the homey surroundings of an officer's club, would not realize the impression they made with their singing. It was impossible to be indifferent towards the gypsies—you either loved them or hated them. Most of us in the regiment loved them, in spite of the threat that was embedded in one of their ancient songs:

He who loves the gypsies boundlessly
Will never go to heaven.

The gypsies sang of love—tender, submissive, or passionately hot—of the joy of meeting, the sadness of parting, and of burning, impetuous jealousy, such as portrayed in Bizet's *Carmen*. An expansive range of emotions was depicted; boldness and freedom were replaced by unexpected submissiveness. And during this evening, free as the wind, the children of the fields bowed their heads before their sovereign, the Great White Tsar.

The chromatic gypsy songs were expressed best of all in minor motifs. But the Tsar did not like them, and for him they sang dashing old songs like, "Heigh-ho! Let the Wine Flow!," "We Are All Gypsies," or the fairly new song and already great hit "Dark Eyes."

Now here is where the Commander stood up. A tray appeared from the office where the regimental silver was kept. On it was a glass of champagne. The Commander approached the Tsar and the choir began to sing:

My silver goblet
is delivered on a golden tray.
To whom do we drink? To whom do we drink?
We drink to our Tsar.
We drink to our people.

At this point the song came to an end. They didn't sing to the Tsar about the friendship or about the hot heads that made up the second verse of the song, since it was remotely possible that it would show lack of respect and offend the monarch.

To the roar of "Hurrah," the Tsar drank the champagne and sat down. He drank with pleasure and with the ease of a Hussar. Yet during his visits with us, neither he nor we allowed ourselves to feel the effects of the alcohol.

The Tsar was chatting with Shishkin, ordering songs, and visibly enjoying himself to the fullest. The officers' club was the only place where he was able to hear the gypsies. He could not invite them to the palace, and of course going to the Black River was out of the question. Song after song was sung. It was already past midnight. We all sat with the monarch—proud of his presence among us. The longer he remained with us, the more we could boast to our neighbors, the Ulan and the Dragoon Regiments, the following day: "Yesterday the Tsar stayed with us till two in the morning."

Finally he stood up, shook hands with the Commander, smiled at us, walked out through the door, got into his open carriage, and left. In the club, the feast continued. Solos were sung: an elderly gypsy woman sang an old ballad, "Yesterday I saw you in my Dream." Another sang "Always and Everywhere With You." Then duets—"Go Away Without Looking," "You Have Forgotten Me," and many, many others—were sung, both on command from the deeply moved, elderly, married captains to whom gypsies were such a rarity, and by request from the young cornets wanting to impress the others with their knowledge of the latest repertoire.

Dawn began to break. The door was opened onto the verandah. The smell of a fresh summer morning hung in the air. We went out to the garden. The gypsies sat down, making themselves completely at home, and began singing a purely Russian song, "Oh Garden, You Are My Garden."

I was not sleepy and did not feel like leaving. But here, with wearied voices, Nikolai Ivanovich and the choir began to sing:

Sleep, sleep, sleep; it is time for us to rest.
Get lost devils; we are deathly tired.

The choir wended its way towards the exit, and in the distance at a table in the reading room sat Volodia[16] Shults, who was in love, and everyone heard him crying out for his Ksiusha.[17] This was one evening in the year when the elderly bachelor Shults was amorous and did not hide his feelings from anyone.

The sun was high in the sky when I was walking home. People were on their way to work. The soldiers were leading the horses to the first manege. But this time I was not ashamed in front of them for staying out all night. "The Tsar was with us!" At home, I plunged between cold sheets, straightened out my tired bones, and with the thought "Life, how wonderful you are," fell asleep with the dreams of youth.

In that year, in the Duma as well as in society, complaints were heard against the Tsar for his frequent visits to the officers' clubs. It was said that he not only took himself away from his work, but he also caused great expense to the officers who were entertaining him. These accusations I have even read in some other memoirs—I think Vitte's.[18]

I do not know how often the Tsar diverted himself from his work, but I remember that once he overstayed at one of our lunches. He was in a

16. Nickname for Vladimir.

17. Nickname for Ksenia.

18. Count Sergei Yul'evich Vitte (1849–1915). He was a Russian statesman—Minister of Communication, Minister of Finance (1892–1903), and Premier (1905). He opened up Siberia by having the Trans-Siberian Railroad built, and encouraged the development of industry.

Tsar with officers in Krasnoe Selo playing "Cups and Ball" (*Bilboka*) in 1906. Olferieff is just to right of Tsar in front row.

particularly good mood and was listening with great pleasure to the singers when all of a sudden, around three o'clock, he recollected something, glanced at his watch, shook hands with the Commander, and started to leave. We followed after him, and surrounding him in the living room, entreated, "Your Highness, please stay—we are expecting the gypsies." The Tsar lingered a second as though he were undecided. Then he waved his hand and said, "I can't. Two ministers are waiting for me."

You may imagine what unkind thoughts we had about those wretched ministers, who did not give the Tsar any rest.

As to the question of the ruinous expense incurred by the officers on account of his frequent visits, that certainly had no basis in fact. The receptions for the Tsar, as well as for all high officials, were subsidized by the so-called housekeeping account, that is, one in which the moneys weren't subject to transfer but were kept for unforeseen expenses under the stewardship of the colonel.

Russian summer vacation with cousins and friends, 1906.

The coming of the monarch to our club was considered a great honor to our regiment. Not only we officers but also the lower ranks were happy to see the Tsar. On the other hand, we observed that he also enjoyed being with us. One explanation for this was that before coming to the throne, he had been one of us—a colonel in the Hussar Regiment. He thought like us; his tastes were the same, he understood us and believed in us more than in anyone else.

But even to us it began to appear that the Tsar was showing favoritism to us during these years. He not only visited us at our club, but also summoned our entire regiment to him at Tsarskoe Selo. I remember such a summons in March 1906.

We had to make a thirty-verst march on a rather poor road—a heavy snow was already melting. We wore helmets. This was my first march in a helmet. I developed a headache from its weight and from the special nature of the leather, which contracted from the cold. I could not understand how our forefathers could participate in military marches and battles in them.

In Tsarskoe Selo we were lodged with the Cuirassier and Hussar Regiments. In the evening we dined with the Tsar and the Empress in the Main

Palace. The familiar faces of the waiters, their silent, skillful service, and swift change of dishes—all this brought back memories of my recent service in the palace. The only difference was that then I stood behind the chair of Her Highness, but now I sat at the same table with her. After dinner, Their Highnesses made the rounds and honored us with gracious conversation.

"Êtes-vous content de votre service à Peterhof?"

"Je suis ravi, Madame."

"Dans quel escadron êtes vous?"

"Dans le deuxième. Nous le nomons Escadron Numero Deux, Madame."[19]

"Number Two," remarked the Tsar, smiling. "You were the page to the Empress last year?"

"Quite right, Your Imperial Highness."

The sun rose, warmed the cornet's soul . . . and it slipped away. How little it took in those days to warm our hearts and sustain the flame.

The next day there was a parade. The Tsar reviewed it on his white-footed mare Trosska, and the Empress stood at the entrance. After filing off, the regiment deployed to the front and faced the Tsar. He thanked us for our loyal service and for the magnificent parade, and then turned and said something to Baron Budberg, who was standing in front of him with a lowered *shashka*;[20] after which the Commander bowed deeply. We realized that our beloved Nikolai Aleksandrovich had been appointed as a member of the Tsar's suite. After that, I observed three officers who, by their posture and concentrated expressions, were clearly hoping to be called up to the Tsar. Stefanovich, our Staff Rotmistr was called, and he bowed deeply to the Tsar. Our Levushka[21] became aide-de-camp. No two rewards bestowed on our regiment could have been greater, since the two recipients were our most beloved men. They shared many similarities: I believe that in their whole lives neither of them would ever act against his conscience, even in a situation when telling the truth would be a clear threat. I do not know how

19. "Are you content with your service in Peterhof?"
"I am very happy, Madam."
"In which squadron are you?"
"In the second. We call it Squadron Number Two, Madam."

20. A special kind of saber.

21. Nickname for Lev.

Nikolai Aleksandrovich's life ended, but Stefanovich was killed in front of me, not wanting to lie to a Kiev mob who had seized him.

Regiments were called to the Tsar not only from Petersburg and its environs, but also from Warsaw and even from the Caucasus. On these occasions they mustered at the Krasnoselsky Camp and were presented to the Tsar, who showered favors upon them.

This measure, of course, served a purpose, and one had to admit that the need for it could not be greater. During these difficult, troubled times, it was above all necessary to reinforce the loyalty of those units most devoted to the throne, because even among them, the men professed a weariness of police duty and disenchantment with military service in general. The officers began to retire in great number, and more than one resigned, not wanting to continue police work, as my squadron commander, Filosofov, made known when leaving. And others left in protest against concessions made to revolution by even such a short-lived representative body as our State Duma. I remember Lieutenant Vinkler-Ulrich, who the day before the October 17 Manifesto[22] declared that he did not wish to serve anyone except His Highness. On the promulgation of the manifesto, he left the regiment that same day.

While visiting us, the Tsar customarily conversed with the older officers. But sometimes he condescended to talk with us. We spoke of parades, campaigns, horse races, bravery, and boldness. The natural exaggeration in story telling by our cornets was not alien to him. I remember once he recounted one of his visits to a regiment in the Caucasus during the time when he was heir to the throne. The story went like this: "The Tsar (Alexander III) sent me to this regiment. Here I was met in the Caucasian manner by being offered a goblet the size of a large bucket. I looked with alarm at the bearded, old captain who was offering it and doubted if I would be able to drink it. The captain evidently noticed my expression, and when the singing

22. This Manifesto of Nicholas II summoned a national legislative assembly (Duma) and extended suffrage rights and freedom of speech, press, and assembly. It created a constitutional monarchy.

stopped, bowed deeply to me and started drinking out of the bucket himself. Without taking his lips from the rim, he drank it all to the bottom, bowed deeply again, and walked away without staggering."

The cornets followed up with a catch phrase: "One must know how to breathe when drinking. See here, our cornet goblet is not large, but to drink bottoms up is very difficult, because it has hollows and ledges inside."

A demonstration goblet was brought in, and everyone had a share in emptying it, tipping it vertically upside down just to the point where the wine didn't spill over while they guzzled.

One occasion finally taught us how deeply the Tsar believed in the supernatural. This was during the difficult days of Tsushima.[23] As far removed as we were from Tsushima, we did not foresee this catastrophe, and the dispatch about it plunged Petersburg and the palace into deep mourning.

Soon after this news, the Tsar had lunch with us for some occasion. There were neither trumpeters nor singers. The lunch was served on small tables in the garden, and since it would have been improper to drink champagne openly at this time, it was decanted from bottles on the sideboard to water pitchers and carried round to the tables like a refreshing soft drink. At the table where the Tsar sat, the "water pitcher" was not served.

This being my duty day for the regiment, I often left the table. When lunch was finished, I returned to the garden and saw the Tsar sitting on the verandah, surrounded by young people. I drew near. The Tsar remarked, "How difficult it is to sit on a horse all morning standing in one spot. Today I got pretty tired reviewing your parades." Petrzhkevich answered, "But Your Highness, during the May parade when it is necessary to stand so long in a helmet, you start to get a headache, because the helmet weighs six pounds."

"Yes, but when I was in India," continued the Tsar, "I saw Fakirs who lie all their lives on nails or stand on one leg." He described how and where these Hindus lay and stood, and it was obvious that he didn't have the least doubt that a person under the influence of a known spiritual strength would be capable of standing on one leg all his life. I listened and could not

23. The antique Russian fleet under Admiral Rozhdestvensky was destroyed by the Japanese in a battle in Tsushima Strait, between Japan and Korea, on May 27–29, 1905.

believe my ears. I wanted to find in his words some inkling of suspicion in what the Fakirs were showing the tourists. But no, he absolutely believed in what he said.

In spite of being a very approachable man, the Tsar was extremely severe towards anyone who showed a lack of tact. I remember how the Commander of the Regiment, General Roop, during supper, instead of waiting until the Tsar wished to smoke, took out a cigarette case and offered him a cigarette. The Tsar took out his own cigarette case, took his own cigarette from it, and rolled it on the table towards Roop.

Another time, one of our colonels, who was not known for tact, was sitting at the dinner table with the Tsar, wishing to impress him with his monarchism and devotion to the Tsar, and made uncomplimentary remarks about the State Duma. The Tsar sharply interrupted his criticisms and asked, "How long did it take you to march from Petersburg to Peterhof?"

Thus we spent those days between patrolling the streets and attending dinners with the Tsar, between fighting drunken sailors and carousing with the gypsies, between the reality of life and a dream world, sliding on the surface of events not knowing or realizing the precipice to which they were pulling us.

An Arshin Eight[24]

During my days in the Corps, I asked a former Horse Grenadier, Misha[25] Ber, a wealthy man who had served for three years in the regiment, retired, and now led a life of idleness in Petersburg, "What does one have to know to be a good officer?"

"Buy yourself a good horse and a good gun," said Misha. "You will gallop and shoot, and you will become a good officer."

I often remembered Misha and subsequently came to the conclusion

24. An arshin eight is a Russian unit of measurement equivalent to three and a half feet. An arshin equals twenty-eight inches. The "eight" stands for eight vershoks. There are sixteen vershoks in one arshin. One vershok equals one and three-quarters inches.

25. Nickname for Mikhail.

that he was right. In the regiment we taught each other horseback riding—the Commander of the Regiment taught the officers, the senior officers taught the junior ones, and we all together taught the lower ranks.

Horseback riding was to some degree a cult. We put all our efforts into it from start to finish. The ideal that we aimed for was to transform the rider and the horse into one solid fighting unit. To accomplish this, the horse had to completely submit to the rider's will, and the rider had to ride in such a way that the horse would give the utmost performance that it was physically capable of giving. This feat was difficult. Just as in any other pursuit, there were differences of opinion concerning the methods of reaching the objective between the upper command and ordinary officers.

Out of France came a new system of breaking in horses, named the Fillis system,[26] which was received with full-fledged enthusiasm by the young people but, conversely, with protest by the old men and by those who had the responsibility of feeding the horses. The old men, who had sprouted paunches and were hardly fit to reeducate themselves, naturally opposed the innovation, saying that the Fillis system exhausted both people and horses, and that even if it were to convert the horseman and the horse into a daring horse gladiator, that fighting unit would quickly collapse from exhaustion.

But the innovators had a powerful supporter: the Most August Commander in Chief Grand Duke Nikolai Nikolaevich, who, in spite of the experience of the Japanese War, which presaged the demise of the cavalry, still continued to believe deeply in its future. He brought into his circle the former commander of the cavalry officers' school, General Brusilov, promoted him to the post of commander of our division, and with him as his man Friday occupied himself with the reforming equestrian training. The basis of their ideas lay in the doctrine that, as a rule, the cavalry in battle would fight on horseback. But since the reality of the battlefield entails the cavalry's dispersal, so that the horseman must then operate on uneven terrain covered by fences and fortified structures, it was necessary first of all for him to learn to cope with these obstacles. Hence once more the demand set before us by Brusilov was that everyone in the regiments of the division was to learn to jump obstacles one arshin, eight vershoks (three and a half feet) in height, singly as well as in formation. To carry out this assignment

26. James Fillis (1834–1913), a well-known English-born French riding master.

we had to have a solid barricade which a horse could not knock over. The performance of this order was supposed to take place in the spring reviews of the squadron's exercises.

The old men began to worry. From experience they knew that they could not fool the Grand Duke, nor consequently Brusilov, and that barrier of one and a half arshins hung over their heads like the sword of Damocles during the course of the entire winter. They knew that it would be the main obstacle to overcome to obtain certification for the regiment.

Meanwhile, we cornets could not wish for anything better: We were given complete freedom to ride horses and arrange contests in jumping. We committed ourselves entirely to this, spending all our days in the riding school preparing the men and horses under the direction of a new graduate of the cavalry officers' school, the best rider in the regiment, Lieutenant Ershov.

Once, Ershov helped me jump my phlegmatic Bunchuk,[27] whom I wanted to ride in the competitions at the Mikhailovsky Riding School. Bunchuk usually did all that was demanded of him very conscientiously as long as he didn't get tired. But as soon as he got tired, just like a donkey, he stopped taking orders.

Ershov, not pleased with the neatness of my style, sent me ten times to the same jump. I felt that Bunchuk was out of breath, but Ershov insisted. Bunchuk approached the barrier at a gallop, and not raising his hoofs, struck it with his chest. I remember how slowly my body rolled over on the other side of the barricade with legs up in the air, and how I flew face first straight into the ground.

I found out later what had happened, after regaining consciousness in the hospital. By my bed sat my childhood nurse, Tatiana Ivanovna, who was visiting me at the time, and she quickly wiped away her tears with a small wad of handkerchief while trying to smile at me. Then I was told that after finding out about my fall, she ran to the hospital, encountered there the Commander of the Regiment, who was coming to inquire about me, called him by name a *bashi-bazouk*[28] who had maimed "her child," and didn't leave the hospital until I regained consciousness.

---

27. A *bunchuk* is a Turkish standard.

28. A member of the Turkish irregulars, a nineteenth-century cavalry troop noted for its brutality; someone depraved.

My wounds soon healed, and I quickly returned to my squadron. Bunchuk didn't suffer in a like manner. Later I learned that after I was carried from the riding school, Ershov mounted him and forced him to jump the barricade.

Spring came. The snow melted. Trees turned green. The cadets' parade ground was covered with tender, green grass. In the lower garden, the fountains gushed, and new faces of female summer residents began to appear. The Palace Guard and the convoy took their posts, and the Court arrived at the Aleksandria residence. It was the beginning of the best time of year in Peterhof. During those beautiful days, a Golgotha—a barrier one arshin, eight vershoks high—was being constructed on the back parade ground.

Despite the intense winter preparations, it was impossible to guarantee the success of the review, because it required riding out in platoons of twelve lines each—that is, almost all the men and horses, amongst whom, certainly, were both men and horses physically unfit to jump.

The barricade was built by the common efforts of all three regiments of the division which was stationed in Peterhof. By agreement of our wise vakhmistrs, who fairly often helped us out of difficult situations regarding the barricade, dirt was spread on the rider's approaching side, which reduced its height, but left it fully an arshin eight from the side where the Chief of Staff was to stand as he reviewed the exercise. We had many practice sessions at this barricade, and to our general satisfaction everything went smoothly and foretold our usual success.

The day arrived for the review of the Ulans Regiment. In command was the then well-known friend of the Tsar, Aleksandr Afinogenovich Orlov, to whom even the Grand Duke was not a threat, and the Ulans felt safe behind his back. The Tsar was expected to be present at the review.

Meanwhile, after several days, Brusilov appeared on the back parade ground with a tape measure, and discovering the craftiness of the vakhmistr, ordered the entire barricade shifted to another location.

On the day of the review, we arrived to watch the Ulans Regiment and placed ourselves on a path directly in front of the barricade. The Second Squadron, under the command of clumsy, fat Vinberg,[29] was taking a lesson. He was a former Lyceum student, an educated fellow, a war historian,

29. Fedor Viktorovich Vinberg (1869–1927).

but Vinberg, by his corpulence alone, was not suited for the cavalry. Nevertheless, the squadron was performing decently, and the Tsar repeatedly gave the "Horse-holders" signal, which denoted praise; and upon this, from the far end of the parade ground came the response, "We are doing our best, Your Imperial Majesty."

The time came for the barricade. The squadron approached it by platoon column, holding a great distance between ranks. Vinberg, who was in the lead, lost his cap and turned back. The first platoon, led by the famous jumper Kolia Poliakov, cleared the barricade smoothly. Niki Skalon's[30] second platoon, following the example of his platoon commander, completely stopped in front of the barricade, and one Ulan, by inertia, was thrown over the barricade without his horse. Everyone turned back to repeat the jump. At the same time, Vinberg was again approaching the barricade and again turned back. Behind him was the third platoon and part of the second, of which half made the jump and the other half turned back. Confusion reigned, and the Ulans, each one separately, tried to turn and jump over the barricade at all costs. The Ulans weren't able to maintain their dignity in front of the Tsar.

At this point it was visible how enraged the Grand Duke was as he spurred on his unfortunate horse with his long legs. The Emperor was engrossed in conversation with Orlov, as though he didn't notice what was happening. Brusilov, tearing away from his place, commanded the squadron to draw aside, and order was restored; and he, together with Staff Commander Afrikan Petrovich Bogaevsky and the fat Chief Adjutant Diagilev, approached the barricade. To the satisfaction of all who were present, Brusilov himself turned back several times before clearing it.

It took a lot of willpower to stand one's ground, thereby clearly risking the goodwill of the Emperor, who especially liked the Ulans and his loyal servant, their Commander. But Brusilov knew the psychology of his patron—the Grand Duke—and was willing to chance it. On this day, the Ulans were saying that in their club, Grand Duke Nikolai Nikolaevich was particularly nice to him, and Brusilov, in a burst of effusive devotion, kissed his hand.

Following the Ulans, our regiment and the Dragoons passed the review

30. Nikolai Dmitrievich Skalon (1886–1945). "Niki" is a nickname for Nikolai.

smoothly because firstly, we had had time to practice jumping the new barricade, and secondly, the seriousness of interest in the task had passed. It became clear that with an all-out effort this obstacle would be surmountable, but for the entire cavalry, it appeared to be the highest possible achievement.

Here it is necessary to state that Nikolai Nikolaevich and Brusilov were not alone among cavalry commanders of other nations in teaching this system. The general tendency of the military school which we patterned ourselves after—the French—was to profess the same theory regarding the use of horses in battle lines. True, this was only in theory, that is, the French were behind us in developing cavalry operations. Much study of this question was being carried on by the Italians, and their cavalry was often used as an example in our studies. In regards to the Germans, they profited by the experience of the Japanese War more than other countries, and as a rule, their cavalry did not enter into battle in equestrian formation.

The review of the squadron's drills that I just recounted was one of the starting points for Brusilov's career, which brought him to the post of Commander in Chief during the war and immortalized his name in history as one of the very few able generals in this painful tragedy for us. Whether it was a result of being born under a lucky star or a consequence of his superior talent, I cannot say, because I personally never served on his staff. I can only say that, not having any patronage, his whole ascent to the eminent post was his own doing. He was an officer of little means from the Tver Dragoon Regiment, and possibly had a connection with the Guards through the Corps of Pages only. He did not graduate from the General Staff Academy, and consequently wasn't canonized as a member of our holy of holies.[31] Both of these facts made his position very difficult, not only in those days when he commanded the Guards' units in Krasnoe Selo,[32] but especially during the war, on account of the opposition of the General Staff,

31. In other words, he wasn't one of the guys.

32. A military camp just outside of St. Petersburg which was used by the regiments of the Imperial Guard for summer maneuvers, Krasnoe Selo, founded in 1765 and located fifteen miles southwest of St. Petersburg, was a permanent camp, practice field, and parade grounds during peacetime. Troops that were stationed in and around St. Petersburg made their summer camps here. It consisted of a huge circle of brightly painted wooden huts, mess rooms, storehouses, stables, halls, and officers' villas. It was a camp of ceremony unique in Europe. In 1925 it became a city. (E. E. P. Tisdall, *The Dowager Empress* [London: Stanley Paul, 1957].)

which continually endeavored to attribute the success on the Southwest Front to everyone except the Commander in Chief.

I remember one maneuver in Krasnoe Selo in which Brusilov commanded the entire advancing cavalry against the designated enemy occupying the Kavelakhty Heights, Laboratory, and the Military Field up to the Mukhalovo Ravines. Being an orderly, I saw how he sat up all night waiting for the report and only gave the order when daylight was approaching.

The whereabouts of the enemy was ascertained, and it was also known that the Emperor would arrive at the Tsar's Bulwark at about the time of the attack. And this circumstance drew all the regiments to the bulwark like a magnet. At the moment of attack, there was complete chaos. The Horse Guardsmen in equestrian formation attacked their own charging Ulans from the rear; the Hussars, instead of being in the north, appeared in the southern part of the military theater. As to the enemy, they raised their flag even though it turned out they were not being attacked by anyone. The Emperor, however, didn't show up at the bulwark. The Grand Duke trumpeted the commanders to assemble. Brusilov and his retinue galloped off towards the after-action review.

The Grand Duke was furious. As usual, he was kicking his horse in the left flank and whirling his whip as if he wished to strike someone.

"I shall begin with this," he thundered, "that I have asked His Majesty and all of the military legation to leave the military field in order not to witness this . . . (his voice changed to a high, screeching pitch) DISGRACE." At this moment, his whip almost hit Brusilov, who was standing in front of everyone, on the nose.

Brusilov lowered his head and remained silent. Voeikov, the future Palace Commandant, and Skoropadsky, the future Hetman of the Free Ukraine, also kept quiet; these two were the main culprits responsible for the confusion, as a result of their wanting to present their regiments to the Tsar. For such people the military field had always been, and always remained, not a place of learning, but a field of court intrigue. They knew that this field belonged to them, and that Brusilov was only there for the temporary amusement of the Grand Duke, who sooner or later would get tired of him.

Those who knew the thorny path Brusilov had traveled in peacetime were not surprised by his audacious behavior during the days of the Emperor's abdication. At the time he was called a "rebellious serf." But wasn't the revolution a mutiny by all those whom we kept in serfdom?

Yanov

"Circle tightly by platoon to the left. Trot!" the harmonious baritone of the squadron's commander, Pavel Vladimirovich Filosofov, resounded on the Strelnetsky drill ground.

The squadron executed the command well with the exception of the second platoon, which piled up and took a long time straightening out its line; and the commander of the platoon, who invariably found himself behind his front line, came out from the flank and stood disconcertedly in the right place.

"Why," bellowed Filosofov, spewing forth his rage, "are all the platoons carrying out the command except the second?" Then, after a pause, he answered himself with sarcasm, "Because the commanders are in front of them."

I was the commander of the second platoon, riding on my gray Orlov-Rostopchin stallion, Svoiak, whom I had purchased from an officer who served on the staff division of our regiment, Andrei Platonovich Stefanovich; and the horse, like myself, had never participated in formation. The more I struggled to make him leap through a temporary opening between the platoons, the more excited he became, and in the end, after some cajoling, he brought me to the center of the drill ground where, succumbing to fatigue, I clung to the saddle with difficulty.

At the conclusion of the exercises, Filosofov announced to me, "I do not intend to excessively tire out the men and horses because of your horse's lack of training. Make the effort to get another horse, and don't ruin my squadron."

There were only a few days left till the review, and to obtain another horse in such a short period would be difficult. I stood with my head lowered in thought and from time to time cast an unfriendly look at my handsome Svoiak, who was completely covered in a lather of sweat as he was led away around us.

Seeing my deep disappointment, Pavel, being a kind person at heart, solved my problem this way: "For the review and for the rest of your training, I will give you my horse Bunchuk, and later, buy yourself another horse."

My day was saved, and the review passed with shining colors. But as a result, when after several months, Filosofov left the regiment and was looking for a buyer for Bunchuk, I could not avoid asking him to sell the horse to me, even though it was not to my taste. After about two years, I sold him to the commander of the infantry regiment for half price.

I brought up this small incident because it had a decisive influence on my future service in the regiment. I realized that receiving officer's shoulder straps was not at all indicative that one was fully prepared for service in the regiment, but that it required great and constant effort even to be on the level of an average officer. It was absolutely essential to learn horseback riding to perfection. Every day I rode my two horses, one an inexperienced government-owned horse such as was issued to each young officer for training, and I participated in all cavalry contests and steeplechases that took place in the garrison. All of this, however, didn't seem enough to me, so during the interim when the regiment was not needed to help the civilian authorities, I was able to arrange my detachment to the Yanov State Stud Farm in order to become acquainted with its operation; but in fact, I went there to gain experience horseback riding.

This farm was located in the province of Sedlets on the outskirts of Yanov, a small Jewish town near the Bela station of the Warsaw-Brest railway. It was the end of April. The Polish spring was in full bloom, and for this inhabitant of the north, the aroma was so fragrant that it almost intoxicated me. By noon the sun was extremely warm, and the woodlarks were soaring high in a cloudless sky as if inviting me to come out to the field, lie in the grass, forget all work, and together with nature take a deep breath of the amazingly pure spring air.

But the assistant to the director of the stud farm, to whom I was referred, a stocky, robust fellow of about thirty-five, belonged to the class of people who could not be influenced by the beautiful spring aroma. This man, who, as was often the case in Russia, bore a surname that made it impossible to ascertain his nationality—Aleksandr Al'bertovich Tsoppi—seemed like one compact, elastic muscle, and he exuded an inexhaustible supply of vigor and energy. Upon our meeting, his face filled with a welcoming smile; he firmly shook my hand with his short, broad hand, and immediately offered to accompany me on an inspection.

In Russia, the government owned horse-breeding farms for two purposes: firstly, to secure the supply of horses for our cavalry, the greatest in the world; and secondly, to improve the bloodlines of our provincial horses. For these reasons, there were stud farms scattered throughout all of southern Russia at which research was conducted to produce the most suitable stock for military use as well as for working, and where the so-called breeding stations maintained choice half-blood stallions for breeding with provincial mares.

In my time, the question of the cavalry horse's breed was resolved—it was settled that the more English blood it had, the more valuable it was for military duty. That is why many prominent stallions were brought from abroad, one of which, by the name of Gal'timor, was bought for 200,000 rubles—a colossal sum of money at that time. Gal'timor, being himself a European winner of Derby, founded a whole line of celebrated Russian steeplechasers such as Gammurabi, Gal'tiboi, and others. A purebred English horse was certainly quite far from ideal for Russia. The ones that worked out were principally half-breeds with a mixture of Russian Steppe, Don, Kuban, and Kirghiz horses. The attempt to mix our Orlov trotter with Arabian blood produced the famous Orlov-Rostopchin breed, which in practice did not gain a good reputation.

At the Yanov State Stud Farm in those days there were several distinguished producers of purebred offspring and a great number of half-bred mares. The latter served mainly as brood mares for supplying the army. A select few of the half-bred colts, upon reaching the age of three and acquiring some training for the development of their muscles, were sent off to breeding centers. Such colts as these were given to me for our mutual training. There were nine of them at the stud farm that year, and I was offered the chance to ride each of them at a gallop two times around the race track every day.

Tsoppi, with all of his optimism, forewarned me: "Of course, at the beginning it is doubtful whether you will be able to gallop more than three a day. But in time, judging from the experience of your predecessors, you will learn to perform the entire task. In any event, the stud farm reckons that these two-year-olds will be ready for dispatching to different centers in two or three months."

Just then a chestnut colored colt with a round, juvenile frame and foal's eyes was brought out. When a saddle was thrown on him and the girth tightened, he began to tremble all over, and when I approached and quickly mounted him, he at first sat down, but then began to buck, trying to throw me off. It all happened just as it does here at the rodeo in America, with only one difference, that here, the main goal of the rider is to remain on the bucking horse as long as possible, but there, it was necessary to force the horse to stop bucking. Two stable boys grabbed hold of the bit and started to pull the colt forward, while a third struck his hind quarters with a whip. As if conceiving what he had to do to get rid of me, he dashed ahead and bolted into the field. I merely tried to direct him so that he would not hit the fence or the wall with full force. Finally he was out of breath and began to slow down. I succeeded in turning him towards home, and he immediately started to trot in that direction.

So gradually I broke all nine horses, and by the end of the month easily galloped all of them around the track. By this time I felt as if power flowed in my veins, and how much easier it had become to master the horses.

I resided in a small cottage in the kitchen-garden of Tsoppi's home. It was engulfed in ivy, and the little footpath leading up to it was almost overgrown with tall lilac bushes. My orderly lived in one of its two small rooms and I myself in the other. Carved with a knife on the doorpost at its entrance were several surnames of some of our famous sportsmen—Nosovich, Ekse, Ershov, and others. And I did not fail to carve my name under theirs.

At the center of all the activity of the stud farm was the riding school, where each day at 10 a.m. all the administrators gathered. There during this time breeding took place, and in the arena a series of concerns were deliberated, plans for the future were rendered, and news was exchanged. There I met Count Nirod[33]—the director of the stud farm, a former Horse Guardsman, and a sullen, grumpy, old man. He showed up there with his wife, who tried to make herself look younger than her years. She was uninhibited, and would sit in an armchair and watch the goings-on in the manege with a shamelessness peculiar to a certain type of female her age.

33. Aleksandr Nikolaevich Nirod, 1847–1913.

After meeting me, she asked me to sit next to her and was obviously getting erotic pleasure out of sitting beside a young officer. It was rumored that Nirod had three homes: one in Yanov, another in Warsaw, and the third in Petersburg. In each of these homes he had a wife, and that he himself was fully subservient to all three. The wives, however, made use of their power only in the confines of their own city.

Occasionally officers were given permission to come to Yanov to acquire horses at the stud farm. They generally stayed in town. Once, two such visiting officers invited me to join them there to dine. It was the first time that I had ever been inside a Jewish settlement,[34] and the little Jewish town of Yanov had a very depressing effect on me with its narrow streets, and old, dilapidated huts with wide open doors, through which the poverty and filth of the dwellings could be seen. On the handrails of the steps hung dirty blankets and mattresses from which bugs had been probably shaken out. I walked in fear of picking up fleas and bedbugs. In the middle of the cobblestone street was a sewer drain where a dirty, foul-smelling liquid flowed from beneath the houses. Here and there Jewish men with their ringlets of hair, wearing long, Jewish gabardines[35] wandered like lethargic flies. Their bodies bore all the signs of malnutrition.

I found my new acquaintances occupied in a very strange sport. Sitting on a bench before a puddle, they were throwing copper coins into the mud, while the Jewish children competed against each other in fetching them from the mire with their teeth. Judging by the ongoing noise and excitement, one might have thought that this pastime gave everyone great pleasure.

We dined in a small restaurant, which was located on the ground floor

34. From 1791, Jews were treated as aliens in their own country and restricted to living in the Pale of Settlement, which was a designated area in western Russia where they had already been living for a long time. They were excluded from the general rights of citizenship, their freedom of movement was denied, and within the Pale, they were only allowed to live in the towns and not the countryside. Permission to leave was only granted to educated or prominent Jews, and even then with much difficulty. The May Laws of 1892 tightened the previous restrictions, and conditions in the Pale became worse and more congested. Life there was full of misery, destitution, and despair.

The pogroms, in which thousands of Jews were murdered and much property was destroyed, originated in Russia in 1881 and continued sporadically till 1917. *Pogrom* itself is a Russian word meaning destruction, devastation.

35. A long, loose, coarse coat or frock for men worn in the Middle Ages, especially by Jews.

of the hotel. We were waited on by the owner, a middle-aged Jew with clever, rapidly shifting eyes, and his two daughters, clothed in dresses which revealed their tawny bodies considerably more than ones proper for a waitress. It didn't take much guessing to determine the nature of the girls' profession as they bawdily eyed the men with come-hither glances. According to the two officers who stayed at this hotel, the owner sold both food and wine and his daughters as well. In fact, when after dinner I was getting ready to go home, he bowed from the waist and invited me to return, openly hinting that his establishment was full of all sorts of comforts.

"Why is there such poverty and filth in Yanov?" I asked Tsoppi. "Because they have no one there to exploit," he replied. "You know—healthy dogs have healthy fleas. But try to remove the fleas and put them under a bell jar; they will not eat each other and will begin to die. In this same way, the Jews in Yanov and in all Polish towns die. We would hire them on the stud farm, but they are afraid of horses. They do not own land, and the landowners, because of their parsimony, will not hire them. But what Jewish fellow is a worker?" he concluded. I was perplexed.

The impression of Yanov and its inhabitants was deeply etched in my memory, and each time the Jewish question arises in my presence, I remember the innkeeper who sold his daughters into prostitution, the flowing of fetid sewage through the streets from which children collected copper coins with their mouths, and the emaciated, gabardine-clad Jews wandering on the streets of the town.

Tempted by Sin

"For him it is merely *shtybno*—he will win by himself," Frank, a forty-year-old stable "boy" told me as he was leading Satanello, a purebred stallion, by the bridle to the starting line. Satanello was the best horse in our regiment at that time, and I was about to ride him in a race at Tsarskoe Selo for the second time since arriving from Yanov.

"What is the meaning of *shtybno*," I thought to myself. "It probably comes from an English word which Frank Russianized." Yet, I hesitated to ask him about it.

On my return from Yanov, the Tsarskoe Selo races were just beginning, and my regimental comrade, Vodia Ber, offered me his Satanello to ride in them. For me, this was a great honor and a pleasure. Having been instructed to spur at the finish and not use the whip, in the first race I had come in second after Ekse, of the Cuirassier Regiment. This time I was given free rein. My main opponent was from the Ulan Regiment, His Majesty Nosovich, and although he was a better-known horseman than Ekse, I still felt ready this day to challenge anyone. But recognizing this didn't diminish my internal quaking, the kind which sometimes doesn't allow one to finish a sentence, and which only those who have participated in public competition know well.

Even though my anxiety was great, I could not get rid of an intrusive thought—there on the platform, when I was leaving to mount my horse, "She" told me, "I will pray for you." And with a wink that I alone noticed, she rested her expressive, gray eyes on me. I could not bear this look, lowered my head, kissed her hand, and quickly left. "Why does she need me," I thought. "She has a husband with whom by all indications she appears to be happy. I never showed her that I liked her . . . but did I like her? Perhaps, because she was the first woman to pay attention to me."

The starter, Aleksandr Ivanovich Zviagintsev, interrupted my thoughts, and instructed us to straighten out and line up by numbers. The horses became excited, and began to rear up and lower their heads trying to pull out the reins and bite at their bits, constantly breaking up the line and making it difficult to choose the precise moment to start. But finally the moment came; Zviagintsev waved a small flag, and the horses, all bunched together, started out at a smooth, bold canter on the soft turf.

There were five of us in all. Nosovich and I were observing each other, and in no time he was next to me. The distance of the race was two versts. We had to pass the platform once, make a complete circle, and finish at the platform. While passing the platform, I thought, "Is she watching me now, or is she already flirting with someone else?" I caught myself in this thought and grew angry.

On the opposite side of the course, I perceived that Nosovich's horse was beginning to lag behind. On the last curve, I was in front of everyone; Satanello was proceeding easily. On the straightaway, however, Nosovich moved his horse out and with several leaps, went ahead of me. I realized that his lagging behind was only a maneuver to put me off guard. I remembered the word, *shtybno*, and without using the whip, leaned forward along Satanello's neck, and thumped him twice with my legs. This produced an effect. Again we were next to each other, but Nosovich was whipping his horse, striving to overtake me.

We were approaching the post, and again I used my spurs several times. It turned out that I had passed the finishing line. I did not know exactly who had won the race, but as I changed my pace and turned towards the platform, I heard the strains of my own regimental march, and from this I understood that I was the winner.

"Today is my holiday," she said when I approached her box seat. "Let's call it 'our holiday,' "I remarked laughingly.

Ber, wishing to celebrate the event, invited all of us to dinner at Ernest. A good dinner, delicious wine, my first success at horse racing, but especially, my success with a woman—all this was so intoxicating, and at times it seemed as if I were dreaming, and I was afraid of waking up. I realized that the awakening would be terrible, that she was the wife of my friend, and the very thought of her as an accessible female was a crime. But here then, I found a sneaking justification: "I didn't start it. I could not tell her, 'Go back to your husband and leave me alone.' Later I may say it, but just not now—today is 'our holiday.' "

After dinner, Vodia, being a sensible man, left us and returned to camp, and we three set out for Strelka, the tip of Elagin Island.

"All" Russian society who had remained in Petersburg for the summer gathered on the very western side of this island where the land ended and the Gulf of Finland began. Ladies in magnificent attire and elegantly dressed, bored men—everyone was drawn to this narrow strip of land with its splendid drives, as if the pale northern sun were a magnet pulling them as it sank in the leaden water of the gulf.

We got out of our carriage and walked to the very end of the spit. The sun was rapidly sinking into the water, and the deeper it sank, the faster it disappeared.

"Why does the sun have to leave?" she said pensively, thinking perhaps of her vanishing youth.

"To get further away from sin," her husband's voice rang out.

The sun passed out of sight. The dim evening glow lit up the horizon. It began to get damp, and gradually the point became deserted.

"It is time to go home," said the husband.

"No," commanded the wife. "I want to have some fun; I want to hear the gypsies."

In the Samarkand[36] we met a large group of former Lyceum students. My friends knew many of them, and we joined them in one of the private rooms, where it was easier for us to play, with a fire which burned brightly.

"Tell me why did I meet you?" sang a gypsy woman. "She is asking my question," I said.

"Why the drama. I do not like drama. This is fate. Do you believe in fate?" she asked. And not waiting for an answer continued, "You know, I dreamed about you last night and knew all this would happen . . . You know, sometimes I imagine that he is you." She ended by focusing her eyes on her husband.

There was nothing more she could say.

"This is impossible," I said, in a desperate attempt to defend myself. "This cannot be."

"All you need is the desire . . . You are dining with me on Sunday."

I parted from the husband and wife in the Samarkand and set out for the Baltic station. But the train had already left. I had to prevail upon the coachman to drive me directly to camp. He raised the top of the calash, and departed at a trot on the road to Ligovo. I curled up on the seat and fell into a deep sleep, as only a very young man can—in all kinds of conditions and wherever exhaustion finds him.

The sun was high when I reached the village of Dmitrievo. The regiment was already on maneuvers, and only the rear was visible, climbing Shungorovo hill. After putting on my ammunition, I jumped on Svoiak, galloped until I caught up with my squadron, and stood in my place with embarrassment.

"Cornet Olferieff, appear at bivouac and report the reason for your tardiness," shouted Ershov, the commanding officer of that summertime squadron. He yelled so loudly that the lower ranks heard him. Afterwards, while on the march, he came up to me and quietly said, "You know how I love races, and yesterday you saw me at Tsarskoe. But I never allowed myself

36. Restaurant.

to be late for duty. If you want to continue racing, you must promise yourself that this will be the last time."

But alas . . . This was not the last, but only the first time.

One day the maneuvers in this camp gathering were particularly drawn out. The cavalry was more fatigued than ever. In conducting the reconnaissance exercises, all the squadrons were required to complete rides of sixty versts in twenty-four hours, and everyone was pretty well exhausted and impatiently awaited the signal to retire.

During this year I was unusually fortunate in my service. Once after exercises, the Commander of the Regiment told me that the Grand Duke was pleased by the attack carried out by the Second Squadron, which he had witnessed accidentally. It happened that on this day he was substituting as Commander of the Squadron. Another time, I received a commendation by order of the division for an important report from the horse patrol. Finally, in that same year, I won the steeple chase at Krasnoe Selo in the presence of His Imperial Majesty.

The latter achievement was quite unexpected, and probably that is why it has remained so well preserved in my memory. This is what happened:

Before the races there was a two-day maneuver in which Orlov, of the Ulan Regiment, was our detachment commander. I was sent to him from our regiment for guard patrol. It was late in the evening. Orlov was sitting in a Finnish hut, and while awaiting the report, was drinking cognac and listening to music. With him sat members of the Ulan Regiment: Prince Engalychev, the oldest colonel; Arsen'ev, nicknamed "Komar"[37]—the Tsar's favorite and his aide-de-camp; Prince Ilia Alekseevich Kropotkin, a boyar, descendant of Rurik, rapidly squandering the income from his ancestral estate in Kazan; Daragan, an accurate adjutant; and Mitia Krupensky, a forty-year-old perpetual cornet who came to the Ulans from the Councilors of State in search of a carefree, idle life and the best possible means of dissipating his incredible income from his Bessarabian estates. All in all, the fellowship was a "serious" one, as every drunk who knew its members would say.

---

37. "Mosquito."

The most interesting among them was Orlov himself. Tall, well-built, handsome, and wearing a creased hussar-style cap cocked on the side of his head, he was the personification of boldness and bravery. Before commanding the Ulans, he had served in the Hussars of His Majesty in the days when the Tsar, as heir apparent, was completing his own training there. In the Hussar Regiment at that time was a group of sincere, unpretentious men, such as Petrovo-Solovovo, Pavlov, Sologub, Orlov, whose whole purpose was to serve the Tsar, the Fatherland, and their regiment. They socialized only within the regiment and aspired to a simple way of life such as that assumed by the soldiers, even outwardly placing themselves on a par with the lower ranks—instead of "yes," they would say "quite right," instead of "all right," they would say "I will obey." And everything was in this spirit. The Tsar himself, being plain and unaffected, was attached to them and became their good friend. It was natural that when he ascended to the throne, he didn't forget them. But Orlov, being the brightest among them, was received into the Ulan Regiment of His Majesty, and became a personal confidant of the Empress. As I previously stated, the Empress, in spite of everything, still felt like a foreigner in Russia and rarely showed trust in any Russian. But to someone who gained this trust, her kindness was unlimited. Orlov was one such person. This relationship did not fail to generate envy towards him. People watched his every move, every minute blunder, and spewed malicious criticism: "There he is, the acclaimed Orlov," people said in a backhanded way; "he is merely a clever courtier. That is why he can get away with everything." He was not wealthy and, it was said, had an unhappy family life. He continued to devote himself entirely to the service, and you would never encounter him in society. Frivolous, corrupt, and envious Petersburg invented complete legends about him, even to the point of saying that he was the father of the heir to the throne, and that [the courtier] Anna Vyrubova divorced her husband so that she could take the place of the Tsarina who left the Tsar.

I remember that one day in Peterhof, while passing through the cadets' parade ground along Peterburgskaia Street with one of my regimental comrades, my fellow traveler pointed out Orlov's carriage, which was parked in front of Vyrubova's house, and asked me:

"Do you know whose carriage that is?"

"I know."

"But did you see the palace bodyguard?"

"I saw. So what?" I asked.

"You doubt the rumors?" my fellow traveler said to me, basing his world view on the novels of Artsybashev[38] and Verbitskaia.[39]

"Perhaps. But admit that even if the Tsarina is there alone, that doesn't confirm the truth of the legend."

"But then couldn't the acknowledged need to have an heir serve as an encouragement to it?"

"No, they're too religious for that."

Severe tuberculosis ravaged Orlov in his youth. He was hastily sent to Cairo, but died en route. Malicious tongues connected this death with the rumors of his closeness to the Tsarina and asserted that he was poisoned.

But at the time of which I am speaking, this same Orlov had begun to go on sprees with his Ulans, listening to singers in a Finnish cottage near Krasnoe Selo.

The Ulan Regiment sang the same songs as were sung by our regiment, but their manner of singing was different. It always seemed to me that it was pretentious and less masculine. Their merrymaking was called a "ball," which brought to mind a polished parquet floor surrounded with delicate lace. But all this was insignificant. From the beginning there was always a close relationship between the regiments in everything, and I never felt myself an outsider among the Ulans.

We were drinking cognac. Orlov was sitting across from me, and noticing that I had a full glass, began to sing:

Horse Grenadier, why no merriment?
Why have you lowered your dear little head?
The others joined in singing:

38. Mikhail Petrovich Artsybashev, 1878–1927, was a Russian writer whose novels were quite popular at the time. His writings of 1905–07 reflected the decadent atmosphere of the period, according to the conservatives who condemned him. They said that his erotic and naturalistic works preached amorality, sexual dissoluteness, and aversion to social ideals.

39. Anastasia Alekseevna Verbitskaia, 1861–1928, was also a popular writer of the time. Her novels were full of sexual motifs and advocated "free" love. One theme was a protest against the abnormal upbringing of women in a bourgeois-aristocratic society.

I feel sorry for the Grenadier
I feel sorry; I feel sorry for him.
I wore out my shoes
By walking to him.

I stood up and gave the only permissible toast for my cornet rank: "To the health of HIS MAJESTY'S Ulans and their Commander."

The glasses were filled and the conversation came to life. The attention centered on me. But the young Kornetik,[40] as Orlov called me, was already a wise old bird, and it was difficult to knock me down.

We stayed up until morning. Finally, the awaited dispatch arrived. Daragan laid open the map. The cognac was pushed aside, and the singers were dismissed. Orlov called me up and gave me a problem to solve; and after saying good-bye to my hosts, I departed in the direction which was ordered, dreaming of completing the maneuver as quickly as possible in order to get to bed.

When I finally reached Dmitrievo, Ershov met me in front of my cottage with his arm in a sling. This was one of his many dislocations, which happened frequently as a result of innumerable falls from the horse and with the horse.

"It's a good thing that I waited for you. You must go now to the races and substitute for me. I'm entered in the three-verst race, but my damned shoulder has slipped out again, and I had to ask you."

"I don't know if I'll be of much help. I've not slept all night," I tried to refuse.

"If you do not participate, our regiment will not be represented at all this year."

There was no further argument. I had to gather all my strength. I washed my face, put on a clean kitel',[41] and urged on a Finnish driver in a two-wheeled cart to get me to the race. Upon arriving, I just had time to run to the stable as the order came to ride out to the starting line. Orlov was the starter.

40. "Little cornet."
41. A uniform jacket.

"Ah, Kornetik. This I like!" he yelled as he caught sight of me. "Now we ought to win this race."

I must admit that I was not at all certain of it, but I just prayed to God that I would remain in the saddle and not disgrace myself.

There were four participants: Poliakov of the Ulans, Trubnikov of the Hussars, Yazikov of the Dragoons, and I of the Horse Grenadiers. At the start, as always, we set out together, but at each barrier I gained at least a body's length. My horse, which I had never seen before, carried me like the "devil" of Gogol's blacksmith, and by the finish I was so far ahead of everyone that in a photo later brought to me by the court photographer, Otsup, I was the only one visible.

The Tsarina personally presented me with the prize. On my arrival at the pavilion, I remembered that I had not shaved and felt very ill at ease standing in a line of officers who were receiving recognition for all the competitions in the course of the current year.

Not having seen the Tsarina since the previous year when I served as her Page, I had the impression that she had gained weight and her manners had acquired a more assured quality. But as before, she continued to carry out her duties with the same seriousness and concentration among crowds of people foreign to her. Orlov was there helping her award the prizes. When my turn came, he said something to the Empress which I could not make out. She handed me a silver vessel and congratulated me on my victory.

After that, I not only knew Orlov, but he knew me, and every time we met, he spared the time to say a few words to me. And during the regimental holiday the following year, the Empress, passing over many of the older officers, came up to me and inquired if I were still taking part in the sport.

In the evening of the day of the races, my comrades honored me in the officers' club, and the Commander of the Regiment himself served me a glass of vodka. This was the most important day of my service in the regiment. I had attained my dream—to be considered a good officer. But alas!—even then it gave me little joy—I felt as if I were becoming more and more entangled in the nets of water nymphs, which I was certain were dragging me to the bottom. Yet, I didn't have the strength to stop and break away from them.

Again, I overslept and arrived late at the riding academy in Old Peterhof. My complete stock of excuses was exhausted. From lack of sleep, my mind worked poorly, yet it was necessary not only to find an excuse, but also to reach the city again by the evening. The problem seemed insolvable, and I had to resign myself to the flow of events—everything would somehow turn out all right.

This was the time when my youth asserted itself and stubbornly hindered my preparation for life. I was twenty-one years of age, but it already seemed to me that I was getting old and would never amount to anything; therefore I needed to get everything out of life that it had to offer . . . come what may.

I was sitting in a deep, soft armchair by the corner window in the living room of the regimental club. It was a gloomy, rainy, autumn day. The living room looked depressing, with its low ceiling and dark furniture, and contributed to my somber, slow-moving thoughts.

From the study, the gentlemen of the first squadron began to gather. As usual, sullen Egershtrom, with a businesslike look, wended his way quickly towards the zakuskas table. He did this just as seriously as when he was riding up to present his squadron in review. He was a kind fellow, a good comrade, and an excellent family man, who lived amicably with his fat, friendly wife. But he was completely devoid of humor, and I never saw him in a happy mood. Aleksei Korochentsev, who had just married a beauty, Lily Volkov, arrived all decked out in style, already imagining how to make use of his uniform, his wife's connections, and the patronage of Aleksandr's brother in order to further his career. Misha Mazing, a large, drunken "bursch,"[42] walked in, striving to carry his title of senior cornet with dignity, and fancying himself to be a formidable-looking leader in his conversation with us young cornets. After him came Durasov, a young cornet from my class, who had still not shed his military school deportment, especially the habit of jangling his spurs noisily.

The first squadron, although it, like all the others, was called "first" in

---

42. A German word which translates as "a German student." It has the connotation of "a vigorous chap with enterprising spirit."

number only, maintained a particular dignity and a certain, hardly noticeable condescension towards the rest of the squadrons.

Very soon from the front hall the sonorous, rich voice of Obermiller, commander of the third squadron, was heard, telling a succession of anecdotes in German to his subaltern officer, Volodia[43] Shults, who had remained a staff captain for too long. Volodia was a hunter and a sportsman, who enjoyed his vodka and zakuskas, but to us he appeared old and sad, as he was a bachelor who was falling in love with a gypsy from the chorus when he was visiting us at the club but once a year. At the time we thought that this fascination was a passing fancy, but obviously nature took the upper hand, and Vladimir Aleksandrovich's annual encounters with the gypsy assumed a greater role, and the outcome was that he married her, retired to the reserves, and moved to his estate in the Caucasus.

Misha Batezatul arrived and was looking around with a devilish smile, seeking out the "elements" to play Preference.[44]

The third squadron brought the atmosphere in the club to life. I was always envious of the happy mood of this squadron. They showed neither rivalry, complications, jealousy, nor conceit. They never wanted anything to stand out or anyone to be amazed by them—they served honestly, and knew how to spend their leisure time joyously and amicably.

The later arrivals were officers who had either come separately from the city or straight from their beds. Kostia[45] Skuratov walked into the living room with his spirited gait, favoring somewhat his right leg, smiling in the same manner at everyone—both old and young. In all the regiments, at all times, there were officers without whom it would be difficult to imagine an officers' club. And, on the other hand, there were officers without whom it would be impossible to imagine the regiment. In our regiment, Skuratov was one of these. In formation he was in the standard platoon of the fourth squadron, and set the direction for the regiment, and in the club he was the center of every enterprise. His popularity among the young attracted the older officers, and his infinite devotion to regimental traditions left no doubt that the cornets were in the right hands.

43. Nickname for Vladimir.

44. A card game.

45. Nickname for Konstantin.

Kostia could not fail to sense my state of mind, and greeting me said, "Blind man, pluck up your courage." Thus, he too chided me for my shortsightedness.

Just before lunch, Adjutant Lev Platonovich Stefanovich arrived. Upon seeing me, he approached, as always, with a friendly, slightly bashful smile, and twitching his shoulder with its golden aiguillette said, "It's good that you're here—the Commander of the Regiment wants to see you."

"What happened?" I asked anxiously, knowing that a lot could have happened that day.

"Nothing special," smiled Levushka,[46] and this smile reassured me.

Finally the Commander of the Regiment, Baron Nikolai Aleksandrovich Budberg, arrived. It was impossible not to like this man, not to respect him, though there was nothing particularly distinguished about him, nor did he even pretend to it. He had served in the regiment starting from the ranks of cornets; the regiment being his whole life, he never married. After taking command of the regiment from the Grand Duke, his only concern was to maintain it just as it had been in his predecessor's time. He did not seek a career for himself. Probably this measure helped him cope with leadership during the difficult times of political agitation and unrest. For all this, we were disposed towards him as if he were one of our own. Nikolai Aleksandrovich shook everyone's hand and called me away to his office. He used the familiar "you" with me since he had known me when I was a boy: "You know, Olferieff, I was a friend of your father's, and I feel that now in his memory I must carry out that which he would have done if he were alive: You must be moved from Petersburg for the time being, and since your squadron is leaving for Livonia,[47] I am reassigning you from the instructional detachment and sending you with the squadron. Remember that I am doing this not for the good of the service, but for your sake. At this point, you need to see Navrotsky; he already knows about this. And now, let's go drink vodka."

We both sighed with relief. The Baron did not like such conduct, but I

46. Diminutive for Lev.

47. Also called Lifliandia, Livland. At the time it was one of the three Baltic provinces of Russia, bounded on the west by the Gulf of Riga, the north by Estonia, the east by the governments of St. Petersburg, Pskov, and Vitebsk, and on the south by Courland.

was happy that the Gordian knot which had racked my brain all morning was so easily cut asunder.

I was thankful to the Commander of the Regiment not only on that day, but also remained thankful to him for the rest of my life, because my mission to Livonia placed me face-to-face with reality for the first time and opened my eyes to much that I had never previously noticed.

My sojourn in Livonia served as the end of my careless youth and as the beginning of a sensible life and a vital struggle.

The Beginning of a Vital Struggle

Livonia

"One good turn deserves another."

We were stationed in Livonia on the estate of Sesvegen, meaning "Seven Roads" in Latvian. It was located on the rail line between the town of Valk and the Shtokmansgof station of the Riga-Orel railway. The castle where we were quartered was a large, new building of gray stone in an oppressive German style with a steep, heavy roof, in one corner of which rose a tower with a conical roof and embrasures. Tongues of soot marks left trails from the embrasures and gave evidence of a recent arson attempt.

The interior of the structure had the same heavy, depressing effect. On the ground floor, the reception rooms were of dark wood adorned with paintings of hunting scenes. Heads of dead wild beasts hung on the walls. The vestibule was enormous, with a huge fireplace; the dining room was gloomy, dismal, and large; and the study, decorated with coats of arms and portraits of knights, was just as gloomy. The living quarters upstairs were suitable but not comfortable. There was neither plumbing nor electricity in the castle.

The estate belonged to one of the richest barons of the Baltic provinces, by the name of Von Volf, whose permanent address was in Berlin. We were met by the young German steward, who was round as a ball and spoke Russian well enough; the elderly housekeeper, who afterwards sat at the head of our table and had great difficulty expressing herself in Russian; a young Polish forester from Poznan; a young doctor; and "Frau Doctor," who was an attractive petite brunette (and knew it well). The last three did not speak Russian. They all were extremely gracious and kind. But where except in Russia could one find such a situation, that the troops of the country defending their own citizens within the country's boundaries had to speak a foreign language to those they were entrusted to protect?

In Sesvegen we replaced one hundred men from the Ataman Cossack Regiment. It was commanded by Captain Petr Nikolaevich Krasnov, who was well-known at that time and was the future Ataman of the Almighty Don Host. He was also the author of the sensational book *From the Two-Headed Eagle to the Red Flag*, which has been translated into many languages. The name "Krasnov"[1] for all intents and purposes entered into the history of difficult times in our native land, and unfortunately, under scrutiny, not always with respect. The opinions of his contemporaries were sharply divided—from high honor for a person who gave his life to save his homeland to deep contempt for a man who betrayed her. At the same time both opinions came from the side of those who fought against the revolution.

Here is my initial impression of this outstanding man: First of all, he justified his last name—he knew how to speak eloquently and write even more eloquently. He wrote patriotic feuilletons[2] in the *Russky Invalid* about the Tsar, the parades, and his loyalty to the Guards, the reading of which produced tears of triumph. These articles were read not only by us young people, but also by those whom he depended on for his career. It was left to him not to make mistakes that would brand him as "out of line" for promotion.

After supper that evening in Sesvegen, as was customary during regimental meetings, toasts were raised to the reigning leader, the chef, the commanders, and finally to the housekeeper, with the singing of "Charochka" and the downing of an incredible quantity of very tasty local beer. On Krasnov's initiative, we gathered in the vestibule around the fireplace, and with maps in hand, he explained to us in detail all his activities in Livonia. His report was short, clear, and businesslike. From it I understood that our task amounted to surveying an area approximately fifty versts in radius, preventing possible revolutionary advances in it, and apprehending the

---

1. The last name "Krasnov" has as its root the Russian adjective *krasnyi*, which besides meaning "red," also means "eloquent," "beautiful," or "fine."

2. Articles in French and other European newspapers in the section devoted to light fiction, literature, reviews, criticism, and general entertainment.

remnants of the organization the "Forest Brothers," who were still hidden in the woods and cellars. We had to survey the region by horse patrols, maintain contact with the neighboring squadrons, and render assistance to the civilian authorities on their request. In general, Krasnov concluded, the situation had quieted down considerably and our job would be fairly easy, leaving time for pursuing tactical field exercises, training horses, and receiving instruction in reconnaissance. He then added, "The fodder is good," and entirely in the manner of a Cossack, looking at our squadron commander while smiling with a wink said, "and easy to get."

In the evening I went to the squadron park. The soldiers were already well-settled in their barracks, which was formerly a large shed. They took over the Cossacks' bunks, bought their extra blankets, and even inherited the young Latvian girls who just walked around the yard with service stripes sewn on their sleeves, and on the appearance of an officer, would come running down the footpath in the soft snow, facing and saluting him with their bright green or red gloves.

The first few days in Sesvegen were broken up by assignments—becoming acquainted with the roads, arranging horse patrol schedules, etc. Fresh air, lots of good country food, and plenty of sleep lifted my spirits and increased my energy.

But then mail arrived. Mother wrote that there were problems in our village, that the peasants absolutely refused to work on the landowners' land, and all our flax remained unharvested. But this was our main source of income, and consequently I again had to expect a shortage of money in that year. I realized that somehow I must help Mother, but it was obvious that my going home would not solve the problem.

Another letter arrived. It was written in small, legible handwriting and had the fragrance of a familiar perfume. It pierced my heart and made me long for Petersburg. But when I started reading it, I was astounded by its insincerity and emptiness, which at a distance clearly revealed the nature of its author and which I didn't want to examine close up. The letter was thrown in the fireplace and remained unanswered.

Meanwhile, a week passed, and another . . . There were no signs of revolution in Livonia, and everything was quiet in Sesvegen. As Krasnov had predicted, we had more time than we knew what to do with. Either there wasn't a library in the castle, or it was located in the locked part of the castle. The local administration was extremely cordial, but kept to themselves, with the exception of the young doctor, who invited us frequently to her home. I liked her very much, but like an old bird, decided to keep a distance between us. I would have to somehow kill time in my circle. Here are a few words regarding this circle:

The commander of the squadron, N., was a baptized Tartar with high cheekbones and slanted, very near-sighted eyes set in a prominent "ram-like" forehead, which as a general rule occurs in very stubborn people. He was about thirty-five years of age. His strong-willed traits were obstinacy and boastfulness. Like all who are self-centered, he talked continuously and constantly bragged. Having finished secondary school, and as a man of substance, having joined the Guards, he did nothing to improve his education, and he never read anything except regimental orders. Reading in general he considered a dangerous business, since many books bore within them the seed of doubt in the justness of the existing order. And criticism, in his opinion, was criminal. He had three ideals: the throne, his own regiment, and his family—precisely in that sequence. He regarded it his sacred obligation to protect them with true Mongolian fanaticism. In the business of commanding the squadron, he looked to two authorities: former Commander K., a very bright and capable individual, who at that time was already retired, and Vakhmistr Poliakov, who knew how to put into words the necessary orders. N., having set himself the goal of commanding the most brilliant squadron in the regiment, and being independently wealthy, spent his own money on buying horses and helping soldiers, frequently evoking resentment from the other commanders. During the war, N. proved himself the bravest officer in the regiment.

In my observation of N. in those days, it seemed that he was in a fog, and was not able to grasp the meaning of all that was occurring then in Russia. Subsequently, when we were shaken by the revolution, a vast abyss, which our life of isolation had lured us into, opened before him; and when his eyes opened to reality, he couldn't bear it—and he dropped dead of a heart attack.

With our squadron lived Divisionnaire Colonel Von K., who was over forty. An Ostsee German, he was well-educated, polite, modest, punctual, and a good executive like the former Regimental adjutant. Intellectually he was different from N. only in that, being the Regimental Adjutant, he did not read but wrote orders for the regiment. As a German bound to Russia only through his suzerain emperor, he looked down upon the Russians and did not like them. He had nothing but contempt for the soldiers. And though he certainly had no knowledge of either Russian poetry, literature, or art, he sneered at them, and considered Russian songs and soldiers singing in formation to be remnants of barbarism. We could not speak Russian in his home since his wife did not understand the language. Only after carefully verifying their noble origins would K. meet and drink with the officers on a first-name basis. He collected coats of arms of the regimental officers and studied their genealogy.

Lieutenant P.'s father was a Lithuanian, but he himself was an Orthodox Russian landowner from the Tula Province, and even spoke with a provincial Tula accent, pronouncing *tri rubli*, instead of *tri rublia*,[3] and inserting a soft sound to the word *pervyi*[4]—*per'vyi*. He was of small stature, frail, and, probably as a consequence of poor health, rather withered. In spite of this, he was a good horseman and a magnificent marksman, and for this he was respected by the soldiers. He never displayed initiative in anything, yet carried out all orders exactly; brilliant solutions to problems would not be forthcoming from him. Lieutenant P. was well-liked in the regiment. He read voraciously and knew the classics well and liked to quote them. He read *Novoe Vremia*, and always knew what Men'shikov was writing in his feuilletons, and in general he studied the newspaper, as they say, "from cover to cover." Nevertheless, from all of his reading, his conclusions were somewhat strange; and he only paid attention to odd things, neglecting the most important events or, perhaps from his own discretion, leaving them to smarter people. I remember once the following conversation at dinner:

"I read here," said P., "that Povolaky Krushevan, a 'not-without-fame' organizer of Jewish pogroms, has arrived in Ivanovo-Voznesensk."

"But why is this important 'in the third place'?" K. asked him, mimicking catechism.

3. "Three rubles."

4. "First."

"Because," answered P., "Povolaky Krushevan is NOT-WITHOUT-FAME."

After this political discussion, if one could call it that, more familiar and understandable subjects were brought up, such as hunting for capercaillie,[5] trapping, etc.

It always seemed to me that if P. had been in the hands of a good commander, he would have become an outstanding officer, but during the war he, like Captain Tushin from *War and Peace*, became a modest hero, who would carry responsibility for everything, and his heroic deeds would be acknowledged on a regular basis. Unfortunately, I do not know about his behavior during the war. I only know that he died in 1915 from injuries received in battle near Warsaw. May you rest in peace, dear comrade.

We also had two young cornets, Vasia P. and Kolia P., both former Pages, and only a year younger than I. It always seemed to me that while Vasia was in the Corps of Pages, he did not like me; and Kolia was his friend, so they kept away from me.

And so, except for morning greetings, I spent most of my time alone, not speaking a word to anyone.

My squadron remained. But consequently, there was nothing to do, since the recruits and the young horses were left in Peterhof, and riding into the field with the reconnoiterers promptly stopped when it began to snow.

Once I had the idea of getting permission from the commander to offer help to the soldiers in their letter writing to their families, and to teach them reading and writing. The response from the soldiers was overwhelmingly enthusiastic, and they opened their hearts to me.

At first I picked out the ones who were completely illiterate. There were only two of them. One was absolutely hopeless, and I had to give up on him. Approximately half of the others had studied for one year in a rural school, and only with great difficulty could they read and sign their names. The other half were literate.

We obtained paper and pencils. Some of them wrote out the alphabet, and some transcribed words which I dictated. In the squadron we found two soldiers' chrestomathies, which we read and reread. Every day I

5. Wood grouse.

completed the lesson with a tale about the history or geography of Russia. I indicated to each soldier his province and town on the geographic map. They learned the different roads, railways, rivers, and sea routes, and compared the progress of our transportation network with the European, our density of population with the German, etc. In the beginning my teaching did not require much effort, but in due time I had to prepare the lessons. The students were like sponges, absorbing and remembering every word.

Since that time, more than half a century has passed, but I remember almost all of my students as if I had seen them yesterday. I remember Dukhov, my senior reconnoiterer; Galaktionov, a teller of tales; Chernykh, a Zaporozhian[6] "philosopher"; Makogon and Eremenko, singers of love and the glory of victory; Shutov, the dancer; Bogomolets, aspirant to the ranks of an officer; Medvedev, the prototype of a future Bolshevik; Popov, Gladky, Litviniuk, Fen'ko . . . How thankful I was to them for their interest in my teaching. They helped me find meaning in my military service and assuaged that spiritually painful experience which befell our lot in connection with our police duty in Livonia.

Much later, I happened to meet some of my students who had already left the regiment. I remember when my train stopped at the Belgorod station, an oiler approached the car, tapping the wheels with a hammer. He was one of the members of our platoon, Zavrazhnyi.

"How are things, Zavrazhnyi?"

"God has mercy, Sir. Just yesterday I passed the examination for conductor and thought of you. Remember when you taught us reading and writing? Until my death I will always be thankful to you."

Once during the war, while passing the Vladimir Ulans Regiment, 13th Cavalry Division, in which I served as the senior aide-de-camp, I heard someone calling, "Sir, Staff Rotmistr Olferieff." Looking around, I saw Dukhov in the Ulan lines.

"How is it that you are here?"

"I was called up from the reserves. And what about you?"

"I am now on the General Staff. You know what, Dukhov? Your Regiment Commander is a former Horse Grenadier, and our Chief of Staff,

6. A Cossack or a man from the country beyond the Dnieper rapids.

Colonel Dreiling, even served in our second squadron. If you wish, I will ask them to transfer you to the staff division, and we will serve together."

"No, Sir. I still remember what you taught us, 'In the service do not force yourself on anyone, but do not refuse your service.'—Remember, then we read? I was called to war here, so this is where I'll stay. Just recently I became a platoon commander. If I leave, it will be difficult to be replaced immediately. Thank you, Sir."

Needless to say, I was proud and happy to receive this answer.

We were in the Molodechno Forest, marching parallel to the enemy front. Suddenly, very close to the location of our troops, we heard a German machine gun. "To the right, in lava,"[7] ordered the commander of the squadron. "In the direction of the first platoon, follow me."

The squadron did not have time to turn about before horses and people began to fall. The battery coming from behind took off with those in the lead and opened fire with grape shot. The clash of combat began.

At the end of the fighting I found the Third Ulan Squadron, but Dukhov was no longer there. "Injured. Just taken away," came the answer. Poor Dukhov did not know, when he spoke of the difficulty of replacing him in the platoon, that he would be replaced that same day. Such is war . . . Such is life . . .

However, my students did not always attain eminence. Among my reconnoiterers was an exceptionally outstanding soldier, Medvedev. He was always the first one to solve a problem and answered questions to the point. He was well lettered and an above-average horseman.

"Why wasn't Medvedev recommended to command school?" I asked the vakhmistr.

"He's a factory worker," answered Poliakov.

Then I remembered that in our day they avoided sending workers to be prepared for the duties of a non-commissioned officer.

"I think that he ought to be encouraged for his splendid work in

7. In a lava formation, "the horsemen function in a molten mass with no regulation, apart from basic interaction with the nearest riders, enabling each to function independently and to the greatest effect." Rossiya Segodnya, "The 'Lava Flows' of the Cossack Cavalry," *Russia Beyond*, https://www.rbth.com/arts/2014/09/10/the_lava_flows_of_the_cossack_cavalry_38175.

reconnaissance. I want to forward his name for lance corporal[8] in a reconnaissance vacancy."

"He drinks, Sir Cornet, and when he's drunk, he becomes rowdy."

"Maybe if he's encouraged, it will help reform his conduct."

Poliakov remained silent. He did not like to take chances on what might or might not be. And I felt that he didn't share my supposition.

But the commander of the squadron agreed with me. My presentation was approved, and Medvedev, to his real surprise, received a chevron.

A year passed. I was on guard duty for the regiment, and during this time was attached to the fourth squadron. N. arrived at the officers' club, and, as always, addressing not only me, but all who were present, said, "Well see here, your Medvedev has been brought before the court. That's right . . . Lance Corporal . . . Look for him in the guardhouse."

I went to the guardhouse. Medvedev disconcertedly stood up and answered my greeting. The chevron was not on his shoulder strap.

"What happened, Medvedev?"

"I roughed up Stashuk yesterday, Sir." Stashuk was his platoon commander and a very good non-commissioned officer.

"How is it that you struck your commander? For this you can be assured of disciplinary battalion."

"He's deserved it for a long time. While we were still in Sesvegen, remember, when you gave me the chevron? He couldn't stand it, and then I restrained myself because of you. But when you left, my life became unbearable. So yesterday I drank and hit him once or twice . . . Why did you leave us?"

"I doubt whether I could help you, Medvedev. You yourself understand that you violated the very foundation of discipline. If we all began to beat our commanders, what would happen?"

Medvedev smiled from the corner of his mouth. It seemed that this idea was not alien to him. He was sentenced to disciplinary battalion, and if he lived to see the revolution, he probably became one of its leaders. And when I was in dire straits in Bolshevik-occupied Kiev, I often thought, "If Medvedev was here, he would rescue me. Or would he?"

8. Russian *efreitor*, from German *Gefreiter*.

———

Already beginning to settle into a routine, life in Sesvegen soon was disturbed by a report from the police that twenty versts from us, a member of the Forest Brothers was hiding in his home. We were ordered to arrest him and turn him over to the civil authorities. It was rumored that we could expect armed resistance. We were given the subject's name, his physical description, and the layout of the farm building in which he lived.

I was dispatched with the platoon to carry out this operation. Poliakov was assigned to help me.

We started out with the intention of arriving at the site of the arrest before sunrise—a time when vigilance would be at a minimum.

It was a clear, frosty January night. The moon shone so brightly that it was possible to read by it. As we approached the farmhouse, I was considering all precautionary measures before the arrest and gave strict orders not to open fire first. Sentries were stationed on all the roads leading from the farm; then Poliakov, the remaining platoon, and I proceeded towards the house. We surrounded the house. Poliakov went to the back door while I knocked on the front door. Soon I heard Poliakov's voice, "Hands up!" And within a minute, they brought before me a tall young blond Latvian in his underwear. Having heard my knock, he had obviously tried to escape by the back door. Leaving sentries outside, I entered the house. We heard a heartbreaking woman's cry, and a young Latvian girl fell at my feet, grasping the flap of my short fur cloak, begging for mercy for her husband. In a cradle, an awakened baby wailed. I ordered the translator to explain to the woman that we were not planning to kill anyone, and began to interrogate the Latvian. He admitted to his name but denied belonging to the Forest Brothers. I explained to him that by order of the Governor General, he must be arrested and sent to Riga.

To this day I am not able to forget the sight of how his wife with trembling hands brought his trousers and helped him put them on, herself wearing a fur coat over her nightgown. I realized that what was happening was disgraceful, and at the same time didn't have a moment's doubt that the situation could have been handled differently.

Twelve years after this arrest, I myself stood in our apartment in Kiev with raised hands, with a revolver pointed at each of my temples. And just like the Latvian's wife, my wife rushed towards me, trying to protect me from what appeared an inescapable death. Although then the only difference was that the ones who came to arrest me roughly cast my wife away, and she fell backwards into the corner of the room. But how could one expect from Kievan hooligans the same manners as from a person who had received what was reputed to be a chivalrous education. The similarity, however, was enough that I recalled then in Kiev the arrest of the Latvian in Livonia.

The wife of the Latvian asked permission to go to Sesvegen with her husband, which I granted, ordering their horses to be harnessed to a sled to carry them both.

Having delivered the prisoner to Sesvegen and written the report, I thought my assignment had been performed, and I would no longer be involved in the affair of the Latvian.

In a few days, N. boasted of how he forced the prisoner to confess by not giving him drinking water and feeding him a single herring. This disturbed me so much that I couldn't bear it, and for the first time told N. how disgusted I was with his behavior, the more so since the interrogation of a prisoner didn't even enter into our obligations. As a result, I no longer had any confidence in the squadron commander.

Then I learned that the order concerning the feeding of the herring, which was given to Poliakov to carry out, never was put into effect. This worthy, reticent, even timid man, who knew exactly where duty ended and mercy began, simply didn't comply with the commander's orders. "I was told to do that," he responded to me. "But I couldn't find the herring . . . And the water stands there where it always has. The captain should have seen it."

As usual, N. was merely bragging. But as a result of this incident, on arrival in Peterhof, I was transferred to another squadron.

When I later learned that Poliakov was killed at the very beginning of the war, remembering my service with this ideal human being, I thought, "Why does war always make victims of the best people?"

Meanwhile, a neighboring landowner and friend of Colonel Von K. invited the officers of the squadron to hunt for a bear who had been seen the day before in his forest. We all went except N.

The landowner's home bore a strong likeness to the usual Russian landlord's home, being in fairly sound condition and decorated in good taste. His family consisted of a wife and two colorless, fair-haired, German daughters, for whom it seemed the officers had been invited.

The ceremony started with a delicious lunch and was accompanied by a good, old vintage wine. The host, a conceited but artificially amiable German, spoke with us in French, frequently inserting Russian expressions in his discourse, by which one could surmise that he knew the Russian language just as well as he knew the French.

After dining we went to the entrance and before us was a surprising sight. In front of the house on both sides of the path, which had been cleared of snow, stood so-called *zagonschiks*[9] with skis in their hands. When we passed them, they bowed, grabbed hold of the landlord's hands, and kissed them. And he benevolently held out his hands to the right and to the left.

They led us to the forest opening and placed us lengthwise to it in numerical order. At the same time, numbers were given according to the ranks of the honored guests. So P. (since K. was not present) got the spot to which the bear was most likely to burst forth. I took the next spot, and so on.

The whole system of hunting was based on the fact that the surrounded animal could not leave the encirclement because he would not want to cross human tracks. This was true for all wild animals. But unfortunately for the landowners, for us, and for others like us, this rule didn't extend to the Forest Brothers. They were not only unafraid of hunters' tracks, but also of guns pointed at them.

This characteristic of an animal allowed the hunter to stand on one side of the forest and wait until the beaters drove it out. On this day it was agreed that only after the first shot, which was intended for the bear, could one shoot a small animal, such as a fox or a hare.

Very shortly we heard shouting, whistling, and clapping of hands from the beaters. I was standing in the clean, white snow, looking in the prescribed direction, praying that the bear would not come out towards me.

---

9. "Beaters." The beater is the one who pushes the beast to the hunters in the raid.

My thoughts were far from even wanting to kill a hare. I remembered the recent arrest of the Latvian, his meager hut, his shabby trousers, which his trembling wife helped put on him, and compared this to the luxurious life of the landlords, and to the servile relation of the agricultural laborers, who did not even own a small piece of land on which they could build their own homes and be secure in the knowledge that no one could evict them. I was contrasting all this to our village, where the peasants had their own homes, though of rather poor quality, and their own plot of land, though very small, from which they could go to work for a landlord or to a factory in town, leaving their family at home. And it became clear to me why the disturbances in the Baltic provinces carried such an embittered spirit. I thought—would I have remained in the position of the Latvians, kissing the landowner's hands, or would I have joined the gang of Forest Brothers? The answer seemed obvious.

Meanwhile, the beaters' voices were coming closer, and along the line a shot was heard, followed by a second and a third. Suddenly, about ten steps from me, I saw a fox, who having noticed me, sank down on his hind legs, and momentarily froze. Instinctively I aimed at the fox, but immediately lowered the gun. This whole process of hunting, which couldn't be called a sport from any quarter, was repulsive to me. The fox vanished, and out of the forest moving towards me came the winded beaters, who at once swiftly departed along the path. Their role was performed, and they would not be so bold as to display an interest in the results of their work.

Shortly, the hunters gathered together, and it was revealed that all the guests, with the exception of me, killed either a fox or a hare. The bear never appeared. Whether he was around and thereby, contrary to a bear's custom, crossed over human tracks was never known.

The landlord was pleased with the general success, and expressed regret that luck was against me. Of course, I never mentioned my encounter with the fox, but Lieutenant P. making a tour around the neighboring fir trees, saw the tracks and with reproach whispered in my ear, "Slept through it."

Having thanked the host for his hospitality, we went directly home.

I remember one more of my assignments, which luckily had nothing to do with either arrests or investigations. The platoon under my command was specially called out to the Novyi Shvaneburg estate, located thirty versts away, for the protection of the arriving landlord. We were ordered to remain there until the arrival of the Guards.

We set forth early in the morning and arrived at our destination about noon. The estate, more beautiful and wealthier than the ones I saw at that time in Livonia, belonged to Baron Sh., whose brother was in the court service of the old Empress.

The manager who met us put the platoon in the manege, which was lit by electricity and decorated with coats of arms which hung on the walls. It was proposed that I go over to the castle, where the footman in livery escorted me to my room and told me that the baron expected me for dinner at six o'clock. In the meantime, I was served a delicious lunch with a carafe of *kummel*[10] and of vodka.

At six I was received by the baron in his study, and we promptly passed through to the dining room, where he welcomed me to dinner with champagne. There were just the two of us in the dining room. It was impossible that the baron, a former officer in the Horse Guards, did not know the Russian language. However, seeing that it was difficult for me to speak German, he switched to French, but not to Russian. But was that action really surprising? Well, there was the very same disdain for the Russian language in the salons of Petersburg and at court. Even in our own village we spoke French so that the servants would not understand.

The topic of conversation ranged from Petersburg, to the nephew of the baron, who was my comrade in the Page Corps, to the Horse Guards, and finally to the superiority of the English purebred horse. Not a word was spoken about the purpose of my visit, and when I mentioned incidentally the day of my departure, the baron immediately changed the subject and spoke of his wonderful manager and his admirable quality of knowing about everything—such was the etiquette. It seemed that if the house we were dining in caught on fire, we would continue to sit there, and conversation about the fire would be considered in bad taste.

With difficulty, I remained a necessary half hour after dinner in the

10. A colorless liquor flavored with caraway, anise, or cumin, made especially in the Baltic area.

baron's study looking at his family portraits, and at the first pause got up to take my leave and went to the manege.

There two unpleasant situations awaited. First, the exalted manager had not thought of heating the manege where the soldiers had to sleep, and they were complaining about the cold. So we notified him, and the fireplace was lit. Thereupon the commander of the platoon, Chernykh, reported to me that the men had nothing to eat except rusks.

"But where are the canned goods that you received three days before departure?" I asked with annoyance.

Chernykh said hesitatingly that the soldiers had eaten all of them before departure. The meat was so delicious that the soldiers ate it like candy.

"Why didn't you check the supplies before leaving?"

Khokhol[11] silently looked at me and from his sly expression, I understood that it was the fault of both of us.

"I have canned goods," he said, "but the majority of them don't—they think that it is easier to carry them in their bellies."

We did some detective work, and ascertained that not too far away was a shop, where all the available sausage was bought, and in the mill on the estate, a case of beer was procured. The rusks were our own. As a result, although late, the men were fed, and the beer improved their spirits. And sitting comfortably on the floor, they carried on a lively conversation.

"Well, Sir, is Livonia and Russia one kingdom?" asked Shutov.

"Of course it is. If you would do a little more studying, you wouldn't ask such questions."

"I know this, but just wanted to say that there are so many different people in Russia, and here they speak a foreign language and look upon their own soldiers as if they were aliens. If our men came to our village, would they have to buy sausage?"

"Is it true that the peasants here don't have any land?" asked the Lithuanian.

"It's true," I answered. And sensing that perhaps the conversation had

11. Chernykh's nickname. *Khokhol* is a nickname given to Ukrainians by Russians. It literally means a crest, a top-knot, a tuft of hair; it was applied to the Ukrainians because of their custom of shaving their heads except for a single tuft of hair.

crossed over to unsteady ground, I told him that during our next lesson we would talk about it.

At that moment the baritone voice of Makogon resounded, supported by the voice of Eremenko, "The wide Dnieper, roaring and sighing."[12]

Makogon knew that this was my favorite song, and he liked it, too.

The raging wind howled
To the valley of tall, bending willows
And rose up with the mountains in a wave.

They both were sitting on the floor with crossed legs, looking right at each other. They seemed completely unaware of anyone or anything except the harmony of tones they emitted. They knew that they sang well. Everyone around them stopped speaking and listened.

The song ended, but the silence continued. They all were hoping that the two would sing another song, but were hesitant to request it. Finally, Makogon shouted, "Hey, Dukhov, now sing a Katsap song."[13]

Under ordinary circumstances, the Khokhols and the Katsaps didn't like each other, and made fun of one another from time to time; but in the regiment, "esprit de corps" came before anything, and there was no animosity between them.

Dukhov was not a soloist, but he had a splendid ear for music and always gave the key for singing in the chorus. He knew his turn would come and had a song ready. He began to sing "Saturday is a rainy day" and everyone joined in.

"It is impossible to work in the field."

This wasn't a soldiers' song at all, but one of hay mowing, winnowing, or harvesting. All the soldiers knew it and had sung it since childhood. I loved it because it reminded me of my village and thus, too, of everything else, transporting me to my beloved Kurchino and precious memories of childhood.

---

12. The song was sung in Ukrainian.

13. This is the Ukrainian slang name for a Russian. It was used by Ukrainians as a term of abuse—something like calling a Russian "butcher."

The song ended on a joyful chord, and after that a dancing song was sung, "Unhappily sowing orach."[14]

The chorus sang and Shutov, having thrown off his short fur cloak, dropped to a squat and began to dance with abandon. He had been a professional dancer from childhood, and having been employed in a performers' traveling tent show, he knew his business. It was difficult just singing to keep up with his tempo, which compelled us to sing faster, when the words of the song were already impossible to comprehend.

Having performed the final skillful spin, he stood up straight as a post and snatched off his cap in salute.

"Shutov, you are a hero," I yelled.

"Happy to do my best, Sir."

It was time to end the evening. Yawning, the men dispersed to the corners of the room. Downstairs in the manege the horses were snorting and chewing on the hay, and once in a while you could hear the voice of the soldier on duty, trying to keep order between two squabbling horses.

The next day the Guards relieved us from duty, and I went directly to Sesvegen without stopping in to see the baron. On the way, Chernykh approached me and cautiously asked, "You are not angry with me, Sir?"

"Why should I be angry with you? I have forgotten about yesterday's food problem, and don't want to think about it anymore."

"No, it isn't over that," he continued. "You see, Petrenko told me that you were from the peasantry. And I said to him this couldn't be. But he kept repeating that you were."

I burst out laughing. "Why does he think this, Chernykh?"

"Well, your last name is Russian, and you know about village life."

It must be admitted that there were many foreign last names in the Guards. And I did know things about village life and peasants' conversations, since I had had the opportunity, probably rare for that time, to grow up in close community with the village where I lived until I was thirteen years of age.

"No, Chernykh, I'm a landowner, but grew up and lived in the village for a long time."

---

14. A plant of the goosefoot family cultivated for use like spinach.

"That's what I thought. You're an officer, and no one except the nobility could become an officer."

"That's not true, Chernykh. During the last maneuvers, we had General Alekseev, who was a peasant. Also, General Ivanov, who was in Kronstadt when we went there, didn't come from the nobility."

"Yes, they probably aren't in the guards"—Khokhol wasn't appeased—"and they wouldn't accept them into our regiment."

I remembered K.'s coats of arms, but could not agree with Chernykh, even here.

"Emperor Peter the Great established the guards, but he paid attention to nothing but business. When it was necessary, he promoted deserving men into the nobility. And he severely punished unworthy noblemen. Since that time the law hasn't changed."

Chernykh held his tongue. But by the expression on his face, it was apparent that my answer did not satisfy him.

"It seems to be true. Maybe so, but it is not." Evidently this was in his Khokhol mind.

Towards evening we arrived home, and I slept in my soft bed in the castle's blue room, which K. called, the "Mädchen Zimmer."

Colonel I. [Isarlov] arrived one morning accompanied by my roommate from Peterhof and a friend, Cornet K.

N. [Navrotsky] secretly informed us that a prisoner had been brought from Riga to stand trial before a field court-martial.

Colonel Iosif Lukich I. commanded our four squadrons in Livonia. He was a wealthy Armenian and one of the oldest officers in the regiment. His character traits were pedantry and moderation in everything—he spoke little, drank little, walked slowly, laughed moderately, and likewise . . . thought but little. It was said that during his younger days he lived according to schedule: on Mondays, he rode his horses, on Tuesdays, he visited friends, etc., and on Saturdays his love would arrive, and when he received her, his orderly in the next room had to start up the organ. So went each week in the course of his entire bachelorhood. When he married, his wife tried by various means to further his career. She even arranged for him to become a member of an English club. Yet, in spite of everything, he was not successful in making a career. With great difficulty, he obtained command of the regiment and led it to war, but very soon he was relieved of his command on account of his total incompetence.

After lunch, I. read to us the Statute of Field Courts-Martial, which I had still remembered from my school days. A field court-martial could only be instituted in an area declared a war zone. The expression "war zone" was avoided at that time and changed to "Area of Extraordinary Protection." The difference was in name only. The field court still had jurisdiction. Following its deliberations there were just two possibilities: the accused was either shot or found not guilty. The sentence was carried out immediately, and the prisoner could neither appeal the decision nor hire a lawyer.

The court was composed of I., the chairman; and N., P., K., and myself, its members.

The session took place in the baron's study in the castle. The prisoner, whom the Guards brought in, was a young man of about twenty-five. He had not gotten a haircut for a long time and was drawn looking—probably due to endless interrogations. (Here it must be noted that except for the external sentries posted at the entry door of the prison where the accused was kept, the Horse Grenadiers had no contact with him. He was completely in the hands of the Guards.) He gave all his testimony through an interpreter, who was a Guard. The indictment was read to him, prepared, obviously, by judicial experts and turned over to I[sarlov]. It was clear from the document that Voldemar Lupik (so he was named), a school teacher, was accused of being a member of the revolutionary band of Forest Brothers, with whom he had committed an attack on a local Orthodox priest, who had been castrated by them and as a result, died.

One must note that the Orthodox clergy in the Lutheran Baltic Provinces were in an extremely precarious position. This was one of the unfortunate mistakes in the policy of our Most Holy Synod towards our Protestant and Catholic borderlands. Their parishes remained empty; the support the priests received from the government was but a beggar's portion, and they were the center of mockery for the entire population.

When Lupik was read the translation of the charge against him, he pleaded not guilty.

At the trial were two witnesses: a forester in the district where the crime had been committed, and the Guard who had arrested Lupik. The forester, a well-educated German, confirmed that the accused belonged to the revolutionary group that called itself the Forest Brothers, and he knew him as an active revolutionary, always delivering incendiary speeches. But he wasn't witness to the emasculation of the priest and could not vouch for Lupik's part in it.

The Guard testified that the crime which the prisoner was charged with was committed long before his arrest; that except for him, all the participants in this assault had already been shot; and that Lupik, according to the testimony of the executed ones, had taken an active part in the attack. However, he could not be found for a long time. Finally, it was discovered that he had returned home and was living in the cellar of his farmhouse. And in that cellar, he had been apprehended by the witness.

When the Guard completed his testimony, I asked I. whether we had the depositions of the executed criminals. There appeared to be none. Lupik was asked why he had hidden from the law if he considered himself not guilty. To this he replied that since everyone knew of his revolutionary activity, he was afraid of being arrested. He again denied his participation in the torture of the priest.

With this, as far as I remember, the judicial inquest ended—Lupik was removed; and I[sarlov] commenced to ask our opinion, beginning with me as the youngest. Again I reminded him that we didn't have the sworn depositions of those executed, and, in my opinion, we could not convict him of the crime without the depositions.

I. stated that since Lupik was sent to us by the Governor General, then, of course, the civil authorities didn't doubt his guilt.

The next one questioned was K., who agreed with me.

I. came out and admitted that the instructions given him excluded any possibility for doubting Lupik's guilt, and, therefore, our duty was to carry out the orders of the civilian authorities. At the same time, he even mentioned something about upholding the honor of the regiment. N. and P. agreed with him, after which I. signed the sentence of military execution. After him, the others signed it. And I signed it.

Later I learned that while the trial was in progress, a grave was already being dug by the local residents under the supervision of the Guards at the edge of the grove, approximately five hundred paces from the castle near the road that led to the station.

An order had come from Riga to hold a public execution, and the Guards were assembling the inhabitants of the volost'[15] at its location.

Many a time after the revolution we had the opportunity to read that, in fairness to the Russian people, the terror in Russia was carried out not by Russians but by foreigners—that at first, the Bolsheviks' power was in the hands of the Jews and depended on the non-Russian troops—Chinese, Latvian, and so forth. And finally, it fell into the hands of a Georgian.[16]

But was it only during the revolution? Is it not possible to say the same thing about the entire history of Russia, beginning with the invitation to the Varangians,[17] followed by the invasion of the Tartars, then, after Peter, the Germans. Remembering Lupik's trial, I can see that even our activity there was not in Russian control. The administrative and economic power was held by Germans, and even the military units were sustained by aliens: Von K. was a German, I., an Armenian, and N. and Cornet K. were Tartars.

Yet can we truly attach any importance to this? Was this the cause of the cruelties that went on and are going on? During the trial, K., the Tartar, was in the minority on the side of acquitting Lupik.

Now, when I look from a distance at Russia's past and at its present, when I recall and see all that conglomeration of names and nationalities, I agree with many foreigners who count all that mass of different races living in the Eastern European plain as "Russian." As a mass, it has its own definite characteristics distinguishing it from the rest of the world's people and from the individual nations that compose it.

The execution of Lupik was carried out that same day. Approximately one hundred local residents gathered at the place of execution. The Guards led Lupik from his prison cell, followed by a Lutheran pastor and surrounded by a convoy of soldiers. He walked with sure steps, holding his uncovered head high. After him came a detachment of our second platoon under the command of lead Cornet Vasia P. Upon arrival at the execution site, Lupik was placed at the edge of the grave facing the soldiers, at

15. A district including several small villages.

16. Stalin.

17. According to the Kievan *Primary Chronicle* of the early twelfth century, the Slavs of Eastern Europe "invited" the Varangians, a Scandinavian people, to come to Novgorod in AD 862 to rule and reign. It was said that the "invitation" was prompted by their need for military assistance to maintain public order and protect lucrative trade routes.

a distance of ten or fifteen steps from them. N[avrotsky] approached him with the sentence in hand and read it in a particularly loud voice. The Guard read the translation.

Could Lev Mikhailovich ever think then that twelve years later his own son would be shot in the same manner by men like Lupik? And did he remember the execution of Lupik when he received word of his son's fate?

During the reading of the sentence, I looked at the detachment of soldiers awaiting the command to kill a human being. To my great surprise it was composed not of men from the second platoon, but was assembled from men of the entire squadron. In the center stood my "protégé" Medvedev. The rest of them were colorless. Since after the execution, we all avoided talking about it, I was never able to find out whether the men were specially engaged in the formation of this detachment because they were, above all, reliable, or were they volunteers? I believe the latter was correct, since Medvedev, in any event, in the eyes of the vakhmistr did not represent a trustworthy element. If so, then his presence among those who carried out the shooting was very interesting.

After the sentence was read, permission was given to Lupik to say some last words. He raised his head, shook his long hair, and spoke in Latvian, which the Guard immediately translated for us:

"I am being shot because I am a revolutionary. This I admit. But I did not commit the crime of which I am accused."

Addressing the soldiers, he asked them not to shoot at his face. The crowd began to drone. N. gave the signal. Vasia gave the order. A rifle volley resounded, and Lupik sank in convulsions towards the grave. A complete silence fell upon the crowd. Our veterinary assistant, in the absence of a medic, approached the fallen body. Having taken his pulse, he reported to the squadron commander that Lupik was dead. The Guards lifted his body in order to throw it in the grave, but at that moment, heart-rending sobs were heard from an elderly woman, who tore off her woolen shawl and begged to have Lupik's body wrapped in it. This was done. The woman was Lupik's mother.

The execution site soon was deserted. But to the very end of our stay in Sesvegen Lupik's grave was always adorned with wreaths, and a footpath was worn towards it, which with the approach of spring grew black and reminded us ever more keenly of our murder. I perceived that this darkened path carried within itself the sentence with which Tolstoy began his novel *Anna Karenina*: "Vengeance is mine; I will repay . . ."[18] I always had a foreboding that after this killing, sooner or later we would suffer a deserved punishment.

Was Voldemar Lupik guilty as accused? Suppose he was. It is possible that any other field court-martial would have found him guilty. I was not disturbed by this fact, but I was conscious that just like Lupik, the Latvian whom I arrested, and all the Latvians openly rebelling against the medieval order at that time in Livonia, against the economic dependence in which they had found themselves among people who looked on them as an inferior race, and against kissing the hands of arrogant barons—were totally right. If I had been in their place, I am sure that I would have joined the Forest Brothers. This reverse side of the coin was so clear to me then that throughout my life, I continued to see it.

In our day when mass capital punishments, inflicted on people sometimes only because they had honestly served their homeland, were considered legal, and when the country which regarded itself as the head of civilization persisted in taking one life after another of its people, the military execution of one Latvian, accused on the basis of circumstantial evidence, would pass completely unnoticed. A half century ago during peacetime, even in our "backward Tsarist Russia" the death penalty for a criminal offense did not exist. That is why for us, the execution then in Sesvegen was an exceptional phenomenon.

My stay in Livonia opened my eyes to the entire bankruptcy and shortsightedness of our politics in the Baltic region. Supporting the big landlords with their contemptuous attitude toward Russia was not only offensive to us Russians, but also dangerous in relation to the war situation. During the war, many of the barons whom we protected, including Von Volf, took Germany's side, and during the revolution, with the aid of Russia's enemies, they strove to recover their land.

HERE I AM NOT SPEAKING OF THE RUSSIAN GERMANS, AMONG WHOM WERE MANY LOYAL TO RUSSIA. THESE PEOPLE WITHOUT RESERVATION CONSIDERED RUSSIA THEIR

18. Tolstoy was quoting the Bible here, Romans 12:19.

NATIVE LAND; THEY TOOK PRIDE IN THEIR RELATIONSHIP WITH THE RUSSIANS AND HEROICALLY GAVE THEIR LIVES FOR RUSSIA IN COMBAT AGAINST THOSE SAME GERMANS. HERE I AM SPEAKING OF A CERTAIN CLASS OF POWERFUL BALTIC BARONS, WHO CONSIDERED THEMSELVES SUBJECTS OF THE RUSSIAN EMPEROR, INASMUCH AS THEIR ESTATES WERE ON RUSSIAN TERRITORY. AND THESE GERMANS, AS A CLASS, ENJOYED EXCLUSIVE INFLUENCE AT COURT THROUGH MANY GENERATIONS. IT RESULTED IN OUR SHORTSIGHTED AND UNJUST TREATMENT OF THE LATVIANS AND ESTONIANS.

For this reason, the heroic Latvian battalions fought with unrestrained bravery against Germany during the war, and with the fall of the old regime, became the principal and much devoted, loyal supporters of Lenin.

Frequently one reads and hears that if in 1905 the administration had placed itself on the path of progress and established a government accountable to the people, there would not have been the horrible terror in the twenties.

Such discussions always remind me of our Vakhmistr Poliakov, who when the word "if" was used would say, "How can you possibly foretell what would have been."

Soon our sojourn in Sesvegen took on a tiresome character as we impatiently awaited orders to load up the train and go home. I decided to make use of this time and asked for leave to travel home to my village in order to straighten out my affairs. It was decided that I could go as soon as the order came to begin loading.

Meanwhile, a robust northern spring made its appearance; the snow quickly melted, green blades of grass began to shoot up on the south-facing slopes of the hills, the larks arrived, and the long evenings were beginning, when one didn't feel like doing anything; even the oppressive boredom of our sedentary life was coming to an end.

During one of these evenings I stepped out of the castle, and without any definite purpose headed up the path towards the squadron. A short time later the air resounded with the singing of our bards at the hitching post, and not wanting to interrupt them, I sat down on a bench and listened.

The sun is low. Evening is near.
Come to me, my sweetheart.

Probably everyone on this warm, spring evening dreamed of his own "sweetheart." For some she was pictured in real life, and for others she appeared hazy, just an imaginary vision . . . "Will I ever have a sweetheart?" I thought. "One who would love me not for my handsome uniform or merely out of loneliness, as it had been till now, but a true love who would share all my thoughts, joys, and troubles. Does she exist?"

At that moment Frau Doctor appeared on the path. Her presence always threw me off balance. But on that evening she seemed especially attractive.

"Guten Abend, Herr Leutnant."

"Guten Abend, Frau Doktor."[19]

"I heard that you are leaving soon, and I shall never forgive you for not stopping by to visit."

"Es waere schlimmer," I told her, "wenn ich eines Tages Ihrem Mann nicht mehr sollte verzeihen koennen, dass er Ihr erster Entdecker war."[20]

As usual, it required a great effort for me to translate my thoughts into German, and I did not know whether she understood me. But like a battle horse hearing the sound of a bugle, she roused herself:

"You are always joking . . . But frequently I am very sad," she said. "You must come to see us before you leave." I promised that I would.

"Do not admire, do not admire another's turtle dove."

"Because another's turtle dove will fly away, fly away."

The soldiers sang, drawling out the words as if in response.

But once again I did not carry out the promise I had given to the doctor's wife. Upon arriving at the castle, I learned that the order for our return had just been received, and that now I could go home on the first train available. This I did not fail to do, the very next day.

Towards evening I changed trains in Shtokmansgof to the Riga-Moscow

---

19. "Good evening, Mr. Lieutenant."
"Good evening, Mrs. Doctor."

20. "It would be worse . . . if one day I didn't have to forgive your husband for being the first one to discover you."

express. The coaches were crammed; not only were the reserved seats all taken, but it was difficult to find a non-reserved one. Finally the conductor took me to a sleeping car where all the upper berths were raised, but below, on one of the straight seats by the window, sat a young woman, who evidently was not planning to lie down and offered me a seat across from her.

My fellow traveler was an attractive girl about the age of twenty. Judging by her dress and by a book of Chekhov lying on her lap, I decided that she was a student. Not to appear nosy, I opened a newspaper and sitting in a half-turned position, pretended to read it, and at the same time had the chance to observe her. This maneuver did not pass unnoticed by her, and she was visibly very amused. I wanted to make her acquaintance, so I tried another ploy: I folded back the upper part of my paper and looked at her over it. She burst out laughing, but immediately turned away, and began to look out the window. I tried to say something, but she didn't answer; the book didn't fall off her lap, and she didn't give me a pretext to speak to her.

At the same time, we were sitting so close together that our knees were almost touching. And she was so pretty and so lively, that I ran the risk: I took her face in my hands and kissed her quickly. She flung herself back in her seat and began to laugh again—I asked, "What is your name?" "Erna," she replied. Thereupon, she very quickly recollected herself and said, "You have no right to converse with me. We have not been introduced." I introduced myself, but the conversation ended here on her request.

Meanwhile, night came, and tiredness with it. I leaned back in the chair and began to doze. A short time later I was awakened by an unexpected act from my fellow traveler: Exactly as I had done earlier, she took my sleepy face in her hands and kissed me. With that, before I could come to, she grabbed her bag and leaped out of the car. I looked through the window. The train had stopped at a small station, and on the platform, illuminated by the slanting rays of the morning sun, she stood with a middle-aged gentleman and lady. By resemblance alone one could not doubt that she was their daughter.

As the train pulled out, our eyes met. And that was all.

So ended the shortest romance of my life.

Soon the train carried me across the border of Livonia, and through the window appeared familiar scenes of undulating plains being plowed by peasants and gaunt little horses; boggy woods; villages with thatched roofs;

and pregnant women at the crossings with flags, surrounded by a great number of children and dogs.

As I neared home, my thoughts of Livonia faded and turned towards the problems at home.

Reaction: 1906–10

The disturbances came to an end. The revolution, having acknowledged temporary defeat, went underground and from there continued to reveal itself by now and then rooting out the most conspicuous agents from the ranks of reaction. Grand Duke Sergei Aleksandrovich,[21] Count Ignatev,[22] Pleve,[23] and Stolypin[24] were some of its victims by assassination.

Having surrounded itself with the visible and invisible walls of protection, the palace lived in isolation from the rest of the country: in winter at Tsarskoe Selo and in summer at Peterhof. The Third State Duma[25] which was rendered harmless by new electoral laws that reduced the voice of the

21. Grand Duke Sergei Aleksandrovich (1857–1905) was the second cousin and brother-in-law of Tsar Nicholas II and commanding officer of the Moscow military region. He was said to be an arrogant reactionary with an unattractive personality. His name was connected with mass arrests of revolutionaries, deportation of Jews, and persecution of the press and legal public organizations. In 1905 he was assassinated in the Kremlin by a Socialist Revolutionary.

22. Count Aleksei Pavlovich Ignatev (1842–1906) was a member of the State Council and an authoritarian general. He opposed the convocation of the State Duma, advocated increased police repression, and strongly promoted Russian nationalism. He was assassinated in 1906 by a Socialist Revolutionary.

23. Viacheslav Konstantinovich Pleve (1846–1904). Some of the positions he held were Director of Police, 1881–84, Vice Minister of the Interior, 1884–99, Minister and Secretary of State for Finnish Affairs, 1899–1902, Minister of the Interior, 1902–04. As a Russian statesman, he pursued ultra-reactionary policies. Jewish pogroms were organized under him and Russification was forced on minorities. In 1904 he was killed by a Socialist Revolutionary.

24. Petr Arkadevich Stolypin (1862–1911) was Premier and Minister of the Interior (1906–11). He fought the revolutionary movement with both extreme repression and social reform. Pursuing agrarian reforms, he promoted the creation of a kulak class in hopes that it would support the Tsarist regime in the countryside. He encouraged the work of field courts-martial, and hundreds were executed under him. Thus came the expression "Stolypin's necktie," which was the hangman's noose. On September 14, 1911, a police agent associated with a revolutionary group shot and killed him.

25. November 1907–1911.

masses and gave disproportionate representation to the gentry, did not even attempt to present itself as a law-making institution. The village police, the district police, and the administrative officers of the counties returned to their posts and took back the reins of government. Pens began to scratch over incoming and outgoing official reports, and by all appearances it seemed that the old order was re-established.

However, this was just a facade. True, the peasants did not get the land. But the landlords were rapidly losing theirs. A new class of wealthy merchants had appeared on the scene, the kulaks, who were buying up land at low prices and establishing their own farms. From these farms came a greater hardship for the neighboring muzhiks. A natural economy was replaced by a monetary one. The new landowners no longer gave land for the peasants to cultivate in return for half the produce in rent, but instead worked it with their own machinery and with hired laborers working for money—money with which it was already difficult to buy the bread of those same kulaks because of short supplies. In an impetuous rush to eradicate the beginning of socialism in the communal possession of land, Stolypin presented a plan which gave each peasant a homestead from the commune's block of land which would be entirely his own. But under this allotment the amount of land did not increase and the muzhiks' poverty did not decrease.

Meanwhile, "His Majesty Capital," in pursuit of cheap labor, moved at a fast pace in Russia. Factories, railroads, and power stations were being built. Electricity lit up the cities, and streetcars began to appear. Coachmen gave way to taxicabs. A fast-growing new society of wealthy, educated merchants, who already were dissatisfied because they had no voice or political influence, demanded recognition through their representatives in the Duma of Guchkov.[26]

There was also a rapidly growing class of people of independent professions who had been indoctrinated in school—doctors, lawyers, scientists, mechanical engineers—who protested against the old regime, formed a political party, the Constitutional Democrats, and with their representative

26. Aleksandr Ivanovich Guchkov (1862–1936), an Octobrist leader, was chairman of the Third Duma.

in the Duma, Professor Miliukov,[27] openly took on the task of introducing a constitution and secretly wished for a republic.

Finally, the growth of the manufacturing industry gave birth to the working class, or proletariat, whose members, while still under the vigilant surveillance of the police and deprived of their leaders, who were hiding out abroad or exiled to Siberia, were concealing their hopes and saving their strength for the approaching decisive struggle.

The development of industry and the growth of capital did not help, and the main body of the nobility, clinging to their privileges, continued to be oblivious to the need to work in order to exist; and losing their land, arranged sinecures for themselves, overfilling the ranks of the already-too-numerous bureaucrats. Thus, after the first outbreak of the revolution, the two fundamental classes on which the Russia of Alexander III was founded—the nobility and the peasants—became the victims. Naturally, the new masters of the situation—the landowners (without the distinction of class status), the industrialists, the manufacturers, and the small but powerful class of intellectuals of various professions—were looking for a new political order.

At the same time there were changes in the army, too. First of all, as a reward for dedicated service in defense of the Tsar and Fatherland from internal enemies, they received . . . new uniforms! However, the greatest contrast came in the remote, poverty-stricken Jewish settlements of our western border, where Hussars appeared in their brilliant uniforms of all colors of the rainbow, and Ulans, with their horse tails and lapels of red, blue, and canary yellow . . . All the Dragoon Regiments received our Horse Grenadier helmets, in which we still take pride, considering that they distinguished us in battle. Even the army infantry officer, who frequently didn't have the means to buy a new skirt for his wife or a pair of shoes for his children, received a breastplate and two additional shiny buttons for his uniform.

A beautiful new uniform, apparently, even in our utilitarian age, holds much greater meaning than we want to believe. Even the most practical power, the Soviets, also dressed its forces in new uniforms when its own existence grew to depend on the army.

---

27. Pavel Nikolaevich Miliukov (1859–1943) was a professor of history and a liberal statesman.

In those days, these expensive reforms, which cost both the Treasury and the officers, were considered imperative to keep the officers in line, inasmuch as they were rapidly deserting. Unfortunately, however, these reforms were not able to retain the needed officers. The only ones who remained were those who could do nothing else. And here one has to profess that these were the ones in charge of command. The Guards suffered from the same malady, only to a greater degree, because an officer of the Guards, having more important connections, was able to easily make arrangements on the side.

Moreover, the new recruits called up in 1906 and later obviously differed from the old soldiers. They still acknowledged the necessity of military service, but already they could easily see the difference between the demands of discipline and arbitrariness of the authorities. I was in charge of conscription in 1907 and remember that the thought often occurred to me then, What if these soldiers had to attack a mob, make arrests, and carry out military executions? Would they obey silently, as the older servicemen did? I thought not.

Family Affairs

God of the cold, God of the hungry
And of the poor far and wide,
God of the unprofitable estates—
There He is, there He is the Russian God.
—VIAZEMSKY[1]

In the spring of 1907, I returned to Kurchino from Livonia and was met with what seemed like insolvable problems. I found that for the past two years, not even one-tenth of the land had been harvested and not one meadow had been mowed. Since there was no food for the cattle, they had to be sold. The manure had not even been removed from the cattle sheds. The only income came from the money paid by the Morozov factory for purchase of the trees in our wooded area, which it cut down and carried away with its own resources. The manager, Andrei Andreevich, was at a loss. According to him, the peasants categorically refused to work on the landlord's land—either for money or for half the crop. And this was not for political reasons, as it later turned out to be, but purely for economic considerations, since we could not compete with the factories in wages paid for work. Even our brickyard closed for this reason.

My first thought was to leave the regiment and return to the land, contract machinery, as it was done on large farms, and begin to till and seed—but soon we had to give up, since in the first place, there was no money to

1. Petr Andreevich Viazemsky (1792–1878) was a Russian poet and literary critic. This verse is quoted from his satirical poem, "The Russian God," written in 1828 and directed against the Tsarist bureaucracy. He was a friend of Pushkin's and also close to the future Decembrists.

provide for machinery and to raise cattle, and in the second, my younger brother and one of my sisters were in school, so mother was obliged to stay in Petersburg.

There was only one thing left to do: sell the property. Mother agreed to this. After the death of my father, she had received from her mother, my grandmother, Varvara Vladimirovna Salova, a settlement which consisted mainly of 40,000 desiatin[2] of black earth in the province of Saratov and then an inheritance of 3,000 rubles a year after the old woman died.

Mother's elder sister, having heard of our decision to sell Kurchino, offered to buy it for the same price that my father had paid for it fifteen years before. Even during his time, it was felt that he had purchased the land at a low price. Aleksandra Fedorovna promised, but not in writing, to save this land for us, the children. After lengthy negotiations and bargaining, in which grandmother Varvara Vladimirovna took part on my aunt's side, mother agreed to sell.

There are two types of people: those who will sacrifice today, while thinking of the future, and the others, just the opposite, who live today reckoning that tomorrow will take care of itself. Rarely does one have these two natures in balance, but in its most extreme manifestations, the former type are called greedy and the latter, prodigal. My aunt, Aleksandra Fedorovna, belonged to the greedy category. She was competent, persevering, and certainly not stupid, but at the same time not egotistical. She wished everyone well, but this was only for those who did not contradict her.

At a very young age she married an army officer from the Rzhev garrison. With no special talents or strengths, he completely submitted to my aunt's every whim and did not impede her from furthering his career. Through her efforts, he was chosen as a marshal of nobility in his district and served nine years, and for this received the rank of councilor of state; and again by her patronage, he became vice-governor and soon after, governor. And when the State Duma convened he attended as a member from the Octobrist Party, or, as Aleksandra Fedorovna cynically called the party, "Where the wind blows."

She had two sons, the elder of whom was disowned on account of his disobedience, and all the favors went to the younger. When the family of

2. Forty thousand desiatin is equivalent to about 108,000 acres.

one of her sisters was orphaned, she took the children in and raised and educated them. But when they could stand on their own two feet and left her home, it turned out that their estate belonged to her, and they had to appeal to their benefactress for every penny. Nevertheless, it must be acknowledged that to the very last day of the old regime she steadfastly took care of them. Our grandmother lived with her, and when she died, all her vast millions were willed to her, and she was obliged to pay her living sisters their share of the proceeds from the estate and the capital. At the same time, the 35,000 rubles which she paid us for Kurchino was subtracted from mother's portion. Since the wish of the deceased was considered sacred, it was not the custom at that time to contest the validity of a will in court if there were no obvious falsifications in it. The will was read and accepted without a word. Only mother's brother stood up and refused his share in favor of his widowed sisters—my mother and Aunt Maria.

And thus, having sold her our estate, we fell into the hands of this woman. I, however, did not protest, because all along I had a foreboding that this might occur, and many others probably felt as I did, but did not wish to think about it.

Five years passed. I was on leave visiting relatives whose estate was approximately forty versts from Kurchino, and I was filled with the desire to look again upon my old home. With a rifle and a dog, I boarded the train and set out for the Chertolino station, and from there I walked through the woods in the direction of the farm.

My heart sank as I emerged towards the ponds and saw the avenue overgrown with birches, which I remembered my father had planted and which led from the ponds to our home. The birch trees had grown so much that it was difficult to see the house. A fresh autumn wind was blowing, and the yellowing crowns of the trees seemed to greet me as they rustled and bowed down before me. The avenue was overgrown with tall weeds and only a small footpath meandered up to the house. I walked along it. There was the device for the Pas de Géant. It swayed a little. There was the bench behind which, through the bushes, you could see the meadow and the ponds, and on which I had seated in turn all the members of my family, the household, and their children, to photograph them with my first Kodak. And here was the house. Once more my heart began to beat fast. The shutters were closed. The first few steps on the verandah were overgrown with burdock. The nest under its roof where the swallows lived from year to year was still there. Here was the coach house, behind which grew burdock and tall thorns. At one time I had boldly hacked my way through them, imagining myself coming to blows with the enemy. And there was the log chopping block, all overgrown with grass, near the kitchen back porch, on which our cook, Nikanor Nikitich, used to chop off the heads of the chickens, in secret, so that I would not demand mercy for them.

I sat down on the steps engulfed in memories. Without my noticing, a stranger approached me, judging from his clothing, an overseer.

"What can I do for you, Sir?"

"I'm a nephew of Aleksandra Fedorovna—Olferieff. I was hunting on her land, shot a hare, and was bringing it to you. I hope that you will not object?"

"Fyodor Sergeyevich! Forgive me! Please come in! We'll have a pot-luck supper, and I'll open the house and light a fire in the stove. You know, I remember you as a child when you came to visit the late Varvara Vladimirovna."

"No, thank you. I'm going to Poltino to see some of my old friends."

"Then we'll hitch the horse to the carriage. You go there, and then you can return home to spend the night."

"No, thank you very much. I'll walk and stay overnight there. Many thanks, again," I said, barely holding back tears, and set out for Poltino.

Cutting across the boundary between the Kurchino land and Poltino, I noticed a new fence made from aspen and birch poles. It followed the same line where remains of the old fence still were visible. Evidently, in putting up the fence, Aleksandra Fedorovna either did not know that a small strip of land beyond it still belonged to her or did not dare move it to its legitimate location.

At the entrance to the village stood a new provincial school in all its glory. And across from it was the same retail store with the same meager merchandise. In all respects, it appeared as though the village had frozen in time—all the same peasant homes, the same sagging roofs, it seemed to me even the same puddles and shallow pits in the road which I always used to see there, and, in spite of the passage of five years, recognized as old friends. It was probably only because I myself had grown that everything seemed smaller and more poverty stricken than I remembered it.

The children playing in the streets did not know me and ran after me in a herd as if I were some sort of freak. I found Iuda Pavlov's izba, and called on him.

"My goodness! Fyodor Sergeyevich! Our dear Sir! What good wind brings you here?" Iuda cried. Instead of being a young fellow, he had become a mature muzhik. His blondish hair, which at one time hung down disobediently over his nose, now was noticeably thinner, and he pomaded it sleekly to his head.

"Holy Mother, how wonderful it is that we're seeing each other again! Here, we think of you often and say, 'He has probably forgotten us. How could he come visit us with his Tsar's service?' We bet that you didn't remember us . . . Well! Well! There you are! Sit down. Agrafena will put the samovar on."

Agrafena, whom I hadn't known, but who undoubtedly had heard about me, came in and stood in the corner covertly looking me over. Two light-haired small children, her sons, were hanging on to her skirt.

"Now then! Iuda Palych,[3] what's your father doing. Where's your dear mother, and how are things in general?"

"Mother died last year, and father is still in Moscow. He never comes home anymore. And things . . . things are not any better, in fact worse. I'm sure you saw the fence that your aunt built. Now, if a horse or a cow, who knows what, jumps over the fence on your land, the overseer takes it and . . . demands two rubles to drive it back. We can't go off to the forest to get wood. We have to pay for everything . . . Surely you remember when we worked on your land, you always shared the crops with us. Now nothing is free. But where can we get the money? Last year we bought an uncultivated plot of land for the cattle to graze. We paid a low price for it, but it was all beard-grass. Even the sheep won't eat it.

"Many of the young men went off to Moscow to work in the factories, and don't even come home in the summer. The women are the only

3. Colloquial, reduced form of the patronymic Pavlovich.

ones here on the land . . . See the school there; it was built thanks to the Zemstvo,"[4] he ended on a conciliatory note.

I slept that night in the red corner under the icons, and awakened at dawn as did my hosts. After bidding them farewell and taking a turn through Kurchino forest, I arrived at the station, boarded the train, and said good-bye forever.

Marusia Grevens

It was on St. Catherine's Day, November 24. After a recurrent unpleasant conversation with Aunt Lodyzhensky, I was sitting in her living room on Gagarinskaia Street plunking out some sort of irritating motif on the piano. The doorbell rang, and in walked a beautiful young brunette. She was simply but elegantly dressed. Smoothly combed dark hair framed her small head, and she was wearing a large hat, as they did in those days. By her olive complexion, she could have been French. She stopped and looked at me inquisitively with her large brown eyes, as if asking, Who are you? I stood up, and the same question ran through my mind. At that moment my aunt walked in.

"Fedia,[5] why have you not asked the young lady to sit down? This is my nephew, Fyodor Sergeyevich Olferieff. —Maria Vladimirovna Grevens."

We sat down, and from the conversation, I realized that my aunt had known the guest for a long time. The visitor was dignified but unpretentious; she spoke ordinary Russian without those artificial airs that were peculiar to Petersburg society. And by her quick and always precise answers, one could perceive that her small head knew how to think. I liked her at first sight, and as she affirms now, it was mutual. But then she was able to

4. The Zemstvo was an elective council responsible for the local administration of a provincial district. It could levy taxes and some of its most beneficial work was in the areas of education and public health. Its electorate was made up of the county landowners, rural communities, and townspeople. The Zemstvo system was founded by Alexander II in 1864 to replace the abolished authority of the nobles, and it became the core of the liberal movement from 1905 to 1917.

5. Nickname for Fedor (or Fyodor).

cleverly conceal it for a long time, which sometimes caused me that anguish known to anyone in love.

On this day, we had dinner with my aunt, and, as my wife tells me today, sitting next to her at the table, I not only forgot to serve her, but having helped myself first, pushed the serving dish to the side.

"And did you like this?" I inquired.

"No, but I forgave you for it."

Apparently there is a proverb used sometimes to justify this reaction: *Ne po-khoroshu mil, a po-milu khorosh.*[6]

"Who is this young lady that dined with us last night?" I asked my aunt.

"Remember Officer Selivanov in Rzhev? She is his niece. Her mother died several years ago, and her father died last year. They both were highly respected people. Well, do you like her?"

"Very much."

"I would be very happy if you married Marusia. But you must leave the regiment and make a living."

"I will never leave the regiment for any Marusia," I said.

"Then forget about her. I am sure that she has enough sense not to marry an officer."

This time it was impossible not to agree with my aunt. Not even mentioning the material side of the question, one could conclude that active service and family life did not mix well. The regiment itself represented a family—in certain respects disciplined, in others unbridled and turbulent, but always friendly and united, demanding from its fellow members complete subordination of oneself. Consequently, the wife's place was in the background. For instance, women and dogs were not allowed in the officers' club. On military assignments, the officer's family situation was not taken into account. Camps, maneuvers, and dispatchings took him away from home for months. The wife was either left to languish alone in Peterhof, to drag her husband from the regiment, or to wallow in that part of regimental life which attracted her: to learn through her husband all the regimental gossip and to entertain officers in her home becoming their

6. "It is not those who are fair that we love, but those whom we love who are fair; One's mistress is never ugly; never was a mistress foul."

semi-comrade—in other words to transform herself into what was known as a "regimental lady." Probably this was the source of the downfall which military service created, which unfavorably influenced young ladies and led some of them to not always go to bed with their own husbands. During this time, we had seven officers' wives in our regiment. I did not wish to place my wife on a par with any one of them.

But I could not keep my mind off of my new friend. I thought about her on the way to Peterhof, in the riding school, in the officers' club, going to bed at night, and upon awakening. And I was immeasurably happy to meet her in the loge of the Mikhailovsky Theater, where she was with my cousin and my cousin's husband.

I sat behind her and could only see her classical, sleek hairdo and a little bit of her neck, which was visible between her hair and her high-necked dress. A strange feeling came over me: I knew that she would be my wife, and, just as certainly, I knew the complete practical unfeasibility of it and tried to drive this thought as far as possible from my mind.

After the theater, we drank tea at her home. She lived in her father's apartment by herself, and she told me, "I am reproached for living alone, but I do not wish to have a lady's companion in spite of people's criticism."

"She is so intelligent," my cousin remarked when we walked into the street leaving her home, "that it is even difficult for me to speak with her."

"In such cases, you don't say 'intelligent,' but 'well-educated,'" her husband noted with annoyance.

Marusia Grevens was an only child. Before her birth her parents lost their seven-year-old son to scarlet fever. She grew up surrounded by the anxieties and protection of her mother, who feared losing her. Her mother kept her away from drafts so that she wouldn't catch a cold. She was not allowed to play with children her own age so that she wouldn't come in contact with disease. Consequently, the cheerful, playful little girl remained at home, as if in a cage, exclusively among adults. She was not even sent to school, but instead tutors came to instruct her at home. Thanks to that, her schooling did not follow a conventional program, and she had the chance to study those subjects which interested her the most. She filled the void created by the absence of playmates and children's games with reading. She liked history, literature, poetry, and art, and her remarkable memory helped her advance further in those domains than other children of her age.

Every summer she traveled abroad with her parents, and there were very few museums and ancient monuments in Europe which she did not go see. All this made her an exceptionally interesting conversationalist. Her parents were not wealthy, but always lived comfortably. In spite of the fact that she was the center of their love and continual concern, she was brought up to obey her elders, to strictly observe tradition, to have a sense of duty, to be faithful to the native land, and to respect religion. And all this occurred during the days when most of the older generation would subject a young girl in her circle to unmerciful criticism if she was allowed such great freedom, and didn't have to ask permission to go where and when she pleased and get acquainted with whomever she pleased.

And so, after such an upbringing, she was left completely alone, with not only the opportunity but also the necessity to arrange her future life. She was enjoying the feeling of this and was not ready to give up her freedom to anyone lightly. Yet, having grown up in complete isolation, she understood neither the nature of people nor the need to struggle for one's existence, which pushes many into lying, cheating, and committing crimes. Being straightforward and honest herself, she was inclined to believe people more than they deserved. And when I became better acquainted with Marusia and listened closely to her, in spite of my youth and comparatively little worldly experience, I was frightened for what the future held for her.

She invited me several times to dinner, and introduced me to her friends, virtually all of whom were elderly people and friends of her father's. We played bridge, which I enjoyed but played poorly. She played well and made fun of me for my lack of concentration. Christmas arrived, and Marusia celebrated Elka[7] twice with her numerous friends. I was invited to both parties, and this was the first time she gave me reason to understand that in my presence she was not bored. We met each other at the theater. In the company of her friends we traveled to the snow at Pargolovo,[8] and we went for drives in coaches. Soon her individual invitations to me consolidated into a single permanent one—come visit me whenever you can. And I again frequented the city, but this time not because I neglected my duty, but, on the contrary, because I treated my service with greater zeal than usual.

7. This term refers to a fir tree, Christmas tree, or Christmas celebration.

8. A village about twelve miles north of St. Petersburg.

We visited the museums, which I had been to previously only on orders from the Corps, and then had contrived to slip away from my teachers and skip off to town. Marusia patiently taught me to appreciate the beauty and to understand the art—we lingered for a long time in the semi-darkness of the Hermitage in front of paintings by Rembrandt, Velasquez, artists of the Primitive School . . . but she had to keep reminding me to look at the paintings instead of at her. She also took me to concerts, where instead of listening to the popular tunes of Varai Panina and Vial'tseva, I heard serious music and realized how banal my musical education was. She often quoted by heart Pushkin and Aleksei Tolstoy, and I was amazed by her memory and by how beautiful this poetry was when she recited it! I had never appreciated it when I read it myself.

Time flew by quickly. Spring was approaching, and Marusia began to make plans for a summer trip to Belgium to visit a friend, and in autumn she intended to make a journey to India. "I want to make use of my independence. There are many places that I have still not seen. And after that . . . I shall return home and see you."

I am sure that she noticed how sad this made me, but I did not think it was right to express my feelings. Once, when she was especially talking a lot about her impending trip and even showed me the luggage which she had bought for it, I must have had a particularly pitiful expression—she looked at me and said in a tone that brooked no opposition, a tone that she often uses now, "I will not live in Peterhof."

I realized that some other reason more real than a wish to satisfy a need for freedom was on her mind, that in spite of the new luggage, the trip to India was far from decided. I realized that she knew how much I loved her.

The time had come for me to think about that which I so persistently avoided thinking about. And it occurred to me that I should go to the academy—this would give me the chance to remain in the regiment, move to Petersburg, and, upon graduating from the academy, also gain that independence which is necessary for a married man.

"I will enter the academy," I said.

She thought about it and affirmed, "Do it."

It was one thing to decide, but another matter to pass a competitive examination in which an element of chance often played a determining role. But I strongly believed that I would be accepted, and she had faith in me.

It was decided that in the summer she would visit her friend in Belgium as planned, and during this time I would pass the examination, and as reward for my efforts, she would become my wife when she returned.

She left to go abroad as my fiancée.

No one in the regiment was surprised when, one fine day, I put on my sword and went to the Commander to ask permission to get married. My behavior had been much too obvious during the past winter, and the information concerning my bride was already in the hands of the Commander. He simply sincerely congratulated me and wished me success in the most serious step of my life. He himself, by the way, was not happy in his domestic life.

Yet when the question arose of my entrance into the academy and of my leave for the summer, Roop objected: "Under no circumstances can I release you before the completion of your regimental studies. Six weeks is plenty for your preparation, and if you do not enter the academy, then I think that the regiment will not lose anything. And this is more advantageous to you. From here you will be able to command a regiment sooner than from the General Staff."

My comrades regarded my intention to enter the academy with great suspicion. "You simply want to play all summer," said Sasha Ershov. "In my opinion, however, there won't be any obstacles to your plans. In the meantime, let's drink a flagon of wine and rehearse for the bachelor party!"

Abroad

In the middle of June, I was granted leave from the regiment. Six weeks remained before the examination, and I needed to find a quiet place where I would be able to study in preparation. My thoughts, however, were always with her. Not a week would go by in which I didn't receive a letter from her and write to her myself. I was counting the days till her return, and it seemed that the only time I would be able to concentrate would be when she was near me. As long as she was there alone, it was impossible for me to go abroad without the risk of incurring the censure of Petersburg's gossips. At any rate, when about two weeks had passed, she met up with her aunt, Galina Aleksandrovna Rodzianko, in Switzerland, and I received an invitation to go there.

I sold my horses, put on civilian clothes, boarded the train, and the next morning crossed the border in Verzhbolovo.

From my first journey through Germany, three things have stayed in my memory. First, the striking difference in the standard of living of the two neighboring peoples divided by a stipulated border, although they lived on the same soil in an identical climate, and even had much in common in racial terms—the Prussians in whom there is a great mixture of Slavic blood, and the Lithuanians who, without doubt, bear a relationship to the Germans. At the same time, a great contrast in lifestyle was evident between these neighbors. On the one side were poor, sparsely scattered villages with their small, wretched, tumbledown thatched-roof huts and filthy, unpaved roads on which shabby, emaciated horses stumbled along, pulling rickety peasant carts. These villages were populated with meagerly dressed people and great numbers of ragged, barefooted, unsupervised children running loose with packs of mongrel, half-starved dogs. And on the other side was a well-fed, self-sufficient Prussian population living in solid, clean structures in small villages, connected by good paved roads. And all this was just on opposite banks of a scarcely noticeable rivulet. This contrast made an indelible impression and instilled heartache and shame for my own native land each time I crossed the border.

The next impression which I have never forgotten came from a company of soldiers who were marching along Unter den Linden[9] street in Berlin to change the guard. Hearing the music, I stepped out of a café, and along with the street urchins, followed the soldiers. The parade was led by a drum major. In Russia, we no longer had drum majors—they had been dropped in the reign of Alexander III because for all their pretension and theatricality, they were not conducive to the spirit of the Russian Orthodox military forces. Here in America, which loves noise, glitter, and all sorts of parades more than any other country, drum majors were swiftly replaced by drum majorettes, with bare legs and gestures that have the sole purpose of arousing sexual feelings in the spectators. The German drum major, on the contrary, performed with the solemnity of a religious rite: in full recognition

9. A famous boulevard in the heart of Berlin, known as one of the finest and most spacious streets in Europe of its day. A double avenue divided by a promenade planted with lime trees, it stretches for about a mile from the royal palace to the Brandenburg Gate and is the center of the city's social and official life.

that he personified the power of his homeland, he carried himself, like all soldiers, ramrod straight, held his left hand on his hip and with his right, majestically raised and lowered his baton. His face, as well as the faces of the others, was frozen in the pompous appearance of greatness. The band which marched behind raised their horns all to the same height so that looking at the flank of the musicians from the side, one could not see the next man's instrument unless it was a different shape.

My father had told me that in his day, when German drill was in full bloom, they were taught to march while balancing a glass on top of their helmet and trying to prevent it from falling for as long as possible. Upon seeing the Germans, I remembered this tale of my father's. We were taught to march with a stomping step. And when we marched along Nevsky towards the Winter Palace for guard duty, we did our best to march as uniformly as possible. But our formation was quite different from the German one. The German company on Unter den Linden performed as a monolith in which individuality did not exist. It always seemed to me that this ability to subordinate their individual being to the mass ranks with the other qualities of the German people that created their nation's power, which was so difficult for all the world to deal with. The big question is, Would the world be able to handle the Germans today?

The final thing that made a very strong impression on me was a small newspaper article that appeared somewhere on the back page of the *Berliner Tageblatt*, which I bought on the train traveling from Berlin to the south. The article said that on the day before, in one of the German towns, a certain blacksmith had been executed for committing murder. It was reported like any ordinary occurrence which did not merit commentary.

In spite of the fact that a short time before this in Livonia, I myself had participated in sentencing a man to death, I could not get over what I had read for quite a while. Even in Livonia, I had protested with all my being against the legitimacy of capital punishment. But there, it was an extraordinary situation which necessitated the suppression of insurrection, even with a reign of terror. Here, in the cultural center of the whole world, the application of the doctrine "An eye for an eye, a tooth for a tooth" seemed completely out of place. Where is the Christian teaching in which civilization takes such pride? From the German paper, I understood that the condemned man was decapitated on the block. The blacksmith walked to the scaffold without support and refused the last rites from a priest. It seemed to me that to refuse was only logical, because for an honest apostle of Christ there is no place in this sort of ceremony, and from a genuine priest, there must not be silent submission, but energetic protest against the ugliness caused by man.

After everything I had to live through and see later on, this entire discussion seems so childish. I am only bringing it up here to illustrate how savage the people became in the twentieth century, by comparison with the humane ideals with which we were brought up in "backward Tsarist Russia" at the end of the last century.

The beautiful landscape of Europe, the Alps, the lakes—especially Vorarlberg—left a wonderful impression. But I felt cooped up in the mountains, and was happy to return to our poor but spacious plains.

Maria (Marusia) Grevens Olferieff with her first daughter, Aleksandra, in 1913.

Mary (Masha), second daughter of Marusia and Fyodor, with her nurse—Petrograd in 1915.

I met my future wife in Basel and, together with her aunt, took up residence in a small town on the shores of Lake Thun. I worked all day; Marusia not only did not bother me, but helped me a great deal with my studies. She took the place of the library in Thun, tutored me in Russian literature and history, and acquainted me with several works of the classics which I had not read. It seemed to me that she knew everything, and with complete trust, I not only accepted what she said, but also used her expressions. In the academy on one of the examinations I was asked to discuss the works of Saltykov-Schedrin.[10] All that I knew about him was what Marusia had taught. I repeated her words exactly and received a good grade.

10. Mikhail Evgrafovich Saltykov (1826–89) was a Russian novelist and satirist who wrote under the pseudonym of Nikolai Evgrafovich Schedrin in the second half of the nineteenth century.

The happy week in Thun, my successful completion of the examinations, a resplendently beautiful wedding at the Page Corps, a honeymoon in Moscow—all this contributed to making these the happiest days of my life, and since they are not different from those of any other bridegroom and are filled with egotism, it would hardly interest others. Here, just from the point of view of the nature of the epoch, I will note that having abandoned the church long before the wedding, I was forced by necessity to involve our regimental priest in a deception, since without a certificate that I had received the sacraments of the church, I could not prove it, and the church would refuse to marry me. Father Andreev looked at me with the expression of an indignant pastor, and making me promise henceforth to carry out all the rites of the church, gave me the necessary certificate. It goes without saying that if the command had kept to the faith, I would not even have been promoted to the next rank without having previously confessed my sins in church. All this, though, has long since passed, and I only bring it up to show that because of the absence of a civil ceremony for marriage in our country, for those who did not celebrate the rituals of the church, it became necessary to lie.

The Imperial Nicholas Military Academy

The General Staff is the brain of the country's armed forces. It is responsible not only for the performance of these forces in war, but also for their makeup, organization, and preparation during peacetime, as well as for the preparation of the theater of military action, the means of communications to it, a workable plan of war, and, finally, for the supply of the army. Naturally, if you assume that the defeat of our army was the cause of the fall of the old order in Russia, then the General Staff was the chief author of this downfall.

There was no doubt that at the end of 1916 the army refused to resist the enemy, and that this refusal came directly from the men on the front, who knew that conditions were such that it was impossible to defeat the Germans. There was also no doubt that the country was so shaken with this unexpected refusal that an insignificant offensive was enough for the entire front to collapse like a house of cards.

But could the course of history have been changed even if there had been an ideal army administration? And a more important question: Could such an ideal command exist under the old regime? The General Staff, as an integral part of the entire old structure, was infected with the same disease by which the whole structure was destroyed.

I entered the academy during the days when the wounds caused by the Russo-Japanese War were still festering, when Petersburg's ruling circles, compelled by the revolutionary explosion, got out of their restraints for a time and tried, in a way that was least detrimental to themselves, to effect needed reforms for the country. The War Department, dependent on the new chairman of the Council of State Defense, Grand Duke Nikolai Nikolaevich, showed signs of particular vigor. Army generals appeared in the capital from the so-called "Manchurian Box,"[1] who, having distinguished themselves in the war, feverishly went to work redoing regulations, making technical improvements in army supplies and armaments, reorganizing their own troops and adapting them to a contemporary war footing. The chief command of the General Staff worked on a new plan of war for the Western Front.

The old General Staff Academy had just been renamed the War Academy and was moved to a magnificent new building on Slonovaia Street, which at the same time was renamed Suvorov Prospect. The purpose of this reform was the desire to bring into higher military education as many of the officers who had served at the front as possible without having to add the graduates to the General Staff, and, conversely, to admit gifted line officers into the General Staff itself. The term of study at the academy remained the same, two years, after which in the course of a year, the officer, having completed his studies with no grade lower than 10, was required to produce and publicly defend three independent works. Only the successful delivery of these works counted as the conclusion of the course of study through the first division and bestowed the right to join the General Staff when there was a vacancy. The requirements for entrance into the academy were not getting lower, but were getting higher, and in spite of the fact that in the year of my entrance more than a thousand sat for the preliminary tests in the districts, only around 250 men were allowed to take the examination, out of which only 150 were accepted. Only seventy-five out of this number graduated in the first category.

The Gospel says, "Many are called, but few are chosen." Yet were these seventy-five the best officers serving in the army at this time? It is only possible to answer this after clarifying first who these one thousand men were

1. During the Russo-Japanese War, the Russian forces were trapped as if in a box in Manchuria. Their navy was bottled up in the mined harbor of Port Arthur, and many ships were destroyed. On land their troops were eventually surrounded by the Japanese and badly defeated. Before the war, Russia had been gaining a sphere of influence in Manchuria, having been granted the right by China to build a railroad through this territory in 1895. However, at the end of the war both Russia and Japan agreed to restore Manchuria to China.

and which regiments sent them for testing in their districts, and second, on what basis the academy itself made its selection.

Unfortunately, the regiments were not interested in sending their outstanding officers to the academy. On the contrary, they tried in every way to discourage them from going. The men who entered the academy were mainly former good students from the military schools, and frequently they came from overburdened families in the hope of improving their material position. Of course the regiments could not hold back ambitious men, men who had a calling to learn military science, men of strong will; but average people also entered the academy, some of whom should not have been there.

The written entrance examinations in the districts, as well as the oral ones in the academy, were very difficult, and so far as human nature permitted, fair: neither regimental uniform, family name, nor patronage had any influence on the outcome. In fact, the examiners in the districts did not know the surnames of those writing the answers. However, the tests evaluated only three traits of those sitting for exams: literacy, memory, and the ability to work. Anyone who mastered all three could be sure that he would be accepted into the academy. There was no additional competition for admission aside from the written exams, so anyone who passed would be admitted. But the examinations were so stringent that usually about one-third failed.

In the academy, as in every military department in those days, intensive work was being carried on to eradicate everything that was considered a cause of our defeat in Manchuria. The clever and progressive-thinking Commandant of the Academy, General Scherbachev,[2] was one of the most energetic supporters of reform. He allied himself with the young professors, some of whom had just returned from detachment to the French Military Academy. One was Colonel Golovin,[3] who lent him special assistance, and

2. Dmitry Grigorevich Scherbachev (1857–1932) was a Russian military leader. He headed the General Staff Academy from 1907 till 1912, when he left to assume command of the IX Army Corps, which fought in the battle of Galicia at the start of World War I and occupied L'vov.

3. Nikolai Nikolaevich Golovin (1875–1944) was a Russian military historian and a lieutenant general. He graduated from the Corps of Pages in 1894 and the General Staff Academy in 1900. From 1908 to 1913 he was a professor at the Academy. In World War I, he

together they led the struggle to abolish scholasticism and introduce practical methods of teaching.

As is always the case, it was much easier to carry on with the old methods. The introduction of new ones, however, invited differences of opinion. There were those who adhered to the French method and French military thinking. Others, on the contrary, did not recognize anything but the German strategy of Clausewitz[4] and Moltke,[5] holding up the latter's strategy and tactics in the War of 1870 as an irreproachable standard of the science of war. A third faction was headed by Professor Bonch-Bruevich,[6] who I think was related to General Dragomirov—a capable but idiosyncratic advisor on military matters to Tsar Alexander III, and following his example, considered that Suvorov's[7] *The Science of Victory* should be the basis of the entire Russian art of war. Finally, the elderly professors like Koliubakin,[8] Khristiani,[9] and others who believed in the holiness of military science

---

was Chief of Staff of the VII Army and of the Romanian Front. His writings on the General Staff and World War I are well regarded.

4. Karl von Clausewitz (1780–1831) was a Prussian general and writer on military strategy of Polish descent. He served Russia in the war against Napoleon. His famous work *On War* was considered a masterpiece and expounded the doctrines of "total war" and "war as a political act," which had a profound effect on military strategy and tactics. In total war he felt that all citizens, territory, and property of the enemy nation should be attacked in every way possible. War itself as a political act was a continuation of diplomacy by other means, in which political leaders of the state must determine the war's scope and objectives and exercise control of its direction.

5. Helmuth Karl Bernhard Graf von Moltke (1800–1891) was a Prussian field marshal known for his military genius. In the Franco-Prussian War (1870–71) his plan of mobilization led to complete Prussian victory. His strategy was elastic and gave his subleaders freedom to make their own decisions. He wrote a number of noteworthy books on tactics, one of which was *The Franco-German War of 1870–71*.

6. Mikhail Dmitrievich Bonch-Bruevich (1870–1956) was a Doctor of Military and Technical Science. He graduated from the Moscow Land Surveying Institute in 1891, the Moscow Infantry School in 1892, and the General Staff Academy in 1898, where he then taught and held staff positions. In the October Revolution of 1917, while chief of the Mogilev garrison, he went over to the side of the Soviet power. In the Soviet Army, he attained the rank of Lieutenant General in 1944. During his life he authored many works on tactics.

7. Aleksandr Vasilevich Suvorov, Generalissimo Prince (1729–1800) was a Russian Field Marshal. He was regarded as the ablest military commander Russia ever produced. Part of his success stemmed from the exceptional psychological rapport he had with his soldiers, and they idolized him. Never defeated in battle, he attributed his success to "intuition, rapidity, impact."

8. Boris Mikhailovich Koliubakin (1853–1924).

9. Grigory Grigorevich Khristiani (1863–1922).

defended the necessity of teaching the philosophy of military thought, assuming that the practical side would come by itself. The strife of all these factions often burst forth openly on the rostrum before an audience, and we followed it with the greatest interest, and subsequently they themselves contested the legitimacy of each other's doctrines out of class. I must admit that we all were on the side of the innovators. Many liked Golovin, his practical methods, and his subject—Service of the General Staff, stated more clearly—management of business in the military staffs. This was new and easy. But it always seemed to me that in the academy, where there was so little time to learn far more important subjects, such as military history, Service of the General Staff could be studied during the practical work. The majority of us realized that it was more important to study Clausewitz in the original than in an interpretation by a little-known professor. We took pride in Suvorov, but laughed at his prophet, Bonch-Bruevich. It would be difficult to find a greater contrast than the one between Suvorov himself and his apologist, the untalented colonel. Our confidence in the old professors was undermined. We regarded them as monuments of a dying era. But we were obliged to listen to them because we had to take their examinations, and their grades had the same weight as all the others. I personally had to defend two subjects before the elderly professors and passed them both well, thanks to the fact that I remembered exactly all of their favorite theses. It was depressing to listen as General Koliubakin, for example, tried for half a year to prove to us that strategy was a science since it possessed its own foundations and first principles. And the more he tried to prove this, the more it became clear that these principles were just as well known to boxers, wrestlers, and even roosters and dogs as they were to the great generals.

By the way, a total of seven great generals were recognized by the academy: Alexander of Macedonia, Julius Caesar, Hannibal, Frederick the Great, Napoleon, Moltke, and Suvorov. However, our teaching system was such that I, for instance, finished the academy in the first division without learning the actual achievements of any of them. In three years, the academy only had time to introduce us to methods of study and the critical approach to history. It was expected that we would learn this very same history later on. Unfortunately, life seldom gave one the chance to find time for this, and as a result, during the war I felt a lack of knowledge of historical precedents.

Nevertheless, in general I am thankful to the academy, for it taught me to work, to master my time, and to regard events critically. If in exile it wasn't necessary for me to take up a broom as a janitor or a pick and shovel, then I owe this to the academy.

About the time I was completing my studies, the conflict between the old and the new directions in the academy intensified, and just as in all of Petersburg's structure, the reaction against the changes strengthened it. More and more frequently everyone had to be told that, really, Kuropatkin and the unfortunate ones whom he commanded had lost the war, that old Russian traditions must not be disturbed, and that the split with the innovators ought to be put to an end. The old men easily found sympathy at Tsarskoe Selo because the Emperor, as was the habit of a Hussar, did not like the General Staff, and regarded the military innovations progressing from it with suspicion. General Scherbachev was appointed Commander of the XII Army Corps, and Golovin was given the Dragoon Regiment. To the surprise of everyone, General Yanushkevich[10] was named Commandant of the Academy.

The appointment of Yanushkevich as Commandant of the Academy, and a year later as Chief of the General Staff, and in that same year, with the declaration of war, as Chief of Staff under the Supreme Commander in Chief, was very typical of that era: Yanushkevich had spent all of his service time in the supply division of the army, never commanded a single unit at the front except a squad, and had never worked in the operative division of the General Staff, which was in charge of the war plan. During the war, however, he appeared at the head of the operative unit of all Russian armed forces. But instead of experience, he had much greater grounds for such a splendid career: he was married to the daughter of the commandant of the Peter and Paul Fortress,[11] General Trotsky, a personal friend of the Tsar,

10. Nikolai Nikolaevich Yanushkevich (1868–1918) was a general of the infantry (1914). Before his appointment as head of the General Staff Academy in 1913, he lectured on military administration there.

11. A fortress in St. Petersburg on Zaiachy Island surrounded by the Neva River. Its foundations were laid at the founding of the city in 1703. Beginning in the eighteenth century, cells built in the walls served as a political prison. Some of the structures on the grounds within the walls include the Peter and Paul Cathedral, which contains the tombs of most of the Russian emperors and empresses from Peter I to Alexander III; the boathouse; the mint, where gold, silver, and copper coins were struck; and the headquarters of the commandant.

and even more important, he was a member of the Union of the Russian People.[12] But malicious tongues also added that Yanushkevich's wife knew how to prepare excellent preserves, which were very much approved by the higher-ups. All my life I remembered my examination on Military Administration, which was administered by Yanushkevich, who was then still a colonel. The question was on supplying the field artillery with shells. This was in the spring of 1912, that is to say, just two years before the war. I, in complete keeping with reality, reported that starting from the ammunition wagon with the guns and ending at the rear depot itself, each gun ought to have one thousand rounds.

Yanushkevich, being satisfied with my answer, and, probably wishing to give me a good grade, asked another question, the answer to which was not in the manual: "Here you say that for each gun there should be not less than one thousand rounds of ammunition, which is absolutely correct. But where does this figure come from? Why not five hundred or one thousand five hundred?" I faltered. "Good gracious, it is very simple. There is no gun built to withstand more than one thousand shots." He smiled superciliously, but did not give me full credit.

In the middle of 1915, at the time of our departure from Poland, when we became aware of our acute shortage of ammunition, which was regarded as the main reason for our retreat, I asked the Commander of the 12th Horse Battery whether the guns could fire more than one thousand rounds. He answered me, an unfortunate "Moment,"[13] as staff officers were called in the army, with a condescending smile. "My gun fired more than one thousand shots long ago. And now all the guns are ready for action. But where is the ammunition? Who told you this?" He waved his hand with

12. The Union of the Russian People was an extreme rightist organization formed from ultranationalist elements in 1905. In its defense of "Mother Russia," it declared war on all sedition and all foreign subversive philosophies. Its purpose was to check revolutionary violence, reestablish order, and rehabilitate the monarchy. Though many so-called respectable, loyal subjects joined its ranks, it also had thugs and men of no moral sense as members. They blamed the revolution of 1905 on the Jews, Poles, Finns, and Balts, and the loss of the war in the East to "long-haired men and short-haired women." The Tsar ill-advisedly accepted honorary membership in the organization. Many others joined not realizing to what extent it was responsible for the pogroms in the country, and that it employed many illegal means to advance its causes. Its excesses went unchecked while the authorities looked the other way.

13. "Moment." Young staff officers were seen as careerists waiting for the right moment to get promoted.

despair. But I did not tell him that I had heard this from the Chief of Staff of the Supreme Commander in Chief in 1912.

I often asked myself, Where did Yanushkevich obtain this information regarding the construction of the gun? It probably came from the artillery department. The only important fact now is that this information was used as a basis for supplying the army just before the war. Was this stupidity or treason? I think that it was quite simply taken on the faith of a statement, as it often happened, made by some representative of the artillery supply, who at the time needed to give a report on his activities. So this figure of one thousand was accepted as an answer by anyone who would not investigate any further.

Professors such as Yanushkevich were an exception to the rule. It was not at all easy to become an academy professor, and just as in the case of the students, patronage could not play a part. It no longer played a part because this employment was not special or enviable. And it was the same in the universities. At the invitation of a professor, the student submitted a paper, and on that basis the professors admitted the post-graduate students to their midst. And this was accomplished after lengthy experience as an instructor and after the public defense of one's professorial work.

Not speaking of the widely known scholars, such as Platonov[14] and Vitkovsky,[15] there was a complete range of young, talented professors, who worked ceaselessly on their subjects, followed each new idea in their domain, and were not dissuaded in their convictions. In addition to this, the replacements assigned to the academy by Scherbachev were not accepted by the Union of the Russian People, and the old pedagogues, having been assured now that the persecution directed at them had ceased, retained their gainful employment.

---

14. Sergei Fedorovich Platonov (1860–1933) was a Russian historian and, after the revolution, an academician of the Academy of Sciences of the USSR. He was a graduate of the University of Saint Petersburg. His work dealt with Russian history from the second half of the sixteenth century to the beginning of the seventeenth, the Time of Troubles. He also wrote on the colonization of the Russian north and the history of the Zemsky sobor.

15. Vasily Vasilevich Vitkovsky (1856–1924) was a geodesist. He graduated from the General Staff Academy in 1885. He worked on geodesic surveys and the triangulation of Finland and the province of Saint Petersburg. In 1889, he began to teach at military and civilian educational institutions, and by 1897 was a professor in the geodesic department of the General Staff Academy. From 1897 to 1905 he was head of the Division of Mathematical Cartography of the Russian Geographic Society.

If Scherbachev and Golovin were unable to introduce a new system of teaching to the academy and to make it more accessible to a greater number of army officers, nevertheless, under the influence of the Japanese War, the very subjects being taught, such as regulations and tactics applying to troops in the battlefield, underwent great changes. Here are the main conclusions that the General Staff drew from this war:

1) A defensive battle is definitely ineffective as a means of gaining victory. There was no position nor fortress which could have withstood the artillery fire. For this reason, the very name "Defensive Action" was changed in the new regulations to "Temporizing Battle," that is, the temporary defense line had to shift to become a line of attack. In conformity with this, entrenched positions of the line, as we saw at Liaoyang[16] and Mukden,[17] ought to yield ground with reinforced "nodes of resistance." This standing order was accepted by everyone, so no arguments arose about this question.

2) Concentrated artillery fire, no matter how strong, cannot decide the outcome of the battle without the forward movement of the infantry for a bayonet charge. To be victorious, the only decisive point is to move towards the enemy, locate him, and destroy him. After all, it was acknowledged that the enemy itself, professing this very doctrine, would not wait for our attack, but would move forward. From this, a new kind of action was introduced into the regulations by the name of the "Encounter Battle," in which the swiftness of orientation and the clever initiative of the commanders who are close to the combat must be the principal factors influencing the outcome of that combat. The thinned-out line introduced into the regulations in order to reduce casualties under fire also required a show of initiative from the most junior commanders including the fireteam commanders. All this necessitated not only changing the regulations, but also re-educating the entire army organization. The lack of school learning and training of the young in the first principles of initiative was acknowledged by every thinking military man, and it was clear that, in preparing for war

16. A province in Manchuria where much of the fighting of the Russo-Japanese War took place.

17. Mukden (or Shenyang City) is the capital of Liaoyang Province in N. E. China. It was developed as a railroad center in the late nineteenth and early twentieth centuries by Russia. During the Russo-Japanese War, it was an important military objective which fell to the Japanese near the end of the conflict.

against Germany, Russia had to overcome an enormous handicap, which required not years, but generations.

3) An increase in the quantity of artillery, introduction of heavy field artillery, and firing from covered positions, as well as the appearance of the automobile, the machine gun, and other technical resources further increased the problem of replenishing the army. Even I, who had received the highest military education, always felt very inadequate when it came to questions of machinery. What could one expect from a recruit, who, in the best of circumstances, could barely read and write, and who, for generations had been mainly accustomed to yielding submissively to his superiors, not thinking, but only taking orders.

With the desire to raise the educational standards of the increasing number of conscripts, and to enlighten them in the spirit of individual initiative—without risk, however, of setting in motion revolutionary propaganda—a story line appeared among military writers that the Russian man, being richly endowed by nature, was able to compensate for his lack of technical knowledge with bravery and native intelligence. Belief in the Russian soldier and belief in God, together with the first principles which Suvorov taught in his *The Science of Victory*—such as, "The bullet is a fool, but the bayonet is a fine chap"—would grant him victory over the enemy, as it had during Suvorov's time. Hence, every measure was taken to raise the spirit in the Russian army, by introducing beautiful new uniforms, having parades, reviews, etc. With this trend, it was necessary to preserve the cavalry as a kind of weapon without any reduction and with little modification of its tactics. Accordingly, in spite of the fact that the experience of war allotted a very small role to the horse on the contemporary battlefield, our new regulations specifically stated that in a future war, the cavalry as a rule would fight on horseback. Just one look at the great abundance of our glorious cavalry would make the enemy forces shudder. All these ideas were evidently approved by Nikolai Nikolaevich, and they lulled the complacent authorities to trust in the invincibility of the Russian Orthodox army. In the academy, Colonel Bonch-Bruevich clouded the minds of his listeners with similar sorts of notions.

The transformation of Japan into a great power in the East and the inevitable approaching conflict with Germany in the West placed us in strategic terms between the hammer and the anvil. It was necessary to foresee the possibility of defending the country by so-called "Interior Operational Lines"—the strategy that was so triumphantly employed by Frederick the Great and subsequently ended with the defeat of Germany in both world wars.

During these days, that is, at the very beginning of the twentieth century, the idea was born to transfer our country's center of gravity, with all its heavy industry, to the Urals—an idea which the Soviet rule has now so successfully actualized. I remember that the professor of strategy, Colonel Elchaninov, who loved to express himself figuratively, said, "It is necessary to erect the Russian Double-Headed Eagle in the Urals, so that with one head toward the west and the other towards the east, he could keep a vigilant eye."

One of the three topics assigned to me was entitled "The Railway and Water Routes of Siberia and Their Interrelation in Case of Complications in the Far East or on the Western Front." I remember that while preparing for this, I read all that either had been written or published on that question. My presentation of the subject went very well and was received with a handshake from the Commandant of the Academy, Yanushkevich, and congratulations before a full auditorium.

I recollect that my inferences regarding the routes in Siberia at that time were dismal, and if the Eagle had then been mounted in the Urals, and Russia had been exposed to attack from the west and the east, then he would have lowered his head, and feathers would have flown from his wings. If my memory is correct, the railroad, with its single-track bridges and with a very complicated piece of construction under way of the Circum–Baikal Railway,[18] could at most only bear the strain of twenty-four pairs of trains in twenty-four hours (of so-called parallel traffic). The situation will become clear to everyone if I mention that the Second Siberian Rifle Division, having sortied from Omsk with the declaration of war, entered into battle for the first time at the end of October, that is, three months later.

18. This was the section of the Tran-Siberian Railroad that skirted the southern edge of Lake Baikal. Though started in 1891, the Trans-Siberian was completed in stages. By 1905, the main part was finished, but the completion of this section, because of the difficulty in building it, occurred in 1915. Until that time, passengers had to cross the lake by ferry or on sledges. For a time, tracks were temporarily laid across the frozen lake in winter, until an engine was lost with the breakup of the ice. It wasn't till 1917 that the all-Russian route through to Vladivostok was finally in operation.

During my time, a project existed on paper to build five parallel railway routes through Siberia, Mongolia, and China. The southernmost trunk line had to go around the Himalayas from the north and come out in Canton. With the aerial and motor communications of today, the need for these routes, of course, is obsolete, but at that time, building them would have been the only means of creating a defense for our borders during a war on two fronts. It is obvious, however, that the realization of this project would take many years.

The advantages of transferring heavy industries to the Urals had already been brought up by Mendeleev.[19] Not only were they solving the problem of transportation by moving the factories closer to the sources of ore, coal, and steel, and also to the breadbasket of Western Siberia, which was then capable of feeding all of Russia; but they also were allowing us freedom of action for our strategies on the western border, where the protection of the Donets Basin[20] and the "black earth" zone[21] served as one of the starting points for all our military plans. All these considerations were entirely justified in the Second World War.

In the course of all its history, one factor in defending our western border played a dominant role. That factor was the presence of a roadless, forested, boggy expanse that was difficult to pass through called the Poles'e,[22]

---

19. Dmitry Ivanovich Mendeleev (1834–1907) was a Russian chemist who is famous for his formulation of the Periodic Law and the invention of the Periodic Table, which organized the known elements into a system. From this he was also able to predict the existence of then unknown elements. A professor at the University of St. Petersburg, he later directed the bureau of weights and measures and served as a government advisor for the development of the petroleum industry.

20. The Donets Basin is an industrial region in Russia whose development began about 1870, and by 1913 it produced practically all the coal and more than half the iron and steel of Russia. It is north of the Sea of Azov and southwest of the Donets River. Other valuable mineral resources of the area include mercury, rock salt, fireclay and gypsum. In the Second World War this area was the scene of heavy fighting.

21. The "black earth" zone, (Russian *chernozem*), contains the best land for agriculture in Russia with its rich humus content. It covers an area of 250 million acres and is located on the southern steppe. It is comparable to the great plains of Canada.

22. The Poles'e lowlands, coextensive with the Pripet (or Pinsk) Marshes, are a swampy, forested area of about 38,000 square miles extending along the Pripet River and its affluents from Brest in the west to Mogilev in the east and to Kiev in the south. This dense network of rivers, lakes, canals, and marshes forms a natural defense barrier and became a battlefield in the First World War.

which divided all the routes from the west into two directions: north towards Moscow and south towards Kiev. Charles XII of Sweden, invading us during Peter's reign, chose the latter route. Napoleon, on the contrary, went towards Moscow. The Kaiser, being tied down during the whole war on his western front, could not move in deep. Later on, Hitler at first struck Moscow, suffered defeat, and went south.

To the west of the Poles'e, resembling the nose of a battering ram, was the so-called "Forward Theater," surrounded by rivers—the Bug and Narew from the north, the Vistula from the west and the swampy rivulet Wieprz to the south. It was defended by a circle of fortresses: Osovets, Zegrzh, Novogeorgievsk, Warsaw, and Ivangorod. In the rear was a fortress-depot, Brest-Litovsk. The routes to Moscow and Petersburg were protected by the Neman River with the fortresses of Kovno and Grodno. And on the routes to the south were the fortresses of Dubno, Rovno, and Lutsk, situated as if on the three points of a triangle.

These lines of defense and arms and ammunition depots were scattered here and there where it was likely that our army would meet the enemy. In the academy, we studied them in full detail and practiced on them in solving tactical problems. Only this part of Russia had relief maps on a two-verst scale[23] of all the roads and villages. Whether the preparation was good or bad, it was the only place where something was done. The strip of land between this region and our border, on the contrary, was eminently prepared to make it difficult for the enemy to advance: the roads were unpaved, there were no storehouses of supplies, and this comparatively sparsely and poorly populated place offered nothing propitious for the concentration of large forces. The apparent result of all this was that the mobilization and concentration of our troops by the calculations of our General Staff would fall behind Germany's by three weeks.

Yet in the senior class of 1913 we began to hear in the lectures on strategy and engineering that almost all of the fortresses there which I have enumerated were officially to be dismantled, because of their age and their complete inability to withstand the fire of contemporary siege artillery. It would be better to have no fortresses, it was said, than to trust in poorly

23. Two versts to one inch on the map.

fortified points that couldn't reasonably be relied upon to hold up. Of all the fortresses, it was decided to save two of the strongest and most up-to-date: Kovno and Novogeorgievsk.

The students of the academy naturally were not privy to the secrets of the war plan, and if the official explanations did not satisfy us we could only make conjectures about them. However, the explanation provided in connection with the decisive spirit of the new regulations seemed satisfactory. It was completely confirmed by the results of the inspection of just one of the two best fortresses, Kovno, where the academy took us after our final examinations in the spring of 1913. During this excursion, in which Yanushkevich himself participated, the commandant of the fortress, General Grigorev, when bidding us good-bye, said, "You are obviously convinced, gentlemen, as to the condition of the fortress. You have seen all its defects, and you must realize that it awaits a superhuman effort for us to hold it."

It puzzled me at the time why after these words General Grigorev could continue as commandant of the fortress, and why it was decided to let Kovno remain as a stronghold. I was not surprised that during the war, Grigorev was not able to hold the fortress in the face of an open attack, but was disturbed when I found out that he was brought up for trial, and that General Yanushkevich, having heard the words of Grigorev with me, escaped punishment for not insisting on Grigorev's replacement as was his obligation, since he was Chief of Staff of the Supreme Commander in Chief when war was declared.

Of course, the dismantling of the fortresses, and the instilling of the spirit of attack at any price, appeared to be not the only consequences of our defeat in the Japanese war. This was due to a much more important fact, which became known to us from Elchaninov's lectures on strategy: Germany radically changed its war plan, having accepted the so-called Schlieffen Plan,[24] which first of all called for striking France with all its might, even violating the neutrality of Belgium in the process, and defending Eastern Prussia with very few forces, even leaving it to be temporarily occupied by Russia.[25] All this was taught us in college in 1913, and it was quite strange that when

24. The plan was developed by the German Field Marshal and strategist Alfred Graf von Schlieffen when he was chief of Germany's General Staff from 1891 to 1905.

25. Then after subduing France, Germany would quickly throw its full weight against Russia, thereby solving the problem of fighting a war on two fronts.

Belgium's neutrality in fact was violated, the world was shocked, as if no one had known about this before. As a result, France demanded that we change our plans and sacrifice ourselves by marching against Eastern Prussia with not less than six corps. Hence, it was necessary to increase the number of our field forces, which we had resolved to build up, having eliminated the fortresses from their borders. What the result of this improvising before the very beginning of military action would be, we shall see later on.

We studied our probable German and Austro-Hungarian adversaries in full detail: their lands and resources, their army organization and its makeup, their tactics, strategy, likely region of concentration, and theater of impending military operations. Our intelligence gathering during peacetime in Germany, and especially in Austria, was outstanding. We observed the German maneuvers and studied their commentaries. For instance, we listened to lectures by Elchaninov, who gave a detailed analysis of the last maneuver before the war in Eastern Prussia, in which the German side destroyed the "Russians" who invaded Prussia, exactly as it happened a year later in reality. WE ALL KNEW THIS IN 1913.

In my last project, I took on the role of commander of an army corps operating forward of Grodno and holding back the Germans who were advancing towards this town. My professor, Colonel Kelchevsky, commanded the German side. My task was to force the Germans to deploy as they came out of the Augustow Forest[26] and to hold them back until the approach of the troops from the Moscow district. Since the professor read my orders beforehand, as was allowed, he burst forth on my flank with an entire division and counted me the loser. True, it had no effect on my grades.

I remember very well one more fact from our schooling regarding the prolonged war that was now imminent. We had a textbook on military

26. The Augustow Forest is located between Augustow and Grodno in what was then Russian Poland. This exercise was prophetic because a major battle occurred there between the Russians and the Germans in the First World War—the Augustow Operation of 1915 (or the East Prussian Operation of 1915). The German 10th and Eighth Armies were on the offensive against the Russian 10th Army and attacked its flanks expecting to surround and destroy it. Though badly beaten, the Russian 10th Army wasn't completely destroyed because of the help it got from the Russian XX Corps, which was engaged in a rearguard action and was surrounded by nine German divisions in the Augustow Forest. By the action of the Russian XX Corps and at great human loss to it, the advance of the German 10th Army was held up for ten days, which enabled the Russian 10th Army to withdraw to the Kovno–Osovets line.

economy written by Professor General Mikhnevich.[27] It started with this sentence: "War demands three things: Money, money, and money." Therefore, our professor concluded, a present-day war could not last very long. I do not recall now whether it was he or someone else who made the prediction that the war must end within three months. But the three-month period firmly sticks in my mind. We remembered this after the war with smiles, only to repeat the same senseless prediction when the Second World War began on the Russian front.

Watching the struggle that is now being carried on by the American Navy Department to preserve its supremacy in pursuit of the country's defense in light of the technical advantages being obtained by the Air Force, I recall a similar sort of battle which was conducted by our cavalry to maintain its right to exist as an essential military resource, in spite of the increasing effectiveness of artillery and machine-gun fire, which excluded any possibility of action in a horse formation against an undefeated enemy.[28] Here this question is debated openly with the participation of Congress. In our country, it was deliberated by the General Staff, but decided arbitrarily by the Grand Duke. Yet, as it was there, so it is here: tradition serves as the main argument in the defense of the old order—the glorious, historical past, which generations of troops have died for while resisting the demands of common sense. How this question will be decided here, we do not know. In Russia at that time, tradition prevailed, and "contrary to reason—in spite of the elements,"[29] it was decided that the cavalry would fight on horseback in the impending war. However, concessions were made to the spirit of the times: a regulation thinned out the cavalry formation, the horses were trained to walk along extremely irregular places with almost vertical slopes,

27. Nikolai Petrovich Mikhnevich (1849–1927) was a Russian military theorist and historian who became a general of the infantry in 1910. He graduated from the General Staff Academy in 1882, and in 1892 taught there as a professor of the history of the Russian art of war. He served as Chief of the General Staff Academy from 1904 to 1907 and became a division and corps Commander in 1907. From 1911 to 1917, he was Chief of Main Headquarters and in 1918 he began teaching in the Red Army. His major writings include *History of the Art of War from Antiquity to the Beginning of the 19th Century* and *Strategy* (2 vols.). The latter had a strong influence on official Russian military thought on the eve of World War I. He looked at military science as a social science and tried to discover the relationship of war and the art of war to economic development and the political structure of the state.

28. This statement was made in the 1950s regarding the US Navy.

29. Quoted from A. S. Griboedov, *Gore ot uma*.

and it came to the point that in the Petersburg district, Nikolai Nikolaevich ordered that the horses be trained to jump across barbed wire, because on the battlefields there would be many barbed-wire obstacles. To what absurdity all these experiments would have gone is difficult to say, since at this point war broke out, putting everyone face-to-face with reality.

Credit must be given to the academy, since the overwhelming majority of the professors looked at this question sensibly. But, unfortunately, the right to decide such questions was not in their power.

The Living Corpse

While in Moscow I saw Tolstoy's *The Living Corpse* at the Stanislavsky Theater. As always, both the production and the performance of the artists made an indelible impression on me. The play itself, with Tolstoy's usual sermons on nonresistance to evil and on Christian love—"I love you for you," etc.—and its criticism of the church, courts of law, authorities, and the entire tenor of life in general, which we now call the Old Order, made me wonder, Whom was Tolstoy calling "the living corpse"?—Could it have been the passive Fedia Protasov, or was it that very same tenor of life, which was enveloping people and already carrying the odor of death?

Here is what was happening in our pattern of life just before the World War:

I worked a great deal in the academy and rarely went out. And the less I saw of what was going on around me, the more astounded I became when I did venture out.

Once, my wife took me to see a traveling art exhibit. There, directly opposite the main entrance, hung a life-size portrait of a man of normal height, approximately fifty years old, in a black, sleeveless undercoat,[30] and high, shining boots. Looking at it, one felt pierced by the gaze of large, burning eyes. The portrait was displayed in such a place that one could not avoid seeing it. We decided that it was Rasputin. We were seized with disgust even though we knew very little about him except by rumor; and that gossip I regarded with suspicion. This portrait invited conversation

30. A type of clothing worn by peasants, *drozhki* drivers, etc.

about it, and here is what Marusia related to me: "You know that M., having recently lost his position as governor in one of the Far Eastern Provinces, was appointed commander of a division of the General Staff. E. I., his wife, a profoundly provincial young woman, had acquired a taste for local intrigues, and was so proud of her success that she told me in full detail how she was able to have her husband appointed to this position. First of all, by some means she obtained an audience with Rasputin, who took her by the chin and said something like, 'Ah, Ah . . . snub nose.'" Later in M.'s home, some relative of Sukhomlinov's[31] wife appeared (Sukhomlinov was Minister of War), and with her was Prince Andronikov, a young man with no definite occupation, who had completed the Corps of Pages and was known among his contemporary pages as a homosexual. With these people, after long bargaining, an agreement was reached; and E. I. paid them five thousand rubles. Soon after that, the appointment, which depended entirely on Sukhomlinov, was made.

There was another instance. The elderly Chairman of the Council of Ministers, Goremykin,[32] while a guest of our good friend, a member of the Council of State, told him that he had received a note from Rasputin with the following contents:

"God's Aged Man, help a small person—let him grab a slice."

"Isn't he impudent," remarked Goremykin, "to address me, a Premier, as God's Aged Man."

Was this "small person" given a slice? History does not mention it. But

---

31. Vladimir Aleksandrovich Sukhomlinov (1848–1926) was a General of the Cavalry. In 1908 he became Chief of the General Staff, and in 1909, Minister of War. He was able to further his career by being a shrewd courtier. He instituted military reforms from 1905 to 1912; but in spite of these efforts, the army was still not prepared for an extended war. In 1915, after many Russian defeats at the front in World War I, he was dismissed. In 1916 he was arrested for treason and various abuses and later was sentenced to a life of hard labor. Because of his advanced age, in 1918 he was released and allowed to emigrate.

32. Ivan Logginovich Goremykin (1839–1917) was a conservative, loyal servant of the Tsar and carried out the will of the palace clique headed by Rasputin. He was Minister of Internal Affairs (1895–99), State Council member (1899), and in 1906 was appointed Chairman of the Council of Ministers. The first State Duma of 1906 opposed his reactionary government, and he succeeded in having it dissolved. His incompetence in handling the Duma, though, led to his dismissal and replacement by Stolypin. In 1914–16 he again served as Chairman of the Council of Ministers. He was killed by the Bolsheviks.

it was typical of Goremykin, the elderly statesman and imperial agent, that what made an impression was not the fact itself that Rasputin had addressed the chief executive, but the form of that address. If Rasputin had started with the words "Your Excellency, I am praying that you not refuse" . . . etc., then all this probably would have gone unnoticed. What Rasputin was trying to say in his own very characteristic way was "All of you are snatching a piece of the Russian pie, so why not give a slice to little old me?"

You tell me, dear reader, that all this is gossip, that this could not have been. I agree. But in this case, it was not the facts themselves that were important to us, but precisely the presence of these scandalous rumors, which reeked with the odor of death from a decomposing regime. And this odor was detected particularly strongly by those who stood at a distance from the helm of power. The gossip traveled far from the limits of Petersburg, and in its transmission, took on a more and more fantastic form. Yet you will tell me that during Peter's reign there were extortioners. What was Menshikov[33] alone worth? Is it not possible to call Peter's government a living corpse? No, for Peter had a vision. At that time a new order was being built; there was a leader, and there was belief in what was being created. In the Russia of Nicholas II, there was neither vision, nor belief, nor creative growth. Absolute power was in the hands of a man who feared this power more than anything, who sought support in his surrounding society, and did not find it; his father's collaborators who worked in the new reign, such

---

33. When Aleksandr Danilovich Menshikov (1673–1729) was exiled to Siberia in 1727 by Peter II, Peter the Great's grandson, the property he managed to gather over the years was confiscated. It consisted of 90,000 serfs, six cities, estates in Russia, Poland, Prussia, and Austria, five million rubles in gold coins, and nine million rubles in English and Dutch banks.

The illustrious career of this Russian field marshal, statesman, and intimate companion of Peter the Great began from lowly origins. As a son of a court stableman, he rose to power through his devotion to Peter and his energetic and superb military and administrative abilities. He directed the building of St. Petersburg and Kronstadt and the shipyards on the Neva and Svir' Rivers. He commanded large infantry and cavalry forces against Sweden in the Northern War of 1700–1721 and headed the country's government when Peter was away. He also served as President of the War College. He was said to be vain and excessively greedy, and even though Peter was on closest terms with him, the Tsar frequently had to punish him with heavy fines to relieve him of a portion of his ill-gotten gains. After Peter died, he was the power behind the reign of Catherine I. When Peter's grandson, Peter II, ascended to the throne, Menshikov was accused of high treason and misappropriation of state funds, which led to his banishment.

as Pobedonostsev,[34] Pleve, Dragomirov . . . continued to do their parts. But when they were no longer there, he did not know how to find replacements. When capable people, such as Vitte, came to him, he quickly began to suspect that they wanted to take away his authority, the retention of which he considered his sacred duty, and he dismissed them. In the mass of other persons around him, he saw only those who were rushing to snatch a slice for themselves, or those who, for all their desire, were not capable of rendering the help that was needed.

Rasputin appeared on the scene. It was the first time in his life that the Tsar had spoken with such a person. The more strangely Rasputin behaved, the more the Tsar was convinced that he was the representative of those 150 million loyal Orthodox peasants whom the Tsar, by the will of God, was destined to govern. The Tsar finally had found a contact with his subjects, and in concurrence with—probably even on the insistence of—his mystical-leaning wife, he drew Rasputin closer to him. Rasputin did not need a chamberlain's position, nor a governor's post, nor a million rubles . . . His very reception by the Tsar in his home was above and beyond anything he heretofore could have possibly dreamed. He, along with the Tsar and Tsarina, had faith in God and participated in prayer; they believed in relics, in the ability of icons to perform miracles and in their healing properties, and in prophecies and signs. Rasputin believed, and convinced his worshippers, that God's grace made allowances for people only when they relinquished their pride. He apparently possessed great hypnotic power and was able to bring under his spell those who went into devout ecstasy with him. How and why the family of the Tsar and Tsarina embraced his zeal was known only to them. The incurable illness[35] of the heir was said to be one of the causes which pushed the family towards religious ecstasy.

---

34. Konstantin Petrovich Pobedonostsev (1827–1907) was a reactionary Russian statesman and jurist. He was Chief Procurator of the Synod (1880–1905) and from this position was able to restrict schools of the district and provincial bodies of self-government and strengthen church schools. As tutor in jurisprudence to the future Alexander III and later his son, Nicholas II, he wielded great power and influence. He championed autocracy, orthodoxy, and Russian nationalism. His methods were to enforce censorship, suppress the opinions of any opposition, persecute religious non-conformists and promote Russification of all national minorities. Until the Revolution of 1905, he was one of Nicholas II's most influential advisors.

35. Their only son, Aleksei, suffered from hemophilia.

But all this happened in their private life, in which they had a right to their convictions. And they believed that their living habits could not go beyond the walls of their chambers.

But that was not so. From the Tsar's chambers Rasputin got into Petersburg's salons, where at the beginning, just as in the palace, he prayed together with inquisitive women. The more the rumors spread, saturated with insinuations and half-truths, the more lewd women came to him, to behold him and even touch the clothing of the elder [*starets*] whom even the Empress herself did not disdain. They adorned Rasputin in silken garments, and they welcomed, escorted, and wined and dined him. He himself finally came to believe in his sainthood, and became more and more arrogant towards a corrupt Petersburg which sprawled before him. Presently, this brought out cheats and swindlers like Prince Andronikov, who, taking advantage of Rasputin's name, began to make shady deals. The two examples which I have given, multiplied by a hundred, gathered in that cesspool in which the Russian ruling class bathed just before the war.

Meanwhile, in my regimental family there was adversity after adversity. As I mentioned before, all of the talented ones among the senior officers left the regiment. The first reason for this was that it became necessary to earn more money in order to live, since the old patriarchal economy, in which the peasants worked for the landlord for a slice of bread, had been consigned to history; and the second was that the standards of military and especially cavalry service were raised so that the fulfillment of them was beyond the capabilities of many "Gentlemen." As a result, all three colonels remaining in the regiment were the kind that no one ever would have hired. All of them, however, in due time were assigned to the regiment, and at the very beginning of the war were relieved of their command because of incompetence. The regimental commander, a capable general, in certifying them, knew very well that he was not acting according to his conscience, but feared to behave otherwise—by this he armed himself against those wealthy powers that stood behind our valiant colonels. But was the damage done worth it? Everywhere it was the same.

At the same time, with the ensuing new demands of the high command and new regulations in the regiment, the young officers carried out extra work, similar to the work being done in the academy, which I mentioned above. The difference was only that there, the commandant of the academy himself announced the restructuring, but here, the initiative came from below. Rotmistr E., a brilliant commander of the squadron, an outstanding sportsman whose name was known to the entire Russian cavalry, a direct descendant of Field Marshall Suvorov, from whom he had inherited his will of iron and military ability, and a charming fellow among his subordinates, provided leadership for that task in the regiment. It seemed as if E. was born to serve in the cavalry: an excellent horseman, who graduated from the Officers Cavalry School with his name engraved on a marble slab, an outstanding commander, who always knew how to demonstrate what was required from his subordinates and achieve the fulfillment of his demands. He organized and developed the sport of horseback riding in the regiment. Our racing stable took part in the races in Petersburg. The entire Russian cavalry spoke about our regiment, and E. grew proud of the regiment and became the idol of our young men.

But all this did not help the prestige of the older officers, nor even the commander. External discipline continued to remain strong—they were saluted, their orders were executed in formation, and in the life of the officers' club, the colonels and commanders of the squadrons remained the masters of the situation. But in questions of training, field duty, horseback riding etc., their demands were met with polite but persistent objections. Frequently a senior officer hesitated to make a reproach, not being sure of its correctness in conformity with the new regulations. When he decided to make such a reproach, it was received condescendingly by those for whom it was intended, and only in that circumstance when it was made. When the elderly colonel approached the regiment's line of formation on his horse riding in the old method with a dancing gait and with the horse's neck tightly arched, it could not but evoke a smile from the young cornets, who were sitting firmly on their purebred horses. Confusion reigned when the regiment, while executing more and more of the strenuous demands of the new regulations, exercised by galloping in the field through intersecting positions, or when officers at the head with their commander advanced towards the obstacle while the older ones circled around that barrier or fell from their horses attempting it. Of course, if all such examinations had been followed by rigorous evaluation, then everything would have been as it should be. But along the way stood patronage, traditions, and connections, which entwined our pre-war order like a spider's web that only a shock could untangle, and that was soon to happen.

Naturally, such a situation could not continue for long. The Commander of the Regiment realized that it was necessary somehow to reestablish the prestige of the senior officers. Knowing, however, that the sympathy of the whole command, beginning with the Grand Duke, was on E.'s side, he decided to act through the colonels and rotmistrs themselves. Making use of a favorable opportunity in which E. displayed initiative bordering on insubordination, he assembled the senior officers and offered each one individually the opportunity to voice his opinion on the question of further measures with regard to E. Anyone who was possessed with envy and injured pride began to speak. Some contended that they must give E. an ultimatum—to either become subordinate or leave the regiment, and one of the envious, Rotmistr C., suggested that they immediately dismiss him from the regiment. This was all the Commander needed to hear. He promptly reported the results of the inquiry of the senior officers to the Commander of the Division. But the Division Commander, who had been a friend of E.'s deceased father, told E.'s mother about this. The next day after dinner in the officers' club, E., looking straight at C., said, "I would like to know who the scoundrel is who wanted my dismissal from the regiment?"

The Trial of Honor

The Duel and the Departure of E. from the Regiment by Judgment of the Trial of Honor

However, it was not possible to reestablish the prestige of the seniors, and it seemed that even basic discipline ceased to exist. Friends of E. stood in open opposition to the Commander of the Regiment, and if it were not for his expeditious promotion and relief of regimental duty, it probably would have been necessary to remove a few more officers.

The newly appointed commander was a childhood friend of the Tsar, Prince D., who tragically was killed along with the Tsar after the revolution. He was humble, well-bred, mild-mannered, and noble in spirit, but of limited capacity. Under different circumstances he could have calmed the mood in the regiment. But for us this appointment came too late. The breakdown was too great. Numerous young people, who were being accepted indiscriminately into the regiment and left to their own devices, led a loose life that far exceeded their means. Indebtedness had reached such a point in the club that many were no longer given credit in the dining room to purchase wine. The club manager himself, having drained all the money he had in his keeping, wrote promissory notes to the suppliers, fearing complaints from their side and hoping somehow to exculpate himself. The amount of the promissory notes grew. Finally, the suppliers went to the Commander, and the scandal was settled by the father of Lieutenant B., who himself went into debt in order to rescue his son.

During this time all Petersburg led riotous lives, as though there was a premonition of its impending doom. Playing the stock market was in full swing. Shady businessmen appeared, pushing even more shady stocks. Such stocks popped up in the hands of our "Great Financiers," cornets. They were sold and traded with other comrades' money, and everyone was promised great riches and a river of champagne.

Meanwhile, champagne was no longer served to many of the officers in the club. Once, at 2 a.m., half-intoxicated cornets were sitting in the dining room. One of them by the name of Doné asked the waiter, Private Kamenev, to bring him a bottle of wine. The latter departed and returned to announce in a loud voice, "Sir, bartender Mochalin gave me orders not to serve you wine."

Such an incredible phenomenon from the standpoint of discipline, that a soldier refused to carry out the request of an officer, was of course the result of the absurd custom of taking club waiters from the ranks of young men who were performing military service. This could have occurred before. But previously, discipline had been ironclad. From the time of the first revolution, the soldier was of a different breed. Bartender Mochalin was drafted in 1909. Modest, a man of action with a great sense of duty, he, being appointed senior in the command of the assembly waiters, quickly adjusted himself to this difficult duty. The officers grew fond of him for his honest, open countenance, and his unfailing readiness to serve them with a constant smile, frozen on his face such as often happens in deaf people. And he was deaf. On account of his deafness he was taken out of the ranks and sent to serve in the club. His enrollment for military service was a mistake of the military's selection committee. The regiment, however, did not like to reject people, since there were always other duties to be performed besides those in the line. And if the individual himself did not protest, and if he were a good soldier, as Mochalin was, then he was very much needed by the regiment. The day was approaching for Mochalin to go into the reserves. After three years of his service in the club, everyone had become accustomed to his cheerful countenance and to a certain degree spoiled him. As it happens in such cases, he came to know exactly what he could allow himself to do—with whom, when, and under what circumstances. Undoubtedly, he considered that he knew club orders better than the newly commissioned cornets.

Cornet Doné, twenty-two years of age, had been promoted into the regiment from the Pages of the Chamber. Very serviceable, he seemed to be correct and disciplined in the traditions of the Page Corps, where obedience, not only to the Commander but also to all seniors, presented itself as the cornerstone of an education. He gave all indications of becoming a good line officer. His character was guarded, and his personal life and family situation were not known to anyone except that, as it came out in court, his mother was in her second marriage, and his stepfather played a part in his destiny. On the tragic day of the murder, Doné was one of the officers who was refused credit to purchase wine. The "Gentlemen Officers" knew who was forbidden to request wine, but the president of the club's managerial committee also knew that one could not rely on the "Gentlemen" to perform accordingly. Therefore, an order was given out to the club "servants" not to dispense wine to the "Gentlemen" until their names were removed from the list of those who had not paid their debts. It created an ugly situation, directly contradictory to the foundation of discipline.

Doné repeated his demand for wine, but the waiter, Private Kamenev, failed to return after receiving the order. Doné, already intoxicated on the wine which he had been treated to by his comrades who were sitting with him, and probably regarding it as his obligation to return the favor, decided to obtain the wine come what may, and went to the bar himself. The bartender, Mochalin, knew that he would not even be held responsible for carrying out an illegal order of an officer. But, here spoke the spirit of the times. In spite of time-honored regimental traditions, Mochalin decided to show the young officer that he was wrong and began to defend the club regulations. Doné once more demanded the wine. Mochalin again personally refused him, and seeing that Doné was approaching the bar, he stood in front of him and barricaded it. Doné made a move to push him aside. Then Mochalin yelled, "help" to Kamenev, a private who was standing close by. Kamenev grabbed hold of Doné's arm. The latter was stopped, and when Kamenev let go of his arm, Doné pulled a Browning out of his pocket and shot Mochalin point-blank, killing him on the spot.

The judgment of the Commander of the Regiment, General Prince D.: The circumstances did not justify murdering the subordinate, even if the latter was at fault. Cornet Doné will be brought up for trial.

The opinion of the Commander of the Division: The need for maintaining discipline required decisive action from Doné, even if he was not right in giving an order to be served wine. The actions of Mochalin do not come under the regulations of guard duty. He does not find substance to Doné's transgression in conduct.

Nevertheless, the Commander of the Corps and, subsequently, the Commander in Chief, Grand Duke Nikolai Nikolaevich, went along with the opinion of the Commander of the Regiment.

At this time I was far away from the regiment. Intensification of my studies at the academy did not even allow me the possibility of going to Peterhof, but I remember how painful it was for me to endure this tragedy in the regiment. The most difficult fact was that the overwhelming majority of the officers proved to be on Doné's side. Whether it was "esprit de corps" or a false exhibition of the need to uphold discipline I don't know. I remember only one thing, that my first impulse was to remove my regimental uniform and request a transfer into the troops of the line. But the recognition that I was an indivisible part of this regiment, and that it would be impossible not to liken myself to a rat running from a sinking ship if I left, forced me to clench my teeth and immerse myself still deeper in academic work.

In the meantime, the grumbling among the rank and file of the regiment, especially in the Second Squadron, to which Mochalin belonged, was held in check with difficulty by the vakhmistrs. A quick and fair trial was necessary.

Doné was brought to trial in the Petersburg Military District Court, which consisted, as it should in such cases, of the General Chairman of the Military Justice Department and three temporary members. The last were all appointed from each of the regiments of our division—these were the most loved and most popular officers in the division. To them the situation was clear. They thought just like their friends, my regimental comrades, and of course, could not go against the wishes of the latter. Doné, who had retained for his defense one of the most brilliant lawyers of that time, Kazarinov, was acquitted. The soldiers in the regiment could hardly expect any other decision. What else could one presume of a trial of "Gentlemen," which itself was composed of "Gentlemen"?

But in spite of the inertia in Petersburg's public opinion during these days, not even it could tolerate such blatant injustice. Just as the military demanded justice, so did the civilian sector of society. Complicated notions of military discipline did not interest them. The military prosecutor, Baron Manteifel'-Tsege, himself a descendant of one of the officers of our regiment, appealed the case. The decision of the court was overturned, and the case was assigned for review in the new Military District Court. This court found Cornet Doné guilty, and sentenced him to imprisonment in the fort for four months.

Here it must be said that our military justice department, even in those days, consisted of the most educated, up-to-date officers of the legal profession. Willingly or not, officers sent to the Military Judicial Academy had to study the people's "rights," and they were so absorbed in this subject of rights that they could not help but learn it. I remember that we, the officers in the ranks, called them socialists, which in those days in our language was a swear word.

The Chief Military Prosecutor did not agree with Doné's previous sentence, and turned the case over to the Main Military Court. The latter, in its administrative session, increased the punishment, and having stripped Doné of his military position, his nobility, and all rights of his rank, condemned him to prison for four years.

But . . . the commander of our regiment, Prince D., was a very close friend of the Tsar . . . The actual report of this affair was given by the Minister of War to HIS MAJESTY THE EMPEROR; upon which, HIS MAJESTY ordered that the sentence be changed, and that Doné be demoted to the rank of private with the right of service, and he was assigned to duty with the Third Novorossiisk Dragoon Regiment.

Thus ended the most shameful episode in the entire history of the regiment, and with this distressing feeling of injustice, the soldiers of the regiment entered the war the following year. But Doné? Believe it or not . . . in the very first year of the war, his officer's rank was restored, and when the White Army went to Serbia, you could meet him there as a colonel.

Yet another small detail: the club waiter, Private Kamenev, who had come to the aid of Mochalin in his attempt to subdue the drunk officer, was sentenced by the Petersburg Military District Court to a disciplinary battalion.

Such was St. Petersburg on the eve of the war. Such was our government, at whose head was an irresponsible, weak old man, Goremykin, and behind the scenes, the all-powerful, uneducated, depraved swindler, Rasputin. Such were our Guards, headed by the "Sovereign Leader," whose prestige was falling lower and lower in the eyes of the people. The State Duma, even though composed solely of noblemen, merchants, and clergy, as the Third Duma was, was powerless to control the government, and as a result was an embittered organization and sought every available opportunity to give vent to its feelings.

Did Russia or the mass of Russian people know what was going on in Petersburg? It was impossible for them not to know. Their own testimony to it was carried from Petersburg to the localities by insulted members of the Duma in regards to their government's attitude towards them, by soldiers of the guards who were leaving for the reserves, and especially by the thousands of young students who had lived in the capital for several years. It was also known and widely taken advantage of by the country's rapidly growing industrial and manufacturing class, which could always bribe whomever was necessary in Petersburg.

Was the situation known by the court nobility surrounding the Tsar in those days? No. there was so much degeneracy that neither then—nor even now, after thirty-five years of exile—did they understand what befell them and why. "I had an estate, a stud farm, and an income," wrote one of these people to me from Paris. "Where did it all disappear? I cannot understand."

Those few like Vitte, Stolypin, Mikhail Rodzianko,[36] who understood the situation and ventured to report it to the Tsar, were immediately slandered for wishing to usurp the Tsar's power and become presidents, and were quickly kept away.

Did the Tsar himself know how the masses of people felt towards him? It can be said with certainty, no. During this time, the old command and administrative process developed to perfection the ability to show only the best side of things to the Tsar and all the other superiors. Parades, ceremonies, well-organized crowds of people yelling "Hurrah" and "God save the Tsar" greeted the Tsar no matter where he appeared. For the last two years before the war, he plainly had to be convinced that Mother Russia, as before, believed in God and was boundlessly devoted to her Sovereign. This took place at the unveiling of the monument to Alexander III in Moscow, the Borodino celebration in 1912, and the 300th anniversary of the House of Romanovs in 1913.

This is how *Novoe Vremia*, which the Tsar read daily, described his arrival in Moscow for the unveiling of the monument: "The majestic moment . . . The people, beholding their TSAR enthusiastically welcomed HIM. For the first time Moscow saw the heir to the crown, Tsarevich and Grand Duke Aleksei Nikolaevich—to this bright hope, this fruit of our fervent prayers, this treasure of the Russian people . . ." Wherever the Tsar went, he was always surrounded by his guards, by a procession with cross and banners, by the Marshal of Nobility, by governors, by administrative officers of the counties, by police, police, police . . . Five thousand volost' chiefs were brought to the Borodino Field alone, from all parts of Russia. The final event in imperial Russia before the war, by strange coincidence, celebrated the tercentenary of the House of Romanov. Petersburg society for

36. Mikhail Vladimirovich Rodzianko (1859–1924) was an important landowner in Ekaterinoslav Province. He was one of the leaders of the Octobrist Party, a member of the Council of State (1906, 1907), Deputy of the Third and Fourth State Dumas (1907–17), Chairman of the Duma in 1911. In the beginning he was linked with court circles and supported the policies of P. A. Stolypin. During World War I, he formed a bloc with the Cadets and opposed the influence of Rasputin. In 1917, after the February Revolution, he headed the Provisional Committee of the State Duma. After the October Revolution and during the Civil War of 1918–20, he served in General Denikin's army. He emigrated to Yugoslavia in 1920 where he died. In 1927 his memoirs, *The Reign of Rasputin: An Empire's Decline* were published.

the last time stepped out in all its finery, with sable furs, and diamonds, and with the guards in their uniforms; even ordinary nobles pulled from their trunks or sewed for themselves their long-forgotten noblemen's uniforms. For the last time before the declaration of war, the Winter Palace opened wide its doors for a triumphal reception. A solemn prayer service was held in the Kazan Cathedral. The opera *A Life for the Tsar* was performed in the Mariinsky Theater, where just as the Emperor appeared in the loge, an unending "Hurrah" resounded, and the hymn "God Save the Tsar" was requested and sung three times by the operatic choir. Finally, there was the ball at which Petersburg's noblemen welcomed their Tsar. The picture in the hall of the Club of Nobility[37] is indescribable. Amidst the glittering throng of the hosts and the guests, the Tsar, with the Empress mother, opened the ball with a polonaise. Following them came the Marshal of Nobility, His Most Serene Prince Saltykov, leading Empress Alexandra by the hand. One more strange coincidence: the legitimate descendant of Saltykov,[38] who by the acknowledgment of Catherine herself was the father of Paul I, walked together with the wife of his illegitimate descendant. The Tsarina, as at all gala events, walked with tightly closed lips and her face showed no sign of happiness. While watching this procession I could not distinguish it from a funeral procession.

Nevertheless, in all these celebrations those who were yelling "Hurrah!" chanting "God Save the Tsar!" and fawning in the Tsar's presence were all the same people: the Guards, the Court, and prominent dignitaries and members of the administrative world. Meanwhile, the city of millions continued to live its routine life, and since most of them did not read *Novoe Vremia*, many knew nothing about our celebration, and others probably did not pay attention to it. One evening as we rode along the Nevsky Prospect to a noblemen's ball, it occurred to me that the appearance of Nevsky Prospect during the last years had changed greatly—electric lights from the

37. In the late eighteenth and nineteenth centuries, clubs of nobility (assemblies of nobility) were founded in St. Petersburg, Moscow, and many provincial and district capitals. They organized balls, masquerades, dinners, and similar activities.

38. Nikolai Ivanovich Saltykov (1736–1816) was a Field Marshal, Count, and Prince. He was one of the many lovers of Catherine the Great. In 1773 he was appointed as guardian to her son Paul, the heir to the throne. He was also made vice president and later president of the Military Collegium, and in 1812–16 served as Chairman of the State Council and Chairman of the Committee of Ministers.

significantly-increasing number of shops, restaurants, and movie theaters doubled the illumination of the very street which coachmen now shared not with old, elegant carriages but with limousines and ever-multiplying numbers of taxis. Along the sidewalks walked crowds of ordinary people, who now enjoyed accessible, low-priced goods in the stores, illusions,[39] and automats-restaurants. More and more, business ceased to depend on the gentlemen and began to respond to the consumption of the masses. Sensitive to this very consumption, factories grew and spread throughout the entire country. His Majesty Capital increasingly stood in opposition to His Majesty the Emperor. The earnings of the masses of people were no longer dependent on the gentlemen or on government service, and people took less and less interest in the Tsar. It is doubtful whether the Emperor and the people surrounding him understood this.

One man close to the Tsar, the clever muzhik Rasputin, understood and could not help but know this. And it was the primary force that kept him close to the Tsar's family. "The Tsar has many enemies, Matushka, but while I am with you, God will not hurt you," was what Rasputin said to the empress, according to the rumors from the palace. And when one of the Tsar's most dedicated men, Prince Orlov, a wealthy, independent individual who became the Tsar's chauffeur in order to protect the Tsar's family while they were moving about, and Fraulein Tiutcheva, who tutored the Emperor's daughters, began to insist that Rasputin be removed, they both were removed instead. And when the president of the Duma, Mikhail Vladimirovich Rodzianko, begged the Tsar to part with Rasputin, the Tsar answered, "It is easier for me to have one Rasputin than ten hysterics."[40] These words reached us through the Rodzianko family, who were related to my wife.

Before lowering the curtain on my reminiscences of Russia prior to World War I, I will say a few words about my last impressions of life in the village before the war.

During the summer, the officers of the academy were sent on a topographical survey. My sector of the survey was near the Serebrianka–Warsaw

39. Cinemas, movie theaters.
40. Referring to the Empress.

railway station, about a hundred versts from Petersburg. Near the railroad bed I found a small house which I was able to rent, and here I lived with another officer. Each of us had two soldiers for field work and each had an orderly. Shortly after that my wife arrived and brought a female cook with her. In all, there were ten people. And our problem was to obtain food. Behind the little house was a village. But there it was impossible to get the most common produce, such as eggs, butter, chickens, and even edible bread—everything had to be brought from the city. Even though ready cash appeared in the village, it did not help its financial situation. On Sundays they had one drunken brawl after another, and when I went out to the field, my orderly always warned my wife not to go alone to the village; and when she did not listen to him, he followed her.

One day while working by the railroad bed, I saw a young lad walking on the tracks towards the station. He walked doubled over as if he were carrying something heavy in his arms—just what, was quickly revealed. Upon reaching the platform of the station, he fell; and when we got to him, he was already dead. Slashed across his stomach was a gaping wound, through which his intestines protruded. He appeared less than twenty years old. The sight of this death I have never forgotten.

Warsaw 1914

In 1914 not to expect war was a delusion limited only to people who were devoid of all powers of observation or were hopeless optimists. In his parting words to us officers graduating from the War Academy in April, the commandant said, "You will soon be required to apply the knowledge which you gained here. We have given you all that science knows of contemporary war. But only continual work and study of all that appears either in military literature or in technology will allow you the possibility of keeping up with the required standards."

I chose for my duty a vacancy on the General Staff in our future forward theater of war in the Warsaw Military District.

But youth took charge. Having just successfully completed the difficult work, with worry and concern left behind and nothing but rainbow-tinted hope for the future, I—and my wife as well—did not have room for any sad thoughts. And happy as never before, we spent my leave in Spa, Belgium, in a small cottage, and took a cruise on a steamer along the Rhine River. Among happy, jovial German youth, together with stout, bearded Germans, we rode on donkeys in the "Sieben Gebirge."[1] While standing on a hill and looking across the Rhine in the direction of France my wife said,

1. Translated from German, "The Seven Hills." A cluster of hills in Germany on the Rhine located about six miles above Bonn. From these hills there are spectacular views of the Rhine and the plain beyond. The beauty of its ruined castles, forests, gentle vine-covered slopes, hills, dells, and craggy escarpments made the area one of the favorite tourist resorts on the Rhine.

"How can there be a war amidst such culture, beauty, and wealth? Is it possible that people will allow this?" And as if agreeing with us, all of Germany through which we traveled appeared rich, strong, happy, and gay.

But my leave quickly came to an end. My wife and I parted in Cologne. She returned to Spa, where our little Shura[2] waited for her, and where she planned to spend the summer until I was settled in Warsaw. At our parting, I was standing in the train looking at my wife, who was standing on the platform. There was nothing more to say to each other; and we both were just smiling and waving when suddenly a violent clap of thunder resounded, and a storm began. The train pulled out. A foreboding of something ominous came over me, and this moment is clearly imprinted in my memory.

Warsaw at that time was a clean, beautiful city that bore a great resemblance to Austrian towns. Judging by its architecture, and especially by its inhabitants, it appeared to be a typical border town between Europe and the Near East.

The European Gothic buildings in the old part of the city at the northern end of the main street, Krakowskie Przedmiescie, stood at once in sharp contrast with the towering Byzantine Orthodox Cathedral, which was surrounded by two-storied state buildings of the time of Nicholas I. The latter housed the district staff and served as the administrative center of the outlying areas. Farther south along Marszalkowska and southwest towards Lazienki there were apartment houses, and the farther south you went, the newer and more opulent they became. This street ended in a beautiful park, in the center of which was the Wilanow Palace. The city, located on the left bank of the Vistula, was connected by three bridges with the suburb of Praga on the right bank, which at one time had served as a fortress, protecting Warsaw from the Russian side. European-type two-horse-drawn cabs rode through the city, and the crowd seemed more smartly dressed than in Moscow or even in Petersburg. However, a large admixture of Jews, with their guttural-sounding speech mixing with the loud sounds of the Slavs, Poles, and Russians, definitely indicated that here was where the West ended and the East began.

2. Editor's note: Nickname for Aleksandra.

During our time, Warsaw was officially the capital of the Kingdom of Poland. The sovereign was declared Emperor and Autocrat of all the Russians, Tsar of the Polish, Grand Duke of the Finnish, etc., etc., etc. But in my day the former autonomy of Poland in this title was coming to an end. It was transformed into the Warsaw General-Governorship, which was ruled on the same basis as the other parts of the Russian Empire.

On my way to Poland, I was warned to be very careful in my dealings with the people, so as not to disturb their feelings of superiority towards everything by reminding them of their subordinate position to Russia. I was prepared for this. But all the haughty attitudes of the city dwellers that I had to face surpassed my expectations. The conductor on the street car, the cashier in the bank, the sales clerk in the store, and the landlady of the apartment, in spite of the similarity of the two languages, and their obligation to learn Russian in school, pretended that they could not understand me. Consequently, I had to take the initiative and remember Polish expressions in order to communicate with them. Conversation with the people of the upper-middle class was carried on in the majority of cases in French. This part of the Polish gentry was extremely polished and kind, and with great discretion accepted us Russians into their circle. For instance, of the two Horse Guards regiments stationed in Warsaw, the Ulans of His Majesty, known to the Poles as the Tsar's Ulans, were received into society as a regiment. The attitude towards the Grodnensky Hussars was another matter; as a rule, they were not admitted into Polish society. The higher-ups in the Polish aristocracy, such as Counts Wielopolski and Przysiecki, and Princes Radziwill and Tyszkiewicz, who had studied with me in the Page Corps and had gotten together with me in Petersburg, were similar to the Baltic barons, who received lavish attention at Court, where it was not even necessary for them to speak Russian; in contrast, they were more loyal than the Germans. Apparently they realized that an independent Poland would assess them much higher taxes than those they paid Russia, and could look for nothing better.

Finally, the peasant population with whom I became acquainted during the war, who, thanks to Russia, had received soil allotments at the same time the Russian peasants were liberated, considered themselves an indivisible part of the Russian people.

In general, the Polish people were completely loyal to us before the war.

But a great number of the Jews, who were similarly persecuted by both the Russians and the Poles, were sympathetic towards the Germans. As we shall see later, the Jews helped a great deal in the German Intelligence Service during the war.

As I mentioned before, up to the very beginning of the war Warsaw continued to be the stronghold of the forward war area. However, according to the war plan, it had to be disarmed. On the exact day of my arrival, its fortifications were blown up. To people not initiated in the secrets of military art, this could not help but make a negative impression:

"Do you want to turn us over to the Germans?" asked my friendly landlady, with whom I was drinking morning coffee, when the blast was heard.

"We don't want to fight near your beautiful city," I said, not being convinced deep in my heart of the soundness of this deed. "We'll defeat the Germans in the Poles'e lowlands, and then we'll return again."

"God willing," she answered. "But we all think that the Yids bribed someone so that it would be easier to give the city to the Germans."

This conversation was in French, but when it came to mentioning the Jewish people, she pronounced the ethnic slur *zhidy*[3] in Polish, with emphasis on the first syllable.

Upon arrival, all newcomers for General Staff duty in Warsaw presented themselves to the district's Chief of Staff, General Oranovsky. I mention him here only because his immediate responsibility was to prepare the plan of survival for the district in case of war. With the declaration of war, he automatically became the Chief of Staff of the entire front line in the fight against Germany. I met Oranovsky in Petersburg. Beginning with his elegant outward appearance, he possessed all the necessary qualities for a good career: He had begun his service in the Horse Artillery Guards, and consequently was known personally by the Tsar; he was married to the daughter of Adjutant General Linevich,[4] who replaced Kuropatkin at the end of

3. "Yids."

4. Nikolai Petrovich Linevich (1838–1908) commanded the allied troops which took Peking in the Boxer Rebellion in 1900–01. By 1903 he was commander of the troops in the Amur Military District and Governor General of the Amur Region. At the beginning of the Russo-Japanese War he temporarily commanded the Manchurian Army. In 1905 he became Commander in Chief of the armed forces in the Far East, but was removed from this post in 1906 for lack of aggressiveness in fighting the revolutionary movement.

the Japanese war as the most popular general in the Far East. Oranovsky possessed as well one of the most essential qualities, that is, cautiousness: he skillfully avoided expressing his opinion in doubtful situations, and he never did anything inadvertently. Ingenuity, boldness in making decisions, and the courage to take responsibility . . . these were not thought about in time of peace. When Oranovsky failed to exhibit these qualities when they were required of him, he was relieved of his duty. Unfortunately, he was removed from his command only after Russia had lost her one-hundred-thousand-man army in East Prussia.

Oranovsky approached me first, listened to my report and said, "Your post is already arranged. You have been temporarily assigned the duty of Senior Staff Adjutant of a brigade of the Cavalry Guards Division. Go immediately to Kolbiel, where the brigade is stationed for a special cavalry mustering, and report to General Mannerheim[5]—he is impatiently waiting for an officer of the General Staff. You will have to begin duty without a senior officer of the General Staff. But you have got to know cavalry affairs. I wish you success," he concluded and shook my hand.

The recently deceased Mannerheim, leader of the Finnish people, now has become an historical figure. Then he was a young, well-built general in the retinue of His Majesty, who had just turned over his duties with the Ulans Regiment and had assumed command of that same brigade. He continued to live and eat with the Ulans Regiment, and he received me in the tent of the officers' mess.

"You have arrived just in time," he said. "General Zhilinsky,[6] who com-

---

5. Baron Carl Gustav Emil Von Mannerheim (1867–1951) was born into a Swedish-Finnish family. He became a prominent figure in the Finnish government and military. Graduating from the Nicholas Cavalry School in St. Petersburg, he served until 1917 in the Russian Army. He commanded a large unit in the First World War and became a lieutenant general in 1917. In 1918 he led the Finnish nationalist forces to victory against the Finnish Bolsheviks and their Russian supporters, and in 1919 he headed the new regime in Finland as regent. He became head of the Finnish defense council in 1931 and commanded the Finnish Army during the Soviet–Finnish War of 1939–40 and again in 1941–44, when Finland was allied with fascist Germany. In 1944 he became president of Finland. He resigned in 1946 because of ill health. The Mannerheim Line, planned by and named after him, was a fortified line of defense across the Karelian Isthmus, which never lived up to its expectations.

6. Yakov Grigorevich Zhilinsky (1853–1918) was a graduate of the Nicholas Cavalry School and later the General Staff Academy. He fought in the Russo-Japanese war as Chief of the Field Staff of Admiral E. I. Alekseev. Though it is said he lacked political and strategic acumen, his close connections to the court led to his appointment in 1911 as Chief of the

mands the forces, will be here any day, and you will have to prepare a tactical task for a review."

His Russian was correct, but he had a strong Swedish accent. A former Horse Guardsman himself, he retained his association with the officers simply as a comrade. But the officers' relations towards him did not exhibit the warmth of the type felt for a favorite commander. He gave me the exact time when I was to appear with my report, showed me the house near the chancellor's office in which I was to live, and ordered me to always let the clerk on duty know of my whereabouts. When he left, my comrades from the Ulans Corps surrounded me, and from my conversation with them, I once again realized that Mannerheim was not their favorite. They only tolerated him. One of my schoolmates even warned me:

"You better watch him. If he makes a mistake, he'll blame you for it. Mannerheim can do no wrong!"

With great interest I watched the drill of the brigade the next morning. Nice and round, well-fed little horses with short gaits were ridden for the drill, calmly, without any overly-cadenced racing movements of the flanks, by which our horses had been exhausted in Krasnoe Selo; all this clearly indicated that the eye of Grand Duke Nikolai Nikolaevich was way off. Mannerheim, however, watched vigilantly for the execution of his commands, and not one irregularity escaped him. His remarks were judicious, even-tempered, and always to the point. It was obvious that he knew his business well.

After the exercises he called me over and began to discuss the impending arrival of Zhilinsky:

"You saw the field, and you saw the small hill where we stood today. There I will station Zhilinsky. Our tactical exercise must be worked out in

---

General Staff. In 1912–13 during negotiations with Chief of the French General Staff, General J. Joffre, he irresponsibly promised to place an 800,000-man army against the Germans immediately after the fifteenth day of mobilization. In March 1914 he became Governor General of Warsaw and commander of the troops of the Warsaw Military District. At the beginning of World War I, he became Commander in Chief of the Northwestern Front. Because of the defeat in the East Prussian operation of 1914, he was removed from that duty in September of the same year. In 1915–16 he was the representative of the Russian high command to the Allied Council in Paris. He was recalled to Russia late in 1916 and placed on the retirement list in 1917. After the October Revolution, he joined the White Guards, and he died in southern Russia.

such a way that all the new battle positions of the mounted cavalry formation as it advances towards the infantry are evident in it. It will be absolutely necessary to complete the cavalry attack close to the hill where the Commander of the Forces will be standing. You think about this today, and tomorrow we will ride to the field and get everything ready."

Thus, the main point of the exercise, and the usefulness which ought to have been derived from it, played no part in the brigade's instruction. It was for display and display only. The designated enemy, that is, the platoons with small flags identifying them as the hostile regiments, could not be given the initiative, and without fail the battle had to end with a cavalry attack, and without fail at the spot where the review board was to stand.

I listened with distress to these instructions, which ordered me to wipe from my brain everything that I had studied during my three years in the academy—all those high-sounding, noble phrases of the professors about the dangers of preconceptions, about the necessity to study and learn only the current situation (whether or not it could be observed by the superiors, who could seek out for themselves a place where they could see the exercise), and about being able to do mechanically in an engagement against the troops only that which had been drilled into them in peacetime. And I received these instructions from a man who had the reputation of being an outstanding cavalry commander!

Yet the order was received, and I decided to apply all my efforts so that even under such circumstances, my assignment would be as close as possible to reality.

But reality, meanwhile, was not forthcoming. The review by Zhilinsky never came to pass. Instead, we were called for the last review which Russia required from us.

To War

Pre-Mobilization Period

In Sarajevo, Archduke Ferdinand is assassinated. Austria presents an ultimatum to Serbia. In Petersburg and other cities, workers riot. News reaches us that the forces are being called out to suppress the disturbances . . .

But for us in Kolbiel, everything goes on as usual. It is Friday, July 11, 1914—St. Olga's day. Exercises are postponed till Monday because the Grodnensky Hussar Regiment is celebrating its regimental holiday. For this occasion their new patron, German Empress Augusta, has sent an oil painting of herself to the officers' club. At the parade she is represented by the Warsaw German consul, who, having removed his high hat, is standing next to Mannerheim during the formal march of the Hussars. "God Save the Tsar" is followed by the German anthem, and then by the regimental march. In the mess tent speeches and toasts are being given in honor of the Reigning Leader and the revered patron. In Berlin the delegation from the regiment presents a bouquet to Augusta. Outwardly everything goes on as it always has. But . . . there is one thing lacking—merriment. There is no enthusiasm and no desire to drink wine.

The official part of the celebration has come to an end, and the club, contrary to other times, is vacated. Both the Ulans and the Hussars, taking advantage of the three-day holiday, depart for Warsaw, and Mannerhiem leaves with them. In the staff of the brigade, I am the only one remaining. On Saturday I work on the impending review by Zhilinsky: I made a few map sketches, went twice to the field, placed guidons[1] where necessary, and in the evening, satisfied with everything and tired, went to bed.

1. A small flag with forked end, carried as a standard by a regiment or other military unit.

The news in the paper began to worry me. The time had come for my wife to return from abroad. In days such as these I thought the singing of the German anthem, the presence of the German consul in his top hat, and the adoration of the "revered" German patron to be strange and inappropriate.

During the night a clerk grasping a telegram awakened me. "Upon receipt of this message, advance the brigade with a machine-gun section, cartridges, and two-wheeled carts in tow to winter quarters." Signed, Lieutenant-General Oranovsky. I signed for the telegram at 3 a.m., July 13, 1914. I remembered this number and did not like it.

All day it poured rain, and we were soaked to the skin as we approached Warsaw. Mannerheim met us on the bridge.

"Good day, Ulans! I congratulate you on the march! . . ."

"We humbly thank you, Your Excellency! . . . Hurrah! . . ."

At this moment there was a loud explosion. It was not like the explosions from the fort that we had grown accustomed to. As we later learned, this one had occurred in the post office, where someone had dropped a package, and this was followed by an explosion in which seven people were killed.

So then—the march. I received an order to report to staff headquarters in the district because the permanent adjutant was being recalled to his position. I sent a telegram to my wife telling her to leave for Warsaw immediately and proceeded to Headquarters.

The city was quiet. The people were still unaware of what had just occurred. The papers were filled with the details of the explosion at the post office; even the news of the Austrian ultimatum to Serbia was moved back to the second page. I was walking along Marszalkowska Street[2] toward Headquarters. Thoughts were swarming in my head: War! Good-bye, happy civilian life which my wife and I had dreamed about when I was in the academy, working day and night. In all three years of our marriage we had lived life to the fullest for only two months while abroad. But is there such a thing as a happy, carefree life? Is it not possible that in each person lies a worm which gnaws at him and compels him to imagine worries and

2. Marshall Street.

complications where none exist? Did I not languish from lack of something to do towards the end of my stay in Spa, and did I not long to return to duty, supposing that something might happen there without me? On the other hand, was it possible to dream of creating a happy life among those cesspools in which our circle was bathing, even in Petersburg? Why would one expect people in Warsaw or in any other city to be more honest and moral? Perhaps war is the very phenomenon which calls people to acts of heroism and should ennoble them. I recalled my conversation with my wife on this subject and how she objected: "War is brutal, and can only make savages of people, not improve them."

Now, even after we have gone through so many misfortunes and horrors that if they had all happened to us at the same time, it is doubtful that any of us would have wanted to go on living, I still cannot agree with my wife. At present I can only state with certainty that a decline in the moral foundations is the first indication of an approaching national calamity.

On the day when I was on my way to the district's staff headquarters, my thoughts were whirling quickly, and one after another was grabbing hold without any order. What is awaiting me—death? Mutilation? Heroic action? Glory? . . . A thick curtain hung over the future, and I faced it straight on. I knew one thing, that I was on my way to perform that job for which I had been preparing all my life. Was I ready for it? Would I have enough will and fortitude to carry it out honorably to the end?

And Marusia? She was the only person who was tying me to the receding past. And I was seized by the irresistible desire to see her once more, even if only for a day, for a few hours, even for a minute. All other thoughts, intentions, and expectations left me, and I resigned myself totally to calculating when she could arrive in Warsaw. On Thursday? Yes, this was the earliest possible time.

At that moment I raised my head and in front of me stood our former regimental commander, General Roop.

"My dear sir! Fyodor Sergeyevich! What good luck brings you here?"

I explained to him that I was on my way to "look for work" at the district's staff headquarters.

"You are already 'hired.' You do not have to go anywhere. I will take care of everything. I must advance with the division to the border, and I do not have a Chief of Staff, for he is absent on leave, nor a Senior Adjutant, for he is in Austria on dispatch. I need you very much. And I am especially glad that it will be you."

I thanked him, although deep down I was not particularly happy to serve under his command. But evidently such was my destiny. He did not ask for my consent.

"When must we leave?" I asked him timidly.

"On Thursday at six in the evening from the Mlawa railway station." "I have a wife . . ." I started to say, but then held my tongue.

After parting with Roop, I went to the Berlin station where I learned that my wife's train was to arrive in the morning. Thus, if she manages to arrive on Thursday, I shall see her. My total preoccupation and all my worries were connected with the preparation for meeting her.

Marusia arrived as anticipated. And the meeting was much less dramatic than one would expect. Because in the first place, she was able to control herself, and in the second, the threatening events were of such immense proportions that the mind probably could not grasp them all at once. In those few hours that we spent together, we walked around Warsaw looking for an area with apartments where we could settle after the war.

Our trains to Petersburg and Ciechanow[3] left at the same time, but from different stations. Having entrusted my friendly landlady to escort my wife to the station, I boarded the train and departed for Ciechanow where the staff of the Sixth Cavalry Division was stationed.

September 1957

Three years have passed since I finished the preceding page and more than ten years since I began to write these remembrances. I have entered my seventy-third year. My strength is quickly waning. And seeing that all the most essential of the extraordinary events that passed before the eyes of a

3. The Russian name for this town was Tsekhanov. For consistency, whenever there is a difference between the Russian name and the English version on a map of that time, I use the English spelling.

most ordinary man still needed to be written down, I decided to make use of every free moment in order to write, write, write . . .

The time of life, the intensive labor of a working man, and life so structured that there are no idle people have led to the fact that people never read nor write. Writers have learned to take, as they say here, "short cuts," that is, to advance towards a goal totally flat out, but readers compete for the speed records by reading 250 and even five hundred pages an hour. After all, those who break records contend that frequently one sentence is enough to understand a page. Children, instead of preparing their lessons, spend all their time sitting in front of capering puppets on television or playing ball. And schoolteachers try to impart to the students as concisely as possible all that standardized material which they are required to teach.

Already, since those days which I am discussing here, a third generation is preparing to take the leading role. The younger people are, the less I understand them. Their views, ideas, tastes, interests—all are completely foreign to me. And it is doubtful whether my recollections will ever interest them.

The population of our planet grows with incredible speed. According to the calculations of statisticians, in about a hundred years, the population of China, for example, will reach two billion; that is, it will almost equal the total population of the earth now. In our far-off California during the thirty-five years that I have lived here, it has increased five times. When the Second World War began in Russia, its population was 175 million; now it numbers 200 million, in spite of the fact that it lost twenty million in the war. Of course, that increase brings with it reorganization in the life of a nation so that the new order acquires a socialistic quality to the detriment of private initiative and individual freedom. In any case, most people—if not all—feel that individualism will soon come to an end. And this angers them. They behave brutally and blame the Soviet regime for everything. There is no doubt that one more, likely last, collision of the two worlds is at hand, and in all probability, it will end that civilization in which we live.

What is the use of my remembrances? In the best case, some bursting bomb will cover them over with dirt, and perhaps in three thousand years some archaeologist will dig them up and try to decipher them as is being done now with hieroglyphics.

Map of East Prussia.

But, by some means or other, all my life I have been used to finishing what I have begun. If my health permits, I will finish this work too.

Mobilization: The First Fiasco

It was a gloomy morning, July 18, 1914. In the small Polish-Jewish town of Ciechanow, the weekday started out as usual. The shops opened; a train arrived from Warsaw and proceeded to Mlawa; two or three wagons loaded with some sort of sacks moved through the street along with the peasants on foot.

Even though the people were aware that at a moment's notice life would have to change, everything still moved at the same pace; and through inertia, the people continued to do whatever they were accustomed to—day in, day out. Just as my wife and I, on the day of our parting, were looking for an apartment in Warsaw where we could live after the war, so too on that day in Ciechanow, and on all subsequent days so long as the guns were not booming, people were neither able to grasp the dimensions of the situation, nor could they realize or believe that the rich, affable Germans living on the other side of the border would suddenly begin to slaughter us, take our beggarly households away, and occupy our poor Jewish towns.

However, the driving engine had already begun to put its gears in motion. In front of their barracks, the Volynsky Ulan Regiment lined up on horseback fully equipped for battle. In front of the regiment stood a pulpit. A priest in sacerdotal vestments was serving moleben and sprinkling Holy Water on the Ulans. On the right flank, where the trumpeters stood, several of the wives, who had lingered longer than allowed, were straining closely towards their husbands' horses. Everyone had a look of concentration and was praying fervently. It was clear that the time had come when God was needed by all.

"Caps on!" the command resounded.

"I congratulate the Ulans on your march," shouted the commander of the division.

"We humbly thank you, Your Excellency."

"I believe that the Ulans justify the trust which the Reigning Monarch and Mother Russia have placed in them!"

"We shall do our best, Your Excellency."

"God be with you, Colonel Kanshin." Roop addressed the Commander of the Regiment, who was standing next to him.

The order sounded, and all the squadrons, as if on parade, behaving as always like a well-tuned engine, drew up in array and followed one another along the dusty road. But then on the same right flank, when the trumpeters set forth, a woman tore herself away from the stirrups of one of them and fell to the ground in hysterics. Other women rushed towards her. The husband stopped his steed instantly, but did not dare dismount, spurred the horse, and stood in rank.

On the border along the road from Mlawa to Neidenburg, close to the border control point, stood a squadron of Glukhovsky Dragoons. Just ahead on the border was one dismounted platoon under the command of an "eastern" man, Cornet Svimanov. The remaining members of the squadron stood with their commander a short distance away, on the other side of a knoll. This was the reconnaissance squadron which, as designated on the mobilization timetable in peacetime, was ordered to cross the border immediately upon the declaration of mobilization.

At the German border control station on the opposite side of the roadblock, life seemingly continued on as usual for the guard's family. Children were running around, chickens were pecking at the grass, and behind the house a cow was bellowing. At a distance of about five hundred feet on the fringe of the forest, two barely visible camouflaged helmets emerged.

Our squadron stood in this position for the greater part of the day. The people and the horses agonized in suspense. The Dragoons took turns going to the field kitchen, where the saddle girths of the horses were released and nose bags were tied on them. However, there was nowhere to water them.

The previous day the order of mobilization had arrived, in which the necessary actions were assigned to the proper person by a timetable. Packets were stored for safekeeping in regimental cash boxes which the commanders had to open immediately upon the receipt of a telegram. In this packet to the Kliastitsky Regiment, the precise orders were that within the course of the first hour, the Horse Sapper detachment of the division, being near the regiment, was to blow up the railroad bridge in Mlawa, and the

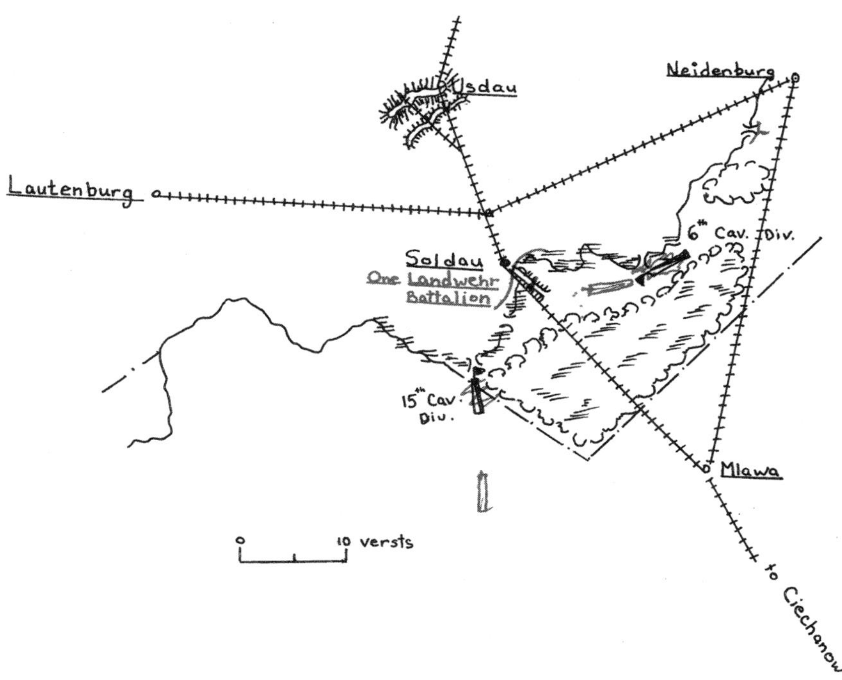

Battle of Mlawa.

reconnaissance squadrons with their designated commanders were to cross the border. Accordingly, the bridge was blown up and the squadrons went forward. But before crossing the border, they were stopped. The next telegram arrived:

"His Imperial Majesty the Emperor orders it agreed not to embark on a single action which could entail unavoidable military engagement."

The commander of the division was obliged from the very first step to violate the plan that had been so carefully worked out in peacetime, and decide for himself exactly what he ought to do or not do in order to carry out the two opposite orders.

It was easy to order that the border not be crossed, but impossible to restore the blown-up bridge. Since the path of retreat had been destroyed, it was also impossible to recover the squadrons from the border.

In the staff division, located in the small house of a Polish nobleman, where there were so many flies that we could not open our mouths without a swarm of them flying in, General Roop was greatly agitated. He consulted for a long time with the recently appointed Provisional Commander of the staff and with me, and after unfastening the buttons of his white summer uniform, made the sign of the cross with a small cross on his forehead beneath his forage cap and on his chest. He was angry at the commander of the Horse Sapper detachment for hastily blowing up the bridge, even though he himself and the rest of us knew that the former did not have the right to do otherwise. And, finally, he made a decision: the reconnaissance squadrons would hold back on the border and not open fire unless an attack was initiated from the side of the Germans. (He dictated "from the side of the enemy," but ordered this scratched out and changed to "from the side of the Germans.") A reprimand was given to the commander of the Horse Sapper detachment for the hasty blowing up of the bridge. This latter action must have served as insurance in case of a possible future investigation.

Here then I arrived in Mlawa with this order, delivered it to the commander of the Kliastitsky Regiment, and after that rode on to the Glukhovsky Squadron on the road to Neidenburg. There my duty was to observe and report to the staff everything that was happening.

After many long, tiresome hours of waiting, at the end of the day a staff division motorcyclist brought both the message that Germany had declared war on us and the order to commence the execution of our first battle scheme.

Simultaneously with the arrival of the motorcycle, the German on the other side of the border control began to hurriedly put his family in a carriage and then drove off in the direction of Neidenburg. Evidently the communication concerning the declaration of war had come to both us and the Germans at the same time. The camouflaged helmets remained on the fringe of the forest without moving, and the cow continued to bellow.

The very beginning of military operations did not proceed without humor. "Rotmistr Sir, how do we start the war?" the squadron commander was asked by Cornet Svimanov, proud of his role as the first to cross the border. And without waiting for an answer, he drew up his platoon in front of the border control station and fired a volley in the direction of Germany. The commander of the squadron approached, ordered the platoon to mount up, send out a patrol, and proceed straight along the highway. Two Dragoons had a difficult time as usual breaking their horses away from formation, and after removing their caps and making the sign of the cross, galloped off over the crossing. The sound of the horses' hoofs reverberated loudly on the paved Prussian road, and for some reason that sound on the foreign road had an unsettling effect on me.

The squadron's march across the border went without opposition, and the helmets facing out from the edge of the forest were concealed.

This is how it went on our front in the Tsar's final attempt to avoid war. Whether it was a sincere desire on the part of Wilhelm to stem a catastrophe at the last minute by a direct appeal to the Tsar, or just a shrewd maneuver to gain time to evacuate the civilian population from the border zone, it is difficult to say. During this time fighting was going on in both France and Galicia, and it was no longer possible to stop the war. It was said that Grand Duke Nikolai Nikolaevich was gnashing his teeth when he received the order from the Emperor. But at that time, still naively believing that we could fight Germany in alliance with Europe and even defeat her, we were angry that we had lost two days, having granted them to Prussia for their own uninterrupted mobilization.

Cavalry Action

There was still another situation at the very beginning of the Soldau operation that caused a delay. The reader will undoubtedly remember from my tale regarding the War Academy that not being able to compete with Germany in speed of mobilization, we prepared to meet her troops in two corridors behind the border on the line of the Bug-Narew Rivers. The entire region between the border and the rivers was purposely prepared to make movement through it difficult. There were no railway sidings, no provisions depots, and no highway. It was surmised that the Germans would move some distance on the line of Novogeorgievsk–Osovets, and there would encounter our army, equipped from the rear, at the contestable points of Osovets–Zegrhz and Novogeorgievsk; and they would be forced to draw up their own rear and narrow our wide-gage railway track for their trains.

The moment mobilization was announced, our cavalry was being brought up to the border. Our tasks were to interfere with German mobilization with a quick invasion into Eastern Prussia, to conduct reconnaissance on a broad front, and to stop the enemy from moving into our frontier.

It must be remembered that in those days the only means of gathering information concerning the enemy was for the cavalry commanders to send out reconnaissance patrols to make a single pass near enemy lines; the commanders relied completely on the initiative of officers. It must also be remembered that we knew about the Germans' Schlieffen war plan and had already been preparing for it for several years. In the course of some of our camp gatherings, we were getting our cavalry ready specifically for combat reconnaissance and on the basis of these preparations, laid the moral support for the reconnaissance squadrons and continual movement forward.

We saw that we were forbidden to cross the border on the first day of mobilization—we lost that day. Now, when the Germans declared war on us, we waited another day, being certain that now they surely would attack us . . . but the Germans did not advance.

In the morning we received the first reports from the reconnaissance squadrons, which informed us that when they reached the Dzialdowo River, they discovered that the enemy had occupied all the crossings, and every populated spot along the border had been evacuated. It seemed that our division should have immediately advanced to support the reconnaissance, but in division staff the question was, What should we do? According to the mobilization plan, the Sixth and the 15th Cavalry Divisions should have joined in Mlawa to form a cavalry corps under the command of the Senior Commander of the division, General Liubomirov. But for some reason the 15th Division was detained, and the cautious General Roop was inclined to wait to meet up with them. Our temporary Staff Commander, Colonel Prokhorov, however, was of a different opinion. Foaming at the mouth, he exhorted the General not to lose time, to cross the border and attack the Germans, because here we would not encounter them. He thought it perfectly logical that if the border population was evacuated, then the enemy did not intend to cross over. He even asked me to convince Roop. "You must know that this is the only chance to prove ourselves. When the infantry battle begins, we will be assigned to the flank or to the rear, and there we will vegetate." In the meantime, the General was saying something else to me. "That 'Khalif of the moment' only needs to earn a small cross, but the responsibility lies entirely on me. What do you think, my dear sir?" he asked.

"I think, Your Excellency," I answered timidly, "that the Staff Commander is right. We must find out as quickly as possible what is going on beyond the Dzialdowo." Roop seemed shaken by my answer, but he could not doubt my sincerity. He called in the Staff Commander, and the order was given to cross the border.

At nine o'clock in the morning the staff division at the head of the main forces crossed the border at the same control point where I had accompanied the Glukhovsky Squadron the day before. The cow continued to graze near the guard house, but the house was empty. Again horseshoes clattered on the paved road, and again the recognition that the road was foreign had an unpleasant effect on me. It was much narrower than ours. A wire fence extended along its sides. Here and there were swampy groves. We passed a small, abandoned settlement, and German "restraint and precision" were visible in everything. Every speck of land was utilized, every shrub preserved, and every small home was clean on the outside and probably on the inside, too.

After passing a marsh, we found a field path leading towards the west and turned onto it, continued into a little forest, and soon came out upon a large, open field. About two versts ahead of us the town of Soldau could be seen, with its small, white houses trimmed with brick. The town was brightly illuminated by the rays of the sun from behind us. To the left as far as the eye could see stretched a swampy forest, isolating us from our border. About half a verst to the right between marshy banks flowed the Dzialdowo Rivulet, which turned south at the edge of the town separating us from it, whereupon it again turned sharply towards the west and disappeared into the forest. We traveled about half a verst forward, and the staff with the General rode out upon a small knoll. To the left on the edge of the forest was our advance guard: two Hussar squadrons and two hundred Cossacks under the command of Hussar Lieutenant Colonel O'Rem. The rest of the units of the division remained in the forest to the rear of us. Roop looked intently towards the town, and we felt that he still was not quite sure of his next move, but it was obvious that we would not leave here without being baptized by the fire of combat. I looked at those around me to see if they noticed how frightened I was. But no one was looking at me; they all were absorbed in their own inner thoughts. At that instant a shrapnel shell whistled above our heads and exploded behind us. Even if Roop had been pondering for a moment what to do next, he had no doubt now. He addressed himself to the Chief of Staff and commanded him to deliver the orders: the advance guard with the 12th Horse Battery will attack the town directly through the field, and the other units of the division will move through the forest circling the town to the left.

Everything that transpired from the time this order was given until the end of the battle—if it could be called a battle and not a massacre—happened of itself, and it was performed in just the same manner as people were accustomed to in peacetime. O'Rem deployed his squadrons and sotnias in a so-called lava formation and trotted towards the town; the horse battery galloped past us, stood in the open position to the right of the half-moon formation, and opened fire on the town. The German battery shifted its fire from us to the advancing half-moon formation, and very soon machine-gun fire was heard, following which we could see horses falling, but all the rest were moving forward, and for some reason concentrating into lines and piling up. At that moment a neighing horse with a blood-stained saddle ran quickly past to the side of us. Galloping up behind her was the wounded Cornet Lomakovsky, his face covered with blood. He dismounted and muttered, "All around us there are swamps." Reeling on his feet and supported by an orderly, he proceeded to the first-aid station.

At that instant I looked at Roop and felt guilty. That responsibility that he so feared may have not been the responsibility towards his superiors, but towards those men whom he led to die.

At this point we followed Roop through the field, trotting towards the left in the direction of the main forces, which remained on the edge of the forest as though they were in doubt whether to venture any further. Along the way, the repelled lava formation streamed back towards us in full disarray. Prokhorov and I began to set in order the Hussars and the Cossacks, who were piled up in a common mass, break them up by platoons, dismount them, and spread them in a half verst lengthwise along the edge of the forest. At this stage we had only one hope, that the Germans would not take advantage of the disorder and descend upon us in attack. I remember that the Hussars completely lacked an understanding of advancing in lines.[4] Whether it was just the result of shock or the absence of preparation, I don't know, but we were obliged to lead and put each soldier in his place. Shashkas, which by regulation we continued to carry in foot formation, dangled between their legs and rendered the Hussars even more helpless.

Near us there were officers who were taking part in the attack in front of the town, where the swampy Dzialdowo was especially wide and passable by just one dam.[5] Beside the dam the Hussars and Cossacks bunched up under machine-gun fire. These officers told us about the events. The commander of the sotnia had pulled out in front, galloping at the head of several Cossacks, almost reaching the opposite bank, but before getting off the dam he was cut down by a bullet, and behind him Cossacks and horses began to fall, and the only crossing to the other shore was covered with the corpses of men and horses. The lava wavered and quickly retreated.

We found out later that our losses were as follows: forty of the lower ranks were wounded or killed, the Cossack Captain was wounded and taken prisoner by the Germans, a Hussar Cornet had a slight injury to his nose, and more than fifty horses were killed—that is, almost 10 percent of the forces who were attacked.

Soon the entire edge of the forest was hastily occupied by units of the division, and I was sent with the horse patrol to meet the 15th Cavalry Division to ask them to make all possible speed to join us. I picked my way straight through bushes and swamps because there was no road, and finally reached the road that Liubomirov was taking, and very quickly met him and his staff at the head of the division. Liubomirov had been previously informed that Roop was planning an attack, and being stationed only ten versts from the battle area, he naturally should have hurried to join up with us. But he was moving at an ordinary pace just as in a peacetime setting, not even dispatching patrols, let alone thinking of setting out to link up with the Sixth Division in battle.

"Your Excellency," I said, "General Roop ordered me to report to you that he now is crossing over with the infantry in an attack on Soldau and is asking you to support him by advancing on this road and doing what is

4. Standing in line with a small distance between each one.

5. The Russian word used here is *gat'*, which translates as "dam" or "fascine way." A fascine way is a structure created of dry brush, twigs and/or timber bound together and laid down to facilitate passage through a swampy area such as this crossing of the Dzialdowo River.

necessary to help take possession of the town. The Germans only have four cannons in that area."

"Tell General Roop," replied Liubomirov, "that I will occupy the position right here," and pointed at the foliage of a copse in front of him. "And if he does not carry out the attack now, then ask him to come to me—I will wait for him here."

"Your Excellency," I tried to object, "General Roop has already begun fighting. Your bursting forth from the other side of the flank . . ."

"I command you, Staff Rotmistr, to transmit what I said to the general." And raising his voice, the General interrupted me, and, addressing himself loudly to his Chief of Staff so that I would hear, said, "Since when must I take orders from any greenhorn?"

The Chief of Staff, Colonel Shnabel, who was my former instructor of tactics in the academy, looked at me reproachfully. There was nothing to do but return to my staff.

Meanwhile, our expectations of a counterattack by the Germans did not materialize, and Roop, evidently waiting for Liubomirov's answer, did not assume the offensive. Day drew towards evening, field kitchens were set up in the forest, and only a few horse patrol units guarded our camp. The commander of the division, having listened to my report, immediately went with the entire staff to see Liubomirov. It was a friendly meeting. General Liubomirov, like Roop, was an officer in the Guards, and as a colleague of the Emperor in the horse artillery during the latter's tenure as heir to the throne, his connection with the higher echelons was strong. Besides this, Liubomirov had another advantage: he and his Chief of Staff had the experience of the Japanese War behind them, which probably had taught them to evade the stumbling blocks in all kinds of surroundings, and not to entangle themselves in uncertain adventures, but to hold back, troubling themselves only with those actions which had future justification. Common sense, having as its basis duty to the Motherland, history of war, science—such people knew all this well in time of peace.

Liubomirov ordered all the units of both divisions to evacuate to our territory in the area of Mlawa. At the conclusion of the order, I heard him say, "If this occurs again, I will bring him before the court-martial," not thinking for one moment that this concerned me. But that night in camp Roop asked me, "What did you say to him, old chap?" After I recounted my story, he did not respond, but merely shrugged his shoulders. And I, likewise, did not ask any questions. So ended our baptismal battle. I was deeply grieved by all that I saw and lived through, but feeling that I was entirely right in my personal incident with Liubomirov, I thought least of all about it. I regretted advising Roop to cross the border, and I was angry both with the Chief of Staff and with myself for not prompting Roop to send the advance guard to Soldau in infantry formation. But the dam was on the map, and if at that time I had not looked at it, I had no one to blame but myself. We pushed him into battle and washed our hands of responsibility. "He is the Commander, so let him command." Another at fault was O'Rem. He could not help but know about the existence of the dam, because during peacetime he was a frequent guest of the German garrison in Soldau. I never had the opportunity to speak with O'Rem, but the gossip was that once during peacetime, after a few drinks in the German Officers' Club in Soldau, he made a bet that with the declaration of war, he would capture the town with a cavalry attack. I did not want to believe this.

I compared the preparation for formation on foot in the cavalry of the Warsaw district with that of our Guards, which occurred in the final years prior to the war. We in the Guards were trained with added emphasis on infantry formation and the art of sharpshooting. What perplexed me most of all was, Why did we return to Mlawa?

Later on, from questioning the prisoners, we found out that the Germans in Soldau had one Landwehr battalion and four cannons. Our division in infantry formation consisted of a battalion. But we had twelve guns, and with the approach of Liubomirov—two battalions and twenty-four guns.

The Second Army Attacks

Evacuating to Mlawa after the attack, we stationed a patrol guard along the border and remained in this position for two days—July 25 and 26. For six days our operation had no news regarding the location, strength, and grouping of the enemy. We knew that its guard units were stationed along the Dzialdowo and that infantry with artillery occupied Soldau. What we did not know was the location of the Germans' western flank—information which was of utmost importance for our entire ability to command.

The Germans, seeing our inactivity, began to harass us with their patrols, and even moved up their battery and opened fire on Mlawa. Our battery, returning fire towards their position, forced them to silence. From one of the German patrol units, several elderly militiamen ran over to us. According to them, no one suffered from our attack on Soldau, the residents had left the town beforehand, and they themselves were quite enraptured by the bravery of the "Russisch Kosaken," who galloped in the open directly towards the machine-gun fire. We did not want to believe their main testimony, that the Soldau-Neidenburg line was defended only by militia units; and that all of the active units had been sent in the direction of Konigsberg and Eydtkunen.[1] If this was true, our four army corps could sweep away the militia, burst forth to the rear of the German forces, which

1. Settlement Chernyshevskoe, Kaliningrad Oblast, Russia.

General Rennenkampf[2] was attacking, and occupy all of Eastern Prussia. My heart stopped from the thought of it, and I wished for a quick, quick arrival of our infantry.

But finally we received our orders: II Army, assume the offensive and attack the enemy on the Allenstein-Osterode Front. Our Sixth Cavalry Division was ordered to tear through the enemy's defense on the Dzialdowo and move north to the rear of the already-retreating I Army of the enemy. A separate message from the army command rebuked us for our inactivity while waiting for further developments of the border operations. The 15th Cavalry Division was ordered to move in the direction of Deutsch-Eylau to defend the left flank of the army.

During this time Colonel Stepanov, our permanent Chief of Staff, returned to the division. He was an old officer of the General Staff with the same Manchurian experience as both Liubomirov and Shnabel. He was a reserved, unassuming fellow, and loved the office and all kinds of written dealings, instructions, etc. He spoke in a whisper with everyone so that others who were present could not hear him. He regarded me with a shade of suspicion as I was a colleague of Roop, and jealously watched so that I would not go over his head, even though I had never given occasion for this. One could obtain very little from him when he was under pressure. With his arrival, the staff increased: six young cornet-orderlies with their servants, who brought packs and camping beds with them. They all were very nice people, but it was not clear to me what purpose was served by taking them out of line duty.

The assignment given us by army order was carried out in this manner: The division crossed the border on the same Neidenburg road, again turned towards the west, and stopped as soon as it received news of the shelling of our patrols at the crossings. A detachment was formed by 300 Cossacks,

---

2. Pavel Karlovich Rennenkampf (1854–1918) was a Russian General of the Cavalry (1910). In 1900 he commanded a cavalry brigade in suppression of the Boxer Rebellion in China, and he later commanded the Transbaikal Cossack Division in the Russo-Japanese War. At the beginning of World War I he led the I Army in the East Prussian Operation of 1914. His failure to aid the II Army and General Samsonov facilitated Hindenburg's victory in Tannenberg. He himself was defeated in the Battle of Masurian Lakes. In 1916 he was made Commander of the Northern Front. After the October Revolution of 1917, he was arrested by the Bolsheviks and shot.

a horse artillery platoon, and a horse sapper unit of the division jointly under the command of Colonel Burkov,[3] Commander of the Eleventh Horse Battery. I was sent as his Chief of Staff. This detachment was ordered to break through across the river and blow up the roadbed of the railroad between Soldau and Neidenburg, which ran parallel to the river. Along this track ran a train carrying the militia to those places where it was needed to prevent our units from crossing the river. This was a kind of mobile reserve, which allowed the forces defending the river to be reduced to a minimum.

After hurrying the Cossacks and spreading them out in rows, Burkov called forth the commander of the artillery platoon and ordered all of us to pull out our revolvers; and together with the rows of Cossacks, we came out on the high bank of the river. The German trenches appeared to be only five hundred feet away on the opposite bank, and were clearly visible. Shooting began, machine guns started popping, and our guns opened fire with "grape shot." The Germans very quickly quieted down. Burkov, ahead of the ranks, descended to the bridge. The Cossacks galloped after him. Several German bullets whistled by, and one of our Cossacks fell. A slain German lay stretched out on the bridge. A little further, on the other bank, lay two more injured. Burkov sent one hundred Cossacks ahead across the bridge. The Cossacks climbed up on the opposite bank; firing began once more, and our group took cover. Again a few shells exploded over the Germans, and they finally fell silent. The Cossacks advanced, followed by the sappers. They attached explosive devices to a small railroad bridge and blew it up.

The assignment had been executed. Burkov dictated the report to me, and we waited for the approach of the division.

In this small junction, I had the opportunity to observe how a German doctor worked under fire, picking up his wounded soldiers. He paid absolutely no attention to us, but approached the bridge and gathered up the corpse of a German lying at our feet. On his sleeve he wore a Red Cross insignia, and not one of the Cossacks thought of hindering him. Burkov even asked him some question, to which the doctor saluted him and answered, "Ich weiss nicht, Oberst."[4]

3. Petr Leonidovich Burkov.

4. "I don't know, Colonel."

At this time neither we nor the Germans had as yet become brutal. In a month such a scene could not have been repeated.

The division we were waiting for never materialized. Then an order came for us to retreat and join up with the main forces. Towards evening the division again returned to Mlawa—entirely as on the military field at Krasnoe Selo—we practiced and then returned home to rest. At the beginning of the war we carried on just as we were accustomed to in peacetime. And this was one of the numerous reasons for our defeat at Soldau.

No matter how beautifully the report portrayed the military actions of Burkov's division, it did not have the desired effect on Samsonov,[5] because it became evident to everyone that the Soldau-Neidenburg line, which he marched to attack with four corps and which three hundred Cossacks so easily broke through, was not occupied by the enemy. Where was the enemy?

Then followed an abrupt order from the Staff of the Army for the cavalry to immediately move ahead and press deep into Prussia, knock out their advance units, and attack them wherever we met. By edict of the Sovereign, we were forbidden to withdraw from combat before the approach of the I Army Corps, which was nearing the border. To see that this command was carried out, Colonel Krymov,[6] who served under Samsonov, was sent to us—the same Krymov, who, during the days of the revolution, having

5. Aleksandr Vasil'evich Samsonov (1859–1914) was a Russian General of the Cavalry (1910). Early in the First World War, as Commander of the II Army, he advanced into East Prussia in order to relieve the German pressure on the French. His army was virtually annihilated by Hindenberg in the battle of Tannenberg, August 14, 1914. His defeat and the defeat of the II Army were thought to be caused by the failure of General Rennenkampf, Commander of the I Army, to come to his support. The inaction of General Ia. G. Zhilinsky, Commander of the Northwestern Front, was also a factor. Samsonov shot himself on the battlefield as part of the II Army was encircled.

6. Aleksandr Mikhailovich Krymov (1871–1917) was a Russian lieutenant general (1917) and son of a noble in the Warsaw Province. He served on the staff of the II Army at the beginning of the First World War and later took up command of the Ussuri Cavalry Brigade (later division) in March 1915, and the III Cavalry Corps in April 1917. He was closely associated with the Octobrist party, especially its leader, A. I. Guchkov. During the counterrevolutionary revolt in August 1917, led by the Supreme Commander in Chief of the Armed Forces of Russia, General Kornilov, Krymov was sent by General Headquarters to Petrograd as leader of the III Cavalry Corps to suppress the revolutionary forces. When the soldiers refused to attack, he went to explain his actions to Kerensky, but he was arrested, and seeing that the Kornilov venture had failed, he shot himself.

been dispatched by Kornilov[7] to Petrograd, either was killed or shot himself in Kerensky's[8] office.

Meanwhile, the infantry of the I Army Corps was approaching our rear, and I was sent as liaison to the arriving staff.

"How goes it, Gentlemen?" called out a bearded reservist. "Damned frightening, I bet?"

"Frightening or not frightening, but they are shooting," the Ulans answered.

"If only to slay the devil, and get something to eat and a little sleep—for two days we have not seen the traveling kitchen; all we did was march and march. And how is your food?"

"When you reach Prussia—there will be lots of food," the Ulans answered laughingly.

I gathered the same impression after speaking with the officers. The third forced march without any organization in the rear had exhausted everyone.

With the approach of the infantry to Mlawa, hostile airplanes began flying over us, including a Zeppelin, which dropped several bombs on the

---

7. Lavr Georgievich Kornilov (1870–1918) was a Russian General of the Infantry and one of the leaders of the Russian Counterrevolution. Early in the First World War he was captured by the Austrians and escaped. From May to July, 1917, he commanded the VIII Army and troops of the Southwestern Front. From July 19 to August 27, 1917, he was Supreme Commander in Chief and attempted to restore discipline among the troops by introducing the death penalty at the front and restricting the activity of soldiers' committees. Conservative elements backed Kornilov in his plans to reconstruct the provisional government on more conservative lines. To accomplish this, he sent troops to Petrograd in August, 1917. Provisional Premier Kerensky feared that Kornilov planned to establish a military dictatorship and dismissed him. When Kornilov refused to accept this, he was arrested. After the October Revolution of 1917, he escaped to southern Russia, where he joined up with General M. V. Alekseev to head the White Guard Volunteer Army. He was killed during an unsuccessful assault on Ekaterinodar and was succeeded by Denikin as Anti-Bolshevik Commander in the South.

8. Aleksandr Fedorovich Kerensky (1881–1970), the son of a nobleman, was educated to be a lawyer. From 1912 to 1917 he was a representative of the moderate Labor party to the Fourth Duma. After the February Revolution of 1917, he joined the Socialist Revolutionary party and became Minister of Justice, then War Minister in the Government of Prince L'vov. In July, 1917, he succeeded L'vov as Provisional Premier, and in August, also became Commander in Chief. His government was overthrown later in 1917 by the Bolsheviks. Kerensky's fall was facilitated by his insistence on remaining in the First World War, his inability to deal with urgent economic problems, and his moderation. In 1918 he fled to Paris and in 1940 moved to the United States.

railroad station, killing and wounding twenty soldiers who were unloading a train. There was total confusion in town and among the units occupying it; everyone who had a gun was shooting at the dirigible, and finally a shell made a direct hit on the gondola, forcing it to land. A large crowd of soldiers gathered around the airship. An ensign ran up to the captain of the vessel, struck him in the face, and knocked him down. There was a moment when we thought the whole crew of the Zeppelin would be torn to pieces, and only with the immediate, great efforts of our horse battery, which was standing right there, were they able to be saved.

In the evening after interrogation in staff headquarters, where the German did not give us any information, we invited him into the staff's tent for supper. He behaved in an eminently arrogant fashion. One of his eyes was badly blackened, and he was visibly suffering physically from the beating. Our brigade officer, Von Brinken, who was sitting next to him, asked him, "Do you really think that Germany is powerful enough to fight with the entire world?"

"Yes," answered the German. And this answer remained in my memory forever. "We may lose the war . . . but not here."

This time we crossed the border towards the west from the line of Mlawa-Soldau in the general direction of Lautenburg-Deutsch-Eylau. The presence of fresh hostile forces was discovered immediately: a horse patrol, cyclists, and a foot patrol of the standing army appeared. Nevertheless, towards evening, without having met opposition, yet surrounded on all sides by German reconnaissance units, we reached Lautenburg, which was deserted. The staff division stopped at a nearby estate, where there was not a soul, but the farm was full of cattle and poultry. I particularly remember a large flock of geese. The owner, naturally, ran off in a hurry. Despite the strict order given to the lower ranks not to touch anything, each member of the Cossack sotnia, in the presence of the staff, soon had a decapitated goose tied to his saddle.

Early in the morning on this day our Dragoons and Ulans were attacked on the western border of Lautenburg, and towards evening we had to abandon the town, having placed a guard close to its eastern border. At the same time, the infantry drew quite near us, and our staff division remained all night on the line which was being patrolled by the guards of the 22nd Infantry Division.

We were quartered in a small, clean village, and like all those in the surrounding area, it had been abandoned by its residents. Having dispatched the orders for the following day, I went out late at night to get a breath of fresh air. All was quiet. Suddenly, I heard an uproar from a crowd and saw that infantry soldiers were looting a grocery and wine shop. An officer impotently yelled at the mob, but no one heard him. I reported this to staff and our guard sotnia was sent to the wine cellar and dispersed the burglars. At that moment, the neighboring house burst into flames, but they were quickly extinguished. Someone shouted that they had found the German who set the fire. An extremely old man, who probably had no place to flee, was dragged out into the street and beaten to death.

Yet one must not forget that all who broke through the barrier of the patrol guard found themselves in immediate combat against our regiments who were already engaged in battle.

I remembered my conversation with General Krymov when we were crossing the border, and I expressed astonishment that the Germans were determined to fight all of Europe.

"Germany is very strong," replied Krymov. "She has strict discipline, and each soldier knows exactly what he is doing. Do not indulge yourself in hope for an easy victory. It will be very difficult to handle her."

I then recalled what the captain of the Zeppelin had said, seeing our confusion in Mlawa: "We may be defeated . . . But not here . . ."

"And His Own Received Him Not"[9]

The II Army was advancing and yielding to the right, securing our left flank on the side of Thorn. Therefore, the I Army Corps, which was moving forward on that same flank, entered Germany last, as at that time the rest of the Corps was already engaged in battle. For the second day, the distant rumbling of guns reached our ears from the right, but today, August 10, the fighting arose in our immediate vicinity, from our rear and a little to the right, towards the 22nd Infantry Division which followed behind us. The supporting unit of this division, after spending the night with us,

9. From the Bible: "He came unto his own, and his own received him not" (John 1:11).

separated and turned towards the shooting. Meanwhile, our regiments of the 15th Cavalry Division occupied Lautenburg again. The enemy who had pushed them out the day before had slipped away during the night. The Sixth Cavalry Division, after completing its assignment, moved to the north. But very soon we received an order from the Staff of the Army: "Attack the Germans who are pressing our advance infantry units in the direction of Soldau." This was evidently the crossfire that we had heard in the morning to our rear. From this order, we also learned that our Army Staff was crossing over to Neidenburg.

We turned directly east to a high point between Usdau and Soldau, from where the shots had come in the morning. There should have been units of our 22nd Division to the right of us but instead, as we discovered later, they proved to be much further south; from the north on the left moved our lateral advance guard—the Kliastitsky Regiment. The area was dry, open, and hilly to the north and swampy to the south. After traversing eight or ten versts, we came out on a field, which bore signs of a recent battle. One discarded gun remained; many spent shells were scattered around; and here and there were quickly dug trenches . . . One could have thought that the Germans had put pressure on our neighbors, as was stated in the orders that we had received, and now were pursuing them to Soldau. At that time we were supposedly to their rear. However, our horse patrols sent south in the direction of Soldau very quickly reported that the enemy was not to the south of us. Stepanov sent me to our lateral advance guard, to order it to dispatch our scouts north. I found Colonel Gamzagurdi[10] at the head of his Kliastitsky Regiment, riding as if on parade. He pointed out to me the obvious position of the Germans, about two versts to the north. At that moment, as if in confirmation of his words, German artillery opened fire on us. In this setting, one hypothesis remained: the enemy, having struck our infantry, had turned east, where heavy cannon fire was coming from. But this was much farther than Neidenburg, where our Army Staff was moving. The whole situation was very difficult to figure out.

It was decided: The Kliastitsky Regiment, entrenched on the heights it had traversed from the front to the side of the Germans who were firing on it, would join with Liubomirov going toward Lautenburg, and send out

10. Gamzagurdi, Sergei L'vovich.

scouts towards the Neidenburg side with orders to link up with the Army Staff who were on their way there. The remaining units of the division were stationed in a small village on the road to Soldau-Usdau, having one battery in position behind the Hussars.

Soon news came from Liubomirov that Lautenburg and the small village where we had spent the night were occupied by the enemy, who had driven them back to the south; and the horse patrol dispatched to the 22nd Division had returned and reported that units of the 22nd Division, which were moving forward, had opened fire on their own watch guards in the morning, giving rise to a vicious battle; panic ensued, and everyone ran towards Soldau. It was during that engagement that they had abandoned the gun we saw on the way out.

Thus went the third week since the inauguration of military action. We already had engaged in battle with the enemy, suffered casualties . . . The Germans were just concentrating their forces and getting ready to repulse us. Where were they? . . . We did not know.

For a long time, I was unable to come to my senses from all I had seen and lived through in the past twenty-four hours. Seeing the instability and our cavalry's unpreparedness for contemporary battle, I waited impatiently for the arrival of the infantry, which would know how to secure the area through which we had passed, and would not return every night to the barracks, as we had been doing. Finally, the infantry approached, and like a locust, destroyed everything in its path, plundered, beat up and killed peaceful citizens, demolished wine shops, got drunk, and with the first shot, retreated in panic. At least in the cavalry there was discipline, of which there was no evidence in the infantry.

Seeing my state of mind, Stepanov said, "You should not get so upset. It can always be rough at the beginning of war. We just don't know, but the Germans probably have the same problems. It is very difficult for all not to have a sense of self-preservation—both us and the enemy. Just wait, everything will even out, and we will begin to fight by entirely correct methods."

"For goodness sake, Colonel, Sir, more than two weeks has already passed, and by our calculations, the war cannot continue for more than three months. When will we have time to get used to it?"

"My dear young man, forget all of these book calculations. Remember that all of our army will be concentrated by Christmas, and only then, of course, will we be able to strike and bring them down.[11] Until then, we will have plenty of time to learn."

As much as I wanted to believe Stepanov, I could not accept that the Germans would allow their soldiers to plunder wine cellars, kill defenseless old men, and beat up a shot-down aviator. Very likely they had disturbances, and people who wrestled with feelings of self-preservation . . . but not at all to the degree that we experienced in the Soldau operation. We had much endurance, bravery . . . But we did not have enough culture, and instead of discipline, the law of the jungle guided us. To be rid of this by Christmas or even by some "future Christmas" after many years—could not be hoped for.

However, I never discussed this with Stepanov. He, like many of us, had not seen anything but Russia, and no matter what I had said, he would not have agreed with me.

Remote Reconnaissance

Liubomirov's retreat from Lautenburg on August 10, under pressure from the enemy, evidently increased Samsonov's concerns for our left flank, because by now our central corps had already traveled more than thirty versts to the north of Neidenburg, and our 15th Corps was attacking the Germans near Hohenstein. They were suffering great losses, but in spite of everything, moving farther ahead. For this reason, on the evening of the tenth, we received an order to reestablish the horse corps under the command of Liubomirov, under whom the staff of the corps was trained, and I was appointed to him as Chief Adjutant. With this appointment I was transferred into the 15th Division, because Liubomirov was still there.

That same evening we received instructions from the Staff of the Army, evidently written earlier: The Sixth and 15th Cavalry Divisions, which have moved out towards the village Loken, will proceed in the direction of the Heilsberg–Zinten front, cutting off the enemy's path of retreat to the Vistula, destroying railroads and bridges, and wiping out the rear supply lines.

11. Literally, "toss them about and wrap them around a ram's horn."

As it often happens, immediately after the formation of the corps the situation caused disunity in the division. Samsonov's quickly growing fear for the left flank of our army and, evidently, the supposition that new German units would come to the aid of the XIII German Army from the other side of the Vistula, generated his order: "The cavalry of General Liubomirov, after turning over one brigade to the I Army Corps for its use, is to defend the army's left flank on the Soldau–Thorn front." At the same time it was said that according to secret service intelligence, the enemy was concentrated in the area of Thorn.

Here I must tell you about our secret service, which I later became acquainted with while serving on the Army Staff. Our secret service was mainly, if not exclusively, based on so-called "double agents," that is, people who served on both sides. Naturally, neither Germany nor we gave them the chance to see or know what we did not want revealed to the enemy, but just the reverse, we took pains to give them only the information that we wanted passed on to our foe. It came to the point that both the Germans and ourselves were sending out falsehoods through the agents, in hopes that the enemy would believe them. I had to bring such an agent from the front blindfolded, interrogate him, pay him hundreds of thousands of rubles, and transport him back blindfolded. I recall a Jewish fellow whose nickname was "The American." He earned the highest pay, as I remember, merely because he was able to lie more plausibly than the others. So this kind of intelligence gathering became a staple of army routine. The Germans could not help knowing that such agents might expose our vulnerabilities—an outcome which we feared most of all; yet, at the same time, use of such agents made a certain strategic sense.

In the execution of this command, General Liubomirov ordered Roop to turn over one brigade to Artamonov, and to guard the nearest flank of the army with the remaining brigade. On the eve of the decisive battle near Soldau, he himself, along with the staff of the corps and the 15th Cavalry Division, advanced in the direction of Rypin–Thorn, which was one hundred versts from Soldau.

Thus, only part of the division was left to guard Lautenburg, from where General [Hermann von] Francois was preparing a death blow to the entire Russian advance into East Prussia. We retreated from there at first as a result of the chaos in the 22nd Division, in which the main forces of this division attacked their own patrol units, then and after that, clearly because of the secret agent's false information about the concentration of Germans in Thorn.

Today is October 4, 1957. I interrupted my writing in order to listen to the news: "Today Soviet Russia sent out the first satellite in space," the radio announced. Not too long ago the Soviets proclaimed that they were the first ones to send up an intercontinental missile. Step by step the Soviets have successfully expanded their border to gain access to the Mediterranean Sea, solving a thousand-year-old Russian problem—freeing the Dardanelles . . . and the people who took part in all this were probably the sons of Pet'ka Kokorev, Van'ka Enamushka, Dukhov, Zavrazhnyi, Medvedev,[12] led by the peasant Khrushchev[13] and commanded by Vakhmistr Zhukov,[14] under whose command "Berlin City" had been taken many years ago.

The Russian peasant had by then obtained a higher level of cultural development, the absence of which prevented him from defeating the enemy in East Prussia in 1914, and now is causing alarm throughout the world.

But I shall continue.

On August 11, we retreated from East Prussia and moved towards the west along the border in the direction of Rypin. The further we went from the booming guns, the more peaceful the area became. The Polish peasants stayed in their homes, and even the majority of the landowners were living on their estates completely in peace. We attributed this to the fact that the

12. These are the soldiers whom the author taught to read and write, as well as his childhood friends from his village.

13. Nikita Sergeevich Khrushchev (1894–1971) was a Russian political leader who rose from the humblest beginnings to become First Secretary of the Communist Party of the USSR (1953–64) and later Premier of the Soviet Union (1958–64).

14. Georgy Konstantinovich Zhukov (1896–1974) was the son of poor peasants who rose to the highest position in the Soviet military. He accepted the surrender of Germany for Russia near Berlin on May 8, 1945. After the war he was Commander in Chief of the Soviets' Troop Group in Germany and head of the Soviet Administration there. In 1953 he became First Deputy Minister of Defense of the USSR, and in 1955 Minister of Defense.

population of the border region had long ago grown accustomed to the idea of remaining in place in the event of war, in contrast to the Prussians, for whom the idea of our invasion was new and unacceptable.

Our retreat from the battle area inevitably led to the thought that we were doing something which we should not have done. We probably all felt this way in the staff. But it seemed that both Liubomirov and Shnabel were trying with great zeal to carry out to the letter all the prescribed orders which came from the rear. It appeared to me that we should have moved through German territory towards Thorn, where better roads emerged on that same flank of our army. And I want to assure the reader that I had this thought expressly AT THAT TIME, and not after all this ended—it was so obvious. I remember I even expressed this opinion to Shnabel in the form of a question:

"Colonel, Sir, which regiment will send the lateral advance guard forward on the German road along the border?"

"As much as is possible, our appearance in Thorn must be a surprise to our enemy," answered my former instructor in the Academy with a condescending smile—"Don't forget that we have a strategic task."

In spite of all the persuasive arguments made by the military theorists that strategy—the science of the theater of war, and tactics—the science of the battlefield, are essentially two separate subjects which should not be confused with one another, they do have one thing in common: common sense. And common sense said that our task was to look for the enemy in the area where he was and, if possible, not move any further away from him, so as to surprise him by our appearance there, where even with the poorest performance of our military skills, this tactic would have shocked him.

But was this really a strategic task? We were ordered to "guard the left flank of the army on the Soldau–Thorn front." To execute this, it seemed that Liubomirov should have sent a reconnaissance squadron to Rypin and Strasburg, and that he himself should have remained in the combat area. But somehow or other we retreated from the battlefield.

The soul grieved, but the body rejoiced. Our staff spent the night on a wealthy Polish estate, surrounded by a dense forest, where our hosts received us very hospitably, as only the Poles can do when they are willing.

An excellent home-cooked dinner, such as I had not eaten in more than a month, the pleasure of ladies' company, which we had been deprived of all this time, a soft bed with two clean sheets on which I settled my weary bones as soon as it was polite to leave for bed—all this helped me to forget for a while.

However, the night did not pass without a slight disturbance. Gunfire resounded from the forest. In the living room where some of our cornets were still dancing with the hosts' daughters, the music stopped, and the sound of running was heard. I dressed quickly and went out to the staircase where I saw my host walking up the stairs in a dressing gown and a night-cap carrying a candle. He was hurrying to see "Pan General." The General, also in his dressing gown, came out onto the landing. From the agitated conversation of the host, I realized that a German patrol, which had been stopping by from time to time ever since the hostilities began, apparently had shown up on the estate. Until now, however, he had not told us of his acquaintance with the Germans.

It was soon ascertained that the German patrol had actually run into our barrier. The horse of one of the German dragoons was killed from under him; he was taken prisoner and brought up to the estate. The dragoon was the same type of militiaman as we had seen on the border during the first days of the war. He was about thirty-five years old. He did not know of any recent concentration of troops in the area where he had been stationed with his squadron from the first day of mobilization, and the fact that the Landwehr was in the immediate vicinity meant that there were no German field forces between Soldau and Thorn.

In the morning, in spite of this, we continued our march to Thorn along that same road, and towards evening arrived in Rypin. According to the inhabitants of the town, there was still no sign of the Germans. Our reconnaissance units who were dispatched to Lipno-Vloclavek[15] reported that the right bank of the Vistula was free of the enemy; but the reconnaissance units who were sent to the border east of Thorn reported that many women were digging trenches on that very border. Liubomirov decided to march in that direction the following morning.

15. The Polish spelling is Wloclawek.

But just as soon as our radio station was set up and revealed our whereabouts, we received an order from the Staff of the Northwestern Front, signed by Zhilinsky, stating the following:

"The 15th Cavalry Division is to set forth immediately in a forced march to Neidenburg by the shortest route and reestablish communications with the Commander of the II Army."

There was a feeling of uneasiness about this order and very little understanding of it. First of all, it was not written in the customary way—it did not give any information on the situation nor on the enemy nor our own troops. It was evident that it had been written in a hurry. And the substance of the order—to reestablish communications with such an eminent force as the Army Staff—carried an ominous implication.

The radiogram was dated August 13. We received it during the morning of the fifteenth. It was one hundred versts to Neidenburg on a straight line. As is known, Samsonov died on the sixteenth of August. If we had not gone so far, maybe we would have been able to save our army commander.

An order was given to saddle our horses. In an hour we turned back on the same road, and after traveling fifty versts, we stopped to feed the horses. From the place where we were quartered on the night of the fifteenth, I was sent to the Staff of the I Army Corps for briefing.

Catastrophe

Very soon after I set out, I rode into a Polish village that had been burned to the ground. There I found our Glukhovsky Dragoons. A group of officers was gathered around the embers of a smoldering house; nearby lay a dead boar, and the very same Cornet Svimanov who had been the first to cross the German border was roasting shashlyk on his sword. Everyone looked tired. They welcomed me with great interest, expecting some news, and were disappointed to hear that I knew less than they. But here is what they did know: The previous day, after intense pressure from the enemy, the left flank of the I Army Corps and a brigade of the Sixth Cavalry Division had retreated from East Prussia. Roop had defended the position a few versts to the east with the Ulans. The Staff of the First Corps was still in Soldau.

The whereabouts of the Second Brigade of our division, and of General Shtempel' and the 11th Horse Battery, was not known.

Not losing any time, I set out for Soldau, trying to get on the road between Mlawa and Soldau, since the road immediately to the north was occupied by the enemy, according to the Glukhovsky Dragoons. The wooded area through which I traveled bore signs of a disorderly retreat: scattered cartridge cases, abandoned two-wheeled carts, a blood-stained cap, and a boot—probably removed from someone who had been wounded. Still at some distance, a sentry challenged me—this was the first infantry unit with which I had come in contact. The soldiers were digging trenches. A very young ensign directed me to the staff of the regiment. From there the person who worked the telephones took me to the staff of the division. The Chief of Staff, not large in stature, with a tuft of beard, long uncut blond hair, and bloodshot eyes (probably due to lack of sleep), came out of a peasant's hut. When I announced to him that the cavalry division was approaching his area, he regarded the news ironically: "What help can we get from the cavalry division? Don't you know what is happening to the right of us? Why are we getting orders directly from the staff of the front? Where is the Army Staff?" Not receiving an answer from me, he said that the Commander of the Corps was probably crossing into Mlawa now.

Finally I reached the road to Soldau, which, as far as the eye could see, was filled with retreating baggage wagons. There were two-wheeled equipment carts of the regiment, the division, and the artillery; wagon trains of the Red Cross transporting the wounded; there were also the slightly wounded, walking along the side of the road. Alternating with the Red Cross carts were wagons carrying personal property—household furniture and effects, including rugs, sofas, gilded picture frames—and, I particularly remember, an upright piano and a pot with flowers. In the course of time, I have thought about this pot quite often, and I wonder—Where were they taking it? No doubt these wagons belonged to the army dignitaries, because the horses were whipped forward by orderlies, and part of the load consisted of military packs.

The further I went the more disorderly it became, and the train of wagons quickly lost ground. Frequently the wagons turned over, scattering their baggage around, and in an attempt to save at least some of the load, the men were transferring it to other wagons. I could hear the rumbling of guns coming ever closer to the right of me, and when I approached the dam that O'Rem's Kliastitsky Regiment had attacked three weeks before, the bullets began whistling over my head. Many of the wagons were crowded together on the dam, and, with difficulty leading my horse by the reins, I crossed to the opposite bank of the Dzialdowo.

At the entrance to the dam, a colonel with a long beard, which was waving in the breeze, was sitting on his horse and cursing non-stop while trying to move the heaped-up wagons along it as quickly as possible.

"Damn you, where are you going? You were told to let the ammunition go ahead. Get rid of this junk!" he yelled as he saw one of the private carts pass by in front of him.

"This, Your Honor, is a cart that belongs to the Staff Corps," answered the baggage master. "This . . ."

"The hell with all of you! Get off the dam!" he said and knocked the cart over.

Next to the Colonel was a young officer who was observing me. I approached closer.

"Gasha! How did this happen? Is our regiment here?"

"No, during mobilization I became an orderly to the Commander of the First Corps. And how about you?"

Gasha Laiming was one of my favorite comrades in the regiment. We embraced, and for a moment were able to block out reality. But this moment was very short. We exchanged our sad thoughts and realized we both had the same opinion concerning the tragedy that was happening around us.

"Take me to the Commander of the Corps."

"He will not tell you anything. You better see the Chief of Staff. Artamonov is mentally disturbed right now. But if you wish, take a look at him yourself."

We entered a building which could have been a school or some kind of public establishment. In the entry hall there were several telephone and telegraph devices, a few communications' operators, and a crowd of officers, who, judging by their appearance, had come from the front lines. The Chief of Staff was not there—he had gone to the front. Gasha opened a door into a hall, and in the corner I saw a pulpit in front of an icon, before which General Artamonov himself was praying.

I recalled how this brilliant colonel on the General Staff had delivered a lecture to us about the Anglo-Boer War in the corps. And this is what I remembered he said, "The first shot was heard—the first blood was spilled."

This sounded so triumphal. And he seemed to us such a fearless hero . . . But now, prostrate on the floor, he was praying to the Russian God, begging Him to vanquish the German God and save his corps and himself . . .

In such a moment all values were re-evaluated.

We left him, and I communicated my order at once to the Lieutenant Colonel of the General Staff, who was running from room to room, and asked him to brief me in as much detail as possible about the present situation.

"General Artamonov is turning over his position as Commander of the Corps to General Dushkevich, who is still on the front. The staff will cross over to Mlawa tonight. The enemy is especially pressing against our right flank. Contact with the Army Staff and the forces to the right of us was lost long ago. The Third Guards Division in the direction of Neidenburg has suffered heavy losses. The Keksgolmsky Regiment has literally ceased to exist. What is going on further to the right of us is not known. Neidenburg is occupied by the Germans, and it will be necessary to look for our Army's Staff further to the east."

With this news I returned to Liubomirov, whom I found south of Mlawa in that very same Polish hut where the war had started for the Sixth Cavalry Division.

At this time Liubomirov already knew more than I did. He had received certain information from the Headquarters of the Supreme Commander in Chief, which began with these words: "In East Prussia our forces have suffered heavy losses . . ."

This is all that remained in my memory from the battle of Soldau. I was not in the heat of combat, but what was happening in my presence gave me the opportunity to form an opinion, perhaps a mistaken one, as to the cause of the catastrophe overtaking us.

It often occurred to me, What would have been the outcome if we had exchanged roles with the Germans at that time and were defending Prussia, and the Germans had attacked us from the Russian side? My deep conviction is that we would have been pushed to the sea and would have surrendered in Konigsberg instead of Tannenberg.

What was our problem? Certainly, the Russian people were not less courageous or self-sacrificing than the Germans. This was later proven in the Second World War. What was the reason for our disgrace?

It was customary to blame our diplomacy for not being able to protect the interests of our country. And fawning before European heads of state, we met their demands by changing our hundred-year-old established plan for defending our boundaries from aggressive adventures—in a locality eminently prepared by us to make attack difficult—and led one hundred thousand peasants into the Prussian swamps, which by nature could not have been better endowed for defense. There is truth in this. But every war is full of surprises; and in the entire history of war, there has never been one that was conducted according to a previously prepared plan. In preparing for war, a country must be able to adapt itself.

Above all, the commanders were held responsible for every failure. Zhilinsky, Rennenkampf, Samsonov, Artamonov, and others were blamed. It was said that Zhilinsky did not lead the army in the right direction. But this operation had been worked out before the war began and was ratified by Grand Duke Nikolai Nikolaevich. Zhilinsky had no grounds to change it.

It is generally accepted that Rennenkampf exaggerated his victory at Goldap, rested on his laurels, and did not pursue the enemy, giving it the opportunity to descend on Samsonov. It was even said that these two commanders were not on friendly terms, and were so jealous of each other that Rennenkampf purposely stopped in order to make victory difficult for his rival.

The victory of the I Army, of course, was exaggerated. But probably that is why he was unable to pursue the Germans vigorously. The personal machinations of these two scapegoats, surely, could not have played a role.

We advanced blindly, not having any information on the strength or the location of the enemy. The Germans knew all about us by reading our reports and orders, which were transmitted over the air without being encoded. Our reconnaissance depended on the cavalry, which, not knowing how to cope with enemy infantry, either remained inactive or were killed in vain during cavalry attacks. The Germans had airplanes and dirigibles—we had only one Farman biplane[16] in our I Army Corps, in which our fearless Cornet Voevodsky was able to fly over the German front and inform General Artamonov of the concentration of von Francois' entire corps behind the left flank of the first line of Artamonov, ready at any minute to attack his rear. For the first time Artamonov opened his eyes to the situation. He was frightened and ordered the corps to retreat from the whole front.

General Roop's First Brigade was assembled in front of Lautenburg where the First German Corps was concentrated. The Second Brigade with Shtempel and the 11th Horse Battery were in the direction of Neidenburg, and 15th Cavalry Division, as we saw, had withdrawn from the battlefield. Ludendorff[17] writes that Artamonov began his retreat solely under the influence of heavy artillery fire, and that there was no infantry attack. This once more confirms that the reason for retreat was fear for our left flank.

Thus our first aerial reconnaissance, instead of saving us, produced a catastrophe.

In the academy we had been told many times of the necessity for individual initiative in present-day war, not only by commanders of large, combined units, but also by all ranks in the army, including the lowest. There was even a phrase coined: "Each rank must take individual initiative." In fact, however, the need to prop up an already-shaky throne demanded that the person appointed to the post of General should above all show infinite devotion to that throne, and absolute submission to the Commander in Chief of the Armed Forces, Chairman of the Council of Defense, Grand Duke Nikolai Nikolaevich. This demand was passed down the line for appointment to all command duties, including those of noncommissioned officers, a rank to which factory workers, for example, would not be appointed no matter how capable they were. The privates too were

16. The 1914 model of this biplane was extensively used for artillery observation and reconnaissance in World War I. It was designed by the Farman brothers, Henri (1874–1958) and Maurice (1877–1964). These aviators were born in Paris to British parents and played an important role in the history of aviation. They merged their interests in the Farman works at Boulogne-sur-Seine in France and manufactured many planes of the pusher biplane type for military and training purposes.

17. Erich Ludendorff (1865–1937) was a German general. A disciple of Schlieffen, he served through the First World War as Chief of Staff of Field Marshal Hindenburg. It is generally believed that Ludendorff was the brain behind Hindenburg's decisions.

educated in that same spirit: They did only what was ordered and only so long as someone was watching them. Often when we advanced across the line of the sentry posts, we could see that at the same time and on the same soil, the German had dug his trench deep enough to fire while standing up, but our guard roughly shoveled the earth barely deep enough to protect his head while firing lying down.

The revolutionary ferment in the nation beginning in 1905 undermined the soldiers' confidence in their officers, and it was very difficult to maintain discipline among the reserves who were called up.

In the battle of Soldau, all the weeping wounds of our sick organism were revealed, like a photographic negative being lowered into the developer. This engagement was the first decisive jolt that helped to overthrow the old regime in Russia, and I deeply believe that even if Russia had concluded peace immediately after it, the revolution would still have been unavoidable.

Our first clash with Germany showed us that our illiterate masses could not achieve victory in Europe, however brave and self-sacrificing they were. "PERHAPS WE WILL LOSE THE WAR," the German prisoner told us at Soldau, "BUT NOT HERE." And at that time we all felt that he was right. After Soldau everyone in Russia recognized this. Yet in the long run no force on earth could hold back Russia's desire for learning. And we see that now even the Bolsheviks cannot ignore a literate populace. It is said that the village schoolteacher, credited as the source of a powerful, united Germany, won the Franco-Prussian War.[18] In Russia before the First World War, such teachers did not exist.

Here I am waiting for an objection: "How can you explain the fact that the same Russian Army, with the same command personnel, and during the very same time, smashed the Austro-Hungarian Army in Galicia?"

The answer to this is that the Austro-Hungarian Empire, by virtue of its social structure, similar to Russia's, was doomed to destruction. In addition to this, with its ethnic composition, Austria-Hungary could not hope to win the war with Russia. The Czechs, Poles, and Galicians, taking the easy way out, surrendered to us and went into our ranks, forming our Polish

18. 1870–71.

and Czech units. Field Marshal Conrad von Hoetzendorff[19] was far from being a poor strategist, and in the area of Krasnik, where his orders were carried out, he was successful. Even in the area of L'vov,[20] where we had three times as many forces, he managed to lead his deeply-suffering army over to the other side of the San River.[21] And as a result, their defeat at L'vov was not as disgraceful as the captivity of our II Army at Soldau.

In the Turkestan Corps

The II Army was destroyed. But the Russian people just scratched their heads and got angry. From the depths of Siberia and Turkestan came fresh forces. And these troops were brand new and of a type that was unknown to me up till that time. Having grown up under harsh conditions from birth, and being accustomed to struggling with nature and showing initiative in that struggle, they knew instinctively how best to attack the enemy and how to defend themselves, without waiting to receive orders from above. The commanders were also different: There was less class distinction between them and the lower ranks than was the case in European Russia. Few of the officers were nobility, and the only difference between the soldiers and the officers was in their degree of education. They spoke among themselves in a simple human language, which at first was even harsh on my ears, because I used to hear such expressions as: "Exactly" instead of "Yes," or "In no way" instead of "No," or a more stupid expression, "I am not able to know" instead of "I don't know." These expressions were not innate to the Siberians or the Turkestanis. Being descendants of people who never knew serfdom, they came to consciously defend their way of life, which suited them and which they did not seek to change.

Even public opinion was taken by surprise, that is, the opinion of that educated part of the population which Petersburg had disregarded up till now. Under its influence, they began to appoint generals to command posts no longer according to their demonstrated fidelity to the monarchy, but

19. Chief of Staff of the Austro-Hungarian forces.
20. Lemberg (German).
21. Approximately seventy miles west of L'vov.

according to their ability. Ruzsky,[22] Alekseev,[23] Polivanov[24] . . . were called in. In an effort to assist the military department, army supply, and the medical division, the Union of Cities and Zemstvo Union were created. Until now, all this had been done as a token of a sincere desire to help the Emperor during difficult days in the defense of the motherland. Our disaster on the front not only did not turn the people against the sovereign, but the reverse; it evoked in them a sense of great devotion to the throne, together with a realization of the need to save the homeland.

All this did not fail to have an effect at the front. In difficult battles near Lodz and at the Bzura River, even though we were not victorious, we held the Bzura and stood in defense of Warsaw.

At this time I had already been given the official duty of subaltern officer

22. Nikolai Vladimirovich Ruzsky (1854–1918) graduated from the General Staff Academy in 1881. He served as Chief of Staff of the Second Manchurian Army in 1904–05. In 1909 he became a general of the infantry and also a member of the Military Council of the Ministry of War. He worked on the development of regulations, including the Field Service Regulations of 1912. When World War I broke out, he commanded the III Army; then from September 1914 till March 1915, the Northwestern Front; and in July–August 1915, the VI Army (with an interruption from December 1915 until August 1916). He later retired on account of his health.

23. Mikhail Vasilevich Alekseev (1857–1918) was a Russian general and Chief of Staff (1915–17) of Nicholas II. Early in World War I, he planned the successful Russian offensive into Galicia and served for a time on the Northeastern Front. He became Chief of the General Staff in August 1915 and assumed control of all Russian armies in the European theater. His job was made difficult by the growing divergence between Russian public opinion and the wishes of the imperial court. Along with other officers, he urged the Tsar to abdicate in favor of the Tsarevich in order to save the dynasty. He was suspended from duty in 1916 when his intention to present the emperor with a peremptory demand for reform became known. When Nicholas abdicated in March 1917, Alekseev was appointed Commander in Chief under Kerensky. He resigned two months later in protest against the provisional government's failure to suppress defeatism and anarchy in the army. After the overthrow of Kerensky's government, Alekseev and General Kornilov organized an anti-Bolshevik force (the White Army) in the south, in the area of the Don.

24. Aleksei Andreevich Polivanov (1855–1920) was a Russian general who was appointed in 1915 as Minister of War to revitalize the sagging Russian war effort. He reorganized the military production and supply system as well as the army's training program. He unsuccessfully tried to dissuade Tsar Nicholas II from personally assuming supreme command of Russia's armed forces in September 1915. In March 1916, Nicholas dismissed Polivanov from his ministry at the instigation of the empress, Aleksandra. He was said to be a capable administrator of liberal sympathies. He later offered his services to the Red Army in February 1920 and was a military expert at the Soviet-Polish peace talks in 1920 at Riga, where he died of typhus.

for errands on the Staff of the I Turkestan Army Corps, which was located in the direction of Mlawa.

The corps was under the command of General Sheideman, who recently had been removed to this duty from his post as Commander of the Army. I did not know the reason for his removal. But judging from his effective performance, which I witnessed in the Turkestan Corps, one must assume that he was a victim of his German name. His Chief of Staff was a young colonel of short stature with a bristly, bushy mustache, quick in his movements and in whatever he did, with a definite Polish accent to his Russian; he wore the uniform of one of the Siberian Rifle Regiments with a St. George's Cross[25] on his chest. His name was Yanuary Kazimirovich Tsikhovich. This man, under whose command I happened to serve, left an indelible impression on my character, and in the course of one year taught me far more military science than all that I had learned in the previous ten years of service. At first I was repulsed by him. But his untiring energy, his evenhanded respect towards everyone—seniors and juniors—his perseverance in carrying out a decision once made, his complete fearlessness in the face of death, his constant willingness to go forward and set an example for others, his particular ability to clearly formulate a given order so that it conveyed its full rationale—these things gave me confidence in his leadership, so that I could follow him into battle without fear. Most interesting of all was that he was not waging war for Russia, because being a Pole, he could not have liked Russia; it was not on account of religion, because when it became necessary, he without hesitation had changed from the Catholic to the Orthodox faith in order to enter the General Staff Academy. As a Pole, he could not have felt respect for the Tsar. He could not have been called a mercenary, because he did not serve for the pay, and he was least of all interested in money. To him, military duty was an art, to which he was devoted as to a favorite sport.

The corps, which grew quickly from five divisions into a small army, was actually under his command. But all the orders were given in the name of, and with the knowledge of, the Corps Commander. Ordinarily, before adopting an operational decision, Tsikhovich listened to the opinions of all of us in the ranks of the operative division, then went to the Commander of the Corps and brought back his instructions, which were immediately

25. One of the highest honors given to a military man.

edited. He himself took each newly arriving officer on his staff to the firing line, and only the ones who carried out his orders calmly under fire gained his trust. Those who could not take the heat quickly disappeared to the rear.

One time Tsikhovich summoned me to compose an order to the division commander, and I included in the order this sentence: "The Commander of the Corps fears for your flank and advises you to take caution to protect it." "Fyodor Sergeyevich, remove from your vocabulary the words *fear* and *caution*," Tsikhovich told me. "Military men can never be afraid of anything! Write: 'The Commander of the Corps considers it necessary . . .' " Since then, to this very day, I have avoided using these words.

Tsikhovich did not know what rest was, slept very little, and demanded from all of us the full measure of our strength.

I arrived at his staff headquarters at eleven in the evening after traveling forty versts on horseback along a muddy road. And this is what I heard from him: "Staff Rotmistr, you have arrived just in time. Sit down here, and I will give you the details of the situation and an order with which you will go to meet the 11th Siberian Rifle Division. I will give you an automobile and you will go immediately."

The idea of getting some sleep in the automobile proved illusory. I was given an American Ford—the only car which could withstand our roads. But in those days, the ride along miry dirt roads roughened by baggage trains was far from inviting. In spite of chains, the wheels ran into the ruts and sank in the mud. The automobile had to be dug out and pushed an endless number of times in order to start the motor. For each car there was a chauffeur and his helper, but in spite of this, they and the passenger became exhausted. It took eight hours to cover the thirty versts which separated Ciechanow from the place where I met the Siberians, and that only thanks to the fact that towards morning the road froze slightly, and instead of raining it began to snow.

The 11th Siberian Rifle Division, which was advancing from Omsk when mobilization was declared, arrived at the front at the end of October. When I met them, they had just disembarked from the train. Heading up the division was the 44th Regiment. In front was a detachment of scouts dressed in sheepskin caps, riding small Siberian horses, led by a very young second lieutenant, whose rosy cheeks were still adorned with peach fuzz. After learning that I was a staff officer, he immediately took me to the

Commander of the Regiment. In his conversation and movements he was the embodiment of youthful enthusiasm. He was clearly proud of his duty as leader of the detachment of scouts, and happily informed me that he had already collected some information concerning the enemy, and had sent reconnoiterers to be in communication with the Turkestanis. On his chest in a micaceous wrapper hung a map marked with red pencil. He was already prepared to describe the details of his future plans of action as we came up to a group of officers, among whom was Colonel Alekseev, the Commander of the Regiment. He was a short, elderly man who, when war broke out, had apparently been serving out his final year before retirement. He had a long, rather narrow goatee, like those depicted on the icons of the saints. And on the whole, he resembled an aged man of God much more than a commander of a regiment. A modest, shy, quiet person, he heard me out and beamed with pleasure when he learned that I had been sent to lead the regiment into the line of fire and to help him orient himself to the surroundings.

"This is excellent. It means you will lead us," he said. "Here is our adjutant, Aleksandr Innokentievich. He will deliver your orders to the battalion." And several times he repeated, "How nice. How nice."

Quite frequently I had to meet with the commanders, who were gladdened by my arrival, because I brought them orders from the top, which relieved them from making their own decisions. Alekseev was one of them. He was neither a Guards' officer nor an officer on the General Staff; he made a way for himself by obedience, expedition, and skill in getting along with everyone. He did not have any pull with the upper echelons. And all this made him especially careful.

In every military union there must be one brain and one will. In the 44th Regiment the brain was Regimental Adjutant Aleksandr Innokentievich. He knew everything, remembered everything, and was even-handed, patient, and polite with everyone. This instilled respect for him. His orders were trusted and carried out faithfully. But there wasn't the will in the regiment to capably make decisions and take risks. And in spite of all the positive qualities of his ranks, the excellent material which the soldiers were made of, the regiment needed this will from without. And it came from Tsikhovich, who told me as he was sending me off, "You know, the Commander of the Regiment there is weak. You will have to prod him all the time. If there is any holding back, report to me immediately." Tsikhovich evidently knew Alekseev, but how he could have judged from the first glance that I, or anyone, was capable of prodding him, was incomprehensible to me. However, these words helped me force myself to do it, and Tsikhovich, being a good psychologist, of course knew this.

After relaying the report of the situation to Alekseev and pointing out the area where he had to deploy, I asked for a horse, and along with the young second lieutenant, rode ahead with the detachment of scouts.

Less than half an hour had passed when a scout came galloping towards us and reported that within a half verst ahead on the road we were traveling was a small village from which shots had been fired at him. We still moved farther ahead, saw the village, and dismounted. A decision was made to pass by the village in lines.

Just as the formation was dispersing and proceeding over a field freshly covered with snow, we heard machine-gun fire from the village, and the line took cover. Close to the road there was a cemetery surrounded by a low brick wall, behind which we hid. I took out my binoculars, poked my head out from behind the wall, and began to survey the village. What I saw was one German after another running over and gathering behind the hut nearest us. I passed the binoculars to the second lieutenant and pointed out the hut to him. He, evidently wanting to show how brave he was, stood up to his full height. I had just twisted around to the other side toward the sergeant major, who was lying down beside me, and started to explain what I had seen, when suddenly I heard a thud to the right of me. I looked around and saw the second lieutenant lying motionless on the ground. A deadly pallor spread over his cheeks, rosy only a few seconds before. There was a small hole near his temple, and just a trickle of blood. Peach fuzz still covered his youthful face. A moan of grief came from the sergeant major. But at that moment the firing intensified, and each of us turned our thoughts to how to protect ourselves.

Shortly after that, to the right and to the left of me I saw the advancing lines of the 44th Regiment, and the commander of the battery creeping towards me with a field telephone. The battle began, and again, just as in the cavalry, everything was carried out as it had been learned in peacetime; but here, in contrast to the cavalry, there was a feeling of stability. It was evident that the regiment was well prepared. The lines ran over and

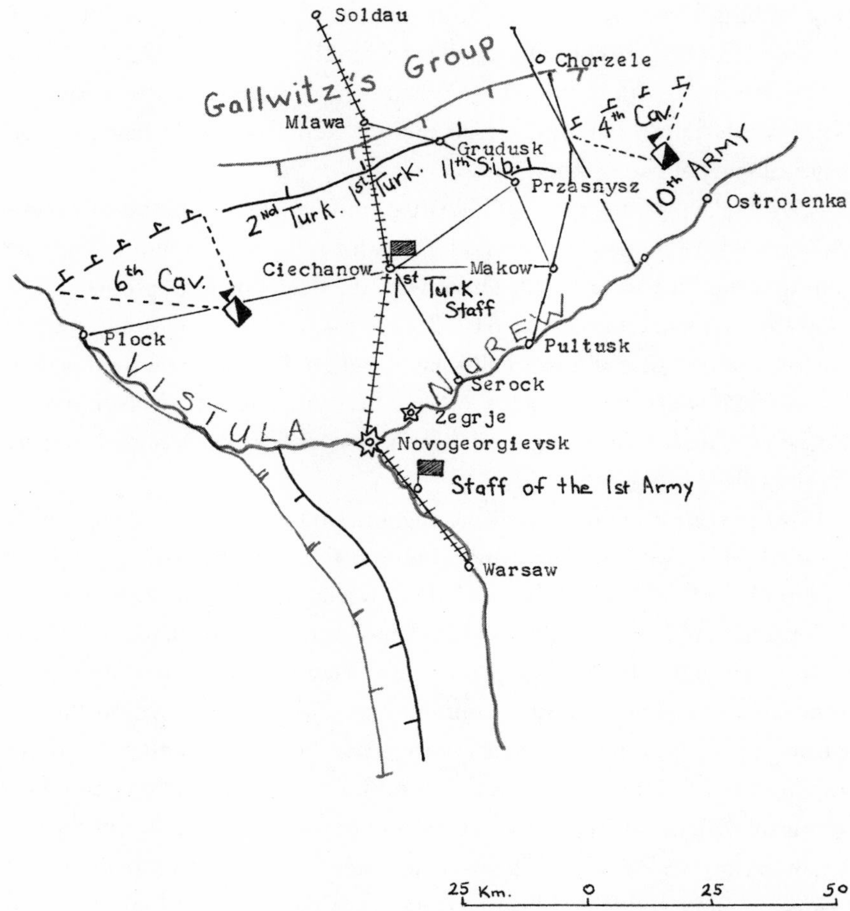

Position on February 1, 1915.

grouped together as in a review, and only little heaps, which no longer moved, remained in places behind them on the white snow. Here and there were wounded men crawling, and towards them crept the stretcher bearers. They crept towards me, too, and carried away the corpse of my young companion in arms. Also approaching us stealthily was the Commander of the Fourth Battalion, Innokenty Innokentievich (I forget his last name), with whom I later frequently played the card game Preference in the dugout. He was a short, dry-witted, swarthy lieutenant colonel with such extraordinarily sparkling eyes. A telephonist crawled up along with him, and so many commanders collected behind the wall with us that one shell could have annihilated us all and stopped our advance. Leaving the gunner in place, we ran over behind a nearby knoll.

At that moment a German plane flew over us in the direction of the Germans. Our gunner promptly set fire to the hut nearest us with a grenade. The German firing became considerably weaker, and the Fourth Battalion approached the village and very quickly and decisively passed through the entire settlement, which had been abandoned by the Germans. We rapidly crossed through there and followed them, along with the Staff of the Regiment. The frightened inhabitants of the huts crawled out from all the crevices and cellars.

The Adjutant notified me that news had come from the Turkestanis that the enemy was retreating in front of them, and I was informed by the staff division that my mission had been accomplished, and that on Tsikhovich's orders I was to return to Ciechanow.

Staff of the Corps

The I Turkestan Army Corps consisted of the First and Second Turkestan Rifle Divisions. Subsequently included were the 11th Siberian Rifle Division, the 63rd Infantry, the Third Turkestan Rifle Company, the Ussuriisk Horse Brigade, and the Sixth Cavalry Division. In this manner the corps was deployed in a small army group whose duty was to defend the approaches towards Warsaw from the side of East Prussia. Likewise, opposite us with a staff in Mlawa, operated the [German] army group of General Gallwitz,[26] whose forces, like ours, changed depending upon the general situation.

As I mentioned before, our corps was under the command of General of the Cavalry Sheideman. He was a serious, well-educated man, who had served a long time in the line and knew well what to expect from a commander subordinate to him and from a private soldier. He was even capable of making a bold decision—a quality which was very rare in our generals of that time. But having just endured a distressing shock in the battles near Lodz, where, it was said, he did not display enough firmness, he completely

26. Max von Gallwitz (1852–1937).

trusted Tsikhovich. Sheideman had a few small faults: he liked comfort, adored attention, and retained three adjutants under him instead of one staff officer. Among the adjutants was his son, who was never there. Not being of illustrious birth, Sheideman knew well the value of patronage and the necessity of pleasing the powers that be. In this instance, he was probably depending upon General Sukhomlinov[27] for his fate. But as a whole, the combination of Sheideman and Tsikhovich was one of the fortunate ones, and was primarily responsible for the only victory in the entire war on the German Front, in February 1915.

I was the youngest of the General Staff officers on the staff of the corps. Lieutenant Colonel Bagratuni was older, but we both played the same role, that is, constantly running about. There were two captains who held the positions of staff clerks, and two ensigns were assigned to help them. Each day from eight in the morning till late in the evening, the officers of the staff sat around a large table with Tsikhovich at its head, so that he could see all of us and vigilantly watch to be sure that no one remained idle. He continually found work for us, and these projects always seemed very necessary.

Of all my colleagues, I remember two who were completely opposite types: Senior Adjutant in the supply unit Captain Ponyrko and Ensign Count Tolstoy. The first one lived near the baggage train beyond the immediate observation of the Chief of Staff and dealt with an aspect of military service which was most useless to the war: collecting and paying out money. Not that the men no longer needed money. It was just as necessary as always. But for the majority, the main concern was survival, and worry

27. Vladimir Aleksandrovich Sukhomlinov (1848–1926) was a graduate of the General Staff Academy (1874) who went on to become Minister of War (1909). He was said to have been responsible for Russia's premature and unprepared entry into World War I. He assured the government of the readiness of the Russian troops, yet as the war continued, operations were hampered by shortages of arms, ammunitions, and supplies, even as he continued to insist that all was well. In June 1915, he was dismissed and replaced by General A. A. Polivanov. Despite Sukhomlinov's close connections with the Tsar, public sentiment forced his arrest in March 1916 on charges from the Duma of corruption, malfeasance, and treason. He was freed six months later at the instigation of the Tsar, but rearrested by the provisional government after the Revolution. He was found guilty in 1917 and sentenced to life at hard labor, which was later commuted to confinement in a fortress. In 1918, because of his advanced age, he was released, and he emigrated to Finland and then to Germany where he died.

about money was not felt as acutely, and the value given it was less. People such as Ponyrko, who lived almost as in peacetime, capitalized on these circumstances. The officers needed the money not on the twentieth of each month, but at the time when they were in the rear. And this Ponyrko took into consideration. Given a receipt, he would provide the money ahead of time. Behind his disbursing office was his apartment, where his friends—and everyone was his friend—could have a drink, a bite to eat, and play a game of cards. Ponyrko himself loved to play and usually won. Subsequently, during the Revolution, I happened to encounter him. At that time he was running a gambling house. But more on him later.

Pavel Mikhailovich Tolstoy was my roommate when I spent the night at staff headquarters. He was less than thirty years of age and was a university graduate in law. Tolstoy belonged to that part of the Russian intelligentsia which recognized that the existing order in Russia must be changed. However, in contrast to his namesake, Leo Tolstoy, even though he was a wealthy man he had no intention of giving away his land or his riches to anyone. He was full of contradictions: As a student, he had associated with an organization which considered terror to be a means of attaining an end, and once was even under investigation for the murder of the governor. He managed to clear himself, but nevertheless his reputation remained tarnished. Moreover, he liked to be addressed as Count, and was exquisitely polite and obliging to those who surrounded him, and these qualities made our poor Turkestani plebeians feel that he was not their sort and that only the war had forced him to associate with them. Like all of us, he was militarily minded, and often allowed himself to criticize the men on the front lines, but instead of joining the line, he stayed in the rear engaged in office duties. For some reason he favored me, maybe because I was the only one on the staff who was not awed by his title of Count.

Whenever I returned from the front, we would exchange impressions. I told him what was going on in the trenches, and he related what orders had been issued during my absence and what information had been received from the other fronts. At that time, we both were extremely optimistic, and wished only to quickly reach the turning point and march into Berlin. The future looked rosy to us, although we disagreed when it came to the question of the organization of this future. It always seemed to me that his stereotyped ideal of a constitutional state modeled on those of Europe would not be suitable for us—and we did not argue about the details. In general I avoided any political discussions with him.

However, more and more frequently, we began to hear unpleasant news from the rear. It came from people whom we called Zem-Hussars, which meant that they were representatives of zemstvo and city unions who, as I mentioned previously, had been organized as a result of the population's patriotic zeal to help the army and the government in their difficult trials. But this help, naturally, entailed control of the persons appointed as representatives; and, of course, this control gave them knowledge not only of such matters as supplies delivered to the front, but also the distribution of troops, their actions, their commanders, and the claims being made by the lower personnel to their superiors. The same thing was happening in the rear, where the same general control collided with the organs of the army and the government. Irresponsible criticism began to spread, and the Zem-Hussars carried the gossip from the front to the rear, and from the rear to us at the front. All this was profoundly disgusting to us military professionals and seemed to have a corrupting effect on the army. Even though Tsikhovich politely accepted the Zem-Hussars, he openly expressed indignation at their attempts to meddle in affairs which did not concern them.

Tolstoy, however, could not understand this, and when one such zemstvo representative, Vasily Vasilevich Vyrubov, who had been his comrade in the university, visited him, I inadvertently witnessed their discussions in our room. Vyrubov was the brother-in-law of the famous Annushka[28] Vyrubova.[29] He himself was married to a very wealthy landowner, Olga Vasilevna Galakhova, and through her played a role in the zemstvo circles. He was a clever politician, always trimmed his sails to the wind, and was a friend to all those who he thought might be useful to him in the future. He, like Tolstoy, was inclined to be progressive, and just like Tolstoy, had no intention of parting with his land. During Kerensky's time, they both made a career: Tolstoy as Kerensky's personal secretary and Vyrubov as his minister on the Staff of the Supreme Commander in Chief.

28. Nickname for Anna.

29. Anna Vyrubova, a young widow, was the go-between for the Empress. A violently emotional friendship existed between them, and she was as much under the spell of Rasputin as the Empress was. (Tisdall, *The Dowager Empress.*)

The conversation between Vyrubov and Tolstoy on political topics regarding the Duma and the Cabinet Ministers, whom I only knew by name, reminded me of the jargon of thieves, and was comprehensible only to the initiated. When the conversation touched on the management of the army, our misfortunes on one front or another, accusations against one commander or another based exclusively on gossip, it began to annoy me, and I strongly objected. I did so not because I did not believe them, but because these questions were beyond their sphere of competence. However, among the many things I learned first from them was that there were rumors of discord between Tsarskoe Selo and the Staff of Grand Duke Nikolai Nikolaevich because they were jealous of the Grand Duke's popularity. There was talk of the crushing of Rennenkampf's I Army and about the treason of Colonel Miasoedov, who might have been the cause of our failure in East Prussia. Finally, they spoke about the suspicions held by the general public toward the Empress, accusing her of being sympathetic to the Germans almost to the point of being a traitor. Having known the Empress, I understood why they reproached her, but at the same time I was deeply convinced that all these accusations were groundless, the kinds of cruelties of which only thoughtless people were capable.

When meeting with the Zem-Hussars I always lost my spiritual equilibrium, and only came to my senses when I was again in the trenches, where from day to day there was an elemental struggle for life, and where, for the time being, there were no other problems.

The Battle of Przasnysz

At the very beginning of 1915, after a series of tenacious frontal attacks at the Bzura River west of Warsaw, the Germans, having thrown reinforcements into East Prussia, conducted attacks on our forces who were occupying the front on the northern shore of the Narew River and on those on the right flank of the Northwestern Front, which had continued to occupy the eastern part of East Prussia.

These attacks, if successful, would expel the Russians from their territory, giving them the opportunity to reach the rear of our armies who were advancing in front of Warsaw by means of a swift movement across the

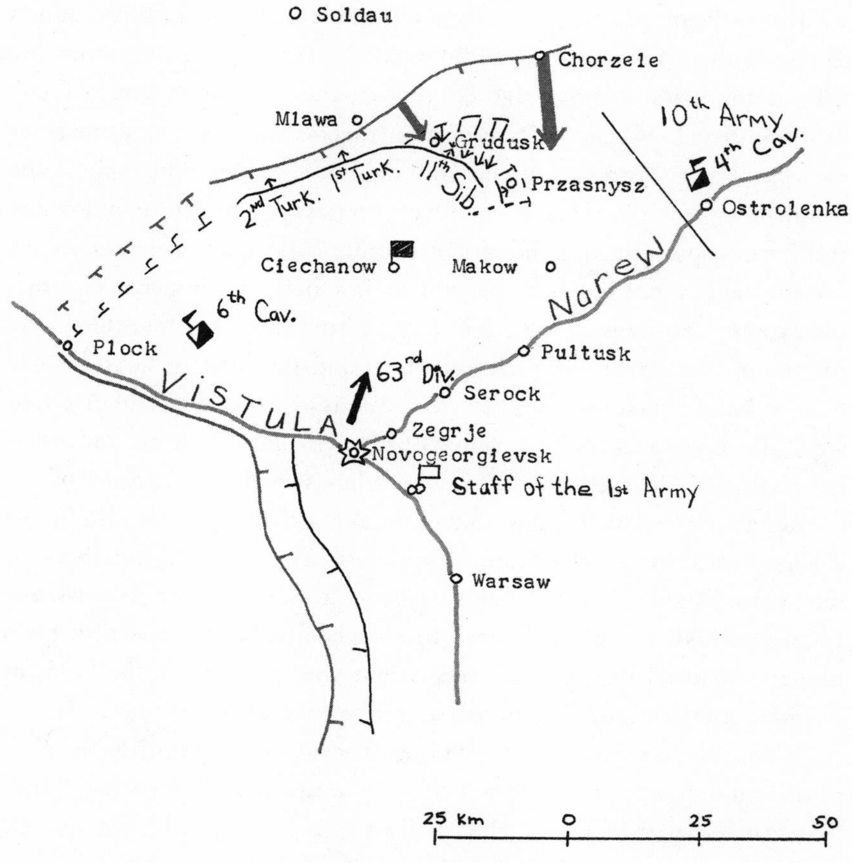

Position on February 10, 1915.

Bug-Narew Rivers and thereby gain the strategic victory that had thus far eluded them.

The first in a series of such blows struck our Turkestan Corps, which had three divisions spread along sixty versts of the front. Our right flank near Przasnysz was at the same time the right flank of our I Army. To the east of Przasnysz was a marshy expanse guarded by one division of the Fourth Cavalry, which formed part of the X Army. This whole area had only one road from the Prussian side, from Chorzele to Makow-Pultusk, which was useless during the summer for the movement of large forces. But in the winter it froze and became passable. All this was known both to the Germans and to us, and Tsikhovich tried to keep in close contact with our

Fourth Cavalry Division; he sent airplanes, which we had now acquired, to patrol the length of this road, and repeatedly emphasized to the Army Staff the necessity of moving the infantry in this direction.

His expectations were soon realized. During the first days of February, the Germans brought down the small town of Grudusk, halfway between Przasnysz and Mlawa, with heavy artillery, wiped it off the face of the earth; and in a night attack, took over our trenches. A major portion of the Fourth Battalion of the 44th Siberian Regiment perished here along with their commander—my partner in the game of Preference in calmer days—Innokenty Innokentievich (I have forgotten his last name).

The entire reserve of the corps was launched towards the heights near Grudusk, and we were able to secure it and hold the road leading to Przasnysz under heavy gunfire.

During this time the aviators informed us that a column not less than a division in strength was advancing towards Makow from the side of Chorzele. These troops could be expected to approach the heights of Przasnysz in twenty-four hours. At approximately this same time the just-formed second string of the 63rd Infantry Division was due to reach Przasnysz from Novogeorgievsk. Thus, on the following day a confrontation between the two divisions could be expected somewhere near Przasnysz.

All day we had no information about the enemy's movement from Chorzele. The Fourth Cavalry Division had apparently broken off from us, evacuating towards Ostrolenka, and if it reported anything, it was reported to the staff of its own X Army. We in the staff of the corps also got no information from our aviation squadron, which was under the command of the Army Staff. As a result, the Commander of the 63rd Division, while passing Corps Headquarters as he was going through Ciechanow, was informed only about what we had learned the previous day.

The division was ordered to occupy and defend Przasnysz. I was ordered to lead the division to Przasnysz and remain with its staff during the operation. I reported to the commander of the division in Ciechanow. The general, elderly, stout, and openly good natured, was looking for support from anyone. The Chief of Staff, a very nervous colonel, was probably not much help to him. It was immediately clear to me that the division was under the command of the Commander of the Artillery Brigade—an even-tempered, sensible colonel with a St. George Cross on his chest. He had the last word

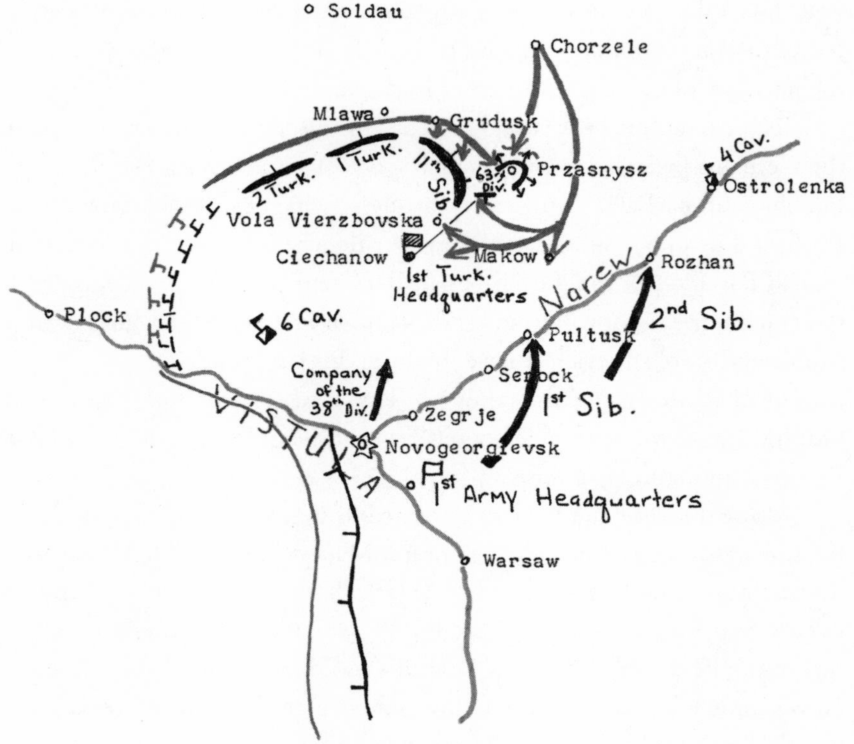

The night of February 13, 1915.

on any decision, and when it was spoken, it became law. It was quite evident that everyone was used to this.

The division was already halfway to Przasnysz when, along with the Colonel of the Artillery, we went forward to reconnoiter.

The sounds of cannon fire from the direction of Grudusk were ever increasing as we rode into the city in the afternoon. The residents had stayed in town—they were already used to the fact that Przasnysz had changed hands several times, but their faces showed grave concern. The Roman Catholic Church was holding mass, and it was filled to capacity. Those who were unable to get inside were kneeling outside around the church and praying fervently.

The city offered no advantage for its defense—it was situated on low ground. To the east and to the north, from where the enemy was expected, were hills and thickets. Opportunities for surveillance and shelling were limited. However, from a strategic standpoint, it was very important as a roadblock, and as a way of supplying the entire right flank of the I Army, which was based in Pultusk. We chose a position towards the north and northeast of the city, on the front facing towards Chorzele. Our left flank intersected the road to Grudusk, where the right flank of the 11th Siberian Division had just retreated. The Staff of the 63rd Division drew up on the road to Ciechanow approximately five versts from Przasnysz. One regiment remained in the division's reserve, which made a stand towards the southeast of the city on that same road to Ciechanow. All these dispositions came from the Commander of the Artillery Brigade. The staff of the division did not provide any news about itself.

The regiments approached Przasnysz late in the evening. Directions were given to their commanders, and they put out a watch guard. The enemy did not disturb us during the night, and we did not receive any new intelligence from either the front or the rear.

We spent the night in Przasnysz in one of the houses with the commander of the brigade. In the morning we were awakened by artillery and gunfire on the entire front of the division. Communication was established with the division's staff, and I found out that the Germans were pressing especially hard on our left flank from the direction of Grudusk. The commander of the division notified me that he was sending his senior adjutant to Przasnysz, and asked me to come to staff headquarters. After traveling about three versts from the city, I met the senior adjutant, Captain Milkhener, who was going towards Przasnysz, and stopped to explain to him where he could locate the commander of the brigade. At that moment two-wheeled cartridge wagons came racing towards us from the direction of Ciechanow, and someone was yelling, "The Germans, the Germans." It turned out that Germans had appeared in the small village where our division's staff was supposed to have been, and were shooting at the baggage train moving through it. The soldiers told us that it was infantry in helmets, that there was not less than a platoon, and that they were moving towards Przasnysz from the direction of Ciechanow. It was very difficult to understand what was going on.

The Ciechanow–Przasnysz road was deep in the rear of the entire

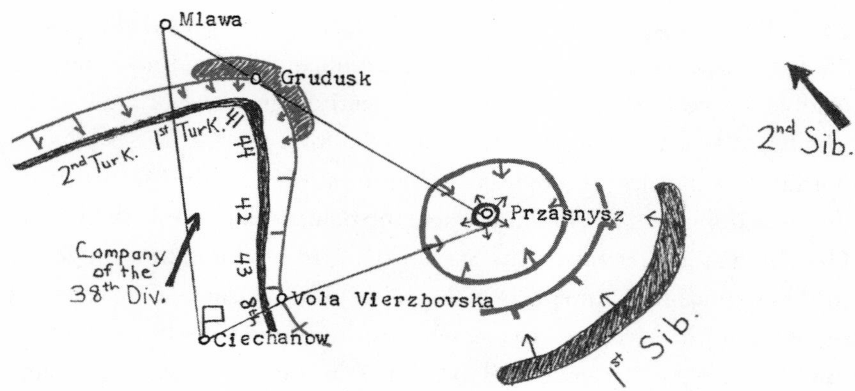

The night of February 15, 1915.

Turkestan Corps' front. A quick decision was necessary, since the small village being occupied by the Germans was only a few hundred sazhen'[30] from us. Seeing a path leading south, Milkhener turned onto it, and the wagon train followed him, but I turned north in the direction of our positions.

After the war I met Milkhener in Odessa, and he told me that a few minutes after we parted, he had been taken prisoner along with the entire wagon train.

In a forest close to the road stood the wagon train of the 11th Siberian Division. I warned them that the Germans were on the road behind them and advised the officer there to move as close as possible to the troops. I myself reached the staff of the 43rd Siberian Regiment and from there notified the staff of the Siberian Division about what had occurred. Headquarters was already in a state of alarm. It appeared that the entire road between Ciechanow and Przasnysz was occupied by the enemy, starting with the village of Wola Wierzbowska, which was only five versts from the staff of the corps. The situation threatened to turn into a catastrophe, since the road to our rear, which led to Pultusk, was in the hands of the Germans, and by crossing the Narew they could open a path for themselves to Warsaw along the right bank of the Vistula. This could lead to not only a tactical but also a strategic defeat of the whole Northwestern Front. At this moment no one knew how strong the Germans were at our rear.

30. A Russian *sazhen'* is equivalent to seven feet.

In the meantime, the 43rd Siberian Regiment, having turned its right flank under pressure from the Germans, lost contact with the neighboring regiment of the 63rd Division. It was clear that the enemy had surrounded Przasnysz, from which direction came a renewed bombardment of cannon fire.

After reaching the Staff of the 11th Siberian Division, I learned that we had also lost communication with the Staff of the Corps. With great difficulty I managed to reach Tsikhovich by telephone through the neighboring Turkestan line, and in speaking with him, I sensed for the first time that he was agitated. He ordered me to wait by the phone, and within a few seconds I heard Sheideman's voice: "Staff Rotmistr, take the division's staff automobile immediately and meet the Eighth Turkestan Regiment, which is approaching Ciechanow. Lead it to Wola Wierzbowska. It is imperative to attack that village as quickly as possible. The Commander of the Army told me that two Siberian Corps were on their way to help us."

The Eighth Regiment did not approach Ciechanow until nighttime, and we reached Wola Wierzbowska just after sunrise. The Germans met us with artillery fire, and when the regiment approached closer, with intense rifle and machine-gun fire along the whole front of our three deployed battalions, it became evident that one regiment would not be enough to seize the village. Upon my report, Tsikhovich ordered the regiment to go into the trenches and wait for the approaching reinforcements. At that moment, except for transport drivers and orderlies armed with rifles who led the supply wagons to the company, there were no reserves in Ciechanow. Even the guard sotnia who were protecting the Staff of the Corps had been sent to Grudusk. "Our spirits are good here, and we are awaiting the Brigade of the 38th Division from the fortification," said Tsikhovich, evidently to reassure me.

Shortly an order came for me to proceed to the Staff of the 11th Siberian Division to replace the Chief of Staff, who had become ill.

The regiments of the 11th Division were thrown into the front line, and led the battle. In the reserves of the division's commander there was only the Cossack sotnia arriving from Ciechanow. At this point the guidance of the fighting on the entire corps' front was transferred to the regiments and companies. The senior commanders, not having any reserves, could not have any influence on it, and I felt that if I could be of some use, it would only be in the trenches.

After obtaining consent from the division's commander, I proceeded to Grudusk.

The Commander of the 41st Siberian Regiment, Colonel Kremenetsky, having united under his command the 41st and the remainder of the 44th Regiments, commanded the combat sector fronting Grudusk. He was a line army officer about forty years of age. The fact that he had been appointed to the regiment from the army already indicated that he must be outstanding, and in my opinion, he was. At any rate, he was not given to second thoughts or to sentimentality. Colonel Kremenetsky had fallen into military service, as most of us had, by being enlisted in the corps of cadets at the expense of the State. He looked upon the service as a duty given him by fate, and as an honest man, performed it conscientiously. He knew his business and treated his subordinates judiciously and uniformly, without ceremony. The regiment believed that its commander was skilled in his work and let him show the way. He regarded war losses philosophically, and his only complaint was that he had not seen any women for a long time. He was a bachelor, of the type that women usually liked.

"Happy to see you, Staff Rotmistr," he said when I presented myself to him. "You undoubtedly know that we cannot retreat from this hill. Tsikhovich just informed us that Przasnysz is still holding and that major reinforcements are approaching us from the other side of the Vistula, and part of them should reach our front by tomorrow morning."

"I know this, Colonel, Sir, and I am asking your permission to remain with you, and I am at your command."

"It's not difficult to understand our situation. The more riflemen and cartridges we have, the more hope that we'll be able to hold these trenches. My whole formation is in the front lines, I don't even have an adjutant, as I have sent him to command a company. Right now there are just two telephonists, my orderly, you, and I here in the dugout. When the assault begins, we'll all go into the trenches and start firing, and from there—God knows."

While we were talking, there was occasional firing in the trenches, upon which it was usually reported that the men were amusing themselves because of boredom. The amusement was cut short by the fact that about three hundred paces in front of our trenches was the road from Mlawa to Przasnysz, where during the night the Germans had tried to take their transport to their troops besieging Przasnysz. At times during the day, they daringly endeavored to rush past on it, but the result for them was frequently not a happy one. The German trenches were approximately 250 steps between us and the road. Naturally, any finger that poked out above a trench—German or ours—demanded to be shot at immediately. And it was clear that before the Germans could turn to the west and sweep our front towards Novogeorgievsk, they needed to take possession of this road. The night before my arrival, two German assaults had been repulsed here.

Soon the commander's orderly came into the dugout and brought each of us a can of Argentinian preserves, a slice of bread, and a can of greasy tea poured into the same can as the preserves. The Colonel reached into a bag and brought out a bottle of diluted alcohol, which he admitted that he had obtained in the automobile detachment of the corps' staff, and we sat down to eat supper.

At that moment, Ensign Tideman, the commander of the artillery platoon attached to the regiment, pulled up to the dugout. He was a Russian-German engineer who had been called up from the reserves, and despite being of German descent, he was one of the most loyal and deserving officers in the corps. Then the adjutant of the 44th Regiment arrived to get the orders for the night, and seeing me, rejoiced as if I were his relative. Finally, the commander of the battalion which was located in front of our dugout walked in. There was enough supper for all, and we had much to talk about.

As strange as it may seem, despite the fact that we all were well aware that there would be a battle during the night, or perhaps precisely because everyone knew this, no one talked about the impending night. Instead, with great animation, we deliberated over the process used to make vodka from alcohol, how much sugar should be placed in the bottom of the bottle, what function the sugar played, to what extent and why vodka made from grain was superior to that made from potatoes, etc. From this, the conversation devolved to the quality of the places of entertainment in Warsaw as compared to those in Moscow. Then Kremenetsky told us of his recent trip to Warsaw and his acquaintance with a Polish singer from a café chantant.[31] With the air of an expert, he compared the qualities of Polish and Russian women. Whereupon he stopped. No one replied. And during this moment

31. A *café chantant* is an intimate cabaret offering sophisticated musical entertainment.

of silence everyone was probably remembering his own "darling." I also remembered. Judging by Marusia's last letter, she should be giving birth any day, and a thought ran through my mind: "Will I ever see her and the new baby?" I even conjectured, "If it is a girl, then I will see her, but if a boy, then no."

"See here, Gentlemen, all of you except me have someone who will feel sorry for you and who thinks of you. And believe me, this is the main cause of the heaviness in my heart."

"But I believe, Aleksandr Petrovich, that a military man should not marry," said the battalion commander.

"Your thinking is incorrect, Aleksei Innokentievich," objected the Commander of the Regiment. "A person will more easily make his peace with death if he knows he will be remembered. That is the surest foundation for initiative."

The conversation had reached a subject which obviously no one wanted to discuss, so it was cut short. The adjutant stood up, said good night to us, and departed. There was so much smoking in the dugout that it became suffocating, so I went outside, and curious as to the news, walked towards the nearest trench, which was on the incline of a knoll facing Grudusk. The night was dark—not a star could be seen in the sky. The men in the trenches were not sleeping. The sentries at the batteries were not so much looking as listening to every sound in front of them. The resting soldiers were sitting in the bottom of the trench holding their rifles, and carrying on a conversation in low voices:

" 'And see here,' he says to the merchant, 'give me the bill,' " one voice was saying. "You see," remarked a listener, "I bet for a big deal." In all of the soldiers' "tales," either a merchant or a priest played a role. The priest was customarily portrayed as a stupid husband, whose wife stepped out with the laborer. And the merchant personified money, which "although not God, nevertheless has mercy." The merchant was a crafty businessman who was difficult to dupe. But in spite of everything, in the end the laborer won over him.

Somewhat further on, an old soldier was teaching a young one how to handle his rifle: "You aim at his feet, or the bullet will fly over him. And watch that your rifle does not fall to your side. Hold it straight, and prop it here on the ground."

"Sir," the teacher addressed me, "yesterday we were sent replacements, but they have never even held rifles in their hands. It is frightening to let them have them. They'll just surrender."

"Don't be afraid, Uncle," a youthful voice answered. "I won't surrender."

There was also a company commander here—a young second lieutenant, who had become an officer probably not more than a year previously, but already spoke with self-assurance. Commander of a company was a position which in peacetime would have taken ten years to attain. He told me, "Fifteen men were sent to the company yesterday, and none of them had seen a cartridge."

At that moment in front of us, where our riflemen were mending a wire, a hand grenade exploded. It was followed by a second and a third. The repairmen ran into our trench, and following after them, heading towards the same parapet, were the Germans. In a twinkling of an eye we were all at the parapet. A German loomed quite close in front of me, and I did not even have time to come to my senses before someone to my right suddenly hit him over the head with a rifle butt, and he fell at my feet.

From the right someone screamed "Hurrah!" and the riflemen started to run forward, pursuing the Germans, who were rushing back, having failed to take us by surprise. The fear that had seized me in the first seconds vanished. I wanted to pursue them and strike them down, strike down as many as possible . . . But then the German machine guns sounded. We hit the dirt. And . . . the impulse did not survive the interruption—we crawled back into the trench.

The telephonist in the trench informed me that I was being called to report to the staff of the regiment. It turned out that the Commander of the Corps was waiting to speak to me on the phone. "Deliver my order to Colonel Kremenetsky to advance towards Grudusk immediately in order to cut off the route of retreat of the Germans, who are beginning to withdraw from Przasnysz towards Mlawa. The First Siberian is having great success at the front. How are things with you?"

"A fierce battle is raging on our entire front. In places the Germans are charging with bayonets. The riflemen are holding up very well."

"That is not enough. Attacking the Germans is their only hope to save themselves from captivity. You must insist that Kremenetsky begin the attack now. I have issued the same order to the Turkestanis."

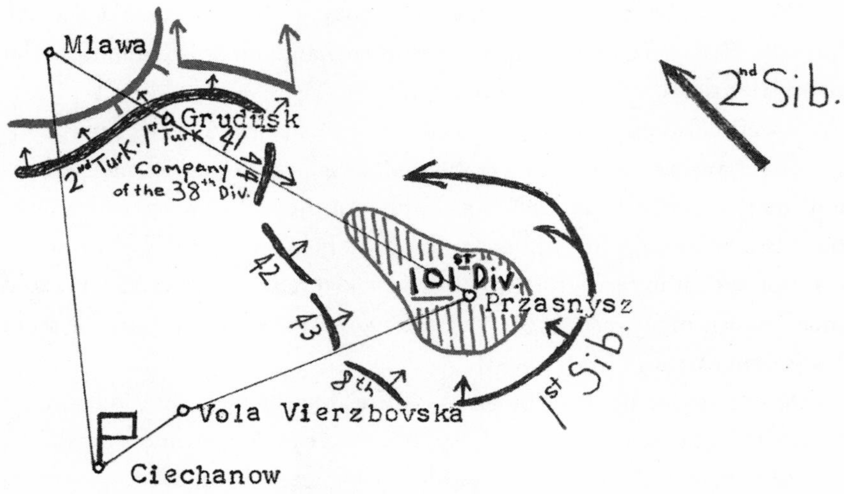

The morning of February 17, 1915.

Kremenetsky had just hung up the phone as I entered. "Attack? I am just this minute stopping the retreat! There are heavy losses in the First Battalion, and the Germans have just taken over its trenches. I have sent two companies of the 38th Division to that area, which have just arrived. You hear fighting along the entire front. With whom do you want me to attack?"

But the situation was clear. The Germans were clearly carrying on a fierce attack against us in order to clear the route to Mlawa for themselves. This was the only road fit for artillery and baggage wagons. The Commander of the Regiment was aware of this and so was I. I stood in silence and looked at him, expecting that he would give another answer. And he gave it:

"Yes, apparently our turn has come. Let's go to the artillery men."

The battery of the 11th Siberian Division was stationed in our sector.

"Have you probed Grudusk with artillery fire to adjust the aim?"

"Yes, it has been probed."

"Open up the most intensive fire. In half an hour I'm hauling out the riflemen. We have orders to take the village. The Germans are retreating."

The commander of the battery did not believe his own ears. Just a short time ago the First Battalion had evacuated quite close to his position, and he was getting ready to gather in the guns.

I reported by telephone to the Commander of the Division about what was happening. He had already been informed about everything by

Sheideman. I called Corps Headquarters. Sheideman answered the phone himself. His voice sounded triumphant. I perceived that the actions on which he had insisted would no longer play an important role. The Germans were surrounded in Przasnysz.

Having concluded the conversation, Sheideman said to me: "Count Tolstoy is standing right here and asked me to relay to you that your wife has presented you with a daughter. Both are doing well. Congratulations."

This is how I learned of the birth[32] of my daughter Masha,[33] whom I didn't see for the first time until September.

Daybreak came. The artillery was bombarding Grudusk. Rifle fire had abated. I went to the trench where I had witnessed the night attack. The slain German was still lying on the parapet. He was a captain. Half of his face had been smashed by the rifle butt. He wore a fur jacket, and from the interior pocket a small booklet protruded. I took it out, and there were his documents with his name and address. As far as I remember, his last name was Hoffman, and his address, it seems, was Stettin. A photograph of a young woman with two children fell out of the book. I took this photograph, wrote down his address, and promised myself that after the war, I would find his wife and give her this picture. Future events, however, prevented me from carrying this out. And now I do not remember where this picture might be.

I raised my head towards the soldiers in the trench and asked them: "Who is responsible for this?"

"Petrenko, there," answered the soldiers. And a young soldier with a wide smile was looking at me.

"But aren't you the one they were teaching to shoot last night?"

"That was me."

A cold winter sun rose. It gazed on us impartially as if saying, "I am not guilty of your war or your quarrels and killings. I am still warming everyone equally and will continue to do so: both you and the Germans." The white snow that had fallen during the night began to cover the little heaps scattered here and there that were the remains of the nocturnal battle's young victims. Stretcher bearers were examining the bodies in the hope of finding

---

32. She was born February 12 (Old Style), February 25 (New Style), 1915.

33. Nickname for Maria.

I began to fly on reconnaissance and experienced all of their troubles myself. One evening I wrote a report on this and delivered it to Tsikhovich. He approved it and sent it to the Army Staff.

Shortly after that our retreat began, and by comparison with the superiority of the German artillery driving us out of Poland, all of our previous concerns seemed so small that I soon forgot about my report.

That winter, when I was already in the 13th Cavalry Division, I was called by the Commander of the Division, an elderly, heavy, Caucasian prince by the name of Tumanov, who said, "Which dear aunt is telling your fortune?[43] You are being appointed to the Army Staff to sleep in a soft bed, to have your dinner on time, and to not even hear the guns. Some people have all the luck!"

The telegram stated that I was appointed to the Staff of the II Army as assistant to the Commander of the Reconnaissance Division and ordered that, upon receipt, I was to proceed to Minsk.

I learned from the Army Staff that I would be taking charge of five flying squadrons which were attached to the army and currently stationed in Minsk. When I presented myself to the Chief of Staff, he told me that it was time to persuade the flyers to do what was needed by the army, and not just what they wanted to do and only when they wanted to do it.

Thus, the aviators were under my supervision, but not under my command. Moreover, I had to force them to do what was needed by the army. Who was their direct commander?

The immediate commander of the entire army's aviation personnel was Grand Duke Aleksandr Mikhailovich,[44] who lived in Kiev and never appeared at the front. However, he knew all the flyers personally and appointed the commanders for each squadron or transferred them from one squadron to another. Aleksandr Mikhailovich jealously guarded this branch of his business so that no one dared to interfere.

---

43. A Russian expression.

44. Grand Duke Aleksandr Mikhailovich ("Sandro"), born in 1866, was the son of Grand Duke Mikhail, the youngest brother of Alexander II. In 1894, he married Grand Duchess Ksenia, eldest daughter of Maria Fedorovna and sister of Nicholas II. He was close friends with his cousin Nicholas, the last Emperor, during the early years of his reign. (Tisdall, *The Dowager Empress*, 10.) In 1929, the Grand Duke visited the author's family, then living in Riverside, California, and took the author's sixteen-year-old daughter, Shura, out to dinner.

The Duty General of the Supreme Headquarters directed the resources unit for supplying the squadrons, and, as I later learned, these two were extremely hostile towards each other.

Finally, the operational leader of the aviation detachments was the infantry commander to whom a given detachment was attached. But, as I have already said, many military units did not know how to make use of the aviators, and therefore left it to the aviators' discretion. In spite of the fact that there were many outstanding, brave officers among the flyers, as a group they were not devoid of human weaknesses and did not put out the full amount of work which they could have performed.

First of all I became acquainted with my new fellow soldiers. I still remember many of their names, even though almost half a century has passed. The airmen had already been informed of my arrival by the Second Army Squadron, which also formed part of my group. They were all happy that they had finally been remembered, and now they would know what duties they were to carry out. Konovalov, Firsov, Yakobashvili, Zverev . . . where are you now, my eagles? I would give so much for the return of those difficult but happy days spent with you!

I asked Quartermaster General Stavrov to obtain permission to transfer the squadrons from Minsk to the front. Having taken up residence with them in the I Army, I gave each squadron its own zone for reconnaissance, and flew with each leader in their designated direction. Each day I noted on the map everything that had been observed by reconnaissance. I flew with the pilots to the positions and became acquainted with the staffs of the divisions and with the regiments, and very soon the troops began to notice us flying. It was early spring, and we were preparing for our advance. Ammunition and heavy artillery were brought to the front. And again we began to dream of the possibility of victory. Once our reconnaissance discovered a large collection of transports in the village of Sventsiany.[45] I decided to make a group flight with bombs. I gathered twelve flying machines, each one with two twenty-pound bombs, and we dropped them all at one time on the train of wagons. I think that this was the first flight of this kind on our

45. This town is called Shvenchenis today (also Svencionys) and is located about 53 miles northeast of Vilna (Vilnius) in Lithuania.

front. The Germans quickly reinforced their combat aviation against us and drew up antiaircraft guns.

Once, when I was returning from reconnaissance with Captain Konovalov, a German fighter plane rose like a candle flame above us. Not having enough speed to get away from him, we tried to turn our Voisin to face the German, so we would have a chance to open fire. The German, however, having twice the agility, always flew to our rear and strafed us with a machine gun. This engagement took place over the very middle of Lake Naroch[46] at a height of two thousand meters. Below us were clouds. Seeing the hopelessness of the situation, Konovalov made a sharp nosedive, and we disappeared in the clouds. Coming out of the clouds, we found ourselves to the rear of the German trenches at an elevation of one thousand meters, and an antiaircraft gun opened fire on us. The bullets were cracking like nuts around us, and to top everything off, our engine stopped. It was a difficult task to glide the plane towards our lines, and Konovalov displayed outstanding skill. We crash landed behind our trenches, breaking the chassis, but fortunately had time to run to a dugout as the Germans opened rapid fire on our plane and destroyed it.

I petitioned to obtain photographic equipment for aerial surveying of fortifications, but I did not receive it during my tour of duty with the Army Staff.

Our advance near Lake Naroch, though both very persistent and besieged by heavy losses, soon petered out, because the winter before, the Germans had built a complete, entrenched "place of arms,"[47] and the only possibility of breaking through was by bringing in new reserves. All such forces were headed toward the Brusilov Front. Notwithstanding, the army formally thanked our flyers and, what especially pleased me, recognized our part in helping the front lines.

During the battles I received a letter from Admiral Fogel, who had formerly been attached to Aleksandr Mikhailovich, asking me to fill a vacancy

46. Lake Naroch is about sixty miles northeast of Vilna (Vilnius) and about twenty-five miles southeast of Sventsiany (Shvenchenis) in the Minsk oblast of Belorussia.

47. A "place of arms," when used in a strategic sense, is an entrenched camp or fortress in which a large army can be collected under cover prior to taking the field. It is a place where they can develop and prepare for a military operation.

on his staff. Without hesitating, I asked permission of the Grand Duke to remain on the front.

In the summer of 1916, the Staff of the II Army was transferred to the town of Nesvizh, near the Baranovichi station, and again a lull occurred.

During the summer, several Nieuport-type[48] fighter planes arrived in our country from France. One of these aircraft was sent to our army and assigned to Lieutenant Kruten. A few days later, he downed two German planes in the space of two hours right over our Headquarters, and we all were able to observe the fight. This was our first battle victory in the air, and it made headlines in all the newspapers. Both of the Germans survived and were treated to dinner and wine in the squadron, and the next day the news was dropped into the German trenches that both men were alive. There was a great spirit of chivalry in aviation in those days.

In August there were rumors among the aviators that five Ilia Muromets-type airplanes[49] had appeared on the Western Front. They were built in Russia according to the design of a young engineer, Sikorsky,[50] who is now

48. This plane was named after the French aviator and aircraft designer, Edouard Nieuport (1875–1911). In 1910 he designed and built the first monoplane with a deep fuselage entirely covered by fabric that protected the pilot from the neck down. In 1911 he and his brother Charles founded the Nieuport Company, which manufactured sesquiplane aircraft that were used by France and Russia during World War I as the basic fighter plane. The plane had a machine gun mounted above the top wing, allowing it to fire clear of the propeller arc. This airplane, with an engine rated at 28 horsepower, set new records for flight speed (120 km/hour) and distance (about 1,000 km).

49. The Russian Ilia Muromets biplane, designed by Igor' Sikorsky, was the world's first heavy bomber. It was a four-engine aircraft, with an engine power of 440 kilowatts (600 hp.), a payload of 1.5 tons, a speed of 100 km/hour, and a wingspan of about 100 feet. It was equipped with aiming devices for bombing with a mechanical bomb-release control, as well as compass and navigation equipment. In June and July of 1914 the Ilia Muromets set a world record by flying from Kiev to St. Petersburg in 14 hours and 38 minutes with one stop. It had a crew of up to eight. The armament on Ilia Muromets planes consisted of four to five machine guns, and some models also had a 37-mm cannon. About 80 were built, and they made four hundred raids on German targets with the loss of only one plane. The Ilia Muromets was first built in 1914 at the Russko-Baltiisky Plant in St. Petersburg. The name "Ilia Muromets" is based on a character in a famous epic Russian poem composed between the twelfth and the sixteenth centuries. This character is identified in the popular mind with the ideal hero-warrior who defends the state from foreign enemies when it is being torn apart by princely feuds.

50. Igor' Ivanovich Sikorsky (1889–1972) was a Russian-born airplane designer and pioneer in aircraft construction. He studied at the St. Petersburg Naval School and the Kiev Polytechnic Institute. In 1908–11, he constructed two helicopters which did not fly. His first airplane was the Model S-2 (1910), and from 1912 to 1914 he constructed several airplanes

an American celebrity. I had never seen these planes myself, but from the description of those who had, they could carry five people and one machine gun. They could not compete with the European machines in speed, quickness of takeoff, nor agility, and they were a much larger target. All this elicited a protest from the aviators, and Aleksandr Mikhailovich took their side. This was enough for Supreme Headquarters; as I already mentioned, being hostile towards the Grand Duke, they showed their support for Sikorsky. Here, too, national feeling and the need to promote the first Russian-built airplane probably played a part.

Somehow or other, the Reconnaissance Division Commander on the Staff of the Front, Colonel Brandt, got the idea of using me for the adaptation of these machines on the front, and I was transferred to the front's Headquarters. This was a new promotion.

How little one had to do in those days to become famous! According to Gorbunovsky's tale, "One will not fly from a good life." The officers on the General Staff mostly sat at Headquarters and carried out chancellor's duties. I am by no means speaking about everyone. There were many brave and worthy men in our midst. Many of them gave their lives on the battlefields. What I am trying to say is that they had a better chance than others to avoid risk. And in those days, flying in itself was considered a risk.

Without bragging I will say that I was thinking least of all about my career. Long before, I had firmly decided that if I lived through the war, I would retire from the military and farm the land. When I thought of this I always remembered Leo Tolstoy: ". . . and will try to farm it as well as possible." Each time I was promoted, I sincerely regretted having to part with the work I was doing. Especially touching was my departure from the II Army, where the aviators arranged a farewell celebration for me.

At the front's Staff Headquarters, Colonel Brandt, whom I had previously met only in passing, told me that he would soon be working out a plan for an air raid on the Germans' rear with five "Ilia Muromets," and that I would have to help in accomplishing this attack. To this I replied that by

including the Grand Russky Vitiaz' and the Ilia Muromets. The latter marked the beginning of multi-engine aviation. In 1919 he emigrated to the United States and in 1923 founded an aviation firm. By 1939 he had designed about fifteen types of airplanes, and he then shifted to designing single-rotor helicopters. He was a pioneer in construction of turbine helicopters, amphibious helicopters with retractable landing gear, and flying cranes.

sending five Muromets groups behind German lines, we would risk losing all of them.

"You are too pessimistic, Olferieff," said Brandt. "We have to make use of them."

With this the conversation ended, and Brandt never brought it up again, but the proposed air attack never occurred. Instead, Quartermaster General Lebedev, my former instructor in the academy, who I remember made me rewrite a report about the supply corps in my last essay on strategy ten times, now made me write a report about the necessity of building hangars for the airplanes for winter.

I wrote him one page in which I explained that standing in the open air, the oil in the delicate engines may freeze and thus damage them. I thought that reasoning was sufficient, but Lebedev was not satisfied. He himself dictated five more pages to me. It was already the end of October and beginning to get cold. Soon snow began to fall, and there was no way to build the hangars.

Upon arrival I presented myself to the Chief of Staff, General Kvetsinsky, and he disappointed me even more. I waited for a long time for him to receive me, and during this time my mind was filled with many questions regarding aviation that I expected to have to answer, and I was prepared to do so. But when he finally appeared and listened to my report, he paid the most attention to the fact that my sword belt was not according to form, and stated that I should have known about the issuance of the new belt and bought it when presenting myself to the Chief of Staff. On this note he concluded the conversation, shook my hand, and dismissed me.

I was not to remain with the staff on the front for very long. At General Headquarters a new post was announced on the staff of aviation officers. And I was appointed to this position as Field Officer for Aviation to the administration of the Quartermaster General of the Supreme Commander in Chief. At the same time I received a letter from Admiral Fogel that Aleksandr Mikhailovich had invited me to visit him in Kiev before I traveled to Supreme Headquarters. And I went there.

The Grand Duke received me with particular cordiality, fed me lunch, and then took me to his study where he began to speak in an aloof manner. The gist of his conversation was that not wanting to overcrowd the already over-populated Mogilev,[51] he was living in Kiev, but that because of the distance, he was not always informed of what was happening at Headquarters, and he wanted me to keep him posted. I asked him whether he was receiving the operational reports from there. He answered that everything he was supposed to receive, he received. He stated this with obvious displeasure in his voice, evidently irritated because I did not understand him. I promised to keep him informed of all that I knew myself. With this, the conversation ended. It did not satisfy him, and I was left with an unpleasant impression and felt that I probably could not live up to his expectations, and if my new duty depended on this, then I surely had not passed the examination.

"We expected you to stay with us," Fogel told me as we were saying good-bye. To this I answered that I sincerely regretted not being able to refuse the battle assignment conferred on me at this time. This answer seemed to satisfy them.

The reason for Aleksandr Mikhailovich's request to keep him informed on the events at Headquarters became clear to me when two weeks later I appeared before Quartermaster General Lukomsky.[52] "What are you planning to do here?" Lukomsky asked having seated me.

"I assumed that you summoned me, Your Excellency. Grand Duke Aleksandr Mikhailovich told me . . ."

"Well, let's not assume," interrupted Lukomsky. "Here you will be doing just what I order you to do. In the Department of the Duty General there is an entire organization which deals with aviation, and an officer from the

---

51. Mogilev was the city where the Tsar's military headquarters was located from 1915 to 1917.

52. Aleksandr Sergeevich Lukomsky (1868–1939) graduated from the General Staff Academy in 1897. During the First World War he served as head of the office of the Minister of War and also as an assistant Minister of War. From October 1916 to April 1917, he was Quartermaster General at General Headquarters. From June to August 1917, he was Chief of Staff for the Supreme Commander in Chief. An active participant in the Kornilov Movement, he was arrested on September 1/14. On November 19/December 2, with the aid of General N. N. Dukhonin, he fled from Bykhov prison to Novocherkassk and took part in the formation of the White Guard Volunteer Army. In September 1918, he became Assistant Commander in Chief of the Volunteer Army and head of the Military and Naval Directorate of General A. I. Denikin. From July 1919 to January 1920, he was Chairman of the Denikin government. In March 1920 he left for Turkey, where he was General P. N. Vrangel's representative attached to the Allied Committee in Constantinople. He later emigrated to France, where he wrote his memoirs and died in 1939.

General Staff is not needed there. I will attach you to the reconnaissance section, and when I need your help with airplanes, I will call you."

On this note, the official conversation ended, and Lukomsky, with whom I was already acquainted, became very amiable and inquired about my wife, and the subject of talk drifted to Petersburg.

The reason for such a reception by Lukomsky became clear to me when I learned that the new regulations on aviation for the officers of the General Staff had been written by Aleksandr Mikhailovich, and being able to report to the Emperor directly, he had asked him to approve this regulation, which was done as a matter of routine. Evidently Lukomsky had not read this document. When it became known that such an officer was to arrive at Headquarters, the administration of the Duty General prepared accordingly for Lukomsky to give me the rebuff.

What especially distressed me in Lukomsky's reception was that he was not even interested in knowing where I had been previously and what I had been doing. However, my one untimely utterance of the Grand Duke's name had inexplicably given me a black mark. The fact that I was assigned to the reconnaissance section was also significant. The Quartermaster General on the Supreme Commander in Chief's Staff obviously was a long way from recognizing that by now aviation had gone beyond being a subsidiary instrument of reconnaissance. In Europe at this time, it had already won an independent position for itself as a powerful fighting element, effective in annihilating hostile reserves and concentrations in the rear, in conducting aerial combat, and adjusting artillery fire; and in the pursuit of reconnaissance, one squadron produced more results than a division of cavalry. He was probably unaware that at that time we already had 1,800 operational planes on the front, and that life itself, in spite of the routine in the rear, created the necessity for establishing some control in the management of them.

What was the cause of the breech between Supreme Headquarters and the Grand Duke?

Although I admit that this question affected me personally, I was not interested in finding out. I firmly resolved to achieve recognition that my work was both useful and necessary through my own efforts, no matter where I was on duty. First of all I decided to learn the exact whereabouts of all the air force units on all the fronts, and I was certain that with this alone, I would bring some help to the situation. After finding a free moment, I saw Lukomsky again and told him of my plan—to make the rounds of all the fronts and bring him a report about the state of aviation on each. Lukomsky willingly agreed to this.

But soon, however, very soon, an event occurred that forced us to forget all of our happiness and adversities, and those who were able to see a little further than their noses understood that the end of everything had come.

The Beginning of the End

When our army had more or less satisfactorily departed from Poland, His Majesty the Emperor proudly bestowed upon Himself the Supreme Command of all the fighting forces.

This event was uniformly highlighted by all the correspondents on the home front, such as Admiral Bubnov, and also later on by the historians of this period, as having a particularly unfavorable effect on both the military operations and the morale of the troops.

As far as military actions, one could only surmise how effective Nikolai Nikolaevich would be in influencing his notorious Yanushkevich[1] and Danilov.[2] We only knew that the responsibility for Soldau, and especially

1. Nikolai Nikolaevich Yanushkevich (also spelled "Ianushkevich") (1868–1918) graduated from the General Staff Academy in 1896, and in 1910 lectured there on military administration. He was a member of the Council of the United Nobility, and Nicholas II was impressed by his reactionary views. In the rapid advancement of his career, he was promoted in 1913 from deputy chief of an office at the Ministry of War to Director of the General Staff Academy. In 1914 he was made Chief of the General Staff—though unqualified for the position. When World War I broke out, he was appointed Chief of Staff under the Supreme Commander in Chief. While he occupied himself with matters of politics and administration, he entrusted all questions of operational leadership to Quartermaster General Yury N. Danilov. In August 1915 he was removed from his post and appointed the Assistant to the Vice Regent of the Caucasus in charge of military affairs. After the February Revolution of 1917, he retired.

2. Yury Nikiforovich Danilov (1866–1937) graduated from the General Staff Academy in 1892 and went on to become General of the Infantry in 1914. Along the way he was Deputy Quartermaster (1908–09) and Quartermaster General (1909) of the main administration of the General Staff. He was a participant in drawing up the strategic plans of

for the exhaustion of our arms and ammunition supply, rested on them. At the same time, Alekseev, Ruzsky, and Brusilov were known to have conducted several successful operations. In regards to the attitude of the troops, that is those combatants in the trenches, who lived from day to day doomed from one minute to another either to give up their soul to God or to become crippled—I can say with certainty that the change of command made no impression on them. The troops were accustomed to knowing that all of the orders always came from the Tsar. And what his position was at the present time, or through whom the orders were given, meant nothing to them.

It was not the change of command that had an influence on the frame of mind of the troops, but the exhaustion of our arms and ammunition supply. Deploying in battle order, frequently from exposed positions under the enemy's relentless artillery fire, lying down in a line and protecting the fleeing refugees and our transports, a soldier knew that, as soon as he fired his five or ten cartridges, he would have to retreat. And here not everyone had the willpower to hold his fire, endeavoring to deal the greatest damage to the enemy with a meager store of cartridges. Many discharged their ammunition as quickly as possible and flowed in with the endless crowd of refugees, blending in with them and disappearing into the sparsely populated, marshy forests of Pinsk. Thus they began to desert. During the summer the fugitives lived in the forests, subsisted on what was given them by the tender-hearted inhabitants, or simply stole the pitiful remains. Towards winter they began to huddle about the railroad stations and crowded on the platforms as if waiting for a train, or they would board a train and travel from one station to another. There were so many of them that neither the railroad officials nor the military police in the rear could possibly check all of them and return them to their units.

But in spite of everything, a significant majority of men remained with their units. These soldiers marched mechanically, fought mechanically, were

World War I, and when war broke out, he was appointed Quartermaster General under the Supreme Commander in Chief. Since the Chief of Staff, Yanushkevich, was said to be totally incompetent, Danilov was virtually acting Chief of Staff. In August 1915, he was appointed Corps Commander and subsequently Chief of Staff of the Northern Front (1916–17) and Commander of the Fifth Army (1917). He emigrated to France after the October Revolution. His writings on the history of World War I are known for their wealth of factual material.

mutilated mechanically, and died mechanically. They had their own companies who did their thinking for them; the companies had battalions, the battalions had regiments, and so on. The established machine, although weakened, still continued to operate. As spring approached, new supplies of cartridges, shells, and guns appeared once more, so the machine came to life again, and we turned it around and went to attack the enemy.

In the summer of 1916 our counteroffensive on all fronts was extremely taxing; we conducted methodically positioned battles in which our troops displayed miracles of self-sacrificing determination to overthrow the enemy, and our losses reached hundreds of thousands. On the Southwestern Front, we moved several tens of versts farther. But . . . all of our efforts did not even earn us the least strategic success. And an involuntary thought arose in the mind of every participant in these battles: "We so easily surrendered a strip four hundred versts in depth to the Germans, and now, in order to retake some thirty versts from them, it has required hundreds of thousands of casualties. How much blood would have to be shed to drive them from our borders? And it seemed that there would not be enough of this blood in Russia. 'Mut verlören—alles verlören.' "[3]

But, you may say, near Verdun, in France, there were even more fierce battles raging. And in World War II, when the Germans reached the Caucasus and almost surrounded Moscow, the fighters' spirit did not waiver. Why did we lose faith in ourselves?

For an answer to this, I will cite an old Russian proverb: "A fish rots from its head."

In the autumn of 1916 when I was transferred to the front's Headquarters, I settled in Minsk with two comrades, Laidoner,[4] from the Academy, and Koko Kruzenshtern, from the Corps. Laidoner, who was subsequently

3. German: "Courage lost—all is lost."

4. Johan Laidoner (1884–1953) was the son of a farmhand who went on to become an Estonian military leader and general. He was educated in Russia for a military career and graduated from the General Staff Academy in 1912. He served in the Russian forces in World War I as Chief of Staff of an infantry division and achieved the rank of lieutenant colonel. In 1918 he became Commander in Chief of the new Estonian Army, which drove the German and Russian occupiers out of Estonia in 1918–19. At the end of 1924, he helped suppress an attempted communist coup d'état. Again in 1934 he led the Estonian Army in putting down an attempted government takeover by the right wing Vap movement, and subsequently headed the military support of President K. Pats's authoritarian regime. From 1937 to 1940 Laidoner was deputy of the National Assembly and member of the State

a Minister of War in Estonia, was a conscientious, capable, and stubborn Estonian, who never elicited sympathy from me. One could feel his dislike of us Russians due to our oppression of his homeland. Kruzenshtern, a German from the Baltic Provinces, was just the opposite—he was very congenial and had above-average training and education. He had been called up from the reserves, and before mobilization, had served as a police officer in the State Duma. All of the staff's officers lived in harmony, and frequently company would gather in our quarters. The conversations always touched on politics. This was during the time when Protopopov,[5] whom Kruzenshtern knew well from the Duma, was serving as prime minister. This appointment provoked an explosion of indignation from us, as it did from all of Russia's thinking individuals, which was far more vehement than those aspersions and rumors which I wrote of in connection with the Turkestan Corps. Earlier, the criticism had been confident; Russians then felt that the power of speaking out was sufficient to overcome all difficulties, that Russia was still very strong, that all would be right again, and virtue would triumph. Now there was a feeling of fright. "Where are we headed?" was the question. And there was no answer to it. The officers spoke of Rasputin and the Tsarina with contempt, and even openly expressed the need to get rid of them in order to save the homeland. And these conversations were carried on among the most loyal element—the officers.

I arrived at Mogilev in the middle of November. The Grand Duke was right: the small town was overcrowded with various kinds of installations. Besides the military, there were representatives of many civilian organizations. This was the country's nerve center, from which all lines of

---

Council. When the Soviets occupied Estonia in June 1940, he was arrested for counterrevolutionary activity, tried, and deported to the Soviet Union, where he died.

5. Alexander Dmitrievich Protopopov (1866–1918) was a Russian statesman, large landowner, and industrialist. He was a member of the Octobrist party and a deputy to the Third and Fourth State Dumas. In 1914 he became Vice President of the Duma, where he sided with the Progressive Bloc. In 1916 he became Chairman of the Council of Congresses of Representatives of the Metalworking Industry. His friendship with Rasputin no doubt had a part in his being appointed in September 1916 as Minister of Internal Affairs. As such, he promoted reactionary policies. He was one of the Tsar's closest advisors, and although he became nearly insane, the Tsarina blocked all efforts to remove him. He attempted to suppress the February Revolution of 1917 with military force, and after the October Revolution he actively opposed Soviet power. He was sentenced and shot by the Cheka.

communication extended to the front and to the rear, and the eyes of the entire nation were turned towards it.

In a small square in the center of town was the Governor's House, which he had been obliged to turn over to the Emperor and his retinue. Next to it was the Provincial Government's quarters, which housed the administration of the Quartermaster General, and this is where Alekseev lived. Opposite, in another public building, was the administration of the Duty General.

The administration of the Quartermaster General was composed of approximately twelve colonels of the General Staff; almost all were recipients of the Cross of St. George, who were evidently select officers from all the fronts. Besides me, there was only one Guards' officer among them—Skalon. I was the only one with the rank of a Captain appointed to the duty of a Colonel—a very rare phenomenon in the General Staff. They accepted me politely but coldly, obviously suspecting me of being an upstart who had managed to steal into the holy of holies, but probably not without the help of the Governor's House, and perhaps even Rasputin himself. Sometimes I noticed how a lively conversation among the officers would cease when I approached. Never in my life had I felt lonelier. And I was unable to figure out why.

I did not have to wait long to understand that the open hostility between those in the Provincial Government's quarters and those in the Governor's House had spilled over onto me. Headquarters was alienated from the Tsar.

After a short period of scrutiny, I no longer felt shunned, and normal relations were established.

One day I had the following conversation with the chief of the operations section, Colonel Baranovsky:

"Yet another unnecessary report, which takes half a day from all of us," he said with annoyance.

"What's the alternative? You know the Emperor has to be informed about the situation of the day."

"Five minutes would be sufficient for that. And even that is not really necessary for him (the Emperor). Indeed, all the events have already been studied and all the instructions transmitted. Live a little longer and you will be convinced."

Each morning at eleven the Emperor arrived for the report. The officer of the day met him with it in hand. Then everyone went upstairs, and there, in Alekseev's presence, the Colonel from each front reported on the situation of the past twenty-four hours, which the Tsar studied.

I remember one such report. During our regrouping the Germans had conducted an attack and caused us considerable losses. The question remained: Was this a show of force on their part or the beginning of the advance, and should we draw our troops away from here or hold on? During the report General Nadezhnyi's[6] name was mentioned. The Emperor, without saying a word, listened to the report. He had long ago grown accustomed to sad news. And the sovereign had delegated the responsibility for solving this problem to Alekseev. But here the name of Nadezhnyi interested the Emperor: "What a nice name. Was he the one who recently introduced himself to me on the occasion of his appointment?" No one who was present knew. After a short silence, one of his attendants said, "Exactly, Your Majesty, he is the one." With this, the procedure ended. Alekseev and the officer of the day left to have lunch with the Tsar.

Counting the preparation of the report by the staff, this took a good half of the day.

The Emperor, as always, treated everyone on an equal footing at Headquarters—with dignified simplicity, and carried out his duty to the motherland as he understood it: by receiving those who presented themselves, listening to reports and signing orders . . . but he kept to himself all that he felt and endured. The difference between his life in the capital and his life in Headquarters was that in the capital, he lived surrounded by the elite aristocracy and his Guards, among whom he had grown up and with whom he spoke a common language. We all knew him as a man, knew his weaknesses, but we zealously protected him from those who stood on the other side of

6. Dmitry Nikolaevich Nadezhnyi (1873–1945) was a son of nobility and later on became a Soviet military figure. He graduated from the General Staff Academy in 1901, fought in the Russo-Japanese War, and served in the Main Directorate of the General Staff. In 1913–14 he was chief of military instruction in Mongolia. In World War I he commanded a regiment, a division, and a corps, and in 1917 was promoted to lieutenant general. He joined the Red Army in 1918 and served in the Ural Region as its military leader. From there he went on to command the Northern and Western Fronts in 1918 and 1919. He defended Petrograd against General Yudenich's White Guards troops in October and November 1919. As time went on he served in various Soviet military capacities and later taught at the M. V. Frunze Military Academy and the S. M. Kirov Military Medical Academy. He retired in 1941 and was awarded the Order of the Red Banner.

us, and guarded that halo of wisdom and justice which from time immemorial the people had attributed to the Tsar. But here the Emperor had stepped outside his circle and appeared face-to-face with his people, represented by their best sons in Supreme Headquarters. Many of them had never seen the Tsar, or had just had a glimpse of him during parades, and their idea of him was a far cry from reality. The longer he lived among them, the more they saw of him, the more disillusioned they became. The Tsar's retinue, who arrived with him, could not have intensified the unfavorable impression of him more. This group included a senile Minister of the Court, Count Frederiks,[7] and his son-in-law, Marshal of the Court Voeikov. Voeikov was a universally abhorred careerist and speculator, who at every opportunity made it known to the members of the staff that, were it not for the war, he would certainly not even deign to converse with them. Then there was a very pleasant, very rich General of the attendants, Petrovo-Solovovo, whose intellectual development had ceased when he turned twelve, and finally Admiral Nilov, who was always under the influence of alcohol.

Critics of Alekseev among our émigrés, who detested him and blamed him for his renouncement of the Tsar, usually say: "But the Emperor gave him complete independence in conducting military operations, so how did the Tsar interfere with him?"

All these people, however, fail to understand that in a nation's armed warfare, the division of authority between the front and the rear, the military and the civilian, does not work. The country must be directed by one brain and one volition. But at that time Alekseev was given permission only to command divisions and battalions on the battlefields, while the movements, supplies, and replenishments of these divisions, the dealings with the allies, and, finally, that most important factor, the support of the nation's spirits, depended on the Council of Ministers, who remained in the power of Tsarskoe Selo, which was in the hands of a religiously crazed

7. Vladimir Borisovich Frederiks (1838–1927) was a large-scale landowner and a Baltic baron who became an adjutant general and then a cavalry general. He was in charge of the court stables from 1891 to 1893. In 1893 he became an assistant minister, in 1897 a minister of the imperial court and in 1905 a member of the Council of State. He was one of the high officials who were closest to Tsar Nicholas II. After the October Revolution he became a White émigré.

woman and an uneducated, odious muzhik; and these good-for-nothings ruled with the most narrow-minded, base standards.

I sometimes wonder, What if in those days in place of Alekseev there had been a willing yet unprincipled man who, in the name of victory, could have stomached shaking Rasputin's hand and entering into the Tsarina's confidence in order to make use of their influence over the Tsar. Perhaps he could have saved the situation. Perhaps. But Alekseev was too honest for this, too open and straightforward. He saw the approaching catastrophe and carried his cross silently.

During the first part of December, I was granted several days leave and went to Petrograd to see my family. I arrived towards evening. At the railway station there were far fewer cabmen than there had been in the past, and their shabby horses had an impoverished, gaunt appearance, their peasant's overcoats were threadbare, and their sledges were unwashed. The city somehow looked unkempt; here and there the snow had not been cleared away, and it seemed that even the streetlamps burned dimly.

My wife was entertaining an elderly man, Simansky, the father of the present Patriarch.[8] The conversation, of course, was concerning the evils of the day, and Simansky maintained that the Lord's Anointed[9] was part of the religion, and he always was, is, and must remain without blame. My wife, with youthful enthusiasm, confirmed that this was so, but that in our difficult days the salvation of our homeland took priority over anything else. I listened to her and was happy that, even though we were living apart, we still thought the same way.

The next day I went to visit Vladimir Gurko,[10] the eldest son of the famous Field Marshal[11] and a member of the State Council, who was con-

8. The author is referring to Sergei Vladimirovich Simansky (1877–1970), who was called Patriarch Alexis. He held the position of Russian Orthodox Patriarch of Moscow and All Russia from 1945 to 1970. His allegiance to the Soviet government helped him strengthen the structure of the church within an officially atheistic country.

9. The Tsar.

10. Vladimir Iosifovich Gurko (1862–1927) and his family were long-time friends of Fyodor and Marusia Olferieff. Their daughter, Shura, and her husband, Sabby, visited his sister, Auntie Leta, in Paris in 1967. Before this, the last time Shura had seen her was when she was five years old.

11. Iosif Vladimirovich Gurko (1828–1901) was known for his talented military leadership in the Russo-Turkish War of 1877–78.

sidered the more intelligent of the brothers, the one to whom the rest went for advice.

"Now then, is the situation serious?" he asked me, speaking with a nasal twang.

"It seems to me that it is much worse here. The further you go to the rear, the more despondent the mood. We are still hoping for victory, but it seems that in your area they have given up the thought of it."

"Yes, but in about two months, God willing, all will be decided."

I concluded then that he knew of preparations for a large-scale advance on the Southwestern Front, where we expected a decisive success, within this frame of time. In the course of time, however, rumors began to spread that on March 11 there was to be a Palace upheaval in which the Gurko brothers, Vladimir and Vasily,[12] would take part. It was said that, in principle, the conspirators had decided to demand the Tsar's arrest, the establishment of a regency of Mikhail Aleksandrovich,[13] and the confinement of the Empress in a convent, and that they were only waiting for the 11th of March, the historic day of the murder of Paul I, to carry out their plan.[14] How much

---

12. Vasily Iosifovich Gurko (1864–1937) graduated from the Corps of Pages in 1885 and the General Staff Academy in 1892, and went on to become a general of the cavalry in 1916. He was a military advisor to the Boer Army in the Boer War of 1899–1902. He also served in the Russo-Japanese War. In 1911 he became Commander of the First Cavalry Division and later he commanded the VI Army Corps, the V Army, and in 1916, the Special Army. From October 1916 to February 1917, he was acting Chief of Staff to the Supreme Commander in Chief. After the February Revolution, he commanded the troops of the Western Front, but in May 1917 was reduced to the rank of Division Commander for both pro-monarchist statements and his criticism of the Provisional Government. He was arrested in July 1917 for corresponding with the Tsar, and in August of that year expelled from the country. Though asked, he refused to take command of the White Guard forces in Russia's north and northwest.

13. Grand Duke Mikhail Aleksandrovich ("Misha") (1878–1918) was the Tsar's brother and son of Alexander III and Maria Fedorovna. In 1913 he contracted a morganatic marriage with Mme. Woulfert and was banished. When World War I broke out he was recalled, and distinguished himself leading the Cossacks. With the 1917 Revolution, he was offered the throne in place of Nicholas II, but he refused it, thus leaving the gap which the Bolsheviks filled. He was murdered in 1918. (Tisdall, *The Dowager Empress*, 13.)

14. Paul I (1754–1801), the son of Catherine the Great and Peter III, was Russian Emperor from 1796 to 1801. He was hostile towards his mother and lived apart from her with his own court and small army. His policies were extremely reactionary. Frightened by the French Revolution and the continual peasant outbreaks in Russia, he imposed strict censorship and police measures to hold progressive social thought in check. In 1800 he prohibited the importation of foreign books and closed down private printing presses. He

of all this was plausible, I cannot judge, but it seemed to me that you could expect Vladimir Gurko to take part in this affair. (I later learned this was true, because Vladimir Gurko told me so himself.)

None of my friends whom I encountered during this visit in Petrograd asked me what was happening at the front as they had in the past, when people would scrutinize my expression and try to foresee when victory would come. Now no one expected it. Only one question remained—when will it end? At our home, food was still available, but we heard complaints from all directions that it was impossible to get anything.

The day after my departure to Headquarters, our poor son, Sergei, was born. He was conceived under the roar of guns, born in the days of painful trials, and grew up in exile and poverty. During the twenty-seven years of his life he received very little from other people, but he gave up his life for them in the Second World War.

During my absence from Headquarters, Alekseev became ill and left for Crimea, relinquishing his duty as commander of a special army to Vasily Gurko. The Emperor set out for Petrograd to attend the State Council. It was quiet at Headquarters, and the mood seemed sadder. On the extreme right flank near Riga, Commander Kuropatkin persistently attacked the Germans with the XII Army, bearing considerable losses.

When I presented myself to General Gurko, he asked me where I had served before my appointment to Headquarters, and after learning that I had come from Baranovichi, became interested. "Well, how is the supply situation there?"

"Three months ago everything was satisfactory."

And I continued as I had said to his brother in Petrograd, "It is better there than here."

"It will turn out well here too," he stated.

In January[15] the Emperor returned to Headquarters. Soon rumors began to spread from Petrograd about the difficulties obtaining food supplies in

defended pro-serfdom landowners and distributed 600,000 peasants among them. By carrying out reforms in the army based on the Prussian Army, he provoked many officers and generals. His character was said to be unbalanced and his petty-minded attention to detail led to dissatisfaction among his courtiers. On the night of March 11, 1801, he was murdered by conspirators.

15. February 22/March 7, 1917.

the capital. We waited from day to day for the recuperation of Alekseev. Reports came from Riga of heavy losses, and the general atmosphere became more and more gloomy. Finally, Alekseev returned, and Headquarters sighed in relief.

At this time I received an invitation from Colonel Tkachev, Commander of Aviation on the Southwestern Front, to go on a tour with him of all the squadrons on his front, to check their work and preparations. Lukomsky added to the assignment by requesting that we make a detailed report to him about what we saw.

The day before my departure I was the officer of the day and in the evening I was seated at the telegraph. About ten o'clock Ruzsky called Alekseev on the Hughes instrument.[16] I do not know what he reported to him because Alekseev took the tape with him. I only saw how he fell back in the chair, grabbing his head, muttering, "Is this the beginning of the end?"

Later I learned that Ruzsky had reported that several units of the XII Army refused to make the attack. They were put in reserve, and the attack did not take place. I remember this fact well because he held the position until the abdication of the Emperor.

On the day of my departure, news came from Petrograd that the population had begun demonstrations there demanding bread. It became known that the city's garrison was unreliable, and the demonstrations took on dimensions that were more and more threatening. The Tsar, fearing for his family in the Imperial Palace, decided to send a battalion of Holders of the Cross of St. George under the command of General Ivanov[17] for their protection.

---

16. The Hughes telegraph was an electromechanical, type-printing telegraph with a piano-like keyboard designed by D. E. Hughes in 1855. The Hughes instrument was a considerable improvement over previous type-printing telegraphs in both speed and accuracy. It was also less liable to mechanical breakdown from wear and tear and from accident. This instrument was for some years extensively used in the United States. Its form was taken up by the French government in 1860 and became extensively used not only in France, but in all European countries.

17. Nikolai Iudovich Ivanov (1851–1919) graduated from the Mikhail Artillery College in 1869. In his career, he was General of Artillery (1908), Adjutant General (1907), and commanded the III Siberian Corps in the Russo-Japanese War. From 1906 to 1908, he was Governor General and Chief Commander of Kronstadt, where he suppressed the Kronstadt uprising in 1906, and from 1908 to 1914, he was Commander of the Kiev Military District. During World War I he led the troops of the Southwestern Front from 1914 to 1916 and

The next morning I arrived in Kiev. People there were living under entirely normal conditions. The shops were filled with provisions, and all of the restaurants were open. I stopped by to see Grand Duke Aleksandr Mikhailovich. And although he had heard of the events taking place in Petrograd, he apparently did not give them particular significance.

Both he and his staff overwhelmed me with the most prosaic questions, the kind we had already stopped thinking about in Mogilev. That same day I went to Brusilov's staff. There I met Tkachev, and on Lukomsky's order, appeared before Brusilov, who had asked me to stop in without fail upon my return and inform him of all that I had seen. In town and on the staff of the front everything was moving along normally, and there was no mention of the happenings in Petrograd. Beside the tracks at the railroad station, I saw several French tanks being guarded by French soldiers.

Here we got into an automobile and went to the front. The railway, which we crossed from time to time, was overloaded with platform cars carrying heavy guns and tanks, which again were accompanied by Frenchmen.

We toured the whole front, all the squadrons, all the staffs, and saw new airplanes and the happy faces of the aviators who had received them.

For several days on the front we did not see one German over our positions, and the aviators were saying, "If someone flies in, we will shoot them down." In Staff Headquarters, we saw large photographs of the German positions displayed. In the headquarters of the II Army, I spoke with comrades from the Academy who all were in good spirits and were full of hope for success. "So long as the Germans don't attack us somewhere first." We saw a German prisoner in Army Headquarters, a non-commissioned officer in active service. Prisoners are always gloomy, but from the few words he spoke to us, we perceived that the situation in Germany was far from easy: There was no hope for victory; the country was starving. "Deutschland Kaput,"[18] he

---

then he was at the Tsar's headquarters. He possessed no abilities as a military commander, but on February 27/March 12, 1917, Nicholas II appointed him Commander of the troops of the Petrograd Military District and sent him with his troops to that city to suppress the revolution, but he failed. He fled to Kiev, and then, after the October Revolution, to the Don Region, where he commanded the White Cossack Southern Army in October and November 1918. This army was defeated at Veshenskaia.

18. German: "Germany defeated."

said, lowering his head. According to him (and this was confirmed by other sources) across the way from the II Army stood a correspondingly large unit of Turkish troops.

I remember visiting the corps stationed in the region of Tarnopol, under the leadership of General Gutor,[19] an able commander, who later served in the Red Army. His staff was situated in a forest. We arrived as the sun set, and here and there its slanting beams broke through the shadows of the tall fir trees, illuminating the tents standing in the regiment's reserve. The soldiers were dining. I was transported mentally to the old, carefree times of peaceful maneuvers, and only the occasional sound of the guns prevented me from forgetting reality. Gutor lived in a beautiful hunting lodge on the edge of a rather large field. After giving us a snack, he took us to evening prayers. On the field the regiment was lined up in the shape of the three sides of the quadrangle. The command sounded: "Caps off for prayers!" And the soldiers began to sing the evening prayer, followed by "God Save the Tsar." This was the evening of March 1. I heard the hymn for the last time carried through the forest from the lips of the soldiers of the Tsar's Army, and again for a moment I forgot reality and tears welled up in my eyes.

Gutor's Corps was on the front lines and was supposed to lead the attack. On saying good-bye he said to us, "Tell anyone who needs to know that we are prepared to carry out the task assigned to us in every detail."

Who could have believed that within less than a year this General would become a Red Commander, and these very soldiers would crush Kiev and slaughter the officers there?

---

19. Aleksei Evgen'evich Gutor (1868–1938) the son of an officer, graduated from the General Staff Academy in 1895. He fought in the Russo-Japanese War and in 1913 became Chief of Staff of the Kazan Military District. In World War I, he was Chief of Staff of the IV Army, Chief of the 34th Infantry Division, and Commander of the VI Army Corps. In April 1917 he became Commander of the XI Army, and from May to July 1917 was Commander in Chief of the armies of the Southwestern Front. He then took a position at General Headquarters. In November 1917 he changed sides and joined up with the Soviets. In August 1918 he became Chairman of the Commission on Service Regulations, and in May 1920 joined the Special Consulting Group of the Chief Commander. In August 1920 he became Assistant Chief Commander for Siberia. He later served as a teacher in the Subdepartment of Strategy at the Military Academy of the Workers' and Peasants' Red Army. He retired in 1931.

The End

"My God, is this really happening? Is it possible that after fifteen years of military preparation and service my dreams will be realized? Victory seemed so close and so possible. If only it could come sooner." These were the thoughts that ran through my mind when, approaching Berdichev, we saw entirely new platform cars with new tanks and guns.

At the Headquarters of the front, I encountered the Commander of the Operations Division, Ivan Ilich Gromyko:

"The Commander in Chief asked me to come see him upon my return to the front."

Gromyko waved his hand dismissively.

"No, he cannot receive anyone now. He is very busy on the telegraph. You know that this minute the Emperor is abdicating his crown in Pskov."

My heart stopped. And what I heard or said after that and how I left Headquarters I do not remember. I came to my senses only on the train, on my way to Mogilev. Around me sat officers of the Guards, who were going to Petrograd on leave. The news of abdication was spreading as if by wireless telegraph, and was the sole topic of conversation. Across from me sat an Ulan of His Majesty, Kostia Apukhtin, an innately intelligent, well-educated fellow.

"Instead of going to Pskov the Emperor should have come to us. We would have never allowed this to happen."

"But you know the Emperor, Kostia. To come to us he would have to be a different kind of Emperor."

Apukhtin kept quiet.

"No, No, No . . . we will stop this. This cannot be . . ." And again he became silent. We did not sleep all night on the journey to Mogilev.

What would have happened if, instead of going to his family, the Emperor had gone to his Guards? From there he could have ordered an advance of the units in the field, which, as Gutor had asked us to relate, were entirely ready to carry out the burden put upon them. If the advance were successful, the revolution could have been held in check, and maybe never would have taken the upper hand. Even if the Emperor had not been able to remain on the throne, the revolution would not have assumed such monstrous proportions as it did subsequently.

Maybe all this was only my fantasy, just a hopeless wish. Maybe we were not ready for an advance; it's also possible that it would not have been successful. I don't know. I am writing here about myself and what I witnessed and experienced during those days, and I am convinced that I was not the only one who thought this way, or who realized that when a combatant's head is chopped off, he is dead. And the subsequent movements of his body are nothing more than posthumous convulsions.

I arrived at Headquarters on the morning when Alekseev received the Tsar's request for the army's opinion of his abdication, and I went directly to the telegraph office. Alekseev was at the telegraph desk, and the entire administration of the Quartermaster General and all of the commanders of the divisions were gathered side by side in the duty room. Alekseev spoke in turn to the Commanders in Chief of the fronts, informing each of them about the progress of negotiations in Pskov and advising them that for the sake of rescuing the front and avoiding bloodshed, they should appeal to the Emperor on behalf of the army to abdicate the throne. These negotiations were conducted after the Emperor asked Guchkov and Shulgin[1] for permission to confer with the army before he abdicated.

---

1. Vasily Vitalevich Shulgin (1878–1976) was a leader of the nationalists, a publicist and author. The son of a nobleman, he contributed to and became editor of the nationalist newspaper, *Kievlianin*. During the February Revolution of 1917 he served on the Provisional Committee of the State Duma. On March 2, 1917, in Pskov, he and A. I. Guchkov presented Nicholas II with the Duma's demand that the Tsar abdicate. After the October Revolution of 1917, he was one of the organizers of the struggle against Soviet power, and he helped create the Volunteer Army. After the Civil War ended, he emigrated.

This answer could just as well have been given by Alekseev, but he decided to remove himself from this immense responsibility and turned it over to the Commanders in Chief. They could no longer say, Go ask someone else; they themselves had to answer. The responses began. The first reply came from Evert[2] in approximately these words: "Being informed by General Alekseev about the existing situation and Your Majesty's desire to hear the voice of the army before making Your decision . . ." and followed by stereotypic phrases: "taking into consideration and proceeding from that," and so on. "As your faithful subject I beg Your Majesty to give up your authority."

When I read this text, I was reminded of Lebedev,[3] a man of many words, and decided that he had composed it.

Ruzsky immediately sent his advice to the Emperor.

An offensively worded, peremptory telegram came in from Brusilov, demanding abdication. It shocked all of us, and I remembered how this man, who was now rising in mutiny, had kissed the hand of the then all-powerful Grand Duke Nikolai Nikolaevich in Peterhof just a few years previously.

On the other hand, General Sakharov, the Commander of Special Forces, which included the Guards, implored the Tsar to remain on the throne.

---

2. Aleksei Ermolaevich Evert (1857–1926) graduated from the General Staff Academy in 1882. In 1914 he was appointed Commander of the IV Army and fought in the Battle of Galicia. He became Commander in Chief of the armies of the Western Front in August 1915. His incompetence as a military leader and his extreme indecisiveness were particularly apparent during the front's summer offensive in 1916 along the Vilna (Vilnius) axis and in the vicinity of Baranovichi. He retired in March 1917 and lived in Smolensk and then Vereia, where he engaged in beekeeping.

3. Pavel Pavlovich Lebedev (1872–1933) graduated from the Alexander Military School in 1892 and from the General Staff Academy in 1900. In World War I, he was Chief of Staff of the III Army, holding the rank of Major General. He volunteered for the Red Army in 1918 and was Chief of the Mobilization Directorate of the All-Russian Main Headquarters from 1918 to 1919. In 1919, he became Chief of Staff of the Eastern Front and then went on to be Chief of the Field Staff of the Republic and of the Staff of the Workers' and Peasants' Red Army in 1919–24. During these latter years, he was also a member of the Revolutionary Military Council of the USSR. From 1922 to 1924, he was Chief of the Military Academy, and from 1925 to 1928 he served as Chief of Staff and Assistant Commander of the Troops of the Ukrainian Military District. He helped plan and execute the operations that defeated Kolchak, Denikin, and Yudenich. Lebedev was awarded the Order of the Red Banner of Labor.

Scherbachev did not write anything, using the fact that he was Chief of Staff of the Romanian King as justification.[4]

Finally, towards morning from the Caucasus came the heartfelt plea of Nikolai Nikolaevich, begging the Emperor to leave the throne.

What objective did the Tsar have in turning to the army for advice? Was it a sincere desire to find out the feelings of his beloved troops, who in the past would always enthusiastically shout "Hurrah" and sing "God Save the Tsar" when they saw him? Or did he secretly hope that over the heads of his generals, he would hear new shouts of "Hurrah," and the troops would invite him to come lead them again? It seems to me that at that time he was not seeking protection from anyone, but he sincerely wanted to fulfill his duty honorably before God and his country to the very last moment of his reign. There was no doubt that he truly believed in the Divine origin of his authority.

Alekseev's goal was to hasten the entire procedure of abdication in order to save the dynasty, and with it the command personnel and the fighting power of the front.

But the revolution was not on hold. The following day Order 1 was issued,[5] and the army, in its final convulsions, took its last breath.

After signing the Manifesto of Abdication in favor of the Provisional Government, the Emperor boarded the train and proceeded to Headquarters.

The next day General Alekseev ordered all members of the staff to be present at the railway station to meet the Emperor. Usually he was met only by the staff commanders. We all stood in line along the railway platform, and at about eight in the evening the Tsar's train slowly approached us. Someone observed, "It's as if we are meeting the deceased."

Alekseev entered the train, and five minutes later the Emperor appeared on the platform. It was painful to look at him. He had aged and grown thin; deep wrinkles lined his face. With his usual gesture of readjusting the left side of his mustache, he shook hands with the general and passed along our rank, as always asking questions from time to time and looking each person

---

4. Scherbachev was appointed assistant to the King of Romania for Military Operations and Commander in Chief of the Russian armies on the Romanian Front in 1917. The Romanian and Southwestern Fronts were combined in December 1917 to form the Ukrainian Front under his command.

5. Order No. 1 by the Petrograd Soviet, which placed military units under the control of elective soldiers' committees.

directly in the eye. This he had been trained to do since childhood, and this he did for the last time. I stood on the very left flank. Approaching me, he asked, "Who is on duty today?" Evidently the same thought went through both of our minds: "What difference does it make now?" Not waiting for an answer, he proceeded to the automobile.

What were my feelings during these moments? I do believe that all of us who were present felt the same. I was very sorry for him, just as one feels pity for a condemned man. But my predominant and much greater sorrow was for our country, with her efforts to defend herself and survive so mercilessly and stupidly ruined. Did any one of us professional officers who was still capable of thinking believe that the Tsar's abdication would bring Russia victory? I can say with certainty, no.

Outwardly, life at Headquarters resumed its normal course; the only difference was that the Emperor did not appear for the operating reports. He was awaiting the arrival of Nikolai Nikolaevich, to turn over the duties of Supreme Commander in Chief to him. At the same time Mikhail Aleksandrovich had refused to assume the throne, and following this the Provisional Government was formed. Empress Maria Fedorovna[6] arrived from Kiev to see her son. The first to leave the Governor's House, like a rat from a ship, was Commandant Marshal of the Court Voeikov. In the meantime there was more and more disturbing news coming from Petrograd. The soldiers' soviet and workers' deputies did not want to recognize the Provisional Government. On the war front, the recently created soldiers' committees began to select their commanders. Here and there a few hated officers were killed. The situation was particularly grave in the Baltic Fleet. Military operations ceased altogether.

One evening while I was on telegraph duty, General Alekseev was called to speak with the Head of the Provisional Government, L'vov,[7] who informed

---

6. Maria Fedorovna ("Minnie") (1847–1928) was the mother of Tsar Nicholas II. She was born Princess Dagmar of Denmark, the second daughter of Christian IX and Louise of Hesse-Cassel. Her elder sister was Queen Alexandra of Great Britain; her brother Frederick became King of Denmark in 1906 and her second brother William ("Willy") was elected as George I of Greece. She married Alexander III ("Sasha"), and was famous as Dowager Empress of Russia from 1894 to 1917. (Tisdall, *The Dowager Empress*, 13.)

7. Prince Georgy Evgen'evich L'vov (1861–1925) was a Russian statesman. A liberal, he played a strong role in the development of the *zemstvo* system of local self-government. He was a deputy of the Constitutional Democratic Party in the Duma and chairman of the

him that Nikolai Nikolaevich was unacceptable as Supreme Commander. Thus Alekseev was appointed, and the Emperor was compelled to leave Headquarters immediately.

As always during the last days, the staff members assembled in the duty room. Among them was Grand Duke Sergei Mikhailovich.[8] The conversation dealt with the possibility of new appointments. They talked about the expected arrival of members of the Provisional Government and about taking an oath to support it. Still clinging to outmoded thinking, the men discussed and quarreled over trivial things such as seniority of ranks, etc.

After being bombarded all day long by the sad news coming from the front and the capital, I could no longer restrain myself and remarked, "In my estimation, all our conjectures and considerations are of no consequence now. Don't you realize that today we are witnessing the beginning of a world social revolution?"

Sergei Mikhailovich, who only a year later was thrown alive into a mine shaft in the Urals, burst out laughing and said, "Indeed you are a pessimist. His Majesty Capital will quickly choke this hydra-headed monster."

I remember that I felt embarrassed, and I held my tongue.

The following day we were all ordered to gather in the administration of the Chief of the Inspecting Department of the War Office to bid farewell to the departing Emperor.

In the large hall the members of the staff were lined up in a square in several ranks. Very soon the Emperor entered the room, escorted by Alekseev. He had evidently had some rest and looked better than on the day of his arrival. In his speech, he thanked us for the help we had given him

---

All-Russian Union of Zemstvos when the February Revolution of 1917 placed him at the head of the Provisional Government. L'vov was an idealist and feared violence, which made him particularly unfit for coping with the turbulent conditions. While he sought to organize a constitutional and democratic government, the Social Democrats gained the actual power by organizing and dominating the workers' and peasants' councils (soviets). In May 1917 agitation for peace with the Central Powers forced the resignation of the foreign minister, Miliukov and the war minister, Guchkov, and L'vov formed a second government. After a Bolshevik uprising was suppressed (July 1917), he resigned, and a moderate Socialist government under Kerensky was organized. L'vov subsequently escaped from the Bolsheviks and settled in Paris, where he died.

8. Grand Duke Sergei Mikhailovich was the youngest son of Grand Duke Mikhail, who was the youngest brother of Tsar Alexander II. His brother, Aleksandr ("Sandro"), was son-in-law of Empress Maria Fedorovna. (Tisdall, *The Dowager Empress*, 15.)

while he was commanding the army and expressed assurance that we would conscientiously perform our duty to the Motherland and not give up arms until we drove the enemy from our borders. He concluded by invoking God Almighty to help us in our service. He spoke sincerely from the heart, and it was clear that no one had written this speech for him. He had not quite finished speaking when we heard a loud clatter, and his Cossack bodyguard fainted. General Petrovo-Solovovo noisily cried like a child. Many others openly wiped tears from their eyes.

What were my feelings at that moment? Here I must do penance for my thoughts then. I was ashamed when I remembered them later, after the Tsar stoically held out for imprisonment, refusing an offer from Germany to save his life, and accepted a martyr's death. At that time I thought, "You so easily sacrificed the homeland for the sake of your own family. For you everything is fine. You will go abroad with your family and live there in peace to the end of your days. You always placed yourself before Russia and you will continue to do so. But you also believed that you were anointed by God, and that without you the homeland could not exist. Why haven't you even made the smallest attempt to hold your power?" I felt sorry for him, but not sorry to be rid him.

Recently I found a loose-leaf calendar with the farewell address from the Emperor to the army, dated March 8, 1917. Here is the translation:

> *It is for the last time that I am addressing you, my fervently beloved troops. After my Abdication from the Throne of All Russia, both for myself and on behalf of my son, authority has been passed to the Provisional Government created through the initiative of the State Duma. May God help it guide Russia along the path of glory and prosperity. And may God help you, gallant troops, defend our Motherland from the vicious enemy.*
>
> *He who thinks now of peace, he who wishes it—is a traitor to his country, its betrayer. I know that every honest soldier thinks this . . . I firmly believe that in your hearts the love for our great land is as great as ever. May the Lord God bless you, and may the Great Martyr, St. George the Victorious, lead you to victory.*
>
> *Nicholas*
> *Supreme Headquarters*
> *8 March 1917.*

The Emperor walked out of Headquarters and entered his Pierce-Arrow, which was decorated with red flags. From that moment on, the Emperor of all Russia was under arrest.

Kerensky's Times: The Inverted Pyramid

Paradoxical as it may seem, the February 1917 event could not be called a revolution. Neither the most conservative merchant Guchkov, nor the impassioned monarchist Shulgin, nor even all of the State Duma desired any forcible change in the existing order of things. On the contrary, the purpose of the Duma was to save this order by all possible means, by replacing the person on the throne. But to everyone's surprise, this throne was so rotten that it was like a termite-infested building crumbling under its own weight. The heir to the throne had an incurable illness; Mikhail Aleksandrovich, conscious of his total inability to take up the reins of government, declined to do so.

As a result, someone had to seize this failing power. And at first we thought that the State Duma was taking it up by forming the Provisional Government.

The representatives of this government, Miliukov, Guchkov, and Kerensky, came to our General Staff Headquarters. All the members of the staff were gathered in a large room, and they addressed us in turn, as if we were the voice of the military establishment. It was as if they were justifying themselves to us for all the goings-on at the highest levels of the government. Miliukov, a professor, interpreted the events from a scholarly point of view. His explanation might have been very interesting if the events had not affected each of us so directly, and had not demanded an immediate solution. Guchkov gave a long and boring speech on how he had tried without success to save the throne, but we did not believe him. Finally, Kerensky came forward. In a stirring, fiery ovation, he expressed that same thought that I had had, that the throne had fallen without any struggle from its defenders or its opponents. The only difference was his firm belief that in reality, power was now in the hands of the Provisional Government. He spoke of the necessity of holding the front and continuing the war until the triumphal end. His speech made a positive impression on everyone—both on the clerks and on the generals. It was met with thunderous applause, and against all logic, I too began to believe that all was not yet lost.

I heard much enthusiastic praise of Kerensky from the administration, and at the same time I learned, among other things, that Colonel Baranovsky, the same one who had spoken with irritation about the Emperor's strategic reports, was Kerensky's brother-in-law. Very soon after that, when Kerensky became Minister of War, Baranovsky became his personal secretary.

Meanwhile, both the General Staff and the Provisional Government took all possible measures to neutralize Order No. 1 from the Soviet of Workers' and Soldiers' Deputies, which decreed that the commanding personnel in the army be changed from commanders to technical advisors and placed in subservience to committees of the troops, in the companies, the battalions, the regiments, etc. It was necessary to acknowledge the existence of the committees, but the election of commanders was prohibited. An order was issued to address the lower ranks as "*vy*" instead of the previously used "*ty*." The very name, "lower rank" was changed, I think, to "soldier." When addressing an officer, instead of "Your Honor" or "Your Excellency," it became "Mr. Captain" or "Mr. General." The practice of saluting the officers remained in force. All these orders came from the Provisional Government, but the army's decay was in full swing, starting from the mortifying abdication of the Tsar.

Once for some reason I happened to be at the railroad station just when a train arrived from Petrograd. The first-class buffet was crammed with soldiers who had come to get a bite to eat. A bearded soldier with an intelligent face was sitting on a divan in the middle of the hall, and did not stand up and salute when he saw me. Among the ranks, saluting the staff was still required, and I reflexively called attention to his infraction:

"Why didn't you salute me? Don't you know that this order still remains in force?" I asked.

Without standing up, the bearded one smiled.

"No, not true. Here, sit down next to me, young man, and we shall discuss it."

After the change of government, the first to disappear from their posts had been the railway police. I could not arrest him, so I had to respond.

"No, I will not sit down, but will listen to you standing up."

"You see, young man, you received your officer's rank by edict of His Majesty. But just where is this 'Majesty' now? One more question—will we give you the rank of an officer? It's best that you don't trouble yourself or bother a comrade soldier. This will be for the best."

Evidently, this was one of the party workers, going to the front in a soldier's uniform. I reported this incident to Lukomsky, who gave me a lecture. "You should have been prepared that a soldier would not listen to you, and you ought to have known that there was no way you could arrest him. You should have pretended that you didn't notice him."

"But, what will the future hold, Your Excellency? How are we going to continue the war?"

Lukomsky shrugged his shoulders.

For a long time neither the officers nor even the Provisional Government grasped the fact that the pyramid had been inverted, and that a commander who answered to no one, His Majesty Comrade Soldier, was above us all.

Meanwhile, everyone who had been living in the Governor's House left Mogilev. As I have already mentioned, the first one, Marshal of the Court Voeikov, disappeared before the departure of the Emperor. The day before the Tsar left, all of his servants departed. Looking out the windows of my own room in Staff Headquarters, I watched the servants with their suitcases exit through all the gates of the governor's small garden and discreetly slip away toward the railway station. I do not know who fed the Emperor on the day of his departure, or even if he had anything to eat. The last to set out for the station was Count Frederiks, an old man. The poor fellow evidently did not quite understand what was going on. It was said that when he arrived at the station, he requested the newspaper *Novoe Vremia*, and when told there was no *Novoe Vremia*, he became infuriated and said that henceforth this paper must always be in the kiosk.

In stark contrast, everything that had been kept in the shadows and suppressed during the reign of the Tsar was now brought out into the open. Once, even before the abdication, while sitting in the staff's dining room, I saw a general of small stature in a rather worn, particularly baggy uniform and unpolished boots, looking as if he had not had a hair cut in several months. He walked along the wall, making his way towards the table where Alekseev sat. I was told that this was the so-called "strategic brain" of Alekseev, General Borisov, and that Alekseev did not make any decisions without first consulting him. Borisov, it was said, had at one time served on the General Staff, but had gotten mixed up in certain political affairs and was dismissed from service.

Before the abdication, Borisov had never appeared anywhere, but afterwards he could be seen everywhere, front and center.

It was soon ascertained that not only the Tsar's entourage was obliged to leave Mogilev, but also all those who directly communicated with him. Alekseev proved to be too conservative and was replaced by General Brusilov,[9] who after the abdication turned decisively toward the side of revolution and delivered stirring speeches defaming the old regime; the soldiers on the Staff of the Southwestern Front carried him through Berdichev[10] in a red chair. Lukomsky was also replaced. Denikin[11] became Chief of Staff and brought with him two quartermasters, Markov[12] and Yuzefovich.

---

9. Aleksei Alekseevich Brusilov (1853–1926) became General of Cavalry in 1912. He graduated from the Corps of Pages in 1872. In his military career he served in the Caucasus in the Russo-Turkish War of 1877–78. From 1912 to 1913 he was Assistant Commander of the troops of the Warsaw Military District. In the beginning of World War I he commanded the VIII Army, and in March 1916 he commanded the Southwestern Front, where the armies made a breakthrough on the Austro-German Front. The "Brusilov offensive" was successful at first, but cost Russia at least a million lives. He was briefly Commander in Chief under the Kerensky regime in 1917, during which time he signed the order introducing capital punishment on the front, to repress the revolutionary struggle of the masses of soldiers. After the collapse of the 1917 June offensive, he was replaced by Kornilov and appointed as a special advisor to the Provisional Government. In 1920 he joined the Red Army's staff in directing the war against Poland. He later (1923–24) served in the central apparat of the Red Army as Inspector of Cavalry.

10. A Ukrainian city on the Gnilopiat' River.

11. Anton Ivanovich Denikin (1872–1947) was one of the main leaders of the all-Russian counterrevolution during the Civil War (1918–20). He graduated from Kiev Infantry Junker School in 1892 and from the General Staff Academy in 1899. During World War I he commanded a brigade, then a division, and from the fall of 1916, the VIII Army Corps on the Romanian front. He was Chief of Staff of the Supreme Commander in Chief in April–May of 1917 and then commanded the troops of the Western and Southwestern Fronts. In November 1917, he, along with General Kornilov, fled from Bykhov prison to the Don River, where he took part in the creation of the Volunteer Army, which he headed after Kornilov's death in April of 1918. The following autumn he became Commander in Chief of the Counterrevolutionary Armed Forces of the South of Russia and Admiral A. V. Kolchak's Deputy Supreme Ruler of Russia. In the summer and autumn of 1919 he led a campaign on Moscow. He was driven back by the Red Army, and his demoralized forces evacuated to Crimea in 1920. There he turned his command over to General Piotr N. Vrangel and departed on an English destroyer for Constantinople. Denikin did not favor restoration of the monarchy. In his political views he sympathized with the Constitutional Democrats (Cadets) and supported a parliamentary republic. He lived in France until 1946 and then moved to the United States, where he died in 1947 in Ann Arbor, Michigan.

12. Sergei Leonidovich Markov (1878–1918) graduated from the General Staff Academy in 1904. He took part in the Russo-Japanese War of 1904–05, served on the General staff from 1908 to 1911, and then taught at the General Staff Academy. During World War I he

Finally, a commission appeared at Headquarters to clean out its counter-revolutionary element, and I, being the protégé of Aleksandr Mikhailovich, was told that my position as an understudy in the administration of the Chief of the Inspecting Department of the War Office no longer existed, and that I had to remain in reserve and wait for a new appointment.

At this time my wife and children left Petrograd for Mogilev because it had become more difficult and dangerous for her to live there alone. Mogilev, not being in the sphere of military actions, was accessible to everyone, and the majority of the members of the staff lived there with their families. But I did not even get a chance to meet with her, because a new vacancy opened on the Staff of the VIII Army, and I had to leave immediately. She had to live in Mogilev alone again, to the great sadness of both of us.

And so, quite unexpectedly, I found myself considered a danger to the revolutionary element because of my connection with one of the members of the Romanov dynasty. I remember another conversation with my colleagues in the staff. It had taken place before the abdication, and although we were only joking, it could have aroused suspicion among people behind my back.

"You know, Fyodor Sergeyevich, perhaps it's only possible to make a career such as yours with the help of Rasputin—to attain the position of Commander of the Regiment with the rank of captain."

"If, in fact, Rasputin solicited for me," I answered, "then he did it without my knowledge."

I met Aleksandr Mikhailovich for the first time in my life in Kiev, and I am sure that he knew nothing about me or my past. But if he was really the one who appointed me to General Staff Headquarters, then it was probably simply because at that time I was the only officer from the General Staff on all the fronts who was taking an active part in live combat aviation. Another possibility is that a comrade from my graduating class at the academy,

---

held staff positions. In April 1917, he became Second Quartermaster General of the Staff of the Supreme Commander, and in June, he became Chief of Staff of the Western Front and in August, Chief of Staff of the Southwestern Front under General Denikin. He was arrested for participating in the Kornilov mutiny, but in November 1917, he fled across the Don and took part in forming the Volunteer Army. He commanded the army's Third Officers Regiment (February–May 1918) and the First Infantry Division (from June). He was killed in battle. Both the First Officers Regiment and later the First Infantry Division of the Volunteer Army were named after Markov.

Disimetier, may have mentioned my name to Aleksandr Mikhailovich when he left the aviator post that he had held at the very beginning of the war to teach in the academy.

I also think that I was not as much a danger to the revolution on the staff as I was to Colonel Gaskel of the General Staff, who supervised aviation in the administration of the Duty General, and who, never having smelled gunpowder during the entire war, did not want me to replace him because he would have to go to the front. All this is nothing more than my personal supposition.

In any event, I was happy to leave Headquarters, where I was quite undeservedly shouldering the burden of other people's sins. I was glad to go to the front in order to be in direct contact with the aviation squadrons again, and more than happy to serve with the VIII Army, which had just come under the command of General Kornilov, a fellow with the aura of a fearless hero, who had escaped from a German prison camp, and who before his captivity had spent the entire war in the very front lines.

The Army Staff was stationed in the capital of Bukovina, Czernowitz.[13]

The Cradle of the White Army

The VIII Army, which Brusilov had led in combat three years previously, which had captured L'vov, traversed through all of Galicia, and never known defeat, was now the only one on the entire German-Austrian Front encamped on hostile territory, at a standstill in the trenches in front of Czernowitz; and not being harassed by the enemy, it was decomposing under the hot summer sun of Bukovina. Slogans brought from Petrograd were heard in the trenches: "Peace without annexation and reparation," "We do not need the Dardanelles," "Peace, come what may." The officers, and those few intelligent soldiers who still had not given up hope of a reinvigorated army, endured, but they were powerless to deal with mass hysteria. It would seem that the Austrians would find it worthwhile to

13. Also Chernovtsy. Bukovina was part of the Austro-Hungarian Empire until 1918. With the dissolution of the Austrian monarchy in that year, the Ukrainian national council at Chernovtsy approved the incorporation of North Bukovina into the West Ukrainian Democratic Republic; later in 1920 all of Bukovina was transferred to Romania.

open fire, so that we would begin to retreat. But the Austrians were as yet unsure of this.

However, the further in the rear the people were from the trenches, the more militant they were; and the safer their position, the more indignant they were about the behavior of the "doomed" in the trenches. It seemed that no one understood why the soldiers would suddenly refuse to continue risking their lives. Well, after three years, they should be used to this risk. Now, when their main oppressor, the Tsar, had abdicated, when they had received their freedom, didn't they understand that they ought to defend this freedom?

"Why do I need this freedom, if I am killed tomorrow?" the soldier answered from the trench. "*And how do I know that it was the Tsar's fault, and not the fault of his Generals, who are sending me to die now?* We will wait, make peace, and after that, we will decide who was right and who was wrong." This was not Lenin's propaganda, but a natural reaction of the people, and by comprehending it, Lenin attained power over the nation.

In the VIII Army I met many of the principal figures of the White Movement: General Kornilov; Captain Nezhentsev, who started the Volunteer Army; General Petr Vrangel, or as he was called in Petersburg, "Piper";[14] General Romanovsky, who later became known as the evil genius of the White Movement, and finally, Colonel Pavel Alekseevich Kusonsky, who wholeheartedly served in the White Army to the very end, only to lose his life as a prisoner of the Germans during the Second World War.

I arrived in Czernowitz on the famous day when Kornilov presented a standard to the first volunteer regiment, which carried his name and was organized by Captain Nezhentsev. They were lined up in front of the Army's Staff. Kornilov was inspecting the regiment, and in response to his greeting, a harmonious and triumphal reply poured forth from hundreds of young men, a response such as we had not heard for a long time. In front stood a lectern and next to it was the standard—black and white. A priest was serving moleben and sprinkling Holy Water on the standard. The regiment marched off in ceremonial order and again warmly cheered the Commander of the Army in appreciation for his gratitude.

14. Baron Petr Nikolaevich Vrangel (1878–1928) was from a noble family of the St. Petersburg province. More is written of him in the narration. He died in exile in Belgium.

The first thing that caught my attention was the youthfulness of the regiment's personnel. It was doubtful that Nezhentsev was more than twenty-five years of age. He was slender, well-built, wore a pince-nez, and rather resembled a typical staff officer, but in his eyes there burned an unquenchable fire of determination and confidence in the righteousness of carrying out his duty. The soldiers in the regiment looked more like military school cadets than common soldiers who had enlisted. They radiated the same spirit of determination as their commander.

A few days after I arrived, before I had time to get acquainted with the units, I was called to see the Commander of the Army. Short in stature, with a patchy beard and hair worn in a typical Mongolian style, Kornilov had probably been nicknamed "clumsy" in military school. But his Kalmuck eyes burned with a great passion, and their gaze penetrated deeply into the soul of those with whom he spoke. This is what he told me:

"I have received an order from Headquarters—here, you read it later—to send an officer from the General Staff with an explicit statement of those measures which I propose to undertake to evacuate the reserve units stationed in Petrograd. You know, before my appointment to the VIII Army, I commanded the Sixth in Petrograd. I don't understand what plans they're expecting to get from me. I tried to instill confidence in me among the reservists, and instead of shooting the soldier who first shot his company commander and started a mutiny, I went to the regiment and hung the Cross of St. George on his chest. However, this didn't help at all, and to the very end of my duty there, I put no plans together and took no initiatives. So now they can carry out whatever they consider to be the most expedient at the present moment. I am sending you because you know all of them there, and it will be easier for you to talk to them."

I must admit that my first meeting with Kornilov left me with an unfavorable impression. He knew the situation on the ground, and Headquarters was waiting for his assistance in resolving problems of the first order—such as evacuating the Petrograd reserve battalions, which, being in total subservience to Lenin, continually threatened to overthrow the Provisional Government in favor of the Bolsheviks. Kornilov did not even express a desire to help Headquarters in this.

During these days, events were moving so fast that when I arrived at Headquarters and briefed Denikin, who had sent written instructions to Kornilov, he [Denikin] had already forgotten who had requested the removal of the battalions. After being directed to see Markov, I learned that the Provisional Government had issued the request. Markov advised us to ignore the request.

Upon my return to Czernowitz, I inspected the aviation squadrons and found the pilots in a negative frame of mind. They complained that the committees were hindering their reconnaissance flights in the direction of the enemy so as not to provoke the Austrians into taking revenge with their airplanes. There were even threats to shell the pilots from our trenches if they dared to fly across the Austrian lines. The officers in some areas did not even trust their own soldier-mechanics, fearing that the latter would sabotage the engines before their flights.

Evidently wanting to forestall our advance on Tarnopol, for which we had begun preparations during the Emperor's reign, the Austrians began their advance on the VIII Army, and without any resistance, pushed it back from the frontiers of Bukovina. Our comrade soldiers quickly retreated to the other side of the Dniester. The Army Staff crossed over into Kamenets-Podolsk. The retreat was covered by a composite of the cavalry corps under the command of General Baron Vrangel.

At a critical moment of the retreat, when news was arriving from all directions that the comrades were refusing to fight, a report came to the Army Staff from Vrangel that he had switched to a counterattack, had crossed the Dniester, and was attacking the Austrians.

Kornilov called me, read the telegram, and said, "Go immediately to Vrangel and verify this report. I doubt that this is true."

When I reached the Dniester, Vrangel's Corps was on our bank, and there was no fighting. According to the staff, in the morning several Cossack sotnias had indeed crossed over to the right bank of the river and pushed back the enemy, but had returned soon after. The report was clearly exaggerated, but the very fact of their crossing, in spite of the unit's small size, indicated that if our comrades had wanted to fight, we would have been able to knock the Austrians back to their old positions. Vrangel spoke very approvingly of the Cossacks' action, and remarked at once, "You should have rallied them there."

When I reported this view to Kornilov, he said, "One more such report and I will remove him from command of the Corps."

In his outward appearance Baron Petr Nikolaevich (Piper) Vrangel always reminded me of Don Quixote—tall, very thin, and always arguing with someone. I first met him in 1906 in Petersburg at Bolshaia Morskaia Street. He had just returned from the Japanese War and was joining the Horse Guards. That day he was very agitated and kept indignantly recounting how a Fabergé jeweler had dared to refuse to give his mother the diamonds he had just sold her unless she left a deposit. The behavior on the part of the merchant seemed entirely normal, but in regard to Baroness Vrangel . . . Ahh, no—It was inadmissible. He was going to Fabergé's to punch him in his snout.

History doesn't tell us how this affair ended. All we know is that Piper remained in the regiment, and Fabergé continued to prosper in his fashionable store.

Initially Vrangel did not intend to enter military service. He graduated from the Mining Institute and was due to become an engineer. But while fulfilling his duty in the Cavalry Life Guards Regiment, he decided to take the examination to become an officer, and was promoted to the rank of cornet in the very same regiment. He had evidently found his calling, for as soon as the Japanese War broke out, he immediately transferred to the theater of war. I do not know how he conducted himself there, but during the war he was promoted out of turn, and in spite of the old Guards' tradition, he returned to the equestrian regiment to saddle up among his comrades. Soon after that he entered the General Staff Academy, from which he graduated with high honors. He was about two years ahead of me, and I remember how he defended one of his graduation projects. He made his presentation not in the manner of a student, but more like a professor who was delivering a lecture. When one of his examining professors dared to contradict him on something, Vrangel proved his point with great skill.

Upon graduation from the academy, he did not go serve on the General Staff, but returned to line duty, since service in the Guards promised him more opportunity for a quick promotion. He soon became commander of a squadron and led it into battle. In Eastern Prussia his squadron stood in reserve during an assault by the Cavalry Guards on the German Infantry. But the minute he felt that circumstances called for an attack, he prevailed upon the Commander of the Regiment to allow him to attack the battery in cavalry formation. Our dismounted units were already approaching this battery, and they would have been taken prisoner without the equestrian attack; but Vrangel, suffering great casualties, reached it first at a full gallop, and for this received the Cross of St. George. Glory to the regiment and glory to Vrangel spread quickly. Soon after that he was named Commander of the Regiment.

One time during the war, on my way to Petrograd, I tried to board an overcrowded train and heard someone call me from the rear: "Come here, there is plenty of room." It was Vrangel, who led me through the coupling towards the lounge car, which was completely empty. How he got into it I didn't ask, because in all likelihood I wouldn't have learned the truth anyway. I stretched out and took a deep breath. But in return for this comfort, I had to listen far into the night to Piper's boastful tales of his real and imaginary triumphs. He told them well and convincingly, and suddenly a thought came to me: What if this very same Piper had been Commander in Chief instead of commander of a regiment? There was no doubt that he had inborn military talent, was well-educated, sure of himself, and not afraid of taking action on a grand scale. He had one more quality that was lacking among many of our generals—he could hold his ground with anyone, be it an English ambassador or a French general, and as an officer in the Guards, could speak the same language with the Emperor. Moreover, it seems to me that he probably would have even made practical use of Rasputin. Anything was possible . . . Yet even though he was promoted very quickly, he was not able to achieve all that he wanted. It was already too late.

In the summer of 1917 there came a time when everyone began to talk of their rights, and no one thought of their obligations. Everyone yearned for self-determination and wanted to elect their own leaders and committees who would protect their interests. In aviation, as I said before, low spirits predominated among the pilots. In addition to that, with the Tsar's abdication, his patron the Grand Duke had departed. Committees had to be organized under the new defender, and a decision was made to call a conference in Moscow of representatives of all the divisions, of the factories that served them, the managers, the warehouses, etc. I was sent from the General Staff.

I left Kornilov's staff just before the advance on Tarnopol, that very same advance whose preparation I had welcomed so enthusiastically in March. During my service under Kornilov's command, I saw him almost every day, and after all that time, he did not impress me as someone who understood the situation. He took no measures which would restore the fighting power of the troops. I do not even remember that he ever went to the front. The organization of the regiment under his command fell entirely to Nezhentsev and the young men who composed it. Kornilov accepted all of this, but did not do an earthly thing to enhance the stature of these volunteer forces. He seemed to follow the line of least resistance. This is why it seems to me that his imminent elevation to the post of Supreme Commander in Chief, his famous trip to Moscow,[15] his speech there, all this was the handiwork of his inner circle—Union officers and people like Zavoiko and an army commissar whose name I have now forgotten. They exaggerated his reputation and went down in defeat along with him.

I shall never forget his unlimited devotion to the idea of fighting for the honor of his native land, his boundless courage, or his ability to lead people, ignoring all danger. But as a statesman, he was not able to broadly comprehend the situation and make the right decisions. This is the reason he so easily fell into the trap set for him by even such a mediocrity as Kerensky.

Action and Counteraction

Moscow in the summer of 1917 reminded me of a bursting dam: torrents of people arriving and passing through filled the streets. On every corner, platform, and square crowds assembled; everyone was speaking, and they talked about everything, but no one was listening to the orators. The very spectacle of the speeches entertained the people. "War until victory," an orator yelled. "You're absolutely right, Comrade," replied an undisciplined soldier from the crowd, knowing of course that there was no one in Moscow to order him off to the front. There were as many soldiers wandering through the streets of towns in the rear as there were on the front, and I often wondered where they all ate and slept. Kerensky's portrait was being auctioned off in front of Pushkin's Monument. It was doubtful that anyone needed it, but again, the very process of the sale amused the people, and the crowd paid

15. The author notes: According to the officers who took part in it, it was staged; they said it openly to me when I went to St. Petersburg to see Burman and Tolstoy.

the salesmen with devalued treasury notes, or *kerenki*. There was no Bolshevist propaganda to be heard, and at this time it is doubtful whether it would have had much success. Everyone seemed cheerful; they did not think of tomorrow, but lived for today, when nobody was shooting at them.

The Muscovites stayed inside their homes, looked out onto the street, and wondered, "What is going to happen?" They were lamenting that there was no Tsar, and were awaiting God's punishment of the people. "Go to church. There in the liturgical prayer the Provisional Government is mentioned instead of the Tsar. But who is this government? A lawyer who specializes in divorce cases—maybe even a Jew! Who wants to pray?" However, a great number of Muscovites continued to behave as before, and the churches were filled with supplicants. The image-lamp continued to burn in front of the Iveron Icon,[16] and the people passing by removed their hats and made the sign of the cross. And all of these people suffered without the Tsar, because he was a part of their religion. Even those who had criticized him and the Tsarina before the abdication were now blaming the army and the generals for allowing him to abdicate.

And it was into this environment that soon after my departure, they brought our Kalmuck,[17] so that the first capital,[18] and with it all of Russia, would support him in his attempt to overthrow the Provisional Government. This entire demonstration was so unexpected and so far from the minds of the inhabitants of Moscow that its failure did not surprise me.

The aviation conference took place in one of the cadet corps in Lefortovo,[19] where approximately five hundred representatives gathered. And since they were all elected, the majority of them, naturally, were from the rank and file, mainly non-commissioned officers who were mechanics. In addition, the pilots and pilot observers were not well-known individuals. A young ensign presided. After the first session, it became clear that no one in the entire delegation was interested in the conference so much as in the chance to take a break in Moscow, and they wanted to extend this respite as long as they possibly could. The delegates were not interested in politics. They were equally indifferent to the elections of committees in the higher

16. The Chapel of the Iveron Icon of the Mother of God. Voskresenskie Gate Square.
17. General L. G. Kornilov.
18. Moscow.
19. A district on Moscow's east side.

administration of aviation. The most important question for consideration was that of wages. Since the delegates were not principally pilots but ground crew airplane mechanics, who were paid less than pilots, the question of comparable wages was raised. This was extremely unjust, because at that time pilots exposed themselves to danger each day and there were a great number of casualties among them, while the situation of the mechanics was no different from that of the baggage masters. This question was examined and deliberated for days. Finally, I asked to be allowed to say a word. As I approached the platform, everyone became silent, probably expecting something special from me, an officer of the General Staff. This was my first public appearance, and I was feeling uneasy. But after a few phrases, I got hold of myself, and since what I said came from my heart, my speech went smoothly.

I told them that at the present time an advance was underway at the front, and that each of us undoubtedly was needed in our detachment, and therefore we should come to a decision as quickly as possible on all questions and return to our posts. I said to them that we ought to be certain that our service to our native land wasn't lost, and that if we failed to come to an agreement now, when this question was settled at some time in the future, everyone would be paid for his time from the day the question was raised. And I further stated that my duty demanded my immediate return, and that I would leave my address with the chairman so that he would be able to call me when my services in my specialty were needed. All this was met with a deathly silence, and I left the meeting.

More than a month passed from the day of this speech, and I received a letter from the chairman asking me to return to the conference. But I did not comply with this request.

In the meantime, many changes occurred on the front. The advance near Tarnopol, whose preparation I had welcomed so enthusiastically in February, turned into a complete fiasco. In spite of the fact that Kerensky came to the front, in spite of all of his eloquence and assurances, he received one answer from the comrades: "If you want to advance, go yourself; we have already had enough war!"

Volunteers formed a strike force battalion, but nothing came of it. Kerensky understood that it would be necessary to do things differently, that improvisation had no place in military action, and that the military machine could only work when it was steered by a machinist. It became necessary to accept the officers' advice to remove the "red" General Adjutant, Brusilov, and appoint Kornilov in his place. The latter took almost all of the Army's Staff with him and left for Mogilev. In Mogilev an Officers' Alliance was organized, and Kornilov's regiment also made its way there. Soon after that, Headquarters dashed off orders to restore authority to the Command Staff. From the other side, the Army Committees, having immediately received instructions from the Soviet of Soldiers' and Workers' Deputies, began to countermand these orders. As a result there was no peace on the front for the command staff.

Events at Headquarters were unravelling at lightning speed. Kornilov's trip to Moscow was clearly received with indifference, in spite of all the efforts by those around him to disguise the fact. When he returned to Mogilev, he awaited Kerensky's arrival at Headquarters, intending to arrest him there. He prepared all these plans in a childish manner, and the officers spoke openly about them.

Verkhovsky,[20] a classmate of mine who was serving then as Governor General of Moscow, arrived at Headquarters, where he conferred with Kornilov, who apparently shared his plans with him. Seeing the carelessness of the plot, Verkhovsky, after taking his leave from Kornilov, went not to Moscow but directly to Petrograd to see Kerensky. As a result, instead

---

20. Aleksandr Ivanovich Verkhovsky (1886–1938) became a Major General in 1917 and a Brigade Commander in 1936. He was born in St. Petersburg into a military family of the nobility. He graduated from the General Staff Academy in 1911 and took part in both the Russo-Japanese War and WWI. During the period of the February Revolution, he was elected Vice Chairman of the Sevastopol Soviet. From July to Sept. 1917, while commanding troops of the Moscow Military District, he cooperated with the Socialist Revolutionaries (SR's) and the Mensheviks and suppressed revolutionary outbreaks among the soldiers. He also opposed the Kornilov movement. From August 30 through Oct. 22, 1917, he was Minister of War, but he resigned because of the preparliament's rejection of measures that he had proposed. (Russia's dropping out of the war, the demobilization of the army, and others.) In November 1917 he attempted together with SR and Menshevik leaders to create at General Headquarters an anti-Bolshevik, "democratic, general socialist government." In 1918 he was arrested for taking part in an SR organization. Having changed his views, Verkhovsky joined the Red Army in February 1919, and beginning in 1920 he was a member of the Special Conference for the Defense of the Republic. During the years 1921–30, he was an instructor in the history of the art of war and tactics at the Frunze Military Academy, attaining the rank of professor in 1927. From 1930 to 1932, he was Chief of Staff of the Northern Caucasus Military District. Subsequently, he served in Vystrel, the higher infantry school of the Soviet Armed Forces, in the General Staff, and in the General Staff Academy.

of Kerensky's coming to Headquarters, an order came to remove Kornilov from his post and arrest him and all his conspirators, among whom were the Commander of the Southwestern Front, Denikin, and all of his staff. In order to avoid excesses, Alekseev was summoned to Headquarters, and with his help, all who were arrested were sent to the prison in the county town of Bykhov,[21] sixty versts south of Mogilev. Outside the prison they were guarded by the Cross of St. George's Battalion of Headquarters, and inside by the Tekinsky[22] Horse Regiment, who were devoted heart and soul to Kornilov. Thus Kornilov was imprisoned, along with his entourage, not so much to isolate him from the ongoing revolution as to save him from his comrades who were angry with him. After that, however, Kornilov was never able to forgive Alekseev for his arrest.

In the meantime, on the Staff of the VIII Army, the following was taking place: By the time I returned from Moscow, Kornilov was already in prison, and probably my completely unnecessary trip to the convention saved me from Bykhov and played a role in my destiny.

The Commander of the Army turned out to be my friend General Sokovnin, the former Chief of Staff of the II Army, who immediately appointed me as Commander of the Reconnaissance Division.

In the Reconnaissance Division at that time there was a French lieutenant, sent to Russia to acquaint us with the methods of reconnoitering used by the French. He did not know a word of Russian, and my assistant, to whom he tried to explain his methods, spoke only Russian. Consequently, they communicated by using signs. The Frenchman was very happy at my arrival and immediately began to complain that we had no information on the enemy. In fact, we had not received reports from the front for a long time, and all that we knew pertained to the time before my trip to Moscow. Besides my assistant, Captain (whose name I have forgotten), there were three clerks in the division who, having nothing to do, sullenly played cards from morning till night.

I went to the front to see how to restore the interrupted reconnaissance reports. Much to my surprise, I saw a completely unexpected scene there.

21. Mogilev on the Dnieper was the capital of the State or "Government" of Mogilev. The "Government" was divided into eleven districts (or counties). Staryi Bykhov was the chief town in one of the districts. It was equivalent to the county seat.

22. From Teke, or Tekintsy, one of the tribes of southern Turkmenistan.

No one had opened fire from the trenches in a long time. Likewise, all was quiet on the Austrian side. The soldiers were making no use of either the communications equipment or the trenches, and were walking around, living and eating in full view of the so-called "enemy." The officers were playing cards in the blindages, and when I asked if they could tell me which Austrian unit was in front of them, a lieutenant colonel answered, "What difference does it make now? I don't think the Austrians are hiding it from us. Why do you need to know?"

"In order to know when they are relieving their own units with others or reinforcing them."

"Well, they aren't going to report this to us. No, but they won't hide. They constantly fraternize with our comrades out in front of the trenches. If new ones arrive, we'll get to know them right away."

Nevertheless I was able to convince the Lieutenant Colonel of the necessity to report immediately everything that he knew about the units stationed across from him.

After making the rounds of the front, the staff division, and the Corps, I had gathered quite a bit of information, and I made arrangements with the Staffs of the Corps to present my report. The Frenchman was very pleased, immediately took out his reference book, compared my numbers of the regiments with the book's, wrote down all the information in columns and calmed down a bit. The work in the division went on, and though the reports yielded very little new information, everyone was satisfied.

Once I delivered a rather harsh reprimand to a clerk who had not carried out my order, and when I spoke to him, I suggested that he get up from his chair. The very next day, the Commander of the Army summoned me, offered me a seat, and said:

"You know that half of the new Army Committee consists of Bolsheviks. Today the chairman came and informed me that in the committee's opinion you don't have enough revolutionary discipline, and you can't remain as Commander of the Division."

"Your Excellency, I don't know what revolutionary discipline is. Yesterday I reprimanded a soldier and requested that he stand when I was speaking to him. I don't know how a commander could behave otherwise, if in general commanders are necessary now."

"Come what may, the responsibility for holding the front—even if only the semblance of it—rests with us. The Allies' success depends on it and consequently so does ours."

"I think that we are fooling the Allies and even ourselves. Yesterday I reprimanded a clerk in the presence of an Allied officer, and I did so at the request of this officer. What else could I have done? And so he sits with us and each day becomes more and more perplexed."

"We all have our cross to bear now. For your safety, my advice to you is to submit a report with a request to enlist in the Reserves. We receive such reports every day. Go to the staff personnel section of the General Staff at Headquarters—they'll direct you on what to do. Remember, I'm doing this to avoid the possibility of further disturbance."

The next day I boarded the train and again went back to Headquarters.

The Revolution Is Deepening

I was sitting in the train and wondering, What is the meaning of revolutionary discipline, the lack of which had gotten me expelled from the Army Committee? How should I have behaved in order to retain my post? The clerk whom I had reprimanded was not a bad soldier. He was always sufficiently disciplined and expeditious. True, he was always morose and looked askance at you, never smiling. Probably he was one of those unfortunate young people who did not have the means to finish school, and all of his life he had remained a second-class citizen. Now, he ardently believed that the revolution had put him on an equal footing with me, and he sincerely felt he was entirely right not to stand up when speaking to me. I of course should have called him aside and tried in private to instill in him the necessity of carrying out my order. It would be unquestionable in battle, I thought. Though at once I remembered that it is not those who are superior who lead in battle, but those who are the most courageous. Thus it has been in all regimes and in all times.

I remembered the past—the bartender in the regiment who was killed by an officer because he did not serve the requested wine; Voldemar Lupik in Livonia, whom we executed as an example to others; our Kurchino peasants, who removed their caps upon seeing us, and knelt down when approaching us with some entreaty. "Vengeance is mine; I will repay . . ."

Thoughts turned to the war, and I saw clearly that in thinking about our obligations to the allies, we were hurting ourselves. The sooner peace was concluded, the better it would be for Russia. It was said that General Evert had offered to the Emperor to open the front. At that time we were disturbed by this. Now it seemed to me that he was right.

There were many officers traveling with me on the train. Probably most of them were from the reserves. This was the period when officers were being persecuted, when each of us had a cross to bear, as Sokovnin said, and no matter where we were headed, our final destination was Golgotha. During these days we elected a defender for ourselves—a person who was an ideal of perfection, in our understanding, a leader; a brave, truthful, selfless individual, whom we were prepared to follow wherever he led us. But, alas, he was like us, and understood neither politics, nor how to lead people or regiments. After his first appearance, he was provoked and landed in prison.

From that moment until the day he was saved by Dukhonin,[23] landed on the Don and was called to action, we had been orphaned.

The question is raised in General Denikin's masterful memoirs: "For what reason did the officers suffer?" They were the same kind of proletarians as the soldiers and workers. Frequently it was more difficult for them to subsist on their sixty rubles a month—to dress, buy shoes, drink, eat, pay rent, and keep up with the fashions—than for a soldier, who on his fifty kopeks needed only tobacco. All this is true. The officers did not suffer because

23. General Nikolai Nikolaevich Dukhonin (1876–1917) became a lieutenant general in 1917. He was from a noble family of the Smolensk Province. He graduated from the Aleksandr Military Academy in 1896 and from the General Staff Academy in 1902. A regimental commander in World War I, he became Deputy Quartermaster General of the Southwestern Front Headquarters in December 1915 and Quartermaster General of the same Headquarters in June 1916. He was Chief of Staff of the Southwestern Front from June to August 1917 and Chief of Staff of the Western Front from August to September 1917. On September 10, 1917, he was appointed Chief of Staff to A. F. Kerensky, the Supreme Commander in Chief. After the October Revolution and Kerensky's flight, on November 3 Dukhonin became acting Supreme Commander in Chief. Relying on counterrevolutionary elements of the headquarters, he took part in attempts to create a counterrevolutionary government headed by the Socialist Revolutionary V. M. Chernov. He refused to carry out the Nov. 7, 1917, order of the Council of People's Commissars to immediately open peace negotiations with the Austro-German command; he was relieved of his post on November 9 and arrested on November 20. Dukhonin was killed at a railroad station by a crowd of soldiers and sailors who were enraged by the news that he had released Generals L. G. Kornilov and A. I. Denikin and other leaders of the Kornilov mutiny from a prison in Bykhov.

they were capitalists, but suffered because with their promotion to officers, they turned into noblemen, became "Your Honor," and metamorphosed into a class hated to the utmost by the people: Gentlemen. They received individual rights, and on attaining the rank of colonel or the honor of the Order of St. Vladimir of the 4th Degree,[24] hereditary rights. Their children received schooling at the expense of the state, and it did not matter if they were capable or deserving of this education, they, too, became officers and received the right to command others. Because of that arrangement, against which the Russian people revolted, we carried a cross and suffered.

In September of 1917, Headquarters, rendered safe from counterrevolution, outwardly seemed to be continuing as usual. But that air of celebration that had been visible everywhere during the days of the Emperor's residence was missing. After Kerensky became the Supreme Commander, Dukhonin agreed to be his Chief of Staff. He was short in stature, a ruddy-cheeked brunette with a small mustache, and he wore the Cross of St. George on his chest. I have no knowledge of his past, except that he served in the staff of the Kiev district and was on good terms with Dragomirov's sons, and as a result had every chance to make a career. Mikhail Konstantinovich Diterikhs[25] was appointed as Quartermaster General of the Staff. More on

24. The Order of St. Vladimir was the last of the Russian orders of merit and was founded by Catherine the Great in 1782. In four grades, it was intended for all classes as a general reward of merit. The badge is in the form of a gold cross with straight arms, enameled dark red and edged with black and gold; in the center, encircled by a thick gold frame, is a circular black medallion bearing a mantle of ermine, surmounted by a crown over the initials of the saint's name. On the black reverse medallion is the date of the foundation, 22 October 1782. The medal is eight-pointed and bears a medallion in the center, in the middle of which is a red cross and around it the four letters C.P.K.B., which stands for Holy Apostle Duke Vladimir. A surrounding inner circlet in red bears the motto of the order, "Prosperity, Honor, Glory." The ribbon is black with a wide stripe of gold. For military merit, the order was complemented with swords between the arms of the cross, which were similarly attached to the star. (Vaclav Mericka, *Orders and Decorations* [London: Paul Hamlyn, 1967], 70.)

25. Mikhail Konstantinovich Diterikhs (1874–1937) was one of the leaders of the Counterrevolution in Siberia and the Far East. He became a lieutenant general in 1919. Born in St. Petersburg, the son of an officer, he graduated from the Page Corps in 1894 and the General Staff Academy in 1900. During World War I in September 1917 he became Quartermaster General of General Headquarters of Supreme Commander A. F. Kerensky; on November 3, he became Chief of Staff of General Headquarters under N. N. Dukhkonin. On November 8, 1917, he fled to Ukraine and soon became Chief of Staff of the Czechoslovak Corps. He was one of the organizers of the uprising staged by the Corps in May 1918. In July–August, 1919, he commanded Kolchak's Siberian Army; in August–September, 1919,

him later. A political section was created within Staff Headquarters as well. At its head was Vasili Vasilyevich Vyrubov,[26] whom I mentioned when I spoke of the Turkestan Corps. The Commander in Chief,[27] keeping for himself the duty of War Minister, remained in Petrograd. From Kornilov's entire staff, Pavel Alekseevich Kusonsky was the only one who was not arrested, and he retained his position as head of the operational section.

I set off to see the chief of the personnel section in the General Staff, Georgy Tityc[28] Kiiaschenko, who had held this position from the very beginning of the war. He was thoroughly pedantic and one-hundred-percent honest. People said that when it came to an appointment to a post, Alekseev might make an exception, even the Emperor might do so, but no one could get around Kiiaschenko.

He was always perplexed with me. The first time I came to see him, I had the rank of a Captain and the duty of a senior staff officer. He was at a loss, but could do nothing about it because the order had already been made out. When I had been relieved from Staff Headquarters at the front, he insisted that I wait for a duty similar to the one from which I had been removed. Since there was no such opening, I insisted that he assign me to the very first available vacancy, and after my lengthy entreaty, he consented. When I arrived this time, he was thoroughly confused, "—Another one. Every day someone arrives. I don't know where to put you." I told him that my wife was living here, and that I didn't need quarters. He calmed down and said, "Ah! This is fine. Go home and wait until you are called—if you are called at all. Your salary will continue as before."

Meanwhile, while I was posted to the VIII Army, my wife had lost the allotment for her lodging at Headquarters, and had had to move to a country house one verst from town, across the street from the railroad station. The house was roomy, and there were outbuildings on the same lot, so there

---

he was Chief of Staff and War Minister; in October–November, he was Commander of the Eastern Front. In 1922, he was elected "Sole Ruler and Commander of the Zemstvo Host" by the so-called Zemstvo Assembly with the support of the Japanese interventionists and declared a crusade against Soviet Russia for the restoration of the monarchy. After the defeat of the White Guards in the Far East, he fled to Shanghai, where he later died.

26. V. V. Vyrubov was Chairman of the Committee of the All-Russian Union of Zemstvos on the Western Front at Minsk.

27. A. F. Kerensky.

28. Colloquial, reduced form of the patronymic Titovich.

was enough room for the two orderlies[29] and my two horses. I unpacked and began to wait.

A call came from Headquarters in less than a week, and I was directed to the political section under Vasily Vasilevich Vyrubov.

"I'm so glad that you're here. My administration is in need of a technical officer as an advisor on questions I know nothing about that pertain to the routine of your military duties."

"Vasily Vasilyevich, I was just fired by the Army Committee for not observing revolutionary discipline. I don't understand anything in regard to revolution or politics, and I'm sure that I won't be of any help to you. Besides, why is it necessary? There's no actual war now. Why are we trying to fool ourselves and others? Discharge me."

Vyrubov was a man of higher than average intelligence, and it was obvious that he understood the situation very well. But above all he was an ambitious person, and the performance of his duty as a commissar at Headquarters promised him a ministerial post in the future. It was only necessary that Aleksandr Fedorovich Kerensky hold on. In any event, he was not risking anything in organizing his administration.

"Do you want me to make you a General?" he asked. "Aleksandr Fedorovich will be arriving, and this is the first thing I will report to him."

"No, thank you. I have the rank granted to me by the Emperor, and I'll die with it."

"I'm asking you out of friendship to help me."

I was obliged to comply. Vyrubov's administration grew quickly. Two supply specialists arrived; one of them was a general. About half a dozen civilians assembled, former colleagues of Vasily Vasilevich from the Union of Zemstvos.[30] An office was set up for a treasurer, a correspondent, and a

---

29. One was an officer's servant and the other a messenger.

30. *Zemstvo* in Russian means County Council. *Zemsky* is an adjective and means county, provincial, territorial. Zemstvo and Municipal Unions were national military social organizations of liberal landlords and merchants, shopkeepers, and businessmen, etc. created in 1914 to assist Tsarism and organize the front for conducting the war of 1914–18. Their formal names were: The All-Russian Zemstvo Union for Aid to Sick and Wounded Soldiers and The All-Russian Union of Cities.

In the beginning they mainly assisted the sick and wounded, performing such tasks as equipping hospitals, hospital trains, and food serving centers, preparing medicines and linen, and training medical personnel. Later, they also fulfilled orders of the main commissariat for clothing and boots for the army and organized aid for refugees. They were financed

janitor, and was furnished with chairs, tables, machines, telephones, etc. During those days nothing was easier than organizing a chancellor's office. No one worried about money; it was printed when needed—and also when not needed—and it was only out of habit that people continued to attach some value to it and exchange it for products. Likewise, there was no lack of personnel. People who had been forced out of their positions and occupations at the beginning of the war still had no idea after the revolution what really was expected of them. They wandered around at the front and in the rear, and stayed in the areas where they were not chased out. My new title was Staff Officer for Assignments to the Chief of the Political Administration under the Supreme Commander in Chief. After a month had passed, it was revealed that my salary was higher than all my expectations, and even though I had not carried out any assignments during that whole month, I received my entire pay. I can only imagine what Vyrubov himself was being paid at this time. True, I received this salary only once.

One day at Administration, much to my surprise, "Piper" Vrangel walked in. It turned out that the committee of his division had found him lacking in understanding of revolutionary discipline. He came to us in order to see Vyrubov, who was a friend from his student days, and probably to inquire as to what was going on.

Vrangel called on us quite frequently. Once, an order came from Kerensky for Vyrubov to go to Bykhov and verify whether Kornilov and his staff were being guarded in a sufficient and vigilant manner. So his mission would carry more weight, he took me along and also invited Vrangel. The entire aim of the excursion was to visit the prisoners and find out if they were satisfied with everything.

I went with a sincere wish to visit friends and do my best to help them communicate with the outside world, to carry out any errands, deliver a letter, or even go see their relatives if requested. It never entered my mind for an instant that any of them would doubt my word. But I was mistaken.

---

from government subsidies, contributions from local organizations of the Union, and donations. The Unions supported the Progressive Bloc.

After the February Revolution, leading figures of the Unions became members of the Provisional Government. They were hostile to the October Revolution and organized counterrevolutionary measures. They were abolished January 4, 1918. The Unions sent their funds abroad and used them to finance the White armies and White émigrés.

The yellow, two-storied prison was surrounded by a stone wall, which blocked the first story windows. At the gate stood a sentry of the St. George's Regiment. After checking our documents, the sentry let us pass, and we entered a rather large courtyard, in the center of which was a row of tables where the gentlemen officers were eating their lunch while orderlies waited on them. The picture was very similar to the gatherings of officers anywhere in bivouac during maneuvers.

Passing through toward the center table where Kornilov was seated, I happily rushed to greet my friends, but their response was cold, and they turned away from me. I felt that I had become their enemy. When we approached Kornilov, he did not shake hands with us. Vyrubov asked him if he could help him in any way. The General cut him short, "No, thank you." Upon seeing me he said, "Oh, you are with them too?"

As we walked back, General Vanechka[31] Erdeli,[32] who knew me as well as I knew myself, stopped me. "Tell me, how did you fall in with Kerensky?" I explained. He gave me a firm and friendly handshake.

Drawing near the gates from the inside, we spotted a Teke. The Regiment of the Teke, with whom Kornilov spoke in their native tongue, would have laid down their lives in battle, just as the Swiss Guards[33] had done for Louis XVI, before anyone could bring harm to their idol. The soldiers of the St. George's Regiment, on the other hand, very quickly went over to the side of revolution, in spite of the fact that, by the will of the Emperor, each of them had been taken from the front for his demonstrated bravery and had been treated kindly by the Tsar, who had ordered the formation of two battalions composed of them to be his personal guard.

Those were the days when throughout all of Russia, the peasants began to oust the landowners from their estates, rob and burn their farms, and divide up their land. "Peace for the huts—War for the palaces," proclaimed Lenin, and the soldiers left the front in droves in order to be in time for

31. Nickname for Ivan.

32. Ivan Georgievich Erdeli (1870–1939) was Commander of the XI Army.

33. The most famous episode in the history of the Swiss Guards was their defense (August 10, 1792) of the Tuileries Palace in Paris during the French Revolution. Threatened by a mob, Louis XVI and his family fled to the Legislative Assembly. The Swiss at the palace resisted the invading mob, but obeyed the King when he sent word to cease fighting. Some 500 men of the regiment were massacred in the ensuing confusion. Their heroic stand is commemorated by the Lion of Lucerne, an impressive monument at Lucerne, Switzerland.

a share of the land. The trains were overcrowded, and the soldiers walked, rode in vehicles, and pillaged the towns through which they passed.

One night my wife awakened me and pointed to a crack in the door to the adjacent room through which the light of an electric lamp was flickering, and footsteps were heard. As I bent down to get my revolver, the bed squeaked, and the footsteps hurried on. I sat on the bed with the revolver in my hands and was ready to shoot if anyone opened the door. Soon the footsteps faded, and we both jumped up and went to the room where the children slept. The nurse and the children were sound asleep; at the back of the dining room, the orderlies were sleeping. But the closet in the hall was open, and all of our clothing had been stolen. At that time it was worth its weight in gold. The next day I reported the incident to the militia, who were totally apathetic, and said, "You had a narrow escape. Thank God you didn't confront them. Last night, right here in town, a Jewish woman began screaming. They killed her and butchered all her children. There's no way we can help you search for your belongings."

During the first days of October, Kerensky arrived at Headquarters and stayed for two days. In the morning Vyrubov asked me to deliver a certain paper for his signature. He told me that Kerensky was resting in the Tsar's bedroom and that I must go in by the back entrance. After going through the passage, I entered a small room from which an open door led to the Tsar's bedroom. A line of people stood in the small room, waiting to be received. Among them was General Borisov. Kerensky, fully dressed, was lying on the Tsar's camp bed and eating an apple. Further behind the wall, someone was speaking to him, but I could not see who it was. "If we could just bring in one Japanese Corps, it would put things in order."

"Yes," answered Aleksandr Fedorovich, smacking his lips as he ate the apple. "But how will you bring it here?"

The generals and colonels standing in line waited patiently and listened to the reasoning of the great statesman. I became ashamed of myself, and turned around and left. I told Vyrubov that there was a long line waiting to see Kerensky and that I felt ill. When he looked at me, I think he probably understood that I would not go back again. "Leave the paper," he said. "I will take care of it myself."

The End Comes to Supreme Headquarters

In the middle of October, Supreme Headquarters resembled a small island in a stormy ocean, threatened at any moment to have every living thing on it washed away by a single wave. In Petrograd, a sailor was breaking up the Constituent Assembly. The Provisional Government barricaded itself in the Winter Palace, which was taken by the Bolsheviks with the help of the crew of the Cruiser *Aurora*; the Cabinet was imprisoned, and Kerensky fled.

October 17, the day of the unsuccessful attempt on the life of Emperor Alexander III,[34] as well as the day of the establishment of the State Duma, now would be remembered as the day when imperial Russia ceased to exist. Lenin declared, "All power to the Soviets." Throughout Russia during this time the landowners' homes were being burned and the peasants were dividing up the land. At the front only a skeleton remained of the staffs and the committees. With guns in hand, the soldiers streamed to the rear, taking advantage of all possible routes, and like locusts, left a wasteland in their path.

At Supreme Headquarters, as before, orders were being written and reports were being received; Dukhonin declared himself Supreme Commander in Chief; the clouds thickened, but life went on, until Lenin gave the order for the immediate conclusion of peace. "The war is crushed," he yelled, and this cry gave him the power to rule the country.

Dukhonin did not accept Lenin's order to immediately send a delegation to negotiate peace with Germany, and it became known that the crew from the Cruiser *Aurora* had set out for Mogilev with orders to destroy the nest of the counterrevolution and to arrest Dukhonin and the seditious generals in Bykhov. Ensign Krylenko,[35] Commissar of the XI Army, was appointed as Supreme Commander in Chief.

---

34. The father of Nicholas II. The year was 1894.

35. Nikolai Vasilevich Krylenko (1885–1938) was a Russian Revolutionist and jurist. He participated in the Revolution of 1905–07 and was a member of the Bolshevik faction in the Duma in 1913. In November, 1917 he was promoted from ensign to Commander in Chief of the Russian forces for the purpose of opening peace negotiations with the Central Powers. He resigned in 1918 and later became a public prosecutor in major political trials and commissar of justice. He was tried in 1938 in the party purge trials and was executed.

During these days there was not one soldier we could depend upon in Supreme Headquarters. Up to now, the St. George's Regiment had not taken any action against us, but it was clear that they did not want to disobey.

Lenin, however, was not sure of this and acted with caution. He ordered the sailors to stop in Orsha,[36] and dispatched messengers with a flag of truce to Headquarters.

Meanwhile, depending on the proximity of the Bolsheviks, the administration at Headquarters began to adapt themselves to receiving them. General Bonch-Bruevich,[37] having already gone over to the side of the Bolsheviks, appeared in Mogilev and began to give instructions on how to select the new committees. One evening General Suleiman gathered all the members of our administration to select a new committee. The chairman of the new committee turned out to be the janitor of our premises, who was an illiterate, elderly private from the reserves. He himself was greatly astounded by his election and asked to be excused, but his request was not granted.

The day before the arrival of the sailors, I was the duty officer at Headquarters. Vrangel came into Dukhonin's reception room, and while he was waiting to be received, we walked back and forth together in the long hall of the Governor's House and exchanged views on the events.

"If the Bolsheviks would accept my terms," said Piper, "I would go with them." What his terms were, he did not say.

That evening Dukhonin called a meeting of the commanders of all the sections of Headquarters. The question under consideration was freeing the prisoners in Bykhov. Colonel Kusonsky was commissioned to carry out this assignment. He was to take a locomotive engine, travel to the Bykhov station and couple it to the already-prepared train, in which all the prisoners were to travel to the Don country. An agreement to accept the prisoners had been received from General A. M. Kaledin,[38] Ataman of the Don troops, long before this.

---

36. A town about forty miles north of Mogilev.

37. A close friend and collaborator of Lenin's.

38. Aleksei Maksimovich Kaledin (1861–1918) was leader of the Cossack counterrevolution in the Don region in 1917–18. He was General of the Cavalry (1917) and was from the nobility. He graduated from the Mikhail Artillery College in 1882 and from the General Staff Academy in 1889. During World War I, he commanded the XII Army Corps and, from

The second question dealt with leaving behind at Headquarters the persons enumerated on a list received from Petrograd, who were threatened with arrest by the Bolsheviks. The first one on this list, of course, was Dukhonin. An automobile was ready for him, and it was obvious that he was thinking of leaving. But in spite of everything, he asked those assembled whether they thought it would be the best possible decision in his case. His closest assistant, General Mikhail Konstantinovich Diterikhs, stood up and said, "Kerensky, a lawyer, could run away from his post, but for a Russian General—the Supreme Commander in Chief of the Russian Army—it would be only proper to remain at his post."

After such high-flown rhetoric, it would seem that Diterikhs, whose name was not on the list, should have remained and stood shoulder to shoulder with his commander. This, however, did not happen. Diterikhs disappeared after the conference.

After listening to Diterikhs, Dukhonin agreed fully with him and decided to remain.

The next morning, after the Bolsheviks arrived at the railroad station, the duty officer at Headquarters, Colonel Chebykin, as he told me later, brought a telegram to Dukhonin. The General was sitting alone and asked, "But, where is Mikhail Konstantinovich? He wanted to be here with me this morning." Chebykin knew nothing about Diterikhs. "What a cautious one he is," said Dukhonin.

I awakened in my own cottage across from the railway station rather late, after being on duty the previous day. The first news I heard from my orderly was:

"Your Honor, General Dukhonin was killed at the station."

"It can't be."

"It's quite true; I saw it myself—he was lying on the tracks, pierced all over by bayonets, and a cigarette was in his mouth."

May 1916 to May 1917, the VIII Army of the Southwestern Front. On June 17, 1917, at the Great Host Council, he was elected Ataman (Cossack Chieftain) of the Don Cossack Host (Executive Body) and became the head of the counterrevolutionary Don Cossack Host government. In August 1917 at the State Assembly, he presented a program for suppressing the revolutionary movement. After the October Revolution, he led a counterrevolutionary revolt, the Kaledin Revolt. Defeat forced Kaledin to acknowledge at a session of the Don Cossack Host government on January 29, 1918, that the situation was hopeless. He relinquished his powers and on the same day shot himself.

When I went to Headquarters, I learned that the new Commander in Chief, Ensign Krylenko, had arrived at the station in Mogilev with a battalion of sailors from the Cruiser *Aurora*, and with him was General Odintsov, who had defected to the Bolsheviks. So as to take control of Headquarters in the least painful way, Krylenko sent Odintsov to ask Dukhonin to come to the railway station for talks with the new Supreme Commander. Odintsov and Dukhonin had been classmates in the Academy. When he arrived at Staff Headquarters, he embraced Dukhonin and assured him that his life was not in danger. Moreover, Odintsov insisted that Dukhonin agree to this, otherwise he could not guarantee anything. Both of them rode in the same automobile to the station. There, without seeing Krylenko, Dukhonin was put in a first-class compartment, and a guard was placed at the door. Odintsov walked out of the compartment. Shortly after that, a crowd of sailors gathered around the train car and demanded that the General be brought out to them because they wanted to make sure that Dukhonin was really under arrest. The guard brought Dukhonin out to the platform. Shouts resounded, "Give him here." He let go of Dukhonin. "Now he wants to escape!" Someone gave him a shove from behind, and he fell on the bayonets of the sailors. The orderly had told me the rest.

Thus ended the First World War on the Russian Front. It was November 20, 1917.

When I walked into Headquarters, I saw our paymaster, who called out to me: "Fyodor Sergeyevich, don't forget to sign in and receive your pay before you leave." He was sitting behind a small table in the antechamber, and in front of him lay packets of red ten-ruble bank notes, carefully bundled with paper bands. I had not recovered after what had just occurred and was dumbfounded at the calm, even cheerful, look of the paymaster, who was carrying out his work as if nothing had happened. I quickly ran upstairs and bumped into General Suleiman, who was carrying a table from one room to another with the help of Colonel Novikov.

"I'm so happy that you're here," said Suleiman. "Vasily Vasilevich has left us, and I'm occupying his room; bring your table in, and you'll be my assistant."

These thoughts ran through my mind:

I'm rather fortunate in my comrades
The vacancies are opening fast.
Some seniors are bypassed and others
are cut down before one's eyes.[39]

The Commander in Chief is murdered, and everyone hurries to elevate himself a step higher.

"What's all this for, Your Excellency? Peace has been declared."

"This doesn't concern us. Our duty is to save the structure of the army."

I was boiling with anger; blood rushed to my head, and I answered him something like this:

"Structure for whom? For these animals and murderers? They don't need your structure, and they don't need you, either. They've already created their own structure, and after what happened this morning, I consider myself freed from my oath and I'm leaving."

"As you wish, Fyodor Sergeyevich. I'm only warning you that if you leave the staff now, you'll be threatened with death."

On my way out, when I was already on the first floor, one of the civilian employees—a Socialist Revolutionary—called out to me from upstairs. He, like the rest of the revolutionaries, had experience in underground living. To my regret, I do not remember his name, but what he did for me saved my life later. He was a charming fellow with a great beard. He played the guitar well and sang gypsy songs.

"Fyodor Sergeyevich, here, take this little book. It may help you." It was a passport. After putting it in my pocket, I firmly shook hands with him and went downstairs to the landing, where the paymaster was sitting. The red ten-ruble notes lying in front of him seemed to be covered with blood. "So now sign and take your money, Fyodor Sergeyevich," shouted the paymaster.

---

39. Quoted from a speech by Colonel Sergei Sergeevich Skalozub in Act II, Scene 5 of Griboedov's *Woe from Wit* (*Gore ot uma*). It symbolized the cynicism of officers whose promotions followed the deaths of their superiors in battle. Olferieff almost certainly read *Woe from Wit* when growing up, for it was a staple of Russian literary culture for the last two-thirds of the nineteenth century. The play was published in an abridged edition in 1833, and in a full edition in 1862. It was first fully staged, though in a censored variant, in January 1831.

I did not answer him. I opened the door and walked out into the street. Just at that moment a column of troops was marching from the station. Ahead of them was a band playing a spirited march. Following them at some distance walked a boy about twelve years of age in a sailor's uniform, which probably was meant to signify the peaceful intentions of the sailors. Next, again at a distance, was a column of sailors with rifles on their shoulders walking very uniformly in cadence. No officers were visible.

These were the very same sailors who had just murdered Dukhonin. I was wearing a colonel's uniform and felt uneasy being so close to them. I looked at their faces—the same faces of ordinary Russian soldiers—faces of young men whom I had grown up with, whom I had taught, served with, and loved, and who, I trust, had loved me. What had happened? What gulf separated me from them? It was clear that they did not understand what they had done, and we were responsible for this ignorance. We had kept them in the dark, exploited their parents in the factories and in the villages, and lived comfortably at their expense. "Vengeance is mine; I will repay . . ."

Maybe I should stay? Perhaps join their ranks and serve them as faithfully as they once served us? No, they will never believe me, and I am no longer needed by them. Maybe later, when everything is settled, my native land will call me again, and I will return and serve once more in the same honest way as, it seemed to me, I had served till now. But, in the meantime, I tried to teach myself not to take revenge on anyone.

The sailors passed by, and I turned toward my house. Thus, unexpectedly, my service to my country ended. I had previously thought of all sorts of possibilities—of being killed, crippled, or retired . . . but to walk out into the street, and by this very action end my service, I never expected. But there was no other way.

With all that was in my past, I belonged to the persecuted—I had been born among them, grew up and served with them, and I did not have the strength to become a traitor to them. However I clearly was still able to see the other side of the coin, probably because in my childhood, all around I had seen the poverty, suffering, and exploitation of the people on whose backs we lived comfortably. And I felt that it was not for us with our dirty hands to take up arms against them. "Should I return and tell Suleiman that I acted too hastily? He will understand and forget the entire incident. No, the die is cast. I am going to the Don to be with my people."

And after this decision, my consciousness of our sins against the people never left me.

Upon arriving home, I had another problem to face—what to do with my wife and children. After what had happened at Headquarters in the presence of the clerk, I expected to be arrested at any moment. But to board the train with my family would be even more dangerous, because the trains were always so overcrowded, they probably would not let us on. They would censure me and most likely put me under arrest immediately, and my family would be left on the street. My wife left the decision to me. I departed alone.

In spite of the fact that everything turned out well and that there was no other way out of the situation, I am always ashamed when I recollect this action. No matter what the justification was, I shamefully ran away from Mogilev, deserting my family, and this continues to haunt me.

From the sublime to the ridiculous is only one step, the proverb says. And from noble effort to dishonorable flight with a false passport is even shorter. Not looking for a justification, I now analyze the flow of my thoughts on that day: More from inertia than sound judgment, I still felt obliged to fight for the honor of my homeland and the army, although I already believed this struggle was futile. I was angry at the cruel injustice meted out to Dukhonin, abandoned at a difficult moment by all of his close subordinates, who in the name of saving the staff were moving tables with the expression on their faces: "My hut is on the periphery,"[40] trying to appear as insignificant small fry in the general stream of events.

But in whom did the sense of self-preservation prevail? In those who remained or in those who fled? I have no answer to this.

Even now, here in exile, we are inclined to criticize those who remained, in spite of the fact that, with few real exceptions, they did not fit in with the new regime, and the majority of them perished. Yet how many

40. Russian idiom meaning "It is no concern of mine."

of them stayed for the same reason I had almost remained, being unable to abandon their families? For this reason it is doubtful that any of us can criticize them.

Before boarding the train, I looked at my passport. My last name was Nikitin—employed by the Red Cross.

Oh my Russia, my dear Russia,
You are unique and indivisible . . .

—V. P. MIATLEV

At the Crossroads

Novocherkassk, December 1917

With great difficulty I pushed my way through the crowd of soldiers overflowing the aisle of the train, found a seat, sat down, and immersed myself in thought. I could not get past the realization that I had done something irreparable, and could not convince myself that I had acted in the right way. The further the train traveled from Mogilev, the more I was tormented with worry for the safety of my abandoned family.

The train stopped at some station, and I mechanically raised my head and saw General Diterikhs sitting in front of me. He was wearing a short fur coat without epaulets or any other insignia belonging to the army, just as I was. He quickly turned away from me, and I felt that I must not show that I recognized him.

This is how we traveled to Kiev, and only as he was exiting onto the railway station platform in the morning did he address me and ask me where I was going. I answered, "To the Don."

"Go see General Alekseev there and ask him if he needs me. I will be grateful if you will convey the answer to me in Kiev." He gave me his address.

Bolshevism had not yet reached Kiev. To all appearances the city continued to live a normal life. There was no shortage of food. Shops, department stores, and restaurants were open, and the militia were still posted on the street corners. In place of the Provisional Government, the Ukrainian Rada[41] had been organized. Executive authority was in the hands of the Ukrainian separatists: Petliura,[42] Grushevsky[43] and

---

41. Ukrainian *Tsentralna Rada*, or Central Council, the Ukrainian legislature.

42. Simon Vasilevich Petliura (1879–1926) was one of the leaders of the Ukrainian counterrevolutionary nationalist movement in 1918–20. He was the son of a coachman. Expelled from theological seminary for his participation in the Ukrainian nationalist movement, he emigrated to L'vov. In 1900 he became a member of the Revolutionary Ukrainian Party. Later he joined the Ukrainian Social Democratic Workers' Party.

Returning to Russia, he worked as a teacher and as a bookkeeper in the Kuban' and wrote for the nationalist Kiev newspapers. In 1906 he became editor of the newspaper *Slovo.* In 1907 he left for St. Petersburg, where he hid from the police. Later he moved to Moscow, where he worked as a bookkeeper and joined the nationalist groups Kobzar' and Hromada. In 1912 he became editor of the newspaper *Ukrainian Life*. Two years later he was drafted into the army. In 1915 he became the chairman of the Main Control Commission of the All-Russian Zemstvo Union for the Western Front. After the February Revolution, he organized and headed the Ukrainian Front Committee. He became chairman of the All-Ukrainian Military Committee of the Central Rada in Kiev, to which he had been elected in May 1917. Later, he served as secretary for military affairs in the General Secretariat of the Central Rada. Under the Hetmanate, he was chairman of the Zemstvo of Kiev Province and of the All-Ukrainian Zemstvo Union. On November 14, 1918, he became a member of the Ukrainian Directory and Chief Ataman (Commander in Chief) of the Army of the Ukrainian People's Republic. He became chairman of the Directory on February 10, 1919. After the defeat of the Directory's forces by the Red Army, Petliura fled to Warsaw, where he entered into an alliance with the government of Poland. He fled abroad in the summer of 1920. After 1924 he lived in Paris. He was assassinated by S. Schwarzbard in revenge for the Ukrainian pogroms against the Jews.

The nationalist movement in Ukraine during the Civil War (1918–20) was called the Petliurovschina. Its base was made up of the Kulaks (rich peasants), local shopkeepers, merchants, businessmen, and nationalistically-inclined intellectuals of Ukraine. Petliura entered into agreements with Kaledin in the Don Region, which turned Kiev into a haven for White Guards, capitalists, landlords and refugees.

43. Mikhail Sergeevich Grushevsky (1866–1934) was a Ukrainian historian and historian of Ukrainian literature, and one of the leaders of the Ukrainian nationalist movement. He advocated autonomy of Ukraine within a federated Russia.

In 1908, after moving to Kiev, he became one of the leaders of the Association of Ukrainian Progressives, which was politically close to the party of the Constitutional Democrats (Cadets). During World War I he favored a German orientation; in 1914 he was arrested by Tsarist authorities and banished to Simbirsk. In March 1917 he joined the party of Ukrainian Socialist Revolutionaries and headed the nationalist Ukrainian Central Rada. With his participation, the Central Rada invited the German interventionists into the Ukraine. After the collapse of the German occupation, he emigrated to Austria in early 1919. There he founded the Ukrainian Sociology Institute. He was permitted to return to his homeland for scientific work in 1924. That year he was elected an academician of the Academy of Sciences of the Ukrainian SSR and became head of the Ukrainian history section of the Academy's

Vinnichenko.[44] The overwhelming majority of the residents of the city had nothing in common with the Ukrainian movement, but they reacted calmly to it, even benevolently, seeing in it the possibility of avoiding the threats from the North.

I met two of my colleagues from the General Staff in the Continental Hotel. Both of them were dressed in a uniform which was unfamiliar to me. It turned out to be the uniform of the Ukrainian Army. They asked me to follow their example.

"We're greatly in need of an officer of the General Staff. They'll make you the Chief of the Zagon."[45]

"What is *zagon*?"

"'Division' in Ukrainian."

"Division of people or cattle?"

"This is no time for jokes. We're preparing to fight for our lives."

"I beg your pardon. Whom are you planning to fight?"

"The Bolsheviks, of course. Either Ukraine defends itself, or Bolshevism will take over all of Russia."

"What about the Germans? It's impossible for you not to know that Ukraine is a German project."

"We need to choose the lesser of two evils. Bolshevism is just as dangerous to the Germans as it is to us. They'll help us."

"No, I can't go along with you," I answered.

Our parting was cold, and in the evening I boarded the train for Rostov.

The train was filled with officers returning from the front. Across from

---

history department. In 1929 he was elected an academician of the Academy of Sciences of the USSR. He worked in Moscow after 1930. He produced a complete work on the history of Ukraine up to the mid-17th Century.

44. Vladimir Kirillovich Vinnichenko (1880–1951) was a Ukrainian writer and statesman. His early naturalistic tales are social in character. His novels set forth his doctrine of human values and his views on the individual's conflict with society. His dramas have been successfully staged in Europe. As an active member of the Ukrainian Revolutionary Party, he was persecuted by the Russian Tsarist government and spent most of the years 1903–17 abroad. In 1917 he became General Secretary of the Ukrainian Central Council, and in 1918 he was named president of the Ukrainian Directorate, for a while heading the Peoples' Republic declared by the Ukrainian nationalists in 1918. His *Rebirth of a Nation* deals with the history of the revolution (1917–20) in Ukraine. After the failure of the revolution, he lived in France.

45. *Zagon* in Russian is a pen for enclosing cattle.

me sat a lieutenant colonel with a very familiar face. He looked at me intently and finally asked:

"Excuse me, did you serve on the Staff of the VIII Army?"

"Yes," I answered, having forgotten that I was supposed to have served with the Red Cross. But immediately I remembered and added, "I served in the Red Cross."

"It seemed to me that you were with the General Staff. Someone who resembled you a great deal came to our regiment to gather information on the enemy. He was a very nice person. He still wanted to continue to fight and didn't believe us that it was already all over. That is when we should have stopped."

I wanted to contradict him but restrained myself in time.

At a small intermediate station just before the Sinelnikovo station, the train stopped, and several sailors from the Black Sea Fleet boarded it. After the train pulled out, they walked through all the cars looking at all the passengers as though they were searching for someone.

It was already dark when the train stopped in Sinelnikovo. From the front car a young officer ran past and shouted at us.

"The sailors are sweeping through the train and removing all the officers who are on their way to Rostov."

Panic descended, and everyone rushed to the exit. I went along with the others, but having thought for a moment while standing on the train landing, I got off on the track side instead of onto the station platform. My brain was working quickly. I remembered that this was the railway junction from which the trains left for the Crimea and for the North. After going around the train I turned toward the platform where the trains were leaving for the North. Luckily a train approached very soon from the Crimea, and I boarded it. I disembarked again at the Lozovaia station, boarded a freight train, and through the kindness of the conductors, and after several transfers, I finally crossed the Donets Basin[46] and reached Novocherkassk from the North. The entire journey took me four days.

46. The Donets Basin is an industrial region north of the Sea of Azov and southwest of the Donets River, a chief tributary of the Don. It covers 24,000 square miles and is a prominent coal-producing and steel-manufacturing area. The development of the Donets Basin began c. 1870, and by 1913 it produced virtually all the coal and more than half of the iron and steel for Tsarist Russia.

I arrived in the evening. The city was in darkness. Later I learned that the workers were on strike at the electric station. With candle in hand, the proprietress led me to my room in the hotel. After freshening up, I went to the officer assembly. A kerosene lamp was burning in the front hall, and at a distance down the hall in the billiard room, playing billiards by the light of two candles, were an Ulan of His Majesty, Vasia Gershelman, my comrade from the corps, and an officer from the communications section at Headquarters, whom I also knew but whose name I have forgotten now.

From my conversation with them I learned that the day before my arrival, Ataman Kaledin had committed suicide. By a previously arranged plan, he had given asylum in Novocherkassk[47] to the generals who had been imprisoned in Bykhov and their volunteers. According to this plan, in which Alekseev had participated, the Don was to serve as the base for the struggle against Bolshevism. But the Cossacks, afraid of attracting the attention of the Bolsheviks to their province, openly protested against the presence of the generals in Novocherkassk, and the Voiskovoi Krug[48] demanded

---

47. Novocherkassk was the chief town of the Don Cossacks. Cossack settlers founded the virtually independent Republic of the Don Cossacks in the fertile steppes along the lower course of the Don River. The host of the Don Cossacks was governed by a popular council, the Rada, and by an elected chief, called Ataman. Their daring raids and exploits attained legendary proportions under Sten'ka Razin in 1670–71.

Though the Don Cossacks gave allegiance to the Tsar in 1614, their self-government was recognized by the Tsar in 1623, and they continued to govern themselves throughout the seventeenth century. Frequent rebellions, however, culminating in that of Pugachev, resulted in the loss of many of their privileges. After the suppression of a revolt in 1707–08, the Don Cossacks lost the right to elect their ataman. The decree of 1835 made them into a military caste with special privileges in return for military service. After 1886, the Tsarist government often used the Don Cossacks to suppress revolutionary movements throughout Russia. After the October Revolution of 1917, the Don Cossacks sought to regain their political autonomy and even strove for independence. They established the Don Military Government and fought the Bolsheviks. Later the Don Cossacks aided the White armies. The Soviet regime abolished Don Cossack army units until the Second World War, when they were reactivated to fight the Germans.

48. The Voiskovoi Krug was the Cossack Assembly. It was the highest administrative and judicial body of the host, and it elected the executives including the Ataman, his two assistants, and a secretary. This Assembly ruled the host. The Don Cossack host was the most numerous divisions of Cossacks in pre-revolutionary Russia, which inhabited the land of the Don host, including present-day Rostov oblast, parts of Volgograd, Lugansk, and Voronezh oblasts, and part of Kalmyk. During campaigns, a campaign ataman was elected and given unlimited authority. The host was divided into 100-man units called *sotni* and 50-man units called *polusotni*.

that they leave the province. Kaledin, a general of the General Staff and former Commander of the VIII Army, was caught between two fires. He felt that he could not go back on his word to the generals, and at the same time, as the Ataman, he could not go against the wishes of his host. His last hope was that the Cossacks returning from the front, and especially the heroic Sixth Regiment under the command of the brilliant Colonel Mamontov[49] (the same regiment, which, in front of my very eyes, had attacked Soldau in cavalry formation), would help him make the Assembly retract its demands. But when this regiment, on entering Novocherkassk, was flying the Red Flag, Kaledin understood that this, his last hope, was lost, and he could find no other way out but to shoot himself.

The temporary vice-ataman of the Cossack Assembly immediately asked the generals to leave the Don province. This occurred the same day I arrived in Novocherkassk.

"Yes," said Gershelman, the son of a former Moscow Governor General. I had known Gershelman since I was fourteen—he had been my father's comrade from the Page Corps as well as mine. He was a brilliant officer, who immediately after graduating from the Corps went directly to fight in the Japanese war. Though an innately kind and an honest man, he continued, "The only thing left for us to do is to answer terror with terror—not to spare anyone—not a brother, not a father, not a wife . . . this is the only way to restore order."

"I don't agree with you, Vasia," I said. "We need to draw the people over to our side. They're not Bolsheviks. I'm convinced that if the peasants know that we will give them the land in their possession, they'll all go along with us."

"Don't spread Kerensky's ideas here," Gershelman said with irritation. "Forget everything that you heard when you were with them in Mogilev." (I felt that this was a jab at me for my service with Vyrubov.) "Well, Kerensky

49. Konstantin Konstantinovich Mamontov (1869–1920) was a White Cossack military commander and a lieutenant general (1919). He graduated from the Nikolai Cavalry School in 1890 and served in World War I as Commander (colonel) of the Sixth Don Cossack Regiment. In the Civil War of 1918–20 he commanded the IV Don Cavalry Corps in the counterrevolutionary armies of Generals Krasnov and Denikin. From August to September 1919, Mamontov led a White Guard cavalry raid along the rear of the Soviet troops of the Southern Front. His corps was routed by S. M. Budennyi's cavalry corps at Kastornaia in November 1919. Because of this, on December 2, 1919, Denikin relieved Mamontov of his command. He died of typhus in Ekaterinodar.

promised them land before the battle at Tarnopol, and how did they answer him? 'The land will be ours anyway. But if you need the war, then go fight it yourself.' "

With a heavy heart I returned to my room, and could not fall asleep for a long time. "Is it possible that they all think the same way here?" And the thought that I had abandoned my family to the mercy of fate in order to join these men whose views I could not share stayed with me all night.

In the morning, even though the weather was gloomy, I was able to survey the city for the first time. It was a typical provincial city of central European Russia, only with a large number of military men in the streets. I was not conscious of any shortage of food in the shops and restaurants where I had been, and everything seemed to be going normally, but the faces of those passing by looked grim.

In a restaurant, I met a colonel of the General Staff whom I remembered from the academy and had encountered many times during the war. I could never remember his name. We began to talk.

"Where does one go to register here?" I asked.

"Nothing's been organized as yet. Go to someone who knows you. You served in Headquarters so you should know them all: Denikin, Markov, Romanovsky . . . I went to see Markov. He wrote down my address and said that he would call when there was a need. But this is of no consequence. Get acclimated and establish yourself. The important fact is that the Dons don't want us here, and the situation is getting worse with each day. You can see that the workers are on strike, and the Cossack Assembly is demanding our immediate departure. The situation is also complicated because Kornilov and Alekseev don't get along. They even live at opposite ends of the city and don't see each other."

"But who is leading the movement?"

"Kornilov is the Commander in Chief. Under him is Nezhentsev, with Kornilov's regiment. They're organizing new units. Officers are arriving every day. There are very few enlisted men. Alekseev is a government unto himself. He's surrounded by Rodzianko, Guchkov, and Boris Suvorin, who have a treasury which they trust only to Alekseev. This is the basis for all the discord among the generals."

"The slogan," he continued, "is 'Loyalty to the Allies, re-establishment of the front, and complete segregation from all internal politics.' But tell me, who is going to decide this political arrangement? The constituent assembly? And where is that? Even if it assembles, who will submit to it? We gathered here merely because there was no other outlet for an honest officer. It is only the belief that truth must triumph that forces us to unite."

"I can see that I've distressed you," he said as he stood up, "but it's better to know everything than to become disenchanted later. We'll look out for each other and look forward to selling our lives as dearly as possible for the honor of our country."

His words could indeed be disturbing. It seemed strange to me, however, that people could prepare themselves for mortal combat in the name of a single idea, with no definite plans for the future, no matter how hard that future might be to achieve. "Only the belief that truth must triumph . . ." All this reminded me of the catacombs in the first era of Christianity, and of Christ himself. And I felt that I myself was still not ready for this kind of sacrifice. I decided to see Alekseev, in fulfillment of the errand Diterikhs had given me. The colonel whom I had spoken with in the restaurant gave me the address of his adjutant, and I went to see him.

The young adjutant, whom I had glimpsed at Headquarters, did not remember me, but he received me cordially and promised to notify the general of my request to see him. He told me to stop by after lunch, at which time he promised to give me an answer. After lunch, however, he said that he did not have time to see the General, and he asked me to go to evening vespers in the cathedral and stand on the right side by the entrance. He would meet me there and give me the answer.

Again the darkness of evening descended. The cathedral was dimly lit with candles and image lamps.[50] There were not many worshippers. I stood where I was directed and soon heard the familiar jingling of Alekseev's spur; one of his spurs was always loose, and sounded as if it were about to fall off. As he passed by, he fixed his gaze on me. I saluted him. He bought a candle and walked ahead.

After the service, the General approached me, shook my hand, and said, "Come now to my home, and we'll talk there."

50. Editor's note: A lamp that burns before an icon.

From all this procedure I understood that since the adjutant did not know me personally, Alekseev, being cautious, wanted to satisfy himself that the name I had given was really my own.

It was a small, dark apartment dimly illuminated by a kerosene lamp in the hall. We walked to his study, where he lit the candles and sat me down across from him. Only here was I able to take a good look at him. He had aged a great deal; was stooped over; and his old, lackluster eyes peered indifferently through his gold-rimmed glasses.

"You served at Headquarters—I remember you."

"Quite true. I was there for a short time during the abdication."

"How can I help you?"

I delivered Diterikhs' message. Alekseev's smile was barely visible.

"Certainly he could be of assistance to me here. We're always happy when someone thinks as we do, but please convey to him that I can't promise him anything." And he repeated what I had already heard from my colleague in the restaurant.

"We're here because there's no other way out for us. I personally have no rosy-eyed hope in the fulfillment of our undertaking, but we prefer death rather than surrender to the mercy of the victors. If Mikhail Konstantinovich agrees with us, then I will be very happy to see him."

"But by what means do you think we could win the population over to our side?"

"We never call anyone to be with us. We believe that all who love their native land will join us. Only with volunteers can we look forward to success. I repeat that I personally have little hope for it. With all the bordering territories currently aspiring to self-determination, wanting to separate from Russia as quickly as possible, we can only hope that the new generation will realize these errors and reunite again."

His dimmed eyes gazed aside. He seemed to be thinking about and visualizing the future. I felt that he was so weary that death itself would be a relief for him.

"Are you going to Kiev?" he asked.

"Yes, if you will permit me. I have to move my family from Mogilev and arrange a safer place for them. I fled from Mogilev."

"Well, may God help you. And then come back with Diterikhs."

I returned to Kiev without incident and immediately informed Diterikhs of Alekseev's reply.

"Who is with him there?" he asked.

I named Rodzianko, Guchkov, Boris Suvorin, and gave him my impression of the mood in Novocherkassk.

"No, the Monarchists aren't for me. You must know, I am a Republican," he said.

Poor Mikhail Vladimirovich Rodzianko: some called him a Republican with a desire to become President, others called him a hopeless Monarchist . . . People see only what they can see and only what they want to see.

Diterikhs' answer was especially interesting considering his behavior later in Siberia and in the Far East, where during the last days of his life he converted Monarchism into a religion—lending truth to the saying: Only paving stones do not switch roles.

I was overcome with mixed feelings from all that I had seen in Novocherkassk. I had enthusiastic admiration for the people who were following lofty ideas, almost without hope of achieving success, seeking to give their lives for a just cause. This admiration was confounded by the recognition that among these honest people, under their white vestments they concealed mean hearts, capable of blackening their sacrificial path. Finally, I felt indignation toward the selfish, shortsighted policy of the population of the Don province, who were bent on getting rid of the generals quickly in order to save themselves.

Thus began the tragedy of the White Movement. Alekseev soon died. Kornilov, Markov, and Nezhentsev were killed in action, and the mean hearts had the upper hand over its remaining leaders.

Terror in Kiev: January 1918

In the city, which was overcrowded with masses of refugees arriving from the north, officers banished from the front, and landowners who had abandoned their plundered estates, it was very difficult to find an apartment. But I was lucky and was able to sublet an apartment in a large new building from the widow of the murdered General Dukhonin, who then moved in with her parents. The apartment was located across the street from the Governor General's Palace in the most fashionable neighborhood of Kiev, called the Lipki[51] district.

Kiev during this time, like Mogilev before its occupation by the Bolsheviks, resembled an island in the middle of a stormy sea, on which people had been rescued from a sinking ship. In the surrounding areas the landowners' estates were being burned and robbed, and the peasant population, not recognizing any authority, divided up their land. For the time being the Ukrainian government was only able to keep order in the city, which is why the exclusively Russian population of Kiev regarded it with indifference. However, there was a feeling that this order was coming to an end. The Bolsheviks were approaching in large numbers from the north. In the Ekaterinoslav area, so-called "Greens"[52] appeared who did not recognize any authority; and from the west, under pressure from the German advance, came the completely demoralized former VIII Army, the one whose Army Committee had expelled me during Kerensky's time for not understanding revolutionary discipline. This horde, with their own interpretation of the slogan launched by Lenin, "Peace for the huts, war for the palaces," left behind a ravaged, dead strip of plundered, half-burned cities with their remaining hungry population. In some areas the trains stopped running completely, in others they ran without any schedule, and made their way through the bands of robbers with difficulty.

The population of Kiev in normal times did not exceed 500,000, and now it was over a million, increasing every day. There were not enough habitable dwellings, the supply of food was exhausted, and prices were going up at an incredible rate.

---

51. The Lipki district was named after the lime trees found there, which were destroyed in 1833.

52. The Greens opposed both the Reds and the Whites—whoever occupied their territory at the moment. The movement arose from the fact that the general attitude of the vast majority of the peasants was a desire to be left in peace to do their work. This was coupled with a strong feeling of annoyance at the various requisitions of food, fodder, carts, and men that both sides subjected them to. Green guerrilla detachments derived their name from the fact that they hid in the green forests, which provided them with cover. The open steppes of Ukraine did not provide any effective hideouts for the Greens, and for this reason there were comparatively few active Green groups in the region. But in the wooded foothills of the North Caucasus there were plenty of Greens. (Gregory P. Tschebotarioff, *Russia, My Native Land* [New York: McGraw-Hill, 1964].)

The government of Petliura was attempting to organize a Ukrainian Army, but was not receiving any support from the peasant population and very little from the officers gathered in the city. So they obtained help from Austria, in the form of specially formed military units made up of Galicians, known as Sich Riflemen[53] for the purpose of alienating Ukraine from Russia. But to begin with, there were not enough of them to defend the city. And furthermore they had hardly any desire to wage war. Finally, with the approach of the Bolsheviks to Kiev, the mob was preparing an internal uprising in that very city, and the Ukrainian Popular Assembly moved politically to the left not in days, but in hours.

In the meantime, after paying my first month's rent for Dukhonin's apartment, I realized for the first time that my financial resources were running out, and that I had no income to look forward to. I even regretted that I had so haughtily rejected the payment of my last wages when I was leaving Headquarters. I had to think seriously about how and where to earn a living for my family.

At this point my wife arrived, cheerfully moving from Mogilev. We were happy that we were together again, and our youth and our belief in truth—our truth—probably ultimately helped us triumph, and for the time being helped us forget reality.

On Christmas day my wife even put up a tree, and invited a guest for dinner—Pavel Alekseevich Kusonsky. He was not a very deep person, but a very sympathetic, incorruptibly honest, and patriotic colonel of the General Staff, the very one who, because of his trusting nature, was subsequently accused in Paris of not preventing the kidnapping of General Kutepov[54] by

53. Ukrainian *Sich* means administrative and military center for Cossacks, and also Cossacks fortification.

54. Aleksandr Pavlovich Kutepov (1882–1930) was a military figure of the Russian Counterrevolution in southern Russia, White Guard general of the infantry (1920). Son of a member of the nobility, he graduated from St. Petersburg Infantry Junker School in 1904. He fought in the Russo-Japanese War of 1904–05 and then served in the Life Guards of the Preobrazhensky Regiment, with which he participated in World War I (1914–18) commanding a company, a battalion, and a regiment and advancing to the rank of colonel. He served in the White Guard Volunteer Army from the moment it was formed, advancing from company commander to Chief of the First Infantry Division. He became Governor General of the Black Sea after the capture of Novorossiisk in August 1918, and carried out brutal repressions against the population there. From the end of January 1919, Kutepov commanded the First Army Corps in Denikin's army and then a corps and the First Army

the Bolsheviks. To the end of his days he remained loyal to the idea of a Great Russia and irreconcilably opposed to Germany, and although almost the entire Russian colony in France cooperated with the Germans during the Second World War, he was taken prisoner by them, subjected to endless interrogation, and died under the strain.

Being a long-time resident of Kiev and a colleague of Dukhonin, Kusonsky introduced me to Dukhonin's widow. And when my financial situation became difficult, with the assistance of Diterikhs, who knew the owner of a dock on the Dnieper, he helped me obtain work unloading barges. Diterikhs had previously been successful in placing officers there.

However, my job did not last very long. We were unloading barrels of prunes from a barge. I had to roll each barrel from the hold up to the starboard side and from there roll it down to the dock. This last part of the work was difficult because you had to restrain the barrel, and the protruding rim scratched the palms of my hands. Nevertheless I accomplished all that was expected of me and unloaded as many barrels as the rest of the professional longshoremen. But one fine day my foreman noticed blood on my palms and called me over.

"Show me your hands." He took my hands in his leathery hands, looked at them for a rather long time, raised his head and said: "Well then, you're not a laborer. You're a gentleman. You better gather up your belongings and go home, or both of us will be in trouble."

"How about my pay?" I asked.

"Come in late on Friday for it. No one will be here, and I'll pay you then."

I remember that this fact especially distressed me because when I was leaving for work that morning, I had heard our Shura ask her mother for a piece of bread, something that we did not have. While walking along Kreschatik,[55] I saw one loaf of French bread in the window of a bakery,

---

in Vrangel's army. After the rout of Vrangel's army in November 1920, he evacuated with the remnants of the White Guard troops to Gallipoli (Turkey); in late 1921 he went to Bulgaria, and he was exiled from there after the September Revolution of 1923. While living in emigration in Paris, he was leader of the supporters of the Grand Duke Nicholai Nikolaievich. After Vrangel's death in 1928, he assumed the leadership of the White Guard Russian All-Army Union (ROVS) and tried to step up its anti-Soviet activity. On January 23, 1930, Kutepov disappeared from Paris.

55. The main street of Kiev.

priced at sixteen rubles. I decided right then that on my way back after receiving my earnings, I would buy it for her. I did not lose hope even though this was probably the only loaf of bread, and it would not last till the end of the day. I figured that I would receive thirty rubles, so even after the purchase of the bread, I would still have fourteen rubles left, which I had already planned to use for our most urgent needs.

But unfortunately, the situation in the city had already changed so much by Thursday that it seemed it would be impossible to go collect my pay in the Podol[56] on Friday.

On my way home I met a small group of young men who were dressed in various outfits which had nothing in common with a military uniform, but who had machine-gun belts across their shoulders and were carrying rifles. After passing me, they took a good look back and walked ahead. Upon reaching the corner of Proreznaia Street and Kreschatik, I saw a big announcement in red on a wall calling all former army personnel to register without delay at the nearest Varta[57] (police station) and enlist in the Vil'ny Kozaki.[58] This was signed by the city's Chief of Defense. Those who did not comply with this order were subject to immediate arrest and deportation from the city. As I walked further along I noticed that these notices were posted on every corner.

Outwardly, life in the streets flowed on as normal. As I approached my home, I met my regimental comrade, Adjutant Levushka Stefanovich, who was coming to invite me to go with him to register.

"I've no intention of registering," I said. "I don't have anything in common with the Ukrainian authority, and I don't intend to."

"Pardon me, but thanks to this authority you're alive today."

"Maybe, but I would rather die than join them."

During the conversation my wife added her thoughts. As in so many times during our life together, which was filled with the most incredible situations, she grasped what was happening with superior intuition:

"Don't go with them, Lev Platonych.[59] You must know, Petliura doesn't

56. The Podol was the quarter of Kiev that was situated on the low ground at the foot of the bluffs. It was the industrial and trading quarter of the city.

57. Ukrainian: *Derzhavna Varta* (1918–19), or State Guard.

58. Ukrainian: Free Cossacks.

59. Colloquial, reduced form of the patronymic Platonovich.

have the army to fight the Bolsheviks. He simply wants to pull out behind your backs, and leave you to take care of them."

But it was impossible to convince Stefanovich. He joined the Vil'ny Kozaki, and after that we never saw him again.

The next day the president of our home committee suggested that everyone fill their bathtubs with water and stock up on candles, because they anticipated a strike by the electrical and water workers. After twelve noon the first grenade exploded over the city. It was followed by a second, a third . . . and soon we were under fire just as during the war. As expected, the city's workers went on strike. The bombardment continued for eleven days, and there was scarcely a house in the city that was not damaged by shelling. By luck, the Bolsheviks evidently did not have heavy artillery, and in firing throughout the city territory, they did no particularly serious damage to the buildings, and deaths from the fusillade appeared to be few. However, during the last days of the shelling, when the attack was concentrated in our area, things seemed rather unsettled at times. Bullets riddled the wall of our house above the room where the children slept. Plaster showered down, and the children began to scream. We carried them to the basement and sat there most of the night.

The next morning a machine gun was placed on the roof of the neighboring house, which was on a level with our windows, and the slightest movement past a window in our apartment was met by a barrage of bullets. All the windows in the living room and our bedroom were shattered by bullets. One of the bullets penetrated the wall above my wife's head while she was still in bed. That day we had to crawl around the house so as not to provoke the gunfire. Only my wife, who evidently had lost all sense of the necessity to save her life, continued to walk at full height, and each time bullets were fired at her.

We learned what was going on outside our apartment from the two brothers who were billeted by the government in one of our rooms. They were true Ukrainians. One of them was a member of the Ukrainian Rada, and the other served in one of the few Ukrainian units loyal to Petliura. Both were Socialist Revolutionaries. The elder held a university degree. According to him, Petliura's government had left Kiev on the first day of the bombardment. The Red Army was only firing at the city, and had not entered it yet, and Petliura's units were fighting in the city against the local rebels. The Ukrainian Popular Assembly, in the meantime, had elected a Bolshevik president and expected the Reds' approval.

The younger brother exhibited extreme cruelty with regard to his non-negotiable political convictions, and yet he displayed sincere kindness and even tenderness towards our children. His unit was quartered in the Lavra,[60] which was besieged from all sides by the local mob, who were armed by the communists. This mob was probably the ones who had placed the machine gun on the roof across from us and were firing through our windows for amusement.

The young Ukrainian visited us several times, and brought all the food he could obtain. Where and how he obtained it he did not tell us, but he was especially concerned about what to get for the children, and watched over them so that they would not be hungry.

Once he arrived all covered with blood: "We killed many of them today. Now they won't be in a hurry to sneak up on us," he said, and with blood-stained hands he passed the children's food to my wife.

Both of the Ukrainians disappeared from our home on the evening of January 11. During the night of the twelfth not one shot was heard, and for the first time in many days we slept tranquilly.

In the morning our devoted orderly, Biberin, knocked on our door, "Sir, the Bolsheviks are making the rounds and arresting all the officers."

I got up quickly and asked him to please leave the apartment. Fortunately for all of us, he had found a sweetheart in the neighboring kitchen and had in fact been living there. I dressed in my civilian clothes and did not have long to wait. My wife had just time enough to throw on her robe when a knock came at the door. I opened it and several ragged-looking men with rifles and revolvers rushed in, ordered me to put my hands up, pressed two pistols against my temples, began to search me, and demanded that I give them all the arms that were in the apartment. Luckily, during the first days of the shooting I had hung my revolver and sword on a rope outside the bathroom window, between the two dwellings. The only thing that remained in the apartment was a small Montecristo pistol,[61] lying on a shelf in the hall.

60. The monastery in the Pechersk district of Kiev.

61. A parlor pistol, popular until the early twentieth century, created by French inventor Louis Nicolas Flobert. In Russia Flobert guns were known as the "Montecristo."

Continuing to hold my hands up, I directed them to it. They thanked me and took it. "What is this?" yelled the man who was searching me. It turned out to be a penknife. They took that also. At that moment my wife ran into the room, and seeing the pistols held at my temples threw herself at me, but one of the thieves grabbed her by her breast and knocked her down with such force that she was unable to get up. I remember the ugly face of this villain. He had a red beard bordering his round, frightful face, red eyebrows, and narrow red eyes. He appeared to be in command of this group, since he gave the orders and they obeyed. He was dressed in a worn-out black overcoat. Over his shoulder was a machine-gun belt, and on his feet were half boots bound with rope. Someone went into the next room where the Ukrainians lived and with great joy ran out with a large bottle of vodka:

"Comrades, a windfall!"

They then went into our kitchen, helped themselves to food, emptied the bottle, and in a totally drunken state, staggered out to the stairway.

Going down the stairs they met a young ensign, a student who had recently been called up for military duty and had just come home from the front. They took him out into the street and shot him in front of his mother. The mother, out of her mind with grief, became hysterical and screamed, "Why him and not the colonel who lives upstairs?" The drunken mob evidently did not hear this; they turned the corner and walked down Institutskaia Street.

This day was far from over—another doorbell and a new search of our apartment. This time the soldiers were from the Red Army.

"Are there any generals or officers living here?"

"No."

"Guns?"

"No."

The soldiers searched the whole house and looked through all the closets. They asked for my documents, and for the first time I showed the passport of Nikitin. At that point the search ended.

The soldiers had just left when the bell rang again. Vera Konstantinovna Stefanovich entered and fell on the couch in hysterics. They had just shot her husband Levuska. Marusia immediately tried to console her as best she could. At that moment the chairman of the house committee came in and announced that I had to leave my apartment at once because my life was in danger. He intimated that if someone asked him who I was, he would tell the truth. I was preparing to leave, but where to? I felt like I was infected with the plague, a danger to the people surrounding me. Everyone was afraid of being too close to me except Marusia. She approached and looked at me, and from the expression in her eyes I understood that if we had to die, we would die together. I looked out the window then and saw a young cadet in a long cavalry greatcoat being led away from the house across the street. One of the soldiers shoved him and the other shot him in the back of his head, and the young man fell face down without moving. There was no place to go.

At that moment the doorbell rang again. A tall, pretty young girl entered wearing a red cross on her sleeve.

"Are you Colonel Olferieff?"

Is she trying to provoke me or not? I wondered. Anyone who did not know me knew me as Nikitin. I did not answer immediately. She understood and said, "Yes, it is you. You cannot remain here. I am Katia Raich. The Verners [parents of Mrs. Dukhonin] know me. I have come to help you hide. Here is a hat and coat. Put them on and follow me."

Addressing my wife she said, "Believe me, we will do everything possible to save him. I will keep you informed. Now, we don't have a minute to lose."

I hugged my wife and followed Raich. "Do not pay attention to anything. Do not speak to me. Walk in silence," she whispered as we were walking down the stairs.

We walked along Elizavetinskaia Street, crossed Kreschatik, and went up Proreznaia Street. The streets were empty except for the patrols that were going from house to house. All the shops were closed. It was a clear, sunny January day, as can only occur in Little Russia.[62] The snow crunched under our feet. It was freezing cold, yet it was warm. Maybe it was the bright sun, maybe it was the presence of the guardian angel I was following that influenced my mood, but the realization that death was possible and so close no longer troubled me.

On the corner of Vladimirskaia Street we entered a large courtyard where one of the largest apartment buildings in Kiev stood. These were

62. The term Little Russia gradually fell out of use by the twentieth century, and the modern term Ukraine started to prevail.

low-rent apartments across from where I lived. The entrance to them was from the yard, and they consisted of three to four rooms. As we approached the door of the apartment where she was taking me, I told her that my passport indicated that I was employed by the Red Cross and that my name was Nikitin. She was delighted with this, since the person I would be living with also worked for the Red Cross. The door was opened by a young woman, who was holding the hand of a girl of about three years of age. Behind her stood a man approximately thirty-five years old, who already knew Raich and was waiting for us. He greeted us with a pronounced Polish accent, and introduced his wife. Then he pointed to a divan in their living room where I was to sleep. Both of them were extremely gracious and kind, as only Poles can be when they want to.

I lived with these good, generous people for more than a week, and despite the fact that by all indications they were not well off, they did not allow me to pay for my room and board. "People will only be happy when they learn to help each other," he said. "People have helped us, and I know that if the need arises again, they will help us again." He not only told me all about his personal life, but spoke of his father and grandfather, who had been shot by the Tsar's Guards during the Polish revolt in 1831—and those Guards, I thought, were my own Horse Grenadier Regiment.

My wife came to see me twice. Before coming through the gate she always stopped and looked back to see if anyone was watching her.

Meanwhile in the city, the extermination of the bourgeoisie, and especially the officers, continued. They killed those who had the red identification papers of the Free Cossacks, and those who had overstayed their leave from the army. In addition, the street mob killed anyone from whom they could remove a good pair of boots or a warm coat. Sometimes the corpses were left on the streets for several days.

In the courtyard of the place where I lived was a small building which had formerly been a police station. Now, according to my landlord, it housed the Extraordinary Commission for Combating Counterrevolution and Sabotage, or as it became known throughout the world, the Cheka.[63]

63. A Soviet security service created on December 20, 1917 by Vladimir Lenin. It was the military and security arm of the Bolshevik Communist Party. Many thousands of dissidents, deserters, and others were arrested, tortured, or executed by various Cheka groups.

Then an order came from the Cheka for all males living in the complex to appear and show their documents. I was very calm when I presented my passport with the name of Nikitin to a man dressed in a military uniform. I was even prepared to give him the whole history of my work on the western front, but he did not request it. That same evening the Cheka included me with eight other residents of the building sent to guard the entrance gate. While on duty we were issued rifles and were ordered to check everyone coming in and going out. I was given a watch from 4:00 a.m. to 8:00 a.m. and from 4:00 p.m. to 8:00 p.m.

Thus, ironically, a fugitive colonel with a fake passport was armed with a rifle and appointed by the Cheka as a security guard. For all their ingenuity, they did stupid things.

This assignment lasted only two days. When I reported for duty at 4:00 a.m. on the second day, I discovered that the members of the Cheka were packing hurriedly, filling a truck with furniture, rugs, some sort of boxes, and other household goods. After loading, they drove off, and other empty trucks arrived and the loading continued. By 6:00 a.m. the Cheka had moved out. They left in such a hurry that they did not even take my rifle. I could not chance leaving my post, since it was possible that they would return. But at 8:00 a.m. when my relief came, we heard a military march being played from the direction of Vladimirskaia Street, and I looked out and saw the Germans marching through the city.

It all seemed like a dream. The body rejoiced at being freed from physical danger, but the soul ached at the sight of the enemies of the ancient capital,[64] the brazen faced Germans, solemnly marching through the streets as the victors.

I returned my rifle to the empty police station, went upstairs, shared what I had seen and grieved together with my new friends. We embraced, said good-bye, and I went home.

64. Kiev was the first capital of Russia; then Moscow became the capital. In 1918 Kiev was the capital of Ukraine.

The German Occupation

In a single day Kiev was reborn. The stores reopened and generals and colonels in their uniforms, merchants and landowners in their fur coats appeared in the Continental Hotel and on the streets. The Ukrainian Council, composed of Communists and Social Revolutionaries, became the Parliament of the Grain Growers, which is to say, it was made up of landlords and prosperous landowners; and Hetman Skoropadsky became its executive leader. He was a former Page, Cavalry Guard, Commander of the Cavalry Guard, General with a retinue, and Commander of the Army Corps in the Tsar's Army. All these events took place without a struggle, resistance, arrests, or executions. The human pyramid turned upside down again, only because military units appeared in the country who did not violate the foundations of public order. It was obvious to all that if the Germans abandoned the region, this order would collapse again, and the same red-headed bully in his top boots who had held a pistol against my temple, and who still lived in Kiev, was waiting for that moment and knew that it would come, at which time he would be able to finish me off, along with the others like me. But the mood of the revitalized bourgeoisie in those days was, "Although it may be just one day, it is ours." Our experience had taught us nothing. All land was being returned to the landlords, and the trade enterprises and factories to the merchants and the manufacturers. The peasant and the laborer again had to watch and wait for the owner to throw him something. The protector of all this order was one German occupation division in Kiev.

However, it turned out that even in those days our whole Southwestern Front was represented by a force of several hundred thousand, and pursued by only one German division and a Cavalry Guard Regiment.

The headquarters of the occupation forces was located in Kiev. It was headed by Cavalry Guard General Alvensleben. All of Petersburg Society who had fled here kowtowed to him, arranged receptions for him and for his officers, and tried to make them believe that the war against Germany was purely a misunderstanding, and that by forming our alliance with the Western democratic countries we had lost our monarchy, for which we were being punished now. Pavel Skoropadsky himself went to pay homage to Wilhelm and upon his return began to imagine himself as royalty.

My wife and I belonged to the Russian minority who suffered upon meeting the Germans on the streets and avoided any contact with them. Sometimes we met people whom we knew who were lobbying for Skoropadsky, and we expressed our outrage at his behavior, and their answer was that this was the only way it would be possible to reestablish Russia. And of course that upon the return of the Emperor, Skoropadsky would immediately subjugate Little Russia to his command. Maybe those saying this were convinced of it themselves. But you had to know Skoropadsky, whose sense of duty was to himself first and then to the motherland. He kept people in the dark when it came to his feelings and convictions. And in any given situation he was capable of doing only what was advantageous to him.

After the German occupation of Kiev, warnings were posted on all the street corners by the German command. They were written in German, Ukrainian, and Russian, telling the peaceful population to continue with their employment and ordering all men who had served in the Russian Army to register immediately at Headquarters. Anyone who failed to follow this instruction was subject to immediate deportation to Moscow.

I did not obey this order. And despite the fact that several of my schoolmates were serving on the Ukrainian General Staff, and knew that I lived in the city and disapproved of their working with the Germans, they did not report me, and I was not arrested. Generally speaking, I must say that the Germans tried to avoid offending the nationalist feelings of the population, and did not bother those who kept away from them. Once a German officer wanted to rent a room from us—the one which had formerly been occupied by the Ukrainians. My wife refused him but did not give a reason. He had full authority to simply commandeer it, but evidently he understood. He excused himself and left.

After we had calmed down a little from all that we had lived through, a more serious problem lay ahead for us: "What to do, where to go, and how to earn a living?" There was no hope of restoring the old regime in the near future or even forming a new one, judging from the arrival of the Bolsheviks in Kiev. Great Russia, by this time, had ceased to exist. Everything was being done to disassociate from her, and the Russian people who found themselves on Russia's peripheries, and even those who had been born here, became outcasts in their homeland if they refused to join the separatist movement. A small group of honest people had fought and sacrificed their lives for the love of their country on the border of the northern Caucasus, without receiving any help from the local population. Alekseev had died, and Kornilov, Markov, and Nezhentsev died heroically in battle. The only one left was Denikin. But in his immediate circle there was a desire for reaction and vengeance, rather than a Christian feeling of sacrifice and love for the homeland.

From the moment the Headquarters fell, I realized that nobody needed me anymore. Now I felt that not only was I no longer needed by these people under whose protection I had lived, but moreover, I was now an eyesore and a hindrance to their efforts to vanquish the shame they felt in betraying their country. The only ones that needed me were my family, and I could not part with them under any circumstances.

I was not alone, however. I found myself in the same situation as tens of thousands of officers who had been exiled from their units by the revolution and who did not dare join the Ukrainian Army.

One day Pavel Alekseevich Kusonsky held a meeting in our apartment which was attended by Lukomsky, Abram Dragomirov, Ya. K. Tsikhovich, a number of young officers, and several of my aviator colleagues, who had just flown in from the front. The question was, Should the officers join the Ukrainian Army? I remember three very specific opinions expressed at this meeting. One young officer, who had been my classmate in the academy and a number one student said, "I think we need to join the Ukrainian Army because we cannot even wear our uniforms now. I'm sorry, but I do not want to wear civilian clothes." When the time came for the older officers to express their opinions, Lukomsky said, "We older officers should not go on duty with the Ukrainians, but you, the young ones, will of course be forgiven in the future."

At that time, it seemed to many of us that the principles and ethics should be the same for the seniors and the juniors. But this was Lukomsky speaking, a military careerist to the very core.

Another characteristic opinion was expressed by my former Chief of Staff, Yanuary Kazimirovich Tsikhovich, "Russia has always rested on three pillars: Faith, Tsar, and the Homeland. Little remains of Faith. There is no Tsar. The remaining pillar, the Homeland, is not stable. Because of this, I am leaving for Moscow."

His opinion expressed neither love for his homeland nor a lack of obligation towards her, but was a choice of the most solid foundation for existence. Tsikhovich was a brave officer and an outstanding Chief of Staff. But he was a professional mercenary soldier, who changed his faith in order to be admitted to the Academy of the General Staff, and being a Pole, could not have had any love for Russia. We parted after the meeting. Lukomsky remained and made his residence with Dragomirov. Tsikhovich left for Moscow. The aviators flew home to wherever they lived, and several of the younger officers went on duty with Skoropadsky.

Mrs. Dukhonin had given up her apartment and the latest landlord raised our rent from 100 to 250 rubles. We did not have the money, and he filed suit to evict us.

Someone referred us to a lawyer, who charged us fifty rubles, and we went to court. The judge solemnly began the hearing in Ukrainian but quickly changed to Russian. Our attorney gave an eloquent speech telling how I had fought not too long ago in defense of our country, and the judge ordered the landlord not to raise our rent.

Soon the time came when we were unable to pay even this amount. One day while walking along the street I met a former senior adjutant from the Supply Corps who had been on the Staff of the Turkestan Corps, Lieutenant Colonel Ponyrko. He was a cheerful, hearty soul who firmly believed that all would be well soon. I told him of my problems, and he immediately offered me work in his restaurant. "We will work together and live to see better days." The restaurant was in Ekaterinoslav,[65] and he suggested that I leave my family here and that both of us go to Ekaterinoslav.

At that time the city resembled an island guarded by a company of German soldiers in the middle of the stormy anarchy of its suburbs. In the environs of this Jewish town were crowds of refugees, just as in Kiev, who were living a full life. Zakharevskaia, the main street, was brightly lit in the evenings, and the theaters, cinemas, and restaurants were going at full speed. One of these restaurants was managed by Ponyrko and owned by a group of officers, among whom were the last Chief of Staff of the Turkestan Corps (I have forgotten his name), a Colonel of the Cavalry Guard, who had been removed from his command of the regiment during the Emperor's time, a Staff Captain of our regiment, and finally our financial

65. The distance from Kiev to Ekaterinoslav (currently Dnipropetrovsk) is 281 miles.

supporters—a Jewish dentist from Kiev and a former jeweler from the same city. The restaurant, of course, did not make money on the food that was served in the front room, but from the card games that flourished in the back room. The Staff Captain served as the croupier, and the General, the former Commander of the Regiment, and I served as the hosts, receiving and accompanying the guests. It was a "typical feast in the time of plague." Money was lost and won in amounts such as I had never seen before.

Sitting in this den, I deeply despised myself and waited impatiently for the first division of the loot in order to return home. One evening I was sitting in the corner after the guests had left and evidently looked very unhappy. I was approached by the dentist who said, "Colonel, don't be so sad. You know that the whole world is nothing but a brothel, and all the people are prostitutes. It is necessary to adapt somehow." This great statement has remained with me to the present day.

As soon as I received my share of several thousand rubles, I said goodbye to my partners and left for Kiev.

During the month of my absence, the mood among the refugees in Kiev had changed noticeably. Instead of the hope of being saved by the Germans, they had begun to doubt their ultimate victory in the war, and threatening news was heard of the successes of the Allies.

News arrived of the loss of the Emperor and his family, and although Ukraine was not officially in mourning, the Sophia Cathedral and all the churches were filled with worshippers. Tears of grief and shame were shed for the innocent family who had suffered for our sins. It was not so much for the fact that we could have saved them, but the fact that in the Tsar's name we had maintained a long-dead system of government that exploited 150 million people. Being aware of these sins, many believed that no matter what might come out of the revolution, we would never be able to restore our position. Very soon after this, as though in confirmation, news arrived of the revolution in Germany and the abdication of Wilhelm.

In the Kirpichev Squad

With revolutionary Germany refusing to interfere in the political affairs of Russia, the sham of Skoropadsky and his Independent Ukraine collapsed like a house of cards. The Galician Sich Riflemen stationed in Kiev left the city immediately—some of them left for home, and the others joined up with Petliura, Skoropadsky's enemy, who was an idealistic Ukrainian and a Socialist Revolutionary. Several of the battalions, the so-called Grain Growers recruited from the prosperous peasants, instilled no confidence in the fight against the revolting peasants, who were from the same villages. The Germans, while maintaining complete discipline, promised before their departure from Ukraine to uphold police order in the area where they were stationed, regardless of which government took the upper hand.

Meanwhile, Petliura, Vinnichenko, and other independence supporters organized the so-called Directory and recruited the Bolshevik soldiers returning from the front. Leading the rebellion against the Hetman during this time, Petliura himself represented only a nominal leader of the revolution that was marching from Moscow, and was inspired by their motto "Peace for the huts—war for the palaces."

Do not forget that all of southern Russia's animosity towards the north was founded not on nationality, but exclusively on economics. "We are feeding you," the Ukrainians were saying. "You are getting rich because of us, and we remain your laborers." The large estates of the same Great Russians in the south inflamed the peasants even more, and it was only a matter of time before the Communist uprising in Ukraine would become perhaps even more brutal than in the north.

Anticipating a possible Allied victory, the government of the Hetman, the troops of the Don Cossacks, and the Crimea attempted to organize the so-called Russian Corps, consisting of officers who had escaped to the south from the front and from the north. They did not want to join up with any armies of the Separatists, and considered the volunteer army to be insufficiently reactionary. Their mission was the restoration of the Monarchy and a unified, indivisible Russia. Many tens of thousands of such officers could have been mustered in the south, the main center being Kiev.

The head of this corps was a popular cavalry general, Count Keller.[66] Each member of the corps wore a tri-color ribbon in his lapel buttonhole and the national flag on his sleeve. Actually, I did not know of any units formed by these officers until Kiev was threatened by the approach of Petliura.

66. Fedor Arturovich Keller (1857–1918).

In Kiev during these days, we were all aware that the primary concern was to save our hides. We and our families were in grave danger, and therefore those who were living in Kiev at that time gathered together and organized a squad led by the same popular Cavalry Guards Artillery General (or maybe Colonel) Kirpichev.[67] He was subordinate to Count Keller, and Keller took the opportunity to use the Hetman's Headquarters to direct us. All the orders came from these headquarters.

I was asked to appear before my company commander, General Grevs,[68] in the barracks just vacated by the Sich Riflemen. It appeared that they had abandoned the barracks in a hurry, leaving lots of guns, ammunition, and carts behind. In one of the rooms was a cash box filled with Ukrainian money, which I was ordered to count and deliver to the Sovereign Bank. Most of the bags were taken by the squad paymaster, Colonel Durasov. One sack, as I recall, contained 250 thousand *karbovanetsi*,[69] and I was ordered to keep this bag and turn it over to squad headquarters.

Grevs, one of the last commanders of the Horse Grenadiers, appointed me as his deputy. There were more than a hundred men in our squad, and most of them were Guards' Officers. The squad was divided into platoons, and commanders were assigned to each platoon. Grevs let us go home until the following morning, at which time we were to take up our positions.

I went to this Squad Headquarters to turn over the money, but no one would accept it. I was told that as soon as a paymaster was appointed they would take the money from me. I left my address and took the money home and placed it under the bed.

The next day we took up our assigned positions, which were on the very left flank across from the settlement of Krasny Kabachek. Our left flank bordered the Dnieper, and the right flank closed up with one of the Grain Growers battalions. In Krasny Kabachek, approximately one verst from our position, we put up a barricade. The whole position formed a half circle with the front towards the southwest. Both flanks of this front were situated along the Dnieper, which acted as a natural barrier against penetration into the town from the northeast.

67. Lev Nilovich Kirpichev (1876–1928?), Major General.
68. Aleksandr Petrovich Grevs (1876–1936), Major General.
69. Ukrainian, plural for *karbovanets*, a unit of currency.

The enemy, whose headquarters were in Belaia Tserkov, was not heard from all day. Towards evening a few shots were fired in Krasny Kabachek. Far to the right a battle seemed to have begun. We attempted to reach the barricades by telephone to ascertain what was happening, but the line was down. When the connection was restored, the commander at the barrier reported that all was quiet at this point. But the tone of his voice seemed strange to us. It sounded as though he was being told what to say and quickly broke off the conversation. A few minutes later we called him again, but again the phone was out of order. I sent out one of our ensigns of the cavalry reconnaissance who was dedicated to us, but the ensign did not return. Then I took a young cavalry guard, Shebeko, with me and went to Krasny Kabachek. Here shots were fired at us. We lay down in the ditch, from where I shouted, "General Grevs wants to speak to Colonel Il'insky." This was followed by silence, even though it was impossible that they did not hear me at the barricade. We spotted people walking towards us from the left, and suspecting that they intended to entrap us, we crawled along the ditch, and after descending from the knoll, went back to our area. It was one of the darkest nights of the southern autumn, when it was impossible to distinguish anything beyond twenty steps. Approaching our positions, we were attacked by machine-gun fire. At this point I identified myself, and the machine gunner stopped shooting. When we approached him, he told us that our patrol had just returned after trying to communicate with the Grain Growers in the neighboring village. He said that the village was empty, and according to the local residents, the Grain Growers had withdrawn from their positions and returned to town. Eight officers stationed at the barricade farther to the right of the village had been slain by the local residents. When I approached Grevs, he already knew about this. I phoned the headquarters of Skoropadsky, and a young officer of the General Staff answered. I did not remember his name, but his voice was familiar to me. He said that the Petliurists were now in the city, the Hetman's Headquarters was closed, and the only measure that he could recommend was to send out truce envoys and abandon our defense. After consulting Grevs, we decided that we should stick together and proceed to the city, and if attacked, resist to the very end. As we walked along Vasilkovskaia Street (the workers' district), we were bombarded with abuse from all sides. When we approached Bessarabka, the area where Kreschatik Street begins, a machine gun opened fire on us from a large food market which had recently been built at the foot of Bibikovsky Boulevard. The cabmen whipped their horses and disappeared immediately, screaming women dashed to the doorways, and the street emptied suddenly. We gradually began to hurry forward along the sidewalk, unable to see from which direction the shots were being fired at us. But at that moment, German soldiers with red armbands exited from one of the neighboring houses one after another and crossed in single file in front of us. A German corporal approached me and said that the German Command would not allow fighting in the streets of the city, and invited all of us to come to their quarters right now, where they would take measures to ensure our safety from the Ukrainians. I delivered the message to Grevs, who agreed, and the company was taken into the German barracks.

The officer on duty offered those who held officer positions a place to stay in the duty room. It was already late in the evening. We had not eaten all day and were very tired from the previous sleepless night. The Germans, foreseeing this, organized a dinner for the whole company in a neighboring restaurant. Upon reaching the duty room after dinner, I immediately lay down on the floor, placed my papahka[70] under my head, and fell sound asleep. Grevs lay down on the sofa, and the rest arranged themselves on the floor the best they could.

During the night the duty officer came in, spoke to Grevs, and left. In the morning we learned that the whole company except those who were in the duty room had been transferred to the Tsarevich Museum on Vladimirskaia Street. All of the Kirpichev squad was concentrated here and was under the double protection of the Germans and Ukrainians.

Six men remained with Grevs in the duty room. We were not sure if we were free to go out. We looked out of the window and saw two sentries standing at the gate. Kreschatik had the look of an ordinary weekday. The stores were open, the cabs were running, and the sidewalks were filled with people. Not wishing to be refused exit by the sentries, we decided to wait for the arrival of the duty officer. But for some reason he did not appear for a long time. Finally a former Life-Dragoon, Vanechka Kuchevsky, who had just married, could not stand it and decided to take the risk. We all asked

70. A tall Caucasian fur hat usually made from sheepskin, also a part of the uniform for the Cossacks, and later for the rest of the cavalry in the Russian Army.

him to cross the street and wave if he was let out without obstruction. He carried out our request and we all went home.

Thus ended one of the attempts by the officers to defend their right to existence. Despite our sincere desire to fight for our rights Petliura occupied Kiev without a struggle. As we learned later, our barricade at Krasny Kabachek had been disclosed to the Petliurists by local residents, who led them to Colonel Il'insky as if to make contact. Il'insky and the entire outpost were seized without a shot, after which the Petliurists ordered the commander of the outpost to report to Grevs that all was peaceful there.

Our neighbors the Grain Growers withdrew from their positions and joined Petliura. Count Keller, to whom the Germans sent a German officer's uniform to save him from being arrested, refused to wear it and was killed with his adjutant, Panteleev,[71] on Kreschatik. The eight officers who were situated to the right in the village were slaughtered by the local residents.

If the urban population at that time treated us indifferently, albeit with distrust, the rural population and the soldiers who had returned from the front were definitely hostile towards us. It was clear that the officers, who had been the main support and defenders of the old order, had no place in the life of the new Russia. And all these Hetmans, Atamans, Krasnovs, Denikins, and Kolchaks could only preserve themselves as long as they were supported by a foreign power: the Germans, the British, the French . . .

But at that time, we were not able to size up the situation—that the Allies needed this support only to secure themselves from the spread of the contagious revolution, and only until such time as their countries reinstated a normal life after the war. The former Great and Mighty Russia was no longer needed by anyone but us.

Everything Is Permitted to a Woman

At the beginning it seemed to us that we were fortunate to have remained in the German duty room. But soon, however, we learned that those under arrest were safer, because they were guarded by the Germans, who took

71. Andrei Andreevich Panteleev (1880–1918), Colonel.

them along when they left. We, finding ourselves seemingly free at the outset, had to go underground again.

When I came to the entrance of the house where I lived in Lipki, a Petliurist was standing in full armor, and asked me how long I had lived in this house. I answered, "More than a year." Luckily he did not ask my name, because I would not have known what to answer him, since the doorman who was also present knew me well. Evidently they were looking for someone else, and I was permitted to go in.

Before I had a chance to speak to my wife, the chairman of the house committee arrived and very politely but firmly stated, "Colonel, it will be safer for you to leave the house, because I am obliged to submit a new list of all the people living here." By this time, I was completely exhausted both physically and mentally. It no longer mattered what would happen to me. My wife understood this and took the initiative in solving our problem.

I was indebted to many that I was still alive: to a young soldier Petrenko, of the 41st Turkestan Regiment, who hit a German officer on the head with the butt of his gun when the officer pointed a revolver at me; to a clerk in the Chancellor's office of Vyrubov at Headquarters, who gave me a passport under the name of Nikitin; to the young girl who took me away from my home during the terror; and finally to the Germans themselves, who came to Kiev and relieved me forever of my service with the Cheka, who sooner or later would have learned of my false identity. But most of all I am indebted to my wife, who with her intelligence, resourcefulness, and energy got me out of Kiev.

First of all, she found shelter for me in the home of our good friend Varvara Nikolaevna Gurko, who lived with her daughter in a small apartment on the other side of town. There again I became "Nikitin." However, barely two days had passed when we were subjected to a search. I showed my documents, which proved satisfactory. In a few days there was another search. I was not at home this time. When I returned, I felt that in spite of all their hospitality, Varvara Nikolaevna could not hide her concern.

My wife was aware of what was going on. It was clear that we had to leave Kiev. But for this we had to have a pass from the Ukrainian authorities. At this time the Chief of Staff of Petliura's forces in Kiev was an officer of the General Staff, and a classmate of mine from the Academy, Colonel Krasovsky. My wife decided to go to him.

Krasovsky accepted her in the evening and came out with a candle in his hand and for some reason was barefoot. Upon learning that she was my wife, he said, "For anyone else, but not for Olferieff—I cannot help him. After all, he is an enemy of Ukraine, and if something happened to me, he would not have any mercy for me."

"I guarantee that he would do the same as you would," my wife answered.

Apparently Krasovsky was not particularly confident in the strength of the regime in which he was serving, and was thinking about how he could risk helping me without getting into any difficulty. He gave me a certificate that gave me the right to travel on all the railroads in Ukraine as an employee of the Red Cross.

It is painful for us to recollect this incident, because after we had gone abroad, we learned that Krasovsky had been captured somewhere by the Whites and shot without a trial.

The certificate given to me by Krasovsky permitted me to return home. Now I had to get rid of the money given to me for safekeeping during the search of the Sich barracks. While it was lying under my bed, it did not give my wife or me any peace of mind. It would be dangerous to carry it to the bank. The Kirpichev squad no longer existed. We could have burned it, but the thought that someone could later accuse me of taking it for myself prevented us from destroying the money. We decided to inquire what paymaster Durasov would do with this money. Through mutual friends we learned that he had no objection to our delivering it to him. My wife immediately took a cab to Durasov, handed over the money, and got a receipt, which she later rolled up and sewed into her dress.

Soon news came that the French had occupied Odessa, and that a train was being prepared in Kiev to send the Czechoslovak prisoners gathered in Ukraine to Odessa. We went to their organization, but were told that the German command allowed them to take only foreigners.

The mind was working quickly. My wife remembered the only foreigner whom she knew in Kiev. He was the Swiss Consul, and through him she was able to communicate with our great Swiss friend residing in Petrograd at this time. She went to him and asked that he give us some sort of Swiss passport.

"Mais, Madame, vous voulez que je fasse une contrefaction?"

"Oui, mais c'est le seul moyens de sauver la vie d'une famille."[72]

Apparently, it was the first time in his life that the honest old man had been put into such a predicament. He understood very little of what was going on around him, but he wished to help this courageous woman. Wanting to make sure precisely what he could do in this case, he said that if the German command would allow him, he would issue the passport.

Not wasting a minute, my wife went to see Alvensleben. She was received by a typical German Guards officer, straight as a ramrod, in full dress uniform with a high collar and a gold band on his wrist.

"You always have been opposed to us. Now you ask me to do you a favor," he said.

"I approach you not in your capacity as the commandant of the German occupation. Rather I come to you as the wife of your comrade in arms, a Guards Cavalry officer of imperial Russia."

The general liked this.

"All right, I will ask the Swiss Consul to help you."

He clicked his spurs and ended the interview.

A day later I was in possession of a Swiss passport which contained my glued-in picture and the seal of the Consulate. Now I was to be called George Agiton. This passport had belonged to a Swiss student who came to Kiev before the war and died there. We still have it in a safe.

But this passport turned out to be insufficient for the Czechs. My wife had to sell her earrings and pay a thousand rubles towards the aid of prisoners who were returning home. After this payment, we were allowed to board the train, and also to bring with us Varvara Nikolaevna Gurko and her daughter, for whom passports were not required.

When we entered the car reserved for us, it turned out that it was not overcrowded with foreigners, but with Russian high-rollers who had been friendly with the Germans during the Hetman's time.

72. "But, Madam, you want me to give you a false passport?"
"Yes, this is the only way of saving the lives of the family."

Odessa 1919

We sit in darkness like prisoners
Still waiting for miracles from the Allies.

—V. P. MIATLEV

A French squadron stands in the port. Sailors with red pompons on their caps, Sinegal Riflemen in red trousers, and Greek and Romanian infantry soldiers walk the streets of the city. Like Kiev, it is overcrowded with refugees. With great difficulty, we find an apartment in Sredny Fontan with a retired captain of the Volunteer Fleet.

We had not had time to settle down before Colonel Nemirok of the General Staff came to see me. He was dressed in a particularly long coat, obviously a hand me down, and requested that I go with him immediately to see General Grishin-Almazov, to be an interpreter between him and [the French commander] General Anselm.

I knew nothing of Grishin-Almazov's past. He impressed me as a very energetic, level-headed young man, who evidently knew how to instill in his subordinates his determination and energy, which in those days was sufficient qualification to become a commander and to play a role in the administration.

He explained to me that he was going to ask the French squad to give weapons, money, and supplies to help the unit that he had organized.

Anselm, an elderly general, received us coldly and even with suspicion, for which we could not blame him. General Grishin's working jacket, without any evidence of a general's rank, and Nemirok's ill-fitting long coat made them look more like robbers. I was dressed in civilian clothes, and my coat was rather worn too. Evidently, the Frenchman's view of the events taking place around us was quite vague. He could not understand why the residents of the city needed arms for defense and against which enemy, since the city was full of troops who had been sent specifically for that purpose. He had heard something about the Volunteer Army, but that was in the Caucasus.

"I have received no instructions regarding arming or supporting your forces. I have to discuss this with Mr. Berthelot, who is in Constantinople, and will let you know."

"There's no time to wait, General Anselm, because you're not always going to be with us," Grishin-Almazov tried to argue. But Anselm interrupted him sharply and called a halt to the discussion.

After that Grishin-Almazov and Nemirok asked me to go to Ekaterinodar to report to Denikin about this conversation with the Frenchman and to get further instructions.

Despite my deep conviction that our game was lost and that the people did not want us under any circumstances, I still wanted to double-check if I was right, and to see what was going on there. I boarded the steamer *Ksenia*, which sailed between Odessa and Novorossiisk, and went to Ekaterinodar. The ship was listing so badly to one side that it was impossible to walk on the deck without holding onto something. Apparently there was not time, nor workers, nor money to repair it. The steamer looked especially pitiful approaching Novorossiisk, as it was gripped by the famous deadly swell of the Black Sea. It groaned, climbing up the crest of the sea swell and then dropping down as if into an abyss. Greatly delayed, we anchored in Novorossiisk.

There was a lot of excitement in the harbor as the goods and guns were unloaded. All this was Russian—probably from Odessa and also what they had managed to bring out from the Romanian Front. It was said that there was a serious typhus epidemic in the city; the only hospital was overcrowded, and people were dying by the dozens every day. Notices were posted on the streets alerting people that they must rid their dwellings and clothing of bedbugs and lice as thoroughly as possible.

I boarded the train and, as always, it was crowded with passengers, and I had the sensation that bedbugs were crawling all over my body. Suddenly I saw a large, juicy bedbug creeping on the seat across from me. I did not dare touch it, and went out onto the platform. While traveling from the station in Ekaterinodar to the headquarters, I met three funeral processions. Denikin was not in the city. I spoke with Lukomsky, who said that negotiations were now underway in Constantinople, that the Allied mission was expected to arrive in Ekaterinodar, and that all questions regarding finances and supplies would soon be resolved.

I learned that my aunts and cousins had gathered in the city, so I called on them. We sat down to dinner and were waited on by the servants. There was an ample supply of food. The essence of the conversation was that soon everyone would return home and begin to live as before. After dinner, Shulgin, a close friend of the family, played the guitar and sang. They were all happy to see me and regretted that I was returning to Odessa. I remembered the old days, and it was sad to realize that what awaited them in the future would bring disappointment.

I decided to take the opportunity to visit Piatigorsk, which had just been occupied by the Whites, and see Vrangel. It always seemed to me that this man somehow had a sixth sense when it came to understanding a situation, and I wanted to ask him what he thought of the present events.

Along the way at each station that had just been liberated from the Reds, soldiers lay dead and dying from typhus on the platforms. There was no medical care. These soldiers were from the Caucasian Army and were on their way home. In Piatigorsk, I learned that Vrangel was ill with typhus and no one was allowed to see him. In the city I met Princess Tumanova, whose husband had just been savagely murdered by the Reds along with General Ruzsky, Bagration-Mukhransky, and ten others. The Bolsheviks made all of them kneel and chopped off their heads with a sword, and before murdering them, forced them to dig their own graves.

On my way back to Odessa I met one of my officer friends, and I shared with him my outrage at the murders of the generals in Piatigorsk. To this he responded that he had been serving under a young White General, Nikolsky, who put captured Red Army soldiers to death in the same manner. He had been a witness to one of these executions himself: A Kuban Cossack was kneeling and looking up at the general saying, "Mr. General, do you believe in God?" "Keep quiet scoundrel, and die!" shouted the general, and ordered the man's head chopped off. My friend was glad he had been able to get away from these horrors.

Farewell Native Land

Upon my return to Odessa, I was called to be a translator to the Chief of Staff of the Allied troops, General Freidenberg,[1] probably an Alsatian (whom the French called Fridanburg). There was no discussion regarding my salary. "Il y a-t-il une récompense plus grande que d'avoir l'honeur de servir sa patrie?"[2] Feeding my family and myself was my responsibility.

When my wife was leaving Petrograd to come to my headquarters, my cousin, who was employed by the Minister of Finance, obtained a cashier's check for her on the Credit Lyonnais in Paris for 10,000 francs, assuring her that it might be of help in the future because it was getting more and more difficult to obtain foreign currency. For a long time during our travels we tried to cash it, but only a speculator in Odessa would take it, probably hoping that he could sell it to the French. That man who finally got the check and tried to exchange it in France probably received nothing, because Crédit Lyonnais was refusing to pay creditors due to the confiscation of its property in Russia by the Bolsheviks. But at this time we found that we had 10,000 of some sort of Odessa money with which we could buy food. This money also enabled us to leave Russia, and we had to leave very soon. For the Allies, the war was over, and no one wanted to continue to risk their lives. Moreover, neither the soldiers, nor the commanders, nor even the generals could exactly size up the situation as to who was right and who was guilty in this turmoil. And the French, represented by their fleet, clearly were on the side of the Revolution.

The Bolsheviks naturally took this fact into account. The expulsion of the Allies from Russia not only raised the spirits of the Red Army, but also created a certain prestige for her in Europe. Shortly after this an appeal began to circulate in Odessa from the Commander of the Red Army, Medvedev, to the French command, that was reminiscent of 1812, demanding their immediate departure. We soon learned that Kherson had been occupied by the Bolsheviks and the land connection with Crimea was disrupted.

1. Henri Freidenberg (1876–1975), eventually a lieutenant general but at this juncture a colonel.

2. "Is there a greater reward than having the honor of serving your country?"

One night during Holy Week we were awakened by the movement of transports along the road which passed by our windows. It was a Romanian convoy moving west. The next morning on my way to Headquarters I ran into Romanian troops who were already moving westward behind the transports. On the road past the railroad station I heard shooting, and Greek infantry were advancing headlong towards the station. Coming out on the embankment, I saw the Red flag flying on the French battleship. After arriving at Headquarters, I learned that the railroad bridge north of the station had been handed over to the Bolsheviks by the French sentry. It was obvious that the Allies would give up the city, and we had to do something without delay.

I went home and found our two-year-old Sergei ill with a cold and a fever. I had the feeling I should take the risk and remain here, but common sense said that it was out of the question, because this was a matter of life or death for the whole family. We decided to pack and attempt to leave with the French, but for this we needed a visa. We went to see Freidenberg. In spite of the fact that I had worked for him and had access without previous announcement, the guard at the door would not let us in. We had to resort to the old method which had worked for us thus far; and here the one hundred Odessa rubles, which outside Odessa were not worth the paper they were printed on, did the job. The guard turned his back to us, and we entered the General's office.

The General, however, flatly refused to give us any sort of visa. "I am strictly forbidden to allow anyone to leave Odessa," he said.

"But I worked for you, and I'll be the first to be arrested." We evidently looked very pitiful, and he took mercy on us and wrote on our passport: "Bon pour Constantza."[3] This was the first port where the transport went to drop off the Romanians. "However," said Freidenberg, "I cannot guarantee that they will let you aboard the transport, because there may not be any room."

Here I must state that the passport I showed Freidenberg was not the one with the name of George Agiton given to me by the Swiss Consul in Kiev, but a passport written by me in a blank passport book. During this time anyone could buy one of these blank passports anywhere in southern

3. Constantza Port in Romania.

Russia. It was still necessary to get someone's signature and stamp. For this, there was a priest on the outskirts of Odessa who would sign it with an illegible signature, perhaps not even his real name, and stamp it with a church seal, applying it in such a way that it was impossible to read. Later on this same passport was stamped with visas by the British, Italians, and Japanese, and I presented it when obtaining papers to enter the United States. I could have written anything I wished on it, and no one would ever doubt its legality. This probably explains why there were so many imposters among the Russian immigrants.

At the station at this time a battle was raging in which the Greek units were trying to hold back the Reds until the departure of the Allies from the port. We had to pass Fontan, which was fairly close to the station, and it was difficult to get a cab. We hired three of them for two thousand rubles to carry us a distance of two versts. We loaded our belongings, sat the children in the cab, and proceeded to the pier. The Greeks had already abandoned a section of the city close to the station through which we had to pass, and the railroad station appeared to be in the hands of the Bolsheviks. The sidewalks on both sides of the street were crowded with workers who had come to meet the Reds. However, no one stopped us, and I only once heard a mocking cry, "Where are you going, you damned bourgeois? There is no place on earth where we cannot find you."

At the pier, the ship to which Freidenberg had directed us was being loaded with Romanians. I tried to go up the gangplank between the soldiers, but the French officer on duty at the top would not let me through, saying that if there was room after loading the troops, he would let us on.

We sat down on the sand close to the gangway and waited. It began to get dark, and the Romanians kept coming and coming. It seemed that there was no end to them. In the city now and then gunshots resounded. We found ourselves all alone between the departure of the old order and the institution of the new terror.

It got completely dark, Sergei fell asleep, and the girls were slumbering between us. Footsteps were heard and before us appeared a French mechanical engineer with a flashlight in his hand, who was apparently going to the ship. Two sailors were following him.

"What are these people doing here with the children?" he asked, addressing the two sailors.

My wife did not wait for their answer and replied in French, "We are waiting to get permission to board the ship."

"The ship is now leaving for the outer harbor. Follow me."

We took the children, the sailors helped with our luggage, and we went up the gangplank. The officer walking in front of us addressed the officer on duty standing at the entrance to the deck, who evidently was the senior officer, and said, "I found this family sitting near the gangplank. They say that they have a visa and were promised a space on this ship."

"But there's no room," answered the senior officer.

"We can't leave them on the shore," insistently argued our savior. "I'll find a place for them."

The senior officer did not reply and ordered the gangplank to be raised.

We were placed around a table in the dining hall of this Turkish passenger steamship, called *Corcovado*, which was overcrowded with troops and with the same kind of fortunate people as ourselves, who apparently had more influence than we did and had managed to board the ship in advance. We left for the outer harbor, where we spent the night. My wife and children arranged themselves on soft benches around a corner table, and I lay down on top of the table, because the floor and all the neighboring chairs were already occupied by sleeping people, and after all the ordeals of the day, we fell asleep.

We were awakened by the rumble of the anchor being raised, and when we went out on the deck, the shore was already quite far in the distance. We walked to the very end of the stern to say a last farewell to our native land. On the horizon the dark gray sea merged with the cloudy sky, and the strip of land became thinner and thinner. I looked at my wife. Tears were streaming down her cheeks, and she did not wipe them away.

Trying to comfort her, I said, "Don't cry. We'll return soon."

She turned to me, and I could tell by the expression on her face that she was suffering physically from being torn away from her native land.

"Never," she answered.

Soon the sea and the sky blended on the horizon. The noise of the water made by the steamship's passage was telling us that we were moving further and further away. Only a few gulls persistently followed us, indicating our proximity to the coast. These were the only creatures who had the right to return home.

It was Easter Sunday 1919 by the Orthodox calendar—the end of the first attempt by outside forces to stop the spreading revolution in Russia. It became clear to the Bolsheviks and to us that this would never happen again. If the outside world should help us in the struggle it would only be with supplies and money. If there was hostility or at least neutrality towards us by the population, the officers, as in previous times, were the only ones who wanted to fight. And no matter how brave and selfless they were, the outcome of this struggle was a foregone conclusion.

A new chapter was opening in the history of Russia, and also of the whole world. After murdering and banishing the ruling class, the peoples inhabiting Russia threw off the Western yoke that they had been under for over two hundred years, the same way they threw off the Tartar yoke at the end of the fifteenth century. On the world map appeared a new 150 million people, who had previously been unknown to anyone and who began to surprise the world with their potential strength, their energy, their perseverance, and their achievements. And over the past forty-five years, people's view of Russia and the Russian people has changed drastically.

And we, having lived out our days in exile, having the opportunity to return home but conscious of our uselessness there, cannot help but be proud of her.

The end.

Russian God[4]

God of potholes, God of snowstorms
God of backroads
God of nights without a place to sleep
Here He is, here is our Russian God

God of the cold, God of the hungry
Of beggars, cripples far and wide
God of unprofitable estates
Here He is, here is our Russian God

4. These verses are only a part of the entire poem. Fyodor probably was quoting them from memory, but they convey a sense of his gloom and hopelessness.

God of all with the Order of St. Anne around their necks
God of menials without boots
God of servants as lackeys
Here He is, here is our Russian God

Stupid fools win grace
Clever men beware of His merciless reign
God of all that is amiss
Here He is, here is our Russian God

—P. A. VIAZEMSKY, 1828

Epilogue: Escape, Travels, and Life in the United States

TANYA ALEXANDRA CAMERON

Fyodor Olferieff ends his memoirs as he and his family escape on a ship from the burning city of Odessa in the midst of revolution. However, the story does not end there. For the sake of survival their travels take them to Constantza, Constantinople, Malta, and then to India, Hong Kong, Nagasaki, Tokyo, and Yokohama. This journey lasted about six months. Another eight months were spent in Japan, hoping that the Allies would invade Russia from the east and the Revolution would be put down. All this was taking place in 1919–20.

Finally, when it became clear that they would not be able to return to Russia, my grandmother, Mary, insisted on first-class tickets to San Francisco. She wanted the family to get as far away from the killing as possible and knew that there were many émigrés from Russia in that city. All through these travels, the Olferieffs lived on the money obtained from selling jewels that my grandmother had sewn into their clothing. The ship they boarded stopped in Honolulu on the way to the United States. When they arrived in San Francisco in June of 1920, they had no immigration papers, only a "Declaration of Alien About to Depart for the United States" issued by the American Consulate General in Yokohama. However, all the first-class passengers were free to get off the ship without much scrutiny. But the

Alexandra (Shura), Mary (Masha), left to right standing, Mary (Marusia), Sergei, and Fyodor seated in St. George, Malta, 1919.

tourist and second-class passengers without papers were not permitted to disembark and had to return to Asia.

The day after they arrived, Fyodor got a job working as a draftsman at the Old Ferry Building. This opportunity came about because while in Japan he had met a fellow Russian who had given him the name of the boss at this office who spoke French. Though my grandparents spoke fluent Russian, French, and German, they did not know much English and had to learn it quickly. Fyodor worked about six months at this job and then went

The Olferieff family in California in the 1920s. Left to right: Aleksandra (Shura), Fyodor, Mary (Masha), Sergei, Maria (Marusia) Grevens Olferieff.

to work for the Associated Oil Company on Montgomery Street as an oil geologist. During this time the family lived in a little hotel on Kearney and Bush Streets.

In 1921, they went to Palo Alto, and he commuted to San Francisco to his job with Associated Oil. At the same time, my grandmother, Mary, taught French at the exclusive Miss Harker's School in Palo Alto, where both my mother, Masha, and aunt, Shura, attended. She was more than qualified to teach, as she had graduated from the Empress Mary School for Young Ladies in Petrograd in 1905 certified to teach French and German at the high school level. One of her professors, a Swiss citizen, Fanny Marie Urech, certified that Mary had spoken French fluently with her parents from her earliest youth. She had studied six hours per week from 1899 to 1905. Under this Swiss professor she finished lexicological grammar and syntax and studied the history of French literature through reading great works of famous writers from all epochs of French literature. Her teacher said she spoke with elegance and was completely fluent in the language, and certified that she was well qualified to be an instructor and lecturer in French in any school or college.

In 1922, the family moved to San Rafael, where Mary taught French at the Dominican College, and where again Masha and Shura were able to attend free because their mother was on staff. The girls boarded there but their brother, Sergei, went to Coleman Elementary School. Again their father, Fyodor, commuted every day to San Francisco to the Associated Oil Company. He took the train, transferred to the ferry across the Golden Gate, and then walked to work. Shortly after this move, he was sent to Tampico, Mexico, on oil business.

In 1925, they moved to San Francisco and lived on the corner of Pacific and Van Ness in a nice apartment. Here the children went to St. Brigid's parochial school, which was founded in 1863 and straddles the Pacific Heights and Russian Hill neighborhoods. In 1926 they moved to Jackson Street near Broderick, and went to the fancy Grant School in Pacific Heights. It was a very wealthy neighborhood. The family also attended the Russian Orthodox Virgin Mary Cathedral on Green Street. They remained in the city till 1928 while Mary taught for the Alliance Française of San Francisco. She would travel to various schools teaching French at the high school level.

At this time Shura graduated from Grant and went to Galileo High School on Van Ness. Then in 1927 Masha fell ill with an acute ethmoid sinus infection. She had to have emergency surgery at the Children's Hospital in San Francisco. My grandparents paid for the operation with a setting of gold dinnerware (fork, knife, and spoon) that they had brought from Russia, because they could not afford the medical bill. When the doctor died, he left the set to my grandparents, and I inherited it from my mother.

Virgin Mary Cathedral congregation on Green Street in San Francisco, 1925. All the Olferieffs except Sergei, who was running around, are in the picture. Third from left in first row in hat is Mary (Masha). Behind her slightly to the left is Alexandra (Shura) also in hat. Behind Shura is Fyodor with Mary (Marusia) in hat to the left of him.

In 1929, Fyodor transferred to Los Angeles. Associated Oil had now become Tide Oil. He worked in Los Angeles while living in Pasadena. On the side, in the early 30s, he also worked in Hollywood, teaching fencing to the movie stars. He looked quite dashing in the role. At this time all the children attended school in Pasadena. Then Mary got a job in Glendora teaching at a private school, and again the family moved. Now it was 1930 and they lived in an orange grove in a house on a hill. The children attended Citrus Union High School. My aunt Shura tells of the time the Grand Duke Alexander, the Tsar's cousin and founder of the royal air force, visited her parents in Glendora. She claimed, "It was one of the most memorable days of my life when he took me to lunch at the Riverside Hotel. At first I was very nervous, but this feeling did not last too long. He was extremely friendly and a brilliant man. He told me a great deal about the time my father served under him during the First World War in Mogilev."

Fyodor Olferieff giving Ivan Lebedeff, a movie star of the time, fencing lessons in Hollywood in the 1930s.

In 1932, the market crash came, and Fyodor was out of a job. So the family moved back to Palo Alto. Masha and Sergei went to Palo Alto High School while Shura attended Sequoia High School, because she was working for a professor emeritus from Stanford whom she nursed and cooked for. She graduated in December 1932 and entered St. Luke's Hospital Nursing School in February 1933. Mrs. Felton was a good friend and helped Shura and the family out.

The rest of the family stayed in Palo Alto at this time. Their good friends Frank and Josephine Duveneck hosted them frequently at their estate in Los Altos, Hidden Villa Ranch. The Duvenecks were from prominent families on the East Coast. They were very involved in social, educational, environmental, and humanitarian activities in the Palo Alto area. In gratitude for their hospitality, Fyodor drew a detailed, beautiful map of the Hidden Villa Ranch and gave it to them as a gift. (It also is the frontispiece in a book later authored by Josephine Duveneck, *Life on Two Levels: An Autobiography*. Its introduction is by Wallace Stegner.) Fyodor also picked tomatoes in the fields and harvested fruit in the orchards of the estate. At this time he did some mapping for others, which provided a little money. In 1932 he gave a lecture at Stanford on "The Red Army." He was commended for presenting the material in "an exceptionally clear and unbiased manner." In addition he wrote a paper, "Soviet Russia in the Orient," that is in the Hoover Institution's archives.

Having graduated from high school, my mother, Masha, was helping out by working for fifty cents a day in a bookstore in Menlo Park. It was at this time that my mother and father met. The house that the Olferieffs were living in was next door to the Delta Upsilon fraternity on the Stanford Campus. My father, Clive Warner, was a member of the fraternity and was the house manager that summer. He had graduated from Stanford and was working on his PhD in history. The future president of the university, Wally Sterling, was a classmate and a friend of Clive's. One of the duties of the house manager that summer was to clean their swimming pool. My father invited Masha to go swimming. The couple eloped in 1934, with my grandmother in hot pursuit because she thought Masha at nineteen was too young to marry. She was coming up the front stairs of the Justice of the Peace's office while Clive and Mary (Masha) were leaving by the back door. At the height of the Depression, they thought that two could live cheaper than one. They lived at this time in a house on Forest Avenue in Palo Alto. In 1938 Clive received his PhD, and he and Mary moved to Santa Monica, where he became professor of history at Santa Monica Junior College and head of the history department.

Also in 1934, Fyodor went to work for the U.S. Coast and Geodetic Survey and made many maps. He corrected maps of the California coastline and went to Pocatello, Idaho, to do map work in that state. He was also sent to Oregon and surveyed the Willamette River, and then was sent to Sacramento to do further work there.

In 1935, Shura graduated from nursing school and worked nights at St. Luke's Hospital. Shura and her father lived in an apartment nearby, on Washington Street between Steiner and Fillmore, while Mary was living in a rooming house in Palo Alto. At this time Fyodor was out of work. They had a can opener in the refrigerator and no food. They would get together with other Russians and pool what little they had. Shura was the only one working, and she was making $50 a month.

Mary (Marusia) with Fyodor at Stanford University with her master's degree in hand, 1938.

In 1936, Mary (Marusia) entered graduate school at Stanford University to get her Master of Arts degree in the Department of Romantic Languages. Her thesis was entitled "Le Féminisme dans les Romans de Chrétien de Troyes." She earned money by teaching in the department, serving as director of the French Table, and working as a cashier in the cafeteria. Remuneration for the quarter was $300 plus lunch and dinner at the French Table five days a week. The students paid five cents a meal extra which covered Mary's meal.

Also at this time, Sergei joined the Merchant Marines. It was a tragic choice, because while they were on shore leave in Manila in December 1941, the Japanese invaded the Philippines, and the cowardly captain of the President Lines ship immediately set sail and left his crew stranded. What happened next is described by the Chairman of The United States Maritime Commission in a document honoring Sergei Olferieff, Quartermaster (deceased), for meritorious service: "[T]he port of Manila was under day and night bombardment by the enemy. The Army was evacuating to Corregidor and Bataan, and thousands of tons of vital supplies had to be transported or fall into the hands of the enemy. All port installations were already in flames, and the waterways between were under constant barrage. To aid in the evacuation of both troops and supplies, a small band of merchant seamen manned four steam launches which towed barges for four days until all were sunk under them. These men then conditioned and manned an abandoned British seagoing tug which performed valiant service between Corregidor and the navigation heads of Bataan until it was sunk at Corregidor on the last day of the tragic operation. They then were issued arms and joined in the defense of beach positions until taken prisoners of war by the Japanese . . ." These brave men were part of the Bataan Death March. They were starved and tortured and later, while they were being transferred to prison camps in Japan, their overloaded, unmarked ship (a red cross on the ship would be a sign that there were prisoners of war aboard) was torpedoed and sunk on October 24, 1944, by an American ship, and most of the prisoners lost their lives. The ship was the *Arisan Maru*, and a documentary called *Sleep My Sons* was made about this event. A survivor remembered Sergei with fondness and said that he was so weak and sick he was unable to swim and save himself. Posthumously Sergei received military honors and a signed letter from the President of the United States to his family. I remember it framed in their dining room in San Francisco.

Mary's degree was awarded in 1938. Shortly before that, in 1937, she moved back to San Francisco and purchased a house on Twenty-fifth Avenue in the Richmond District, and Fyodor went into the real estate business. He got his broker's license, but he wasn't a successful salesman because he took pity on people and rarely collected his commissions because his clients couldn't afford them. Meanwhile, Mary gave private lessons in French in San Francisco. Fyodor's first office was on Irving near Eighth and then he rented a space for the business on Geary Blvd. Through these years Shura and Masha helped the folks financially.

Later, the President Lines Company sent insurance money to the families of the crew that the captain had abandoned on shore in the Philippines. With this money, the Olferieffs sold their first house and made a down payment on a house in the Sunset District on Twenty-third Avenue. I

Russian military friends at Officer's Club in San Francisco, 1967. Fyodor is third from left.

remember both of these homes with fondness. The first one had a basement full of canned goods just in case of another revolution or hard times. It was like a store with lots of Campbell's Soup. The second house no longer had stockpiled food. Times were better.

Fyodor also enjoyed fellowship with his Russian émigré military friends at an officers' club in San Francisco. In 1955 on the fiftieth anniversary of his graduation from the Page Corps and his entrance into the Horse Grenadiers Regiment, he was given a beautifully painted icon of St. Fyodor. Later, on the fiftieth anniversary of the Revolution, in 1967, the group gathered to mark the occasion.

My grandfather was a kind man and loved children and animals. My fondest memories as a child were the walks with him and his dachshund, Chiquita, in Golden Gate Park and our trips to the Fun House and the San

Francisco Zoo. He had a sense of fun, and he taught my sister and me card games including Solitaire. He also loved to play songs of the Red Army. My grandmother loved the opera and was always studious and reading. My mother frequently called me "little Babushka" because my personality and behavior must have been similar.

Fyodor worked till he was eighty, and at eighty-six passed away from colon cancer in 1971. Mary died at ninety-three from arteriosclerosis in 1977.

A Broken Life

GARY M. HAMBURG

I

Historians of Russia have long debated the causes of the Russian revolution and civil wars. Did Russians consciously prepare their revolution from 1825 on, as Martin Malia asserted in his magnificent biography of the early socialist Aleksandr Ivanovich Herzen?[1] Did the Empire's class antagonisms combine with Vladimir Il'ich Lenin's leadership to make the revolution, as Trotsky maintained in his 1931–1933 history, or as the Soviet scholar Isaak Izrailevich Mints contended in his 1967 narrative of the revolutionary year?[2] Or was Russia even as late as 1913 further from socialist revolution than from capitalist democracy, as Wayne Dowler has asserted?[3] Was the Russian revolution therefore the result of the war mobilization that occurred between 1914 and 1917, a mobilization that the Bolsheviks perpetuated in the civil war, as Peter Holquist has argued?[4] Or were the events of 1917–1921 byproducts of a Bolshevik coup d'état and of the party's ruthless campaign to defeat its adversaries, as Richard Pipes has claimed?[5]

Whatever interpretation we may adopt, it is clear that the civil strife between 1917 and 1921 fundamentally changed Russia, even if not every social group experienced an improvement in its condition. As Mark D. Steinberg has noted, urban streets transformed from sites of labor protest into a "realm of refugees and the homeless (many of them children), beggars and criminals, and of people selling or bartering their belongings for food." Meanwhile women, who had from 1914 to 1917 played key roles in the rural economy and village government were, after 1917, "shoved aside in striking manner."[6] The formal granting to women of political equality by the Provisional Government and the Soviet administration did not demolish traditional gender roles.

Nevertheless, the revolution and civil war encouraged revolutionaries and utopians of various types. Steinberg has written touching portraits of the poet Vladimir Vladimirovich Maiakovskii and of the Marxist Aleksandra Mikhailovna Kollontai, who "refused to accept the limitations of the present in theory or practice."[7] Richard Stites has even described the entire period as an age of "revolutionary dreams," of "utopias in the air and on the ground."[8] Not all revolutionary dreamers were spectators. Michel Heller and Aleksandr Nekrich have labeled the Bolshevik regime as "utopia in power."[9] Andrzej Walicki has analyzed the development of Lenin's "totalitarian communism" as a utopian attempt to accomplish "human liberation from the blind necessities of economic and social life." According to Walicki, Lenin feared that any concession to bourgeois freedom would vitiate the workers' material welfare by subjecting toilers to exploitation at the hands of propertied interests.[10] Lenin therefore sought a revolutionary dictatorship and the resolution of Russia's problems by coercion: he called for "cleansing the Russian land of all sorts of harmful insects, of crook-fleas, of bedbugs—the rich and so forth."[11] In the end, Lenin and his party obliterated the former ruling classes and sought to replace them with a community of toilers—that is, to destroy old class identities and to create a "new identity for all."[12]

Even though Russia's process of social transformation proved halting and thus fell short of utopian hopes, the dramatic changes that occurred constituted a temporal rupture, a fracture in time. In a series of contests over the language of citizenship itself, over public symbols, and over images of Russia's enemies, the old regime and its symbolic system were delegitimized, then destroyed.[13] Many of Russia's elites—its nobility and "bourgeoisie" (the term "*burzhui*" came to connote "all non-workers," "anyone dressed in city clothes," "anyone who wears a hat and has a 'seigneurial face' ")[14]—were victimized, chased out of the country or killed, depending on their political attitudes, on the degree of their opposition to the new ways of life, or simply on their vulnerabilities. The writer Ivan Alekseevich Bunin's diaries from 1918 to 1919 complained about the vicissitudes of life in Soviet-controlled Moscow and Odessa, when, in his terms, "the terrible unspoken truth about human nature was revealed." As the authorities measured each room of his home before confiscating it for collective housing space, Bunin lay on his sofa with heart palpitating.[15] By early June 1918, he felt: "I am simply dying, physically and spiritually, from this life."[16] The playwright Mikhail Afanas'evich Bulgakov tried to capture the human reality of the nobility's exodus from Russia after the civil war in his play *Flight* [*Beg*] (written 1928, revised 1933–1937, first published 1962).[17] The play recounts eight dreams set in various locales—Tauride province, Crimea, Constantinople, Sevastopol', and Paris—from late 1920 to fall 1921. It is almost as if Bulgakov's *dramatis personae*, lacking a solid reality in which to live, have already begun to see their days as darkly lit memories.

Perhaps the most shocking image of the revolutionary period can be found toward the end of the poet Osip Mandel'shtam's *Second Book* [*Vtoraia kniga*] (1923), in the poem entitled "Age" [*Vek*]. Mandel'shtam chose the word *vek* for his subject because it connotes "the span of a human life," "a historical age or epoch," and "century." He likened his life/age/century to a wild animal, its spinal cord severed, its vertebrae bound together by blood: "Your spinal cord has been crushed, my splendid, pitiful age, and you with senseless smile look about, cruel and weak, just as a feral beast, once agile, reposes on the traces of its own paws."[18]

II

Until his granddaughter Tanya Alexandra Cameron translated his memoirs, Fedor Sergeevich Olfer'ev was a figure virtually invisible to history. He was one of the tens of thousands of Russians who fled their country for safety in the West amid revolutionary and civil conflict. A privately organized online genealogical site, All-Russian Genealogical Tree [*Vserossiiskoe genealogicheskoe drevo*] contains a fragmentary entry for him: "Olfer'ev Fedor Sergeevich (?–7 Aug[ust] 1971, San Francisco, California, USA. Colonel of the General Staff. Educated in the Corps of Pages, began service in the Life Guard Cavalry Grenadiers Regiment. In 1914, graduated the Academy of the General Staff. Through the First World War—a staff officer at Supreme

Command [*Verkhovnaia Stavka*]. After the revolution, moved to San Francisco, where he headed the Union of the Life Guard Cavalry Grenadiers Regiment and the Union of Pages."[19]

The entry does not specify his birth date. From this obituary, we might infer that Olfer'ev came from an educated, probably well-to-do family; otherwise, how else could he have qualified for entrance into the Corps of Pages? But it tells us nothing about his childhood education. Did his parents teach him to read at home? Did they hire tutors? We might guess from the obituary that in 1914 he was a promising military professional, and that he left turbulent Russia after 1917 to live most of his life (over half a century!) in California. We learn here nothing about his politics: was he a conservative, a nationalist, a liberal, a socialist? Did he join the Volunteer Army in 1918? The fact that he joined a military society in San Francisco hints at continuing psychological ties to the imperial army—a likely indicator of participation in the White movement—but possible correlation is no proof.

From accessible documentary sources we can construct a better but still fragmentary picture. The service registry, *List of General Staff Officers* [*Spisok general'nago shtaba*] for 1914 carries an entry for "Olfer'ev Fedor Sergeevich," giving his birthday as August 2, 1885, his religion as Orthodox, and his entry into military service as September 1, 1903. The service directory also mentions that Olfer'ev received his first commission as *kornet* [French *cornette*; English equivalent "second lieutenant"] on April 22, 1905. Because we know he received his formal education at the School of Pages, we can deduce that he graduated in 1905, just before being commissioned. The service directory further reports his graduation from the General Staff Academy in 1914 and his concurrent commission as *poruchik General'nago shtaba* [junior officer of the General Staff] in the Warsaw Military District.[20] The military historian A. V. Ganin has compiled a list of General Staff officers from 1917 to 1922. The entry, "Olfer'ev [Fedor Sergeevich]," gives his rank as *podpolkovnik* [lieutenant colonel] as of August 15, 1917, and informs us that, as of November 11, 1917, Olfer'ev was "staff officer for supplies under the supervision of the assistant to the Supreme Commander in Chief of the Russian army."[21]

In addition to this information from service directories, we have a bibliographic rarity, the mimeographed *Miscellany of the Union of Pages* [*Sbornik Soiuza pazhei*], published in Paris from 1955 to 1965. In 1964, the

Miscellany carried a brief excerpt from Olfer'ev, recording his "first steps" in the School of Pages and also analyzing his classmates, teachers, and the school's curriculum.[22]

In the guide to the Hoover Institution Archives in California, there are additional clues to Olfer'ev's life. He deposited there a copy of a paper he had written in 1932 on "Soviet Russia in the Orient"—an overview of Soviet military defenses in the Far East in the 1920s.[23] In the same repository, in the papers of Antonina von Arnol'd, there are letters to Olfer'ev concerning the disposition of the von Arnol'd family property.[24] The *pater familias*, Roman Apollonovich von Arnol'd, had served as an officer in the Russo-Japanese War and later became police chief in Harbin before emigrating to the United States. Both sets of documents—the paper on Soviet defenses and the letters linking Olfer'ev to the von Arnol'd family—point to Olfer'ev's military career in Russia as a marker of his identity in the United States.

The Hoover Institution Archives also contain letters from Olfer'ev pertaining to the National League for American Citizenship.[25] The League, founded in 1913 by Nathaniel Phillips, promoted naturalization, voting rights, and employment for immigrants.[26] By the mid- to late 1930s, when Olfer'ev became actively interested in its activities, the League had the reputation of a reformist group, trying to increase the number of immigrants to the United States and to better their treatment once they were here.[27]

In the late 1960s, M. Lyons acknowledged Olfer'ev's assistance in a book on the Russian Imperial Army. The book appeared under the imprint of Hoover Press in 1968.[28]

Finally, from the Social Security Death Index, we also know that, in the United States, Olfer'ev changed his legal name to "Theodore Olferieff."[29]

Thus, from extant sources we know that Olfer'ev lived from 1885 to 1971. His formal education occurred in the Imperial School of Pages from 1898 to 1905 (the curriculum was seven years of study) and the Imperial General Staff Academy from 1911 to 1914 (a two-year curriculum, plus an additional year of independent study). He was promoted rapidly during the Great War from junior officer to lieutenant colonel. We can infer that he saw action in the field in the Warsaw Military District before being advanced to Stavka (Russian military headquarters) in 1917 or before. His life in emigration bore earmarks of a traditionalist outlook (membership in the Union of

Pages) and continued interest in military affairs (the 1932 paper on Soviet defenses in the Orient, and the 1968 publication on the Russian Imperial Army), but also suggested a commitment to fair treatment of immigrants in the United States, and to possible reform of American laws on immigration. This picture of Olfer'ev's life would have remained a thumbnail sketch were it not for publication of the present volume.

III

The Russian-language original of Olfer'ev's memoirs is an untitled typescript consisting of 395 pages. The first forty-three pages are typed in Cyrillic script, single-spaced, on unlined paper, with several of the early pages perforated three times on the left-hand side, an indication they were bound in a three-ring binder. Someone—probably the author—has entered French and Latin terms by hand, either written in script or printed. In this portion of the manuscript, there are few corrections to the Russian text. Most frequently, typing errors are crossed out with typed x's over the mistakes. In one case, the author has crossed out an entire paragraph by hand, and has entered substitute lines in Cyrillic script. The handwriting is in careful, old-style (prerevolutionary) orthography. In a few other cases, the author has crossed out entire paragraphs and provided no replacement language.

Most of the remainder of the original is typed, double-spaced, again with three perforations on the left side of the pages. A substantial portion of the manuscript (pages 44 to 153) carries few corrections, but other portions (pages 154 to 185, for example) appear rougher. Here the author has scratched out words by hand, entered missing words in Cyrillic above some of the lines, and corrected dates by hand. Pages 185 to 193 shift back to single-spacing, but much of the remaining manuscript is double-spaced. Beginning with page forty-four, most pages are lined, three-hole notebook stock.

In the portion of the manuscript devoted to the Great War, the author has inserted several hand-drawn maps, giving military dispositions and distances, either in *versts* [a prewar unit of distance] or kilometers. Railroad lines and rivers are marked. The maps are drawn in one, two, or even three colors, with red used either to clarify a military position or to indicate a unit's movement. The absence of topographic indicators suggests these maps were Olfer'ev's originals, perhaps drawn from memory. Olfer'ev's maps do not seem technically precise, but they help the reader imagine the military encounters described in the memoirs.

The sum of the evidence—typed and hand-corrected memoirs, written with different spacing on different stocks of paper—is that Olfer'ev wrote his manuscript over a long period of time, that he was a conscientious writer who wanted to get details right, and that he likely produced different versions of the "original text" and collated them.

It is not clear when Olfer'ev began to write the memoirs, but the text provides us clues. In the chapter, "To War," in a subsection entitled "September 1957," Olfer'ev notes: "Three years have passed since I wrote the preceding page [on the coming of World War I, before mobilization], and more than ten years since I began to write these remembrances. I have entered my seventy-third year." This remark indicates that Olfer'ev started writing his memoirs in the aftermath of World War II: the phrase "more than ten years" may mean "after September 1946" [more than ten years, but not eleven years]. The context—a passage interpolated into a discussion of World War I—may imply that Olfer'ev considered the two world wars' impact on Russia as decisive events in its history. Further along in the same subsection, he commented: "Already, from those days I am discussing here, a third generation is preparing to undertake a leading role . . . [Growing population] brings with it a reorganization of the life of a nation so that the new order acquires a socialistic quality to the detriment of private initiative and individual freedom. In any case, most people, if not everyone, instinctively feel that individualism will come to an end. And this angers them. They behave brutally and blame the Soviet regime for everything. There is no doubt that one more, likely last, collision of the two worlds is at hand, in all probability, it will end that civilization in which we live."

This apocalyptic passage redefined the historical context that inspired Olfer'ev's memoirs. After 1945, he took up his pen to remember his previous life, before the Great War, the Russian revolution, and civil war fractured it.

Two paragraphs in Olfer'ev's memoirs offer a glimpse of his mood in the late 1950s. One mentions the launch of the satellite Sputnik, the first successful test of an intercontinental missile, and the southward expansion of the Soviet border, toward the Mediterranean. He then adds: "And the people who took part in this [border expansion] were all probably the sons of Pet'ka Kokorev, Van'ka Enamushka, Dukhov, Zavrazhnyi, Medvedev . . . led by the peasant Khrushchev and commanded by *Vakhmistr* Zhukov, under whose command 'Berlin city' had been taken many years ago." The other paragraph asserts: "The Russian peasant had obtained that stature, the absence of which prevented him from defeating the enemy in East Prussia, and is now causing alarm throughout the world."

Here Olfer'ev's apocalypticism combines with his pride in Russian achievements in the international sphere. His observation about Russian cultural attainments in the 1950s is an oblique criticism of the class order that had obtained in the pre-1914 days. The concluding passages of Olfer'ev's memoirs forcefully state his perspective:

> *A new chapter was opening in the history of Russia, and also of the whole world. After murdering and banishing the ruling class, the peoples inhabiting Russia threw off the Western yoke that they had been under for over two hundred years, the same way they threw off the Tartar yoke at the end of the fifteenth century. On the world map appeared a new 150 million people, who had previously been unknown to anyone and who began to surprise the world by their potential strength, their energy, their perseverance, and their achievements. And for the past forty-five years, people's view of Russia and the Russian people has changed drastically.*
>
> *And we who have lived out our days in exile, having the opportunity to return home, but conscious of our uselessness there, cannot help but be proud of her.*

This passage indirectly discloses when Olfer'ev finished his memoirs: sometime in 1962. If 1917 was the "new chapter" in Russia's history, and forty-five years had passed since that time, then the final paragraphs of his book must have been completed in 1962. It may be that he finished the book in late summer/early fall 1962—a moment of optimism in the Soviet Union because of Khrushchev's efforts to de-Stalinize the Soviet system, but also a time of better relations with the United States. The fragile hopefulness of this period came to an abrupt end in October 1962 with the Cuban missile crisis. After that crisis, Olfer'ev might not have confessed so much pride in Russia, and he certainly would not have been so confident of the possibility of returning to Russia.

Therefore, the timeline for Olfer'ev's memoirs must be this: he started to write in 1946, in the wake of World War II and at the beginning of the Cold War; he finished writing in 1962, likely before the Cuban missile crisis. His dominant emotions—astonishment over the advance of socialism and pride in Russian achievements—were to some degree contradictory. He did not anticipate publication of the memoirs, and, in fact, he did not expect them to be understood. "What is the use of my remembrances?" he asked. "In the best case, some bursting bomb will cover them over with dirt, and perhaps in three thousand years some archaeologist will dig them up and try to decipher them as is being done now with hieroglyphics."

No, Olfer'ev wrote not to be understood by contemporaries but to understand himself and to record his broken life for posterity.

IV

Every memoir is an imaginative reconstruction of an individual's life story, of moments private and public, related from a particular perspective. Some of the best Russian memoirs—for example, Aleksandr Ivanovich Herzen's wonderful *Past and Thoughts* [*Byloe i dumy*], Boris Nikolaevich Chicherin's pungent *Memoirs* [*Vospominaniia*], Vladimir Galaktionovich Korolenko's *History of My Contemporary* [*Istoriia moego sovremennika*]—have drawn on their authors' diaries, correspondence, and published writings, as well as public records. These memoirs therefore feel reliable to readers alert to the documentary foundations just under the surface of the narratives. Yet many other extraordinary memoirs—Lidiia Korneevna Chukovskaia's *Conversations with Anna Akhmatova* [*Zapiski ob Anne Akhmatovoi*] and Nadezhda Iakovlevna Mandel'shtam's *Hope Against Hope* and *Hope Abandoned* [*Vospominaniia*] are good examples—depend to a large extent on remembered conversations, yet they seem no less authentic to readers. Olfer'ev's memoirs may belong to a third type, combining lyric impressions of childhood, acerbic sketches of personalities from the Corps of Pages and the General Staff, and *tableaux vivants* of historical events based on personal observations and (very occasionally) historical documents. Olfer'ev sometimes juxtaposes his remembrances with others' accounts, thus enabling him to bolster the authenticity of his own narrative or to make critical distinctions. His memoirs therefore shift in texture and tone, from the dreamy subjectivity of childhood, to the informed sensibility of a career officer, to the apocalypticism of old age.

Olfer'ev divided his memoir into thirteen chapters and supplied fifty-one titles for subsections. He likely composed the text sequentially (that was surely true for the second half of the book), but corrected and polished earlier chapters as the book's remainder took shape. He may have planned the book in three parts: recollections from childhood to 1914; memories of the Great War and the Russian revolution; and a concluding section on the civil war and on circumstances of his exile from Russia. But these three broad sections are a guide for moving through the fifty-one subsections, as through a detailed outline, with each subsection devoted to an event or theme. Whatever his compositional plan, Olfer'ev managed to write a continuous narrative from his first memory as a three-year-old boy in 1888 to his departure from Russia in 1919 at age thirty-four.

V

Olfer'ev was born in 1885 to a noble family living in Zubtsovskii district in Tver' province, near the confluence of the Volga River and its small tributary, the Shutinka, a stream only three kilometers long. The family house, called Stolypino, sat near a small village of a few dozen houses (thirty-six of them in 1859, forty-nine in 1888), an Orthodox church, and a small market. In Zubtsovskii district, the nobility held over 70 percent of privately owned land; in 1888, the average estate comprised roughly 750 desiatins.[30] As a general rule, the local nobles farmed their properties using local peasant laborers.[31] The annual salary of peasant laborers was between eighty-four rubles for women and 103 rubles for men—that is, from thirty to thirty-six kopecks a day.[32] In 1888, just under half of families had one member who was literate. Less than 13 percent of the district's populace could read. The literacy rate for males in Stolypino township was 25 percent, but it was much lower for females: less than one percent of females could read or attended school.[33]

Olfer'ev's childhood memories—all related in the present tense—are disconnected but not untypical for a young gentleman in the countryside. He recalls a small nuclear family: a mother who acted as caregiver and disciplinarian, a father who paid little attention to him but commanded his respect; a sister and an "orphan" playmate; a nanny who was close to God. He remembers tearful visits to church and punishment for stealing consecrated bread as moments in his religious upbringing. He calls to mind encounters with a French governess. Two of Olfer'ev's earliest memories—nearly drowning under an overturned carriage in the local river, and watching the family's "big house" burn to the ground—remind us that Russian country life was perilous even for the elites. Fear of drowning haunted the eighteenth-century childhood of Sergei Timofeevich Aksakov, whose memoirs recounted a terrifying experience.[34] Fear of fire was omnipresent in rural Russia, especially among peasants, as the historian Cathy Frierson has shown.[35] But nobles were also vulnerable: the Tambov landowner Boris Nikolaevich Chicherin's animal shed and barns burned in August 1885, and his mansion Karaul lost two rooms to fire in 1900.[36]

In 1891, Olfer'ev's family moved to Rzhev, an old Russian city established in the twelfth century, which was contested ground in the struggle between Moscow and Tver', and also between the Muscovite and Lithuanian states. During the Church schism of the seventeenth century, Rzhev became a stronghold of the Old Believers. In Olfer'ev's time, over half the city's inhabitants were Old Believers—a fact he does not mention in his memoirs, probably because Rzhev's Old Believers were priestless and could therefore worship without a dedicated sanctuary.[37] Thus their presence was not manifested in the eighteen Orthodox and two Uniate churches in town.

Olfer'ev's faith was influenced less by the local priest than by his nanny Tat'iana Ivanovna. She taught him: "God will not forget you, if you think of others." She preached forgiveness to all. Her brand of other-directed Christianity was common among Russian peasants in the nineteenth century. Nine-year-old Fedor Dostoevskii, frightened by a wolf in the forest, was comforted by a peasant named Marei, who showed him "almost maternal tenderness."[38] In his autobiographical narrative *Childhood* [*Detstvo*], Lev

Nikolaevich Tolstoi describes the "gentleness and diligence" [*krotost' nrava i userdie*] of his house servant Natashka, who died "within genuine Christian patience," "pardoned all offenses," "never feared death and accepted it as a blessing. . . . Her whole life was pure, uncorrupted love and self-sacrifice."[39]

Olfer'ev recalls the local Orthodox church near his house, in which worshippers were divided between local civilians and soldiers. Probably the soldiers struck him as romantic figures: he soon resolved "to become a soldier, ride on horseback, jump over obstacles, and go to war with the Turks." This resolution was also influenced by the orderly magic of parade-ground exercises and by his father, who said: "Soldiers exist to protect us from enemies who might attack us."

In 1893, at age eight, Olfer'ev moved with his family to Kurchino, a substantial new estate—885 desiatins of land—in Rzhev district. There his father was the first to hold the post of land captain [*zemskii nachal'nik*]. This office, created by the counter-reform of 1889 but only slowly implemented, conferred broad supervisory authority over peasants, especially in helping resolve land disputes between them and local landowners or over their duties to those lords. Land captains also had authority over peasant institutions, such as village and township assemblies and township courts. Because they also supervised the district police force, land captains were often regarded as officers of the law. They could fine violators of the civil and criminal codes; in certain circumstances, they could jail violators for up to a year.[40] Through childhood eyes, Olfer'ev recounts a meeting between his father and fifteen peasants led by the township elder [*volostnoi starshina*], who hoped to make a good impression on the new land captain. Olfer'ev notes, now from an adult perspective, that the land captains were considered by Russia's liberal intelligentsia as "obstacles" to progress, but he insists that his father commanded the peasants' deference. This observation, along with Olfer'ev's youthful religiosity and patriotism, indicates that he was a "conservative" on the Russian political spectrum. He notes that local peasants probably could not imagine life without masters—another indication of his paternalistic outlook.

Olfer'ev's family established "neighborly relations" [*dobrososedskie otnosheniia*] with the local peasants. As a child, he hit it off with older peasant boys, but it is clear that he called them by their familiar names—Pet'ka, Van'ka, Os'ka—a liberty allowed to the masters; while they called him by his formal name and patronymic—Fedor Sergeevich—or by the generic "master" [*barin*]. This system of address was one of the many remnants of serfdom that persisted in the countryside three decades after its abolition.

Olfer'ev does not gloss over the poverty of peasant life. He recalls, for example, their squalid housing, the village's endemic alcoholism, the prevalence of spousal abuse, the peasants' lice-infested clothing, their starchy diet based on rye flour. He recalls as well childbirths in unhygienic conditions, and the peasants' fatalistic acceptance of death. He reports the scarcity of medical resources near the family's estate: a ten-room hospital over ten kilometers from Kurchino, and only two doctors for the entire district.[41]

As local authorities invested money in the medical infrastructure, this situation gradually changed for the better, but Olfer'ev's description of peasant life captures the main difficulties confronting rural authorities before 1914.[42] In pondering the effects of this rural poverty on Russia's historical fate, Olfer'ev concludes that poverty helped peasant soldiers to endure awful conditions in 1914, but also deprived them of the cultural sophistication required to win the war.

In a passage that demonstrates the peasants' land hunger, Olfer'ev depicts the drama surrounding a local land surveyor attempting to clarify the legal boundaries between peasant communal land and his family's estate land. Olfer'ev reports the incident first from his childish perspective and then from an adult vantage point. According to the child, the Olfer'evs could have afforded to permit the peasants to encroach on estate property. But to the adult Olfer'ev, the peasants, once in possession of the disputed acreage, would only have extended their claims to manorial land, because they wanted to till all the land as their own. Yet, he supposed, they would not have tilled it efficiently. In Olfer'ev's mature opinion, there was in fact no good solution to the problem of peasant land hunger, other than having poverty force young peasants to move into the city. Olfer'ev knew, of course, that peasant migration to urban factories would generate an urban proletariat and therefore increase the threat of revolution. In any case, according to Olfer'ev, the idea of breaking up communal lands to permit more efficient farming, as enacted by prime minister Petr Arkad'evich Stolypin after 1906, "failed to resolve the basic problem of the lack of land."[43]

Olfer'ev remembers the landed gentry of Rzhev district not as wealthy parasites but rather as a mixture of hardworking farmers (for example, the

Kossopolianskii family), lessors of small estates (Aleksandra Nikolaevna Zagarina, Aleksei Pavlovich Ignat'ev, and Petr Aleksandrovich Potemkin were his examples), and owners of summer dachas (Mitrofan Vasil'evich Ivanitskii and the family of the future communist authority Andrei Aleksandrovich Zhdanov). Olfer'ev notes that in certain respects, such as educational level, poorer landowners could not be distinguished from peasants. He does not say so explicitly, but the petty gentry's relatively low material and educational condition was a long-standing feature of Russian country life.

Olfer'ev puts his neighbor Sergei Leonidovich Ivin in a special category. He sees Ivin as a "petty tyrant," a social type he recognized after reading Ivan Sergeevich Turgenev's *Sketches from a Hunter's Album* [*Zapiski okhotnika*]. "[W]hen I read Turgenev's description of Russian landowners such as Chertopkhanov and Nedopiuskin, in my imagination Chertopkhanov always bore the face of our Ivin." In Chertopkhanov's willfulness, cruelty, and self-destructiveness—traits that frightened his fictional neighbors—Turgenev highlighted disagreeable sides of gentry life and obliquely criticized Russia's social hierarchy. We do not know whether Olfer'ev agreed with Turgenev's critique of the landed nobility, but the memoirs make it clear that he resented his neighbor Ivin for "stealing" the family's governess, Mademoiselle Blanche.

Olfer'ev's connection of Ivin to Turgenev's Chertopkhanov is a clue to the way he shapes his childhood memoirs. He organizes his childhood recollections in concentric circles: himself and immediate family in the innermost circle; then friends from peasant stock in the next circle; local peasant life and land questions in the next; and finally neighboring gentry. At several points, he takes inspiration from Russian literature. He alludes to Aksakov and to Tolstoy in comments on family life; to Turgenev in treating the landed gentry. Olfer'ev's memories were simultaneously "literal" and "literary." His manner of blending social and literary types was common among educated Russian elites at the end of the old regime.[44]

Toward the end of his chapter on childhood, Olfer'ev depicts three pillars of Russian life: faith, tsar, and country [*vera, tsar', i otechestvo*]. He distinguishes the people's firm faith in God from their awareness of the sinfulness of the local clergy, such as the drunk Fr. Mefodii. He suggests that just as most Russians "could not imagine a world without God, they could not imagine a sovereign state without a sovereign." In his opinion, because the tsar was essential to Russian life as a symbol of continuity, Aleksandr III's unexpected death in 1894 was experienced by the common people less as personal tragedy than as the symbolic loss of a distant father figure. Olfer'ev doubts that Russians' love of country was as well-defined as that felt by Frenchmen or Germans. Because Russia was a vast imperial polity, its people were more tolerant toward foreigners and its nationalism was more abstract.

Olfer'ev's evidence for the Russian understanding of faith, tsar, and country rests on childhood memories—of prayers and priests, of the tsar's death, and of the peasants' reluctance to pay taxes. But these memories are structured around a variant of Sergei Sergeevich Uvarov's traditional formula of "Orthodoxy, Autocracy, Nationality"—a formula that was the foundation of Russian state ideology in the era of Nicholas I. To apply this formula to Russia through 1917, as Olfer'ev did, was to insist on the continuity of the peasant *mentalité* over the entire old regime. Moreover, he also used it to describe Soviet habits of mind. In his opinion, communists constituted a secular clergy, Stalin was the "red tsar," and Soviet nationalism shifted the object of popular loyalty from the Empire to the Soviet polity.

Olfer'ev concludes his remembrance of childhood with a discussion of two aspects of education: the inculcation of literacy in the common people, teaching that usually occurred in peasant huts rather than in school buildings; and his own experience with domestic tutors at Kurchino. He notes the rapid growth of literacy in the late nineteenth/early twentieth century, particularly among young people. He saw that learning to read and to write "was done entirely on the initiative of the peasants themselves," but also that literacy instruction focused mainly on children between the ages of eight and ten. Both these observations are consistent with the findings of the great Russian social historian Boris Nikolaevich Mironov, who pointed to high rates of literacy among military recruits (45 percent were literate in 1894–1903, 62 percent were literate in 1904–14), much lower literacy rates among young women (only 22 percent were literate in 1897), but also to recurrent illiteracy—that is, young people who forgot how to read and to write.[45]

Olfer'ev's childhood educational experience was entirely different. He quickly acquired near native fluency in French and a reading knowledge of

German, along with command of his native Russian tongue. For him, the crucial factors in education were not so much cognitive as attitudinal. He felt the contradiction between the "nihilism" of his tutor Nikolai Nikolaevich Turchaninov, who rejected God and tsar, and the "conservatism" of another tutor, Mikhail Vasil'evich Sadikov, who followed a prescribed syllabus in grammar, arithmetic, and sacred theology. Olfer'ev surely felt confused over the clash of his tutors' worldviews, but that clash helped him in two ways: first, Turchaninov rejected anti-Semitism, and this criticism of religious intolerance may have taken some of the edge off Olfer'ev's country-squire conservatism; and second, his tutors' disparate ideologies prepared him for the polarized politics of Petersburg.

VI

In 1898, thirteen-year-old Olfer'ev moved to Petersburg to enroll in the School of Pages. There he studied for the next seven years, graduating in 1905 amid the street protests of that turbulent year.

By the late imperial period, the School of Pages was the longest-lived and most prestigious military boarding school in Russia. Although it did not assume its distinctive shape until 1802, under Tsar Aleksandr I, its roots can be traced to 1711, when Petr I created the foundation for a European-style court consisting in part of educated aides. By 1712, Petr supported a school where a handful of young men studied languages (French and Latin), mathematics (arithmetic and geometry), geography, history, and military science.[46] By 1898, over three thousand young men had completed their studies at the school. One of them was Olfer'ev's father, Sergei Nikolaevich, who graduated in August 1876.[47] In the late 1890s, admission to the school required completion of entrance examinations in French, German, Russian, theology, and mathematics, but candidacy for admission was often the result of a legacy system, which gave previous graduates the right to nominate their sons as candidates. Olfer'ev claims that this system of recruitment fostered a "closed society" of students. He noted that most students were either Russian or Baltic German by ethnicity, and that three-quarters of the Russians came from old princely and boyar families or from families whose ancestors had served the state in the eighteenth century. All the Russians admitted in his day were hereditary nobles. Tatars were underrepresented at the School of Pages; Jews, Finns, and most peoples from Central Asia were not represented at all.

The school's curriculum aimed to provide both broad general education and more specialized courses in military science. Classes in general education included theology, languages (Russian, French, German), mathematics, science (natural science, physics, and cosmography), geography, history, law, calligraphy, and art. Measured in hours of instruction, the curriculum concentrated heavily on languages and mathematics, with an average of eighteen hours a week spent on these subjects.[48] Students spent an average of nearly thirty class hours a week on the general curriculum. The school's official program also mandated participation in extracurricular activities: military drills, gymnastics, fencing, swimming, dancing, music, and singing. The government limited hours of instruction in extra-curriculars to thirteen per week.[49] Given the prescribed general and extracurricular program, there was little time left for military science, even though in 1881 a government commission had insisted on "prioritizing the theoretical and practical study of military subjects in combination with those subjects of advantage to the officers' general development."[50]

According to Aleksei Alekseevich Ignat'ev, who enrolled in the School of Pages in 1894, four years before Olfer'ev, the classes in military science were excellent. In the lower forms, students learned elementary tactics from Colonel Vladimir Aleksandrovich Dediulin; later, General Tsezar' Antonovich Kiui [Cui] taught artillery and fortification, General Grigorii Grigor'evich Danilov taught topography, and the future war minister Aleksei Andreevich Polivanov taught military administration. Ignat'ev thought the level of instruction in military history "very modest." Practical instruction was much better.[51]

Olfer'ev notes the absence of an applied component in general education courses. Future officers learned abstract, not applied, mathematics; they learned Russian and global history, but "nothing about the history of war." Although General Nikolai Alekseevich Epanchin, the school's director from 1900 to 1902, was a military historian, he was distant from the students and so did not shape their instruction. The students learned something about military matters from their drill instructors, from their mechanics teacher, and from their law instructor, who taught them military jurisprudence. Otherwise, students benefitted from a general education designed to transform them into courtiers. In retrospect, having duly noted the flaws in his education, Olfer'ev regretted "how much was given to us and how little we grasped."

During the late imperial period, there were twenty or so military schools in Russia, each with roughly six hundred students divided into seven classes. This meant that there were a few dozen students enrolled in each class at the School of Pages: Olfer'ev counted seventy-seven students in his class photograph. Because students spent so much time together, they knew each other well. This familiarity was reflected in their habit of addressing each other by the second person singular pronoun *ty* [thou]. As Ignat'ev, observed: "This form of reference was maintained not only in the Corps of Pages, but among former pages, even those of high rank who noticed on the uniform of an official the small white Maltese cross that signified school membership."[52]

The bond among class members was also fostered by common experiences, some of them unpleasant. Olfer'ev compared the school's psychological environment to that of a "correctional institution" [*ispravitel'naia tiur'ma*, literally, a "prison"]. Students routinely concealed their comrades' escapades from their superiors. They internalized the school's status system—its division into classes and its privileging of older students [cadets] over younger or newer ones, who were referred to in student jargon as "animals" [*zveri*]. One consequence of students' *esprit* was their difficulty in accepting outsiders, anyone whose demeanor or attitude did not fit the collective mold. As Olfer'ev makes clear, the students brutally marginalized a classmate named Aleksandr Ivanovich Verkhovskii. As a result of some relatively innocent remarks, they excluded him from their midst and forced him to leave school before graduating. Their actions may have pushed him to the political left: in 1917, Verkhovskii proved an enthusiastic supporter of the February revolution. Shunning by his peers may also have hardened Verkhovskii's will to resist group tyranny: confined to a Soviet prison in 1931–1934, he declared hunger strikes against his jailers, whom he accused of unjust treatment.[53] The Verkhovskii affair showed that, in spite of intense pressures to conform, not all students did so.

Students at the school carefully guarded their privacy. Ignat'ev maintains: "Each cadet had two worlds: his own inner world connected with his family, which he could not share with anyone else; and the other external, temporary cadet world, which he wanted to end as soon as possible." For most of the students, faith was a private matter. Ignat'ev contends: "No one spoke about religion and no one was interested in it; rather for the overwhelming majority going to church was simply a boring service duty."[54] Olfer'ev does not directly address the question of religion at the School of Pages. He likely identified more closely with the Church than did other students, because he was so sympathetic to the faith tradition of his nanny and of the Tver' peasants. Still, his knowledge of Christian scriptures was superficial, as illustrated by his embarrassing failure to respond to Grand Duke Konstantin Konstantinovich's question about the four gospels.

How did the School of Pages prepare its students for political life in Russia? The curriculum aimed to educate students to serve the state in two senses: first, to ready them to serve the monarch; and second, to train them as future army officers. Before graduation, senior pages attended members of the royal family at court rituals. As Olfer'ev notes, assignments depended on class rank. The class valedictorian attended the tsar, the salutatorian the empress, and so on. As second student in class rank, Olfer'ev attended Empress Aleksandra, but, in her absence in 1904, he waited on Grand Duchess Ol'ga Aleksandrovna. His duty was to carry the train of the grand duchess's dress at the christening of Tsarevich Aleksei. Performance of such ceremonial tasks afforded pages the opportunity to meet the emperor and royal family and to bond with them. The intimacy between courtier pages and the royal family helped the royals to assign graduates of the School of Pages to fitting positions in the army. In other words, the School of Pages was a key institution in Russian politics, because it advanced the careers of loyal monarchists.

Yet the school did not always uphold the royal family's best interests. Ignat'ev, who studied at the Kiev Military Academy before entering the School of Pages, pointed out that the Kiev academy produced better-prepared military technicians. He observed, by contrast, that many graduates of the School of Pages were "dimwits [*temnye lichnosti*] who chattered splendidly in French, possessed excellent manners and, to my great surprise, subsequently made their way in higher circles."[55] Ignat'ev, whose first ceremonial assignment was attending the Moscow coronation ceremony in 1896, also notes Tsar Nicholas II's political shortcomings. Ignat'ev calls Nichols II a "soulless sphinx" for his indifference to the tragedy at Khodynka Field, where a crowd trampled to death many people gathered for the celebration.[56] For his part, Olfer'ev had mixed feelings toward the tsar. Nicholas II impressed him at their first meeting, but those feelings later changed to indifference. Olfer'ev had little sympathy or affection for Empress Aleksandra. Her conversations struck him as "discharging a burdensome and uninteresting duty." In his opinion, she did not understand the Russian people as well as the Dowager Empress Mariia Fedorovna did.

Olfer'ev's memoir suggests that, by 1905, political currents outside the government had divided the sentiments of students at the School of Pages. Apparently, most of his classmates were monarchists. "We were all educated to devote ourselves to the throne," he wrote, "but perhaps because of our closeness to the court, we neither deified the monarch nor had a slavish attachment to him, as did many monarchists who knew the tsar only by his portraits or by reading newspapers." Olfer'ev and his classmates did know the history of their school and thus were aware of the political activities of previous graduates. Olfer'ev admired the anarchist Petr Alekseevich Kropotkin, an 1862 graduate of the School of Pages, whose resistance to the Russian political system was legendary. Some of the school's alumni entered rightist political groups. Olfer'ev cites the examples of Senator Fedor Fedorovich Trepov, General Vladimir Mikhailovich Bezobrazov, and Aleksei Pavlovich Ignat'iev, all of whom joined the Russian Assembly [*Russkoe sobranie*], one of the first right-wing political organizations to appear after 1900. In late 1904, the Russian Assembly sent a delegation to the tsar to signal its support for throne and altar. In 1906 it transformed itself from a voluntary society into a political party.[57] Other alumni, such as Boris Aleksandrovich Engel'gardt and Mikhail Vladimirovich Rodzianko, participated in the Russian Liberation movement, and after 1905 in the Octobrist party—a center-right group that played a crucial role in Russian politics to 1917.

In retrospect, Olfer'ev expresses surprise over classmates and other contemporaries who joined the revolutionary cause. He criticizes Aleksandr Verkhovskii for complaining in 1905 about pages having "to drag around women's skirts"—to carry their trains at court ceremonies—and for asking soldiers in the Mounted Grenadiers whether senior officers beat them. Olfer'ev regards Verkhovskii's remarks as breaches of discipline and as markers of political disloyalty. Olfer'ev says nothing in the memoir about Aleksei Alekseevich Ignat'ev except that the latter "can be judged by his memoirs"—a comment meant to signal that Ignat'ev had discredited himself by serving Soviet power after 1917. In fact, Ignat'ev, who fought in the Russo-Japanese War, returned to Petersburg a critic of autocracy and a supporter of the October 1905 manifesto promising national elections and the provision of civil rights.[58]

These differences in political outlooks that were already manifesting themselves among the pages in 1905 testify to the splintering of support for the old regime.

VII

Olfer'ev personally witnessed several important incidents in the 1905–1907 revolution. The first occurred on January 6, 1905, in conjunction with the annual Blessing of the Waters, when a unit of the mounted artillery guard fired a "salute" to the tsar. Shrapnel from exploding shells fell near the raised platform on which Nicholas II and the royal family were watching the ceremony. Palace security assumed the incident was a deliberate attack on the tsar. According to Olfer'ev, Nicholas himself asked: "So my own battery fired at me?" After the incident, the Petersburg official Ivan Aleksandrovich Fullon, who was formally in charge of security arrangements, was dismissed from office, but Grand Duke Vladimir Aleksandrovich, the unit's commander, was not. As Olfer'ev notes, the incident was hushed up, but the shelling was a prelude to the scandal just three days later on Bloody Sunday, when political protestors were met by gunfire on the capital's streets.

In April 1905, Olfer'ev received his officer's commission. He left Petersburg with the Mounted Life Guard Grenadiers to protect the Imperial Palace in Peterhof. In early fall, however, the government stationed the Grenadiers and the Finland Guards regiment in Petersburg itself. At first, as Olfer'ev noted, the Grenadiers patrolled the streets and sometimes lined up in battle formation to prevent street disorders from getting out of control. In one instance, the Grenadiers confronted an unruly crowd. According to the memoirs, Olfer'ev's unit faced two hundred students and workers who were assembled close to the university and moving toward the Stock Exchange Bridge. His squadron blocked the crowd from crossing the bridge by repeatedly riding through it, but without drawing weapons. Olfer'ev's unit obeyed orders from its commander, Pavel Vladimirovich Filosofov, to maintain a peaceable disposition unless threatened by the crowd, even though the crowd taunted the Grenadiers by calling them *oprichniki*, a reference to Ivan IV's dreaded enforcers. According to Olfer'ev, the incident passed without bloodshed.

Olfer'ev recorded this event but did not assign it a date and did not sketch its historical context. Perhaps it was the event that occurred on October 2, 1905, a point when feelings ran high in university circles because of the sudden death in Petersburg of Moscow University's liberal rector, Sergei Nikolaevich Trubetskoi. He was a hero to many students and professors across Russia, because he had extracted a promise from the ministry of education to restore administrative autonomy at Russian universities, but also because he had appealed to the tsar to establish a constitutional regime.[59] After Trubetskoi's death on September 29, Petersburg University students resolved to honor him by assembling in Znamenskaia Square in central Petersburg. They then marched back toward the university on St. Basil's Island, singing the Marseillaise. In front of Kazan' Cathedral they were met by armed cavalry who directed them across the Palace Bridge toward the university precincts. In the square in front of the university, a portion of the crowd headed toward the Stock Exchange Bridge, where they were pushed back by armed city police and mounted cavalry, possibly Olfer'ev's Grenadiers. A contemporary description of this encounter claimed the cavalry's action caused "panic" and chaos in the crowd.[60]

The use of the Grenadiers on Petersburg streets was part of a broad counter-insurgency strategy in which the government employed troops against civilians. The historian John Bushnell has counted nearly 2,700 occasions when troops assisted civilian authorities to restore order between January and late October 1905.[61] The government's reliance on the military to police civilian conduct shook soldiers' loyalty to the government. Bushnell has pointed out that between mid-October and the end of December 1905, there occurred eighteen mutinies in the Petersburg region alone.[62] Olfer'ev mentions his unit's exposure to hostile crowds in 1905 and again in 1906, when protestors threw rocks at the Grenadiers. He records no mutinies in the regiment but admits that relations between officers and soldiers were strained.

After Bloody Sunday, Olfer'ev saw the royal family again on a number of occasions. Shortly after the sinking of the Russian fleet at Tsushima Strait in late May 1905, Nicholas II arranged lunch with the Grenadiers. Olfer'ev recalls the tsar's stoic demeanor over the event that had "plunged Petersburg and the Palace into deep mourning." The memoirs recount two meetings with the tsar at the Petersburg officers' club frequented by his regiment. There Nicholas II listened to gypsy musicians and happily drank to toasts by the Grenadiers.

In March 1906, Nicholas hosted the Grenadiers at Tsarskoe Selo. Olfer'ev saw that this meeting, ostensibly convened to honor his regiment, also had a political purpose—namely, to sustain the morale of officers who "served as the only support of the old order." Even among these officers, some "professed weariness with police duty and disenchantment with military service in general." At this meeting and at others, the tsar displayed his personal tact. He deflected criticisms of the State Duma, even though he may have shared the critics' perspective.

Tsarskoe Selo was a settlement on territory formerly belonging to the Swedish crown that had become, by the mid-eighteenth century, a wealthy town with its own church and an ensemble of buildings for the royal family and courtiers. Before 1727, the settlement had been under the jurisdiction of the Chancellery for Equestrian Affairs [*kantseliariia koniushennykh del*], but later it fell directly under the sovereign's personal supervision. From the early nineteenth century, the settlement's layout encompassed a large field for martial maneuvers. Olfer'ev's Grenadiers could exercise their horses there, or, in inclement weather, at the royal stables [the Manège].[63] In 1841, the government built a road from Tsarskoe Selo to Kolomiazhskoe Pole, where a pavilion and a gallery were constructed from which spectators could view horse races. In the mid-nineteenth century, these two-verst races attracted large crowds from Petersburg, but by the early twentieth century the races also had military purposes. Olfer'ev claims to have taken part in races with fellow officers, but does not supply a date for the competition. During the races, he may have stayed at the regular officers' quarters, or perhaps in one of the four "cavaliers' houses" [*kavalerskie domiki*] constructed by Empress Elizabeth.

Olfer'ev describes the tsar's inspection of the Grenadiers' parade that occurred in spring 1906. Nicholas signaled approval of regimental horsemanship by hand-signals, and patiently encouraged underperforming officers to control their balky horses. According to Olfer'ev, the riding drills had a serious military purpose: to bolster the cavalry's ability to maneuver past, or over, obstacles in the field. The 1906 parade-ground success of General Aleksei Alekseevich Brusilov, the long-time head of the Petersburg Cavalry School, led to his April 1906 appointment as commander of the II Guards Cavalry Division. Olfer'ev saw the promotion as "one of the starting points of Brusilov's career, which brought him to the post of commander in chief during the war."[64] According to Olfer'ev, Brusilov may also have owed the promotion to his patron, Grand Duke Nikolai Nikolaevich, who in these days was much loved by the tsar. Years later Brusilov agreed with that assessment.[65]

Even in 1905–06, the Grenadiers did not devote all their efforts to military drills and street patrolling. At one point when his unit was "not needed to help civilian authorities," probably in April 1906, Olfer'ev arranged to be sent to a state-supported horse stud farm in Poland to study its operations and to ride its horses. This was the famous stud farm at Janów Podlacki, near what Olfer'ev called "a small Jewish town" of the same name, and not far from the somewhat larger town of Siedlce. The Janów stud farm had supplied horses to the Russian cavalry since 1817. Since its functioning was crucial to Russia's war readiness, Olfer'ev's assignment to the farm made good military sense, at least by the logic of the General Staff, who, even in the age of heavy artillery and machine guns, clung to cavalry horses as an element of tactical consequence. In visiting the stud farms, Olfer'ev admitted little interest in military considerations, but as a young officer, sought to test his skill as a rider of Janów's fabulous crossbred horses.

While visiting the farm, Olfer'ev stayed in Janów, a town with less than three thousand inhabitants. The town first appears in historical sources in 1423, and by 1465 had become the seat of a Catholic diocese. In the late seventeenth century, the local bishop established a seminary [*seminarium duchownego*] there that functioned until 1939. Jews settled in Janów in the late seventeenth century; indeed, according to the 1897 census, almost 80 percent of the town's residents were Jewish. Early in the twentieth century, some local Jews had begun to support Zionism; others emigrated from Poland to the United States.[66]

Olfer'ev recalls Janów's narrow streets, its old and dilapidated huts, its filthy dwellings with dirty blankets and bedbugs, and its open sewers. He compares Janów's Jewish men to "lethargic flies," while describing the town's children as filthy but lively. He suspects that the middle-aged Jewish innkeeper in the local restaurant is prostituting his two daughters. Olfer'ev claims that in the future, whenever the Jewish question arose in conversation, he remembered the innkeeper, the prostituted daughters, and the town's terrible poverty and filth. His image of Janów's Jews acknowledges the town's poverty, but it is also invidious to Jewish men. He does not address Russia's responsibility for Janów's plight, nearly a century after the imposition of tsarist rule.

From Olfer'ev's memoirs we do not know whether he spent any time in Siedlce, just to the west of Janów. The question is important because from September 8 to 10, 1906, just a few months after his visit to the area, the so-called Siedlce pogrom took place. Fifty locals were killed, many of them Jews, a hundred more were injured, and property in the Jewish quarter was destroyed. While most historians of this incident have classified it a pogrom, in a recent essay, Artur Markowski has argued that the violence did not follow the pattern of other pogroms, in which Christian civilians tended to be the main perpetrators.[67] He maintains that what occurred in Siedlce was "an armed clash with the mainly Jewish revolutionary movement (the Bund), as a result of which the Jewish quarter was looted." Markowski attributes the decision to initiate violence in Siedlce to Russian military leaders and to the region's acting governor, who saw the action as "pacification."[68] Olfer'ev evidently failed to sense these tensions or to understand the Jews' situation in Russian Poland. Instead, after visiting Janów, he felt "bewildered" by the Jews' condition.

After returning from Janów, Olfer'ev and his unit moved with other Russian guards units to Krasnoe Selo, a settlement near Petersburg founded by Peter I in 1714. Beginning in 1765, under Catherine II, Krasnoe Selo had become the site of large-scale military maneuvers during the summer, often in June and July. By the mid-nineteenth century, Nicholas I regularly arranged parade-ground maneuvers there. The town was soon known as the summer military capital of the Russian Empire, because nearly 120,000 soldiers were typically quartered there. Common soldiers usually slept in white field tents, and officers in wooden barracks. According to Iurii Vladimirovich Makarov, an officer of the Semenovskii Life Guards regiment who lived at Krasnoe Selo at the same time as Olfer'ev, officers' barracks were equipped with spring mattresses, writing tables, and comfortable soft chairs. Young officers often socialized with women whose families had come to spend the summer at Krasnoe Selo dachas.[69] Thus life in Krasnoe Selo was governed by the same masculinist norms that regulated social life in Tsarskoe Selo and Petersburg.

Officers generally spent the month of May practicing with firearms and conducting maneuvers with their squadrons. June was reserved for larger-scale field maneuvers. Sometimes these maneuvers were observed by visiting dignitaries from Europe or Asia: in 1913, for example, by the French general Marshal Joseph Jacques Césaire Joffre and members of the French military mission.[70] In 1906, the year when Olfer'ev encamped at Krasnoe Selo, the guests of honor were the Greek King George I and Queen Ol'ga Konstantinovna, formerly a Russian grand duchess, who in 1920 briefly served as regent in her adopted country.

The main events of the social season in Krasnoe Selo were the horse races [*krasnosel'skie skachki*] and riding competition that usually occurred in early July. These races were thought at the time to be one of the most outstanding sports competitions in Russia. Thousands of spectators watched the races from the royal pavilion, and the winners—Olfer'ev was one—received their prizes from a member of the royal family. Olfer'ev received his award for winning the steeplechase from Empress Aleksandra. He called the event "the most important day of my service in the regiment," a remark that is redolent with pride but that reads strangely in light of the regiment's other services to the crown.

In mid-July 1906, Olfer'ev's Grenadiers helped suppress a rebellion at the Kronstadt Naval Base. His memoirs date the order to depart Petersburg for Kronstadt to an "autumn evening," but without saying whether it was in 1905 or 1906. In fact, while an uprising did occur at Kronstadt on October 26–27, 1905, the specific incidents Olfer'ev subsequently describes belong not to the fall 1905 disorder but to one nearly a year later, in July 1906.

On arrival in Kronstadt, Olfer'ev's detachment was met with "deadly silence," which was soon broken by "a mob of sailors looting a liquor store." When the Grenadiers surrounded part of the crowd, the sailors insulted and attacked them. After subduing the drunken rebels, Olfer'ev's Grenadiers escorted the rebels back to the harbor. There they discovered the corpses of seven naval officers who had been killed by the mutineers. The next day, the Grenadiers, who at that point constituted the only loyal military on Kronstadt, were reinforced by troops under the command of General Nikolai Iudovich Ivanov. The joint forces suppressed the mutiny and restored order on the naval base. Olfer'ev's unit remained on Kronstadt for a month.

According to the memoirs, the entire first night on Kronstadt, the Grenadiers "did not remove our weapons and ammunition or unsaddle our horses"—an indication that the troops were on high alert. Olfer'ev reports that soldiers in his unit thrashed the intoxicated sailors, and that, during the Grenadiers' first week on the base, "sailors were caught in the streets and, whether innocent or guilty, were beaten mercilessly with riding crops."

This rebellion of Kronstadt sailors was one of fourteen that occurred in the Russian armed forces between July 9 and 23, 1906; indeed, it was part of a planned rebellion by the entire Baltic Fleet. The Kronstadt militants awaited an uprising in Helsinfors, after which they planned to seize control of the island's forts and of the vessels in its harbors. The rebels' end game was an attack on Petersburg, in which they would depose the government and convene a Constituent Assembly.[71] The Kronstadt mutiny began on July 19 with arming of the sailors in the First and Second Fleet divisions and the arrest of their officers. The mutineers seized the Kronstadt arsenal but did not manage to capture the fortress's artillery—a failure that enabled Olfer'ev's Grenadiers to land at the naval base without peril.

Olfer'ev's memoirs do not give a full picture of the violence that occurred at Kronstadt. He reports seeing the corpses of seven officers murdered by the rebels. The victims included two officers from a sappers' detachment, three from a naval mine group, an aide to Admiral Nikolai Aleksandrovich Belemishov, and a supply captain. During the mutiny's first two days, there were at least nine killed and twenty wounded.[72] By July 20, the government had already begun to restore order on the naval base. Between July 20 and September 21, military tribunals ordered the execution of thirty-six rebel sailors. In addition, eight mutineers were sentenced to life terms at hard labor, and 183 rebels were sentenced to terms of four to twenty years at hard labor. Eventually, the government sent a total of 458 sailors to terms of two to four years at hard labor.[73]

As the historian William C. Fuller Jr. has shown, the government's repressive tactics in late 1905/early 1906 were engineered by Sergei Iulievich Vitte, who reproached the army for its indecisiveness in confronting revolutionaries and called for more ruthless action against Russia's internal enemies. In 1906, army units were deployed over 2,500 times to repress disorders.[74]

Returning from Kronstadt in late August, Olfer'ev plunged back into the social world of elite Russian officers. This interlude in fall 1906 amounted to a coming-of-age event. He fell in love with an older, married woman. He drank too much and burned the candle at both ends. For connoisseurs of Russian literature, Olfer'ev's amatory experiences in 1906 recall passages in Tolstoy's *Anna Karenina* depicting Vronskii and Anna. For historians of Russian culture, Olfer'ev's memoirs depict a type of Russian masculinity cultivated in universities and elite schools from the reign of Nicholas I on. Officer candidates learned to endure physical pain, to control their emotions and their speech in public, to identify with their reference group—in Olfer'ev's case, with his squadron.[75] Olfer'ev's drinking did not violate the norms of this masculine culture, nor did his illicit sexual liaison, until his exhaustion started to interfere with his military duties. The memoirs suggest that the royal family and his superior officers tacitly sanctioned these activities—Nicholas II's love of gypsies and of alcohol even constituted an endorsement of them. Nevertheless, Olfer'ev's commander Baron Nikolai Aleksandrovich Budberg put a halt to his excesses by sending him to Livonia. Olfer'ev noted at the time that Budberg acted paternalistically, "not for the good of the service, but for [my] sake."

Livonia was a portion of the Baltic region encompassing areas in Estonia and Latvia. Olfer'ev was stationed "on the estate of Sesswegen" [*imenie Sesvegen*]. This estate, called *Cesvaine* in Latvian and *Sesswegen* in German, had been held by the Livonian Knights and then by the bishop of Riga since the early thirteenth century, but had been twice sacked by Russian armed forces in the Muscovite period. In 1815, Cesvaine became the property of Baron Adolfs Heinrichs fon Vulfs. Late in the nineteenth century, Baron Adolfs Gerhards fon Vulfs financed construction of a large palace in Tudor-Renaissance style. Olfer'ev mistakenly refers to the palace's architecture as "an oppressive German style" [*postroika . . . v tiazhelom nemetskom stile*]. He noted on its embrasures "soot marks" that "gave evidence of a recent arson attempt."

We cannot determine from Olfer'ev's memoirs precisely when he was at Cesvaine. He mentions "a clear frosty January night" there, without indicating the year. He also reports that he later returned from Livonia to Kurchino in Tver' "in spring 1907." Since his unit relieved another commanded by the Don Cossack Petr Nikolaevich Krasnov, who led a guards regiment in the region from 1906 to early 1907, Olfer'ev probably served at Cesvaine several months in early 1907.

From late November 1905 to early 1907 there was considerable violence throughout the Baltic provinces of Estland, Livland, and Kurland. According to the historian Andrejs Plakans, in Estland and northern Livland (the Estonian portion) 167 manor houses were burned, while in southern Livland and Kurland (the Latvian portion) another 413 manor houses were torched. Plakans cites an estimate that, during 1905 alone, "about 40 percent of manorial properties in the Baltic provinces were destroyed or seriously damaged."[76] Plakans' calculations of damage from the so-called "Baltic troubles" [*pribaltiiskaia smuta*] roughly match those of Liudmila Mikhailovna Vorob'eva, according to whom 230 estates in Livland and another 229 estates in Kurland were put to the torch.[77] In the period 1905 to 1907, the Russian authorities in the Baltic area executed as many as 2,500 people; they sentenced another 700 to hard labor, and another 2,600 to exile in the Russian interior.[78] In Latvian territory alone, according to Vorob'eva, between December 1905 and May 1908, approximately 1,500 faced trial under martial law; of these, the courts sentenced 595 to death, acquitted 183, and sentenced the remainder to hard labor, prison, or exile in Siberia. Vorob'eva points out that most of those sentenced to death were tried by temporary military courts; military field tribunals sentenced ninety-five people to death.[79]

Olfer'ev's assignment was to protect landlords' property in the Cesvaine region and to reestablish order for a radius of fifty versts (roughly fifty-five kilometers) from Cesvaine. When briefed by Krasnov, Olfer'ev learned "the situation [in Cesvaine] had quieted down considerably" since early 1905, but there were still peasant guerrilla bands—the "Forest Brothers" [*lesnye brat'ia*] operating nearby. The Forest Brothers were especially numerous in

Kurland, in Friedrichstadt and the Illuks districts, but they also operated in nearby Cesvaine in Venden district. Olfer'ev's unit was told to arrest the remnants of this organization. At first, according to his memoirs, "there were no signs of revolution in Livonia, and everything was quiet in Sessvegen." He took advantage of the lull in activity to teach illiterate soldiers in his unit to read, and semi-literate soldiers to write. He reports the soldiers' gratitude for his teaching, but also notes that his literacy groups had "assuaged the spiritually painful experience which befell our lot in connection with our police duty in Livonia."

What he meant by the phrase "spiritually painful experience" [*tiazheloe dukhovnoe perezhivanie*] is apparent from his description of two incidents. During the first, his unit raided a farmhouse to arrest one of the Forest Brothers. The unit surrounded the farmhouse at night and apprehended the accused Latvian man, in his underwear, in front of his young wife. Olfer'ev felt the arrest "disgraceful," because it could have been handled differently, with less force. He recalls this same farmhouse arrest years later, in 1918, when "Kievan hooligans" captured him at gunpoint and his own wife "rushed to protect me from what appeared an inescapable death." Olfer'ev also reports that military authorities had issued orders to coerce a confession from the Latvian prisoner by withholding water from him. In the event, the order to withhold water was not carried out, because Olfer'ev's subordinate, Lieutenant Poliakov, refused to obey it. Olfer'ev's testimony points to the Russian army command's ruthlessness in dealing with peasant partisans. We do not know the backstory of this particular arrest, but, as a general rule, German landowners made lists of Estonian or Latvian peasants whom they suspected of partisan attacks or of membership in the Forest Brothers; the landowners then denounced the peasants to the Russian authorities. Sometimes militia acting under landowners' direction, so-called "self-defense organizations" [*Selbstschutz*], burned down peasants' houses. Forest Brothers could be killed on the spot, without trial.[80]

The second "spiritually painful" incident was the field court-martial of a prisoner who had been transported from Riga to Cesvaine to stand trial for membership in the Forest Brothers and for murdering a local Orthodox priest. In 1905, attacks on clergymen, whether German pastors or Orthodox priests, were not uncommon in Riga, and by 1906 they had spread to the countryside. These attacks entailed elements of Latvian nationalism, of class warfare, and also of revolutionary assault on symbols of autocratic authority.[81] In the Cesvaine trial the prisoner, Voldemars Lupiks, admitted his involvement in "revolutionary activity": he had made "incendiary speeches" against the local authorities and had participated in the Forest Brotherhood. Lupiks denied any role in the murder, by castration, of the Orthodox priest. Olfer'ev interprets Lupiks' "revolutionary activity" as Latvian resistance to the "administrative and economic power held by [Baltic] Germans"—that is, as a nationalist and class-based protest against the local ruling minority.

Olfer'ev reports his own discomfort over the proceedings against Lupiks. Olfer'ev sat as one of the four officers in the military court. At twenty-two years of age, he was likely its youngest member. He decided that the prosecution had not proven the murder charge against Lupiks, because it did not produce depositions proving his involvement. Olfer'ev's superior, Colonel Iosif Lukich Isarlov, dismissed this objection by pointing out that the civil authorities in Riga "didn't doubt his [Lupiks'] guilt." Besides, Isarlov insisted, the duty of the field tribunal "was to carry out the orders of the civilian authorities." As a matter of Russian law, Isarlov's assertion was mistaken: the field court-martial could have found Lupiks innocent. To Olfer'ev's future regret, he signed the death warrant for Lupiks, who was shot and buried in a grave prepared before the trial had ended.

For most of the nineteenth century, executions had been rare in Russia. Reflecting on Lupiks' execution, Olfer'ev considers the morality of capital punishment. He now grasps "the entire bankruptcy and shortsightedness" of imperial Russian politics in the Baltic region. It was clear that the Petersburg government had supported the region's German landlords, who had for generations treated Latvian and Estonian peasants unjustly. Olfer'ev admits that, had he grown up as a Latvian peasant, he would likely have joined the Forest Brothers. Later, from 1914 to 1918, his sympathy for the indigenous people of the Baltic region helped him understand why Latvian peasants sympathized with revolution in the Russian Empire.

VIII

At the end of the fourth chapter of his memoirs, Olfer'ev includes a short section entitled "Reaction: 1906–10." Here he argues that, starting in

1906, "the revolution . . . went underground." Meanwhile, the inhabitants of the royal palace sought "isolation from the country" by moving outside the dangerous city of Petersburg: they wintered at Tsarskoe Selo and summered at Peterhof. According to Olfer'ev, the Third State Duma (which convened in 1907) "did not even attempt to represent itself as a law-making institution"—suggesting that it allowed the executive to rule Russia without protest. In rural Russia, Olfer'ev contends, representatives of the prerevolutionary elites—the village and district police and township officials—"returned to their posts and took into their hands the reins of government."

This restoration of the old regime, according to Olfer'ev, was superficial, because, under the surface, Russian industrialization was rapidly transforming society. The nobility split between those landowners who continued to work the land with their own machinery and through hired labor, and other landowners who abandoned the countryside altogether. This latter group either sold their estates or rented their lands to peasants or to merchants. Between 1906 and 1910, Prime Minister Petr Arkad'evich Stolypin introduced a series of reforms designed to facilitate peasant families' exit from communal land arrangements and to aid their consolidation of previously fragmented allotments into individual farms. Olfer'ev makes the important point that, under the Stolypin land reforms, the total amount of land being tilled by the peasants did not significantly increase. Therefore, both nobility and peasantry "became the victims" of the Stolypin reforms. The "victors" of this so-called period of reaction, Olfer'ev maintains, were wealthy merchants, wealthy peasants [*kulaks*], industrialists, professionals, and intellectuals, all of whom were "looking for a new political order."

Olfer'ev's view of the "reaction" is curious, for several reasons. First, as the Russian original of his memoirs makes clear, he was uncertain of its dates. The typescript fixed the reaction as beginning in 1907, but Olfer'ev later crossed out that year and inserted 1906 instead. The difference between the two dates is not trivial. One might argue on political grounds in favor of 1907 as the beginning of the reaction: Stolypin mandated a change in Russia's electoral laws on June 3, 1907, and it was under the new electoral procedures (the so-called Third of June System) that elections to the Third and Fourth Dumas occurred. The Stolypin electoral law, enacted by royal decree, was indeed a moment of executive ascendancy over the Duma. However, a strong case can also be made for 1906 as the year when the "reaction" commenced. That year witnessed the widespread use of field tribunals, of summary hangings and jailings of revolutionaries. It also saw the dismissal of the First State Duma in July—an act that demonstrated that the tsar did not intend to govern in collaborative partnership with a left-leaning legislature. The Vyborg Manifesto in late July, an appeal by Constitutional Democrats and Trudoviks to engage in civil disobedience, failed to change the executive's course of action. In November 1906, Stolypin promulgated the first steps toward the dissolution of the land communes and the creation of independent peasant agriculture on the West European model. Probably because Olfer'ev places heavy emphasis on the Stolypin land reforms and on the birth of a capitalist rural economy in Russia, he chose 1906 rather than 1907 as the commencement of the "reaction."

It is also worth noting that Olfer'ev soft-pedals the police and military repression that marked government policy throughout 1906 and early 1907. His formulation—"the revolution . . . went underground"—obscures the effect of the repression, in which his own military unit was involved in Petersburg, Kronstadt, and the Baltic provinces, and which he acknowledges elsewhere in the memoir.

The section on the reaction of 1906–10 has the feel of a retrospective account drawn from reflection on historical sources, rather than the spirit of contemporaneous personal observation. The term "reaction" appears as a staple in the histories of the Duma period written by Bolsheviks, Mensheviks, and Socialist-Revolutionaries, but in the period 1906–10 Olfer'ev was not affiliated with any of these groups. Indeed, although he recognized the government's isolation, he did not support the revolution in the cities or the countryside.

That said, Olfer'ev's view of the period ends with a question about the political reliability of common soldiers recruited circa 1907: "Would they obey silently as the older servicemen did," if ordered "to attack a mob, perform arrests, and carry out military executions?"

In 1907, Olfer'ev's mother Tat'iana Fedorovna [*née* Salova] sold the family estate Kurchino, in Tver' province, to her sister (Olfer'ev's aunt) Aleksandra Fedorovna. Olfer'ev mentions several reasons for this sale: the collapse in farm revenue during the 1905–1907 revolution, "when not even one-tenth of the land had been harvested and not one meadow had been mowed"; his family's inability to pay farm workers enough to compete with factory wages; his mother's prodigal spending. Olfer'ev laments that the sale made his immediate family dependent on the good graces of Aunt Aleksandra, but he acknowledges that his family was still enormously wealthy. His mother had also inherited an estate in Saratov province and an annuity of three thousand rubles. Although he claimed to have had a "foreboding" of the estate's sale, the reality hit him hard, as his memory of a 1912 visit to the abandoned manor house shows. His meeting with an old overseer and his stroll through a nearby peasant village "with its sagging roofs" and pitted roads are the stuff of other memoirs about Russian estate life of the era. His account resembles the narrative in Ivan Bunin's *The Village* [*Derevnia*] (1910) and in that writer's nostalgic *Life of Arsen'ev* [*Zhizn' Arsen'eva*] (1930–1933).

The sale of Kurchino in 1907 apparently forced Olfer'ev to think about his immediate future. If he could not retire from the military to lead the life of a country gentleman, then he might as well remain in the army and become a career officer. This second path became complicated for him when he fell in love with Marusia Grevens, the niece of a family acquaintance from Rzhev. Although he admired her intelligence and liveliness, Olfer'ev hesitated to propose marriage. He recognized that, should he remain in military service, his attention would be divided between her and his unit, which now seemed to him like a surrogate family. He also feared that marriage might compromise his "independence" in the service and thus thwart his ambition. After hesitating, Fedor and Marusia nevertheless decided to marry.

IX

Olfer'ev does not disclose the precise date of his entrance into the Academy, but he took final examinations there in spring 1913. The curriculum demanded two years of study, often "theoretical" in nature, devoted to tactics, strategy, military administration, statistics, military history, geodesy, and cartography. For students like Olfer'ev who succeeded academically in the two-year curriculum, the Academy offered a third year, or "supplemental year," of independent research on practical military problems.[82] Olfer'ev completed the third year of study in 1914, so he was part of the last class to graduate before the Great War.[83]

If he completed the Academy's three-year program in 1914, Olfer'ev must have entered as a first-year student in 1911. It is not clear from the memoirs when he sat for the entrance examinations. He might have done so at any point between late 1908 and mid-year 1911. He mentions that when he entered the Academy, the war ministry was "dependent on the new chairman of the Council of State Defense, Grand Duke Nikolai Nikolaevich." Olfer'ev also refers to one of the Academy's professors, the distinguished Nikolai Nikolaevich Golovin, who "had just returned from detachment to the French Military Academy [*École supérieure de guerre*]." Since the Grand Duke served as chair of the Council of State Defense from 1905 to 1908, and Golovin returned from France in 1908, perhaps Olfer'ev finished his entrance exam in late 1908 or early 1909. If so, he stayed with his unit for two or three more years after passing the entrance exam. The timeline of his career before entering the Academy was not unusual: junior officers generally served five years after their first commission before becoming eligible for the Academy.

Olfer'ev's purpose in studying at the Academy was to win a post on the General Staff. The Academy had opened its doors in 1832 as the Academy of the General Staff and had been renamed in 1909 the Imperial Nikolaevan Military Academy [*Imperatorskaia Nikolaevskaia Voennaia Akademiia*]. Since the military reforms of Dmitrii Alekseevich Miliutin in the 1860s–70s, the General Staff had been the army's nerve center, and the Academy had been a key institution in supplying the army with well-trained officers. According to Olfer'ev, the Academy only accepted 150 men each year, and of those only seventy-five graduated in the "first category"—that is, with eligibility to join the General Staff. His estimate of the number of students was perhaps high: at the century's turn, the historian Andrei Vladislavovich Ganin counted 314 officers-students in all three years of course work.[84]

Olfer'ev expresses doubt that candidates for the Academy were in fact the best young officers in the Russian army. In his estimation, most students had good records from military schools, but there were also mediocre students, and those who "should not have been there." Ignat'ev, who studied at the Academy from 1899 to 1902, makes a similar observation:

"in the Guards and the army, the Academy was thought a special preserve for careerists and opportunists."[85] However, both Olfer'ev and Ignat'ev regarded the Academy's entrance examinations as "very difficult." Olfer'ev estimates that only six of every ten candidates who sat for the exams passed them. Ignat'ev offers a description of the questions posed in each field and of the traps laid by demanding examiners.[86] The impression is that those admitted to the Academy had to have orderly minds, the ability to improvise, and a solid fundamental education in history, mathematics, Russian language, three European languages, and geography.

Before the Russo-Japanese War, classes at the Academy were more theoretical than practical, in spite of the efforts of General Nikolai Nikolaevich Sukhotin to get away from what he considered the "scholastic system" of teaching there.[87] As a result, according to Ignat'ev, graduates of the Academy were oriented toward "passive, positional defense" rather than toward a war of movement. They were "incompletely acquainted with contemporary technical means of waging war." They did not know the best ways to position field artillery or machine guns. They tended to be "ignorant of social questions"—that is, of the psychology of the lower classes and how that outlook might affect army morale.

During Olfer'ev's time at the Academy, young instructors drew lessons from the Russo-Japanese debacle and strove to update Russian war strategy. The leader of this effort was Golovin, who tried to shift instruction toward contemporary military practices by devising an elaborate series of war games that were actually based on maps from earlier wars. By 1914, Golovin had attracted ten other instructors into his "circle."[88] Before the Great War, Golovin published *Service in the General Staff*, a book based on lectures that Olfer'ev attended in 1911.[89] Later, as an émigré during the Soviet period, Golovin wrote authoritative histories of the Russian front in the World War,[90] a pioneering study of the early civil war,[91] a meditation on Aleksandr Vasil'evich Suvorov's *Science of Victory*,[92] and a theoretical work on military science focused on sociological factors in warfare.[93] Golovin and his circle were supported by General Dmitrii Grigor'evich Shcherbachev, the head of the Academy from 1907 to 1912, and by Grand Duke Nikolai Nikolaevich, who in 1914 served as the Supreme Commander in Chief of the Russian army. In spite of their protectors in high places, Golovin and company faced resistance from within the Academy. As Olfer'ev notes, skepticism came from old-fashioned scholars like Boris Mikhailovich Koliubakin and Grigorii Grigor'evich Khristiani; from adherents to Suvorov, such as Mikhail Dmitrievich Bonch-Bruevich; and also from defenders of German military theory as articulated by Karl von Clausewitz in *Zum Kriege* and by Helmuth Karl Bernhard Graf von Moltke in *Geschichte des deutsch-französischen Krieges von 1870–1871* (1885). According to Olfer'ev, the traditionalists had the ear of Tsar Nicholas II, who distrusted Golovin and the "innovators," and who therefore engineered the appointment in 1912 of Nikolai Nikolaevich Ianushkevich as head of the Academy.

Olfer'ev and many of his student peers sided with the Golovin circle, and therefore learned the "main conclusions" of the General Staff concerning the Russo-Japanese War: first, that under modern conditions, defending fortresses and fixed positions is impossible except as a temporary expedient, and thus war planning should focus on offensive maneuvers; second, that concentrated artillery fire must be accompanied by forward infantry thrusts in which infantry commanders must take the initiative to locate and destroy the enemy; and third, that the increasing importance of machinery in warfare demands new attention to battlefield supply of critical war machines.

From the perspective of Russia's future war plans, the first of these conclusions—about the indefensibility of fixed positions and of fortresses—was of greatest immediate significance. The General Staff had lost confidence in the army's ability to defend the Empire's western fortresses. Even the strongest fortress, at Kovno, looked vulnerable to General Ianushkevich in 1913. Olfer'ev's last assignment at the Academy was a war-game defense of Grodno—a key position on the German front. According to Olfer'ev, Russian doubts about the army's defensive capability arose in part from memories of the Far Eastern debacle in 1904–05, but also from military intelligence about German maneuvers in Eastern Prussia in 1913. The Germans assumed, just as Russian planners had done, that in the event of a two-front war, Germany would be attacked through East Prussia by the Russian army. What is ironic is that due to the sporadic trench warfare on the Russian front from 1914 to 1916, Russia and its allies often found themselves fighting not a war of maneuver but a war of attrition over what amounted to fixed points.

Olfer'ev asserts that the second conclusion—about coordination of artillery and infantry attacks—presented a profound challenge to the Russian army. Heretofore, Russian infantry actions had been predicated on strict soldierly discipline, not on small group or individual battle initiatives. To take the initiative in mass battles—so-called "encounter battles" [*vstrechnye boi*]—Russian authorities would have to recognize the need for "reeducation of the entire army" [*neobkhodimost' . . . perevospitaniia vsego armeiskago organizma*], and they would have to do so despite the fact that infantrymen had inadequate instruction in schools and little sense of initiative generally. This was risky business, Olfer'ev observes, because encouraging individual initiative might lead to dissemination of "revolutionary propaganda" in the armed forces. In other words, the effort to save the Motherland from the Germans and Austrians might well result in its destruction by Russian revolutionary forces.

Olfer'ev seems to think that the need to improve the delivery of technically sophisticated war materiel might also be an obstacle, because Russian soldiers might not know how to use the machines on which their lives would depend. This was a reasonable concern, but Olfer'ev fails to note two more compelling worries: inadequate supplies of war materiel proved nearly fatal to Russia's war effort in 1915; and Russia's peasant soldiers turned their arms against the government in 1917.

Olfer'ev makes several important observations about official decisions that may have prompted soldiers to become revolutionaries. First, he contends, the government made a superficial attempt to shore up soldiers' morale by giving them new uniforms and by preaching a combination of nationalism and populism that identified the people with the tsar. Second, he notes, the generals decided to maintain the cavalry. This was less a technical military decision than a show of power. Olfer'ev does not mention that the cavalry embodied the class superiority of the nobility over the foot soldiers drawn from the common people. In the writings of military theorists, such as Andrei Georgievich Elchaninov, the cavalry performed a political function in addition to its military duties.[94] Elchaninov assumed that the unity of tsar and people would be unbreakable in wartime.[95] According to Olfer'ev, General Bonch-Bruevich also "clouded the minds of his listeners with like notions."

Olfer'ev and the Golovin circle apparently invested some hope in the likelihood that a war with the Germans "could not last very long"—perhaps not much more than three months. Olfer'ev connects this assumption with

Nikolai Petrovich Mikhnevich, a war historian at the Academy.[96] This assumption was the Russian variant of what Lancelot L. Farrar calls "the short war illusion,"[97] an illusion that kept the Russian General Staff from facing up to the danger of revolution in the Russian army, since the generals expected the war to end before a revolution could occur.

X

Olfer'ev sketches aspects of the Russian "pattern of life before the World War" in a short chapter that borrows its title from Lev Nikolaevich Tolstoy's unfinished drama *The Living Corpse* [*Zhivoi trup*]. Olfer'ev watched the six-act play in Moscow, at the Moscow Art Theater, probably during its premier run which began in late September 1911, a year after Tolstoy's death.[98] *The Living Corpse* stirred intense debate at the time and even became a pretext for determining the great writer's public legacy. Was Tolstoy's story of a failed marriage a vehicle for his moralism, to condemn the "license" and egoism of Russia's elites? Or did it imply a rejection of Russia's backward system of divorce law, with its reliance on both ecclesiastical and secular courts to police morality? Olfer'ev saw the play both as one of Tolstoy's "usual sermons on nonresistance to evil" and as a "criticism of the Church, courts of law, authorities and the entire tenor of [Russian] life in general"; and he wondered whether the Russian monarchy and Russian privileged society now constituted "a living corpse."

Analyzing the last years of the old regime, Olfer'ev cannot help mentioning Grigorii Efimovich Rasputin, the controversial peasant-courtier and subject of countless shadowy rumors. Olfer'ev recalls seeing a portrait of a fifty-year-old peasant, clad in a black undercoat [*poddevka*] and tall boots. The peasant's large burning eyes mezmerized viewers. The portrait in question was surely Aleksandr Dmitrievich Raevskii's 1912 canvas, "Portrait of an Elder" [*Portret startsa*], displayed at that year's spring exhibition by the Academy of Arts in St. Petersburg. We know from contemporary accounts that thousands of Petersburgers visited this exhibition, and that it was controversial.[99] The portrait disgusted Olfer'ev and his wife Marusia, but Rasputin reportedly was pleased by the likeness.[100] It is likely that the very features that upset the Olfer'evs—the subject's luminous eyes, nervous self-possession, and commanding presence—were the things that appealed to Rasputin and his many followers.

Since 1910, rumors of Rasputin's immorality had circulated in the palace and imperial court.[101] The allegations against him included the charge that, in 1909, he had raped the royal housemaid Mariia Ivanovna Vishniakova—a charge that Empress Aleksandra dismissed.[102] In March 1910, the newspaper *Moscow News* [*Moskovskie vedomosti*] carried a series of articles about Rasputin's womanizing, political ambitions, and religious charlatanism. The articles' author, Mikhail Aleksandrovich Novoselov, repeated his denunciation of Rasputin in a short book.[103] There was enough noise surrounding Rasputin in 1910 that Prime Minister Stolypin ordered a secret investigation of him. However, when Stolypin reported the findings to the tsar in early 1911, Nicholas rejected them.[104]

In late 1911/early 1912, Rasputin's enemies tried to drive him from the capital. On December 16, 1911, Bishop Germogen (Dolganev) and Hieromonk Iliodor (Trufanov) and others confronted Rasputin over his "ungodly" behavior and demanded he never again set foot in the royal palace. On January 11, 1912, Germogen publicly accused Rasputin of "depravity" and of membership in the ecstatic but reputedly subversive Christian sect, the *khlysty*.[105] On January 25, Iliodor wrote a denunciatory letter, which he intended for the emperor's eyes, but which quickly leaked to the press. In it Iliodor made a series of lurid claims that Rasputin was a rapist and also the empress's lover.[106] In support of this last charge, he appended a letter written by Aleksandra to Rasputin—a letter that, if innocent, was at the very least ill-advised in its wording and compromising to the royal family's prestige.[107] Worst of all for Rasputin, the originals of this denunciation and the supporting letters wound up in the hands of Minister of Internal Affairs Aleksandr Aleksandrovich Makarov, and copies found their way to the Duma politician Aleksandr Ivanovich Guchkov. Makarov presented Iliodor's letters to Nicholas II. Meanwhile, Guchkov launched a sensational investigation of Rasputin in the Duma commencing on January 26. On February 1, 1912, Nicholas and Aleksandra refused to expel Rasputin, and on February 11 they received him in the palace—a signal of continuing imperial favor.[108] Under pressure from Church and state authorities, Rasputin voluntarily left Petersburg for his village home in Pokrovskoe on February 18. Strangely enough, on the very next day

Rasputin's portrait was displayed for the first time at the Academy of Arts exhibition, although Rasputin was not identified by name as the subject. On February 26, the chairman of the State Duma, Mikhail Vladimirovich Rodzianko, confronted the tsar over Rasputin; on March 8 Rodzianko sent Nicholas a written report on Rasputin's philandering and "crimes."[109] On March 9, in an open session of the Duma, Guchkov described Rasputin as a "vestige of the Dark Ages" who, with a "gang of supporters," was endangering the Church and the state. Guchkov accused the Ober-Procurator of the Holy Synod of turning a blind eye to the threat emanating from Rasputin.[110]

If Olfer'ev visited the Academy of Arts exhibition in the month between mid-February and mid-March 1912, he must have been aware of Rasputin's notoriety. Olfer'ev remembered "knowing nothing about Rasputin" but "distrusting the rumors" about the elder [*o Rasputine my nichego tolkom ne znali i k slukham o nem ia otnosilsia s nedoveriem*]. However, he and Marusia had also heard gossip about the corrupt sale of offices through Rasputin's network. The conduit of this corruption was Prince Mikhail Mikhailovich Andronikov, a junior official in the ministry of internal affairs and editor of the newspaper *Voice of Russia* [*Golos Rossii*]. Andronikov was an intriguer and able flatterer said by Stepan Petrovich Beletskii to know "almost all department heads of almost all ministries and many other officials, who were thought to have influence over ministers."[111] Apparently, Rasputin often visited Andronikov's apartment, and Andronikov visited Rasputin's place. Andronikov may have introduced Rasputin to Prime Minister Ivan Logginovich Goremykin.[112] One of the regular visitors to Andronikov's apartment was Natal'ia Illarionovna Chervinskaia, a relative of Ekaterina Vikent'evna Sukhomlinova—the wife of Minister of War Vladimir Aleksandrovich Sukhomlinov. A photograph of the Sukhomlinovs hung from Andronikov's walls.[113] These details render plausible the "gossip" reported by Olfer'ev that Andronikov helped arrange the sale of a post on the General Staff for five thousand rubles, and that during the war Rasputin corresponded with Prime Minister Goremykin about the appointment to office of one of Rasputin's protégés. To his credit, Olfer'ev classified these stories as unverifiable rumors [*Vy skazhete mne, chto nichego podobnogo moglo i ne byt'. Soglasen*]. In relating the rumor about the sale of office, he did not mention the name of the alleged purchaser.

Olfer'ev nevertheless described Andronikov as a "cheat and swindler . . . who, taking advantage of Rasputin's name, began to make shady deals." What lay behind this animus was perhaps Olfer'ev's knowledge of Andronikov's links to prominent military figures: to General Sukhomlinov; to General Aleksei Andreevich Polivanov, who served as assistant minister of war until his dismissal in 1912; to Captain Nikolai Pavlovich Sablin, a naval officer close to Nicholas II; and to General Timofei Mikhailovich Beliaev, an artillery commander who also served as vice-chairman of the right-wing Russian Assembly.[114] Olfer'ev may have also heard rumors that Andronikov had received government funds (true), that he had channeled some of them to Rasputin (also true), and that he had access to various banks (true again) as well as to money from private parties petitioning the government for assistance. The best historian of right-wing salons in Petersburg has pointed out that Prince Andronikov's circle was but one of thirty-one salons or societies lobbying for influence,[115] and that Andronikov's circle had relatively little impact on the tsar.[116]

Olfer'ev was certainly right to conclude that Rasputin seriously damaged the royal family's reputation. The "scandalous rumors" linked to Rasputin "reeked with the odor of death from a decomposing regime." In wartime, the rumors about Rasputin fed the perception that the Empress Aleksandra was both an "unfaithful wife" and a "traitor" to Russia.[117]

In his picture of Russia before the Great War, Olfer'ev points to symptomatic problems in his regiment and in the Russian officer corps. He notes that talented officers of noble origins sometimes left his regiment because "it became necessary to earn more money in order to live," and that other politically connected noble officers remained in the unit, even though they were not as competent. In Olfer'ev's judgment, the first phenomenon was a consequence of the abolition of serfdom and of the disappearance of the "old patriarchal economy." The second was a result of a collision between the patronage-client system that had traditionally characterized the Russian army and the meritocratic system of promotion instituted by the military reforms of the 1870s. According to the historian John W. Steinberg, in 1912 roughly half the Russian officer corps came from noble families, but in 1914 there were more non-noble officers serving on the General Staff than officers of noble origins. Steinberg attributes the latter development to War Minister Miliutin's efforts in the 1870s "to create a meritocracy."[118]

The promotion of competent officers of non-noble origins held the long-run promise of greater military efficiency, but in the short term the cadre of non-noble officers threatened the prestige of senior commanders, not because the younger officers breached discipline but rather because they insisted on conformity to recent regulations as opposed to the traditional norms. Olfer'ev reports the case of a certain "Rotmistr E" who, during maneuvers, "displayed initiative bordering on insubordination," and who was later forced by a trial of honor [*sud chesti*] to leave the regiment. Olfer'ev describes this affair circumspectly, without mentioning the name of the regimental commander, but notes that soon after "E's" trial of honor the commander was replaced by "Prince D.," a "childhood friend of the tsar . . . who tragically was killed along with the Tsar after the revolution."

From these hints, we can reconstruct at least part of Olfer'ev's story. The two regimental commanders were Vladimir Khristoforovich Roop, who commanded the Grenadiers Regiment from 1907 to 1912, and Prince Vasilii Aleksandrovich Dolgorukov, the very Prince D. who was killed by the Bolsheviks on July 10, 1918 in Ekaterinburg. Because the succession of command occurred in March 1912, the "court of honor" that dismissed Rotmistr E must have convened late in 1911 or early in 1912. We do not know the identity of "E" but Olfer'ev tells us that he was "a brilliant commander of the squadron and a direct descendant of Field Marshall [Aleksandr Vasil'evich] Suvorov."

In 2002, the historian Boris Vasil'evich Galenko compiled a genealogy of the Suvorovs, based on the research of Colonel A. Z. Miklashevskii.[119] However, neither Mikhlashevskii, who completed his research on Suvorov's family tree in 1900, nor Galenko provides enough data on the post-1900 Suvorovs for us to determine the real name of Rotmistr E. The only clue from their work is that two Molostovs, both Suvorov's descendants in the male line, were attached to the Life Guard Grenadiers at one point.[120] Either one might have been the mysterious "E."

Olfer'ev also reports a more serious affair—the shooting of a bartender named Mochalin in the Petersburg officers' club by a drunken cornet named Doné. According to his account, the regimental commander, Prince Dolgorukov, decided that the cornet had no justification for using a weapon against a subordinate; he referred the case to a military tribunal. When the issue reached trial at the Petersburg Military District Court, however, the killer was acquitted thanks to a brilliant defense by Mikhail Grigor'evich Kazarinov. (In 1917, Kazarinov defended former War Minister Sukhomlinov against charges of treason and bribe-taking.)[121] As Olfer'ev observes, the case provoked disagreement up the chain of command. Grand Duke Nikolai Nikolaevich sided with the regimental commander in demanding the killer's punishment; the tsar overturned the acquittal. Cornet Doné was stripped of his officer's rank and was demoted to the rank of common soldier. However, the tsar neither took away Doné's noble rank nor sent him to prison. Olfer'ev calls the incident "the most shameful episode in the entire history of the regiment," probably because it showed the divergence between regimental "honor" and military justice: a gentleman-officer could kill a subordinate and receive only a minor punishment for doing so.

During this time, Olfer'ev claims, the government was out of touch with the population at large. He cites a series of orchestrated celebrations designed to demonstrate popular support for the tsar: the 1912 unveiling of the monument to Aleksandr III, the 1912 centenary celebration of the battle of Borodino, and the 1913 tercentenary of the Romanov dynasty.

In the last decade of the old regime, two monuments to Tsar Aleksandr III were unveiled in the Russian capitals. In 1906, the Italian sculptor Paolo Troubetzkoy completed the design for a bronze equestrian statue to be set on a red granite foundation. The casting of the bronze required more than eighteen months, and the labor to erect the monument took several more months. Even before the monument was unveiled on May 23, 1909, it triggered controversy. Nicholas and Aleksandra approved Troubezkoy's life-size model, but Grand Duke Vladimir Aleksandrovich initially criticized it as a "caricature" of the tsar before finally agreeing to the project.[122] After the unveiling, the monument became the target of ridicule. The artist Boris Mikhailovich Kustodiev wrote his wife on the day of the unveiling: "[The monument] is most ridiculous and awkward, a horse without a tail, with open mouth as if loudly screaming, a horse holding itself back and not wanting to advance, and he [the rider] awkward and ungainly, and viewed from behind—a very comical impression! A spine like a woman's breast and a colossal tailless rear end."[123] In spite of the monument's strangeness, it survived the 1917 revolutions and the Soviet period. It now stands in front of the Marble Palace, as part of the Russian Museum complex.

Olfer'ev comments on the second monument to Aleksandr III, which was designed by the architect Aleksandr Nikanorovich Pomerantsev and the sculptor Aleksandr Mikhailovich Opekushin. This monument, funded by subscription after the tsar's death in 1894, was constructed from 1900 to 1912 in front of the Cathedral of Christ the Savior in Moscow. It was unveiled on May 30, 1912 in an elaborate ceremony at which Moscow Metropolitan Vladimir (Bogoiavlenskii) presided jointly with Nicholas II. The unveiling revealed a bronze statue of the emperor seated on the throne, his head elevated fifty feet above the ground. The crowned emperor held in one hand the scepter of office and in the other the orb of sovereign authority. He was dressed in a tsarist mantle. Beneath him on the granite foundation reposed four bronze, two-headed eagles. The monument carried the inscription: "To the Most Venerable, Most Autocratic, Majestic Sovereign Aleksandr Aleksandrovich of All Russia"—an evocation of the crown's might and a reminder of the autocratic nostalgia that still persisted in Russia just on the eve of the Great War.

Although Olfer'ev did not attend the monument's unveiling, he would have seen the covered scaffolding when he visited Moscow early in 1912. He cites a Petersburg newspaper account of the unveiling ceremony, which referred to the ceremony as a "majestic moment," but he suggests that the event in fact insulated Nicholas II from what the common people really thought about him, since the tsar was surrounded by "police, police, police." It is worth mentioning that the statue symbolically linked state and Church, since it was incorporated into the cathedral's grounds. The link specifically to the Cathedral of Christ the Savior also pointed in various ways to Russia's victory over Napoleon in 1812, as the cathedral had been planned as a memorial to the Russian victory. Its dedication in 1883 occurred during the coronation of Aleksandr III.

The monument was later enshrined in public memory for two reasons: its demolition on Lenin's orders in 1918, and the cinematic reenactment of its demolition in Sergei Eizenshtein's 1927 film, "October."[124]

The Borodino centenary celebrations took place from August 25 to 30, 1912, the first three days on the battlefield itself, and then from August 28 on in Moscow. According to the historian Richard Wortman, the Borodino festivities enabled the tsar temporarily to ignore contemporary political difficulties and "to evoke the grandeur of the battle and the heroism of his ancestors."[125] At Borodino, the tsar reviewed troops from units whose predecessors had fought the French, received a religious procession bearing the wonder-working icon of the Smolensk Mother of God, and met 4,550 peasant elders from all over Russia. According to Moscow's provincial governor, Vladimir Fedorovich Dzhunkovskii, "the rapture with which the peasants greeted their monarch defies description."[126] In Moscow Nicholas II again encountered rapturous crowds—first at Khodynka Fields and then in the square outside the Dormition Cathedral. On the square, the crowd knelt with the royal family as a large choir sang a prayer in honor of Aleksandr I.[127] Olfer'ev devotes only one sentence to this national pageant, and in general he dismisses it as contrived: "parades, ceremonies, well-organized crowds of people yelling 'Hurrah,' and 'God save the tsar.'" He is surely right to point to the government's hand in orchestrating the Borodino celebrations. As the Moscow historian Galina Ul'ianova has observed, the Borodino centenary had been in the planning stages for five years.[128]

The tercentenary of the Romanov dynasty was celebrated in three stages: a jubilee in Petersburg on February 21–24, 1913; a pilgrimage by the tsar to Volga cities linked to the Romanov family in May; and a visit to Moscow on May 24–27. The organizers sought to highlight the dynasty's role in the development of the Russian state and in the advancement of Russian society. Therefore, as Ul'ianova has noted, these events were interpreted "not only as an event for the dynasty and its retinue [but] as an important marker in the nation's history."[129]

In Petersburg, according to Wortman, on February 21 there were twenty-five processions of the cross. The three largest converged on the Kazan' Cathedral, where roughly four thousand people had gathered in the royal presence. Nicholas II, reposed on a marble throne, listened to the reading of a manifesto proclaiming the union of tsar and people as the key to Russia's growth and future success. Later that day, he met descendants of boyar families whose ancestors had signed the 1613 document announcing the election to the throne of Mikhail Romanov.[130] He also accepted congratulations from courtiers, officials, and military officers, and heard a brief valedictory by Mikhail Rodzianko, who spoke for the State Duma. On February 22, the royal family attended a performance of Mikhail Ivanovich Glinka's opera *A Life for the Tsar.* On February 23, Nicholas and Aleksandra danced at a ball organized by the Petersburg nobility. According to Wortman, Aleksandra "was distant at the ball. [She] looked haggard and left early, inflicting more wounded feelings."[131] Ul'ianova notes that Aleksandra followed the protocol of dancing the first dance with the Petersburg noble marshal, Ivan Nikolaevich Saltykov.[132]

Olfer'ev attended the tercentenary in Petersburg and was present at the ball on February 23. He calls the celebration "the final event in imperial Russia before the war," a moment when "Petersburg society for the last time stepped out in all its finery." He observes the irony of the empress's dance with a descendant of the Saltykov line (Prince Nikolai Ivanovich Saltykov, Catherine the Great's rumored lover, being the purported father of Emperor Paul I). Olfer'ev maintains that Aleksandra "walked with tightly closed lips" and that "her face showed no sign of happiness." He compares the solemnity of the entire occasion to a "funeral procession." This may have been an exaggeration, but it resonates with Wortman's commentary on the empress's demeanor.

Olfer'ev formed his last impressions of prewar Russian village life while doing a topographical survey of the area near the Serebrianka-Warsaw railroad station, roughly 159 kilometers from Petersburg. According to the 1897 census, this region—the Luga district—was among the least densely populated areas in Petersburg province.[133] The two villages near the railroad station, Bol'shaia Serebrianka and Malaia Serebrianka, comprised less than one hundred fifty inhabitants in 1838,[134] and scarcely two hundred at the turn of the century. Olfer'ev reports that in the village "it was impossible to get the most common produce . . . even edible bread." That was surely true, for two reasons: agriculture in the Luga district generated little income and was hardly above subsistence level; and local peasants would not likely have sold their food to outsiders in the months before fall harvest. Olfer'ev also observed "one drunken brawl after another" on village streets, and he witnessed the death of a young man who had been cut across the stomach in a knife fight. His account of village life suggests the deep poverty, restiveness, and even murderousness of the villagers, in contrast to the official narrative that celebrated the people's Christian faith and political loyalty to the crown.

XI

When Olfer'ev graduated from the General Staff Academy in April 1914, he anticipated a war in Europe. "Not to expect war," he writes, "was a delusion limited only to people who were devoid of all powers of observation or were hopeless optimists." If this was his frame of mind, then his decision to apply for a post in the Warsaw Military District was precisely to put himself "in our future forward theater of war." His brief leave of absence before reporting to Warsaw—a leave spent in Belgium but also in transit across Germany—must have seemed unreal. His wife's question, "How can there be a war amidst such culture, beauty, and wealth?"—reflected the incredulity of many civilians in 1914 who, having been raised in a golden and largely peaceful period of European history, could not quite imagine that war could be imminent.

Apropos the impending war, Olfer'ev and his wife Marusia argued about whether it might be a good thing. Her notion, that "war is brutal and can only make savages of people," was not untypical in liberal Europe, but in Russia it was an opinion confined largely to Tolstoyans and a few pacifist intellectuals, and to untold numbers of peasants, who regarded army life as a horrific burden. Olfer'ev took the view that war is a fact of the human condition, that, as a national calamity, it springs from a "decline in the moral foundations" of society, but also that "war is the very phenomenon which calls people to acts of heroism and should ennoble them." His opinion, widely held in military and conservative circles, had been forcefully expressed by Vladimir Sergeevich Solov'ev's character, the general, in the compelling philosophical dialogues *Three Conversations* [*Tri razgovora*] (1900).[135]

In fact, therefore, the Olfer'ev family's debate over the war's purported inevitability and its potential value in regenerating society was far from naïve. These questions were also disputed among diplomats and responsible statesmen of the day in other parts of Europe. According to the distinguished historian Gordon Craig, in the first months of 1914 the German Chancellor Theobald von Bethmann-Hollweg thought the fragile European peace could be maintained; however, by July 1914, Bethmann became gloomily preoccupied by the Russia threat, which, he said, "grows and grows and hangs upon us ever more heavily like a nightmare."[136] After the assassination of the Austrian Archduke Franz Ferdinand on June 15/28, Bethmann clung to the narrow hope that Germany's mobilization would intimidate the Russians. Failing that, he wished the war would be short. As Craig aptly remarks, Bethmann's policy in 1914 "can be fairly described as whistling to keep one's courage up."[137] In fact, the German chancellor internalized the terms of the war debate, as he careened from hope that war could be avoided to the conviction that it was virtually inevitable.

From the perspective of Russian statecraft, the European situation looked unstable by October 1912, when the government began to prepare itself for the possibility that the Balkan war might escalate into a general conflict. As the historian Dominic Lieven has demonstrated, Nicholas II considered mobilizing infantry units in the Kiev and Warsaw military districts, but, after meeting with the Council of Ministers in December 1912, he decided not to issue the mobilization order.[138] Yet the signing of the Treaty of Bucharest on July 28/August 10, 1913 did little to allay Russian anxieties, because, as it seemed to Foreign Minister Sergei Dmitrievich Sazonov, the treaty fueled the expansionist ambitions of Bulgaria and Serbia and therefore made future collision between Russia and Austria more likely, rather than less so.[139] To avoid war, Sazonov would have had to properly "manage" Serbia in 1913 and 1914, but he and his colleagues proved unable to do so.[140]

The Russians' alarm over the Balkan situation only increased in winter 1913–1914, when the German government sent a military mission to the Ottoman Empire. To the Russians, the idea of a German officer commanding units of the Turkish army raised the prospect of a German protectorate over Turkey and of de facto Austrian-German domination over the Black Sea.[141] Bethmann's remarks in 1913 that the European peace was in danger because of Slavic hostility toward Germany, along with Kaiser Wilhelm II's musings that the Slavs must be made to submit to German authority, suggested that a pan-European conflict might be inevitable after all.

On February 5/22, 1914, the grand marshal of the Russian court, Pavel Konstantinovich Benkendorf, wrote his brother: "No one here wants war or adventure, but for a number of months now the feeling that war is inevitable has spread more and more in all classes."[142]

A sense of war's inevitability haunted the famous memorandum to

Nicholas II by the leading rightist politician in the upper house of the Russian legislature, Petr Nikolaevich Durnovo.[143] In this memorandum, Durnovo called armed conflict between Germany and England "unavoidable" [*neminuemo*]. He warned that if this conflict did occur, it would likely involve Russia as one of the powers aligned with England.[144] The consequences for Russia would be disastrous. The main burden of fighting the Germans would fall on Russia, Durnovo thought, even though Russia lacked the armaments to sustain a prolonged war and even though its transportation network was inadequate to fight a European war.[145] Durnovo asserted that war with Germany would damage the prestige of both the German and the Russian monarchies.[146] Given the hold of "unconscious socialism" on the Russian masses,[147] he predicted the war would "inevitably stimulate the socialist movement" and would "plunge Russia into darkest anarchy." Durnovo worried about the possibility of "social revolution with an unforeseeable outcome."[148] The only way out of this blind alley was for Russia to align itself with Germany instead of with England and France—a shift that Durnovo thought logical, since Germany was a "conservative" power like Russia.[149] However, he conceded that Russia's rivalry with Austria over the Balkans stood in the way of Russian-German alliance. Indeed, he observed that Russia's anti-Austrian policy had driven Germany to become Turkey's protector. His memorandum therefore can be read in two ways: as a last-ditch attempt to persuade the tsar to jettison a decade of Russian foreign policy, or as a prophecy of coming social revolution.[150]

We do not know whether the emperor read Durnovo's memorandum, but Lieven argues that he probably did so.[151] A more interesting question may be how many people outside of ministerial circles had access to Durnovo's view. Because of his role in the ministry of internal affairs and his position in the State Council, Durnovo's opinions mattered. He spoke enough in the State Council to make known his attitudes toward England, Germany, and Austria.[152] It is therefore conceivable that Olfer'ev knew the substance of Durnovo's "prophetic" memorandum, either through his contacts in the General Staff or through his wife, who had family ties to the Duma leader Rodzianko.

The other issue debated by the Olfer'evs—whether war brutalizes or ennobles its participants—had a surprising currency in 1914 and in the early war period. In one of his first essays after August 1914, the German belletrist and novelist Thomas Mann welcomed war against France as a moment of poetic inspiration: "War! It was purification, liberation, what we needed, and untrammeled hope."[153] However, Mann's brother Heinrich, also an essayist and novelist, considered the war a disaster, a result of Germany's hypocrisy and corruption.[154]

Russian idealizations of war came from various sources. As Melissa Stockdale has shown, a common tendency was to regard the armed conflict as "transformative"—with political reformers seeing the war as time for turning subjects [*poddanye*] into citizens [*grazhdane*], peasants imagining it as the moment when they might achieve equality of rights and gain land, and religious thinkers seizing on the conflict as a moment for individual and collective spiritual rebirth.[155]

Among religious philosophers, the idealization of the war commenced even before the guns of August had fired their first salvos. In a 1912 essay entitled "The Old National Messianism and the New," Evgenii Nikolaevich Trubetskoi sketched a utopian notion that the old, narrow nationalism must give way to an all-encompassing "Pentecostal" messianism, in which national particularities would be affirmed but nations would come together in the kingdom of God.[156] As Randall Poole has argued, Trubetskoi's messianism informs his lectures in the fall of 1914, especially his "War and Russia's World Task," delivered at the Vladimir Solov'ev Religious-Philosophical Society.[157] In that lecture, Trubetskoi maintained that Russians felt connected by a "liberating mission" that would "serve all humanity."[158] The mission was "supra-national, universal—the task of universal political regeneration of all oppressed nationalities."[159] Trubetskoi conceived of this mission less in terms of physically defeating the Germans—he was certain of victory on the battlefield—than of lifting the moral banner of "spiritual unity,"[160] of striving for a "spiritual Jerusalem."[161]

XII

Olfer'ev might have supposed the war would cleanse and ennoble Russia, but the reality he encountered in Poland was scarcely uplifting. Certain groups in Warsaw—Polish aristocrats and Poles from the upper-middle class, for example—treated the Russians billeted there with respect, but common Polish city dwellers did not. Olfer'ev remembers Warsaw's Jews as "sympathetic to the Germans" and therefore ill-disposed toward the Russians.

Besides being jarred by the suspicion from the locals, Olfer'ev found fault with his superior officers. To Nikolai Aloizievich Oranovskii, commander of the First Cavalry Brigade, he attributed an excess of caution and a deficit of imagination. In General Carl Gustav Emil von Mannerheim, he found much military discipline, but only of the sort useful in parade-ground maneuvers. Olfer'ev did not meet the Warsaw Military District commander, General Iakov Grigor'evich Zhilinskii, but he had little respect for Zhilinskii's judgment.

At the war's outset, Olfer'ev was posted as senior staff adjutant to the so-called Ulans Regiment—the sixth regiment of I Brigade in the VI Cavalry Division. His immediate divisional superiors were Vladimir Khristoforovich Roop and General Pavel Petrovich Liubomirov. The division maneuvered as part of General Aleksandr Vasil'evich Samsonov's II Army but answered to Zhilinskii.

The VI Cavalry Division's initial charge was to cross the Polish-German border near Mlawa into East Prussia, to prevent German units in the region from mounting an offensive, and to conduct reconnaissance on German movements. In a brief attack on the small town of Soldau near the Dzialdowo River, Olfer'ev's unit lost forty soldiers without capturing its objective. His eagerness for battle, evident when he pressed superiors for a full assault on Soldau, diminished quickly in the face of the heavy casualties. He saw first-hand the unsuitability of mass cavalry attacks on enemy positions that were fortified by machine guns. He realized that not all Russian forces were capable of responding with appropriate tactics to enemy counterattacks, and he learned that, in battle, the morale of Russian soldiers could easily waver. He also grasped that coordinating the battle efforts of two different units could be exceedingly difficult. These problems, especially the last, manifested themselves on a large scale in maneuvers of I and II Armies near the Masurian Lakes. According to the military historian David R. Stone, General Pavel Karlovich von Rennenkampf's I Army was ordered to engage the German VIII Army north of the lakes, with the goal of pinning the Germans in place, Meanwhile, Samsonov's II Army was to advance east, then circle around the lakes to attack the Germans from the rear. If the two actions had worked according to plan, the Russians would have caught the Germans in a pincer.[162] The objective was not necessarily to defeat the Germans at one blow, but rather to force them to divert manpower from the western front. Rennenkampf's I Army invaded East Prussia and beat the VIII Army into retreat, but then lost contact with it, so that on August 13/26, Rennenkampf did not know the location of the Germans' main force.[163] Meanwhile, Zhilinskii assumed that the VIII Army had retreated westward, so he ordered Samsonov's II Army to advance rapidly to block the German exodus. On August10/23, he told Samsonov that he should "meet the enemy retreating before Rennenkampf and cut off the German retreat to the Vistula."[164]

In retrospect, Zhilinskii's faulty assumption about the Germans' position proved a fatal blunder. The center of Samsonov's army marched straight into the German VIII Army, which had relocated itself south of the Masurian Lakes. Russian forces—VI, XIII, and XV Corps—fell under devastating fire. At Tannenberg, the Germans annihilated the II Army, forcing its remnants to surrender. On August 17/30, Samsonov committed suicide. Contemporary estimates of Russian losses at Tannenberg reached as many as seventy thousand casualties and over ninety thousand prisoners of war.[165] The debacle at Tannenberg forced Rennenkampf's I Army to retreat from East Prussia to a line forty kilometers inside the Russian prewar border. Military historian David Stone has suggested that I Army lost eighty thousand troops by mid-September. If that figure is accurate, Russia's total losses in the East Prussian campaign were nearly a quarter of a million troops.[166]

In the attack of II Army, Olfer'ev's regiment played a small role. Its first assignment was to cut through German defenses near Dzialdowo and then move north to cut off the German retreat. Part of this assignment involved blowing up a railroad bridge between Soldau and Neidenburg, a task his unit accomplished. The second assignment was to join I Corps on Samsonov's left flank and to advance into Prussia toward Lautenburg-Deutsch-Eylau. On August 10/23, Olfer'ev's regiment approached Lautenburg before receiving an order to turn and engage a German unit to their rear, close to Soldau. His regiment sustained casualties from artillery fire, but then lost contact with the Germans. On the evening of August 10/23, Olfer'ev was assigned to XV Cavalry Division under General Liubomirov. He was now ordered to advance toward Rypin, an advance that was supposed to protect Samsonov's left flank but failed to do so. The XV Cavalry and I Corps lost contact with the body of Samsonov's II Army. Olfer'ev reported his doubt about the wisdom of Liubomirov's decision to advance toward Rypin, and, in retrospect, he wondered whether, properly directed, his cavalry unit might have saved Samsonov from defeat at Tannenberg.

After escaping captivity or death at Tannenberg, Olfer'ev took part in his unit's disorderly retreat across the prewar border between Soldau and Mlawa. Close to Dzialdowo, he came across General Leonid Konstantinovich Artamonov, commander of I Corps, as the general prayed before an icon to save his soldiers and himself. Artamonov was well-respected, due to a diplomatic mission to Ethiopia in 1897–1898, his exploration of the Nile in 1898–1899, and his role in the Russo-Japanese War. Seeing the general in fervent prayer, however, Artamonov's own officers concluded he was "not in his right mind" [*Artamonov seichas ne v svoem ume*]. All around Artamonov on the Soldau-Mlawa road were retreating troops, wagons of wounded soldiers, equipment carts with the pathetic spoils from Russia's invasion of East Prussia. Olfer'ev's sketch reminds us of the passage in Tolstoy's *War and Peace* on the Rostovs' departure from Moscow in 1812.

Olfer'ev acknowledges the various factors that contributed to Russia's catastrophic defeat in East Prussia: diplomatic agreements that compelled Russia to invade Prussia before its mobilization had been completed; the "blindness" of Russia's advance and the Germans' interception of Russian wireless messages; the incompetence of Russian army commanders and the lack of initiative at every army rank; common soldiers' skepticism toward their officers. Ultimately, he believed, Russian soldiers could not achieve victory in Europe because so many of them were illiterate or culturally backward. The Russian Empire had foundered in 1914 because during the two preceding generations, the government had not supplied the villages with enough schoolteachers. Olfer'ev therefore posited that Russian peasant soldiers lacked "culture."

Olfer'ev's interpretation of the Tannenberg defeat sees illiteracy as a contributing factor to the lack of training, low morale, and the absence of battlefield initiative. He also suggests that the peasant soldiers' primitive outlook had surfaced in their mistreatment of the German Zeppelin pilots at Mlawa, in the looting of a small village grocery store, and in the overall conduct of Russian infantrymen who, like so many locusts, "destroyed everything in their path, plundered, beat up and killed peaceful citizens, demolished wine shops, got drunk and, with the first shot, retreated in panic." In Olfer'ev's estimation, in August 1914 Russian soldiers were guided not by discipline but by "the law of the jungle." He therefore asserts that if the Russian and German armies had changed positions, the Germans would still have defeated the Russian forces. He adds that Tannenberg laid bare the sickness of Russia's old regime and provided the "first jolt" of revolution.

XIII

In the wake of Tannenberg, Olfer'ev may indeed have sensed the Empire's doom, but he still hoped, perhaps irrationally, for military victory over the Germans. Like many other Russian officers, he welcomed the appointment on September 3, 1914 of General Nikolai Vladimirovich Ruzskii as commander in chief of the Southwestern front; the promotion on September 24 of Mikhail Vasil'evich Alekseev to general of infantry; and the advancement in July 1915 of General Aleksei Andreevich Polivanov to the post of war minister. According to Olfer'ev, these appointments were based not on loyalty to the monarch, but rather on the generals' reputations for military competence. He also noted that the appointments took "public opinion" into account. He meant that they reckoned with the views of "the educated portion of the population heretofore neglected by Petersburg."

Olfer'ev implies that each of these generals had a political coloration. In the first months of the war, Ruzskii earned a reputation for independence of judgment on the battlefield.[167] He carefully protected that reputation, in part by cultivating friends in the liberal opposition. In 1915, he contributed to the "spy mania" in the capital that liberal "patriots" like Guchkov did so much to inspire. Inside the war ministry, his patron was Polivanov, who on July 30, 1915 proposed that Ruzskii replace General Ianushkevich as chief of staff to the supreme commander of Russian armed forces.[168] Ruzskii did not receive the appointment, but instead became commander in chief of the northern front on August 18, 1915. During his brief tenure there, Ruzskii proposed the removal of all Baltic Germans from administrative posts in the region and the exiling of Lutheran pastors from the Baltic provinces.[169] In the political crisis of late 1916/early 1917, Ruzskii was probably the first general to align himself with the Progressive Bloc's oppositional demands.[170] He played a key role in the tsar's abdication.

Like Ruzskii, General Alekseev valued the prerogative of field commanders, especially front commanders, to set strategy based on military considerations. Yet Alekseev likewise did not ignore political concerns. In writing Russia's war plan in 1912, he insisted that military calculations take into account the aspiration of Slavic peoples to achieve national independence—a political premise that set him at odds with War Minister Sukhomlinov.[171] In August 1915, when Nicholas II assumed command of Russian armed forces, he named Alekseev chief of staff. So far as Alekseev was able, he kept strategic decisions outside the influence of courtiers; however, he had to work with public figures. This meant collaborating with members of the State Council and State Duma, among them politicians such as Aleksandr Ivanovich Guchkov—a prominent Octobrist who, in 1915, became head of the Military-Industrial Committee and, in August, a founder of the Progressive Bloc. Guchkov was known in public circles for his hostility to Rasputin, a hostility he shared with Alekseev. According to General Anton Ivanovich Denikin, then an officer on the General Staff, Alekseev told the tsar he would resign his post if Rasputin were to be present at military headquarters in Mogilev.[172] In 1916, Alekseev tried to brief Nicholas II on the dangers to the throne posed by Rasputin. He also suggested the adoption of a ministry responsible to the Duma.[173]

In mid-August 1916, Guchkov sent an open letter to Alekseev complaining about the deficiencies of the Petrograd cabinet's support for the war effort.[174] Later, in December 1916 and early 1917, Guchkov apparently sought Alekseev's cooperation in removing Nicholas II from the throne. Alekseev's answer to this entreaty is a matter of controversy. According to Denikin, then a lieutenant general on the General Staff, Alekseev told the would-be conspirator that an attempted coup d'état in wartime would be disastrous.[175]

At this juncture, Polivanov was politically the best connected of the three generals and was perhaps the shrewdest among them. A military strategist and intellectual of some celebrity—in the 1890s he served as a chief editor of the publications *Military Affairs* [*Voennyi sbornik*] and *Russian Invalid* [*Russkii invalid*]—Polivanov rose to commander of the General Staff during the Russo-Japanese War. For six years, starting in April 1906, he was assistant war minister, a post that entailed collaboration with politicians from the Council of Ministers, the State Council, and the State Duma. From 1907, he met frequently with the Duma Commission on Defense, where he encountered Guchkov. He and Guchkov shared information about the army's needs, about the Duma's perception of defense policy, about the military budget, and about Russia's strategic position in the Balkans. In 1908, for example, Polivanov listened carefully to Guchkov's concerns about Ottoman aggression in that region.[176] In November 1909, Guchkov suggested to Polivanov a template for army reorganization, which the latter summarized for his colleagues in the war ministry.[177] In 1912, Polivanov's collaboration with Guchkov probably compromised him in the eyes of War Minister Sukhomlinov and was a factor in his dismissal as assistant minister.[178] In September 1913, Polivanov heard from Guchkov direct criticisms of the government, including a reference to the need for a national assembly of the land [*zemskii sobor*].[179]

Polivanov was instrumental in involving the Red Cross in the care of troops—a move controversial in governmental circles. When Polivanov was named war minister in 1915, he collaborated with the Duma minister in urging creation of a joint commission on military supply.[180]

It is likely that Olfer'ev approved of the appointments of Ruzskii, Alekseev, and Polivanov not because he saw them as "liberals in uniform," but rather because he valued their competence and pragmatic patriotism.

Olfer'ev seems ambivalent about the activity of the Union of Zemstvos and Union of Cities in facilitating military supply and medical care at the front. The two unions, which had been created in the first days of the war, joined together in August 1914 as Zemgor, under the leadership of Prince Georgii Evgen'evich L'vov. Zemgor staffed over two thousand field hospitals, established medical relief stations at major railroads, and by early 1916, had cared for over 750,000 men.[181] On the other hand, representatives from Zemgor struck Olfer'ev as untrustworthy. These so-called "zemhussars" [*zem-gussary*] "carried gossip from the front to the rear and from the rear to the front." They undercut troop morale, and "meddled in affairs that did not concern them." Minister of Internal Affairs Nikolai Alekseevich Maklakov complained that Zemgor wanted to weaken the autocracy.[182]

The evidence buttressing Olfer'ev's suspicion that Zemgor was untrustworthy included a conversation between the leftist intellectual Pavel

Mikhailovich Tolstoi, a staff officer in the I Turkestan Army Corps, and Vasilii Vasil'evich Vyrubov, a member of the main committee of Zemgor and in 1916 manager of zemstvo affairs at Stavka under General Alekseev. As Olfer'ev notes, both Tolstoi and Vyrubov later played sensitive roles in the Provisional Government—Tolstoi as an aide to Aleksandr Fedorovich Kerenskii, and Vyrubov as assistant minister of internal affairs in the L'vov cabinet. In 1915, Olfer'ev was present when Tolstoi and Vyrubov discussed Duma politics, the tensions between Tsarskoe Selo and Grand Duke Nikolai Nikolaevich over the latter's unsatisfactory performance as army commander in chief, and the alleged treason of Colonel Sergei Nikolaevich Miasoedov.

All three topics named by Olfer'ev were touchy issues. Discussing Duma politics raised the fraught relationship between the executive branch, which sought to assert its control over wartime policy, and the legislature, which since July 1914 had felt sidelined and therefore unable to contribute properly to the war effort. From late July 1914 to late January 1915, and again from February to mid-July 1915, the tsar refused to call the Duma into session. The result was extraordinary tension between the Duma leadership and the imperial cabinet. In the Duma sessions from July 19 to September 3, 1915, liberals demanded the replacement of a cabinet appointed by the tsar with a "government of confidence"—that is, with a slate of officials acceptable to the liberal Progressive Bloc. Olfer'ev mentions that Tolstoi's vision for the future was "a constitutional state modeled on those of Europe." This desideratum was uncontroversial for certain Russian intellectuals, but it should not have been raised in an army unit.

The second topic, the performance of the army's commander in chief, was an issue deserving consideration by the tsar and governmental leaders, but for obvious reasons should not have been raised in staff-level meeting of the I Turkestan officer corps. Grand Duke Nikolai Nikolaevich had had virtually nothing to do with writing Russia's war plan, and he was not even named commander in chief until after the commencement of hostilities in July 1914. He was nevertheless being held responsible for many of the army's early defeats. When Tolstoi and Vyrubov alluded to tensions between "Tsarskoe Selo" and the grand duke, they probably referred to the Empress Aleksandra's well-known antipathy to Nikolai Nikolaevich. At a secret meeting of the Council of Ministers on July 16/29, 1915, the council chairman

Ivan Logginovich Goremykin warned his colleagues that Aleksandra had "stored up dissatisfaction against the grand duke," had opposed his appointment, and considered him "the sole cause of the misfortunes that we are experiencing at the front."[183] The hostility between Tsarskoe Selo and the grand duke reached its apogee on August 6/19, 1915, when the tsar informed Polivanov that he intended to remove Nikolai Nikolaevich from office and to take personal command of the army.[184] The tsar persisted in this decision even though Polivanov and other ministers sought to dissuade him.

From Olfer'ev's memoirs, it is not clear whether Vyrubov had access to confidential sources at court or in the cabinet, or whether Tolstoi and Vyrubov were merely repeating "gossip" from the capital: that the empress was unhappy with Nikolai Nikolaevich had been an open secret since summer 1914, and the tsar's inclination to take command of Russia's armed forces had long been rumored.[185]

Perhaps the most dangerous topic raised by Tolstoi and Vyrubov was the question of Miasoedov's treason. Unsubstantiated rumors of the gendarme Miasoedov's corruption had circulated since 1907, when he served as a border inspector on the Petersburg-Warsaw railroad. Public accusations of espionage had assailed him in 1912, when Guchkov and others had suggested that Miasoedov was working for the Austro-Hungarian General Staff. The distinguished Russian historian Kornelei Fedorovich Shatsillo has argued that Guchkov used the 1912 accusation against Miasoedov to weaken War Minister Sukhomlinov, so as to make the appointment of Polivanov more likely.[186] Shatsillo has also maintained that there is no evidence of Miasoedov's guilt: a treason case against him went nowhere in 1912. Yet, in spite of three investigations by different governmental agencies, Miasoedov was never fully vindicated.[187] During the war, Miasoedov worked as a translator interrogating German prisoners. On February 18/March 1, 1915 he was arrested and imprisoned on treason charges fabricated by a double-agent, Iakov Pavlovich Kozlovskii.[188] Miasoedov was hanged on the order of a military tribunal on March 20/April 2, 1915, even before General Ruzskii had confirmed the sentence against him.[189] Shatsillo has called the Miasoedov affair a "bloody farce," which certain tsarist officials used to their advantage.

Grand Duke Nikolai Nikolaevich was pleased at the verdict, because he could point to Miasoedov's ties with Sukhomlinov and thereby weaken the hated war minister. General Mikhail Dmitrievich Bonch-Bruevich received two promotions in the wake of his role in seeking Miasoedov's prosecution. Because the Miasoedov affair undercut Sukhomlinov's credibility, it made likelier Polivanov's eventual promotion to war minister.[190] The execution of Miasoedov as a traitor gratified Guchkov and his political allies, who aimed to discredit the war cabinet but also to prove that the tsarist regime, without guidance from the educated public, would betray Russian interests and lose the war. Indeed, as William C. Fuller has noted, Guchkov received letters of gratitude citing his opposition to the "traitor" Miasoedov. The socialist Kerenskii also circulated a letter praising progressive Duma politicians for supporting Russia's defense and for opposing the "real traitors" inside the government.[191]

In the short run, the losers in the Miasoedov affair were Miasoedov himself and a number of his friends who were arrested on suspicion of aiding the enemy. At least twenty-five people stood trial in June 1915 for their alleged complicity—fourteen of them in Warsaw, eleven in Dvinsk. Four were hanged.[192]

Tolstoi and Vyrubov could scarcely have mentioned Miasoedov's alleged treason until after his arrest in mid-February, but it is likelier they would have taken the risk of discussing it only after his execution in late March. If we take all three topics together—executive relations with the Duma, the hostility of Tsarskoe Selo toward Sukhomlinov, and Miasoedov's supposed treachery—the likely date of the conversation with Olfer'ev was late March to mid-summer 1915. Since all three themes had a potentially negative impact on army morale, their discussion was problematic. No wonder Olfer'ev accuses Tolstoi and Vyrubov of speaking in "the jargon of thieves."

XIV

After Tannenberg, Olfer'ev served with the remnants of II Army under General Sergei Mikhailovich Sheideman. On October 28/November 10, 1914, the II Army defended Lodz against an assault by the German IX Army, an assault that by November 1/14 put the Russian forces in a desperate position.[193] By November 12/25, Russians forces had driven the Germans back, but were quickly compelled to withdraw themselves, to the Bzura River between Lodz and Warsaw. There between November 19/December 2 and December 20, 1914/January 2, 1915, they were caught in the so-called battle of four rivers—actually the early stages of a six-month struggle on the Bzura-Rawka line that developed into trench warfare. By 1915, Russian casualties at Bzura reached two hundred thousand troops. According to Olfer'ev, while the Russians were not victorious at Lodz and Bzura, they helped hold Warsaw.

Although the II Army had fought bravely and had stayed intact, General Ruzskii decided to relieve Sheideman of command and to demote him to leader of the I Turkestan Army Corps—Olfer'ev's unit. Olfer'ev suspected that Sheideman "was the victim of his German name," but Ruzskii's decision was actually based on disappointment over the II Army's failure to conduct a successful offensive against the Germans.[194] Olfer'ev found Sheideman a capable leader: educated, experienced in the field, capable of bold action, politically savvy. He regarded Sheideman and Colonel Ianuarii Kazimirovich Tsikhovich [Cichowicz] as an excellent team.

The aggressive spirit at Army Headquarters [*Stavka*] led to a decision on January 4/17, 1915 to attack the Germans along a broad front from Plotsk in the south to Masurian Lakes in the north. Stavka also planned a simultaneous attack on the Southwestern front aimed to knock Austria out of the war. According to David Stone, Stavka's determination to move on two fronts amounted to a failure to choose, and therefore duplicated the blunder in Russia's original war plan.[195] By February 1/14, 1915, Olfer'ev's unit had been repositioned to the north of the Vistula River, near Mlawa—that is, to the same area where his cavalry had fought in the war's first days. There they confronted German troops under General Max Karl Wilhelm von Gallwitz, who, on February 5/18, launched a two-pronged assault on Przasnysz. After nearly two weeks of bitter fighting, the Russian forces—the I and II Turkestan Army Corps and the I and II Siberian Corps—drove Gallwitz's troops out of Przasnysz. Olfer'ev calls the Przasnysz campaign "the only victory in the entire war on the German front."

Olfer'ev's account of the February 1915 battle at Przasnysz is one of the finest set pieces in his memoirs. He describes the danger facing Russian troops: a German advance to the rear of Russian units, with the possibility of strategic victory on the Polish front. Then he turns to battle details: the German artillery's bombardment of the small town of Grudusk, which "wiped it from the face of the earth"; the Russians' ignorance of enemy movements; Olfer'ev's commission to occupy Przasnysz on the night of February 13/26; the faces of Przasnysz's concerned citizens as they huddled in prayer; German artillery fire along the entire divisional front on February 14/27; the confusion of Russian units on the Ciechanow-Przasnysz Road when surrounded by the Germans on the night of February 15/28; the dramatic fight at Grudusk on February 16/29. Olfer'ev recalls the nighttime conversation among officers gathered in a dugout—a conversation that ranged from the brewing of home-made vodka, to places of entertainment in Warsaw and Moscow, to the charms of Polish and Russian women, to resignation at the prospect of death. He contrasts that dialogue with snatches of conversation by common soldiers about handling rifles, about the determination not to surrender, about social roles in soldiers' tales. His account of the Przasnysz battle concludes with the Germans' flight from the town and their mass surrender to Russian forces. In one battle sector, Olfer'ev counted "nearly four hundred men who had surrendered." Overall, he estimated the number of German prisoners at Przasnysz at fourteen thousand.

Olfer'ev's recollection of battle displays many features of good military writing. It captures the battle's scale (thousands of troops engaged along a front of sixty versts, or sixty-four kilometers), its ferocity (a small town "wiped off the face of the earth"), and its confusion. He records officers' and soldiers' talk, making clear their class distinctions. His narrative makes unobtrusive use of Lev Tolstoy's techniques of narration, such as the slowing down of action, sudden shifts of scenery, "making strange" the accustomed ways of battle. He also alludes to difficulties that would hobble Russia's war effort in 1915 (the peasant soldiers' discussion of how to handle rifles) and the innovation of air reconnaissance.

XV

In spite of the victory at Przasnysz, the Russians' strategic situation on the northwestern front was not good. General Faddei Vasil'evich Sivers [*Thaddeus von Sievers*], commander of X Army, fell under attack from the Germans' X Army on January 26/February 7, 1915. By January 30/February 11, Sivers had ordered a retreat. On February 8/21 thirty thousand Russian troops, mainly from XX Corps, surrendered at Augustow Woods. Stone has estimated that, in winter fighting, the Russian Imperial Army sustained as many as two hundred thousand casualties.[196]

This was a serious blow to Russian hopes for success in the war, but it paled in comparison to the damage done by fighting in summer and early fall 1915. By late September 1915, the Russians had lost Galicia and had withdrawn from Poland and Lithuania. Stone has put the losses of the Russian army in the "great retreat" at roughly a million soldiers.

The German advance began on April 19/May 2, 1915, when General August von Mackensen's XI Army attacked Russia's III Army southeast of Cracow. By April 22/May 5, Russian forces faced disaster: indeed, on April 27/May 10, III Army was in full retreat. After Mackensen had reorganized and resupplied his forces, he launched a new attack on May 10/23. This one forced the Russians to surrender the fortress at Przemysl. Another attack on May 31/June 12 pushed the Russians back to L'vov. By then, the German offensive had cost the Russian army another half-million men.[197]

These German victories opened the possibilities of an advance into Lithuania and the chance to drive the Russians out of Poland. By July 11/24, General Alekseev had ordered withdrawal to the east, and on July 23/August 5 the Germans took Warsaw. Meanwhile, the Germans' reinforced X Army forced the Russians to surrender Vilnius on September 3/16. Only between September 5/18 and September 12/25 did the Russians finally stabilize the front.[198]

The causes of Russia's great retreat were not mysterious. Russian intelligence did not disclose the scale of Mackensen's attack on the Southwestern front near Gorlice. Russian supplies of artillery shells and rifles were insufficient to counter Mackensen's heavy artillery. The German shelling of Russian infantry lines was devastating, because Russians had not dug deep enough trenches and had not prepared proper fallback positions. In a postwar analysis of the retreat, General Aleksandr Aleksandrovich Neznamov pointed to Russia's "poverty in technical means" [of waging war] and to its "cultural backwardness"—factors that forced the generals to compensate for shortfalls in armaments by committing manpower to gaps in the front. Yet Russian soldiers, once committed in the fight, lacked the ammunition to maintain their defenses. In Neznamov's opinion, this amounted to a "vicious circle," in which Russia made an "enormous sacrifice" in men.[199]

In a contemporaneous assessment of the Russian defeat in Galicia, General Nikolai Iudovich Ivanov underlined German artillery superiority as the key factor, "resulting in colossal losses of [Russian] men," and "rapid gains" by the Germans.[200] On August 21 /September 3, 1915, the very same General Ivanov wrote a personal letter to Grand Duke Nikolai Nikolaevich describing the "horrors" of the great retreat and expressing fear for the country's future. According to Neznamov, Ivanov's letter reflected the "nervousness" of many field commanders and also their growing conviction of the "impossibility of contending with the Germans" [*nevozmozhnost' borot'sia s nemtsami*].[201]

In the political sphere the great retreat had far-reaching consequences. With some exaggeration, the historian Joshua A. Sanborn has characterized the small Carpathian town of Gorlice, where Mackensen launched his attack on April 19/May 2, 1915, as "a graveyard, not just of men, but of the Russian Empire as well." The retreat entailed "a massive dislocation of civilian populations."[202] By April 1915, the Russian military authorities had already ordered deportations beyond the Vistula River of ethnic Germans and of "Jews and all suspicious people."[203] After the German capture of Gorlice, Russian commanders decided to "cleanse" war zones of everyone deemed unreliable and also to deny the Germans economic resources—railroad lines, crops, fodder for livestock, food supplies.[204] This scorched-earth policy backfired on the army, by driving refugees onto the roads, thereby complicating the soldiers' retreat: the army had to clear blocked avenues of retreat but also to stem the flood of refugees into rear areas. The policy also made soldiers the enemies of local inhabitants, whose houses were burned on army orders. By mid-1915, the war zone had become inhospitable, dangerous, and "nearly uninhabitable."[205]

Sanborn has argued that the façade of Russian political unity had begun to crack as early as February 1915, but that in summer of that year "the real fracture of the political system occurred."[206] The symptoms of the political fracture included popular dissatisfaction with the war effort, the search for those deemed guilty for Russia's military defeats, sharp ethnic antagonisms on the part of Russians against ethnic Germans and Jews, and the breakdown of the superficial comity between political parties and the government. In Sanborn's opinion, the recall of the Duma on July 19/August 1, 1915 was an effort by the government to mollify oppositionist sentiment without submitting to it. The decision on September 3/16 again to prorogue the Duma was a symbolic admission that the opposition could not be bought off so easily.[207] Sanborn's conclusion is that the events of summer 1915 "fundamentally crippled" Russian society, economy, and politics.[208]

In February 1915, buoyed by the Russian success at Przasnysz, Olfer'ev still thought the army's situation "entirely satisfactory." He did not anticipate the ammunition shortage of the spring, nor did he foresee the ferocity of artillery fire that would come on June 30/July 12 from the Germans outside Przasnysz. He admits that, when the shelling occurred, the Russians' helplessness to respond demoralized the soldiers in his unit. He blamed army chief of staff Ianushkevich and those around Ianushkevich for the shortsightedness behind the ammunition shortage.

In August 1915, Stavka split the Northwestern front into two commands. On August 4/17, Olfer'ev met General Alekseev, now the commander of the northern front. Alekseev, a broad-shouldered man of average height, struck him as a "typical common Russian man" [*tipichnyi russkii prostoliudin*], a thoughtful person whose lack of affectation inspired confidence in subordinates. According to Olfer'ev, Alekseev grasped, without saying as much, the necessity to retreat on the northern front, to abandon Kovno and other fortresses.

Olfer'ev found the retreat "far from easy," because troop transports got tangled with civilians, and because "no one had any hope of our return to Poland." The Russian rear guard screened the larger body of retreating troops. Soldiers carried their own ammunition and also artillery shells, and then passed the shells to units in immediate need of them. The Russian army withdrew four hundred versts (about four hundred twenty-five kilometers) inside the Empire's prewar borders. In Olfer'ev's verdict, the country survived because of its "profound depth."

XVI

After the battle at Przasnysz, Olfer'ev took an assignment that required him to travel by air to a difficult-to-reach destination. He flew in a plane belonging to the II Army Aviation Squadron [*2-oi armeiskii aviaotriad*], piloted by staff captain Evgraf Nikolaevich Kruten'. Olfer'ev became acquainted with the air squadron members, came to like them, and began to think about the military potential of aviation. During the winter of 1915/1916, General Georgii Aleksandrovich Tumanov informed Olfer'ev that he had been appointed to the staff of II Army, as assistant to the commander of reconnaissance. He would supervise five aviation squadrons, which were headquartered in Minsk. By pulling him out of a fighting unit, this appointment may have saved Olfer'ev's life.

The background to Olfer'ev's encounter with Russian fliers is fascinating. Since the late 1860s, the Russian government had been investigating the military potential of lighter-than-air vehicles, and in 1902–1903 it established a small group of balloonists to conduct aerial surveillance and to direct artillery fire. General Sukhomlinov, then the commander of the Kiev military district, assigned the young Aleksei Alekseevich Ignat'ev to this unit.[209] A decade later, in August 1912, the government created the Air Wing [*Vozdukhoplavatel'naia chast'*] of the General Staff to supervise field balloons, dirigibles, and heavier-than-air vehicles. Thus, the establishment of Russian military aviation coincided with Olfer'ev's tenure at the General Staff Academy.[210]

Before the war, the Empire had four factories producing airplanes, but the government still bought many of the army's airplanes from French firms—Nieuport-Duplex or its successor, Société Générale d'Aérolocomotion. Olfer'ev recalls flying the Voisin [*Vuazen'*] biplane, a rear-engine craft, that was designed and built in prewar France but was later manufactured in Russia. Olfer'ev probably flew the Voisin Type L, but may have also flown the Voisin Type III.

At Second Squadron, Olfer'ev met some outstanding airmen. Nikolai Kirillovich Kokorin was a daring reconnaissance pilot and, after August 1915, one of Russia's first ace fighter pilots [*istrebiteli*] credited with five "kills." The Frenchman Alphonse-Flavien Louis Poirée, whom Olfer'ev describes as "born in the Pyrenees, probably a Basque," was actually from Aisne in northern France; in prewar France Poirée had attracted a popular following as an aerial acrobat. He flew a hundred combat missions with the Second Squadron. The most remarkable of these pilots was Kruten', a young nobleman who became famous for conducting night bombing raids on German bases. From November 1916 to March 1917, Kruten' led a group of Russian fighter pilots who were sent to France for special training.

By his death on June 19, 1917, he had published eight books on aviation and was credited with five "kills."[211]

While with the Second Squadron, Olfer'ev himself flew reconnaissance—a natural assignment for a cavalry officer who in the past had been tasked with surveillance of enemy lines. He discovered the deficiencies of the low-flying and unwieldy Voisin aircraft and the relative superiority of the German Fokker planes. He also saw more clearly the utility of air reconnaissance and became frustrated that Stavka did not take pilots' reports more seriously.

Control over army aviation was vested in Grand Duke Aleksandr Mikhailovich, the fourth son of Grand Duke Mikhail Nikolaevich and the grandson of Emperor Nicholas I. The grand duke had a remarkable career behind him. An intrepid sailor, at age twenty he circumnavigated the world. Early in the reign of Nicholas II, Aleksandr Mikhailovich advocated strengthening the navy in the Pacific, and in the succeeding decade, he advanced projects for increasing naval armaments and enhancing commercial maritime trade. In 1909, he became a vice-admiral and in 1915, an admiral.

The grand duke became an advocate for aviation—establishing a flying school in Sevastopol' and promoting aviation's military potential more generally. Olfer'ev notes that Aleksandr Mikhailovich thought of Russian military aviation as his private fiefdom, "jealously guarding this branch of his business so that no one dared to interfere." The grand duke was an extraordinary figure, whose brilliance and willfulness earned him many enemies, both in the Committee of Ministers during the Russo-Japanese War, and at Stavka during the Great War. Olfer'ev reports "intense hostility" between the grand duke and the duty general at Stavka, Aleksandr Sergeevich Lukomskii.

While at Minsk, Olfer'ev supervised five flying squadrons that flew reconnaissance and combat missions. In winter 1915–16 he obtained permission to transfer these squadrons to the front in rural Belorussia. He himself flew reconnaissance over Sventsiany (Svencionys)—a town of roughly eight thousand people where units of the German army were staged. He ordered a bombing mission to destroy German ground transports in the region. The memoir does not mention the date of the bombing raid, but the sortie must have occurred at Lake Naroch, to the southeast of Sventsiany, between March 5/18 and March 17/30, 1916.[212] Olfer'ev believed the bombing raid to be "the first flight of this kind on our [northern] front."

Around the time of the Baranovichi offensive, which took place from June 20/July 3 to July 12/25, 1916, Olfer'ev was transferred to the village Nesvizh [Niasvizh], an ancient town first mentioned in the thirteenth century in conjunction with the great battle with the Mongols on the River Kalka. At the turn of the twentieth century, its population barely exceeded ten thousand people. Olfer'ev mentions that, near Baranovichi, Kruten' shot down two German planes. He does not note that during the Baranovichi battle, Russian airmen were unsuccessful in providing correction to artillery fire on German positions; nor does he mention that Russian ground forces sustained eighty thousand casualties at Baranovichi.[213] Much of the blame for this debacle fell on General Aleksei Ermolaevich Evert, whose bad leadership earned him a reputation for indecisiveness, even incompetence. The military historian David Stone has charged Evert with "criminal passivity" during this time.[214]

The forces under Evert's command in summer 1916 were supposed to direct the main blow against the Germans as part of a coordinated attack in which the northern and southwestern front commanders would stage diversionary offensives. As it transpired, General Aleksei Alekseevich Brusilov broke through Austrian defenses on the southwestern front. His tactically brilliant attack, originally meant as a diversion, opened out into a four-month offensive lasting from May 22/June 4 to September 7/20, 1916. The Brusilov offensive succeeded in meeting one of its chief aims—reducing German pressure against the French army at Verdun. However, it stalled out before Austria could be forced out of the war, and so Brusilov did not manage to change the war's strategic balance. The estimated Russian casualties ran to well over a million men—a staggering loss that the imperial army could not recoup.

XVII

Between October 1916 and February 1917, Olfer'ev gained a new perspective on Russia's military prospects. He was transferred from western front headquarters in Minsk to Stavka itself, in Mogilev. During the transfer process, he was again alerted to the tensions between Grand Duke Aleksandr Mikhailovich and Stavka. This tension was evident in late October, when the grand duke asked Olfer'ev to keep him informed about what was happening at Stavka; and again in mid-November, when General Lukomskii gave Olfer'ev a cold reception under the impression that he was a tool of the grand duke. Olfer'ev decided he was "not interested in finding out [the cause of the breach between Stavka and the grand duke]."

Part of this tension stemmed from Stavka's irritation over the grand duke's highhandedness, as we have already noted, but the antagonism also had more serious causes. According to the grand duke's memoirs, in early May 1915 his aviators had warned Stavka of General Mackensen's concentrated artillery between Tarnow and Gorlice. The Russian army could not counteract this artillery because of the shell shortage then affecting imperial forces. Even though the grand duke considered the obvious course of action a quick retreat by the Russian army, Stavka had not drawn that conclusion. Later, in the fall of 1915, after the tsar assumed supreme command of the Russian army, the grand duke faulted chief of staff Alekseev for "enmeshing himself in political plots with the enemies of the existing system who hid under the guise of representatives of Zemgor, the Red Cross, and the Military-Industrial Committee." The grand duke accused these political radicals of going to Stavka not to take stock of the army's needs, but to "link themselves with army commanders [such as Alekseev]."[215] According to Aleksandr Mikhailovich, Duma representatives pressured him to criticize the empress for her "treason" and to denounce Rasputin to the tsar—pressure the grand duke resisted as wrongheaded in the case of the empress and pointless in the case of Rasputin. The implication of the grand duke's account is that he found Stavka hidebound in 1915, and also politically compromised by its ties to Zemgor and the Duma in 1916.

Olfer'ev assumes that, from early in the war to August 1915, there were tensions between the army's supreme commander Grand Duke Nikolai Nikolaevich and the "notorious" chief of staff Nikolai Nikolaevich Ianushkevich, whose competence Olfer'ev had doubted since his time at the General Staff Academy. Olfer'ev implies that much of the blame for the Tannenberg disaster rested with Ianushkevich and with his aide Iurii Nikiforovich Danilov.

An indication of Russia's military problems in 1915 was the beginning of mass desertions from the army. Olfer'ev traces this phenomenon to the demoralizing ammunition shortages that accompanied the great retreat of

1915 and to the devastating German artillery fire that year. In summer and winter 1915, he encountered deserters in the forests and in the railroad stations near the front. He claims that by late 1915 there were so many of these "fugitives" [*bezhentsy*] that "neither the railroad officials nor the military police in the rear could possibly check all of them and return them to their units."

In the summer of 1916, Olfer'ev saw, up close, the horror of total war. In his words, "soldiers marched mechanically, fought mechanically, were mutilated mechanically, and died mechanically." The troops "displayed miracles of self-sacrificing determination," but they could not help but ask: "How much blood would have to be shed to drive [the Germans] away from our borders?" By late 1916, in spite of the army's inertial discipline, the soldiers' inner faith in the war effort was on the verge of collapse.

Olfer'ev does not ascribe responsibility for this situation to Nicholas II's August 1915 decision to assume command of the Russian armed forces. He explicitly disagrees with "all the correspondents on the home front, like Admiral Bubnov, and . . . historians of the period," who saw the tsar's decision as having "a particularly unfavorable effect on both the military operations and the morale of troops." Olfer'ev's reference here is to Admiral Aleksandr Dmitrievich Bubnov, a flag officer of the Naval Administration [*Voenno-morskoe upravlenie*] in Stavka, who, after the 1917 revolution, taught briefly at the Naval Academy before becoming a prominent figure in the civil war and in the Russian emigration. In his memoirs, Bubnov describes the tsar's decision to replace Nikolai Nikolaevich as "ruinous" [*pagubnoe*]: "The replacement of the grand duke dealt a heavy blow to Russian society . . . and thus deepened the chasm which, after short-lived unity at the war's beginning, came more and more to divide the throne and the people, and which ultimately toppled the entire edifice of the great Russian Empire."[216]

If, as Olfer'ev contends, the demoralization of the troops had other causes, nevertheless the tsar's 1915 decision had dire consequences: it created or widened the gulf between him and many of the officers at Stavka. That breach had a number of dimensions.

First, according to Olfer'ev, some of the junior staff officers, such as the Estonian Colonel Johan Laidoner [Ivan Iakovlevich Laidoner] and the Baltic German Colonel Otto Akselevich von Kruzenshtern, frequently talked politics. Laidoner, von Kruzenshtern, and Olfer'ev himself objected to the conduct of Aleksandr Dmitrievich Protopopov, who served as minister of internal affairs from September 16, 1916 to February 28, 1917. Protopopov was a member of the Third and Fourth Dumas, and after 1914 the vice-chairman of the Fourth Duma and a member of the Progressive Bloc. But he was rumored to be a friend and client of Rasputin, and to have explored the possibility of a separate peace with the Germans in an unauthorized June 1916 meeting in Stockholm with Fritz Warburg, an advisor to the German embassy. On October 19, 1916, a group of Protopopov's Duma colleagues arranged to meet him at Rodzianko's apartment in Petrograd. They demanded that Protopopov resign from the cabinet, and they criticized him for his ties to Rasputin and for releasing the fallen war minister Sukhomlinov from prison.[217] Olfer'ev does not reveal on what grounds his circle at Stavka condemned Protopopov, but he leaves a tell-tale indication: "The officers spoke of Rasputin and the Tsarina with contempt, and even openly expressed the need to get rid of them [*neobkhodimost' pokonchit' s nimi*] in order to save the homeland." Since Rasputin was murdered in Petrograd on the night of December 16–17, 1916, the conversations at Stavka about "getting rid of him" must have occurred between Olfer'ev's arrival at Stavka in the first half of November and the middle of December.

Second, Olfer'ev speaks about the "open hostility" between those who lived in the provincial governor's house [*gubernatorskii dom*]—that is, Nicholas II and his retinue—and those in the provincial administration building [*gubernskoe pravlenie*]—General Alekseev, his aide General Vasilii Iosifovich Gurko, and a dozen colonels and staff captains attached to the General Staff. Some of this hostility arose from irritation over the wasteful daily ritual of briefing the tsar about the military situation on each front. Staff captain Vladimir L'vovich Baranovskii, who from late September 1916 served as administrative officer under Lukomskii, told Olfer'ev that making and delivering these reports cost "half a day," when five minutes should have sufficed. Baranovskii dismissed Olfer'ev's argument that the emperor "has to be informed about the situation of the day." The problem was that Stavka had already issued orders before most briefings occurred, and that the tsar merely listened passively to them.

Olfer'ev might have noted that Baranovskii probably harbored other reasons for irritation at the tsar. Baranovskii's sister Ol'ga L'vovna was married to the Duma socialist Aleksandr Fedorovich Kerenskii, an outspoken critic of the royal family and of the executive. Under the Provisional Government in July 1917, Baranovskii would serve Kerenskii as chief aide in the war ministry. In any case, Olfer'ev discovered that the tsar's daily briefings were empty rituals.

Another source of hostility was that the emperor was out of his element at Stavka. In Petrograd and at Tsarskoe Selo, Nicholas II was surrounded by aristocrats and military aides, "with whom he spoke a common language." As Olfer'ev could testify from his own experience, these courtiers "knew [the emperor] as a man, knew his weaknesses . . . but zealously protected him" from those who stood outside the charmed circle. In the provincial governor's house in Mogilev, Nicholas's retinue included the senile Count Vladimir Borisovich Frederiks, the corrupt general and palace commander Vladimir Nikolaevich Voeikov, the light-minded Boris Mikhailovich Petrovo-Solovovo, and the alcoholic Admiral Konstantin Dmitrievich Nilov, none of whom possessed sufficient gravitas to protect the tsar. Meanwhile, in the officers at Stavka, the emperor confronted the best "sons of the Russian people," and, according to Olfer'ev, "the longer [Nicholas] lived among them, the more disillusioned they became."

Essentially, Olfer'ev contends, in wartime the normal division of authority between military and civilian officials does not work. The military ethos requires a single will to direct the energies of country and army. Nicholas II tried to provide that unity of will by becoming supreme commander. He failed because he was out of his depth and because he did not share Stavka's worldview, but also because he did not cede civilian authority to Alekseev. Instead, the emperor allowed that authority to rest with the empress and Rasputin—as Olfer'ev put it, "in the hands of a religiously crazed woman and an uneducated, odious *muzhik*."

In other words, Olfer'ev argues, the Russian situation temporarily demanded a military dictatorship. His conviction probably drew on historical precedents, such as Petr I's leadership of the Russian army in the Northern War against Sweden, and Field Marshal Mikhail Illarionovich Kutuzov's leadership against Napoleon in 1812. It was also rooted in Olfer'ev's elite military training. Did Olfer'ev think the situation justified the removal of the emperor? Wasn't that the conclusion of a logic that "spoke openly" of getting rid of Rasputin and the empress? Olfer'ev seems to admit as much when he agrees with his wife Marusia that "saving Russia stood higher than anything else."

XVIII

Olfer'ev recalls taking several days leave from the front in December 1916 to join his wife in Petrograd. He may have been mistaken about the date of the leave. When he departed Stavka, Olfer'ev recalled that Alekseev was still serving as chief of staff; in fact, Alekseev was absent from Stavka with an illness. He recuperated in Crimea from November 10/23, 1916 to February 19/March 4, 1917. Therefore, Olfer'ev's leave must have begun in early November, not early December.

In Petrograd, he found dimly lit streets, gaunt horses, people shabbily dressed, a breakdown in public services. On this visit to the capital, he did not note significant difficulties with food supply.

On the eve of his arrival, he met Vladimir Andreevich Simanskii, the father of the bishop of Tikhvin, Sergei Vladimirovich Simanskii. Vladimir Simanskii was a venerable old man, a graduate of the law faculty at Moscow University, who had worked in the Moscow Foundling Home, in the office of the Moscow governor-general, and since 1891 had worked in the office of the Holy Synod. Simanskii and Olfer'ev adverted to "the questions of the day" [*na zlobu dnia*]—that is, to the question of whether the tsar should be removed from office. Simanskii cautioned Olfer'ev: "The Lord's Anointed [*pomazannik Bozhii*] . . . always was, is, and must remain without blame [be immune from accusation]." The biblical term *pomazannik Bozhii* referred to any king of Israel, but it was used in Russia as a descriptor of the tsar. Simanskii was therefore reminding Olfer'ev of the Orthodox duty to obey the powers that be.

The next day, Olfer'ev visited Vladimir Iosifovich Gurko, a staunch monarchist, who in 1906–1907 had served as assistant minister of internal affairs, but who by late 1916 had become an outspoken critic of Nicholas and Aleksandra. Olfer'ev maintains that during their conversation Gurko promised him: "In about two months, God willing, all will be decided" [*nu, mesiatsa cherez dva Bog dast vse razreshitsia*]. Olfer'ev initially mistook

Gurko's comment as a reference to a coming military offensive, but later came to believe it was an obscure allusion to a coup d'état in which Vladimir Gurko and his brother, General Vasilii Gurko, were to take part. The timetable for the coup envisioned the tsar's arrest on March 11—the day 116 years earlier of the arrest and murder of the Emperor Paul. Olfer'ev claims that Vladimir Gurko later confirmed the existence of the plot.

As the historian Sergei Petrovich Mel'gunov demonstrates, the period from summer 1915 to early 1917 was replete with conversations about the tsar's forcible removal from office through a palace revolution. The instigators of these conversations included the leader of the Constitutional Democrats, Pavel Nikolaevich Miliukov; the head of *Zemgor*, Prince Georgii Evgen'evich L'vov; the Octobrist Aleksandr Ivanovich Guchkov and his allies, Mikhail Ivanovich Tereshchenko and Nikolai Vissarionovich Nekrasov (these three were known as "the triumvirate"); and the grand dukes Dmitrii Pavlovich and Kirill Vladimirovich.[218] Guchkov's conversations with his confidants began in mid-November 1916 and focused on the possibility of a guards' unit arresting the tsar at a train station in Novgorod province. The idea was to avoid moving against the tsar at Stavka, where the coup would be riskier to carry out.[219] Guchkov confided this plan to General Petr Aleksandrovich Polovtsov, who recorded it as follows: "There existed a plot. It was proposed to persuade the tsar to send guard cavalier regiments to the capital for rest and to uphold order [there], then to lure the tsar from Stavka and, with the help of the cavalier guards, to effect a palace coup, to extract an abdication in favor of the tsarevich and a regency. All this was to occur in mid-March [1917]."[220]

After the revolution, in testimony to the Provisional Government's Investigative Commission, Minister of Internal Affairs P. A. Protopopov mentioned that General Vasilii Gurko was involved in the plot: Gurko was supposed to post guards loyal to the plotters to make the arrest.[221] That the guards in and near Petrograd had been strongly affected by revolutionary propaganda was confirmed by the diary of Major-General of the Emperor's Suite, Dmitrii Nikolaevich Dubenskii.[222]

If Olfer'ev arrived in Petrograd in the first half of November 1916, he may have been among the first to hear an allusion to Guchkov's conspiracy.

XIX

At several junctures in his narrative, Olfer'ev claims that, in late 1916/early 1917, the mood in Petrograd was more ominous than elsewhere in Russia, even than at Stavka. His assertion about the relative optimism at Stavka seems strange, until we recall certain facts: the relative weakness of the Austrian army and Russian superiority over the Central Powers in terms of the number of battalions; the hope fostered by General Brusilov's 1916 offensive that a new Russian breakthrough might occur in 1917; and the optimism of Russian commanders, especially Brusilov, concerning prospects on their respective fronts.[223] At a conference of front commanders on December 17/30, 1916 that reflected this optimism, General Ruzskii argued for a wide attack in the north but for an especially powerful thrust toward Riga.[224] Brusilov sketched out a multi-dimensional advance in the southwest to vanquish the Austrians, but he also suggested the possibility of a drive to the south to seize Istanbul.[225]

The commanders' hope in December 1916 for a strategic breakthrough waned quickly. Writing from Crimea on January 9/22, 1917, General Alekseev criticized the front commanders for producing an incoherent plan for spring 1917.[226] In early January, the northern front offensive toward the Jelgava Road made initial progress but petered out when units of XII Army mutinied. According to Stone, some mutineers "denounced the tsar and the high command as traitors."[227] By February 1917, Stavka heard reports of food shortages and of breakdowns in transport at the front. According to the military historian Andrei Medarovich Zaionchkovskii, in February 1917, for the first time, the high command faced the issue of "collapsing morale among the troops, of indiscipline, and of the spread among soldiers of powerful propaganda against the war and against the existing system."[228] Summarizing the difficulties confronting the army in February 1917, Zaionchkovskii wrote: "A third year of burdensome war without conspicuous successes, without proper preparation of the technical means to wage it, but with demoralized personnel, with the loss of experienced officers, and with commanders whose appointments were for the most part unwarranted—such a war could not fail to affect the morale of the entire army. [According to General Ruzskii,] the army had come to resemble a volunteer militia, in which many elements used the first pretext for encouraging indiscipline and spreading propaganda in a group threatened by food shortages. . . . Echoes of the mood and of events within the country reached the officer corps and did not remain without impact on its worldview, or on its morale. At the front, one felt a kind of oppression of the spirit, a sort of calm before the storm, an apathy and indifference like that often preceding a catastrophe."[229]

XX

Olfer'ev's account of events in early 1917 is accurate in most, but not all, respects. Let us review the crucial points in that account and then analyze them in the context of other sources.

According to Olfer'ev, in December the tsar had left Stavka for Petrograd "to attend a governmental conference" [*na gosudarstvennoe soveshchanie*] and had returned to Stavka in January. Rumors circulated at Stavka about difficulties obtaining food in Petrograd, and reports of heavy military losses came in from Riga. The atmosphere at Stavka "became more and more gloomy. Finally Alekseev returned and headquarters sighed in relief." None of the developments mentioned above, save for the tsar's supposed return to Stavka in January, is precisely dated.

Olfer'ev goes on to report: "The day before my departure I was the officer of the day and in the evening was seated at the telegraph. About ten o'clock [General] Ruzskii called Alekseev on the Hughes instrument. What he [Ruzskii] reported to him, I do not know . . . I only saw how [Alekseev] fell back in his chair, grabbing his head, muttering: 'Is this the beginning of the end?' "

Later, Olfer'ev claims: "I learned that Ruzskii had reported that several units of XII Army [on the northern front] refused to go on the attack. They were put in reserve, and the attack did not take place. I remember this fact well, because he held the position until the emperor's abdication." As in the previous instance, Olfer'ev supplies no date for this event. We do not know from the memoirs when Olfer'ev departed from Stavka.

Finally, Olfer'ev reports, "on the day of my departure, news came from Petrograd that the population had begun demonstrations there demanding bread. It became known that the city's garrison was unreliable, and the demonstrations took on dimensions that were more and more threatening [to the government]. The tsar, fearing for his family in the Imperial Palace, decided to send for their protection a battalion of soldiers of the Cross of St. George under the command of General Ivanov."

This paragraph obviously refers to the first days of February/March revolution—February 23/March 8 to February 27/March 12—that is, from the food protests of February 23/March 8 to the decision to send General Ivanov's unit to Petrograd on February 27/March 12. As in the earlier portions of the account, however, there are no dates assigned to events, and Olfer'ev only alludes to the events, vaguely and sometimes inaccurately.

Beginning with the tsar's departure from and return to Stavka, Olfer'ev's story needs some correction. In fact, Nicholas II left Stavka rather abruptly, on December 19, 2016, not to attend a conference of state but primarily to be with his family. He remained with his family at Tsarskoe Selo and returned to Stavka late in February, on February 22/March 7—just as the Petrograd protests took shape. Because Nicholas's stay in Tsarskoe Selo largely overlapped with General Alekseev's convalescence from an illness in Crimea from November 10/23, 1916 to February 19/March 4, 1917, the absence of the two principals from Stavka had left General Gurko, junior staff officers like Olfer'ev, and (from a distance) the front commanders to run the military machine.

Well before the February return of the tsar and of General Alekseev, there were rumors of food shortages in Petrograd, reports of heavy losses near Riga, and a deterioration of the general atmosphere at Stavka. Olfer'ev is accurate in recalling these developments, which are attested in many sources. He is also right about the sigh of relief that accompanied Alekseev's return to Stavka. As the historian Kirill Aleksandrov has pointed out, "in Stavka, Alekseev enjoyed respect and authority." Indeed, one junior officer, Dmitrii Nikolaevich Tikhobrazov, called Alekseev "the Russian Moltke."[230]

Olfer'ev's description of the telegraphic exchange between Ruzskii and Alekseev concerning the loyalty of XII Army is confusing for several reasons. The phrase about several units of XII Army refusing to attack reminds one of the mutinies near Riga in January. However, there was a much later transmission from General Ruzskii to the tsar on February 27/March 12 that was received at Stavka at 9:35 p.m.—a near match to the time Olfer'ev served as duty officer. As chief of staff, Alekseev would have received the telegram and, since it was intended for the tsar, he would not have left the text for Olfer'ev's inspection. In the telegram, Ruzskii wrote of the "pressing crisis and the disturbances in Petrograd" that "might in the future foster very unfavorable conditions [in the army]." Ruzskii warned the tsar and Alekseev of the "absolute necessity to adopt immediate measures to calm the population [in Petrograd] and to inculcate in it trust and resiliency of spirit, faith in itself and in the future." The adoption of these undefined "measures" might raise soldiers' fighting spirits, Ruzskii thought. However, he concluded: "In the current circumstances, measures of repression may well enflame the situation rather than provide the necessary, prolonged respite [the country needs]."[231]

In this carefully worded telegram, Ruzskii told the tsar and Alekseev not that XII Army had refused orders to suppress the Petrograd disturbances, but that the Petrograd disorders *might spread to the army at the front*. He also suggested that repressive measures would be counterproductive. Ruzskii's vague reference to "immediate measures to calm the population and to inculcate in it trust and resiliency of spirit" was a coded plea for a new government. In the circumstances, a new government could be the long-awaited "ministry of confidence," consisting of public figures with the Duma's support, or it might be a regency: the ouster of Nicholas II in favor of his son Aleksei, and the temporary tutelage of Grand Duke Mikhail Alekseevich or of the Grand Duke Nikolai Nikolaevich. Ruzskii did not spell out the choices, but he did not have to do so. Ruzskii's message of February 27/March 12 was therefore more far-reaching than a disclosure that elements of XII Army had supposedly refused an order. That was probably why Alekseev muttered: "Is this the beginning of the end?"

Olfer'ev mentions "news from Petrograd that the population there had begun demanding bread. It became known," he wrote, "that the city's garrison was unreliable, and the demonstrations took on dimensions that were more and more threatening."

The Petrograd population had endured food shortages of increasing severity starting in fall 1916. In response to this problem, the acting Minister of Agriculture, Aleksandr Aleksandrovich Rittikh, requisitioned grain from the provinces to supply the capital. As the historian Tsuyoshi Hasegawa has pointed out, by mid-February 1917, the situation "did not improve. On the contrary, it got worse."[232] On February 19/March 4, 1917, the Petrograd City Duma decided to introduce bread rationing, a decision that, predictably, caused a panic.[233] No doubt the bread shortages in winter 1916–17 contributed to labor unrest, which manifested itself in strikes for higher wages, in food protests, and the like. Hasegawa describes the strikes on February 20–22 /March 5–7 involving several thousand workers as "the rumbling of thunder, sure signs of the approaching storm."[234]

Most historians of the revolution consider February 23/March 8 its first day, partly because of the strikers' militancy, partly because of vandalism directed at bakeries, partly because on that day Cossack mounted units hesitated to use force against demonstrators. Petrograd security forces, led by city police chief Aleksandr Pavlovich Balk and commander of military reserves Vladimir Ivanovich Pavlenko, mobilized local resources to contain the demonstrators. However, Minister of Internal Affairs Protopopov, who telephoned Tsarskoe Selo to inform the empress of the disorders, told her he expected the city to return to calm the next day.[235]

On February 24/March 9, the strikes spread from the Vyborg district to other parts of the city, and Duma leaders called for an emergency meeting with the cabinet to discuss the food crisis. The commander of the Petrograd garrison, Sergei Sergeevich Khabalov, decided to ask for cavalry units from Pskov to be sent to the city as reinforcements for the police.[236] Khabalov admitted that the I Don Regiment of Cossacks "had not effectively dispersed the crowd, had attacked [it] weakly—that is, had approached the crowd and stopped instead of driving it off."[237] This was a first hint of a potential mutiny in Petrograd military detachments. Protopopov notified Stavka and the tsar on the evening of February 24/March 9 that Petrograd's food shortage had unleashed "disorders" among workers, but that, so far, the "workers' movement was not organized." Protopopov claimed that the "soldiers called [to restore order] are honorably performing their duty." He covered up the unreliability of the I Don Regiment.[238]

On February 25/March 10, roughly two hundred thousand workers left their factories to participate in what was now a general strike. Hasegawa notes that soldiers began to support the demonstrators against police in certain places in the city.[239] Near Liteinyi Bridge, a crowd of protestors killed a local police captain, Mikhail Petrovich Shalfeev, and workers in the Vyborg district drove the police from their stations.[240] Again the I Don Regiment showed no disposition to fire on demonstrators. On Znamenskaia Square, a former soldier and Cossack junior officer murdered the police officer Mikhail Evgen'evich Krylov.[241] By the evening, the police chief admitted that the security forces had lost the day in all respects. He and General Khabalov met the Council of Ministers to summarize events. The ministers pronounced the situation "most ominous" [*groznym*]."[242] In his memoirs of the revolution's "five days," Balk, the Petrograd police chief, recounts a meeting with his subordinates late in the day: "Those dealing with these matters were depressed and confused." He himself saw "a picture of the government's collapse. The troops were not resisting the rebels, were crossing over onto their side, or in the best case were doing nothing . . . Police officers were changing from their uniforms into civilian clothing."[243]

According to Hasegawa, news of serious disturbances in Petrograd "reached Nicholas in Mogilev for the first time on February 25/March 10 through a telegram from the empress and from the report of the palace commandant, Major-General Nikolai Ivanovich Voeikov, who had kept up with Protopopov."[244] Hasegawa has in mind Aleksandra's letter of Saturday evening, February 25/March 10, in which she reported: "Strikes and disorders in the city are more than provocative [*bolee chem vyzyvauiushchi*] . . . This is simply a hooligan movement. Young boys and girls scurry about and shout they have no bread simply to stir up trouble, and workers block other workers from working."[245] In response to the news, the tsar ordered Khabalov to crush the disturbances by force.

On February 26/March 11, 1917, soldiers from three units—the Semenovskii, Pavlovskii, and Volynskii Regiments—fired on demonstrators, killing at least fifty people.[246] The shootings provoked a mutiny in the Pavlovskii Regiment involving a hundred soldiers, who then took up arms and fired on police. Other regiments—Volynskii, Litovskii, Moskovskii—followed suit. Under Khabalov's order the Petrograd security authorities ordered the arrest of the Pavlovskii mutineers. Khabalov chose not to report the mutiny to Stavka.[247] The tsar learned of the mutiny from Duma chairman Rodzianko, who disclosed that, "in places, troops are firing at each other." The tsar dismissed the report as "nonsense."[248] Rodzianko also sent a telegram to Generals Alekseev and Ruzskii at 9:00 that night. He asserted that, because of the food shortage, "the starving crowd is embarking on the path of anarchy and license." He maintained that the crowd exhibited "complete lack of faith in the government, which has proven incapable of extricating the country from the crisis." He asserted: "The government finds itself in a state of complete paralysis and helplessness to restore order." Rodzianko called for a new government "possessing the trust of the population"—code for a ministry drawn from the Duma leadership and commanding the Duma's confidence. Like Khabalov, however, Rodzianko neglected to mention the mutiny in the Pavlovskii Regiment.[249]

On February 27/March 12, 1917, soldiers in the Volynskii and Litovskii Regiments mutinied, and some members of other regiments joined the demonstrators. Elements of the Moskovskii Regiment, besieged in their own barracks by the Volynskii Regiment, were coerced into joining the rebels.[250] Insurgent soldiers emptied the Kresty prison and the Shpalernaia House of Detention. By the end of the day, the insurrection had affected soldiers all over the city.[251] Select troops under the command of General Khabalov were never deployed. Khabalov's order to use armored cars against the insurgents was disobeyed.[252] Shock troops from the Preobrazhenskii Regiment tried to create a defensible perimeter inside which the disintegrating government could operate, but hostile crowds surrounded the Preobrazhentsy.[253]

At noon on February 27/ March 12, Khabalov reported to the tsar the mutinies in the Pavlovskii and Volynskii Regiments.[254] At 10 p.m. Khabalov sent a second telegram to General Alekseev confessing his inability to reestablish order.[255] He admitted: "The majority of units have betrayed their duty and have refused to fight the insurgents," while others "have fraternized with the insurgents and have fired on troops loyal to the government."[256] Meanwhile, at mid-day on February 27/March 12, Rodzianko had notified the tsar: "The government is completely impotent to suppress the disorder. No hope can be placed on soldiers in the garrison. Reserve battalions of the guards have been carried away by the insurrection. Officers have been killed . . . A civil war has begun and is spreading."[257]

Olfer'ev's report about the day of his departure from Stavka runs together developments in Petrograd over several days: demands for bread had echoed since winter 1916 but were especially loud in the strikes of February 20 and 21; the unreliability of the city's garrison had become known at Stavka only on February 27; the mutinies of February 26 and 27 in the Petrograd garrison were the justification for sending General Ivanov's select battalion to Petrograd on February 27. Olfer'ev implies that the only reason

Nicholas dispatched Ivanov was to protect the royal family at Tsarskoe Selo; in fact, Ivanov was being sent to Petrograd as a kind of military dictator. According to Alekseev's instructions, Ivanov would possess "full emergency powers" [*chrezvychainye polnomochiia*].[258]

Olfer'ev's account of the February days shows awareness of certain developments—food shortages, worker demonstrations, garrison mutinies, the dispatch of military units—but not of their chronological sequence. He interprets General Alekseev's reaction to General Ruzskii's telegram on February 27 as a response to disobedience in XII Army, when in fact Alekseev must have been reacting to a nascent revolution. Olfer'ev's impressions highlight the virtual impossibility of gauging others' thoughts from behavioral clues. The memoirs also remind us of the mutability of memories, even when the events being recalled are life-altering.

XXI

Olfer'ev testifies that he left Stavka for Kiev on the same day that Alekseev ordered General Ivanov's select military unit to go to the Petrograd region to restore order. That order was issued late at night on February 27–28/March 12–13, so Olfer'ev likely departed Stavka on February 28/March 13. The journey from Mogilev to Kiev—440 kilometers—would have taken six hours by train. So an early morning train would have arrived in Kiev just after midday.

During this journey, Olfer'ev would have missed the latest developments in Petrograd: first, the telegram from members of the State Council to the tsar warning that, unless the Council of Ministers resigned, the likely outcome would be "destruction of the legal order, military defeat, the end of the dynasty, and profound misfortunes for Russia";[259] second, the notification from General Mikhail Alekseevich Beliaev, the new war minister, that troops in the Petrograd garrison "under the influence of propaganda, are throwing down their arms and either joining the rebels or adopting neutrality. [Meanwhile,] the normal functions of government and of the ministries have come to a halt."[260] These developments made it clear, if it were not already, that Petrograd was in the throes of revolution.

Arriving in Kiev, Olfer'ev saw "normal conditions"—its well-provisioned shops and open restaurants standing in contrast to Petrograd's squalor. Olfer'ev's instructions sent him to Grand Duke Aleksandr Mikhailovich who, according to Olfer'ev, "had heard about the events taking place in Petrograd [but] apparently did not assign them particular significance." However, based on the grand duke's own memoirs, it is likely that he saw the Petrograd situation as a terrible disaster but did not disclose that assessment to the visiting junior staff officer. In early February 1917, Aleksandr Mikhailovich had told Empress Aleksandra, face to face, that "revolutionary propaganda has penetrated deeply into the populace," that "all classes of the population of Russia are hostile to your politics," and that "perhaps in two months not a stone upon a stone will remain in Russia to remind us of the autocrats sitting on the throne of our forebears."[261] Therefore, as soon as he learned about armed clashes between the crowd and soldiers of the Petrograd garrison, the grand duke offered to join the tsar at Stavka. "I remembered the traitor-generals who surrounded the sovereign and felt I should go to Stavka without permission." During these anxious moments the grand duke visited the Dowager Empress Mariia, whom he found plunged into "agitation and sorrow." Aleksandr Mikhailovich testified that his visit to the dowager empress occurred on the day after Nicholas II left Stavka by train to go to Tsarskoe Selo.[262] Since the tsar's conveyance departed from Stavka at 5 a.m. on February 28/March 13, the grand duke knew the full seriousness of the crisis on March 1/14—that is, on the day after Olfer'ev arrived in Kiev. Still, by February 28/March 13, the grand duke was fully aware that the throne was in peril.

After he met with the grand duke, Olfer'ev visited General Brusilov's headquarters in Berdichev, some 180 kilometers from Kiev. On February 28/March 13 at 2 p.m., Brusilov had received a long telegram from Alekseev summarizing developments in Petrograd since February 25, with special emphasis on the mutinies occurring in the Petrograd garrison, and on the formation of a "revolutionary government" [the Petrograd Sovet] in the Mariinskii Palace.[263] On February 28, when Brusilov met Olfer'ev, the general was already informed about the Petrograd crisis. In Olfer'ev's memoirs there is no indication of a substantive discussion between him and Brusilov; indeed, Olfer'ev reports that at headquarters "everything was operating normally and there was no mention of events in Petrograd."

On March 1/14, Olfer'ev went by automobile to visit army positions near Tarnopol [Ukrainian *Ternopil*], two hundred seventy kilometers due west from Berdichev. There General Aleksei Evgen'evich Gutor presided over the singing of the evening prayer and of "God Save the Tsar." This was the last time Olfer'ev recalled hearing that hymn sung by the tsar's soldiers. The irony of this event, according to Olfer'ev, was that Gutor later served in the Red Army. Irony aside, according to the military historian Andrei Vladislavovich Ganin, over 40 percent of graduates from the General Staff Academy served the Red Army in the civil war.[264] Gutor's path to the Red Army was therefore not anomalous.

Olfer'ev claims that after arriving in Tarnopol, he and his companions spent "several days there without seeing a single German [flier] over our position" [*Za neskol'ko dnei na fronte my ne videli ni odnogo nemtsa nad nashim raspolozheniem*]. If this claim is accurate, Olfer'ev's timeline here must be mistaken: had he spent several days near Tarnopol, he could not have returned from Tarnopol to Berdichev by March 1.

Olfer'ev returned by train to Berdichev, where he learned from the commander of the operations division, Ivan Il'ich Gromyko, that the tsar was abdicating the throne. Stunned by the news, Olfer'ev decided to take a night train to Stavka in Mogilev, a journey of over five hundred kilometers that would have lasted eight hours. Olfer'ev claims that he and his fellow officers "did not sleep all night on the journey to Mogilev." He arrived at Stavka "on the morning when Alekseev received the Tsar's request for the Army's opinion of his [pending] abdication." Olfer'ev describes the reactions of each of the front commanders.

Is this account credible?

At roughly six o'clock in the morning on March 1/14, the chairman of the State Duma Rodzianko telegraphed General Alekseev that, "since the former Committee of Ministers had been removed from governance, ruling authority had passed to the Provisional Committee of the State Duma."[265] Alekseev did not respond at once to Rodzianko, because he was unsure of the tsar's location: Nicholas had left Stavka for Tsarskoe Selo and, because railroad workers had blocked access, the imperial train had not reached its destination. By early afternoon, Alekseev learned that disorders had spread from Petrograd to Moscow. Just before 4 p.m., Alekseev therefore sent a telegram to the tsar alerting him to the situation in Moscow. Alekseev added that revolution in Russia would "become inevitable as soon as the disorders began to affect [military] resources," and "would mean a shameful end of the war with disastrous consequences for Russia." Yet Alekseev predicted that putting down the disorders by force "would lead Russia and the army to destruction." The general asked Nicholas "to place at the head of government a person whom Russia trusts and to charge him with forming a new cabinet." Alekseev asserted: "If Your Imperial Highness does not act, by tomorrow power will pass into the hands of extreme elements, and Russia will experience all the horrors of revolution."[266]

Between 5:15 and 6:20 p.m. on March 1/14, General Vladislav Napoleonovich Klembovskii, the assistant to Alekseev at Stavka, notified all front commanders that the Provisional Duma Committee under Rodzianko had replaced the Petrograd cabinet, and that Alekseev had asked the tsar for a new head of government "commanding the confidence of the populace."[267] Thus, by early evening on March 1/14, Alekseev had given the tsar an ultimatum to form a new cabinet that could command the public's trust—a message to heed the demands of the Duma leadership and the Progressive Bloc.

By eight in the evening on March 1/14, the political situation had further deteriorated. A rebellion had broken out on the Kronstadt Naval Base, and it threatened to spread throughout the Baltic Fleet. Alekseev, who had not yet contacted the tsar about the situation in Kronstadt, asked Rodzianko to help restore order on the railroads and in telegraphy.[268] At 10:20 p.m., Alekseev sent the tsar still another telegraphic message. This one demanded "immediate publication of a sovereign act strong enough to calm minds, something possible only by means of recognizing a responsible ministry and entrusting its composition to the chairman of the State Duma [Rodzianko]." Alekseev included in his telegram the words of the manifesto he expected the tsar to sign.[269] Thus the telegram at 10:20 p.m. not only repeated the early evening ultimatum but made an even more radical demand—namely, that the tsar create a "responsible ministry" (one elected by the Duma and responsible to it) rather than a government of confidence.

In neither of these telegrams did Alekseev explicitly ask the tsar to abdicate the throne. How then did Olfer'ev and his fellow officers in Berdichev come to suppose that on the evening of March 1/14 the tsar, sitting in a railroad car in Pskov, was abdicating his crown?

Here we can only speculate. One possibility is that Olfer'ev's narrative of events in Berdichev was a false memory. True, he might have known at the time that the tsar's train was in Pskov, because General Lukomskii shared that fact with General Mikhail Fedorovich Kvetsinskii, chief of staff of the army on the western front, at 7:43 p.m.[270] Presumably that news spread among front commanders, although we cannot know for sure. But it *was* widely known in the upper officer corps that Nicholas's train was heading to Pskov, so military men might have assumed that it had arrived. Nothing of the substance of the discussion between the tsar and General Ruzskii in Pskov was revealed to front commanders on March 1/14. Olfer'ev and his fellow officers in Berdichev therefore could not have known for certain that the tsar was abdicating his throne.

A second possibility is that Olfer'ev and others *assumed* the abdication was in process at Pskov. That assumption, which took hold ahead of General Alekseev's actual demand for establishment of "responsible ministry" under Duma chairman Rodzianko, was natural enough under the circumstances: the collapse of government authority in Petrograd, months of rumors about removing the tsar and empress from power and about imposing a regency, Nicholas's passivity at Stavka, and the urgent need for a credible government as Stavka anticipated another year of hostilities with Germany and Austria.

Another factor that may have contributed to the assumption of an imminent abdication was the attempt in Petrograd to involve the Grand Duke Mikhail Aleksandrovich in the solution to the political crisis. On February 27/March 12, Rodzianko persuaded the grand duke to petition the tsar to create a new government under the chairmanship of Georgii Evgen'evich L'vov.[271] Rodzianko also advocated that the grand duke take the initiative by establishing a quasi-dictatorship in the capital and by recognizing the authority of the Provisional Committee of the Duma to replace the discredited Petrograd authorities. The grand duke refused to do so, believing that such a momentous change required the tsar's approval.[272] As of March 1/14, Grand Duke Mikhail Aleksandrovich supported the creation of a responsible ministry under Rodzianko, but without the tsar's abdication. Nevertheless, Rodzianko's effort to co-opt the grand duke into a political deal may have fostered the impression in Petrograd that the tsar intended to abdicate the throne. Olfer'ev mentions that his nocturnal conversation with other officers involved "news" that "was spread as if by wireless telegraph."

In other words, the "news" spread by rumor. Perhaps a rumor that the tsar intended to abdicate spread from Petrograd to Berdichev before the night of March 1/14, when Olfer'ev departed for Stavka?

A decisive moment in the history of the revolution was the telegraphic conversation between General Ruzskii and Rodzianko at 3:20 a.m. on March 2/15, 1917.[273] In this exchange, Ruzskii reported that the tsar had agreed to form a responsible ministry. Ruzskii asked Rodzianko to send him the text of a manifesto to be promulgated later that day—March 2/15. Rodzianko replied that the situation in Petrograd had worsened to the point there had occurred "the awesome demand for abdication in favor of the son [Aleksei Nikolaevich], under the regency of Mikhail Aleksandrovich."[274] Rodzianko, professing a "broken heart," thus for the first time demanded the tsar's abdication. Through his aide General Iurii Nikiforovich Danilov, Ruzskii reported this conversation to Alekseev two and a half hours later, at 5:48 a.m.[275]

At roughly 9 a.m. on March 2/15, Alekseev asked his assistant, General Lukomskii, to telegraph Pskov, where the duty officer was to awaken Nicholas II with the news that Rodzianko had asked for the tsar's abdication. In this telegram, Lukomskii informed General Ruzskii of his conviction that "there is no choice, abdication must occur." Lukomskii pointed out that the royal family in Tsarskoe Selo was in the hands of mutinous soldiers, so, if the tsar did not agree to abdicate, "there will occur further excesses, which will threaten the tsar's children, and then a civil war will begin, Russia will perish under Germany's blow, and the dynasty will also perish." Lukomskii implied that Alekseev had decided to ask front commanders for their opinions on abdication, so that military authorities could then "send the necessary communiqué to the army."[276]

Sometime between 9 a.m. and 10 a.m. on March 2/15, General Ruzskii reported to the tsar the contents of his late-night conversation with Rodzianko. According to the courtier General Sergei Nikolaevich Vil'chkovskii, who witnessed the exchange, Ruzskii gave Nicholas the transcript of the fateful telegraphic conversation.[277] The tsar read it, then arose and looked out the window of his train car. He told Ruzskii he was ready to abdicate, but expressed this fear: "The people will not understand."[278]

Between 10 and 11 a.m. Alekseev sent telegrams to front commanders in which he described Rodzianko's demand for the tsar's abdication and for a regency under Grand Duke Mikhail Aleksandrovich. Alekseev expressed his own support for the abdication and made clear that he saw no alternative to it. He asked his commanders for their endorsement of the abdication. To General Aleksei Ermolaevich Evert, commander of the western front, Alekseev declared: "The Sovereign is vacillating, [so] the unanimous opinions of the front commanders may arouse him to make the decision that is the only possible way to save Russia and the dynasty."[279]

Although it would have been possible for a front commander to reject the option of abdication, Alekseev's note made difficult any course of action other than support for the tsar's removal from office. Alekseev asserted, in so many words, that the crisis in Petrograd was forcing the generals to "save" Russia and the dynasty. Alekseev must have known he was party to a soft coup d'état.

Olfer'ev remembers arriving at Stavka on the morning when Alekseev asked the front commanders to support the tsar's abdication. Olfer'ev went from the Mogilev train station straight to the telegraph office, where "Alekseev spoke in turn to the commanders in chief of the fronts." (This account, if true, would have required Olfer'ev to have left Berdichev by midnight or 1 a.m. for the eight-hour trip to Mogilev.)

According to Olfer'ev, Alekseev might have spoken for the army without consulting his commanders, but he consulted them nonetheless because, in his view, securing their assent for abdication was the only way to persuade the tsar to give up the throne. Olfer'ev describes various generals' responses. General Evert, after pronouncing himself "infinitely devoted to Your Majesty," begged Nicholas to abdicate the throne "for the sake of the country and the dynasty." General Brusilov told Nicholas to abdicate in favor of his son Aleksei under the regency of Grand Duke Mikhail Aleksandrovich, for "otherwise, he [Nicholas] will call down on himself an incalculably catastrophic result." Olfer'ev underscores that Grand Duke Nikolai Nikolaevich "on bended knees" [*na koleniakh*] asked Nicholas to abdicate "to save Russia and your successor . . . There is no alternative." These responses would have arrived at Stavka before 2:30 p.m.—that is, four hours after Alekseev had solicited the commanders' opinions but before he dispatched a new telegram to the tsar begging Nicholas not to delay a decision "which will foster a peaceful and favorable outcome to the crisis that has developed." In the new telegram General Alekseev included the opinions of the other front commanders.[280]

Having read the new message from Alekseev, the tsar agreed in principle to abdicate. Between 2:45 and 3:00 p.m., Nicholas drafted two telegrams—one to Rodzianko and one to Stavka—announcing his "readiness" to abdicate in favor of his son Aleksei.[281] At that juncture, the official decree of abdication had yet to be written and signed.

Olfer'ev regarded the tsar's abdication as a step that Nicholas undertook to discharge his duty to Russia, and that Alekseev hastened "to save the dynasty . . . and the fighting power of the front." However, Olfer'ev was skeptical that the abdication would have these effects, and blamed the tsar for contributing to Russia's impending military defeat.

After abdicating the throne, Nicholas returned from Pskov to Stavka on the evening of March 3/16. The tsar's approaching train led one officer at the Mogilev station to quip: "It is as if we are meeting the deceased." On seeing Nicholas—now aged, withered, and thin—Olfer'ev felt sorry for the former tsar, but he felt sorrier for the Russia that Nicholas had "so mercilessly and stupidly ruined." The Executive Committee of the Petrograd Soviet ordered Nicholas's arrest on the very day of his return to Stavka. The Provisional Government issued its own arrest decree on March 7/20. It is instructive that the Provisional Government did not call for "the tsar's arrest," but rather used euphemistic language requesting "deprivation of freedom of the former emperor" [*lishenie svobody byvshego imperatora*].[282]

On March 8/21, just before the tsar left Stavka for the last time, he delivered to a select group of senior officers at Stavka a "farewell address to the armed forces" [*proshchal'nyi prikaz armiiam*]. According to Olfer'ev's version of the text, Nicholas noted that authority had passed from him "to the Provisional Government created through the initiative of the State Duma," and he invoked God thrice. He said: "May God help it [the government] guide Russia along the path of glory and prosperity. And May God help you, gallant troops, defend our Motherland from the vile enemy." At the speech's end, Nicholas rejected talk of an easy peace with the enemy, called on every soldier to express love of country, and then he said: "May the Lord God bless you, and may the Great Martyr, St. George the Victorious, lead you to victory." Olfer'ev claims to have found the text of the address "in a loose-leaf calendar," probably one in which he had recorded the words from memory.

According to the archivist Vladimir Nikolaevich Khrustalev, the actual text read as follows:

> *For the last time I address you, my ardently beloved army. After abdication of the Russian throne for myself and for my son, power passed to the Provisional Government, which arose at the initiative of the State Duma. May God help it lead Russia on the path of glory and prosperity. And may God help you, glorious army, to defend our Motherland from the wicked foe. For two and a half years, we have borne every hour the heavy burden of military service, much blood has been shed, many efforts have been made, and the hour is already near, when Russia, in league with our glorious allies, by common striving for victory, will break the enemy's will. This unprecedented war must be fought to complete victory.*
>
> *Whoever thinks now of peace, whoever desires it, is a traitor to the Fatherland, its betrayer. I know that every honest soldier thinks the same. Carry out your duty, defend our glorious and great Motherland, obey the Provisional Government, listen to your superiors, remember that any weakening of discipline in service only strengthens the hand of the enemy.*
>
> *I firmly believe that infinite love for our great Motherland will never be extinguished in your hearts. May the Lord God bless you, and may the Great Martyr George, the bringer of victory, lead you to victory.*
>
> *Nicholas*
> *8 March 1917*

Immediately after Nicholas signed this address with the intention that Alekseev print it and distribute copies to the armed forces, Guchkov forbade its distribution. According to Dmitrii Nikolaevich Dubenskii, the editor of the journal *Chronicle of War* [*Letopis' voiny*] and the official historian in Nicholas's circle, "in Stavka, this address was held in utter secrecy, and was known to only a few people."[283]

Olfer'ev's immediate response to the farewell address was to criticize Nicholas for his selfishness when in power and for his weakness in failing to retain that power. Later, Olfer'ev felt shame over having entertained these ungracious thoughts.

XXII

Although the February/March days had witnessed the abdication of the tsar and the end of the dynasty, Olfer'ev did not classify the "February event" as a revolution. In his opinion, those political actors who had deposed Nicholas II wanted merely to replace the tsar with another royal, and thus to save the throne. Yet the self-appointed conservators of royal power could not have succeeded in this plan, Olfer'ev thought, because the throne "was like a termite-infested building crumbling of its weight." As Olfer'ev saw it, the Romanov dynasty's collapse from within did not constitute revolution, but it was a necessary precondition of revolution: after the abdication, the ensuing political vacuum was filled first by the Provisional Government, then by the Bolsheviks.

Olfer'ev calls the first phase of the revolution "*Kerenshchina*"—an untranslatable term that can be rendered by the locutions "Kerenskii's time," or "the Kerenskii period," keeping in mind that the Russian suffix *–shchina* is pejorative. The historical linguist Aleksandr Zelenin has noted that the suffix *–shchina* enjoyed wide currency in the revolutionary press after 1890 and became especially common in the émigré press after 1917. The term *Kerenshchina* was used often in the 1920s to designate Kerenskii's inept leadership.[284] Olfer'ev appropriates the term to convey the émigrés' condemnation of the Provisional Government.

Olfer'ev calls the first section of his analysis of the *Kerenshchina* "Inverted Pyramid" [*piramida vverkh dnom* = literally, "pyramid turned upside down"]. This expression refers to a metaphor for the Russian social order often found in the leftist press before 1917—a pyramid depicting the wealthy at the apex and toilers at the base of society. The leftists pictured a revolution as the inversion of the social pyramid. With a revolution, "the world turned upside down" of European carnivals would be realized. Olfer'ev may also have been thinking about another source of this metaphor—Lev Tolstoy's *War and Peace*, in which Napoleon and other dignitaries at the social pyramid's apex proved to be furthest from controlling historical events. Perhaps Olfer'ev's reference to this Tolstoyan trope was ironic?

Olfer'ev mentions a visit to Stavka by representatives of the Provisional Government—Kerenskii, Guchkov, and Miliukov. Their visit occurred on March 18/31, a little over two weeks following the tsar's abdication and only ten days after Nicholas's farewell address. In the interim, General Alekseev and other staff officers had sworn allegiance to "the fatherland" [*otechestvo*] rather than to the Provisional Government, even though Alekseev also pledged that everyone would work with the new government for Russia's sake. On March 7/20, Alekseev had lobbied the Provisional Government to appoint Grand Duke Nikolai Nikolaevich to a second stint as supreme commander in chief of Russian armed forces, but Prince L'vov and Guchkov balked at that step. On March 11/24, the Provisional Government had named Alekseev "acting" supreme commander in chief—with the emphasis on "acting." Behind the scenes, there was opposition to Alekseev on the grounds that he represented a "dictatorial" approach to strategic decisions. For his part, Alekseev pointed to the effects of the "domestic political disturbance on our reserve units" and to "moral disorientation in the army" that he suspected would delay the army's full staffing for three or four months.[285] These developments indicated wariness from both sides: the Provisional Government had its doubts about Alekseev and Stavka, and Alekseev returned the sentiment.

The meeting at Stavka on March 18/31 had multiple purposes. The principals wanted to negotiate the timing of a spring offensive against the Germans and Austrians. They wanted to discuss Russia's war aims in light of tsarism's collapse. They sought to find a modus vivendi on which Stavka and the Provisional Government could build in succeeding weeks. General Alekseev recommended delaying the spring offensive, given difficulties with food and ammunition supply and problems with railroad transport. Guchkov acknowledged these obstacles to launching an offensive, but he nevertheless urged the army to prepare to advance. At the Stavka conference, the authorities made no formal changes in Russia's war aims. However, Miliukov, the new minister of foreign affairs, pressed the navy to seize the Bosporus and Dardenelles. The head of the naval staff, Admiral Mikhail Vladimirovich Bubnov, approved the naval operation, as did General Alekseev, but Minister of War Guchkov blocked it.

But Olfer'ev's account focuses on efforts by Kerenskii, Guchkov, and Miliukov to explain their recent political actions to the General Staff. Olfer'ev had little sympathy for Miliukov's scholarly perspective on the revolution and less for Guchkov's "long and boring speech" justifying his conduct as an attempt to save the monarchy. Olfer'ev and other officers who had long been aware of Guchkov's conspiratorial opposition to the royal family "did not believe him." In other words, they regarded Guchkov as a brazen liar and his speech as a tissue of falsehoods. Olfer'ev agreed with Kerenskii's explanation that the throne had collapsed of its own inadequacies and observed that Kerenskii's patriotic fervor "made a good impression on everyone—both on the clerks and on the generals." Olfer'ev came to believe that, "contrary to reason, not all is lost [in the war effort]." Kerenskii's pose as a patriot uniting all patriots was, as the historian Boris Kolonitskii has noted, deliberate mimicry of the remark by Kaiser Wilhelm II in 1914: "For me there are no more parties, only Germans."[286] The remark also reflected Kerenskii's conviction that social progress in Russia depended on military victory.[287]

Although the Provisional Government and the generals at Stavka aimed for a modus vivendi, the tensions between them increased rather than diminished over time, for several reasons. First, the infamous Order No. 1, issued by the Petrograd Soviet on March 1/14, put supervision of soldiers' political activities under the aegis of the Soviet rather than of army officers. The order forbade officers from engaging in "vulgar communications" with soldiers, and it vested control over ammunition not in officers but in soldiers' committees. Many on the General Staff believed that Order No. 1 undermined officers' authority over the troops and therefore undercut military discipline. Olfer'ev complains that army leaders were transformed by the order "from commanders into technical advisors, and were placed in subservience to committees of the troops."

Second, at War Minister Guchkov's urging, the Provisional Government not only blocked the reappointment of Nikolai Nikolaevich as supreme commander in chief but also, on March 22/April 4, removed Grand Duke Aleksandr Mikhailovich from leadership of the Russian air force. According to Olfer'ev, the removal of members of the royal family as "counterrevolutionary elements" led to his own reassignment, for as a person linked to Aleksandr Mikhailovich, he was regarded as a danger to the revolution.

In other words, by late March/early April 1917, the officers at Stavka like Olfer'ev sensed that the Provisional Government was conducting a purge of politically "unreliable elements" in the military.

Third, the Provisional Government's suspicion of Stavka's "counter-revolutionary" tendencies was part of a broader popular suspicion toward the army officer corps. This suspicion was expressed both by soldiers' committees and by elements of the Petrograd Soviet. On March 14/27, the Bolshevik Iurii Mikhailovich Steklov declared that a soldier had the right to kill a reactionary general if the general should raise a hand to discipline the soldier.[288]

Guchkov used popular suspicion toward officers to justify his own distrust of the generals and to motivate a review of their performances. As early as March 6/19, Guchkov tried to persuade Alekseev to remove "incompetent generals . . . at one stroke."[289] This was a strange demand in view of the fact that Alekseev had long exercised his prerogative to promote able field commanders and to sidetrack feeble leaders. Guchkov put his old ally General Polivanov in charge of a special commission that would make lists of underperforming generals. According to Mel'gunov, by late March Guchkov had marked for removal roughly one hundred twenty generals out of eight hundred.[290] On April 29/May 12, 1917, Guchkov boasted that he had acted "mercilessly" toward his targets.[291]

Fourth, in early March the Polivanov commission drafted Order No. 114, which abolished lower army ranks, abolished officers' titles, forbade officers from addressing off-duty soldiers as they might on-duty soldiers, and eliminated disciplinary rules for off-duty military personnel. This new order, which had the effect of permitting soldiers to engage in political activity as other citizens did, accelerated the "politicization" of the army to which officers at Stavka objected.[292] The tension over Order No. 114 led the Polivanov commission on March 9/22 to draft another document, the "Declaration of Soldiers' Rights," which contributed to soldiers' expectations that army regulations would assume a new, humane character.[293] Olfer'ev interpreted all these developments as evidence of a revolutionary "inversion" of the pyramid.

XXIII

Once he had been dismissed from Stavka, Olfer'ev was assigned to VIII Army, which since April had operated under the command of General Lavr Georgievich Kornilov. Olfer'ev does not record the date of his arrival in Chernovtsy [Polish *Czerniowce*, Ukrainian *Chernivtsi*], where VIII Army was stationed, but he recalls the occasion as "the famous day when Kornilov presented a standard to the First Volunteer Shock Squadron [*udarnyi otriad iz dobrovol'tsev*], which carried his name and was organized by Captain Nezhentsev." The presentation of the banner occurred on June 10/23, 1917. The "Captain Nezhentsev" who received the banner was Mitrofan Osipovich Nezhentsev, a decorated officer and schoolmate of Olfer'ev's at the General Staff Academy.

Olfer'ev describes the complex situation confronting VIII Army in summer 1917. On the one hand, VIII Army had performed well during the Brusilov offensive and indeed, had staved off defeat at that time. Furthermore, the command staff of VIII Army carried itself with a swagger. General Kornilov was a forceful, charismatic leader "whose Kalmuck eyes burned with a great passion, and their gaze penetrated deeply into the soul of those with whom he spoke." General Petr Nikolaevich Vrangel had graduated from the General Staff Academy in 1910, the year before Olfer'ev's entrance. Vrangel had first distinguished himself in the Russo-Japanese War, winning a decoration for bravery. Early in the Great War, on August 6, 1914, he won the Cross of St. George, and, in October 1915, he was commended for his leadership on the southwestern front. Olfer'ev lauds Vrangel for his orderly mind and confident bearing: "He could hold his ground with anyone." Another important figure in VIII Army was General Ivan Pavlovich Romanovskii, a graduate of the General Staff Academy in 1903, who had served as Kornilov's chief of staff since the latter's appointment to VIII Army. Romanovskii earned praise for his conduct under fire in June 1915. Colonel Pavel Alekseevich Kusonskii had graduated from the General Staff Academy in 1911, the year of Olfer'ev's matriculation at that school. Kusonskii served in VIII Army from 1915. In October 1916, he was decorated for "zealous and distinguished service." All these officers subsequently played key roles in the White Army.

On the other hand, as Olfer'ev notes, in mid-1917 VIII Army "was decomposing under the hot summer sun of Bukovina." Officers still hoped for victory in the war, but, according to Olfer'ev, they "were powerless in dealing with mass hysteria." Most frontline troops remained loyal and determined to fight, but the reserves were less eager to see battle and even resented the grit of "doomed" trench fighters. Although Olfer'ev's assessment of the officer corps was positive, he also pointed to its shortcomings. Kornilov did not know how to cope with the chaotic situation in Petrograd or how to incorporate into the VIII Army the reserve battalions sent from the capital. According to Olfer'ev, Kornilov "took no measures which would restore the fighting power of the troops." Olfer'ev implies that Kornilov was a man with little substance and one without bearings, who took credit for Nezhentsev's organizational skill. Worse yet, when Kornilov was offered the post of supreme commander in chief of the Russian armed forces on July 19/August 1, 1917, he negotiated with the Provisional Government for three days, following not his own agenda but the advice of his "inner circle." Olfer'ev also criticizes Vrangel, for falsifying a report to Kornilov claiming that Vrangel had sent units across the Dniestr River to attack the Austrians. According to Olfer'ev, Vrangel was a fantasist prone to spending hours telling "boastful tales of his real and imagined triumphs."

Olfer'ev's own duty at Chernovtsy was to inspect the air force. He found its officers depressed and unhappy over interference from the soldiers' committees, which blocked Russian fliers from conducting reconnaissance on enemy positions, apparently because the committees feared that Russian overflights would trigger Austrian artillery fire on Russian positions. Olfer'ev left Chernovtsy "just before the [army's] advance on Tarnopol"—that is, on June 23/July 6, 1917. If Olfer'ev's memory is accurate, his term of duty at Chernovtsy was less than two weeks, from June 10/23 to June 23/July 6.

VIII Army's attack on Austrian troops was initially successful. Russian forces took eight thousand prisoners in the offensive's first two days. The Russians advanced beyond Kalush, a small multi-ethnic city in Austrian Poland. However, German troops halted the Russian advance in mid-July, then drove VIII Army back.[294] The operations by VIII Army were part of the so-called "Kerenskii offensive," an unfortunate, politically inspired campaign demanded by Russia's allies and carried out, in spite of Russia's military deficiencies, because Kerenskii hoped for a victory that would put an end to the army's demoralization.[295] In any event, by early August 1917 the Russians had withdrawn from Austrian Galicia.

XXIV

That same summer, Olfer'ev was ordered to Moscow to participate in an "aviation conference." This was the First All-Russian Aviation Conference [*Pervyi Vserossiiskii aviatsionnyi s"ezd*], which convened on July 10/23, 1917. According to one participant, the conference's members divided into "leftists" and "rightists." The latter, comprising a majority of delegates, supported the platform of "war to a victorious end" and elected a steering committee reflecting that view.[296] The conference remained in session more than a month before it succeeded in establishing the All-Russian Council of Aviation [*Vserossiiskii sovet aviatsii*].[297]

Olfer'ev describes the conference as a dilatory affair involving five hundred delegates, most of them non-commissioned officers, who were less interested in politics than in securing higher pay for themselves. When he addressed the gathering several days after the conference began, he called on the delegates to resolve their disagreements quickly so that they could return to their units. This message was so unwelcome that the delegates received it with "deathly silence."

By the time Olfer'ev returned to VIII Army in late August/early September, Kornilov had been appointed supreme commander in chief and had left VIII Army for Stavka. Kornilov served in that post just over a month—from July 19/August 2 to August 27/September 9, 1917—and then was arrested. Olfer'ev's return to the staff of VIII Army occurred after Kornilov's arrest—that is, in late August/early September. Olfer'ev provides no details of the *Kornilovshchina,* that is, of the supreme commander's purported attempt to seize power and to depose Kerenskii.

According to the historian Rex A. Wade, July and August 1917 "were months of almost continual government instability," during which the extreme left and extreme right strove to discredit and topple the Provisional Government.[298] On July 3/16, Petrograd workers and soldiers tried to seize power, but this effort collapsed on July 5/18. On July 21/August 3, Kerenskii threatened to leave the Provisional Government, but on July 23/

August 5 he decided instead to form a new cabinet. Meanwhile, Kornilov and his allies in the army criticized the "chaos" in Petrograd, and demanded capital punishment not only for disobedient front fighters, but also for those sowing discord "in the rear." At the Moscow State Conference from August 10/23 to 13/26, Kerenskii pleaded for delegates' support, but rightist critics of the Provisional Government seemed more impressed by Kornilov's campaign for army discipline. According to Wade, Kerenskii and Kornilov tried to reach a modus vivendi to restore order. From Kornilov's point of view, the Provisional Government's "weakness" would have to be mitigated by purging socialists from ministerial positions, by reducing the Petrograd Soviet's influence on it, and by arresting the Bolsheviks. Kerenskii saw these steps as unnecessary and undemocratic, although he was prepared to seek the army's support if it became necessary to impose martial law in Petrograd.[299]

The distrust between Kerenskii and Kornilov reached its apex on August 27/September 9, when Kerenskii dismissed Kornilov as supreme commander in chief. Kornilov responded by sending troops to Petrograd "to restore order"—that is, to impose a political solution favorable to him and his allies at Stavka. The failure of this mission undermined whatever remained of officers' faith in current political arrangements and, in the eyes of the left, it further discredited the "counter-revolution." As Wade has observed, the "winners of the Kornilov Affair were the radical left."[300]

Kerenskii offered an *apologia* for his conduct in July–August 1917 in a book called *The Kornilov Affair*.[301] Like much of Kerenskii's writing, his account is dramatic, full of revolutionary invective aimed at his "counter-revolutionary enemies." The book is also logically contradictory and, at moments, implausible. Kerenskii himself had appointed Kornilov commander of VIII Army and later supreme commander in chief of Russian armed forces, but in his book, Kerenskii nevertheless maintains that "the entire period from July 3 to August 27 can be divided into three stages: first, preparatory work by various [rightist] groups and their coalescence into a united whole; then the organization of forces and of the means to exploit the Moscow State Conference; and finally the decisive attempt to seize power under the guise of struggle against the Bolsheviks. The [rightist] movement's goal was military dictatorship."[302] Thus, Kerenskii's own testimony portrays him as spectator, if not an accomplice, to Kornilov's attempted counter-revolution.

Olfer'ev's explanation of the July–August crisis is simpler. In his opinion, Kerenskii was a "mediocrity" whose insistence on launching an offensive in summer 1917 was bound to fail so long as the army lacked discipline. Kerenskii had appointed Kornilov supreme commander in chief because General Brusilov had failed to restore order. Meanwhile, Kornilov did nothing to restore army discipline and "did not have the skill to broadly grasp the [political] situation and to make the right decision." According to Olfer'ev, Kornilov should have bolstered the volunteer "shock" unit of VIII Army and perhaps used it to restore military discipline. Instead, Kornilov followed the advice of his "inner circle"—his adjutant Vasilii Stepanovich Zavoiko and his commissar Maksimilian Maksimilianovich Filonenko—to seek a political accommodation with Kerenskii.

Kornilov's failure led to his arrest and the arrests of his sympathizers and co-conspirators, such as General Anton Denikin. Because Olfer'ev had been in Moscow at the aviation conference, he was not held responsible for abetting Kornilov's coup, and he therefore avoided arrest.

Olfer'ev's next assignment, commander of reconnaissance [*nachal'nik razvedyvatel'nago otdeleniia*] in VIII Army, confirmed his picture of lax discipline among frontline troops. He did not remain in this post for long. The army committee overseeing headquarters at VIII Army relieved him of duty for his "lack of revolutionary discipline."

XXV

In the portion of his memoirs entitled "The Revolution Is Deepening," Olfer'ev tries to explain the process by which revolutionaries displaced Russia's traditional elites even before the Bolshevik seizure of power on October 25/November 7, 1917. He suggests that this process entailed a radical redefinition of the concept of discipline. The imperial armed forces had demanded obedience of soldiers to officers, and of officers to the emperor. This code of discipline began to fracture in the mass defections of 1915, and the fracture widened in 1917 after the publication of Order No. 1 and the code of soldiers' rights. The break between Nicholas II and the "political" generals at Stavka constituted a fatal blow to traditional military discipline. That is why Olfer'ev describes the emperor's abdication as the moment when the army's "head was cut off." Indeed, "the subsequent movements of [the] body are nothing more than posthumous convulsions." In July and August, Kornilov wanted to restore army discipline by imposing the death penalty on deserters and those who betrayed the fatherland, but he did not succeed—and perhaps could not have succeeded—in doing so.

By degrees, "revolutionary discipline" replaced the traditional kind. Elected army committees, often dominated by politically active soldiers, exercised their informal authority to remove objectionable officers from their units. Whereas Kornilov and many other generals abhorred the soldiers' committees, Kerenskii considered them as an expression of "revolutionary democracy" and as a check on the generals. Olfer'ev attributed his own dismissal from VIII Army to a soldiers' committee dominated by Bolsheviks.

Pondering the source of the demand for "revolutionary discipline," Olfer'ev concludes that it stemmed from the people's resentment over past social injustices and, more generally, from resentment over Russia's legacy of social inequality. He recalls several examples of this rank inequality: the unjustified killing of a bartender by an officer in his unit before the war, the wrongful execution of Voldemars Lupiks in Latvia, and the forced deference that peasants had to show toward landowners. These phenomena, still fresh in his memory, caused him to question the moral legitimacy of Russia's old social order. At the same time, he agreed with Denikin's observation that most officers suffered privations no less onerous than those experienced by common soldiers and peasants. The difference, as Olfer'ev saw it, was that when someone was promoted to officer rank, he was regarded as a nobleman and transformed into a member of a hated social class—the "lords." The officer, if he rose to a high rank conferring hereditary nobility, then enjoyed the privilege of educating his children at the state's expense, thus transmitting his privileges to the next generation. In other words, Olfer'ev thought, the new "revolutionary discipline" was also an expression of the common people's desire for future social equity. In addition, the desire for revolutionary discipline was part of a more general aversion to a system that had mired peasant soldiers in the senseless mass slaughter of the Great War, a war that Russia could no longer win.

In spite of understanding the case for "revolutionary discipline," Olfer'ev could not bring himself to break ties with the old military code and with the traditionally constituted officer corps. He looked on Kornilov as his leader and defender, almost as his surrogate father. How else to explain Olfer'ev's description of himself as an "orphan" during the time Kornilov languished in prison at Bykhov?

Kerenskii prevailed on General Alekseev to arrest Kornilov and Kornilov's allies. Denikin called these arrests "the liquidation of Stavka."[303] Alongside these arrests, there occurred other developments: Kerenskii's assumption of the title "supreme commander in chief"; the appointment of General Nikolai Nikolaevich Dukhonin as chief of staff at Stavka on September 10/23; the appointment of Mikhail Konstantinovich Diterikhs as quartermaster general at Stavka on September 6/19; the appointment of Vasilii Vasil'evich Vyrubov as head of the newly created political section of Stavka, also in mid-September. As Olfer'ev pointed out, only Colonel Pavel Alekseevich Kusonskii was held over from Kornilov's staff. From Kerenskii's perspective, the liquidation of Stavka was necessary to guard the Provisional Government against "counter-revolution." Kornilov and his officer allies might have resisted arrest by fleeing to the south to prepare for civil war, but when Kornilov surrendered to Alekseev, most of the *kornilovtsy* decided to share his fate, "even if it meant death." As Denikin observed, the collapse of Kornilov's movement signified the end of hope: "At Stavka, everything was psychologically finished."[304]

On September 17/30, 1917, Olfer'ev asked General Georgii Titovich Kiiashchenko for a new assignment. Within a week—that is, roughly on September 23 /October 6—Kiiashchenko commissioned Olfer'ev to Vyrubov's political staff. The new assignment was awkward. Vyrubov wanted Olfer'ev to act "as an advisor on questions I know nothing about that pertain to the routine of your military duties." He offered to put then-lieutenant colonel [*podpolkovnik*] Olfer'ev up for promotion to general. Vyrubov was in fact recruiting Olfer'ev to join the ranks of the army's "revolutionary democrats," with the quid pro quo being a promotion jumping ranks. This tactic represented the liquidation of Stavka by other means. Olfer'ev rejected the offer, citing his ignorance of politics and his lack of enthusiasm for promotion beyond the rank granted him by the tsar. Olfer'ev saw Vyrubov as a revolutionary careerist; Vyrubov saw Olfer'ev as a staunch monarchist.

Olfer'ev recalls that Vyrubov then presided over a sham office, with tables, chairs, and a budget but no real tasks to perform. When Olfer'ev took Vyrubov's commission "out of friendship," he did not realize that his first assignment would be visiting Kornilov and other arrested generals in Bykhov to discover whether they were being well treated. At Bykhov, Olfer'ev found twenty-one prisoners, among whom were ten generals. According to Denikin, the prisoners were "of various views, most being apolitical." They developed their own esprit and lived completely apart from the outside world during their six weeks of confinement. Denikin recalled visits by "the commissars Vyrubov and [Vladimir Konstantinovich] Stankevich," who did little to change the regimen under which the prisoners were held."[305] Olfer'ev offered to help the arrestees "communicate with the outside world." Kornilov spurned the offer and refused to shake Olfer'ev's hand, because he suspected Olfer'ev of being "with them [the revolutionaries]." Indeed, Kornilov no doubt suspected Olfer'ev of being a revolutionary spy.

The exchange with Kornilov, quite painful to Olfer'ev, was symptomatic of Russia's political polarization. And so was Olfer'ev's repulsion at Kerenskii, who in early October, during his stay at Stavka, lounged in the tsar's bedroom.

By the fall of 1917, the old order was collapsing on the streets of Petrograd. The Petrograd social disorders, which had begun earlier in the year, reached the Mogilev region. Thieves dressed in the stolen garb of well-to-do citizens committed robberies in broad daylight.[306] One October night, as Olfer'ev and his wife lay abed in a small town (perhaps Palykavicy) on a railroad line just outside Mogilev, thieves rummaged through their closets and made off with the Olfer'evs' clothing.

XXVI

Olfer'ev's treatment of the October revolution is confused in some respects, but his confusion is historically interesting.

The first paragraph of the section in the memoirs entitled "The End Comes to Supreme Headquarters" [*Konets Stavki*] depicts Stavka as "a small island in a stormy ocean, threatened at any moment to have every living thing on it washed away by a single wave." Meanwhile, in Petrograd, Olfer'ev tells us, "a sailor dispersed the Constituent Assembly [*matros razognal Uchreditel'noe sobranie*]," while the Bolsheviks, aided by the Cruiser

Aurora, barricaded the Winter Palace, arrested the members of the Provisional Government, and forced Kerenskii to flee Petrograd.

Olfer'ev's narrative coheres around nautical imagery: turbulent ocean, waves, a sailor singlehandedly dismissing the long-awaited Constituent Assembly, the semi-mythic *Aurora* firing a salvo to intimidate the cornered remnants of the Provisional Government. Olfer'ev associates the October Revolution with rebellious sailors, a link that made sense to him in view of the role played by Bolshevik sailors from Kronstadt and the socialist sailors in Petrograd itself.[307] However, Olfer'ev erred in his date of October 17 for the dismissal of the Constituent Assembly [*Uchreditel'noe sobranie*] (which was elected in November 1917, then dispersed on January 6, 1918 by Pavel Efimovich Dybenko, a representative of the Baltic Fleet). The organization that was actually dismissed in October 1917 was the Provisional Soviet of the Russian Republic, the so-called "Pre-Parliament," which had gathered on September 23/October 6, 1917 in the Mariinskii Palace in Petrograd, and which was locked out of its assembly hall on the morning of October 25/November 7.[308] The Pre-Parliament was widely understood as preparing the legislative way for the actual Constituent Assembly. Olfer'ev probably linked the Pre-Parliament's dismissal to a sailor because on October 25/November 7 several squadrons of sailors from the Baltic Fleet surrounded the palace and prevented the Pre-Parliament's delegates from entering. Incidentally, General Alekseev was among the delegates turned away that morning.[309] The leaders of the Pre-Parliament issued a declaration that the body had not ceased to exist, but its operations had been temporarily suspended.

After erroneously dating the dismissal of the Constituent Assembly and the fall of the Provisional Government to October 17, Olfer'ev then links those events with two other events that occurred in October in previous decades: the purported assassination attempt on Tsar Aleksandr III in October 1888; and the establishment of the State Duma in October 1905.

The first event occurred on the night of October 17–18, 1888, when the imperial train derailed during the royal family's return from Crimea to Petersburg on the Kursk-Khar'kov-Azov rail line. The emperor's train car collapsed at either end, and he held up the ceiling until his family exited the carriage. Immediately after the terrible incident, rumors circulated that terrorists had planted a bomb on the tracks. An investigation led by the jurist

Anatolii Fedorovich Koni established that the derailment occurred because of other factors: the train's excess weight, its bad brakes, and faulty tracks. In spite of Koni's findings, the rumors about a terrorist attack established themselves as "fact." When the tsar died in 1894, it was said that he succumbed, in part, to the psychological effects of the 1888 assault.[310]

The second event was proclamation of the October Manifesto on October 17, 1905. The manifesto promised the people civil rights, national elections, and establishment of an elected State Duma. The legislation that actually created the electoral system and the Duma did not appear until 1906.

Tying together these events—the dismissal of the Constituent Assembly, the overthrow of the Provisional Government, the assassination attempt, and the manifesto, Olfer'ev asserts that October 17 "would be remembered as the day when the Russian state ceased to exist" [*stal pamiatnym dnem kontsa sushchestvovaniia Rossiiskago Gosudarstva*]. In his mind, the end of statehood was accompanied by Lenin's slogan, "All power to the Soviets," by the burning of landlords' homes, and by peasants dividing the land. The paragraph in his memoir about October 17 thus illustrates a myth-making process, linking a terroristic attack on the tsar, the de facto end of autocracy (the October Manifesto), and the end of the imperial state itself. Olfer'ev's reference to the "Russian state" is perhaps an unconscious allusion to the historian Nikolai Mikhailovich Karamzin's *History of the Russian State* [*Istoriia Gosudarstva Rossiiskago*], which many educated Russians from privileged backgrounds read growing up.

Olfer'ev maintains that the end came to Stavka on November 20/December 3, 1917, with the murder of General Nikolai Nikolaevich Dukhonin, the Supreme Commander in Chief of the Russian armed forces. According to Olfer'ev, Dukhonin's death and Stavka's effective dissolution constituted the "end of the First World War on the Russian front."

To follow Olfer'ev's logic, we must keep in mind Stavka's role from mid-1915 on. Starting in summer 1915, under Nicholas II, Stavka became a locus of political authority as well as Russia's strategic hub. In February–March of 1917, Stavka and the Duma leadership persuaded Nicholas to abdicate the throne, then from early March till late August/early September, Stavka competed with Petrograd for sovereign ascendancy in Russia. From early September to late October/early November, Kerenskii temporarily eclipsed Stavka's political influence by assuming the title of supreme commander in chief, but when the Provisional Government collapsed on October 25/November 7 and October 31/November 13, Stavka stepped in to rally supporters of the Provisional Government against the Bolsheviks. On November 1/14, when Kerenskii conferred the title of temporary commander on Dukhonin, he made Dukhonin and Stavka the de facto center of Russian sovereignty outside the Petrograd Soviet. Stavka also became the main potential locus of military resistance to the Bolshevik government.

As the army's new commander, Dukhonin found himself in an almost impossible political situation. On November 1/14, Kornilov wrote him from Bykhov: "You face a moment when people must stand firm or retreat, for otherwise they will bear responsibility for the country's disorder and shame for the army's final collapse. Based on the fragmentary information I have received, I think the situation critical but not yet irreversible. But it will become so, if Stavka is seized by the Bolsheviks or if you voluntarily recognize their authority." Kornilov then outlined a six-point program of armed resistance to the Bolsheviks, the substance of which required positioning forces presumed loyal to Stavka near Mogilev. Dukhonin expressed doubts about these units' loyalty. In response to Kornilov's call for concentration of arms and troops to defend Mogilev, Dukhonin wrote tersely: "That may give rise to excesses."[311]

Dukhonin followed Kornilov's advice in one respect. He refused to recognize the authority of the Soviet of People's Commissars.[312] Meanwhile, Dukhonin listened to entreaties by politicians from the moderate left and from Ukraine who sought Stavka's support. From November 4/17 to November 11/24, the right Socialist-Revolutionary Viktor Chernov and Mensheviks such as Fedor Il'ich Dan tried unsuccessfully to put together a non-Bolshevik but all-socialist cabinet under Stavka's protection. At the same time, on November 6/19, two delegates from the Central Rada in Ukraine, Dmytro Ivanovich Doroshenko and Oleksandr Gnatovich Lotots'kyi, tried to persuade Dukhonin to support the reorganization of the army, for Russia's sake but also Ukraine's. The declaration of the Ukrainian People's Republic on November 7/20 complicated Dukhonin's task, because his goal was to keep the Russian army intact, not to splinter it.[313]

Dukhonin's biggest challenge came on November 8/21 from the Bolshevik government, which ordered him to initiate preliminary ceasefire negotiations with the Germans. When he refused on the grounds that he was no diplomat, the Soviet government relieved him of his command, pending the arrival in Mogilev of Nikolai Vasil'evich Krylenko.

A greater contrast than that between Dukhonin and Krylenko can scarcely be imagined. Dukhonin came from the Smolensk nobility, and was educated in the Kiev Military Academy, the Aleksandr Military Academy, and the General Staff Academy. He fought bravely in the Great War and was awarded several decorations for meritorious service. He rose in the army to the rank of lieutenant general. In spite of his traditional pedigree, Dukhonin belonged to the new type of staff officer eager to assess the shifting political scene, to seek out allies but without initiating any novel political combinations. Kerenskii credited him with "understanding the necessity [of soldiers' committees and commissars]." He wrote: "Dukhonin was a broad-thinking, open and honest person, one far from political game-playing and machinations."[314]

Krylenko was born into an intelligentsia milieu: his father was a newspaper editor in Smolensk. He attended classical gymnasium in Lublin, then enrolled in Petersburg University, where he split his time between studying history and engaging in political protests. In 1904, he joined the Bolsheviks, in 1911 worked for the party newspaper *Zvezda*, in 1913 was arrested and exiled from Petersburg to Khar'kov. He did prison time from November 1915 to April 1916. Upon his release he was assigned to military duty as an ensign [*praporshchik*]. He was arrested again in July 1917, and he then faced treason charges before General Verkhovskii ordered his release in September. Whatever else might be said of Krylenko, he was neither a professional soldier nor an adept of military science. One of his biographers described his real profession as "revolution."[315]

On November 9/22, 1917, Lenin informed Russian soldiers of the new government's intention to negotiate a separate peace with the Germans. On November 13/26, Krylenko, accompanied by fifty-nine armed sailors, took a train to Dvinsk to begin those negotiations. Dukhonin decried the negotiations as "insanity," and in his own telegram to the troops, he pleaded "for time for true Russian democracy to form a government and an administration that will give us and our allies a swift peace."[316] By November 17/30, Dukhonin knew that the Soviet government had sent three squadrons of sailors—about three thousand men—toward Stavka. In a telegram to the commander of the Romanian front, Dmitrii Grigor'evich Shcherbachev, Dukhonin listed his options: "First, to fight; second, to move [Stavka's] operations quickly to another location—for example, to Kiev, if we can reach an agreement with the Central Rada. To the third option—bloodless surrender of Stavka—I shall not resort."[317]

Dukhonin's preference was to shift Stavka's operations to Kiev, but that option proved unworkable when local Bolsheviks from the Mogilev Soviet prevented the transfer of Stavka personnel in motorcars, and the Central Rada failed to issue authorization for the relocation. On November 19/ December 2, Dukhonin ordered Colonel Kusonskii to go to Bykhov to release Kornilov and other arrestees. Dukhonin told friends that when he authorized Kornilov's release, "I signed my death warrant."[318]

In Olfer'ev's account of Dukhonin's murder on November 20/ December 3, 1917 at the Mogilev train station, the general was accompanied by Major-General Sergei Ivanovich Odintsov, one of Dukhonin's classmates from the General Staff Academy. According to Olfer'ev, Odintsov's role was to help "take control of Stavka in the least painful way." In other words, Odintsov reassured Dukhonin only in order to betray him. Olfer'ev describes Odintsov as having "defected" to the Bolsheviks. In fact, although Odintsov had offered in mid-November to serve on a commission of military experts to negotiate with the Germans, and although he later fought with the Red Army against the Whites, he was likely more of an opportunist than an ideologue. In any case, Odintsov's role as intermediary between Dukhonin and Krylenko, albeit treacherous, was a formality: the local revolutionary committee had placed Dukhonin under house arrest the previous evening.[319]

Olfer'ev learned of Dukhonin's murder from Colonel Pavel Aleksandrovich Chebykin, who reported that the general's corpse was now "lying on the tracks, pierced all over by bayonets." Denikin, in his memoirs, gives this account: "A mob of sailors—savage, angry—tore at General Dukhonin as 'Supreme Commander' Krylenko looked on and [the mob] cruelly mutilated his corpse."[320] The murder of Dukhonin and the purge of Stavka constituted the liquidation of the Soviet government's main competitor for sovereignty in Russia. But the respite was temporary, because the subsequent civil war were a prolonged contest for authority involving dozens of political and social entities. Yet as Olfer'ev testifies, for Russia the murder was a marker of the end of the Great War. The road from the Mogilev station to Brest-Litovsk was short.

After Dukhonin's killing, Lieutenant General Nikolai Aleksandrovich Suleiman requested that Olfer'ev take up the role that General Diterikhs had played for Dukhonin. But Olfer'ev decided to leave Stavka. He told Suleiman he would not fight "for the animals and murderers" of the new regime. He felt "freed from his oath [of allegiance]."

This scene awkwardly closed Olfer'ev's professional military career. Like Dukhonin's death, Olfer'ev's decision to leave the General Staff constituted one of the many costs of the revolution that Russians were only beginning to pay.

XXVII

Olfer'ev broke irreconcilably with Soviet authorities over Dukhonin's murder. He had already fallen under suspicion for his ties to Grand Duke Aleksandr Mikhailovich and for his lack of revolutionary discipline. His remarks about the army's new masters, whom he described as "animals and murderers," could be neither forgotten nor forgiven. Nevertheless, abruptly leaving the army caused him shame. His precipitous abandonment of his wife and children after the murder, even if it was necessary to save himself, haunted him.

Strangely, however, Olfer'ev did not extend his condemnation of Russia's new rulers to the sailors who had actually shot Dukhonin and mangled his corpse. "It was clear," he writes, "they [the sailors] did not understand what they had done, and we [privileged Russians] were responsible for their ignorance. We kept them in the dark, exploited their parents in the factories and in the villages, and lived comfortably at their expense." Olfer'ev quotes St. Paul's *Letters to the Romans* 12:19—"Vengeance is mine; I will repay"—as a reminder to himself that he should not hold a grudge against the killers.

In a sense, Olfer'ev's attitude toward the common people is an honest reckoning with his guilt over the oppressive past of the ruling class, and thus constitutes an attempt to put in practice, under difficult conditions, Dostoevsky's notion of universal responsibility for sin. Yet we should also register in Olfer'ev a degree of condescension toward the brutal sailors who killed Dukhonin. Was it not evident that these young revolutionary servicemen knew exactly what they were doing, and precisely why?

Incidentally, General Denikin also sensed that murderous resentment against the masters had built up over the centuries among the common people. Unlike Olfer'ev, the general found this hatred simply terrifying: "Above all, boundless hatred flowed everywhere—toward [privileged] individuals as well as ideas, toward everything that was socially and intellectually above the crowd, that had attained the smallest trace of distinction, even in uncontroversial subjects—that had earmarks of a certain culture that was alien to, or inaccessible to, the crowd . . . The crowd's psychology manifested no attempt to rise to the level of higher forms of living: instead there was the overwhelming desire to seize or to destroy. [They wanted] not to advance themselves but to reduce to their own level anything or anyone that stood out. A general apologia for ignorance."[321]

Olfer'ev fled Stavka on a false internal passport identifying him as "Nikitin," a member of the Red Cross. He took a train from Mogilev to Kiev, and he intended later to travel to Novocherkassk to meet leaders of the nascent Volunteer Army. Because very prominent "Bykhov generals"—Kornilov, Sergei Leonidovich Markov, Aleksandr Sergeevich Lukomskii, Ivan Pavlovich Romanovskii—had stationed themselves in Novocherkassk, Bolshevik agents were searching southbound trains for officers in disguise. On his way to Kiev, Olfer'ev, now regarding himself as "persecuted" [*gonimyi*], tried to blend in with civilian travelers by wearing a short fur coat without army insignias. Aboard the train, he spotted General Diterikhs, who was similarly attired. Each refrained from speaking for fear he might give away the other's disguise. Olfer'ev's passage to Kiev was the beginning of his fugitive life.

Olfer'ev offers a complex account of his tenure in Kiev. He reports that sometime after his arrival, he left Kiev for Novocherkassk, where he disembarked on January 30/February 11, 1918 after a four-day train journey. Olfer'ev claims to remember this date because it was the day after Cossack Ataman Aleksei Maksimovich Kaledin committed suicide. Yet Olfer'ev also describes the Bolshevik siege and occupation of Kiev—beginning with the storming of the Kruty railroad station on January 15/28, through the Bolsheviks' entrance into Kiev on January 26/February 8, to their withdrawal from that city on February 16/March 1, 1918. If Olfer'ev had taken a train to Novocherkassk from January 26 to 30 /February 7 to 11 and had then spent some time in that city meeting with officers of the White Army, he could not simultaneously have remained in Kiev to witness the Bolshevik occupation. It is possible that he slipped out of the city shortly after the Bolsheviks occupied it. By doing so, he might have avoided being arrested or killed in Kiev, but would have risked being arrested by Bolshevik agents while traveling by rail. However, as we shall see, this scenario is inconsistent with other passages in the memoirs, which have him held at gunpoint in his own apartment immediately after the Bolsheviks entered Kiev, then moving with Marusia to a safer place in the city.

It is therefore likelier that soon after arriving in Kiev and relocating his wife and child there, he visited Novocherkassk for a short time before returning to Kiev. In this scenario, he would have seen General Alekseev and the other White generals sometime in late December 1917/early January 1918—that is, shortly *before* Kaledin's suicide and before the Bolsheviks' occupation of Kiev.

In any case, Olfer'ev's first impression of Kiev was positive. He saw it as still relatively prosperous, a city with a functioning commercial district, open restaurants and food shops. He saw no sign of the acute food shortages or of the brazen criminality that had beset Petrograd for the past months. After stepping off the train from Mogilev, he evidently took a room in the Continental Hotel, an elegant four-story hotel on Nikolaevskaia Street in the city center, just four blocks from the Dnepr River. He quickly moved to the nearby Lipky district, to an apartment house located across the street from the governor-general's palace. There he sublet an apartment from Dukhonin's widow—an arrangement that, in the short term, benefitted them both. Once settled in his sublet, Olfer'ev contacted his wife Marusia, and she managed to join him there.

As he surveyed Kiev more carefully, Olfer'ev learned that the city's economic and political situation was shakier than he had originally thought. He now estimated that the city's population had doubled since the 1897 census—from half a million to a million inhabitants. In fact, according to the census the city's population in 1897 was just under a quarter-million residents. The population might have reached 600,000 by 1914, but subsided by 1917 to under half a million people. In any case, when Olfer'ev surveyed the city in 1918, he realized the working-class quarters were overcrowded, and he notes: "[By 1918] there were not enough habitable dwellings, the supply of food was exhausted, and prices were going up at an incredible rate." Because he had by then exhausted most of his cash, he took a job as a stevedore, unloading barges at the river docks, in the section of the city called Podol [Ukrainian *Podil*]. He quickly lost the job when the foreman noticed that his hands were those of a gentleman, not of a manual laborer.

At the Continental Hotel, Olfer'ev met two unnamed colleagues from the General Staff, both of them now dressed in the uniform of the newly established Ukrainian army. One of them may have been Iakov Vasil'evich Safonov, who had served Grand Duke Nikolai Nikolaevich at Stavka. Safonov belonged to XXXIV Army Corps, a unit reorganized in late August/early September 1917 as I Ukrainian Army Corps. Another officer may have been Georgii Akimovich Mandryka, from the Russian VI Army Corps, which on November 29/December 11, 1917 was Ukrainized in the II Zaporozhian Sech' Corps. These officers tried to persuade Olfer'ev to join the Ukrainian army to fight the Bolsheviks. He refused to do so, on the grounds that "Ukraine is a German project"—that is, he regarded independent Ukraine as a polity artificially sustained by the Germans.

Olfer'ev observed that political authority in Ukraine had passed to the Central Rada and to the faction of "separatists" [*separatisty*]: Symon Vasyl'ovych Petliura, Mikhailo Serhiyovych Hrushevsky, and Volodymyr Kyrylovych Vynnychenko. According to Olfer'ev, the majority of Kiev's residents "had nothing in common with the Ukrainian movement, but they reacted calmly to it, even benevolently, seeing in it the possibility of avoiding threats from the North" [i.e. from the Bolsheviks]. If, *pace* Olfer'ev, Kievans saw their separatist government as a firewall against Bolshevik control, then they did support the movement at least tacitly.

Kievans' soft support for the separatist government did nothing to stop the Bolsheviks and their local sympathizers from trying to capture the city. The military clash was unavoidable, for two immediate reasons: the ongoing political disagreement between the Central Rada and the Petrograd government over control of Ukraine; and the Bolsheviks' concern that the "Ukrainized" army would not resist the Germans in the event that peace negotiations failed. To these immediate causes of the Bolshevik attack on Kiev we can add a third, deeper concern—namely, that the separatist Ukrainian government had turned a blind eye to the effort by former Russian army officers to organize a counter-revolutionary force in Novocherkassk. In any case, as the historian Jonathan D. Smele has noted, in December 1917/January 1918 the Kievan authorities were in a weak position to resist the Bolsheviks. The government's efforts to Ukrainize units of the old imperial army were "incomplete and a separate command structure had not yet emerged." Other elements of the government's defense plan—the establishment of a popular militia and support of "Free Cossack" formations—remained on the drawing board or were of marginal effectiveness.[322] Yet despite its relative weakness, the Central Rada managed to thwart a coup by Ukrainian Bolsheviks and Kievan workers on November 30/December 13—just ten days after Olfer'ev's arrival in Kiev.

From December 6/19, 1917, the Petrograd government considered itself in a state of war with the Central Rada. On December 12/25, delegates of the I All-Ukraine Congress of Soviets proclaimed a new government—the People's Republic of Soviets—as a rival to the Central Rada. On December 15/28, in reaction to the Soviet military and political threats, the Kiev government took steps to accelerate the formation of a Ukrainian army, but it reversed these steps in early January 1918 by the Law on Formation of a Ukrainian Popular Army, which sought to form a militia instead. Olfer'ev was incensed by the Ukrainian authorities' program to "register" army personnel for Kiev's defense, on pain of "immediate arrest and deportation from [Kiev]," and he refused to obey the order. His wife Marusia saw the measure as motivated by cynicism and desperation. She remarked: "Petliura doesn't have the army to fight the Bolsheviks."

Bolshevik forces approached Kiev from the north. They defeated Ukrainian units at the Kruty railroad station on January 15/28, 1918. A short time later, they began shelling the city of Kiev.[323] According to the jurist Aleksei Aleksandrovich Gol'denveizer, the bombardment of Kiev from the river's left bank near Darnitsa lasted over ten days. It killed relatively few people but caused "appalling destruction." For example, a six-story home on Bibikovs'kyi Boulevard caught fire and burned; the city's waterworks ceased to operate, and the fire department failed to extinguish this blaze and others.[324] Inside the city, Gol'denveizer testified, "chaos and disorder [*khaos i sumiatitsa*] reigned. The 'Free Cossacks' defending the city licensed various excesses; in the courtyard of our home they shot everyone they deemed somehow suspicious."[325]

According to Gol'denveizer, after the Bolsheviks entered Kiev on January 26, there followed "days full of terror and blood. The Bolsheviks systematically killed anyone linked in any way with the Ukrainian army, especially officers." Anyone with an army registration card faced "inevitable death." "Soldiers and sailors with machine guns conducted house searches, and they led away [Ukrainian] soldiers. In the courtyard opposite military headquarters, they held a brief trial, and there in the royal gardens, exacted revenge. Thousands of young officers died in those days." The head of the Bolshevik military force in Kiev, Mikhail Artem'evich Murav'ev, proclaimed that the Bolsheviks "had brought the idea of socialism at bayonet point."[326]

Olfer'ev's account of the January days is consistent with Gol'denveizer's. He reports eleven days of artillery bombardment, shattered windows, walls pock-marked by shell fragments and bullets, and a lack of water for drinking and sanitation. When the Bolsheviks took control of the city on January 26/February 8, they searched the Olfer'evs' apartment and put a gun to his head. They knocked down Marusia when she tried to interpose herself. They looted the apartment house. On their way out of the building, they shot a young ensign in the face. Another search group shot a young cadet in the back of the skull. The Olfer'evs survived only because of their false identity papers and because relatives of General Dukhonin moved them to a safer apartment, near the corner of Proreznaia and Vladimirskaia Streets, just two blocks from the Holy Wisdom Cathedral in the city center. The Olfer'evs lived there "more than a week" with a family of Poles.

Olfer'ev remembers "the extermination of the bourgeoisie" continuing, with victims now including "anyone from whom they [the street mob] could remove a good pair of boots or warm coat." Across the street from the Olfer'evs' new place was a small police station, which became the temporary headquarters of the Cheka. Olfer'ev was compelled to present his (false) papers to them. The Cheka and Bolshevik occupiers fled the city when the German army entered it. The Bolshevik administration—the People's Secretariat—left the city on February 14–15/27–28, 1918. Bolshevik military forces withdrew from Kiev on February 16/March 1, 1918.[327]

XXVIII

As noted above, Olfer'ev's departure from Kiev to Novocherkassk probably occurred sometime in late December 1917/early January 1918—not on January 26/February 8, 1918, as he recalls in his memoirs. En route to Novocherkassk, he evaded Bolshevik sailors only by disembarking his train at Sinel'nikov station in Dnepropetrovsk region, and again at Lozovaia Station in Khar'kov province. His trip took four days.

Olfer'ev found Novocherkassk full of political intrigue. The White camp was divided into two groups: one organized around General Alekseev, the second around Kornilov and the Bykhov generals. Alekseev was the senior figure in terms of service rank and also the best connected of the generals in the political world. One of Olfer'ev's contacts described Alekseev as "a government unto himself" [*Alekseev—eto vrode pravitel'stvo*]. Alekseev's coterie consisted of politicians—the Octobrists Rodzianko and Guchkov—and of the journalist Boris Alekseevich Suvorin. Alekseev relied on Rodzianko and Guchkov to advise him about political circumstances, and yet, according to Olfer'ev, Alekseev tried to keep the Volunteer Army from adopting a clear domestic political program. At this stage, the watchwords of the movement were loyalty to the Allies, reestablishment of the front, and avoidance of internal politics [*polnoe otmezhevanie ot vsiakoi vnutrennei politiki*]. At the same time, Alekseev invited Suvorin to print a newspaper in Novocherkassk.[328] Alekseev had raised money to support the newspaper and to subsidize the living costs of the officers involved in the White cause. According to Olfer'ev's friend Colonel Vasilii Sergeevich Gershel'man, the disposition of Alekseev's war chest was "the basis for all the discord among the generals."

The Bykhov generals had a number of reasons to distrust Alekseev. Kornilov and Alekseev did not get along, according to Gershel'man. The distance between the two generals was partly rooted in the denouement of the Kornilov affair in September 1917, when Alekseev, acting on behalf of the Provisional Government, had arrested Kornilov. There was also tension between them as a result of Kornilov's demand on December 18/31, 1917 that he, not Alekseev, exercise "full authority over the Volunteer Army."[329] Their positions as members with Kaledin of the "triumvirate" overseeing the

Don region made them allies but also competitors, and this also likely deepened their mutual distrust. Denikin also felt that the biggest problem facing the White movement at the turn of the year 1917/1918 was the disposition of the treasury that Alekseev controlled: Alekseev had raised 800,000 rubles in Moscow, and Rostov merchants had contributed another six million rubles to the Volunteers—a substantial amount, but not nearly enough to finance the Whites' activities.

For whatever reason, Alekseev remained detached from the other generals and wary of strangers. Olfer'ev met him at vespers in the Novocherkassk Cathedral, the seven-cupolaed Cathedral of Ascension [*Voznesenskii Sobor*] on Ermak Square, one of the tallest and most magnificent church buildings in Russia. The two men walked from there to Alekseev's modest flat, a small apartment illuminated by a single kerosene lamp in the hallway and by candles in the living room. Olfer'ev took away the impression that Alekseev had little hope for victory in the civil war, principally because territories on Russia's periphery, such as the Don region, desired self-determination, not a united Russian state. Sometime later, Olfer'ev reported to General Diterikhs his conversation with Alekseev. Diterikhs noted that Alekseev's inner circle included Rodzianko, and therefore concluded that Alekseev wanted to restore the monarchy.

For his part, Olfer'ev had three major reservations about the White cause. The first was that, while he admired the leaders of the White forces personally, the movement lacked political objectives—that is, it was "without definite plans for the future." He could not see how the White movement could compete with the Bolsheviks and sustain itself without an ideology that could appeal to the masses. Second, the distrust among the White generals suggested that, whatever the nobility of their cause, the leaders harbored selfish motives: they had "mean hearts, capable of blackening their sacrificial path" [*zlye serdtsa sposobnye omrachits' ikh krestnyi put'*]. Third, judging by the opposition to the Volunteer Army's officers on the part of many Don Cossacks and non-Cossacks, Olfer'ev saw significant, if not insuperable, obstacles to White victory. He therefore regarded participation in the civil war as virtually suicidal.

XXIX

On February 5/18, 1918, pursuant to an appeal for assistance from remnants of the Central Rada, German military forces began to advance into Ukraine. They moved quickly toward Kiev via armored trains, arriving there on February 16/March 1, 1918. The German authorities ordered their troops not to requisition grain in the countryside, and to treat the Ukrainian population in friendly fashion, but meanwhile to enforce the Brest-Litovsk agreement with the Rada. That agreement required Ukraine to supply the Germans with foodstuffs—one hundred thousand carloads of grain by the end of June.[330] To accomplish these objectives, the German army supported the Rada against the Bolsheviks. One of the key figures in the German occupation of Kiev, General Wilhelm Gröner, understood his task as follows: "To put the Ukrainian government back in power, to support it with German arms, and to extract from it grain and other foodstuffs—the more the better."[331] Even though the German authorities in Kiev committed themselves to supporting the Rada, they did not much respect it. One of Gröner's aides called the Ukrainian government an *Operettestaat*—a "comic opera government."[332]

A fault line developed in relations between the Rada and the German authorities because of the Germans' desire to ensure the provision of grain through the expansion of cultivated land in Ukraine, and because of their plan to restore land confiscated during the Ukrainian revolution to the nobility. The Rada, dominated by Socialist-Revolutionaries, resisted the German program for two reasons: it undercut the Rada's authority, and it sowed counter-revolution in Ukraine. As the historian Oleh Fedyshyn has observed, the Rada's policy was "nationalization of large estates for the benefit of the peasants." When the Rada refused to yield to German demands for grain, German troops tried to collect it by force. When Ukrainian peasants refused to meet supply quotas, or when they murdered German field agents, German soldiers arrested or killed them in retaliation.[333] Something like partisan warfare soon developed in the countryside.

By April 5/18, 1918, the German ambassador in Kiev, Baron Philip Alfons Mumm, had decided the Rada was an unreliable partner and would have to be replaced. Later that month, on April 15/28, the Germans reached an agreement with Pavlo Petrovych Skoropads'kyi to establish a new regime, in which Skoropads'kyi would act as ataman or hetman.[334] In any case, on April 16/29, 1918, Skoropads'kyi and his allies seized power "to save the country from chaos and lawlessness."[335]

Although Hetman Skoropads'kyi fancied himself a dictator, and although the German authorities did their best to support him, he was unable to restore social stability in Ukraine. Peasants continued to resist German efforts to collect grain. Socialist politicians expressed unhappiness with the hetman and his policies. On July 17/30, 1918, the Russian Socialist-Revolutionary Boris Mikhailovich Donskoi assassinated Field Marshal Hermann von Eichhorn in Kiev. While the Germans did not blame the hetman for this act, it also did nothing to settle nerves. Eichhorn's killing provoked anti-Ukrainian articles in the foreign press.[336] On August 21/September 4, 1918, Skoropads'kyi visited Berlin, where he met Kaiser Wilhelm II and officials responsible for German occupation policy, but this visit did not positively affect the situation in Kiev.[337] The economic agreement between the hetman's government and the German and Austrian governments, an agreement concluded on August 28/September 10, 1918, required that Ukraine export over a third of its grain to the Central Powers.[338] This compact forbade the occupation authorities from requisitioning grain using their armies, but it made Skoropads'kyi's officials do so in the Germans' and Austrians' stead—not a recipe for the hetman's long-term domestic popularity.

The Germans' ambiguous attitude toward the hetmanate—their formal support and simultaneous suspicion of the hetman's pro-Russian tendencies—contributed to Skoropads'kyi's decision on November 1/14 to proclaim Ukraine's union with Russia. But this proclamation, designed to shore up the hetman's domestic popularity, only encouraged his critics to rise against him. A month after the proclamation, on December 1/14, 1918, Petliura drove the hetman out of Kiev.

Throughout the period from April to December 1918, the Volunteer Army organized itself. Even though the army attracted officers who wanted to save Russia from both the Bolsheviks and the Germans, many officers saw fighting the Germans as pointless. They realized that embarking on such a campaign would eventually necessitate scrapping the Treaty of Brest-Litovsk and opening an unpopular guerrilla war against the Germans.[339] Meanwhile, as Fedyshyn has noted, Kiev became "a mecca for all the Russian rightists," and "as much a center of Russian political life as it was a Ukrainian center."[340] The German attitude toward the Russian monarchists in Kiev was double-edged: the occupation authorities preferred a Ukraine attached to Russia to a completely independent Ukrainian state; on the other hand, the Germans could not permit Russian nationalists like Count Aleksei Aleksandrovich Bobrinskii and General Fedor Arturovich Keller openly to recruit a pro-monarchist Russian army, at least not without an understanding that Russian forces would not turn against Germany.[341]

Olfer'ev's account of the occupation emphasizes the German authorities' support for merchants and for landowners belonging to the Agrarian League—the so-called "Grain Growers" [Russian *khleborobortsy*; Ukrainian *kliborobortsy*]. This re-inversion of the social pyramid revitalized the landowning classes, at least for a time, but at the cost of their dependence on a foreign power. Olfer'ev notes that displaced Russians from Petrograd vied with one another at officers' receptions to curry the favor of the German General Werner von Alvensleben—a sure sign of that dependency. Meanwhile, Olfer'ev saw the Ukrainian hetman Skoropads'kyi as an opportunist, as a man "whose sense of duty was first to himself and only then to the Motherland [Russia]."

Olfer'ev estimated that "tens of thousands" of former army officers had been exiled by the Russian revolution to Ukraine. He reports an emotional debate at his apartment among some of these officers. They articulated three different opinions: some resolved to join the Red Army, others wanted to join the Ukrainian separatists, and still others expressed a commitment to remain apart from both these groups. Olfer'ev perceived an absence of genuine Russian patriotism in those who felt allegiance toward the Red Army. He associated Ukrainian separatists with misguided military professionalism—that is, with aversion to civilian life and an overwhelming desire to be in uniform. Olfer'ev saw himself in the third group—that is, he was a "despised outsider" who felt that the Russian old regime could not be restored, and who lacked faith in an independent Ukraine.

Like Olfer'ev, several thousand Russians remained neutral toward both the Red and Ukrainian armies—a posture that did not endear them to some Kievans. Olfer'ev reports that the family's Ukrainian landlord attempted to raise the rent on their apartment in a scheme to evict them for nonpayment. The Olfer'evs won a reprieve only by appealing their rent in court. Still, they found it hard to make a living in hostile Kiev. Olfer'ev worked for a month at a restaurant in Ekaterinoslav, as the host of a backroom gambling parlor. He regarded the job as demeaning, but learned from his business partner the adage that "the whole world is nothing but a brothel, and all people are prostitutes." This perspective was one that Olfer'ev could not easily accept, given his position as the son of a privileged Russian landowner, as a believing Christian, and as a former military professional. Yet the adage struck him as worth remembering in a revolutionary age, when circumstances had pressed so many individuals to abandon their moral compunctions.

Olfer'ev's memoirs do not say when he worked in Ekaterinoslav, but he provides two temporal clues: first, the circulation of rumors that the Western allies might defeat the Germans; and second, the arrival of news of "the demise of the [Russian] emperor and his family." Doubts concerning the Germans' ultimate victory in the Great War may have surfaced after the collapse of the German army's offensive at the Marne in mid-July 1918. The launching of the Allied offensive in early August triggered rumors that Germany would be defeated. These two military events roughly coincided with the execution of Nicholas II and his family at Ekaterinburg on July 3-4/16-17, 1918. If these developments occurred during Olfer'ev's absence from Kiev, he must have been in Ekaterinoslav in early summer 1918—perhaps from late June to late July.

On returning to Kiev, Olfer'ev saw churches filled with worshippers who were shedding tears of shame "for the innocent family [the Romanovs] who suffered for our sins." For his own part, Olfer'ev suspected that the royal family could not have been rescued. He lamented the fact that "in the tsar's name we had maintained a long-dead system of government that exploited 150 million people."

One of the most interesting sections in Olfer'ev's memoirs concerns the defense of Kiev against Petliura's attack on the hetman's government—a defense orchestrated by the "Kirpichev retinue" [*Kirpichevskaia druzhina*] of volunteers. Members of the so-called "Directory," consisting of Petliura, Vynnychenko, and other socialists, were the supposed leaders of the attack. Yet Olfer'ev regards Petliura as only the "nominal leader" of the revolutionary movement: in his opinion, the real energy behind it came from the Bolsheviks. Olfer'ev insists that the Ukrainian revolution "was founded not on nationality, but exclusively on economics." In other words, he considered its driver to be peasant hatred of rural landowners and worker hatred of factory owners and the "bourgeoisie." Thus, from Olfer'ev's vantage point, Petliura was one of the Ukrainian faces of a countrywide communist uprising.

Olfer'ev could not recall whether Kirpichev was a "guards Artillery General or perhaps a colonel." His lack of clarity suggests he did not know Kirpichev well. In fact, Lev Nilovich Kirpichev had graduated from the Konstantinovskoe Artillery School in 1899, had served in the imperial army for nearly two decades, and had been promoted to the rank of major-general in August 1917. The Kirpichev retinue, which the general formed in fall 1918, was supposed to consist of several hundred men divided into ten detachments [*otdely*]: five infantry groups, a cavalry squadron, an engineering squadron, and three reserve detachments. Apparently, the three reserve detachments were never populated with actual troops.[342] Olfer'ev belonged to the fifth detachment, which was commanded by Aleksandr Petrovich Grevs, a graduate of the Nikolaevskii officer school in Petersburg and a veteran of the Life Guards Cavaliers Grenadiers Regiment. It is unclear how many soldiers served in the fifth detachment, but the historian Aleksandr Sergeevich Puchenkov has estimated its size as roughly two hundred men.[343]

Not much is known about the operations of the Kirpichev retinue or about its links to the wider Volunteer Army movement. Olfer'ev recalls that Kirpichev "was subordinate to Count [Fedor Arturovich] Keller, and that Keller took the opportunity to use the hetman's headquarters to direct us. All the orders came from these headquarters." Here Olfer'ev implies that the retinue was linked both to the pro-monarchist Russian forces and to Hetman Skoropads'kyi. Historian A. S. Puchenkov has observed that two prominent Russian politicians then in Kiev regarded the Volunteer Army as the "center" around which the future "All-Russian government" was forming.[344] Moreover, General Denikin recalls granting permission to "Kievan formations" to bear the flag of the Volunteer Army.[345] Indeed as Olfer'ev notes, each member of Count Keller's volunteers "wore a tri-color ribbon in his lapel buttonhole and the national flag on his sleeve." (The tri-color ribbon took its colors from the Russian national flag, adopted in 1696: the flag had three horizontal stripes—white over blue and red. The Volunteer Army kept these colors. Meanwhile, the Council of Peoples Commissars replaced the old banner with a red flag in spring 1918.) Thus, the Kirpichev retinue had connections with pro-monarchist military forces (through Bobrinskii and Keller), with Russian non-Bolshevik politicians then in Kiev (Sazonov and Miliukov), and with the wider White movement (through Denikin). The retinue also identified with the Russian imperial cause (via the tricolor). Yet its chief goal, according to Olfer'ev, was "to save our hides."

In late November 1918, Olfer'ev acted as Grevs's deputy in the retinue's fifth detachment. The group was sent to the village Krasnyi Kabachok on November 30/December 13 to defend it against an attack by the Directory's forces. According to Olfer'ev, the fifth detachment set up with its left flank guarded by the Dnepr River and its right flank guarded by a detachment of Grain Growers. There was intermittent firing by the Directory's forces in the evening, then friendly fire from machine guns. Late that same night, he received the news that Petliura's forces had entered Kiev. At daybreak, the fifth detachment retreated north into Kiev along Vasil'kovskii Prospekt—through the workers' district, where it "was bombarded with abuse from all sides." At Bessarabka, the detachment took cover from machine gun fire and received an escort from German army units still in the city.

Olfer'ev's detachment survived because a group of German soldiers then escorted it to the "German barracks"—probably the officers' quarters at the junction of Bol'shaia Street and Trekhsviatitel'skaia Street, not far from the Andreevskii Theological Academy and from the Mikhailovskii Monastery. If the detachment had been taken to the Tsarevich Museum [*Muzei tsesarevicha*] (also called the Pedagogical Museum) on Vladimirskaia Street, Olfer'ev would likely have been murdered along with more than a hundred other officers of the Kirpichev retinue being held there.

Olfer'ev mentions that at Krasnyi Kabachok, peasants killed eight officers. He also notes the murder in Kiev of Keller and of Keller's aide, Colonel Andrei Andreevich Panteleev, while they were being escorted from the Mikhailovskii Monastery to Luk'ianovskii Prison. These murders at the hands of Petliura's troops occurred near the monument to Bohdan Khmel'nits'kyi on Wisdom Square, on December 8/21, 1918. Other memoirists have also reported serial killings of officers without benefit of trial. Mariia Antonovna Nesterovich-Berg, a sister of mercy whose personal vocation was looking after Russia's invalided veterans, especially officers, noted street placards bearing the photographs of thirty-three tortured officers: "I had seen a whole group of officers shot to death by the Bolsheviks, their bodies stacked like kindling in the mortuary of one of Moscow's hospitals, but those were victims of gunfire. Here [in Kiev] I witnessed something else. The nightmare of these Kievan corpses is impossible to describe. It was apparent that, before killing them, the perpetrators horribly and cruelly tormented the victims. Eyes plucked out; cut-off ears and noses; severed tongues; gaping wounds to the chest in place of St. George's crosses; exposed intestines; strangulation marks on necks; stomachs packed with dried leaves. Whoever was in Kiev then remembers the burial of these victims of Petliura's army."[346] Other accounts mention the killing of wounded officers in hospitals, mass burials of corpses without funeral rites, the intimidation and the deliberate starvation of the remaining officers held at the Tsarevich Museum.[347] Some officers at the museum survived, but only because of the intervention of German troops and because of the Allies' diplomatic pressure on Petliura.[348]

XXX

In the first weeks of the Directory, the new authorities promoted Ukrainian nationalism by insisting that merchants display signs written in Ukrainian rather than Russian, and by conducting frequent inspections of apartment houses to identify "suspicious" ethnic Russians like Olfer'ev with links to the Kirpichev retinue. Gol'denveizer found the new government's Ukrainian language campaign "perplexing," because Petliura had seized control of what to Gol'denveizer seemed to be "a completely Russian city." The police's and militia's searches for suspicious Russians were accompanied by seizures of valuables from private safes. Thus the national agenda to make ethnic Russians uncomfortable was linked to a war on private property—that is, to what Gol'denveizer calls the Directory's "leftist competition with the Bolsheviks" [*sorevnovanie s bol'shevikami v levizne*].[349] The Directory's sponsorship of the Workers' Congress [*Trudovoi Kongress*] in January 1919—a meeting at which every effort was made to reduce the representation of professionals and intellectuals—was also an indication of the regime's leftism.

Meanwhile, the police turned a blind eye to open street criminality (petty thefts, assaults) and armed burglary. Gol'denveizer characterizes the Directory's tenure as "an age of hooliganism [*epokha khuliganstva*] *par excellence*."[350] The regime's strident Ukrainian nationalism, leftism and toleration of crime contributed to a climate of violence in which anti-Jewish pogroms became more likely.[351] Most of the period's pogroms occurred outside Kiev, as Lidiia Miliakova and Nicolas Werth have shown in their study of anti-Jewish violence.[352] However, in January 1919, Kiev's Central Jewish Committee issued a proclamation offering "material, economic and spiritual assistance" to victims of pogroms in Kiev itself.[353]

According to Gol'denveizer, the inhospitable Directory and the violence it fostered drove exiled Russians—"all Moscow" and "all Petrograd"—to flee Kiev. "Pessimists" joined departing German soldiers in transit through Poland to Berlin. "Optimists" sought safe haven in Odessa. Russians ransomed their valuables and paid large bribes to obtain travel documents to escape from Kiev.[354] Nesterovich-Berg also observed that the violence of Petliura's men caused "panic and flight from Kiev."[355] She herself received a warning to "flee Kiev at once." She took a train to Odessa and remembered traveling "with many officers in civilian disguise."[356]

After his narrow escape from death on December 1/14, Olfer'ev returned briefly to his apartment in Lypki, then "went underground" with his wife and children. Marusia obtained false passports for the family with the help of Lieutenant colonel Mikhail Iakovlevich Krasovskii[357] (Olfer'ev's old classmate from the General Staff Academy), the Swiss consul in Kiev, and a German general, Alvensleben. To board a train to the south, the Olfer'evs paid a thousand rubles, ostensibly to assist Czechoslovak prisoners being transported from Kiev to Odessa. Olfer'ev remembers his train being crowded not by foreigners escaping Kiev, but by "Russian high-rollers" who had consorted with the Germans during the hetmanate [*tem russkim khailaifom, kotoryi druzhil s nemtsami vo vremia getmana*].

Olfer'ev does not mention when he left Kiev, but his narrative suggests that he lingered only a few days after the installation of the Petliura government. Thus, he must have departed Kiev within the month—between December 2/15 and 8/23, 1918.

Once in Odessa, Olfer'ev saw Colonel Nikolai Zakhar'evich Neimirok, who had previously been active in the White underground in Kiev, and General Aleksei Nikolaevich Grishin-Almazov, then Odessa's military governor.[358] Grishin-Almazov asked Olfer'ev to translate for the General Philippe Henri-Joseph d'Anselme, commander of French operations in Western Ukraine. Olfer'ev found d'Anselme to be poorly informed about the developing crisis in Odessa, peremptory in dealing with Grishin-Almazov, and lacking the independence to make decisions. According to the historian J. Kim Munholland, d'Anselme found the Russian volunteers unimpressive and too identified with the Russian old regime.[359]

Grishin-Almazov and Neimirok asked Olfer'ev to go to Ekaterinodar to report to Denikin on his exchange with d'Anselme. Thus, Olfer'ev became one of many couriers who carried information between the Odessa volunteers and Denikin's headquarters.[360] Olfer'ev's steamship *Ksenia* stopped in Novorossiisk, and his report of a serious typhus outbreak in that city enables us to fix his time there as some point in late December 1918 or early January 1919. The Novorossiisk city council initiated countermeasures against typhus starting on December 13/31, and by late December/early January the city was under quarantine, with all hospital beds and barracks requisitioned for patient treatment.[361] Later, at Ekaterinodar, Olfer'ev passed his message not to Denikin (who was out of the city) but to General Lukomskii, then serving as Denikin's assistant. In Ekaterinodar, Olfer'ev dined with his aunts and cousins, who at that juncture were refugees from their central Russian estates. The rightist politician Vasilii Vital'evich Shul'gin, a family friend who happened to be in Ekaterinodar, joined the dinner party.

From early December 1918 to mid-March 1919, Shul'gin played a pivotal role in the politics of the White movement. On December 8/21, 1918, he lobbied Denikin to confirm General Grishin-Almazov as military governor of Odessa.[362] Soon he took a position as Denikin's liaison in Odessa and as a political advisor to Grishin-Almazov. Shul'gin's two-room suite in Odessa's London Hotel became the site of a political salon for Russians from the north, and also for "counter-intelligence" against Odessa's Bolsheviks.[363] In January and February 1919, Shul'gin published a newspaper, *Rossiia.* He served as its editor and was the author of articles arguing for the Russian nationalist cause and against any compromise with Ukrainian separatists.[364] In Olfer'ev's memoirs, the content of his Ekaterinodar conversation with Shul'gin is unclear. But Olfer'ev's assessment—"I remembered the old days and was sad to realize that what awaited them [his relatives] in the future would bring disappointment"—suggests that he was less sanguine than Shul'gin was about prospects for the White movement.

On his journey, Olfer'ev visited Piatigorsk, a fourteenth-century settlement that by the mid-nineteenth century had become a health spa and resort town of some nine thousand people. The community had grown rapidly over the last decades of the old regime, achieving a population of over thirty thousand before the Great War.[365] In October 1918, roughly two months before Olfer'ev's arrival, citizens of Piatigorsk had witnessed an atrocity. According to the account given to Olfer'ev by Princess Tumanova, "her husband had just been savagely murdered by the Reds along with General Ruzskii, Bagration-Mukhranskii, and ten others. The Bolsheviks made all of them kneel and chopped off their heads with a sword."

Evidence of this atrocity was assembled by the Special Commission for Investigation of Bolshevik Atrocities [*Osobaia komissiia po rassledovaniiu zlodeianii bol'shevikov*], a group operating under Denikin's charter. According to their findings, between late August and early October 1918, the Bolsheviks arrested 160 people—military officers, wealthy Russians, and Cossacks—and held them as hostages, in the Hotel Novoevropeiskaia, in a private home on Ermolovskii Prospekt, and in the Piatigorsk prison. On October 21/November 3, 1918, the Piatigorsk Cheka announced the execution of fifty-nine hostages in "retaliation for the killing of [our] good comrades, of members of the Central Executive Committee [of the Soviets], and others." On October 31/November 13, the Cheka announced the execution of forty-seven others.[366] Included in the first list of executed hostages were twenty-two generals (among them Prince Georgii Aleksandrovich Tumanov, Princess Tumanova's husband), thirteen colonels, a lieutenant colonel, one admiral, one senator, a former minister of justice, five princes, a baron, and a count.

According to the Cheka, the hostages were executed by shooting, but the investigation suggested another mode of execution. The prisoners were taken to the Cheka's headquarters. They were stripped of their clothing except for underwear, their arms were bound behind their backs, and they were escorted to the city cemetery. From the cemetery gates, groups were taken to already prepared graves. The prisoners were forced to undress, and then the executioners struck them with sabers [*shashki*]. The sabers did not kill all the prisoners immediately: for example, General Ruzskii required five blows.[367] One of the executioners described his method as severing arms and legs, then beating the prisoner's torso with a whip, then cutting off the head.[368]

Olfer'ev's reception of Princess Tumanova's story about the Piatigorsk executions tells us something about the moral climate of Russia's civil war. The execution narrative itself identifies the event as an atrocity—a "savage," "bestial" murder [*byl zverski ubit krasnymi muzh vmeste s generalom Ruzskim, Bagration-Mukhranskim i desiat'iu drugimi*]. However, the number of victims was understated rather than exaggerated. It was as if Princess Tumanova could not fathom the scope of the killings. Olfer'ev heard the report "with outrage" or "indignation" or "revulsion" [*ia podelilsia svoim vozmushcheniem*]—that is, he registered both strong emotion and moral abhorrence. This was because he knew General Ruzskii personally, and because he realized that many of the victims came from professional military backgrounds and/or from Russia's elite classes. But Olfer'ev was also offended because the code of Russian soldiers did not permit mass slaughter of defenseless people, especially "hostages," even if that code allowed for field executions of "rebels." In relating the story to an officer friend, Olfer'ev learned that the White Army had conducted similar executions. The friend cited the execution of a young Kuban Cossack by General Vladimir Pavlovich Nikol'skii, the future chief of the military administration of Southern Russia. Olfer'ev probably mentions the White atrocities because he was opposed to brutal executions by any of the belligerents in the civil conflict. In his opinion, such phenomena issued from Russia's moral corruption, for which he blamed the Empire's social elites.

On returning to Odessa, Olfer'ev worked as a translator for General Henry Freydenberg, chief of staff to General d'Anselme. Olfer'ev points out that he worked gratis for Freydenberg, but he says nothing about the business he helped Freydenberg transact. We know that by February 1919, the French authorities, including Freydenberg, were pessimistic about the chances for success of their intervention. They complained about the hostility of the local population toward them, and also about "intense Bolshevik propaganda" directed at them.[369] By early March 1919, French troops had surrendered Kherson and Nikolaev to Hetman Nikifor Aleksandrovich Grigor'ev, who was then an ally of the Bolsheviks[370] but also an ally of the Left Ukrainian Socialist Revolutionaries, the so-called *bor'bysty* [Russian *bor'bisty*]. Grigor'ev's advance toward Odessa flooded the city with refugees, making its defense ever more difficult. French authorities in Odessa believed that Grigor'ev's forces were well-disciplined and numerically superior, and they feared a popular uprising inside the city from Grigor'ev's sympathizers.[371] The French appealed to their government in Paris for reinforcements, but when the request was denied, decided they could not sustain the occupation. On March 20, 1919, General Louis Franchet d'Espèrey recommended that the French troops evacuate Odessa and end their intervention.[372] On March 29, President Clemenceau authorized troop withdrawal from Odessa.[373]

The civil war historian Peter Kenez has suggested that the French withdrawal from Odessa was the result of bad planning (the French did not bring to Russia a force sufficient to occupy Odessa and Southern Ukraine), of ineffective fighting at Kherson in mid-March, of Bolshevik propaganda inside Odessa, and of confusion and panic in the city. In Kenez's opinion, "primary responsibility for the Odessa debacle belongs to the French. They embarked on an ambitious scheme without clear goals, without an understanding of the consequences, and with insufficient forces. Their combination of ignorance, arrogance and cowardice made their policies extremely unattractive."[374]

Although the French authorities in Odessa knew by March 20, 1919, that they would have to withdraw forces from the city, they did not immediately inform their Greek allies or the Volunteer Army of their intentions. Because they kept their plan of evacuation secret until the last minute, its implementation on April 1 sowed further panic in the already panicky city. General Espèrey ordered the evacuation completed in seventy-two hours—that is, by late on April 4. In fact, the last ship did not depart Odessa until the evening of April 6.

Although Olfer'ev had worked with General Freydenberg, the latter apparently did not inform him of the planned evacuation. According to the memoirs, Olfer'ev deduced that the Allies "would give up the city" from evidence of the movements of Romanian and Greek troops and from the Bolsheviks' appearance at a railroad bridge near the city embankment. He therefore only learned of the evacuation at the last possible moment. Freydenberg initially refused to give him and his family safe passage out of Odessa; however, Freydenberg later relented and supplied the Olfer'evs with a visa to Constanza, Romania—the destination of the Romanian troops being transported from the city. The Romanians began to evacuate on April 4. Most of their units left by train, but the rear guard departed on ships.

According to Olfer'ev, he and Marusia had to plead with the French duty officer at the port and with ship officials to gain access to the steamship *Corcovado*. This was the SS *Corcovado*, built as a passenger vessel for the Hamburg-America Line in 1907. It sailed under Turkish flag as the *Sueh* in 1915, and by 1918 had become part of the German Black Sea Fleet. The French authorities commandeered the vessel in 1919.

The ship left port late on April 6—that is, Easter Saturday. It then embarked from Odessa's outer harbor the next morning, Easter Sunday. Olfer'ev marked the occasion by reflecting that Western governments would never again intervene militarily against Bolshevik rule. He thought any anti-Bolshevik army recruited from the lower classes could not succeed, because "the officers, as in previous times, were the only ones who wanted to fight. And no matter how brave and selfless they were, the outcome of this struggle was a foregone conclusion."

XXXI

The Olfer'evs traveled first to Europe, then to Japan, and finally, in 1920, to San Francisco. As Tanya Cameron notes in her epilogue, the Olfer'evs anglicized their names: Fedor Sergeevich Olfer'ev became "Theodore Sergeyevich Olferieff," his wife Marusia became "Mary Olferieff." They both found jobs in the Bay Area. He worked with an oil company, then as a ranch hand, then as mapmaker for the US Coast and Geodetic Survey, and last as a real estate agent. She taught French at the Dominican College in San Rafael—one of the oldest universities in California (founded 1890) and first Catholic college in California to grant degrees to women. In 1938, Mary earned her master's degree in Romance Languages with a thesis on Chrétien de Troyes.[375] Her interpretation of Chrétien highlighted his "feminism"—a notion also explored by one of Mary's contemporaries in the United States,[376] and by succeeding scholars.[377] It is possible that Mary Olferieff's research was inspired by the work of Myrrha Lot-Borodine (*née* Miropiia Borodina), a Russian expatriate who, starting in 1909, published a series of books and articles on Chrétien, on Arthurian legends, and on the role of women in courtly literature.[378]

The Olferieffs provide an excellent example of an émigré family adapting to American conditions. They changed their names, so their peers in California could pronounce and spell them; they took jobs suitable to their skills, adapting themselves to the local labor market; meanwhile, they maintained links to Russia by living in the Russian community in northern California.[379] As noted elsewhere in this essay, Olferieff followed Russian military developments in the Pacific region and lectured at Stanford's Hoover Institution on the subject. Olferieff's interest in the assimilation of émigrés into American life was also a link to Russians abroad.

Yet at the heart of the Olferieffs' American experience were wounds that would never entirely heal: memories of a life broken in Russia. They meditated on the haunting question: "What went wrong?" For more than fifteen years after World War II, Fyodor Sergeyevich explored his memories of the "old world" in an attempt to answer that fatal question. He and his wife had been raised in privilege. Russia's common people silently resented them, their educations, and their social advantages. Like other privileged Russians, they served a regime that by 1914 was a "living corpse," and a throne "infested by termites." The war hastened the throne's collapse but did not cause it. The Russian civil war grew out of class antagonism, political disorder, and the people's low cultural attainments—that is, out of hatred, chaos, and ignorance. The Olferieffs' broken life was, in short, a product of the machinations of the "Russian God" mentioned in Petr Andreevich Viazemskii's 1828 poem: a merciless deity of "menials without boots," of "beggars, cripples far and wide," a "God of the cold," a "God of the hungry."[380]

Notes

1. Martin E. Malia, *Alexander Herzen and the Birth of Russian Socialism, 1812–1855* (Cambridge, MA: Harvard University Press, 1961).
2. L[eon] Trotskii, *Istoriia russkoi revoliutsii, v dvukh tomakh* (Berlin: Granit, 1931–1933); Isaak Izrailevich Mints, *Istoriia Velikogo Oktiabria, v trekh tomakh* (Moscow: Nauka, 1967–1971).
3. Wayne Dowler, *Russia in 1913* (DeKalb: Northern Illinois University Press, 2010), 279.
4. Peter Holquist, *Making War, Forging Revolution: Russia's Continuum of Crisis, 1914–1921* (Cambridge, MA: Harvard University Press, 2002).

5. Richard Pipes, *The Russian Revolution* (New York: Knopf, 1990); Pipes, *Russia under the Bolshevik Regime* (New York: Knopf, 1993).
6. Mark D. Steinberg, *The Russian Revolution 1905–1921* (Oxford: Oxford University Press, 2017), 15, 200–201.
7. Steinberg, *The Russian Revolution*, 289–349, here 293.
8. Richard Stites, *Revolutionary Dreams: Utopian Vision and Experimental Life in the Russian Revolution* (New York, Oxford: Oxford University Press, 1988).
9. Michel Heller, Aleksandr Nekrich, *L'utopie au pouvoir. Histoire de l' U.R.S.S. de 1917 à nos jours* (Paris: Calmann-Levy, 1985).
10. Andrzej Walicki, *Marxism and the Leap to the Kingdom of Freedom: The Rise and Fall of Communist Utopia* (Stanford, CA: Stanford University Press, 1995), 269–396, here 278, 290.
11. Lenin, quoted in Walicki, *Marxism and the Leap to the Kingdom of Freedom,* 307.
12. Vladimir N. Brovkin, *Behind the Front Lines of the Civil War. Political Parties and Social Movements in Russia, 1918–1922* (Princeton, NJ: Princeton University Press, 1994), 403.
13. Orlando Figes and Boris Kolonitskii, *Interpreting the Russian Revolution: The Language and Symbols of 1917* (New Haven, CT: Yale University Press, 1999), 187.
14. Figes and Kolonitskii, *Interpreting the Russian Revolution*, 177–78.
15. Ivan Alekseevich Bunin, "Okaiannye dni," entries for April 24 and 25, 1918, *Proza,* ed. D. M. Magomedova (Moscow: Slovo, 2000), 612–13.
16. Bunin, "Okaiannye dni," entry of June 11, 1918, *Proza,* 651.
17. Mikhail Afanas'evich Bulgakov, "Beg. Vosem' snov," *Sobranie sochinenii v 10-i tomakh,* tom 5. *Bagrovyi ostrov. P'esy, povesti. Chernovye tetradi romana "Master i Margarita"* (Moscow: Golos, 1997), 218–300.
18. Mandel'shtam, "Vek," *Vtoraia kniga,* 72–73.
19. *Genealogicheskii forum VGD, Nekropolistika. Istochniki i literatura. Nezabytye mogily. Rossiiskoe zarubezh'e*, tom 1, forum.vgd.ru/341/74254/10.htm?a=stdforum.
20. *Spisok general'nago shtaba* (Petrograd: Voennaia tipografiia Imperatritsy Ekateriny Vtoroi, 1914), 673.
21. A. V. Ganin, "Spisok General'nago shtaba. Ispravlen po 1 marta 1918," in Ganin, *Korpus ofitserov General'nago shtaba v gody Grazhdanskoi voiny 1917–199 gg. Spravochnye materialy* (Moscow: Russkii put', 2009), 475.
22. "Iz vospominanii F. S. Olfer'eva (1905 g.), *Sbornik Soiuza pazhei. no. 30 (1964)*, 1–9.
23. See "Overview of the Theo Olferieff typescript: Soviet Russia in the Orient (1932)," ZZ116, Hoover Institution Archives.
24. "Financial Records. Will," Register of the Antonina R. von Arnold Papers, Box 3, Folder 3, Hoover Institution Archives.
25. "Register of the Antonina R. von Arnold Papers, National League for American Citizenship, 1938," Box 10, Folder 7.
26. See for example Harold Fields, "Where Shall the Alien Work?" *Social Forces* 12:2 (December 1933), 213–21; Fields, "Closing Immigration Throughout the World," *American Journal of International Law* 26:4 (October 1932), 671–99; "Nathan Phillips, 91, Helped Immigrants," *New York Times,* September 10, 1976.

27. See, for example, "Biographical Note," Alice Winifred O'Connor Papers, Lawrence History Center. O'Connor was an immigration reformer in Massachusetts.
28. M. Lyons, *The Russian Imperial Army: A Bibliography of Regimental Histories and Related Works* (Stanford, CA: Hoover Institution, 1968).
29. See "Theodore Olferieff in Social Security Death Index," www.fold3.com/record /78026093-theodore-olferieff.
30. See especially "Otdel VI. Chastnovladel'cheskoe khoziaistvo," in *Sbornik statisticheskikh svedenii o Tverskoi gubernii,* tom 7. *Zubtsovskii uezd* (Moscow: Tovarishchestvo A.A. Levenson, 1891), 238.
31. "Otdel VI. Chastnovladel'cheskoe khoziaistvo," 239.
32. "Otdel VI. Chastnovladel'cheskoe khoziaistvo," 245.
33. "Gramotnost'," in *Sbornik statisticheskikh svedenii o Tverskoi gubernii,* 52–53.
34. Sergei Timofeevich Aksakov, *Detskie gody Bagrovo-vnuka, Sobranie sochinenii S. T. Aksakova,* tom 2, ed. A. G. Gornfel'd (St. Petersburg: Tipo-litografiia Tovarishchestva "Prosveshchenie," 1909), 196–200.
35. Cathy A. Frierson, *All Russia Is Burning! A Cultural History of Fire and Arson in Late Imperial Russia* (Seattle: University of Washington Press, 2002).
36. See letter of October 17, 1900 from B. N. Chicherin to A. N. Chicherin, TSGAOR/ GARF, fond 1154 [Chicherinykh], opis' 1, delo 66, "Pis'ma B. N. Chicherina k A. A. Chicherinoi, A. N. Naryshkinoi, i A. V. Stankevichu (1883–1900 gg)," ll. 342–43.
37. See D., "Rzhevsk," *Entsiklopedicheskii slovar' Brokgauza i Efrona,* tom XXVIa (St. Petersburg: 1899), 672–73.
38. Harriet Murav, "Dostoevskii in Siberia: Remembering the Past," *Slavic Review* 50:4 (Winter 1991), 858–66, here 858.
39. Lev Nikolaevich Tolstoi, *Detstvo,* in *Polnoe sobranie sochinenii,* tom 1 (Moscow: Gosudarstvennoe izdatel'stvo "Khudozhestvennaia literatura," 1935), 35–36, 94–95.
40. On the counter-reforms, see Petr Andreevich Zaionchkovskii, *Rossiiskoe samoderzhavie v kontse XIX stoletiia: politicheskaia reaktsiia 80-kh–nachala 90-kh godov* (Moscow: Mysl', 1970). For the memoir of a land captain from Tambov province, see Aleksandr Ivanovich Novikov, *Zapiski zemskago nachal'nika* (St. Petersburg: Tipografiia M. M. Stasiulevicha, 1899).
41. On the efforts of local land councils to improve medical care, see Natal'ia Mikhailovna Pirumova, *Zemskaia intelligentsiia i ee rol' v obshchestvennoi bor'be do nachala XX v.* (Moscow: Nauka, 1986). On the scarcity of doctors and on efforts to professionalize physicians, see Nancy Mandelker Frieden, *Russian Physicians in an Era of Reform and Revolution* (Princeton, NJ: Princeton University Press, 1981).
42. The classic book on peasant life of the era is Andrei Ivanovich Shingarev, *Vymiraiushchaia derevnia: opyt sanitarno-ekonomicheskago issledovaniia dvukh selenii Voronezhskago uezda* (St. Petersburg: Tipografiia "Obshchestvennaia pol'za," 1907).
43. On the Stolypin land reforms, see Viktor Grigor'evich Tiukavkin, *Veliko-russkoe krest'ianstvo i stolypinskaia agrarnaia reforma* (Moscow: Pamiatniki istoricheskoi mysli, 2001).
44. For an analysis of the way that literature, philosophy, and national values ran together in the early nineteenth century, see Sergei Anatol'evich Nikol'skii and Viktor Petrovich

Filimonov, *Russkoe mirovozzrenie. Smysly i tsennosti rossiiskoi zhizni v otechestvennoi literature i filosofii XVIII–serediny XIX stoletiia* (Moscow: Progress-Traditsiia, 2008), especially chapter ten on Turgenev, 287–354.

45. Boris Nikolaevich Mironov, *Rossiiskaiai imperiia: ot traditsii k modernu, v trekh tomakh*, tom 3 (St. Petersburg: Dmitrii Bulanin, 2015), 478–80.
46. Dmitrii Mikhailovich Levshin, *Pazheskii korpus Ego Imperatorskago Velichestva za sto let* (St. Petersburg: Tipografiia "Khudozhestvennoi pechati," 1902), 27.
47. For a list of graduates, with their service biographies, see Otto Rudol'fovich fon-Freiman, *Pazhi za 183 goda (1711–1894)* (St. Petersburg: Tipografiia Aktsionernago Obshchestva, 1894), here 682.
48. Levshin, *Pazheskii korpus,* 652.
49. Levshin, *Pazheskii korpus,* 653, 656.
50. Levshin, *Pazheskii korpus,* 626.
51. Aleksei Alekseevich Ignat'ev, *Piat'desiat let v stroiu* (Moscow: OGIZ, 1948), 54–55.
52. Ignat'ev, *Piat'desiat let v stroiu,* 52–53.
53. On Verkhovskii during the war, see Iurii Safronov, *Dnevnik Verkhovskogo* (Moscow: Veche, 2014), and Aleksandr Ivanovich Verkhovskii, *Rossiia na golgofe: iz pokhodnogo dnevnika 1914–1918 gg.* (Moscow: Gosudarstvennaia publichnaia biblioteka Rossii, 2014); and Sergei Nikolaevich Poltorak, *Voennaia i nauchnaia deiatel'nost' Aleksandra Ivanovicha Verkhovskogo: pamiati professora V. I. Startseva* (St. Petersburg: Ostrov, 2014).
54. Ignat'ev, *Piat'desiat let v stroiu,* 45.
55. Ignat'ev, *Piat'desiat let v stroiu,* 39, 53.
56. Ignat'ev, *Piat'desiat let v stroiu,* 63.
57. For a history of the organization, see Iurii Il'ich Kir'ianov, *Russkoe sobranie. 1900–1917* (Moscow: ROSSPEN, 2003).
58. Ignat'ev, *Piat'desiat let v stroiu,* 294.
59. Sergei Nikolaevich Trubetskoi was a distinguished philosopher, a follower of Vladimir Sergeevich Solov'ev. In June 1905, he spoke to Nicholas II about the need for popular representation in Russia. He also advocated establishment of university autonomy, a policy shift the government approved on August 27, 1905. Trubetskoi died suddenly in Petersburg on September 29, 1905. See Oleg Timofeevich Ermishin, *Kniaz' S. N. Trubetskoi: zhizn' i filosofiia: biografiia* (Moscow: Sintaksis, 2011).
60. D. [pseudonym], *1905 i 1906 god v Petersburgskom universitete. Skhodki i mitingi (Khronika).* (St. Petersburg: Izdanie Balashova, 1907).
61. John Bushnell, *Mutiny Amid Repression: Russian Soldiers in the Revolution of 1905–1906* (Bloomington: Indiana University Press, 1985), 52.
62. Bushnell, *Mutiny Amid Repression*, 141.
63. See S. N. Vil'chkovskii, *Tsarskoe Selo* (St. Petersburg: Tovarishchestvo R. Golike i A. Vil'borg, 1911), 1–63, *passim.*. See also "Podbel'skogo shosse. Tsarskosel'skii ippodrom," in *Spravochnik organizatsii g. Pushkina. Entsiklopediia Tsarskogo Sela*, tsarselo.ru.
64. On Brusilov, see Georgii Alekseevich Kumanev, ed., *General A. A. Brusilov: ocherki o vydaiushchemsia russkom polkovodtse* (Moscow: Institut rossiiskoi istorii RAN, 2010); Ivan Ivanovich Rostunov, *General Brusilov* (Moscow: Voennoe Izdatel'stvo, 1964); Sergei Nikolaevich Semanov, *Brusilov* (Moscow: Molodaia gvardiia, 1980); and

Aleksei Alekseevich Brusilov, *Moi vospominaniia* (Moscow: Veche, 2014). Brusilov himself attributed his 1906 promotion to Grand Duke Nikolai Nikolaevich.

65. See Brusilov, *Moi vospominaniia*, 39.
66. *Yad wa-shem. Pinskas ha-kehillot Polin. 'ensiklopedyah shel ha-yishuvim ha-Yedudiyim le-min hiwasdam we-'ad le-ahar sho'at milhenot ha-'olam hsheniyah.* Kerek 7 (Jeruslaem: Yad Vashem, 1999), 265–66.
67. Artur Markowski, "Anti-Jewish Pogroms in the Kingdom of Poland," in *Polin: Studies in Polish Jewry*, vol. 27, *Jews in the Kingdom of Poland, 1815–1918*, ed. Glenn Dynner, Antony Polonsky and Maran Wodzinski (Portland, OR: The Littman Library of Jewish Civilization, 2015), 219–56, especially 230–33.
68. Markowski, "Anti-Jewish Pogroms," 231.
69. Iurii Vladimirovich Makarov, *Moia sluzhba v Staroi Gvardii, 1905–1917* (Buenos Aires: Dorrego, 1951), 44–48.
70. See Aleksandr Vladimirovich Luzhbin, "Iz Krasnogo Sela–na voinu. Iz istorii rossiiskoi imperatorskoi konnitsy," *Istoriia Peterburga,* no. 2 (18), 2004, 59–64, here 60.
71. Bushnell, *Mutiny Amid Repression,* 212–16.
72. Oleg Gennad'evich Nazarov, "Nedovol'stvo sredi moriakov . . . ," *Voenno-istoricheskii arkhiv* 2017, no. 3 (207), 134–35.
73. L. I. Andreev, "Revoliutsionnoe dvizhenie v voiskakh severo-zapanykh okrugov," in *1905. Armiia v pervoi russkoi revoliutsii. Ocherki i materialy*, ed. Mikhail Nikolaevich Pokrovskii (Moscow-Leningrad: Gosudarstvennoe izdatel'stvo, 1927), 70–71.
74. William C. Fuller Jr., *Civil-Military Conflict in Imperial Russia 1881–1914* (Princeton, NJ: Princeton University Press, 1985), 138–44.
75. See Rebecca Friedman, "Masculinity, the Body, and Coming of Age in the Nineteenth-Century Russian Cadet Corps," *Journal of the History of Childhood and Youth* 5:2 (2012), 219–38; Friedman, *Masculinity, Autocracy and the Russian University 1804–1863* (New York: Houndmills, Basingstroke, Hampshire, 2005).
76. Andrejs Plakans, *A Concise History of the Baltic States* (Cambridge: Cambridge University Press, 2011), 271.
77. Liudmila Mikhailovna Vorob'eva, *Istoriia Latvii: ot Rossiiskoi imperii k SSSR, v dvukh knigakh. Kniga 1* (Moscow: Fond "Istoricheskaia pamiat'"; Rossiiskii institut strategicheskikh issledovanii, 2009), 72.
78. Plakans, *A Concise History of the Baltic States,* 273–74.
79. Vorob'eva, *Istoriia Latvii . . . Kniga 1*, 75.
80. Vorob'eva, *Istoriia Latvii . . . Kniga 1*, 73–75.
81. Vorob'eva, *Istoriia Latvii . . . Kniga 1*, 69.
82. K. K. [Vladimir Dmitrievich Kuz'min-Karavaev], "Nikolaevskaia akademiia general'nago shtaba," *Entsiklopedicheskii slovar' Brokgauza i Efrona*, tom XXI (1897), 1010–102. The best study of the curriculum is in John W. Steinberg, *All the Tsar's Men: Russia's General Staff and the Fate of the Empire, 1898–1914* (Washington, DC: Woodrow Wilson Center Press, and Baltimore: The Johns Hopkins University Press, 2010), 37–75, 192–231, especially 223–29.
83. His graduation was confirmed by *Spisok general'nago shtaba* (Petrograd: Voennaia Tipografiia Imperatritsy Ekateriny Vtoroi, 1914), 673.

84. Ganin, "Imperatorskaia Nikolaevskaia Voennaia Akademiia," *Entsiklopediia. Vsemirnaia istoriia,* www.histrf.fu; *ibidem., Zakat Nikolaevskoi Voennoi Akademii 1914–1922* (Moscow: Knizhnitsa, 2014), especially chapter 1.
85. Ignat'ev, *Piat'desiat let v stroiu,* 100.
86. Ignat'ev, *Piat'desiat let v stroiu,* 101–10.
87. Ignat'ev, *Piat'desiat let v stroiu,* 112.
88. Ganin, "Imperatorskaia Nikolaevskaia Voennaia Akademiia," *passim.*
89. Nikolai Nikolaevich Golovin, *Sluzhba general'nago shtaba* (St. Petersburg: Ekonomicheskaia tip-litografiia, 1912). Golovin also wrote an important monograph on the French military academy that introduced the school's structure and curriculum to Russian readers. See Golovin, *Frantsuzskaia Vysshaia Voennaia Shkola* (St. Petersburg: Izdatel'stvo Imperatorskoi Nikolaevskoi Voennoi Akademii, 1910). For a study of the Russian General Staff with attention to Golovin and the military reformers, see Steinberg, *All the Tsar's Men, passim.*
90. Golovin, *Iz istorii kampanii na russkom fronte v 4-kh tomakh* (Paris: Izdanie glavnago zarubezhnago Soiuza russkikh voennykh invalidov, 1926–1940).
91. Golovin, *Rossiiskaia kontr-revoliutsiia v 1917–1918 gg, v 5-i tomakh* (Paris: Biblioteka "Illiustrirovannoi Rossii," 1937).
92. Golovin, *Suvorov i ego "Nauka pobezhdat',"* (s.i.: Knizhnoe izdatel'stvo "Vozrozhdenie," 1931).
93. Golovin, *Nauka o voine: o sotsiologicheskom izuchenii voiny* (Paris: Signal, 1938). At the end of this volume, there is a bibliography of Golovin's works. See *op. cit.,* 229–37.
94. Andrei Georgievich Elchaninov, *Geroi-polkovodtsy 1812 goda* (Moscow: Tipografiia I.D. Sytina, 1912); Elchaninov, *Otechestvennaia voina* (Moscow: Tipografiia I.D. Sytina, 1912).
95. Apropos the Russo-Japanese war, Elchaninov writes: "The feats of Russian soldiers are a great joy to the Sovereign, and he ardently takes pride in them and believes that they will never drop the Russian standards." Elchaninov, *Tsarstvovanie Gosudaria Imperatora Nikolaia Aleksandrovicha* (Moscow: Tovarishchestvo I.D. Sytina, 1913), 98.
96. See Nikolai Petrovich Mikhnevich, *Istoriia voennago iskusstva s drevneishikh vremen do nachala deviatnadtsatago stoletiia* (St. Petersburg: Parovaia skoropechatnia O. Iablonskago, 1896); Mikhnevich, *Glavnyi shtab: Istoricheskii ocherk* (St. Petersburg: Voennoe Ministerstvo, 1896); Mikhnevich, *Strategiia* (S. Petersburg: Tipo-litografiia A.E. Landau, 1899).
97. Lancelot L. Farrar, *The Short War Illusion: German Policy, Strategy and Domestic Affairs, August–December 1914* (Santa Barbara, CA: ABC Clio, 1973).
98. Tolstoy wrote the play's first draft between January and August 1900, then revised it several times. He left it in December 1900 to concentrate on other projects, and in spite of several subsequent references, never completed the revisions. The play appeared in print posthumously, on September 23, 1911, in the newspaper *Russian Word* [*Russkoe slovo*]. The co-founder of the Moscow Art Theater, Vladimir Ivanovich Nemirovich-Danchenko, had heard of the play in October 1900 and had asked Tolstoy to license its production, even before its completion. In 1911, Nemirovich-Danchenko

directed the production, and the great Konstantin Sergeevich Stanislavskii appeared as one of its characters. Writing through staging, the project showed the Moscow Art Theater's entrepreneurial side. See Sergei Dmitrievich Balukhatyi and V. S. Mishin, "Kommentarii. Zhivoi trup," in Lev Nikolaevich Tolstoi, *Polnoe sobranie sochinenii, v 90-ti tomakh*, tom 34 (Moscow: Gosudarstvennoe izdatel'stvo khudozhestvennoi literatury, 1952), 533–42.

99. Anatolii Aleksandrovich Mordvinov, "Poslednii imperator, vospominaniia fligel'-ad"iutanta A. Mordvinova," *Otechestvennye arkhivy 3–4* (1993), tom 4, 49–50.
100. Douglas Smith, *Rasputin: Faith, Power and the Twilight of the Romanovs* (New York: Farrar, Straus and Giroux, 2016), 261–62.
101. Smith, *Rasputin,* 155–157.
102. Edvard Radzinsky, *The Rasputin File* (New York: Anchor Books, 2010), 126–30.
103. The articles were collected by Mikhail Aleksandrovich Novoselov, *Grigorii Rasputin i misticheskoe rasputstvo*, (Moscow: 1912). The police confiscated copies of the book before it could be distributed.
104. Smith, *Rasputin,* 181–82, 200.
105. Smith, *Rasputin*, 228–29, 235.
106. Smith, *Rasputin*, 244.
107. Smith, *Rasputin,* 246.
108. Smith, *Rasputin*, 255–59.
109. Smith, *Rasputin*, 266–71.
110. Smith, *Rasputin,* 271–73.
111. Quoted in Dmitriii Igorevich Stogov, *Pravomonarkhicheskie salony Peterburga-Petrograda (konets XIX–nachalo XX veka)* (St. Petersburg: Dmitrii Bulanin, 2007), 249.
112. Stogov, *Pravomonarkhicheskie salony*, 252–53.
113. Stogov, *Pravomonarkhicheskie salony*, 254.
114. On regular visitors to Prince Andronikov's salon, see Stogov, *Pravomonarkhicheskie salony,* 252–53. In September 1911, just after the assassination of Prime Minister Stolypin, a group of right-wing parties sent a memorandum to his successor, Vladimir Nikolaevich Kokovtsov, demanding the government's adoption of policies in the interests of the Russian nation. This memorandum was signed by Beliaev. See "Dokladnaia zapiska riada pravykh partii na imia prem'era V. N. Kokovtsova [sentiabr' 1911 g.]," in *Pravye partii 1905–1917 gg. Dokumenty i materialy, v dvukh tomakh*, ed. Iu. I. Kir'ianov, (Moscow: Rossiiskaia politicheskaia etsiklopediia. ROSSPEN, 1998), tom 2, *1909–1917 gg.*, 46–53.
115. Stogov, *Pravomonarkhicheskie salony*, 293–301.
116. Stogov, *Pravomonarkhicheskie salony*, 260.
117. Boris Kolonitskii, *"Tragicheskaia erotika." Obrazy imperatorskoi sem'i v gody pervoi mirovoi voiny* (Moscow: Novoe literaturnoe obozrenie, 2010), 289–325.
118. Steinberg, *All the Tsar's Men,* 282.
119. Boris Vasil'evich Galenko, *Sem'ia i potomki Suvorova. Biografii blizhaishikh rodstvennikov i potomkov polkovodtsa* (St. Petersburg: GVIM A. V. Suvorova, 2002).
120. Galenko, *Sem'ia i potomki Suvorova*, 58–61.

121. On the Sukhomlinov trial, see William C. Fuller, Jr., *The Foe Within: Fantasies of Treason and the End of Imperial Russia* (Ithaca, NY: Cornell University Press, 2006), 215–56.
122. Graf Sergei Iul'evich Vitte, *Vospominaniia. Detstvo. Tsarstvovanie Aleksandra II i Aleksandra III (1849–1894)* (Petrograd: Knigoizdatel'stvo "Slovo," 1923), 413–20.
123. "[Boris Mikhailovich Kustodiev] k Iu. E. Kustodievoi, 23 maia 1909 [Peterburg]," Kustodiev Boris Mikhailovich. Sait khudozhnika. Pisma, http://kustodiev-art.ru/pismaa_103.
124. See Mike O'Mahony, "Bringing Down the Tsar: 'Deconstructing' the Monument to Tsar Aleksandr III in Sergei Eisenstein's *October*," *Sculpture Journal* 15:2 (2006), 272–78.
125. Richard S. Wortman, *Scenarios of Power: Myth and Ceremony in Russian Monarchy from Peter the Great to the Abdication of Nicholas II* (Princeton, NJ: Princeton University Press, 2006), 380.
126. Vladimir Fedorovich Dzhunkovskii, *Vospominaniia*, tom 2 (Moscow: Izdatel'stvo im. Sabashnikovykh, 1997), 34–37; quoted in Richard G. Robbins, Jr., *Overtaken by the Night. One Russian's Journey through Peace, War & Terror* (Pittsburgh: University of Pittsburgh Press, 2017), 192.
127. Wortman, *Scenarios of Power,* 382.
128. On the bicentennial of Petersburg in 1903, the bicentennial of the battle of Poltava in 1909, the centennial of Borodino in 1912, and the tricentennial of the Romanov house, see Galina Nikolaevna Ul'ianova, "Natsional'nye torzhestva," *Rossii v nachale XX veka*, tom 1, serii "Rossii XX vek. Issledovaniia" (Moscow: Novyi khronograf, 2002), 542–651.
129. Ul'ianova, "Trekhsotletie Doma Romanovykh," in "Natsional'nye torzhestva."
130. Wortman, *Scenarios of Power*, 384–87.
131. Wortman, *Scenarios of Power,* 388–89.
132. Ul'ianova, "Trekhsotletie."
133. *Pervaia vseobshchaia perepis' naseleniia Rossiiskoi imperii, 1897 g.* tom XXXVII. *S.-Peterburgskaia guberniia* (St. Petersburg: Izdanie Tsentral'nago statisticheskago komiteta ministra vnutrennikh del, 1903), iv–v.
134. *Opisanie Sanktpeterburskoi gubernii po uezdam i stanam* (St. Petersburg: Gubernskaia tipografiia, 1838), 40.
135. Vladimir Sergeevich Solov'ev, *Tri razgovora, s predisloviem avtora* (Munich: Izdatel'stvo Milavida, 1900).
136. See Gordon A. Craig, *Germany 1866–1945* (New York: Oxford University Press, 1978), 333–34; original in Kurt Riezler, *Tagebücher, Aufsätze, Dokumente,* ed. Karl Dietrich Erdmann (Göttigen: Vandenhoeck & Ruprecht, 1972), 183.
137. Craig, *Germany 1866–1945,* 333–38, here 333.
138. Dominic Lieven, *The End of Tsarist Russia: The March to World War I and Revolution* (New York: Penguin Random House, 2015), 265–69.
139. Lieven, *The End of Tsarist Russia*, 277–83.
140. Lieven, *The End of Tsarist Russia,* 283.
141. Lieven, *The End of Tsarist Russia,* 284–85.

142. Quoted in Lieven, *The End of Tsarist Russia,* 290.
143. See "Zapiska N. Durnovo," in *Svet i teni Velikoi voiny. Pervaia mirovaia v dokumentakh epokhi,* Anatolii Vital'evich Repnikov, Elena Nikolaevna Rudaia, Andrei Aleksandrovich Ivanov, sostaviteli, (Moscow: ROSSPEN, 2014), 58 -73; originally published in *Krasnaia nov'* 1922, no. 6 (10), 182–99.
144. "Zapiska N. Durnovo," 58.
145. "Zapiska N. Durnovo," 62–64.
146. "Zapiska N. Durnovo," 70–71.
147. "Zapiska N. Durnovo," 70.
148. "Zapiska N. Durnovo," 71 -72.
149. "Zapiska N. Durnovo," 73.
150. On Durnovo as "prophet," see the remarks by Andrei Aleksandrovich Ivanov and Boris Sergeevich Kotov, "'Predvidenie neobychainoi sily': o 'prorocheskoi' zapiske N. Durnovo," *Svet i teni Velikoi voiny,* 51–57.
151. Lieven, *The End of Tsarist Russia,* 307.
152. Lieven, *Russia's Rulers under the Old Regime* (New Haven, CT: Yale University Press, 1989), 207–30.
153. Thomas Mann, "Gedanken im Kriege," *Die Neue Rundschau. Band 25, 1914,* 1471–84, here 1475.
154. See Heinrich Mann's great novel, *Der Untertan,* begun in 1914, published in Russian in 1915, in German in 1918. See also his critique of authoritarianism in the essay, "Zola" (1915).
155. Melissa Kirschke Stockdale, *Mobilizing the Russian Nation: Patriotism and Citizenship in the First World War* (New York: Cambridge University Press, 2016), 4.
156. Evgenii Nikolaevich Trubetskoi, "Staryi i novyi natsional'nyi messianizm," *Russkaia mysl' 33* (March 1912), 82–102.
157. Trubetskoi, *Voina i mirovaia zadacha Rossii,* 2nd edition (Moscow: I. D. Sytin, 1915); Randall Poole, "Religion, War, and Revolution. E. N. Trubetskoi's Liberal Construction of Russian National Identity, 1912–20," *Kritika: Explorations in Russian and Eurasian History* 7:2 (Spring 2006), 195–240.
158. Trubetskoi, *Voina i mirovaia zadacha Rossii,* 6–7.
159. Trubetskoi, *Voina i mirovaia zadacha Rossii,* 11.
160. Trubetskoi, *Voina i mirovaia zadacha Rossii,* 17–18.
161. Trubetskoi, *Voina i mirovaia zadacha Rossii,* 21.
162. David R. Stone, *The Russian Army in the Great War. The Eastern Front, 1914–1917* (Lawrence: University of Kansas Press, 2015), 62–70.
163. Stone, *The Russian Army in the Great War,* 67.
164. Stone, *The Russian Army in the Great War,* 69.
165. Stone, *The Russian Army in the Great War,* 76.
166. Stone, *The Russian Army in the Great War,* 76–80, here 80.
167. Maksim Viktorovich Os'kin, "Nikolai Vasil'evich Ruzskii," *Voprosy istorii,* 2012, no. 4, 53–72, here 57.
168. Os'kin, "Nikolai Vasil'evich Ruzskii," 60–62.
169. Ol'kin, "Nikolai Vasil'evich Ruzskii," 63.

170. Os'kin, "Nikolai Vasil'evich Ruzskii," 66; Evgenii Ivanovich Martynov, *Politika i strategiia* (Moscow: Finansovyi kontrol', 2003), 177.
171. Alekseev argued that the supreme commander should focus on "strategic problems" rather than other issues, which could be left to the General Staff. See Vasilii Zhanovich Tsvetkov, "Mikhail Vasil'evich Alekseev," *Voprosy istorii*, 2012, no. 10, 23–47, here 26–27.
172. Anton Ivanovich Denikin, *Ocherki russkoi smuty*, tom 1. Vypusk pervyi (Paris: J. Povolozky & Cie., 1921), 34.
173. Denikin, *Ocherki russkoi smuty*, tom 1, 35.
174. Tsvetkov, "Mikhail Vasil'evich Alekseev," 29–30.
175. Denikin, *Ocherki russkoi smuty*, tom 1, 37.
176. See diary entries of April 9/22 and May 27/June 9,1908 in Aleksei Andreevich Polivanov, *Iz dnevnikov i vospominanii po dolzhnosti voennago ministra i ego pomoshchnika. 1907–1916 gg., v dvukh tomakh,* edited by Andrei Medardovich Zaionchkovskii (Moscow: Vysshii voennyi redaktsionnyi sovet, 1914), prozhito.org.
177. Diary entry of 17/November 17/30, 1909, in Polivanov, *Iz dnevnikov*, prozhito.org.
178. Diary entry of April 20/May 3, 1912, in Polivanov, *Iz dnevnikov*, prozhito.org.
179. Diary entry of August 28/September 10, 1913, in Polivanov, *Iz dnevnikov*, prozhito .org.
180. Polivanov left a memoir on his career as war minister, *Deviat' mesiatsev vo glave Voennago ministerstva (13 iiunia 1915 g.–13 marta 1916 g.)*. The first five chapters, published in Polivanov, *Iz dnevnikov i vospominanii po dolzhnosti voennagoministra i ego pomoshchnika 1907–1916 gg.* (Moscow: Vysshii voennyi redaktsionnyi sovet, 1924), covered the period from June 13 to August 21, 1915. The remainder of the memoir appeared as "Russkaia armiia v Velikoi voine: Polivanov A. A. Deviat' mesiatsev vo glave Voennago ministerstva (13 iiunia 1915–13 marta 1916)," edited by Vladimir Vasil'evich Polikarpov, *Voprosy istorii*, 1994, Nos. 2, 3, 5, 7, 9, 11.
181. See William Gleason, "The All-Russian Union of Towns and the All-Russian Union of Zemstvos in World War I," Ph.D. diss., University of Michigan, 1972; Thomas Earl Porter with Lawrence W. Lerner, *Prince George E. L'vov: The Zemstvo, Civil Society, and Liberalism in Late Imperial Russia* (Lanham, MD: Lexington Books, 2017), 169–73.
182. Vladimir Petrovich Semennikov, *Monarkhiia pered krusheniem, 1914–1917* (Moscow: Gosudarstvennoe izdatel'stvo, 1927), 95–96; quoted in Porter, *Prince George E. L'vov*, 173.
183. "Zasedanie 16 iiulia 1915 goda," in *Tiazhelye dni. (Sekretnye zasedaniia Soveta ministrov 16 iiulia–2 sentiabria 1915 goda),* compiled by A. N. Iakhontov, *Arkhiv russkoi revoliutsii,* tom XVIII (Berlin: Slowo-Verlag, 1926), 21.
184. "Zasedanie 6 avgusta 1915 goda," in *Tiazhelye dni*, 52–53.
185. See the remarks of the Acting Minister of Internal Affairs Prince Nikolai Borisovich Shcherbatov, "Zasedanie 16 iiulia 1915 goda," *Tiazhelye dni*, 53–54.
186. Kornelii Fedorovich Shatsillo, "'Delo' polkovnika Miasoedova," *Voprosy istorii* 1967, no. 2, 103–16, here 107–8.
187. Shatsillo, "'Delo' polkovnika Miasoedova," 108.
188. Shatsillo, "'Delo' polkovnika Miasoedova," 112–13.

189. Shatsillo, "'Delo' polkovnika Miasoedova," 114–15.
190. Shatsillo, "'Delo' polkovnika Miasoedova," 115.
191. Fuller, *The Foe Within,* 140–41.
192. Fuller, *The Foe Within,* 147–49.
193. Stone, *The Russian Army in the Great War,* 115–19.
194. Stone, *The Russian Army in the Great War,* 121.
195. Stone, *The Russian Army in the Great War,* 126.
196. Stone, *The Russian Army in the Great War*, 130–37.
197. Stone, *The Russian Army in the Great War,* 151–62.
198. Stone, *The Russian Army in the Great War,* 167–72.
199. Aleksandr Neznamov, *Strategicheskii ocherk voiny 1914–1918. Chast' IV* (Moscow: Vysshii Voennyi Redaktsionnyi Sovet, 1922), 67.
200. Quoted in Neznamov, *Strategicheskii ocherk voiny 1914–1918. Chast' IV*, 55. See also Stone, *The Russian Army in the Great War, passim.*
201. Neznamov, *Strategicheskii ocherk voiny 1914–1918. Chast' IV,* 123–25, here 123.
202. Joshua A. Sanborn, *Imperial Apocalypse: The Great War and the Destruction of the Russian Empire* (Oxford: Oxford University Press, 2014), 65–66.
203. Sanborn, *Imperial Apocalypse*, 75.
204. Sanborn, *Imperial Apocalypse,* 77–78.
205. Sanborn, *Imperial Apocalypse*, 87.
206. Sanborn, *Imperial Apocalypse*, 92–93.
207. Sanborn, *Imperial Apocalypse*, 98–106.
208. Sanborn, *Imperial Apocalypse,* 108.
209. Ignat'ev, *Piat'desiat let v stroiu,* 137–39.
210. For an analysis of Russia's early military aviation infrastructure, see Sergei Viktorovich Averchenko, "Aerodromno-tekhnicheskoe obespechenie voennoi aviatsii Rossii v 1910–1914 gg.," *Voenno-istoricheskii zhurnal* 2016, no. 10, 3–12.
211. "Kruten', Evgraf Nikolaevich," in *Aviatory-kavalery ordena Sviatogo Georgiia i Georgievskogo oruzhiia perioda Pervoi Mirovoi Voiny 1914–1918 godov. Biograficheskii spravochnik,* ed. M. S. Neshkin and V. M. Shabanov (Moscow: ROSSPEN, 2006), 156–57.
212. See Vladislav Napoleonovich Klembovskii, *Strategicheskii ocherk voiny 1914–1918 godov. Chast' V* (Moscow: Gosudarstvennaia tipografiia, 1920), 18–24; Stone, *The Russian Army in the Great War*, 236–37.
213. Stone, *The Russian Army in the Great War,* 251.
214. Stone, *The Russian Army in the Great War,* 256.
215. Velikii kniaz' Aleksandr Mikhailovich, *Kniga vospominanii. Prilozhenie k "Illiustrirovannoi Rossii" za 1933 god,* 3 vols. in 1 (Paris: Biblioteka "Illiustrirovannoi Rossii," 1933–1934), chapter XVII, *passim.*
216. A[leksandr Dmitrievich] Bubnov, *V tsarskoi Stavke. Vospominaniia admirala Bubnova* (New York: Izdatel'stvo imeni Chekhova, 1955), 159–60.
217. Aleksandr Blok, "Prilozhenie V," in *Poslednie dni imperatorskoi vlasti (po neizdannym dokumentam)* (St. Petersburg: Alkonost, 1921), 144–57.
218. Sergei Petrovich Mel'gunov, *Na putiakh k dvortsovomu perevorotu (Zagovory pered revoliutsiei 1917 goda)* (Paris: Knizhnoe delo "Rodnik," 1931).

219. Mel'gunov, *Na putiakh k dvortsovomu perevorotu*, 146–47.
220. Petr Aleksandrovich Polovtsov, *Dni zatmeniia: zapiski glavnokomandiushchego voiskami Petrogradskogo voennogo okruga generala A. Polovtsova v 1917 godu* (Paris: Knigoizdatel'stvo Vozrozhdenie, 1918), 38; Mel'gunov, *Na putiakh k dvortsovomu perevorotu*, 148.
221. Mel'gunov, *Na putiakh k dvortsovomu perevorotu*, 148–49. See "Pokazanie A. D. Protopopova ot 31 avgusta [1917 g.]," in *Padenie tsarskogo rezhima*, tom 4 (Moscow: Gosudarstvennoe izdatel'stvo, 1925), 81–94.
222. D[mitrii] N[ikolaevich] Dubenskii, "Kak proizoshel perevorot v Rossii. Zapiski-dnevniki," *Russkaia letopis'. Kniga 3* (Paris: s. n., 1922), 12–13; quoted by Vladimir Nikolaevich Khrustalev, "Brat'ia Gurko v istorii Rossii. Zhiznennyi put' generala Vasiliia Iosifovicha Gurko (1864–1917)," in Vladimir Gurko, *Tsar' i tsaritsa* (Moscow: Veche, 2015), fn. 68.
223. Stone, *The Russian Army in the Great War*, 272–75.
224. Andrei Medardovich Zaionchkovskii, *Strategicheskii ocherk voiny 1914–1917gg.. Chast' VII. Kampaniia 1917 g.* (Moscow: Vysshii Voennyi Redaktsionnyi Sovet, 1923), 19.
225. Zaionchkovskii, *Strategicheskii ocherk voiny 1914–1917 gg. Chast' VII*, 26–27.
226. Zaionchkovskii, *Strategicheskii ocherk voiny 1914–1917 g. Chast' VII*, 29.
227. Stone, *The Russian Army in the Great War*, 277–78, here 277.
228. Zaionchkovskii, *Strategicheskii ocherk voiny 1914–1917 gg.. Chast' VII*, 33.
229. Zaionchkovskii, *Strategicheskii ocherk voiny 1914–1917 gg.. Chast' VII*, 38.
230. Kirill Aleksandrov, "Stavka nakanune i v pervye dni Fevral'skoi revoliutsii 1917 goda: k istorii vzaimootnoshenii imperatora Nikolaia II i russkogo generaliteta," *Zvezda* 2017, no. 2, https:// magazines.gorky.media/zvezda/2017/2/ stavka-nakanune-i-v -pervye-dni-fevralskojrevolyuczii-1917-goda.html.
231. "Telegramma glavnokomanduiushchego severnym frontom gen. Ruzskogo tsariu 27 fevralia 1917 g.," in "Febral'skaia revoliutsiia 1917 goda (Dokumenty stavki verkhovnogo glavnokomanduiushchego i shtaba glavnokomanduiushchego armiiami severnogo fronta), *Krasnyi arkhiv*, 1925, tom 2 (Moscow-Leningrad: Gosudarstvennoe izdatel'stvo, 1927), 3–78, here 13.
232. Tsuyoshi Hasegawa, *The February Revolution: Petrograd, 1917* (Seattle: University of Washington Press, 1981), 198–99.
233. Hasegawa, *The February Revolution*, 200.
234. Hasegawa, *The February Revolution*, 210–11.
235. "Pokazaniia A. D. Protopopova," "Gospodinu Predsedateliu Chrezvychainoi komissii . . . ot 31 avgusta 1917 goda," in *Padenie tsarskogo rezhima, v 7-i chastiakh. Chast' IV*, ed. Pavel Eliseevich Shchegolev (Leningrad: Gosudarstvennoe izdatel'stvo, 1922–27), 87–101, here 96.
236. "Dopros gen. S. S. Khabalova 22 marta 1917 goda," in *Padenie tsarskogo rezhima. Chast' I*, 182–219, here 188–89.
237. "Dopros gen. S. S. Khabalova," 188.
238. "Pokazaniia A. D. Protopopova," "Gospodinu Predsedateliu Chrezvychainoi komissii . . . ot 31 avgusta 1917 goda," 98.
239. Hasegawa, *The February Revolution*, 247.

240. Hasegawa, *The February Revolution,* 249.
241. On Krylov's identity, see Nikolai Vladimirovich Rodin, "'Pristav Krylov': opyt istoriograficheskoi identifikatsii i materialy k biografii," *Peterburgskii istoricheskii zhurnal,* 2017, no. 4 (16), 77–99. Krylov was misidentified by Hasegawa and several other historians of the February revolution.
242. Arkhiv Guverovskogo Instituta voiny, revoliutsii i mira (SShA, 1929), "Gibel' tsarskogo Petrograda: "Fevral'skaia revoliutsiia glazami gradonachal'nika A. Balka," "Pokazaniia general-maiora A. Balka tovarishchu prokurora Petrogradskogo okruzhnogo suda G. Kostenko, 9 aprelia 1917 g.," *Russkoe proshloe. Istoriko-dokumental'nyi al'manakh, Kniga 1* (St. Petersburg: Svelen, 1991), 19–23, here 21.
243. "Vospominaniia A. Balka . . . Poslednie piat' dnei tsarskogo Petrograda (23–28 fevralia 1917 goda," *Russkoe proshloe. Kniga 1,* 26–62, here 49.
244. Hasegawa, *The February Revolution,* 263.
245. See "Perepiska Nikolaia i Aleksandry Romanovykh. 1916–1917 gg.," *Krasnyi arkhiv.* 1923, no. 4, 208–10; Vladimir Nikolaevich Khrustalev, ed. *Dnevnik Nikolaia II i Imperatritsy Aleksandry Fedorovny, v dvukh tomakh,* tom 1 (Moscow: Vagrius, 2008), 183–85, here 184.
246. Hasegawa, *The February Revolution,* 267–70.
247. Hasegawa, *The February Revolution,* 273–74.
248. Hasegawa, *The February Revolution,* 275.
249. "Telegramma predsedatelia Gosud. Dumy Rodzianko gen. Alekseevu 26 fevralia 1917 g.," in "Fevral'skaia revoliutsiia 1917 goda," *Krasnyi arkhiv,* 1927, no. 2, 5–6.
250. Hasegawa, *The February Revolution,* 279–86.
251. Hasegawa, *The February Revolution,* 284–94.
252. Hasegawa, *The February Revolution,* 296–97.
253. Hasegawa, *The February Revolution,* 298–300.
254. "Telegramma gen. Khabalova tsariu 27 fevralia 1917 g.," in "Fevral'skaia revoliutsiia 1917 goda," 8.
255. It is possible that Olfer'ev mistook General Khabalov's telegram to the tsar and Ruzskii's telegram to the tsar and Alekseev, because Khabalov referred to troop indiscipline in Petrograd. However, this seems less likely, because Olfer'ev recalled the unusual circumstance of an exchange between Ruzskii and Alekseev.
256. "Telegramma gen. Khabalova tsariu 27 fevralia 1917 g.," in "Fevral'skaia revoliutsiia 1917 goda," 15–16.
257. "Telegramma Rodzianko tsariu 27 fevralia 1917 g.," in "Fevral'skaia revoliutsiia 1917 goda," 6–7.
258. "Telegramma gen. Alekseeva gen. Beliaevu 27 fevralia 1917 g.," in "Fevral'skaia revoliutsiia 1917 goda," 10–11.
259. "Telegramma vybornykh chlenov Gosud. Soveta 28 fevralia 1917 g.," in "Fevral'skaia revoliutsiia 1917 goda," 18.
260. "Telegramma gen. Beliaeva gen. Alekseevu 28 fevralia 1917 g.," in "Fevral'skaia revoliutsiia 1917 goda," 20.
261. This was the so-called "long conversation in the bedroom with Aliks," mentioned in Nicholas's diary. See "Dnevnik Nikolaia Romanova," *Krasnyi arkhiv* 1927, no. 1 (20)

(Moscow-Leningrad: Gosudarstvennoe izdatel'stvo, 1927), 123–52, here 133 (entry of February 10/23, 1917).

262. See Velikii kniaz' Aleksandr Mikhailovich, *Kniga vospominanii* (chapter 17).
263. "Telegramma gen. Alekseeva glavnokomanduiushchim frontami 28 fevralia 1917 g.," in "Fevral'skaia revoliutsiia 1917 goda," 22–24.
264. Andrei Vladislavovich Ganin, *Korpus ofitserov General'nago shtaba v gody Grazhdanskoi voiny 1917–1922 gg. Spravochnye materialy* (Moscow: Russkii put', 2009), 134.
265. "Telegramma Rodzianko gen. Alekseevu 1 marta 1917 g.," in "Fevral'skaia revoliutsiia 1917 goda," 36.
266. "Razgovor po priamomu provodu podpolk[ovnika] Baranovskogo s podpolk[ovnikom] Mediokritskim (Pskov), 1 marta 1917 goda," in "Fevral'skaia revoliutsiia 1917 goda," 39–40, here 40.
267. "Telegramma gen. Klembovskogo glavokomanduiushchim armiiami 1 marta 1917 g.," in "Fevral'skaia revoliutsiia 1917 goda," 40–41.
268. "Telegramma gen. Alekseeva Rodzianko 1 marta 1917 g.," in "Fevral'skaia revoliutsiia 1917 goda," 44–45.
269. "Telegramma gen. Alekseeva tsariu 1 marta 1917 g.," in "Fevral'skaia revoliutsiia 1917 goda," 53–54.
270. "Razgovor po priamomu provodu gen. Lukomskogo s gen. Kvetsinskim 1 marta 1917 g.," in "Fevral'skaia revoliutsiia 1917 goda," 50.
271. See Vladimir Mikhailovich Khrustalev, *Velikii kniaz' Mikhail Aleksandrovich* (Moscow: Veche, 2009), 350, entry in Mikhail's diary for 27 fevralia 1917 goda.
272. On the history of this conversation, see Sergei Petrovich Mel'gunov, *Martovskie dni 1917 goda,* http://azbyka.ru/ otechnik/Sergei_Melgunov/martovskie, 358–63.
273. "Razgovor po priamomu provodu gen. Ruzskogo s Rodzianko 1 marta 1917," in "Fevral'skaia revoliutsiia 1917 goda," 55–59.
274. "Razgovor po priamomu provodu gen. Ruzskogo s Rodzianko 1 marta 1917," in "Fevral'skaia revoliutsiia 1917 goda," 56–57.
275. "Telegramma gen. Danilova gen. Alekseevu 2 marta 1917 g.," in "Fevral'skaia revoliutsiia 1917 goda," 62–63.
276. "Razgovor po priamomu provodu gen. Lukomskogo s gen. Danilovym 2 marta 1917 g.," in "Fevral'skaia revoliutsiia 1917 goda," 75–76, here 76.
277. See Sergei Nikolaevich Vil'chkovskii, "Prebyvanie Gosudaria Imperatora v Pskove . . . po rasskazu gen. Ruzskogo," *Russkaia letopis'. Kniga 3* (Paris: Izdanie "Russkogo ochaga," 1922), 161–87, here 177.
278. Vil'chkovskii, "Prebyvanie Gosudaria Imperatora v Pskove," 178.
279. "Razgovor po priamomu provodu gen. Everta s gen. Klembovskim 2 marta 1917 g.," in "Fevral'skaia revoliutsiia 1917 goda," 67–68.
280. "Telegramma gen. Alekseeva tsariu 2 marta 1917 g.," in "Fevral'skaia revoliutsiia 1917 goda," 72–73.
281. Mel'gunov, *Martovskie dni*, 459–60.
282. See Khrustalev, ed., *Dnevniki Nikolaia II i imperatritsy Aleksandry Fedorovny*, tom 1, 184–85.

283. See Khrustalev, *Dnevniki Nikolaia II i imperatritsy Aleksandry Fedorovny*, tom 1, 354–55.
284. Aleksandr Zelenin, *Iazyk russkoi emigrantskoi pressy (1919–1939)* (St. Petersburg: Zlatoust, 2007). See section 1.1.1. Suffiksatsiia abstraktnykh sushchestvitel'nykh.
285. On these points, see Vasilii Zhanovich Tsvetkov, *General Alekseev* (Moscow: Veche, 2014), chapter 4, section 2, "Vo glave armii i flota. Verkhovnyi glavnokomanduiushchii."
286. Kolonitskii, " 'Tovarishch Kerenskii': anti-monarkhicheskaia revoliutsiia i formirovanie kul'ta 'vozhdia naroda' (mart–iiun' 1917 goda)," (Moscow: Novoe literaturnoe obozrenie, 2017), electronic version, location 3623.
287. Richard Abraham, *Aleksandr Kerensky: The First Love of the Revolution* (New York: Columbia University Press, 1987), 149.
288. Mel'gunov, *Martovskie dni*, 618.
289. Mel'gunov, *Martovskie dni*, 772–73.
290. Mel'gunov, *Martovskie dni*, 776.
291. Mel'gunov, *Martovskie dni*, 779.
292. Mel'gunov, *Martovskie dni*, 794–95.
293. Mel'gunov, *Martovskie dni*, 821–22.
294. Stone, *The Russian Army in the Great War,* 288–91.
295. See Stone's pithy remarks about Kerenskii's fantasy of "revolutionary greatness and popular acclaim" in Stone, *The Russian Army in the Great War,* 287–88.
296. See the website, "Militera.lib.ru," which reproduces military memoirs. See "E. I. Akhmatovich. Pervye dni," http:// militera.lib.ru/memo/russian/ sb_zvezdy_na_kry lyah/01.html.
297. See Sergei Pavlovich Eliseev, "Sokhranit' vse aviatsionnye shkoly dlia trudovogo naroda," *Voenno-istoricheskii zhurnal,* 2012, no. 6, 10–15. On the history of the naval airforce in the revolution, see Kirill Nazarenko, *Flot, revoliutsiia i vlast' v Rossii: 1917–1921* (Moscow: Kvadriga, 2011).
298. Rex A. Wade, *The Russian Revolution, 1917* (Cambridge: Cambridge University Press, 2000), 194.
299. Wade, *The Russian Revolution, 1917*, 202–3.
300. Wade, *The Russian Revolution, 1917*, 203–5, here 205.
301. Aleksandr Fedorovich Kerenskii, *Delo Kornilova* (Moscow: Zadruga, 1918).
302. Kerenskii, *Delo Kornilova,* 53.
303. Anton Ivanovich Denikin, *Ocherki russkoi smuty v 5-ti tomakh* (Paris: J. Povolzsky & Cie, 1921–1926), tom 2, 73.
304. Denikin, *Ocherki russkoi smuty*, tom 2, 75–76.
305. Denikin, *Ocherki russkoi smuty*, tom 2, 86.
306. Tsuyoshi Hasegawa, *Crime and Punishment in the Russian Revolution: Mob Justice and the Police in Petrograd* (Cambridge, MA: Belknap Press of Harvard University Press, 2017), 171–73.
307. On revolutionary politics of the navy, see Mikhail Aleksandrovich Elizarov, "Levyi ekstremizm na flote v period revoliutsii 1917 goda i grazhdanskoi voiny: fevral' 1917–mart 1921 gg." Dissertatsiia na soiskanie uchenoi stepeni doktora istoricheskikh nauk, St. Petersburg, 2007.

308. See Svetlana Evgen'evna Rudneva, *Predparlament. Oktiabr' 1917 goda. Opyt istoricheskoi rekonstruktsii* (Moscow: Nauka, 2006).
309. Rudneva, *Predparlament*, 221–22.
310. Ol'ga Edel'man, "Krushenie tsarskogo poezda," *Otechestvennye zapiska*, 2002, no. 2, https://magazines.gorky.media/oz/ 2002/2/krushenie-czarskogo-poezda.html.
311. Denikin, *Ocherki russkoi smuty*, tom 2, 137–38, here 138.
312. See Sergei Nikolaevich Bazanov, "Poslednie dni general-leitenanta N. N. Dukhonina v Stavke," *Voenno-istoricheskii zhurnal*, 2001, no. 11, 54–60.
313. See Irina Mikhutina, *Ukrainskii Brestskii mir. Put' vykhoda Rossii iz pervoi mirovoi voiny i anatomiia konflikta mezhdu Sovnarkomom RSFSR i pravitel'stvom Ukrainskoi Tsentral'noi Rady* (Moscow: Evropa, 2007), chapter 2, *passim.*
314. Kerenskii, *Rossiia na istorichiskom povorote. Memuary* (Moscow: Respublika, 1993), 297. See also the sketch of Dukhonin in Bazanov, "Poslednie dni," 54–57.
315. Marina Nikolaevna Simonian, *Ego professiia–revoliutsiia: Dokumental'nyi ocherk o zhizni i deiatel'nosti N. V. Krylenko* (Moscow: Znanie, 1985).
316. Bazanov, "Poslednie dni," 56.
317. Bazanov, "Poslednie dni," 57.
318. Bazanov, "Poslednie dni," 58–59.
319. Bazanov, "Poslednie dni," 59.
320. Denikin, *Ocherki russkoi smuty*, tom 2, 45.
321. Denikin, *Ocherki russkoi smuty*, tom 2, 147–48.
322. Jonathan D. Smele, *The "Russian" Civil Wars, 1916–1926: Ten Years That Shook the World* (Oxford: Oxford University Press, 2015), 54–55, here 55.
323. See Oleksandr Dmytrovich Boiko, "Bii pid Krutamy: istoriia vivchennia," *Ukrains'kyi istorichnyi zhurnal*, 2008, no. 2 (479), 43–54.
324. "Iz kievskikh vospominanii (1917–1921) A. A. Gol'denveizera," *Arkhiv russkoi revoliutsii*, tom VI (Berlin: Izdatel'stvo "Slovo," 1922), 161–303, here 204–5.
325. "Iz kievskikh vospominanii (1917–1921) A. A. Gol'denveizera," *Arkhiv russkoi revoliutsii*, tom 6, 161–303, here 205.
326. "Iz kievskikh vospominanii (1917–1921) A. A. Gol'denveizera," *Arkhiv russkoi revoliutsii*, tom 6, 206.
327. Viktor Anatol'evich Savchenko, *Dvenadtsat' voin za Ukrainu* (Khar'kov: Folio, 2006), ch. 3, http:// militera.lib.ru/h/savchenko_va/index.html
328. Boris Suvorin, *Za rodinoi. Geroicheskaia epokha Dobrovol'cheskoi Armii 1917–1918 gg. Vpechatleniia zhurnalista* (Paris: O.D. i Ko., 1922), 5.
329. Denikin, *Ocherki russkoi smuty*, tom 2, 188–89.
330. Oleh S. Fedyshyn, *Germany's Drive to the East and the Ukrainian Revolution, 1917–1918* (New Brunswick, NJ: Rutgers University Press, 1971), 76, 87–104.
331. Wilhelm Gröner, *Lebenserinnerungen,* ed. F. F. H. vom Gärtringen (Göttingen: Vanderhoeck & Ruprecht, 1957), 385; quoted in Fedyshyn, *Germany's Drive to the East,* 107.
332. Richard Merton, *Erinnerungswertes au meinem Leben, das über das Persönliche hinausgeht* (Frankfurt am Main: Fritz Knapp, 1955), 44; quoted in Fedyshyn, *Germany's Drive to the East,* 111.

333. Fedyshyn, *Germany's Drive to the East,* 124–25.
334. Fedyshyn, *Germany's Drive to the East,* 140–42.
335. Fedyshyn, *Germany's Drive to the East,* 141–44, here 144.
336. Fedyshyn, *Germany's Drive to the East,* 166; Ruslan Iakovych Pyrig, "Fel'dmarshal German Aikhgorn: Sluzhba ta smert' v Ukraini (kviten'–lypen' 1918 g.)," *Ukrains'kyi istorichnyi zhurnal,* 2017, no. 3, 24–45, especially 43–45.
337. Fedyshyn, *Germany's Drive to the East,* 168–69.
338. Fedyshyn, *Germany's Drive to the East,* 193.
339. Peter Kenez, *Civil War in Southern Russia, 1918: The First Year of the Volunteer Army* (Berkeley: University of California Press, 1971), 71.
340. Fedyshyn, *Germany's Drive to the East,* 244.
341. On Keller, see Sergei Vladimirovich Fomin, *"Zolotoi klinok Imperii." Svity Ego Imperatorskogo Velichestva general ot kavalerii graf Fedor Arturovich Keller,* 2nd edition (Moscow: Forum, 2009); Andrei Sergeevich Kruchinin, "General ot kavalerii graf F. A. Keller," in Kruchinin, *Beloe dvizhenie: istoricheskie portrety* (Moscow: OOO "Ast," Astrel', 2011), 297–365.
342. Sergei Vladimirovich Volkov, *Beloe dvizhenie v Rossii: organizatsionnaia struktura: materialy dlia spravochnika* (Moscow: Biblioteka, 2000), swolkov.org.
343. Aleksandr Sergeevich Puchenkov, *Ukraina i Krym v 1918/ nachale 1919 goda: ocherki politicheskoi istorii* (Moscow, St. Petersburg: Nestor-Istoriia, 2013). See the chapter "Padenie getmanshchiny," http:// www.krimoved-library.ru/books/ukraina-ikrim-v -1918-nachale-1919-goda-ocherkipoliticheskoy-istorii.html.
344. See "Beseda s S. D. Sazonovym," *Kievskaia mysl',* 1918, 20(7) (noaibria), and "Beseda s N. Miliukovym," *Kievskii golos,* 1918, 10 (noiabria), in Puchenkov, "Padenie getmanshchiny," krimoved-library.ru.
345. Denikin, *Ocherki russkoi smuty,* tom 4, 272; quoted in Puchenkov, "Padenie getmanshchiny," krimoved-library.ru.
346. Mariia Antonovna Nesterovich-Berg, *V bor'be s bol'shevikami* (Paris: Imprimérie de Navarre, 1931), 195–96.
347. Puchenkov, "Padenie getmanshchiny," krimoved-library.ru.
348. See Roman Borisovich Gul', *"Ia unes Rossiiu: Apologiia emigratsii,* tom 1, *Rossiia v Germanii* (Moscow: B. S. G. Press, 2001), 56–57; quoted in Puchenkov, "Padenie getmanshchiny," krimoved-library.ru.
349. "Iz kievskikh vospominanii (1917–1921) A. A. Gol'denveizera," 232.
350. "Iz kievskikh vospominanii (1917–1921) A. A. Gol'denveizera," 234.
351. "Iz kievskikh vospominanii (1917–1921) A. A. Gol'denveizera," 231.
352. See Lidia Miliakova, Nicolas Werth, *Le livre des pogroms. Antichambre d'un genocide. Ukraine, Russie, Biélorussie 1917–1922* (Paris: Calmann-lévy, 2010); for the Russian original, see Lidiia Miliakova, ed., *Kniga pogromov* (Moscow: ROSSPEN, 2006).
353. "Proclamation du Comité central juif d'aide aux victimes des pogroms à la population juive de Kiev," in Miliakova and Werth, *Le livre des pogroms,* document 10.
354. "Iz kievskikh vospominanii (1917–1921) A. A. Gol'denveizera," 234–35.
355. Nesterovich-Berg, *V bor'be s bol'shevikami,* 195–96.
356. Nesterovich-Berg, *V bor'be s bol'shevikami,* 197–98.

357. See Ganin, *Korpus ofitserov General'nago shtaba v gody grazhdanskoi voiny 1917–1918 gg.*, 254; *Spisok general'nago shtaba, ispravlen po 1 iiunia 1914 goda,* 674.
358. On Grishin-Almazov in Siberia, see Vladimir Ivanovich Shishkin, "Komanduiushchii Sibirskoi armiei general A. N. Grishin-Almazov: Shtrikhi k portretu," in Shishkin, et al., *Kontrrevoliutsiia na vostoke Rossii v period grazhdanskoi voiny (1918–1919 gg.). Sbornik nauchnykh statei* (Novosibirsk: Institut istorii SO RAN, 2009), 126–95.
359. J. Kim Munholland, "The French Army and Intervention in Southern Russia, 1918–1919," *Cahiers du monde russe et soviétique,* vol. 22, no. 1 (January-March 1981), 43–66, here 48.
360. Another courier was Dmitrii Vsevolodovich Neniukov, formerly vice-admiral of the Russian Fleet and, during the civil war, commander of the Volunteer Black Sea Fleet. See Dmitrii Neniukov, *Ot mirovoi do grazhdanskoi voiny. Vospominaniia 1914–1920,* ed. Anton Viktorovich Posadskii (Moscow: Kuchkovo pole. Gornye tekhnologii, 2014).
361. Sergei Shilo, "Novorossiisk v gody grazhdanskoi voiny," http:// www.novodar.ru/index.php/novohistorypunkt/4000-nvggv-0702011.
362. Aleksandr Sergeevich Puchenkov, "'Bol'shoi gorod daet vozmozhnost' razvernut'sia': Iz istorii frantsuzskoi interventsii v Odesse," *Trudy istoricheskogo fakul'teta Sankt-Peterburgskogo universiteta,* no. 14 (2013), 125–57, here 125.
363. Puchenkov, "'Bol'shoi gorod daet vozmozhnost' razvernut'sia,'" 127, 129–30.
364. Puchenkov, "'Bol'shoi gorod daet vozmozhnost' razvernut'sia,'" 136–37; and V. V. Mikhailov, "Bor'ba politicheskikh napravlenii v Odesse v dni frantsuzskoi interventsii," *Voprosy istorii,* 2012, no. 6, 93–104, here 97.
365. On Piatigorsk and surrounding areas, see Grigorii Georgievich Moskvich, *Illiustrirovannyi prakticheskii putevoditel' po Kavkazu* (St. Petersburg: Izdatel'stvo putevoditelei Gr. Moskvicha, 1913).
366. "Osobaia komissiia po rassledovaniiu bol'shevikov, sostoiashchaia pri glavnokomanduiushchem vooruzhennymi silami na iuge Rossii. Akt rassledovaniia," in *Krasnyi terror v gody grazhdanskoi voiny: po materialam Osoboi komissii po rassledovaniiu zlodeianii bol'shevikov,* ed. Iurii Fel'shtinskii (London: Overseas Publications Interchange, 1992), 18–32, here 22–24, history.org.ua.
367. "Akt rassledovaniia," 25–26.
368. "Akt rassledovaniia," 26.
369. Munholland, "The French Intervention in Southern Russia," 50.
370. A. V. Mishina, "N. A. Grigor'ev–ataman povstantsev Khersonshchiny," *Novyi istoricheskii vestnik,* 2007, no. 1 (15), nivestnik.ru.
371. Munholland, "The French Intervention in Southern Russia," 53–54.
372. See "Note sur la question d'Odessa," March 20, 1919, Archives du ministère des Affaires étrangères francais; "Au General Franchet d'Espèrey à M. Ministre de la Guerre, 15 avril 1919," in AMAEF; both quoted in Munholland, "The French Intervention in Southern Russia," 56.
373. Munholland, "The French Intervention in Southern Russia," 57.
374. Peter Kenez, *Civil War in Southern Russia, 1919–1920: The Defeat of the Whites,* vol. 2 (Berkeley: University of California Press, 1977), 187–91, here 191.

375. Mary Olferieff, "Le feminisme dans les romans de Chrétien de Troyes," master's thesis, Stanford University, 1938.
376. See Ruth H. Shull, "Chrétien de Troyes: A Feminist of Twelfth-Century France," master's thesis, Butler University, 1933.
377. See, for example, the discussion by Lynn Tarte Ramey, "Representations of Women in Chrétien's 'Eric et Enide': Courtly Literature or Mysogyny?" *Romantic Review* 84:4 (November 1993), 377–86.
378. See Marianne Mahn-Lot, "Ma mère, Myrrha Lot-Borodine (1882–1954)," *Revue des Sciences philosophiques et théologiques* 88:4 (October–December 2004), 745–54. For her early work, see Myrrha Lot-Borodine, *La femme et l'amour au XII-e siècle* (Paris: A. Picard et Fils, Éditeurs, 1909); Lot-Borodine, *Trois essais sur le roman de Lancelot du Lac et la quête du Saint Graal* (Paris: Librairie ancienne honoré champion, 1919); and Lot-Borodine, *Chrétien de Troyes, Erec et Enide, roman d'aventures* (Paris: E. De Boccard, 1924).
379. See Michael William Tripp, "Russian Routes: Origins and Development of an Ethnic Community in San Francisco," master's thesis, San Francisco State University, 1980; Emil Theodore Hieronymus Bunje, H. Penn, and Frederick Joseph Smith, *Russian California, 1805–1841* (San Francisco: R. & E. Research, [1970]; Terence Emmons, *Alleged Sex and Threatened Violence: Doctor Russell, Bishop Vladimir, and the Russians in San Francisco, 1887–1892* (Stanford, CA: Stanford University Press, 1997); Amir Aleksandrovich Khisamutdinov, *Russkie volny na Pasifike: Iz Rossii cherez Kitai, Koreiu i Iaponiiu v novyi svet* (Vladivostok: Rubezh, 2013); Khisamutdinov, *Russkii San-Frantsisko* (Moscow: Veche, 2010); Lydia B. Zaverukha, Nina Bogdan, *Russian San Francisco* (Charleston, SC: Arcadia Publications, 2010).
380. See *Polnoe sobranie sochinenii Kniazia A. Viazemskago*, tom 3, *1808–1827 g.* (St. Petersburg: Tipografiia M. M. Stasiulevicha, 1880), 450–53. There are actually two poems under the title "Russian God" ["*Russkii Bog*"]: the first, slightly longer, begins with the line "Do you really need an explication?" [*Nyzhno li vam istolkovan'e* . . .]; the second begins "God of potholes, God of snowstorms" [*Bog" ukhabov", Bog" miatelei* . . .]. Olfer'ev quotes the second variant, which we have "from a manuscript of Prince [Vasilii Andreevich] Dolgorukov." The 1880 *Polnoe sobranie sochinenii* dates the poem to 1827. However, Soviet literary scholars have dated it to 1828. See Petr Andreevich Viazemskii, *Stikhotvoreniia,* 3rd edition, ed. K. A. Kumpan (Leningrad: Izdatel'stvo Sovetskii pisatel', 1986), 219, 491–92. The variant reading quoted by Olfer'ev appeared in this edition on 427; its source was a "copy in the archive of the brothers Turgenev."

Gary M. Hamburg is Otho M. Behr Professor of History at Claremont McKenna College, in California, specializing in Russian intellectual, cultural, and political history. He is the author of sixty journal articles or book chapters and the author or editor of twelve previous books. The most recent, *Russia's Path toward Enlightenment: Faith, Politics, and Reason, 1500–1801* (Yale University Press, 2016), won the Marc Raeff Prize in Eighteenth-Century Russian Studies. He is coeditor with Semion Lyandres of the *Journal of Modern Russian History and Historiography* (Brill).

Hamburg is currently writing a study of politics and communities in Russia from the Pugachev Rebellion of 1773–74 to the peasant emancipation of 1861. The working title is *Russia's Road toward Justice, 1773–1861.*

Tanya Alexandra Cameron grew up in California and majored in history at Stanford University. In order to help run the Montana cattle and sheep ranch of her husband's family, Cameron also earned a degree in business at Montana State University. In the early 1980s Cameron computerized the financial operations at the ranch, and for thirty-seven years she served as its CFO while also volunteering for various community organizations.

In 1969, Cameron promised her grandfather that she would do something with his memoirs, which she received after his death. Thus began a lifelong project that led her to study Russian and Russian history, travel extensively to the Soviet Union to follow in her grandfather's footsteps, and begin the translation. Finally, in retirement, she finished this labor of love and learning.

Index